C0-FXD-227

The Mystery Hidden for Ages in God

American University Studies

Series VII
Theology and Religion
Vol. 161

PETER LANG
New York • Washington, D.C./Baltimore • San Francisco
Bern • Frankfurt am Main • Berlin • Vienna • Paris

Paul M. Quay, S.J.

The Mystery Hidden for Ages in God

PETER LANG
New York • Washington, D.C./Baltimore • San Francisco
Bern • Frankfurt am Main • Berlin • Vienna • Paris

BX
2350.2
.Q38
1995

Library of Congress Cataloging-in-Publication Data

Quay, Paul M.
The mystery hidden for ages in God / Paul M. Quay.
p. cm. — (American university studies. Series VII, Theology and religion; vol. 161)
Includes bibliographical references and index.
1. Spiritual life—Catholic Church. 2. Catholic church—Doctrines. 3. Sin, Original. 4. God—Love. 5. Salvation. 6. Mystery. I. Title. II. Series.
BX2350.2.Q38 230′.2—dc20 93-17286
ISBN 0-8204-2221-5
ISSN 0740-0446

Die Deutsche Bibliothek-CIP-Einheitsaufnahme

Quay, Paul M.:
The mystery hidden for ages in God / Paul M. Quay. - New York; Berlin; Bern; Frankfurt/M.; Paris; Wien: Lang.
(American university studies: Ser. 7, Theology and religion; Vol. 161)
ISBN 0-8204-2221-5
NE: American university studies / 07

The paper in this book meets the guidelines for permanence and durability of the Committee on Production Guidelines for Book Longevity of the Council on Library Resources.

© 1995 Peter Lang Publishing, Inc., New York

All rights reserved.
Reprint or reproduction, even partially, in all forms such as microfilm, xerography, microfiche, microcard, offset strictly prohibited.

Printed in the United States of America.

To Mary,

Seat of Wisdom and Mother of the Church

who, in her Son, has brought forth

the New Testament from the Old.

Contents

PART II
RECAPITULATION IN CHRIST

PART III
THE CHURCH, THE NEW ISRAEL

Acknowledgments

My first glimpse of the pastoral importance of the thought of Henri de Lubac, S.J. and of the profound effects it could have in the spiritual lives of ordinary Catholics came through conversations with R.P. Winoc de Broucker, S.J., in 1964 and again in the summer of 1969. Great encouragement for the further development of my thoughts in this domain was given me by conversation with Father de Lubac himself at Fourvière that latter summer, when he indicated that the mere sketch I then had in mind for this project was very possibly sound and that he knew of no one else working on it.

Rev. Paul V. Robb, S.J. gave me the opportunity to present these ideas in a fuller and more structured form during a six-week workshop at the Longwood Cenacle, Chicago, in the summer of 1972. Rev. John C. Futrell, S.J. led me to develop them as a course in graduate spirituality at St. Louis University. Through the kindness of Dr. Peter Cataldo, I was invited to present a summary of my thought to the Dawson Conference in St. Louis in June of 1982; he also saw to having it published it in the Proceedings of that meeting. Mr. John J. Mulloy shared most generously with me his own great knowledge of the thought, private as well as public, of Christopher Dawson, and gave me much other help and encouragement.

Loyola University of Chicago granted me an unpaid academic leave for a year to complete the book and Rev. Robert Harvanek, S.J., graciously offered the Jesuit community's support for that period. Dr. Arnold Vander Nat and Dr. John Bannan of Loyola's Philosophy Department enabled me to exchange teaching assignments during one further semester to finish the work.

I am deeply grateful also to my mother, Mrs. Eugene (Effie Alley) Quay, and to Rev. Mitch Pacwa, S.J. for their careful reading of earlier versions of the manuscript and for their sound advice for its improvement. I owe a large debt of gratitude to Rev. Joseph W. Koterski, S.J. for his careful and helpful editorial reading of the quasi-final form of several chapters as well as for many helpful suggestions and encouragements during its writing. I offer my sincere thanks also to Rev. John J. Kilgallen, S.J. for his careful reading of chapters 7 and 8 and for the excellent advice he gave on how to improve them. Special thanks are due to Rev. Robert T. Sears, S. J., who performed the painful task of checking the whole manuscript for typos and for theological consistency. The flaws that remain are my own contribution and indicate how bad things might have been without such good help.

Abbreviations

AB	The Anchor Bible, Garden City (NY): Doubleday (1964 ff.)
BAG	*A Greek-English Lexicon of the New Testament and Other Early Christian Literature,* trans. & adapted from 4th German ed. of W. Bauer by W. F. Arndt & F. W. Gingrich, Chicago: University of Chicago Press (1957)
CCL	Corpus Christianorum, Series Latina, Turnholt: Brepols, 1953 ff.)
CSEL	Corpus Scriptorum Ecclesiasticorum Latinorum, Wien: C. Geroldi filium *et al.* (1866 ff.)
DS	*Enchiridion Symbolorum, Definitionum et Declarationum de Rebus Fidei et Morum,* ed. H. Denziger, rev. A. Schönmetzer, 33rd ed., Freiburg im Breisgau: Herder (1965)
DTC	*Dictionnaire de théologie catholique*, ed. A. Vacant, A. Mangenot & E. Amann, Paris: Letouzey & Ane (1902 ff.)
EM	*Exégèse Médiévale: les quatre sens de l'écriture*, (4 vol.), Henri de Lubac, Paris: Aubier (1959–1964).
GN	Gregorii Nysseni Opera, Leiden: Brill (1952 ff.)
HE	*Histoire et Esprit: L'intelligence de l'Écriture d'après Origène*, Henri de Lubac, Paris: Aubier (1950)
JBC	*The Jerome Biblical Commentary*, ed. R. E. Brown, J. A. Fitzmyer, R. E. Murphy, Englewood Cliffs (NJ): Prentice-Hall (1968)
LPGL	*A Patristic Greek Lexicon*, G. W. H. Lampe, Oxford: Clarendon Press (1961)
NJBC	*The New Jerome Biblical Commentary*, ed. R. E. Brown, J. A. Fitzmyer, R. E. Murphy, Englewood Cliffs (NJ): Prentice-Hall (1990)
PG	Patrologiae cursus completus, series graeca, ed. J. P. Migne,

	Paris (1857 ff.)
PL	Patrologiae cursus completus, series latina, ed. J. P. Migne, Paris (1844 ff.)
SC	Sources chrétiennes, Paris: Éditions du Cerf (1946 ff.)
ST	*Summa Theologiae*, St. Thomas Aquinas
TDNT	*Theological Dictionary of the New Testament,* edd. G. Kittel & G. Friedrich, tr. G. W. Bromiley, Grand Rapids: Eerdmans (1964 ff)

Sigla:

( )	When used to enclose a scriptural reference, parentheses indicate that the text referred to was taken from the *Revised Standard Version of the Bible*, copyright 1946, 1952, 1971 by the Division of Christian Education of the National Council of the Churches of Christ in the USA, with 'thee' and 'thou' replaced by 'you' along with corresponding changes in adjectival and verbal forms. Used by permission.
{ }	When used to enclose a scriptural reference, braces indicate my own or some other translation of the text in question.

Chapter 1

The Problem

A. A Question

This book took its origin from a question put to me back in the mid-50's by a friend I'd first come to know in Fiji during the Second World War. Alfred Shatkin was Jewish but firmly non-believing, a convinced atheist, intellectually honest, of quick wit and slightly barbed tongue. He would needle me on occasion about my faith as a Catholic; sometimes we would get into a long discussion—always fruitless as far as either's changing the basic position of the other, but always fruitful, at least for me, in sharpening the mind and opening up questions and approaches that were new or interesting.

The first time I passed through New York after being mustered out of the Army and finishing the early years of Jesuit formation, Alfred met me at the train station and we went walking and talking for a pleasant while, finally taking a seat on a bench near the Public Library. Of course, we had been talking matters philosophical and theological, though about what in particular I have no memory. But then he told me of a Catholic who lived in his apartment building, a man apparently devout and in good standing in the Church, who went to Mass every Sunday, but who was also well known in the building for beating his wife mercilessly and otherwise proving himself a very immoral man, whether by my standards or Alfred's. So, Alfred asked me, "With all the gifts from God that Catholics supposedly have, how is it that they are frequently worse in their morals, or only indistinguishably better, than us atheists?"

How I answered then, I do not remember. But the question remained with me, and over the years of theology and priestly ministry I have given it some thought. Evidently, there are at least two elements to be considered: are Catholics' morals in fact pretty much as he indicated? and if so, why are they not, on some sort of average at least, better than they are?

Questions related to Alfred's have arisen from other sources also. Why should spiritual growth, my own and others', be so slow? Why do some priests or religious seem to go backwards rather than forwards? Why do many Catholics, even priests and religious, seem to lack the close personal relationship with Jesus Christ that is so visibly operative in the lives of many believing Protestants despite the greater spiritual opportunities given the Catholics? After Vatican II, why did so many priests and religious leave their consecrated life to live as laymen—or even abandon the Church altogether—and this, after many reasonably productive and apparently contented years under their vows? Why are Christians often more easily led into moral evil by the surrounding culture than are, say, Orthodox Jews? Again, all these are simple variants on the basic question: how *should* Christians grow spiritually, how *do* they, and why the difference?

This question, however, cuts more deeply and more terribly than at first appears. Our century has been drowned in blood: the hundreds of millions of infants aborted; the far fewer, though still many millions, slain by Stalin, Mao, Hitler, and Pol Pot; the other millions killed in the two World Wars and the swarm of lesser conflicts; to say nothing of the victims of the internal collapse of family life and its replacement with gang life, drugs, and 'virtual reality.' The sight of a Christianity seemingly no more powerful to save from such evils than any secular moral system has contributed more to modern atheism than have scientific progress, the achievements of technology, and philosophical argument together. The question, "When confronted by such evils, where is Christianity and its vaunted power to change the hearts of men?" is answered quickly by "Nowhere" or "Collaborating with the evildoers." But what is nowhere is discarded as nonexistent; what collaborates with evildoers is fought aggressively in order to destroy it. Hence, the current mixture of indifference and hostility.

If this book, then, may be said to deal with spirituality, it is not with practical guidance for an individual's daily life that it is concerned or merely with theological study of the scriptural and doctrinal bases for the spiritual life of Christians. Rather, it is concerned with this fundamental question: is there a Christian spiritual life that is, except for superficialities, different from the spiritual life of a man of any religion or none? And if so, whatever the theory of this life may be, can it in fact be lived by ordinary Christians in a way that makes any difference at all in the world? In sum, is Christianity what it has always claimed to be: the mystery hidden for ages in God that has now been revealed so as to bring about man's salvation, if not from all external evils, at least from the evils of his own heart? If so, where is the evidence?

B. A WAY TOWARD AN ANSWER

One who looks at Christianity from without sees it divided into the Catholic Church, autocephalous Orthodox and other Eastern churches, and a multiplicity of Protestant denominations. This division among those who claim to follow Christ has assuredly weakened the effectiveness of Christianity in the world. Yet if one looks within these churches, one finds that another reason for this ineffectiveness is the chasm that has opened slowly over the past several centuries between the intellectual life of the West and the moral and spiritual life of Christians. Christian intellectuals tend to despise as "fundamentalists" those holding firmly to identifiably Christian practice and devotion; the latter, to distrust the former as covert apostates. All sense the chasm, however, much as many prefer to deny or ignore it.

a) One response to this sundering of Christian thought and life, an attempt by the intellectuals to re-establish contact with the ordinary Christian, was *la Nouvelle Théologie* of the late '40's and the '50's. Bent on recovering and updating patristic thought, its vigor and excitement came from the realization that such an approach could produce an effective medicine for the great wound in the Christian soul that divided the mind from the heart.[1]

Vatican II was convoked in order to meet this same problem; the search for its solution motivated most of the conciliar decrees. Yet the true thrust of the Council has in large measure been lost in the turmoil stirred by the misunderstandings and misrepresentations of the conciliar documents effected by the pandemic "liberalism" of the West.

The Council recognized that the catastrophes marking our times represented a challenge, not only to the West and not only to Christianity but to the whole world, to ponder seriously the source and the way to man's salvation: How can we and our earth be saved from an ever more infantile individualism working through an ever more mature technology, seemingly hell-bent on destroying civilization—not just that of the West but of the other great cultures as well? Hence came the importance of the Council's insistance that the purpose of God's revelation was to make known His decrees concerning man's salvation.

By implication, every valid theology should be governed by the same over-arching purpose and justify itself through its contribution to Christians' spiritual lives, even though each theology might highlight a different aspect of revealed truth and of God's will for us. Though metaphysical, psychological, historical, and other approaches to theology have their place, this place is always to be validated by its potential helpfulness to our life in Christ.

This book, then, attempts to show how one might recast the whole field of theology so as to make clearly visible its rationale as contributory to a living faith and Christian action.[2] If the whole of theology is to be thus restructured, this is not in order to despise or discard the varied schools and legiti-

---

[1] Cf. Walter J. Burghardt, S.J., "On Early Christian Exegesis," *Theological Studies 11*, 78–116 (1950). Excessive claims made by some in the movement led to a justifiably sharp response from the Vatican (*Humani Generis*, [1950] DS 3875–3899) though in some respects this response, too, was excessive, as shown shortly thereafter at Vatican II, in many ways prepared for by *la Nouvelle Théologie.*

[2] A small attempt at such a restructuring in moral theology is given by my book *The Christian Meaning of Human Sexuality*, San Francisco: Ignatius Press (1988).

mate approaches of the past. Rather, it is to make systematically evident the universal subordination of theology to revelation and to the spiritual life of the Christian. Nor will a recast theology necessarily be less technical; a glance at the various patristic works *Contra Eunomium* would suggest the contrary. What is in question is orientation and clarity of purpose.

b) If Christianity is to have a greater practical efficacy in achieving its mission in the world through a clearer focus on God's purpose in revelation and through taking fuller account of patristic approaches, it becomes necessary to examine the way Scripture, the primary locus of this revelation, is understood today. For the split between theology and Christian life is in large measure a split between those methods of scriptural interpretation characteristic of the patristic period and those which see the Scriptures primarily as a set of religious documents from another time and culture, to be understood simply by what current biblical scholarship can derive concerning the intentions of the writers. Or, to use a traditional terminology, the 'literal' sense and the 'spiritual' sense of the Scriptures have been severed.

Unsurprisingly, any effort to find in the biblical text a meaning for the reader that was given not solely by the writer but by God raises at once the hermeneutic question for Catholics as it did long since for Protestants. Hence, despite radical differences, there exists a sort of analogy to the problematics of such Protestant theologians as Barth, Gogarten, Bultmann, and Tillich: is there anything that modern man can take from the Old Testament (or even from the New) for his life and growth as a Christian that he may honestly see to be God's word *to him* or *for him*?

Even in the 2nd Century the Church had to respond to such questions. Convinced that the mode of exegesis and interpretation which constituted her response and which was universal among Christians until the Reformation could not be discarded without thereby abandoning the core of Christian belief, such scholars as de Lubac, Daniélou, Martelet, and von Balthasar sought to recover this mode of understanding for modern times. Building upon their work, I try to show how this original Christian hermeneutics—this study of "typical" meanings—can prove useful today, without the arbitrariness or even fancifulness that rightly brought the interpretion of types into discredit.

The spiritual sense cannot be found, however, apart from an accurate understanding of the literal sense. Hence we are not dispensed from but required to take full advantage of modern scriptural studies for whatever they can contribute. Using these studies, then, to present the basic types and to control their interpretation, I try to show something of what can actually be accomplished through the use of typology rather than merely to state what someone else ought to do about the problems mentioned.

c) Finally, from New Testament times on, Christians have described spiritual growth in terms of an increase in virtues, natural and supernatural. Often, however, the theological framework and the understanding of human nature implied were drawn too extensively from philosophical sources, while the Scriptures were relegated largely to serving as the subject matter for one's prayer. More recently, spiritual growth has been simply identified with psychic development. As a result, grace (and much else of which faith speaks) is now largely ignored in favor of "religious experience." Moreover, except in existential psychology, the most important of natural factors in psychological development, the freedom of human decisions, has also been ignored.

This book seeks to give due weight to what is sound in each approach but without conflation or compromise. Rather, through the teachings of the Fathers of the Church, transcribed into modern language and systematic form, the processes of nonfree psychic growth and healing are distinguished from the Christian's freely accepted spiritual maturation while yet both are shown to be necessary and interwoven aspects of one's living in Christ by grace. The systematic framework and conceptual basis are, moreover, drawn from the Scriptures themselves and not from philosophy, psychology, or other human science.

I have written primarily for professional theologians, but also for mature laymen seriously interested at a theological level in the questions mentioned above. Seeking the answers on the basis of the Church's own perennial teaching about mankind, herself, and her Lord, I have tried, where possible, to avoid technical language and style. Certain new ideas, however, require more careful and extended treatment than would be needed if they were already accepted or at least discussed among Christians.

Chief among the new developments are the following:

a) A theory of original sin is presented which would give full weight to the Church's traditional teachings, yet with which the best of modern psychology, genetics, and paleo-anthropology seem compatible.

b) It is shown how one may see the order of origination of the three divine Persons and the oppositional relations between them as a pattern of Personally characteristic loves between the Three. This, taken with a much neglected scriptural name of the Spirit, makes possible some understanding of the procession of the Spirit from the Father through the Son that has not been available hitherto. From this, a resolution is found for the centuries-old controversy between Orthodox and Catholics concerning the *Filioque*, doing full justice to both sides, not by compromise but by deepening the doctrine.

c) There is a development of a notion I have called 'reflection,'[3] analogous to the classical notion of 'mission,' in terms of which one can see the intratrinitarian relations manifested in the created order and can understand more deeply the role of Christ's humanity in His unique mediatorship.

d) The recovery of a full doctrine of the spiritual sense of the Scriptures is shown to depend essentially upon the patristic doctrine of recapitulation. Through this, the crucial importance of the Old Testament for the spiritual growth of Christians is established, as well as the need—if they are to reach the fulness of the Christian life—for their growth to be patterned in accord

---

[3] I use single quotes when naming a word or concept. Thus, in the next line, "notion of 'mission,'" is equivalent to "notion labeled by the term 'mission,'"

with the spiritual sense, in Christ, and not merely with the literal sense.

Where technical treatment of some point is necessary, it is given in an Excursus, set apart from the body of the text. The most difficult material, unfortunately, comes early (Part I, Chapters 3 through 5); but there are summaries at the beginning or end of these chapters to enable one to skip the details of the argument till later.

Given the range of material covered (the book is already thick enough and annotated enough to cause some a certain dismay), I have taken positions on a number of controversial points without adverting to the controversy, offering the reasons for the position I take, or referring to the variety of opinions in dispute. My reasons, however, for declining to use so-called "inclusive language" will be made clear in Chapter 20. On the other hand, the newness of the approach here taken (even though the doctrine is quite traditional) has called for frequent reference to a wide range of previous thinkers. Such seeming eclecticism could cause a theologian a certain discomfort. My purpose, however, is not to pretend to integrate these different systems and modes of understanding. I refer to them, rather, for particularly clear or well-stated witness to one or other aspect of a position under discussion; but the theological argument that I make, taken as a whole, is my own responsibility.

C. The basic principle of the spiritual life

Adam was created in that Image of God which is Christ and according to that Likeness of Father and Son which is the Holy Spirit. The "in-the-Image"[4] was his nature, for Jesus is the sole, complete and undamaged exemplar of man's natural being. The "in-the-Likeness" was his life in Jesus, the Christ, i.e., "the Anointed" by the Holy Spirit. Through the Spirit, he was made son of the Father and brother to Jesus, living by the divine life itself. Being in Christ, he was like God.

But man is no longer as God created him in the beginning. As a result of original sin, we enter the world spiritually dead, without likeness to Christ and wounded in nature, His image in us damaged and deformed. Yet Christ still remains the model for all that we are and have, by nature and by grace. Only by coming integrally to image Christ and to reflect without falsification His likeness can we become what God destined us to be at the beginning. Only if once more enabled to live in Christ, can we be saved.

The restoration of the integral person does not, however, begin with the rebuilding of our sin-shattered nature so that it becomes a fitting and suitable recipient for grace.[5] Rather, the divine likeness is infused first, as pure gift to

[4] The language here is that of Diadochus of Photike, though his meaning is slightly different. For him, the in-the-Image is equivalent to man in grace but at the beginning of his spiritual life, while still in that portion of the Christian life I shall call 'recapitulative.' The in-the-Likeness refers to man as being led in all things by the Holy Spirit, living fully in accord with the New Testament, no longer simply recapitulating the Old.

[5] This seems to have been implicit in the insistence of the Judaizers of St. Paul's day that a Gentile become a Jew before he could be made a Christian. In any case, some such thought seems

one who is by nature and sin unfit to receive it. The Holy Spirit thereby makes him, in Christ, a son of the Father. The Spirit's persevering building up of Christ's likeness then gradually re-forms and reshapes the broken vessel of our nature.[6] This restoration, admittedly, is never complete in this life. Most evident in the inescapable weaknesses and illnesses of our bodies, our never-ending need for healing is even more painfully present in our psychic troubles and disorders. Yet no greater mistake can be made by anyone seeking to live a true spiritual life than to invert the order of nature and grace by concentrating on the healing of his psychic wounds rather than on his life in Christ.

If we are to live in Christ, we must live in Him in accord with the pattern of His own life, a pattern it will be our concern to sketch out and develop. Following St. Irenaeus, the traditional designation of this pattern is '*recapitulation.*'[7] In its strongest form, recapitulation names a process intended to shape the entire life of the Christian:

God intends that, through the action of His grace, each Christian

(a) relive in Christ, during the first portion of his life, all that God led His people through from the fall of Adam to Christ's death and resurrection, and,

(b) thereafter, live as son of God in Christ in the full freedom of the Holy Spirit, so as to glorify the Father in the Church by making Him known to all men through the Spirit's power.

The transition from the life of recapitulation of the Law and Prophets to a life like that of the apostles and the saints of the New Law corresponds to Jesus' passage out of this world to the Father. In language perhaps more familiar to today's Catholics, the transition from the life characterized by active prayer and growth in the moral virtues to a life that is freely directed by the Spirit and characterized by the passivity of infused contemplation and the total domination of charity reflects Christ's transit though death on the cross to His taking His seat at the right hand of the Father and pouring out His Spirit upon His disciples.[8]

Without the gift of the Holy Spirit, through whom we share Christ's life, this process of spiritual and, also, psychological growth would take as long as the time from Adam to Jesus. But by His gift, the entire process is compressed from hundreds or even thousands of millennia into the short span of an ordinary Christian's life. Part of our effort will be to develop this seem-

---

to motivate those today who are more concerned with psychological remediation than growth in Christ. How the life in Christ, if put first, effects such remediation is the burden of much of this book.

[6] Cf. Paul Agaësse, S.J., "La règle et le sens," *Christus* 56, 496–507 (1967).

[7] This consecrated, though somewhat cumbersome, term was borrowed by Irenaeus from Eph.1:10 to designate this vastly complex concept, which served as the key to his refutation of the gnostic heresies of his day. As will be seen later, 'recapitulation' includes much more for Irenaeus than just this one aspect.

[8] Living one's life in Christ means more, then, than occasional choices to imitate the Master on this point or that. It means embracing an entire pattern of life whose main parts reflect these two stages.

ingly simple notion in sufficient detail and with enough applications to show its importance both for theology and for the spiritual life of Christians.

D. Structure of spiritual growth from conception till death

For each of us, the spiritual journey begins at the same moment as our natural life. Thus Catholic doctrine about the causes and nature of original sin is explicitly tied to conception, though its effects and remedies are generally discussed in connection with birth.[9] When we first came into being, newly conceived in the body of our mother, we were, like Adam after the fall, bereft of grace, by nature children of wrath (Eph.2:3), already doomed by sin to wander in the desert of this world, with neither hope nor desire for the goal for which our very nature was made and without which it can have no meaning, till we die in thirst (Am.8:11–12) and despair.

But though that is where each of us began his life, God's goodness was not content to leave us there. Instead, He has called us to rejoice forever in that knowledge and love of Him by which the divine Persons know and love each other. From death of both body and spirit we are called to share eternally in the life of the Most Holy Trinity in heaven.

Any true understanding of the spiritual life, then, must know accurately our condition when we began, the state to which God has called us, and the way between them. Though mapped by God's revelation and described by saints and spiritual authors, this journey is still difficult and hazardous enough that those who would be of help to others by way of spiritual counsel and direction must labor much to acquire a detailed understanding of the way, along with knowledge of the signs that indicate where each individual is and where he should seek to go next.

This book is in consequence divided into three parts. Part I deals with our starting point, our conception in original sin. After a brief sketch of the Church's puzzling and seemingly inconsistent teachings on the matter, I indicate the methodological flaw that has given rise to the vigorous controversies of the present day. To gain a better understanding, it is necessary to grasp the structure of the love of which original sin is the trait-by-trait contradiction. This requires consideration of the structure of divine love within the Trinity and of the structure which that implies for the charity of Christ in which we share by grace. One can then show how original sin, as the privation of this charity at conception, initiates an ever-spreading psychic damage that impels one towards actual sin.

But from the Church's doctrine on the Trinity is it possible to discern a structure of love between the Persons within the Godhead? This somewhat technical problem requires that we address in detail the nature of the proces-

[9] E.g., Trent, Decree on Original Sin, DS 1513: "*origine...et propagatione*"; Decree on Justification, DS 1523: "*dum concipiuntur.*" One aspect of the great importance of the dogma of the Immaculate Conception of our Lady is its underlining of this precise point.

sion of the Holy Spirit and its difference from that of the Son. The key to a solution lies in a little used but scriptural name of the Holy Spirit, noted only in passing by the Greek Fathers, seemingly unrecognized in the West. This name will be shown to ground an intrinsic understanding of how the generation of the Son by the Father differs from the procession of the Spirit from the Father and why this latter must take place through the Son. More important for our present purpose is the insight so obtained into the inner structure of the divine love.

Since we are in no way able directly to imitate the Trinity and since Christ is our sole mediator, we consider how the trinitarian structure of the divine love is reflected in Jesus, and how this is mediated by Him to us. We will then see the basic traits of human charity as it is meant to exist in each of us and also glimpse in a general way how we are intended to live our lives in Christ through sharing these characteristics of His life.

It is then not difficult to see the consistency of the Church's teaching on original sin—it is sin because it is a nullification of those aspects of charity that are the created reflections of the Trinity. Consideration, then, of the psychic growth of the fallen infant before birth and of what the grace of God, if fully felt in its true nature, would do for a child's psychic development gives some understanding of the terrible effects produced by this privation of charity from the moment of conception. Since these effects are built into us from conception, the psychic damage perdures even after the sin itself is removed. Personal maturation and individual spiritual growth, though intended by God to occur together, remain unsynchronized because of the residual psychic effects of original sin even after the restoration of grace.

That mode of the life in Christ that we called "recapitulation" gradually heals this damage to our nature. Part II, then, considers this healing process, the path of true spiritual growth that leads from our sinful state at conception to the life that is led in the full power of the Holy Spirit. Even as Jesus was the perfect Jew, who relived all the stages of the life of Israel, rectifying what was done amiss and perfecting all else, so each Christian who lives by the grace of Christ is able to relive Israel's life in and with Jesus. Only by such a life does he become able eventually to live as befits a son of God, directed in all things by the Holy Spirit.

This process of recapitulation—of reliving the life of Israel as given us through the Old Testament—requires that the Old Testament (and, also the New) be understood not only according to the sense intended by its human authors (the 'literal sense') but also in accord with its 'spiritual sense': the meaning given by God Himself to the persons or events ('types') referred to by the text. To ascertain this meaning, then, requires that one know what, in fact, the text says and means. One need not fear that the historical-critical methods of the last 250 years will have to be discarded. Rightly employed, they are essential if one is to arrive without arbitrariness at the spiritual sense, which invariably signifies some aspect of the mystery of Christ, who revealed the existence of this sense to His disciples.

Yet, assuming we can find both literal and spiritual senses with some fullness, how can God's revelation in the Old Testament be something still alive and operative for us? If it is the record of God's word, spoken once for all and long ago to the human authors of the texts, how may we legitimately consider these texts as His word speaking to us now? Granted that the Old Testament is needed to provide us with some understanding of the Jewish religious, cultural, and terminological background of the New, can it have other relevance today, when Christianity is already well established? Or, to recast the question from the perspective in which it was first posed in the 2nd Century by Marcion: If the New Testament contains the fulfilment of the Old, why should Christians continue to read the often dull, obscure, or even barbarous texts of the Old?

The answer to be offered here to this hermeneutic problem corrects, I think, the distortions—mostly small though gigantic in their cumulative effect—that have long made this problem seem intractable. For although the hermeneutic problem has long had a clear answer for Catholics, embodied in the doctrines and practice of the Church, this answer is now largely rejected by Protestants and ignored even by Catholics. This basic doctrine of the Christian faith, then, is set out at the beginning of Part II; but, rather than leave it as a merely abstract matter of principle, I show how it is to be applied in the spiritual lives of us all through our recapitulation in Christ.

Since this process is not merely individual but radically social, Part III considers how the Christian's growth is mediated by the Church and modified by his culture. Since both Church and culture are, in their turn, incessantly modified by the actions of individual Christians, the spiritual development of the Church herself is analysed as she interacts, through her members, with diverse cultures. It is then shown why the Church must always be, of her own nature, intensely involved in the building up of the cultures in which she is planted. The spiritual role and value of the so-called "institutional Church" is set out, making clear why a revolt against this is directed not only against the Church and the revelation she transmits but against human nature itself.

The tight linkage between the spiritual lives of individuals and the development of cultures permits an analysis of the religious decline of the West and the consequent disintegration of Western culture itself during the last 600 years. This regression can be traced to a gradual loss by Christians of the true understanding of the spiritual sense of the Old Testament. Only through the recapitulation deriving from this sense can Christians be rightly formed in those basic human virtues that establish genuine individual, sexual, and social identities. With the loss of the spiritual sense, the Old Testament ceased to be seen as a Christian book, which this sense alone can show it to be. The New Testament then came gradually to float in the air, as the solid foundation for its teaching that God had provided through the Old Testament, dissolved. Yet, if this analysis of the cause of Christian weakness in the West is correct, the means lie ready to hand for a reversal of the decline.

Part I

ADAM AND CHRIST: ORIGINAL SIN

Chapter 2

Original Sin and the Structure of Charity

Though Adam's sin occurred at the dawn of human time, it is not itself a starting-point for theological understanding.[1] Sin, Adam's or any other's, puzzling and baffling as it is, is not, strictly, a mystery at all.[2] The genuine mysteries of faith blind us by the excess of their light. Sin is the darkness of an irrational negation of all mysteries. Sin's incomprehensibility comes not from an infinite fulness of being, as with the true mysteries of God, but by defect, by an unintelligible nullification of being and eradication of the likeness to Christ that should be present.[3]

---

[1] As Pope John Paul II has remarked, "Only the perspective of the redemption justifies the reference to the beginning," General Audience of Dec. 3, 1980, #3, in *Blessed Are the Pure of Heart*, Boston: Daughters of St. Paul (1983), *p* 193.

[2] The "mystery of iniquity" {II Thess.2:7} does not refer directly to human sin, original or actual, but to the whole plan of Satan for human perdition, in mocking antithesis to *the* Mystery: God's plan of salvation for man in Christ—cf. Gregory J. O'Kelly, S.J., (unpublished) Commentary on II Thessalonians, *ad locum*. So also, when Pope John Paul II deals with "the Mystery of Sin," he goes on at once to speak of "the factors at work which place it beyond the merely human," and makes clear that he is not considering sin as a mystery except in terms of the true mysteries of faith (*On Reconciliation and Penance in the Mission of the Church Today*, Boston: St. Paul Editions [1984], *pp* 46–7).

[3] Therefore, one can expect nothing but problems if one chooses to look at original sin in separation from the rest of the doctrine of faith (cf. DS 3016, I Vatican). If one remembers, for example, the doctrine of Mary's conception without taint of original sin, the inadequacies of those explanations which reduce original sin to some "sin of the world," i.e., a sin-filled and otherwise evil situation throughout the world into which both she and we are born, become at once apparent.

If, then, we are to understand sin at all, it is at that positive aspect of reality which is destroyed by sin that we must look. We can learn the "nature" of a gaping wound, assess the degree and kind of damage it has inflicted, determine what treatment is likely to preserve life and eventually to help the wound to heal, and even infer something of the agent which produced it only by comparing the body's wounded configuration with what we know of the structure and functioning of the uninjured body. In like manner, we shall not understand much about sin by attempting to focus on it in itself but only by considering what it was that sin has destroyed and by scrutinizing the bounds and limits of destruction, the configuration of the wounds, and the losses of power and function that have resulted.

A. Original sin: the problem

Original sin, if not remedied by God's mercy, totally blocks the attainment of the supernatural goal that is our sharing in the inner life of the three Persons. Anyone who dies while still in the state of sin in which he was conceived is intrinsically, essentially, incapable of the life of heaven: the immediate vision of the Trinity and the all-consuming love that floods forth from that sight.[4]

Hence, we may gain some understanding of original sin if we consider it, first and foremost, as the negative and destructive counterpart to the charity of God that is poured into our hearts by the Holy Spirit when once we have been sanctified and the Trinity comes to dwell within us.

In the case of an actual sin, we can usually remember, to some degree at least, our status before the sin and can compare it with our condition afterwards. But we have never experienced that prior state from which Adam fell. We were in sin from the moment of our conception till our baptism or conversion of heart. At no time have we been free from the consequences of original sin. We cannot, then, distinguish by experience what is due to original sin in us from what is ours by nature.[5] Of course, we do sense profoundly within ourselves that we are broken, that we are at odds with ourselves and with our world, and this, often enough, without being simultaneously at odds

---

[4] For reasons not clear to me, this doctrine has often been misinterpreted as implying that those in heaven have no further contact or community of life with those in limbo. But whatever the merits of the doctrine of a limbo for the unbaptized infant, it in no way implies such a separation. The inability to see God directly, as He is in Himself, need no more separate the just from the unbaptized than the inability to perceive the difference between green and red need separate the color-blind from the rest of men.

[5] Hence those who subject faith to "experience" not only tend to slight the doctrine of original sin but quickly to cease to live as Christians. For it is not uncommon, even among those for whom the goal is clear and truly sought, to have very false notions of their situation in this world, thinking that the powers, desires, motives, psychic structures, and the like which they find in themselves, are trustworthy guides and helps on the journey, not realizing in what way original sin has damaged us nor how the enemy of our human nature makes use of such damage to gain access in order to destroy us.

with God, i.e., without present actual sin.

Clearly, our knowledge of a state that was damaged or destroyed by original sin, even that there is or was such a state, can only be based on revelation. Only through faith can we know that man has fallen, that Jesus is the New Adam, who is the revelation in word and action of man unfallen though in a world both fallen and redeemed, and that it is Mary, immaculate from her conception, who is the New Eve, mother of all who live in Christ.

We take, then, as our basic data those doctrines that have been defined as of Catholic faith since part of God's revelation. To go back no further into the list of such definitions, we find that the Council of Trent defines original sin to be a "sin which is the death of the soul" (DS 1512), which no human power can take away (DS 1513), which needs to be expiated, which involves guilt, indeed, our own guilt (DS 1523), and which has that intelligible (or in this case, unintelligible) structure (*ratio*) that truly and properly belongs to sin. Thus, it is unlike concupiscence, which, at least in the reborn, does not have this *ratio* (DS 1515). It is, however, also Catholic teaching that original sin is contracted without one's consent (DS 780).[6] Neither is it the result of any act by which anyone since Adam turns his will away from God (DS 1948–49). In the state of original sin, although one's will is not set against God or in opposition to Him, neither is it inclined, as by nature it should be, towards Him.

Thus, though original sin is truly and properly sin, it differs greatly from our actual sins. A look at some of the differences will help us get our bearings before we seek to enter the central mystery.

Original sin has not been committed by anyone since Adam (DS 1950–1951). It does not result from our violating any norms. Since it is neither an act of ours nor free, God cannot be rightly said to forbid or prohibit it. The obvious question, then, is: how can this condition of soul be truly and properly sin and bear the guilt and punishment proper to sin if it has not come from one's own free choice and is not even voluntary? How can one be blamed for a sin that he did not commit, did not even have the power to commit, that is not, strictly speaking, commitable at all since not an act but a state of soul inherited from Adam?

The great heresies of the 16th and 17th Centuries responded to such questions by making original sin, however mysteriously, largely equivalent to grave, personal, actual sin, a radical corruption of our nature. Catholics replied that original sin is sin in an analogous sense only, that it must be sharply distinguished from actual sin, that it is a distinct genus and kind of sin.

Yet our prime analogate for the understanding of grave sin is actual mortal sin. This is sinful because by it the created will sets itself in free and knowing opposition to God's will, the creature acting as if it were the Creator. Evidently, actual sin involves the use of one's natural powers contrary to the directionality given them by their nature, a violation of natural law. But,

[6] Condemnation of Baius. Note, however, DS 371 concerning damage to freedom of the will.

more importantly, grave actual sin is a direct attack on the divine majesty. It denies God's supremacy at least by denying the creature's subjection by its very nature to God. As a refusal of God's will, even at the price of destroying the created life of God within us, actual sin is the free choice of an attitude that is in inner contradiction to charity, the love of God above all things and of one's neighbor for His sake.

God created man to share not only in the aspects of His divine nature manifested *ad extra* but even in His inner, trinitarian life. This sharing in His inner life exists in us through the complex of supernatural powers or virtues that Scripture calls faith, hope, and charity. By faith, we know God and not merely about God. For, faith is a participation in the knowledge and understanding which the Three Persons have of Themselves and of all things else.[7] Hope is a sharing in what we may for the moment consider as the power of Their mutual trust and total reliance upon Each Other for Their very being. Charity is the essence of God's own inner life, for "God is love" (I Jn.4:8, 16); and our charity is a living share in the love of the three Persons for One Another.

Without charity, some aspects of faith and hope may continue for a time; but they are "dead", so disintegrated and decayed as to be quite incapable of bringing us to salvation. Yet even their dead presence is not negligible; God can by His grace use even their remains to bring about repentance and the regeneration of the divine life in us. But though eternal life is given to us *in* and *through* faith and hope, it is not given *by* faith and hope. It is only by the love that is charity that God's life is ours. For charity *is* eternal life, already possessed though still inchoate and not yet total. The supernatural understanding that is faith is given us for the sake of charity, which is the love we have for God and for creatures precisely because of what faith shows us of them and not because of their current attractiveness to us. Hope gives us the strength to act in accordance with our faith, to take the risk of loving all men, whatever their sins, because and as God does.

Charity, then, through which we are saved, is a created sharing in the divine life of Him who is love. As a supernatural power that is made part of our very being, charity enables us to love in the manner and mode in which God loves and in accordance with the pattern of His love. We are enabled to love what He loves, for at least some of the reasons for which He loves it, on the basis of the knowledge of it which He has and shares with us by faith, and to act from this love in accord with the ways in which He acts towards each object of His love. In brief, our love for God Himself and for each of His creatures, from angels to stones, has the same intrinsic structure as God's love for that same being.

Grave actual sin[8] not only destroys this supernatural life but, as we are all

---

[7] Hence, though the "objects of faith" are those truths knowable only by faith, there is no human experience and no natural intellectual knowledge that does not call for illumination by faith or that can be rightly and adequately understood independently of faith.

painfully aware, our own free choice of what we know to be wrong injures us at a psychic level. Every sin leaves its marks in our attitudes and dispositions. But, as anyone who tries it quickly discovers, there is little point in trying to track down all the strongly interconnected intellectual, volitional, emotional, organic, biochemical, and physical aspects that we sum up as "formation or alteration of character," "change of attitude," or "development of habit."

"Habits of sin," then, are due not to any loss of freedom of the will itself (a metaphysical impossibility) but to the psychological set given the whole person by his sins. Especially at the largely animal level of feeling and emotion, where body-chemistry, especially brain-chemistry, is determinative, this emotional set reinforces and solidifies prior decisions. By the strength of its influence, it makes further free choice of evil seemingly inevitable. Difficult as it is to trace all the patterns here, one of the few things that seems clear is that, in all cases, our power to love is somehow affected for the worse. We become more self-centered, less rightly concerned for the true good of others, and, by very definition, uninterested in loving God. Charity has been replaced by selfish desire.[9]

Yet original sin is in some ways more deadly than the great majority of mortal sins that men commit. For in original sin, *all* aspects of supernatural life are absent. Not only is there no charity, but there is no trace of either faith or hope. We are spiritually dead at our conception, and then still-born into a world where the devil rules through our fear of bodily death (Heb. 2:14), the seeming extinction of the only life left us. Original sin is the total absence of divine life in one whose very nature was created "in the Image of God," that is, in Christ, but who lacks totally "the Likeness of God" through sanctifying grace that would make him supernaturally like the Son in His relation to the Father.

In other ways, however, it is less deadly than actual sin. Though both original sin and mortal sin, if not remedied by grace, deprive men of eternal life, yet only unrepented actual mortal sin condemns one to never-ending flame in hell. Further, original sin is the more easily remedied. For, baptism constitutes a true remission and cleansing away of all sin by a rebirth into the divine life (DS 1514) and can do this without the knowledge or consent of the recipient.[10]

But some of the harm done us by original sin is not remedied at the

---

[8] So-called 'venial sin' is not here in question, not because it is unimportant but precisely because it does not destroy God's life within us, though rendering it less vigorous and less operative.

[9] In American culture, it is often overlooked that one can be intensely selfish and yet altruistic at the same time. If the self is the object of one's love and desire, any activity so motivated is selfish, even if the concrete desire involves choosing the good of others. Thus, if one has chosen to be an altruistic person solely because he likes people of that character and wants to rival or surpass them, his altruism is tainted at least with selfishness.

[10] This remediation takes no time, being an instantaneous operation of divine power. It is, moreover, complete in the sense that, once done, the person is ready for heaven, possessing already the principle of eternal life.

moment of baptism. What is not remedied is, presumably, something not directly touched by the supernatural activity and power of grace. For surely God does not refuse out of mere arbitrariness to heal us completely in this life. Rather, given the sort of beings we are, begotten from fallen Adam, some of the effects of his sin continue in us through material damage to our bodily nature and existence. Therefore our healing, apart from the gift of new life in Christ, takes place slowly, over time, and may affect one aspect of our composite being much more strongly at a given moment than other aspects.[11]

We have something here, then, that seems analogous to the psychic damage done to us by actual sin. But even more than actual sin, original sin has altered our characters, modified our temperaments, changed our dispositions, weakened our powers. Whatever natural dispositions and temperamental attitudes our genes determine for us, this gene-determined personality is damaged at its core, differently in each according to his genetic traits, yet similarly in each in accord with one basic destructive pattern.

Even though through original sin we are born under the power of the devil (Eph.2:2–3, I Jn.5:19), the damage is not done by any positive principle of evil at work within us.[12] The warping and distortion of the psychic (and indeed the physical) is neither freely chosen nor voluntary within us. It is present like a withered hip-muscle, whose weakness lets the normal growth and use of other muscles curve and twist the spine, leading by their very health to greater deformity and, eventually, illness. But it is more serious than that, being like one of those terrible diseases originating in the lack of a single gene, one that was meant to regulate some aspect, say, of fat metabolism, whose absence leads inexorably to painful death precisely through the healthy activity of a body that becomes the more diseased the more it grows in otherwise normal fashion.

Lacking the divine life for which this nature of ours was made, the psychic structure of the unborn infant develops on its own, without the influence of grace.[13] Each aspect of the psyche, all made by God to support the life of charity, comes to develop without the regulation and governance of that which alone can make the whole organism one in Christ. God's good gifts of temperament and attitude become, by the absence of grace, a "nature" that is progressively organized in such manner as to make the life of grace ever more

---

[11] Does a miracle remove from time altogether, i.e., is it a strictly instantaneous action? Or does it simply speed up the process enormously? Cf. Jules Lebreton, *Tu Solus Sanctus: Jésus Christ vivant dans les saints: étude de théologie mystique*, Paris: Beauchesne (1948), *pp* 96–97 & 101. Cf. also the suggestive remarks of St. Augustine *(Sancti Aurelii Augustini In Johannis Evangelium Tractatus CXXIV*, ed. R. Willems, CCL 36, Tract. 8, 1–2 & Tract. 24, 1) and St. Irenaeus *Adversus Haereses* III, 11, 5 (Irénée de Lyon, *Contre les hérésies III,* SC 211, edd. A. Rousseau & L. Doutreleau). *(*

[12] Cf. also St. Caesarius of Arles, Sermon 229 (##1–3), CCL 104, 905–908; also, the Council of Trent (DS 1511 & 1512).

[13] One does not find, however, in current discussions of original sin (nor even in earlier ones) very much said about the spiritual significance of the the period between conception and birth.

difficult.

If a long-withered hip-muscle were miraculously healed, still the rest of the body's deformity would remain. To rectify this would require the gradual restructuring a skilled chiropractor might effect if coupled with persevering and steady exercise by the patient according to a prescribed regimen. So, also, this deformation of the psyche is not undone simply by the infusion of grace, even if this take place at birth. Baptism restores the divine life. Yet during our time in the womb, the lack of this life actively damaged our individual nature as it developed from conception onwards, dynamically forming a psychic antithesis to charity within us. Further, since grace must "enter," since its original mode of union with the human person is absent, since the structures of the psyche created for it at the beginning have grown awry, its presence is not usually felt. Hence, it has, initially at least, little effect at the psychic level. Rather, the whole psyche must be restructured and strengthened in chiropractic fashion if one is to take full advantage of this newfound vitality. The science and art involved in spiritual asceticism and direction are meant to provide the understanding and skills needed for this endeavor.

The psychic damage that remains unhealed after baptism has traditionally been called "concupiscence." As the name of this abiding defect of character suggests,[14] and as the analogy with the effects of actual sin indicates, it is primarily the basic psychic structure of our power to love that is deranged by original sin, a derangement that shows itself through disordered desires, lusts, and longings—traces of genuine love gone rotten. The native structures made for charity have been turned into a jumble of disorderly cravings.

When grace is absent, this psychic disorder is but an external manifestation of the decay of a dead soul.[15] But when grace has brought one spiritually to life, this remanent disorder retains nothing that is truly and properly called sin although it arose from original sin and inclines and disposes us to actual sins (DS 1515). In what aspect of our being, then, was concupiscence so grave a wound when grace was absent if it can nonetheless persist when grace is present, yet without being any longer (properly speaking) sinful?

B. Original Sin: The Love That It Negates

What I have sketched as a possible way of understanding original sin is, thus far, too general to be very useful. We must show how such a psychic disorder can rightly be called 'sin,' how it can cease to be 'sin' without being eliminated, how it is transmitted from one generation to another by birth, and a number of other problems.

---

[14] *Concupiscentia* in Latin and *epithumia* in Greek are roughly equivalent to 'desire' or 'craving.'

[15] Cf. DS 1512. We may already surmise that it is due to original sin that faith, hope, and charity appear to us as "accidents" (in Thomistic language), however exalted, rather than as part of our very substance—for they can come and go in our lives on earth while leaving what we ordinarily call our nature relatively intact.

The first of these questions can already receive a partial answer. Grave sin of any sort is an opposition to God that results in a privation of the divine life within us. Original sin meets easily enough the criterion of privation. It is the element of opposition to God that seems to be missing in it, since the infant's will is not opposed to Him.

In accord with the approach to the "mystery" of sin sketched above, I wish now to examine the internal structure of our intended participation in the divine life, considering it from that aspect which seems most radically the opposite of sin, i.e., the free and God-given, supernatural love of God and neighbor which is charity, since this is the true life of the soul without which even faith and hope are dead.

The divine love is not simply an external action of God upon His creatures, for God *is* love. This love that is the inner life of God is the life of the Father, Son, and Holy Spirit. Charity is our participation in the holiness and justice of God but, still more deeply, in the life of the Trinity. Charity, then, must have a structure that can only be adequately expressed in trinitarian terms.

Sin shows itself most sinful when it shows itself as resolute hostility to the Trinity. Original sin is just such a hostility, even though nonfree, within us: an abiding though unwilled opposition to the Trinity in our psychic structures, quite unbalanced by any countervailing action of grace.

The patterns of our being, as first created in Adam, made us exist wholly for the Father's glory in Christ. They included a connatural imprint of the divine love upon our physical being, and a dynamic structure of drives, passions, feelings, and emotions that would support and serve the action of charity.

All these psychic patterns have been inverted, reversed, turned inside out. Deformed into their contraries, they are dark now where they once were light. They are convex where they were concave. In each detail they are the antithesis of grace. Their inner dynamism has been so altered that, once we are old enough to act freely, they incline most of our choices toward sin. From before birth, our natural and spontaneous tendencies to love have become the exact inverse of the impulses of divine charity, inverses that cancel, trait by trait, our similarity on the created level to the uncreated love within the Trinity.

Such firm antagonism to the Triune God, built into the psychic traits of each individual, even though nonfree and incapable, in itself, of setting the will against God, at least by analogy well deserves the name of 'sin.'[16] At this point, if we are to know what original sin negates in enough detail to be of use to us later, we would do well to consider the basic teachings of our Lord on the matter. This we do in the rest of this chapter.

---

[16] That all this must be connected with a fundamental derangement of faith and hope is clear. The exact nature of this derangement, will be considered in *Ch* 6.

C. JESUS' TEACHING ON CHARITY

We turn now to consider the traits of created charity and begin with love of our neighbor—where the infant's love presumably first becomes active. But to deal with this, we shall need very quickly to move to the love of God within the Trinity.

Given the connection that both Jesus (Mt.22:39–40; Mk.12:31; Lk.10:28) and the Pharisees (Mk.12:33–34 and Lk.10:27) saw between the Great Commandment and that which "is like it" (Mt.22:39), our love for our neighbor should not only originate from and be caused by our love for God[17] but should in some way be like it in nature or in internal structure. But neither commandment describes the structure that is the basis of their likeness. It is, rather, in the sublime beauty of His discourse at the Last Supper with its concluding prayer to the Father that Jesus sets forth explicitly the nature and structure of charity and how love of neighbor should be related to love of God.

Yet the more carefully one reads His words, the harder it is to find a legitimate meaning for some of His statements. If we remember who is speaking and who His Father is, even if we take every mention by Jesus of Himself as referring to Himself only in His humanity, we must find the seeming incommensurability between what He commands us and what we, even with grace, seem capable of doing an incomprehensible paradox.

1. Thus, He says, "A new commandment I give to you, that you love one another; even as I have loved you, that you also love one another" (Jn.13:34); and again, with renewed emphasis, "This is my commandment, that you love one another as I have loved you" (15:12).

2. But He has told us how He loves us: "As the Father has loved me, so have I loved you" (15:9).

3. Finally, He speaks to the Father: "[You] have loved them even as You have loved me" (17:23).

4. Shifting His point of view from the action of love itself to its result in a union of persons, He prays, "Keep them in Your name, which You have given Me, that they may be one, even as We are one" (17:11); and again, "That they may all be one; even as You, Father, are in Me and I am in You, that they also may be in Us,...that they may be one even as We are one, I in them and You in Me, that they may become perfectly one" (17:21–23). So, also, "You will know that I am in my Father, and you in Me, and I in you" (14:20).

Is it really possible, even with grace, for any of us to love anyone else as Jesus loves each of us? As the Father loves Jesus? And can even the Father love *us* even as He loves His Son? The mind staggers; yet Jesus' words are meant for us and have a sense we are meant to grasp.[18]

---

[17] As, e.g., I Jn.4:7, 11, 21, makes explicit.

[18] Strictly, we should ask, "How did Jesus wish His apostles to love each other?" As will be

Evidently, there can be no question of comparable intensities in these loves or of comparable purities or comparable worths.[19] The love of the Father for the Son, or even for us, is incomparably greater in being and in intensity, in purity and in worth, than even the created sharing in that love that exists in Jesus' Heart. Yet this latter love is so great in comparison with the smallness of our loves that we find it hard to imagine how it can be less than the Father's.

In these statements of Jesus, the word "(even) as" (*kathōs* in Greek) is central.[20] The sense of the relation so designated is what we have to seek. *How* does the Father love His Son, His Son love us, and the love of charity extend from one of us to another?

One might reply, of course, that all these loves are mediated by, in, and through the Holy Spirit. But true though this is, it does not seem to be the point our Lord is making. He talks about the Spirit many times in this discourse, but only once in conjunction with a passage concerning charity.[21] Nor, with the same single exception, is *kathōs* used in connection with the Spirit or His action[22]—a use that might help us discover the relationship *kathōs*

---

seen later (418–419), serious misunderstandings have arisen from taking what Jesus said to His contemporaries as though said *to* us rather than *for* us. Justification for any such alteration of context must be provided any and every time it occurs. Here, given proper understanding of what He said, we need only find the structure of the love He commands the apostles in order to learn the structure of created charity itself. There is nothing in the apostolic office that would alter that basic structure.

[19] Raymond E. Brown, S.S., in *The Gospel according to John (xiii–xxi)*, (AB, vol. 29A), Garden City (NY): Doubleday (1970), rather too quickly compares or even conflates these loves and speaks of "intensity" with neither definition nor justifying argument. E.g., "The Father's love for Jesus is the basis for Jesus' love for his disciples both as to origin and intensity. The Son loves his disciples with the same divine love the Father has for him" (*p* 663). "In what way is Jesus' death for others held up as an example for (and the source of) the disciples' love? It is clearly to be a model of the *intensity* of their love, but I Jn.3:16 would seem to interpret it also as a model for the *way of expressing* love...[an understanding that] became one of the great justifications for the Christian martyrs" (*p* 682). One must suppose that Brown is referring to intensity as judged by actions since beyond laying down one's life in torment, as the Lord indicates in 15:13, there is no further intensification of external action possible. But to the inner intensity of Jesus' love, no reasonable comparison is possible.

[20] Brown, *op. cit.*: "For John *kathōs* is not only comparative but causative or constitutive, meaning 'inasmuch as'..." (*p* 663). "The 'as...so' construction sets up a parallelism between what the Father has done for Jesus and what Jesus does for the disciples." (*p* 762). "*kathōs* has both a comparative and a causative force here [17:21]...heavenly unity is both the model and the source of the unity of believers.... The model of unity is the mutual indwelling of Father and Son" (*p* 769).

[21] We shall see that St. Gregory of Nyssa takes Jn.17:22 as referring to the Holy Spirit as the bond of unity between the disciples. It would be quite proper, on this interpretation, to see *kathōs* there as implying that the Holy Spirit is the common element in the comparison and even its cause. But such passages as 15:10 make clear that this specificity of meaning comes, if at all, from the context and not from itself.

[22] If, as Gregory argued, *doxa* here refers to the Spirit, this only makes the comparison more paradoxical, as being based on the unity between Father and Son established by the giving of the

expresses. Rather, the Spirit is presented as One who is known, who teaches, reminds, witnesses, convinces and convicts, who, as the Spirit of truth, leads into all truth, announces future things, and declares what belongs to Christ. It is not our Lord but St. Paul (Rom.5:5) who speaks of the Holy Spirit as the one who pours out the love of God in our hearts.

As to a causative aspect,[23] this seems strong in 14:31, weak in 17:18, absent in 15:4, and as exemplary cause only in 15:10. But in all passages one finds a relation indicated by *kathōs* that arises from a comparison built on a likeness of structure between what the linked clauses (themselves usually in parallel) assert or deny.

I shall take it, then, that all uses of *kathōs* in this discourse are concerned with some sort of quasi-structural comparison. I shall argue that each love to which Jesus refers has an internal shape, form, or structure that makes it comparable with the others despite the far more obvious differences. When this task has been completed, we shall be able to say much more about how the ground of comparison involves mediation by the Holy Spirit and a common cause.

I have suggested that original sin is, on the psychic level, a trait-by-trait nullification of that created share in the life of the Trinity that is constituted by charity. It is necessary, then, to pause to consider what has been revealed to us concerning the inner life of the Trinity, inasmuch as this is the model and "form" for charity. This will be our study in Chapter 3. Secondly, since we go to the Father only through Jesus, we need to see how the loves of the three Persons are mediated to us by Jesus, something we shall look at in Chapter 4. Finally, we will be able in Chapter 5 to discover what the principal traits of charity are in ourselves. Only then (Chapter 6) will we be able to see concretely how original sin affects us, how it cancels out the traits of charity within us, and how it can, without violating anything due to our nature, yet damage our nature profoundly.

Holy Spirit.

[23] Cf. Brown, note 20 above.

Chapter 3

The Inner Structure of Uncreated Love

At this point, to discuss at length the intra-trinitarian structure of charity in order to learn more about original sin might seem to be using a cannon to shoot at sparrows. But before we finish, we will have abundant use for the cannon. Not only will it be important for the analysis of original sin towards which it is first directed, but we should keep in mind that whatever we learn of the Trinity is something learned about our final goal—for it is in the radiance of God's light that we shall see light and be given to drink from the river of His delights. Moreover, since our spiritual life is a sharing in that of Christ, the more aware we are of His relations to the Father and to the Holy Spirit, the more we can of set purpose follow Him and become like Him. I shall, then, turn at once to the Church's trinitarian doctrine, without attempting to derive it anew, and shall use it to see what more can be found of the inner structure of the divine Love Itself.

Among Western theologians, a particular psychological imagery, based on the processions of interior word and love, has come to overshadow all other ways of thinking of the Trinity. Marvellously developed by St. Thomas on the basis of some remarks of St. Augustine, it continued to develop in our own days through Lonergan's work. The imagery, also psychological, that Augustine himself preferred was that of a lover, his beloved, and the love between them. This, too, was developed and extended in the Middle Ages, especially by Richard of St. Victor. Richard substituted, however, for the love between the lover and his beloved, the presence of a friend of the beloved given by the lover lest their love be closed on itself. This current of thought also has continued to exert much influence till the present.[1]

In strong contrast, the careful language of the great ecumenical Councils of the Middle Ages used no psychological imagery at all. Why this should have been the case, I leave to historians of dogma. But the austerity of the conciliar texts is extremely helpful to anyone seeking to develop further imagery, since they highlight key elements of structure that must be found in any suitable image.

Yet given the importance of the mystery, strangely little has been done, at least in the West, in a strictly theological way with other sorts of images, many of which are found in great richness in the Eastern Fathers of the Church.[2] Their imagery, however, was left largely at the level of suggestiveness and intuitive insight. Not much was done by them, or by others since, in the way of systematic development of their insights.

Our concern with such development here will be governed entirely by the conviction that charity is the created reflection of the divine Love Itself and that what God has revealed concerning His own inner life must throw some light on the mysteries connected with our sharing that life. Our investigation will be focussed by the questions we have already indicated: Is there a "trinitarian structure," if one may so speak, that created charity possesses in virtue of its being a sharing in the uncreated Love? And since "God is love" (I Jn.4:8, 16), in what way, if any, could such a structure (i.e., the order of the Persons) be understood as a love between Them?

In Section I, I propose a way to see the "active" and "passive" generation of the Son as forms of Personal love. Then, emboldened by the relative ease of that task, I seek in Section II to carry out an analogous task concerning the Holy Spirit. This, however, calls for an effort to find some new imagery for the Holy Spirit still hidden in the Scriptures. Such imagery is pointed out by some remarks of St. Gregory of Nyssa. Then, guided by the medieval councils, we can see something of how the Spirit may be said to love the Father and the Son, and conversely. Finally, I discuss briefly such reasons as I can see why this imagery for the Spirit received so little attention from the Fathers. That done, in the following chapter I shall apply the insights gained to the structure of created charity, after which we will be ready to turn back to the

---

[1] One thinks here of Heribert Mühlen's earlier work in which he describes the Holy Spirit as subsistent We-Relation coming forth from the Father as subsistent I-Relation and the Son as subsistent You-Relation (*Der heilige Geist als Person,* 2nd ed., Münster: Aschendorff [1966]); or of Edmund Fortman's arguments for 'Friend' as Personal name for the Holy Spirit, in parallel with 'Father' and 'Son,' on the basis of a phrase of Augustine's and some development by Albert the Great (*Activities of the Holy Spirit,* Chicago: Franciscan Herald [1984], *pp* 175–183).

[2] The Scriptures offer us many images of the lesser mystery that is the Church. Often in seeming conflict, all are needed to describe her. Yet, they are not simultaneously applicable without generating objectively unfounded but still, for us, insuperable contradictions. Cf. II Vatican Council, *Lumen Gentium,* ##3–9. For the way in which such seemingly incompatible diversities are to be dealt with by the theologian, cf. Henri de Lubac, "How Is the Church a Mystery?", in *The Church: Paradox and Mystery,* tr. J. R. Dunne, Staten Island: Alba House (1969), *pp* 13–29, originally published as *Paradoxe et mystère de l'Église,* Paris: Aubier (1967). *A fortiori,* we may expect greater diversity of imagery concerning the mystery that underlies all others, the Trinity.

problem of original sin as the innate nullification of this structure.

A. The loves between Father and Son

At the center of trinitarian theology is the ancient doctrine of the *monarchia*, "the most august topic of the preaching of the Church of God," as Pope St. Dionysius called it (DS 112). All three Persons are not merely equal but absolutely one in all that pertains to the divine essence: majesty, wisdom, love, glory, power, and all other divine attributes. Yet there exists an order of origin, immanent within the Godhead, such that the Father is the sole First Principle, the sole Source, who has Himself no source or principle. Both Son and Holy Spirit proceed from Him; the Son, from Him alone; the Holy Spirit, from Him through the Son; each, therefore, ultimately from that sole unoriginated Principle from which all that is, in heaven or on earth, has its being.

Given this inner order of the Persons in the Godhead, then, since "God is love," we may speak of the Father as unoriginated Love; the Son, as originated Love; the Spirit, as Love breathed forth from both, from the Father through the Son. Yet there is but the one Love, the one inclination of the one divine will. Since one with the divine essence, this Love is common to all three Persons.

A love that is common to all, however, cannot be the love characteristic of any Person. For, *what* the Father is, is indistinguishable, even logically, from *what* the Son is and *what* the Spirit is. Each of the Persons, then, is that act of infinite Love.

Yet there does exist a perspective from which one may speak of a love for the Son that is characteristic of the Father, of the Son for the Father, of the Spirit for Both. Indeed, such a perspective is imposed upon us as soon as we consider our Lord's words at the Last Supper no longer in economic terms but immanently,[3] no longer as referring to His human nature only but to His Person. Any such love must, of course, as a Personal characteristic,[4] be definable ultimately in terms of *who* each Person is. And among the Persons, we recall, there can be no other distinctions than those of the structure or order of origination.

There is only one act of generating, and this belongs to the Father alone, not to the Son nor to the Spirit. There is but one act of breathing forth, which belongs to Father and Son but not to the Spirit. And so for all Personal characteristics. Since God is love, the question we need to address is, "In what way can one see, in the inner logical structure of each of these Personal

---

[3] Cf. R. E. Brown, *The Gospel according to John (xiii–xxi)*, (AB 29A: Garden City [NY]: Doubleday, 1970) 632.

[4] This term is awkward, and 'personal property' would be easier. But the latter has become a consecrated term for use solely of the relations of Paternity, Filiation, etc. What we are principally concerned with here, however, are what St. Thomas calls the *actus notionales*, e.g., generation or procession.

characteristics, a structure that of itself bespeaks love or has a structure that we can legitimately identify with love?" How, for example, do generation and spiration form two distinct kinds of love, each characteristic of the Father? True though it is that the Father is generative or unoriginated or spirative Love, nothing in "generative" or "unoriginated" or "spirative" of itself suggests love; yet it is in such adjectives that the structure of the divine Love must somehow be hidden.

It is not hard to show that what is "generative" has a logical structure that, with one proviso, is clearly identifiable as a type of love.[5] If one takes care that each of the Personal loves has exactly that relation of origin (and, all together, the same order) as the Persons themselves, no theological harm is done. One is doing no more ultimately than seeing under a new formal light the same characteristics that have long been known and accepted by all Christians.

But, in matters where language is so weak an instrument, it will be better to break off statements of purpose and show by the doing what I intend.

1. The Father's Love for the Son

The great medieval Councils give the basic statements concerning the generation of the Son by the Father. But though these Councils speak of the generation of the Son and of His being born, they translate these into a language of giving and receiving. Thus, the ecumenical Council of IV Lateran states: "The Father, by begetting the Son from eternity, has given His own substance to Him...[W]ithout any diminishment, the Son by being born has received the substance of the Father" (DS 805). The Father gives the divine nature in its fulness to the Son without its being thereby diminished in the Father. The whole divine nature is given to the Son; and the Son is God because He receives the one divine nature from the Father. The Son is identically *what* the Father is, but is not *who* the Father is.[6] The Father wills, then, the infinite Good, the Godhead itself which He Himself is, to the Son, in an act of total love, for among men the language of gift is a language of love.St. Thomas sets out this connection well:

> A gift, properly speaking, is 'a giving without a return'...that is, which is not given with an intention of some return; thus it involves a gratuitous handing over. The intelligible structure, however, of a gratuitous handing over is love; for on this account we give something gratuitously to someone, that we will some good for him. The first thing, therefore, that we give him is the love by which we will him the good.[7]

---

[5] Evidently, to speak of the Persons' characteristics as love, it is necessary always to assume, at least implicitly, a reference to the particular Person's willing of this characteristic. For generation, say, to be love, it must be an act that, whatever its logical structure, is willed or assented to by the One who generates. This guarantees, then, reference to the one will of the Three and their common love. Something similar is done by St. Thomas (in *ST* I, 45, 6 c) when he remarks: "[P]rocessiones Personarum sunt rationes productionis creaturarum, inquantum includunt essentialia attributa, quae sunt scientia et voluntas."

[6] *ST* I, 31, 2 ad 4.

One need add only that every gift is seen as a good not previously had by the recipient, though the love that motivates the gift is already directed to the recipient.

To love is to will what is truly good for the one beloved. But the Father wills to give all that belongs to Him, except to be Father, to the Son(cf. DS 1301). Since this gift contains the infinite goodness of the divine essence, the Father can be said truly, as Father, to love the Son. The goodness of the Son, then, by which He is equal to the Father, is a given goodness. The giving is logically prior to this goodness as it is in the Son; the Giver is its Source. Thus, this love is logically antecedent to the Son's worthiness of it; and the Recipient could not have it except by this gift.[8]

Since the Father's love for the Son is logically antecedent to the gift of the divine essence, which latter alone makes the Son worthy of the Father's love, it is clear that the Father's love is an unoriginated love. It is a love not stirred in response to some good other than the Father's. It does not have its origin in any way elsewhere. Nor is it drawn by an antecedent goodness of the Son. It involves no principle of origination other than the Father, and flows spontaneously only from the goodness of the Father Himself.

The Father begets the Son by giving Him all that the Father is[9] (except to be Father). As mentioned, then, the Father's willing for His Son of the good that is the divine nature is logically prior to the Son's being worthy of such love. Therefore, it is not inasmuch as the Son has the divine nature that the Father gives it but that the Son may have it. The good that is the divine nature in the Son is not logically antecedent to the Father's love but consequent upon it—if one may use such language so as to seek to express something of the intrinsic order of origin within God.

Thus the Father does not love the Son because the Son is good but the Father makes the Son good because He loves Him. The Father does not love the Son *because* the Son could in some way be thought to be and actually be infinite Goodness—hence infinitely worthy of the Father's love—anteced-

---

[7] *ST* I, 38, 2c

[8] "The divine essence is the gift which the Father gives to the Son," St. Thomas Aquinas, *ST* I, 38, 1, obj. 2, where he refers this doctrine back to St. Hilary's statement: "Major utique donans est, sed minor jam non est, cui unum esse donatur." Hilary's entire chapter, however, is concerned with this discussion of the gift and the giving of the glory of the Father to the Son, a glory we shall speak of later as "intrinsic glory." Thus, Hilary goes on to say: "Si autem in ea gloria donatur ei esse qua Pater est, habes et in donantis auctoritate quia major est, et in donati confessione quia unum sunt. Major itaque Pater Filio est. Et plane major, cui tantum donat esse, quantus ipse est." Sancti Hilarii Pictaviensis Episcopi, *De Trinitate* 9, 54. Ed. P. Smulders (CCL 62A), *p* 433. (PL 10, 325). So also, in *de Synodis* (PL 10, 520C): "Omnibus creaturis substantiam Dei voluntas attulit; sed naturam Filio dedit ex impassibili ac non nata substantia perfecta nativitas."

[9] This double "object" manifests the character of the act as love. Cf. e.g., St. Thomas' remark: "An act of love is always directed to two things, namely, to the good which one wills for someone and to him for whom one wills the good.... And to this extent, love is said to be a unitive force even in God.... For that good which He wills for Himself is not other than Himself, who is good by His own essence." *ST* I, 20, 1 ad 3.

ently to the Father's gift to Him. Rather, because the Father loves Him, therefore He constitutes Him Son.

It is this pattern of giving that defines the characteristic love of the Father. In loving the Son (though not freely) He chooses (albeit necessarily) to be One who makes the gift of all that He is to this Other. Inasmuch, then, as the Father gives, seeking no return other than that the gift be accepted, His act is, though not free, perfectly voluntary and gratuitous.

But this gratuity is not merely psychological, seeking no return. It is also metaphysical since, as in human generation, the Father gives existence to one who, therefore, has no antecedent claim whatever upon it. The Father loves before (in merely logical priority) there is any goodness present in the one loved that could coerce, draw, or even invite His love. Even, then, in the absolutely necessary love of the Father for the Son, one can discern the gratuity that love requires.

2. *The Son's Love for the Father*

The Son, also, "love[s] the Father" (Jn.14:31), with His human will indeed, and with the divine will in the love common to all the Persons; but He can also be said to love the Father with a love that is a personal characteristic of the Son. But in what way can mere reception be considered as love? Among men, to be begotten is a great good, but it is hardly love. What good is thus willed to the Father by the Son?

If He who is Father, the Unoriginated, is constituted Father only by His gift of His being to the Son, then He is Personally constituted only by the Son's reception of His gift of the divine essence—for a gift is formally a gift only insofar as it is received. Hence, the Son's will to receive the gift is a will that the Unoriginated be Father to Him. He wills to receive, even as the Father wills to give, the divine essence, so that the Unoriginated have the goodness of paternity and that He, the Son, be like His Father in everything except for origination.

As mentioned earlier, "by being born, the Son has received without any diminishment the substance of the Father."[10] Hence, the Son not only receives but chooses (though not freely) to receive all that He is without changing or altering it in any way. He seeks in no way to be different from His Father except by being His Father's Son, i.e., by receiving all, in perfect sameness except for what pertains to origination. The Son does not have or seek to have in or of Himself any independent root of being, neither independence of origin nor diversity of attribute. He wills this reception precisely in order that He be, consequently and not antecedently, a worthy Son of such a Father.

Humanly speaking, we may receive a gift in several ways. **a)** We may recognize it as contributing to our good, accept it accordingly, but regard it as no more than we deserve. **b)** Or we may receive what is given but refuse, for whatever motives, the love it implies. For we may consider this love as not genuine; we may see it, say, as an effort to resolve a dispute or to buy a favor

---

[10] IV Lateran (DS 805).

or to ingratiate the giver with us. Or we may sufficiently dislike or even hate the giver, so that we want no love from him no matter how genuine. **c)** Or we may receive the gift and the love that gives it but see this reception as also a humiliation, since it manifests that there was something we truly valued or desired that was both lacking to us and supplied by another who was, thus, in some way better than we. **d)** Finally, there is the reception we speak of as 'grateful acceptance.'

All but the last way of receiving a gift fail, on scrutiny, to be full acceptance of the gift as a gift. The first treats what is given as merited and, therefore, not as a gift at all but as one's due. The second way takes, in fact, not the gift but only the thing that is given, considering it either as being without the love that 'gift' implies or refusing that love as unworthy or rejecting it as from someone disliked. The third way may be a true reception of the gift; but it is an inadequate one. Too conscious of ourselves, we attend to other things than the giver and his gift. However much we prize the good that is given, we see our receiving of it as somehow an evil. The love that gives it is mistrusted or depreciated as insufficiently considerate, sensitive, or wise—for it has slighted our self-esteem.

That a gift be received, the recipient must be pleased both with the thing given and with the love of the giver, each in truth and right proportion, yet always both together. Thus, the love behind the gift may be much greater than the goodness-to-the-recipient of the thing given, which then serves chiefly as a token and sign of this love. Conversely, we know of gifts we prize but which came with relatively little love. Assuming right proportion, we can say that gratitude is an intrinsic and constitutive element in the acceptance of any gift. Without gratitude, no gift is ever truly accepted; only when suffused with gratitude can a receiving be regarded as full acceptance of a gift.

The response, then, of Him who is Son to the gift of the divine essence is, as perfect acceptance of this infinite and perfect gift, an infinite gratitude. He receives the divine essence as wholly His own and as possible for Him only as gift, and accepts the characteristic love that the Giver of His being has for Him. But gratitude has the form or structure of love, since one way of willing another's good is to be pleased with his goodness as expressed in his gift.

Perfect gratitude does nothing to change or alter the gift, for the gift represents the giver. And one who accepts another's love, loves this other. One accepts the Giver's estimate of what the gift should be, hence, of what is good for oneself and of the goodness of his love for one.

But the will to accept a gift is logically prior to its being received. Hence, the Son wills to receive the gift antecedently to His having any good, while still "unworthy" *in signo primo* of the Father's love. Thus, He accepts as one who has no claims on the Giver, for He has nothing to offer of His own. He can do no more than receive. He cannot make a return in kind. He has no way to offer a gift in return, because to give the divine essence is precisely to be Father, not Son.[11]

Though the Son's will to accept is logically prior to the actual acceptance, this will to accept is not antecedent to the gift's being offered. Therefore the Son's acceptance is, as just described, taken in relation to the Son; yet it must also be consequent upon the Father's goodness in giving and upon the goodness of what is given.

Willingly to receive oneself from another, then, is an act of love; and the Son loves the Father *as* His Son, i.e., as One defined by His receiving of His whole being directly from the Father.

B. The Love of the Spirit: the Glory of Father and Son

The conciliar texts say far less about the Holy Spirit than about the Father and the Son; and the information they give about the procession of the Spirit is not comparable to what they give about the generation of the Son. The language used is singularly colorless. Apart from the Scriptural "proceeds," the Councils use only such words as "has" or "is from." Moreover, some of what is said about the Spirit serves only to manifest an equivalence of meaning underlying a diversity of language.[12] Elsewhere, what is stated is merely negative, denying that the Spirit proceeds as from two principles or by two spirations.[13] Such statements are important for what they show of structure of relationships between the Persons, but shed very little light on the inner nature of the Spirit's procession.

The conciliar language does serve, however, to underline the fact that the personal characteristic of the Spirit is to proceed. Though mentioning (active) "spiration" as personal characteristic of Father and Son,[14] the Councils go out of their way through careful circumlocution to avoid any positive utilization of this notion.[15] (Passive) "spiration" seems nowhere to be used of the Spirit, any apparent ambiguity on this point in Florence[16] being removed by

[11] I would now wish to alter what I wrote in *The Christian Meaning of Human Sexuality*, *pp* 62–63, concerning the Trinity, where I used "gift" and its cognates of the Persons indiscriminately. A better statement, I think, can be found in Joseph A. Bracken, *What Are They Saying About the Trinity?*, New York: Paulist (1979), *p* 17. As he indicates on *p* 22, however, there are some serious weaknesses even in his formulation.

[12] "[Q]uod...Patres dicunt, ex Patre per Filium procedere Spiritum Sanctum, ad hanc intelligentiam tendit, ut per hoc significetur Filium quoque esse secundum Graecos quidem causa, secundum Latinos vero principium subsistentiae Spiritus Sancti sicut et Patrem" (DS 1301). This is to be taken, of course, in conjunction with DS 1300; cf. infra note 16.

[13] "Spiritus Sanctus aeternaliter ex Patri et Filio, non tanquam ex duobus principiis, sed tanquam ex uno principio, non duabus spirationibus, sed unica spiratione procedit" (II Lyons, DS 850).

[14] Cf. II Lyons, ibid.

[15] E.g., "Spiritus Sanctus ex Patre et Filio aeternaliter est, et essentiam suam suumque esse subsistens habet ex Patre simul et Filio" (DS 1300). Or again, "Et quoniam omnia, quae Patris sunt, Pater ipse unigenito Filio suo gignendo dedit, praeter esse Patrem, hoc ipsum quod Spiritus Sanctus procedit ex Filio, ipse Filius a Patre aeternaliter habet, a quo etiam aeternaliter genitus est" (DS 1301). And again, "Spiritus Sanctus quidquid est aut habet, habet a Patre simul et Filio" (DS 1331).

[16] "[E]x utroque aeternaliter tamquam ab uno principio et unica spiratione procedit" (Florence,

reference to the earlier and uncontested assertion in II Lyons.[17] Hence procession must be the characteristic love that we seek.

Now, the theological difficulties attendant on the procession of the Spirit are notorious. Apart even from the dispute over the *Filioque*, there is the problem of distinguishing the procession of the Spirit from the generation of the Son. The *words* are different. But since each action has the Father as Source and terminates in a distinct Person who has the whole of the divine essence, giving the words a different content has not been easy, except for the fact of some type of mediation by the Son in the procession of the Spirit.

Closely connected to this problem are the questions concerning the logical order of the constitution of the Persons. Why, for example, must spiration take place "after" rather than "before" or even "along with" generation?[18] Or, since the Unoriginated cannot be said, precisely inasmuch as He is Father, to love the Spirit (or He could not give this power to the Son), is there any way to speak of a characteristic love of the Father for the Spirit or of the Son for the Spirit or of the Spirit for either?

More positive content for the conciliar statements and the further insight needed for dealing with the above difficulties would seem to be obtainable only from a return to the other revealed designations for, or names of, the Holy Spirit. 'Holy Spirit' must remain, in my judgment, the principal name for the Third Person. But there seems to be no reason not to supplement what we already know by quarrying further in what God has given us for our profit.

In this part, then, I shall try to show that there is another name for the Spirit, given in the Scriptures and known to the Fathers (though singularly little used by them for reasons we shall have to consider), that enables us to offer somewhat fuller answers to the questions mentioned.

What we need for our present purposes especially is:

a) a designation that clearly relates to the Third Person;

b) that relates to His existence in the bosom of the Trinity (prior, that is, to His being sent);

c) that implies clearly His distinction from the Father and the Son by relations of origin in mutual opposition;

d) that shows procession under an aspect other than those mentioned by the Councils; and

e) such that this aspect may rightly be seen as a characteristic love belonging to the Holy Spirit and that, by oppositional relation, points to a correlative love belonging to the Father and the Son, united as one principle.

The designation 'Holy Spirit' or simply 'Spirit' meets the first three

---

DS 1300)

[17] Cf. note 13.

[18] Cf. the theory of Francois-Xavier Durrwell, (*Holy Spirit of God: an essay in biblical theology*, tr. Sr. B. Davies, OSU, London: Geoffrey Chapman [1986], *pp* 140–148) where he seems to attempt to justify this last position, insisting that "The entire activity of the Father is to beget the Son.... *He [the Spirit] must therefore be this begetting.... He is the begetting*" (*pp* 140–141).

requisites easily. For, the Spirit (τὸ Πνεῦμα, that is, the Breath) proceeds from (ἐκπορεύεται, Jn.15:26) the Father. This procession constitutes a personal characteristic of the Spirit, founding a "*relationis oppositio.*" For, whatever proceeds from or goes forth from is distinct by relational opposition from that from which it proceeds; and the Breath stands in relational opposition to the Breather.

The fourth requisite merely states what we are looking for, since the Councils use 'Holy Spirit' but no other name. As to the fifth, it is hard to see that one may speak usefully of loving one's own breath, still more if this is shared, e.g., as one breath from two nostrils, or as one breathing forth from the lungs through the nose, or even in artificial respiration, in a sort of criss-cross, the breathing-out of one being the breathing-in of the other.

St. Paul makes clear, of course, that 'spirit' often means the intelligent, immaterial, but substantial principle of life, especially when speaking of the Holy Spirit (e.g., I Cor 2:11). If the spirit is not equivalent to the person, it is at least the principle by which he is a person. Now, one does love one's life, one's own soul (cf. I Sam 18:1 & 3 concerning Jonathan's love for David). So, this analogy might be helpful for active spiration. But how would it avail for procession? Does one's life love one? Or a person's soul love the person? Indeed, the going forth of the spirit suggests death, not life.[19]

1. Gregory of Nyssa: the Spirit Is Glory

In one of his minor works, St. Gregory of Nyssa argues briefly that the Spirit is called 'glory' by our Lord in His prayer to the Father at the Last Supper (in Jn.17:5):

> I think that He there [Jn.17.22] calls the Holy Spirit 'glory,' (that Spirit) which He gave to the disciples through His breathing on (them). For there is no other way for those who are divided from one another to be made one if not conjoined by the oneness of the Spirit...[Rom 8:9]. But the Spirit is the glory, as He says elsewhere to the Father, "Glorify me with the glory which I had from the beginning beside You before the world was". For God the Logos, having before the world the glory of the Father, since in the last days He became flesh, it was necessary for the flesh, through compenetration by the Word, to become that which the Word is.[20] But this happens from the taking of that which before the world the Word had. But this was the Holy Spirit, for there was nothing else before the ages except Father, Son, and Holy Spirit.[21]

---

[19] Thus Jesus "delivered up the spirit" {Jn.19:30} and "He sent forth the spirit" {Mt.27:50}. In the other Gospels, the less expressive "ex-spired" is used, but with the same association.

[20] There is an interesting parallel to this sentence in St. Hilary: "The Son, now made flesh, was praying that the flesh might begin to be to the Father what the Word (is); so that that which was temporal might receive the glory of that brightness which is apart from time, so that the corruption of the flesh might be absorbed into the power of God and transformed by the incorruption of the Spirit." But this is followed by examples that seemingly tie it entirely to the created order. Cf. *De Trinitate* 3, 16, *p* 88.

[21] *Opera Dogmatica Minora, II*, "In Illud Tunc et Ipse Filius," ed. J. K. Downing, (GN 3/2, 1987), *pp* 21–22 (PG 44, 1320D)

Toward the end of the last of his great sermons on *The Song of Songs*, Gregory again remarks that the Spirit is called 'glory' by our Lord in Jn.17:5 & 22.[22]

> But the bond of this oneness is 'the glory'. But that the Holy Spirit is called 'glory' no one would deny who reflects upon the Lord's own words, 'for the glory,' He says, 'which You gave to Me, I gave to them' [Jn.17:22]. For, of a truth, the One saying to them 'Receive the Holy Spirit' gave to the disciples such glory. But He received this glory, which He always had before the world was, when He was clothed about by human nature. Once (this nature) had been glorified through the Spirit, the glory of the Spirit was distributed to all those of the same (nature), beginning with the disciples.

Now, in contrast to Gregory's undeveloped and somewhat casual interpretation of Jn.17:5, we find carefully, even elaborately wrought arguments in St. Hilary and St. Augustine for very different interpretations. Further, this same *v* 17:5 is simply unmentioned by Gregory in his major works on the Trinity, by St. Gregory of Nazianzen in his *Theological Discourses*, and by St. Basil in his *Treatise on the Holy Spirit*. Nor apart from two very minor allusions, to be mentioned below, does St. Augustine comment upon it in his *de Trinitate*. Leaving till later an attempt to understand such strange facts, here let us simply take our cue from the passages from Gregory of Nyssa cited above and examine the relevant portion of Jesus' prayer (Jn.17:1–5) in detail.

2. *The Glory that Jesus Desired*

An obvious parallelism exists between the beginning of Jesus' prayer in Jn.17:1–5 and the beginning of His discourse in Jn.13:31–32.[23] In the latter, to judge from both its own content and its context, the glory in question arises from the Lord's suffering and death in their ordering to His resurrection and ascension. Through the preaching of the Church, the salvation He has wrought is made known to all the world, and this redounds to the glory of the Father, made known in the fulness of His love for men. But this passage refers as well, and principally, to the Father's seating Jesus beside Himself at His right hand on the throne of His glory (Mt.25:31, with Rev 3:21), so that Jesus as King might bring all things to the Father—a Johannine parallel to 1 Cor 15:24–28. Our question here is to what extent these understandings apply to 17:1–5.

The parallelism mentioned above is evident. In both passages, Jesus indicates the singular nature of the present moment, speaks of His being glorified in it in order that the Father be glorified, and then speaks of the Father glorifying Him in return. In both, the language, simple as it is, gains special solemnity and elevation by our Lord's extensive referring to Himself in the third person instead of the first.[24]

---

[22] *In Cantica Canticorum*, ed. Hermann Langerbeck, Oratio XV, (GN 6, 1960), *p* 467.

[23] This parallelism takes on special importance in St. Hilary's treatment of our passage.

[24] Between 13:32 and 17:1 there is only one instance of this stylistic trait (a fleeting reference to "the Son" in 14:13), a trait we shall look at in more detail below.

Yet despite these and other parallels between these passages,[25] the differences are major:

a) In 13:31–32, Jesus speaks of Himself only as the "Son of man"; in chap 17, only as "(Your) Son."

b) In chap 13, the Son of man has just now been glorified; in 17, the Son speaks of "the hour" that has come and requests that He be glorified as a result.

c) "God" glorifies the Son of man; the "Father" is to glorify His Son.

d) God is glorified *in* the Son of man;[26] in chap 17, the Son glorifies the Father.

e) In chap 13, glorification has just taken place or is to do so in the immediate future; in chap 17, Jesus' glorification lies in an indefinite future, not on earth.[27]

Even the solemnizing use of the third person instead of the first differs significantly in the two passages.

Jesus often, even habitually, spoke of Himself in the third person. In the majority of cases, He did so by speaking of Himself as "Son of Man," far the most common of the third-personal self-designations scattered throughout all the Gospels. In the Synoptics, though rarely, He also spoke of Himself as "Bridegroom" (Mk.2:19–20), "your Lord" (Mt.24:42), "the King" (Mt.25:34, 40), "Son (of God)" (Mk.9:7; cf. also Mk.14:61–62, Mt.26:63–64), and, of particular interest here, "Christ" (Mt.23:10 with the article, Mk.9:41 without the article).

This use of third-personal designations, while giving His ordinary speech a characteristic objectivity and calm elevation of tone, serves two other purposes as well. In some places Jesus seems to speak this way for the discomfiture of His enemies, to assert things of Himself certain to make them bristle yet which they cannot accuse Him of saying of Himself unless they make manifest that they have fully understood what He has been saying to them. His references to Himself before Caiaphas are examples of this usage. In other places (or sometimes the same ones) He speaks in this way when saying things that He wishes to be matters of public record or things to be made part of the preaching of His followers. His calling Himself "Son" in the baptismal formula of Mt.28:19 is an example.

For the most part these designations are separated from one another by references to Himself in the first person. When He does make use of this trait of style *in extenso*, He seems to wish to emphasize the solemn gravity of the

---

[25] Cf., e.g., Brown, *John*, 745.

[26] This peculiar locution occurs nowhere else in this Gospel; cf. Brown, *John*, 606. Of itself, it would seem a common hebraism, better translated as 'by.' Yet it seems to be a sign that the glorification spoken of is at the created level; cf. what is said below (*pp* 38, 57–59) about Augustine's notion of the glorification of the Father and Jesus among men.

[27] Many other passages, e.g., Jn.12:23, make clear that such differences cannot be pressed independently of context; our purpose here is only to avoid neglect of differences and unjustifiable conflation.

message. So, with the account of His Second Coming (Mt.24:27–31, 36–44) and the Judgment of the nations (Mt.25:31–46). John reports the same usage, but in cases where its use *in extenso* seems based on the loftiness of the content rather than, as in the Synoptics, on its awesome fearfulness.[28]

In Jn.13:31–32 at the beginning of the great discourse, Jesus refers to Himself not as "Me" or "I" but only as "the Son of man," resumed five times by the third-personal pronoun. Similarly, in 17:1–3, He refers only to "your Son" and "the Son." Then, after four third-person pronominal forms referring to Himself, this usage reaches its climax in *v* 3, when He refers to Himself by name and title, "that they may know...Him whom You have sent, Jesus Christ."[29]

Yet how strikingly different is the effect in the opening *vv* of chap 17! Their singular power (again considering only this one feature of His manner of speech) comes from our Lord's using the second person to speak to the Father with the utmost of familiarity and tenderness while yet, in profound reverence before Him, referring to Himself in the third person. This contrast, to my knowledge, is found nowhere else in any of the Gospels.

The prayer begins simply yet solemnly, "Father, the hour has come; glorify your Son that the Son may glorify You" (17:1). Verse 2 (concerning the Son's mission to make eternal life available to all flesh) and *v* 3 (specifying what eternal life is) both serve to make clear that the glorifying of which He speaks is indeed to be accomplished among men. The third-personal self-references indicate not only a content of sublime importance, as mentioned above, but also that what He is saying is, in one form or another, to be part of His disciples' future teaching.

Abruptly and with the emphasis provided by explicit use of the personal pronoun, Jesus returns to the first person: " *I* glorified You upon earth, having accomplished the work that You gave Me to do." He has anticipated the morrow's sacrifice in the Eucharist just established (cf. the possible echoes in Jn.19:28, 30 of the accomplishment, completion, or fulfilment mentioned here).[30] He has already glorified the Father upon earth; that task is, in principle, finished. He is now looking forward to His glorification at the right hand of the Father.

Jesus continues in the first person (*v* 5) with a peculiar intensity of

[28] Note especially the long passage Jn.5:19–23, 25–29. The reference throughout is to "the Son," except for once explicitating that He is "the Son of God," and one comment that He is also "Son of man."

[29] One may wonder if it is not the influence of this unforgettable sentence that led St. Paul and early Christians generally to call our Lord "Jesus Christ" by preference, rather than "Jesus, *the* Christ," which would seem the expression of greatest utility in preaching, especially to their fellow Jews. In any case, in the light of Jesus' typical manner of self-reference, this naming of Himself, though extraordinary, is not out of character or implausible, given the extraordinary nature of this whole prayer, despite the opinion of some that this line must be a later insertion, e.g. Brown, *John*, 741. Cf., however, C. K. Barrett, *The Gospel according to St. John*, 2nd ed., Philadelphia: Westminster (1978), 503–504.

[30] Cf. Barrett, *Gospel* 553.

longing. "And now, Father, do You glorify Me alongside Yourself (i.e., in your presence, beside and with Yourself) with the glory which I had alongside You before the world was." He yearns to be with the Father; yet He expresses this indirectly. What He asks for directly is that the Father glorify Him along with Himself (the Father) with the glory that He (Jesus) had before the world began. No longer is it a matter of being glorified Himself that He may then glorify the Father; the glory He is homesick for belongs eternally to the Father also.

Whatever interpretation one may offer for the first clause of this verse, the remainder requires an interpretation that satisfactorily answers the question: "What glory did Jesus have with the Father before the world began?"

Though we shall see that Hilary and Augustine both have difficulty in finding a satisfactory answer to this question, modern commentators, like most of those before them, expound the text as its stands and pass quietly by the theological problem thus presented. Brown says little on the point, but cites two translations he seems to regard as competent, pointing out that they "refer to pre-creation glory in the fellowship of the Father and the Son," and then asks, "Does this imply that the glory that Jesus has after his exaltation in the flesh will be the same as the glory he had before the incarnation?" This he leaves unanswered; but his unhappiness at the prospect of an affirmative answer would indicate that he sees the problem.[31] Barrett takes the verse in much the same sense but without hesitation: "παρὰ σεαυτῷ, that is, by causing me to return to the position I enjoyed before the incarnation."[32]

Now, as Gregory of Nyssa argued, since the Son had this glory before creation and since all that He has comes from the Father, this glory of the Son proceeds eternally from the Father. But this glory cannot be the glory that is the divine nature itself, i.e., the common glory of all three Persons. For, this is not something that Jesus lacks as God nor that His humanity is capable of receiving, *pace* St. Hilary.[33]

Nor was it the *lumen gloriae* that He sought. For this stands in essentially the same relationship to His human nature as to ours. He was to be given the complete enjoyment of the *lumen gloriae* (if He did not already have it);[34] but so are we in our small measure. Yet we cannot make this part of His prayer our own. This glory that pre-exists the world is identifiable neither with the

[31] Brown, *John*, 742–743. In his more general comments, he is quite explicit: "[T]he glory that Jesus requests is identified with the glory that Jesus had with the Father before the world existed" 753.

[32] Barrett, *Gospel*, 504. The glory in question is, for Barrett, not the Holy Spirit (*pp* 500–501) but what I shall call Christ's "intrinsic glory," as is clear from his comment on *v* 17:24, "This means the glory of Christ within the Godhead, his glory as God" (514). Brown states that there is no reference in chap 17 to the Holy Spirit (*John* 741). Yet, though his remarks referred to above (743) suggest that he also takes the pre-creation glory as "intrinsic glory," it seems that all his comments explicitly concerned with 17:5 could be also interpreted in accord with the identification of the Spirit as the Glory.

[33] Cf. *pp* 56–57 below. This seems to be Barrett's error also—cf. note 32.

[34] Cf. DS 3645

Father nor the Son, but is that by which the Father glorifies the Son along with Himself.

To paraphrase *v* 5 under Gregory's interpretation, I would suggest this: "And now, do You, Father, let Me be made glorious in my humanity alongside Yourself by the Holy Spirit, who is that Glory which I had with You eternally as Son before the world was." The making glorious of the humanity here relates to the Spirit's part in Jesus' enthronement and the Spirit's work in the world as He glorifies both Father and Son among men.

It is not hard to see the plausibility of Gregory's identification of this glory with the Holy Spirit. There is but the one glory, of the Father and the Son alike, as there is but the one Holy Spirit, who proceeds from the Father (15:26) but whom the Son had alongside the Father before creation. If this glory that the Son has eternally belongs to the divine nature, then His humanity cannot long for it or receive it. But if the glory is another divine Person, neither Father nor Son, then the humanity can be glorified with this Glory in whatever way it is intrinsically capable of being glorified while also the Son is glorified according to His divinity within the Godhead. Our problem will then be to discern something of this latter glorification.[35]

But if one accepts the identification of the Spirit with the glory that Jesus desired, the question remains, "What can possibly be meant by 'glory' in this context?" The most obvious meanings are already excluded. 'Glory' here cannot mean the intrinsic glory of the Godhead. Neither can it mean some merely created glory—though this was Augustine's opinion, who drew "from the ancients" the definition: "Glory is someone's widespread and laudatory reputation"[36] and applied it in his commentary on Jn.17:1–5 both to the glory the blessed offer God in heaven and to the glory given Him in the present age.

St. Basil the Great, however, in an important passage suggests that the sort of laudatory glory favored by Augustine might indeed have an eternal and uncreated counterpart. Basil begins by noting:

> [The Spirit of Christ] alone worthily glorifies the Lord. For "He will glorify Me," He [Jesus] says, not as creation [does], but as "the Spirit of truth," clearly making the truth shine forth in Himself and, as Spirit of wisdom, revealing in His own majesty the Christ, the power of God and the wisdom of God. And as Paraclete, He expresses in Himself the goodness of the Paraclete who sent Him, and in His own dignity He manifests the grandeur of Him from whom He came forth. There exists, then, one glory which is natural, as light is the glory of the sun; another which is extrinsic, judiciously offered by deliberate choice to those thought worthy.

---

[35] Confirmation of the identification of the Spirit with glory can, I think, be found in a number of NT passages e.g., Rom.3:23; 6:4 with 8:11; Eph.1:14; Rev.11:11, But the theologically helpful results of this identification seem to me more likely to open one to conviction than too quick a rehearsal of scriptural passages taken in a new or forgotten interpretation. In any case, I am concerned here only to make plausible Gregory of Nyssa's suggestion, not to try to nail it down irrefutably.

[36] "[F]requens de aliquo fama cum laude," *In Johannis*, Tract. 105, *p* 605.

Basil indicates that the glory he is speaking of does not lie solely in the created world, not only by his negative reference to creation but by designating the Spirit's office as "another Paraclete" as an expression of the goodness of Christ and the grandeur of the Father in a manner that is interior or intrinsic to Himself.

Then, having distinguished clearly between intrinsic ("natural") and laudatory ("extrinsic") glory, he goes on to divide the latter into a "servile" glory, given by creation, and a "familial" one given by the Spirit.

> This [laudatory glory] also is twofold. For, "a Son," [Malachy] says, "glorifies His Father, and a slave his Lord." Of these two, therefore, the servile glory is rendered by the creation; that glory which is, might I so speak, familial is brought to fulness by the Spirit.[37]

In view of the carefully designed parallelism of the third sentence, one might at first assume that, as the creation is the agent of the servile glory as it brings its praises before its Lord, so the Spirit would be the agent of familial glory, the Glorifier within the Godhead.[38] Such an interpretation, however, would destroy the initial assertion that it is the Son who glorifies His Father.

Rather, though creation 'renders' or 'proffers' the servile glory, the very different word ἐκπληροῦται is used to say what is done by the Spirit. When the Son glorifies (δοξάζει) the Father, He does so in a familial manner, in contradistinction to all created activity; therefore, within the Trinity, by means of the Spirit. Thus, the role of the Spirit is that of Glory. The Son laudatorily glorifies the Father with a glory that is 'filled up,' 'fulfilled,' or even 'constituted' by the Spirit.

What Gregory, who was Basil's brother, did was to argue that it was of *this* glory that Jesus was speaking in His prayer; and Basil's explanation of Jn.16:13–14[39]—the Son glorifying the Father with the eternal Glory that is the Spirit—may be seen as reciprocal to Gregory's interpretation of Jn.17:5.

3. *Glory as Relational: Human Glory*

But a question remains: can 'glory' be used relationally at all, in such manner that it could, in principle at least, be used of One of the three Persons without including the Others?

What does one man do who 'glorifies' another? What is human 'glory'? Unfortunately, in our day these words, like 'honor' and 'piety,' have undergone a great denaturing and fallen from use almost completely except in religious contexts. So, it will not be out of place to examine more carefully just what 'glory' and 'glorification' signify. 'Glory' may be defined as a superlative

---

[37] Διπλῆ δὲ καὶ αὕτη. Υἱὸς γὰρ, φησὶ, δοξάζει Πατέρα, καὶ δοῦλος τὸν Κύριον αὐτοῦ. Τούτων τοίνυν ἡ μὲν δουλικὴ παρὰ τῆς κτίσεως προσάγεται· ἡ δὲ, ἵν' οὕτως εἴπω, οἰκειακὴ, παρὰ τοῦ Πνεύματος ἐκπληροῦται. Basile de Césarée, *Traité du Saint-Esprit*, (SC 17, ed. B. Pruche, Paris: Éditions du Cerf, 1946), *c* 18, 46, *pp* 195–196.

[38] So Pruche seems to understand the passage in his translation, ibid.

[39] The context, it is true, mixes together both created and uncreated glories, but does so only in the effort to show the uncreated nature of "the Spirit of Christ."

fame and renown for one's excellence, issuing from admiration and praise that are universal among those who know of and are competent to judge of this excellence—what belongs to one "when all men speak well of you" (Lk.6:26).[40] Linguistically, this meaning is the most basic one, from which the others we shall discuss are derived.

If, then, one person is to glorify another, (i.e., to be the source of his glory in the laudatory sense just defined) he must first perceive the intrinsic excellence and goodness of the other. This excellence is also oftentimes called 'glory' (I shall refer to it as 'intrinsic' or 'nonrelational' glory). Evidently, one may 'glorify' someone with this glory also, by being the source of the excellence for which he is glorified in the laudatory sense.

The images characteristic of this nonrelational, substantive glory seem by preference related to external splendor, brilliance, and radiance. What is glorious manifests its excellence by its splendor. For, its goodness must be seen or perceived by the eye or the mind. The substantive glory of objects of great value, such as a gold, gems, or crowns, so long associated with kingship, make the association easy enough to understand.

The one who glorifies responds to this perceived excellence by exulting in it and declaring, to himself and to any and all who will listen, its goodness and greatness. Glorification, then, results from a non-selfreflective impulse of appreciation and from an awareness of what is excellent as excellent, without any concern for oneself by way of comparison. One praises a good man for his perceived goodness alone. Yet by this praise, one becomes a better man oneself.

This exultation in the excellence perceived is expressed in English (but not in Greek) by another cognate: 'to glory in' the perceived excellence of another.[41] 'Glorying in' is the necessary paroxysm of the glorifier's love of goodness that brings into being the praise and fame that constitute this relational glory. To glorify someone, then, is exultantly to proclaim his excellence, precisely as his own, or joyfully to give credit and honor to him for his prowess or splendor, of action or of being.

If the same excellence is perceived in more than one person, so that it is not seen as unique to the one who is being glorified but as shared with others, then either it belongs to the one being glorified in a way not found in the others or else the glorifier will glory equally in this same excellence in each. But he will still glorify any one of these persons with a glory other than that of the others. For, one does not glorify someone's excellence but glorifies *him* for this excellence.[42]

---

[40] Since among men such glory may be to greater or lesser degree hollow, as is implied in this remark of our Lord's, no corresponding excellence being truly present, there is a parallel usage that implies this hollow fame, especially where it has been sought or promoted by the person being praised. The fuller term is 'vainglory', i.e., *vana gloria*, empty glory. This pejorative usage we shall not need to consider further.

[41] One glories only in someone's excellence, but not in him.

[42] Some qualifications to this paragraph will be needed. Cf. *pp* 46–49 below.

Glorification requires that one man perceive the exalted excellence of another (his intrinsic or substantive glory) and esteem it and praise it as such. Hence, the one who glorifies must be capable of a true and sound judgment about this excellence, if the glory he offers is not to be vainglory. Conversely, one's praising of another's excellence is logically consequent upon the glorifier's being illumined and irradiated by the splendor that is the nonrelational glory of the one being glorified.[43]

Glorification is formally such only when one's glorying-in 'comes forth,' i.e., ceases to be private and merely one's own so as to become public, i.e., fame. The glorifier praises to others, perhaps also to the one being glorified, the latter's intrinsic goodness and greatness. Glory is what results. Relational or laudatory glory, therefore, exists only in the act or process of glorification, even as does thought, which exists only in its activity.

Thus, laudatory glory is not like a gift, i.e., a thing, something substantive. So, when one speaks of "giving (laudatory) glory" to someone, it is not a handing over of something pre-existent or logically prior. "Giving glory to" is either synonymous with 'glorifying' or signifies a permission to glorify others on the same grounds as oneself, to share in one's fame or in the excellence at its base (cf. Is 42:8; 48:11, "I will not give My glory to another.")

Obviously, glory can be reciprocal, i.e., the one glorified can glorify his glorifier while the latter is glorifying him. If the excellences in each are of the same kind, the glories given by each to the other could in principle also be the same.

To sum up, if one man glorifies another, 'glorify' means either that (i) the glorifier gives the person glorified a certain excellence that, insofar as manifest, makes him glorious and henceforth shines out from him; or that (ii) he perceives and truly appreciates the other's excellence, glories in it, and so proclaims it to himself and to others. The activity of glorification is intrinsic to the glorifier; the glory, however, is not, but proceeds from the glorifier, though subsisting in his activity as its connatural effect, especially insofar as conjoined to the glory given the same person by others. Glory, obviously, is also other than the one glorified, neither part of him nor in him.

Correspondingly, 'glory' refers either (a) to the manifestation of someone's intrinsic but splendidly manifest excellence; (b) to this excellence in itself; (c) to the state of affairs resulting from the enthusiastic appreciation and praise of his excellence by others. One notes that this appreciative or laudatory glory of someone exists only relationally, i.e., it does not exist as his possession or property but it subsists in the actions of others in a particular relation of praise to some excellence in him. This excellence itself is his glory in sense (b), a nonrelational or substantive glory. His glory in sense (a) is the radiant shining forth or effulgence that manifests his proper excellence, called glorious because of this radiance.

---

[43] The element or aspect of praise in glorifying is necessary to distinguish it from a simple manifestation of goodness, which could be made to others without any of the personal involvement required for praise and glory.

4. Glory as Relational: Divine Glory

The same three notions of 'glory' recur in the Scriptures, along with the following, strictly religious enrichments:

(A) 'Glory' is an overwhelming brilliance and splendor, especially that which is the characteristic manifestation of the divine presence.[44]

(B) Often 'glory' is taken as the glorious being itself. Thus, the angels are called "glories" {Jd 8; II Pet 2:10}. More frequently, "glory" refers directly to the LORD Himself, to God. 'Glory' in this latter sense is proper to the Godhead as such. Since proper to the divine essence, this glory is nonrelational. Many passages in both OT and NT use this sense only. The same is true of liturgical usage.

(C) Thirdly, 'glory' as widespread renown among men of the LORD's excellence, is common in both Testaments. In the New, especially in John's Gospel, it refers, as St. Hilary and St. Augustine emphasize, to the acknowledgment of Jesus by all the world, angels as well as men, as Christ and LORD through His incarnation and, most especially, by His crucifixion, resurrection, and ascension; hence, to creatures' consequent praise and adoration of the Father.

One sees, despite the difference of imagery involved, that glory in sense (C) results from the recognition and praise of the intrinsic glory of sense (B), perceived through the radiant glory of sense (A). Glory in senses (A) and (B) is, then, in some way, substantive, belonging to or being itself the glorious; whereas notion (C) involves a relationship with others who recognize and respond properly to the excellence that constitutes the glorious one as such.[45]

But radiant glory (sense (A)) is relational as well as substantive, since it shines forth from what is glorious and, so, is distinguished from the glorious by a relational opposition, as coming forth from it. This relationality of radiant glory is to be carefully distinguished from that belonging to laudatory glory (sense (C)). This latter is relational only. It proceeds not from something glorious but from those to whom the glorious has been made manifest.[46] This laudatory glory, then, subsists only in its going forth from the glorifiers.

In which of these meanings, then, may 'glory' be used correctly of the Holy Spirit as Person, immanent within the Godhead?

If one takes 'glory' as intrinsic or substantive, i.e., as the divine excellence itself, then glory cannot be restricted to any one Person but is a divine

---

[44] Cf. the comment of Brown (*John 29A*, 751): "'[G]lory' has two aspects: it is a *visible* manifestation of majesty through *acts of power*."

[45] Durrwell would seem to argue, as do others, that the Spirit is to be named Glory on the basis of many passages in the OT as well as in the NT. But it is not easy to see most of these passages as referring to the relational Glory that the Spirit is.

[46] Evidently, as based on an appreciated excellence of another, this relational glory can also be said to 'come forth' from the appreciated excellence itself, inasmuch as this acts as occasion for the former. Such a usage is unsuitable here since it would have (relational) glory 'coming forth' from that which is not its active source.

attribute belonging to all three Persons without possibility of distinction. This does not obviate, of course, the possibility of appropriating 'glory' to the Spirit, even as 'holiness' and 'love' are appropriated to Him.

If one takes 'glory' as radiant, i.e., as the uncreated effulgence of the intrinsic glory that is the divine essence, there does exist an an opposition of relations, i.e, a relation to the Glorious of what shines forth from it and an opposite relation to what shines forth on the part of the Glorious.

This is, indeed, a Person-constituting opposition. But evidently neither the Glorious nor its Effulgence could be the Spirit.[47] For these relations, as the Fathers never ceased to point out, are those spoken of by Hebr 1:3, between the Effulgence and the (intrinsic) glory from which it shines forth, i.e., between the Son and the Father. The Father is the Glorious One, whose intrinsic glory is manifested by its Effulgence which is the Son. For, the Father glorifies the Son, in this context, precisely by giving Him the Father's own excellence, so that the Son is the manifestation and Image of the intrinsic glory of the Father.

Now, I have suggested, apropos of Gregory of Nyssa's remarks, that the glory Christ asks for in Jn.17:5, is appreciative or laudatory glory of renown. What I am proposing is that this renown and appreciation are not restricted in 17:5 to the created order, as they are in *v* 4 and, perhaps, *v* 1 but, rather, that they refer exclusively to the uncreated. The Holy Spirit is the reciprocal, laudatory Glory of the Father and the Son.

If, then, one speaks of the Spirit as laudatory or appreciative Glory, i.e., as the uncreated praising of the two Persons by One Another, then, as seen above, a new set of opposing relations of origination is to be considered. For relational glory, in general, comes forth from one person, has another as object, and is identifiable with neither.

Translating, then, what has been said already into the language of glory, we see, firstly, that the Father 'glorifies' the Son in sense (i) (i.e., that He acts as the source of the Son's excellence) by giving Him the Father's own intrinsic glory, i.e., the divine essence. Secondly, the divine essence is manifested to the Father (i.e., as radiant glory, if sense (A) be extended to the uncreated order) as the Son's own excellence and to the Son as that which is the Father's. But how to translate properly the interrelations of Father, Son, and Spirit that are implicit in laudatory glorification (sense (ii) extended to the uncreated order) calls for some care.

5. *The Holy Spirit as Glory of Father and Son*

We assume two things: that the Glory that the Son had before creation is the Holy Spirit; and that this Glory is laudatory or appreciative in nature.

The Spirit is, on this interpretation, the Father's exultant praise of the Son in admiration of the Son's exalted excellence. The Father perceives fully the excellence of the Son as equal to His own; and His praise of the Son is the

[47] There is no serious problem in speaking of the Spirit as (radiant) glory on the created order; indeed, there is much to commend it.

result of His appreciation of the Son's divinity, a praise offered by the only one competent to appreciate and good enough rightly to love such excellence. The Father then glories in His Son's excellence precisely *as* in Another's than the Father's. The resultant Glory subsists only in the act itself, as the Father's glorying expresses itself "publicly," not on the created order but still "outside" the Father, that is, as proceeding from the Father.

Since the Glory is laudatory, for the Father to glorify the Son with Himself, Father and Son must both be already constituted, with purely logical priority, as Persons (though it is by the one mind and one will of the divine nature that the Father glorifies the Son.)[48] Secondly, the Unoriginated, already constituted as Father, duly appreciates what He has given to His Only Begotten and what the Son has perfectly received. This gift from the Father (the divine essence) is the Son's intrinsic glory. It is manifest to the Father as His radiant glory, as the perfect effulgence and image of the Father's own intrinsic glory. For the Son is the effulgence of the Father's glory by His receiving of the divine essence and is perfect image of the Father by His having the divine essence as already received.

Now, if the Father is to glorify the Son appreciatively alongside Himself with the Spirit, then the Father must (first) glory in the excellence of the Son. He glories, then, in the Sonship of the Son, i.e., in the perfection of His likeness to the Father, a likeness of simple identity of essence, for there is no other Source or root of being than the Unoriginated. The Father, then, rejoices over and praises exultantly His Son, and this Glory proceeds from the Father as the very Breath of His life.

The words of our Lord in Jn.17:1, "Father, glorify Your Son that the Son may glorify You," suggest a further aspect of this Glory that we must consider, that is, its reciprocity. A line from St. Hilary expresses these things well (though Hilary expressly and repeatedly refers it solely to man's glorifying of Christ and the Father): "All praise of the Father is from the Son, because in whatever things the Son is praised, this praise will be the Father's."[49] If we extend this to uncreated Glory, then, in all in which the Father glorifies the Son, this Glory will also be the Father's.

If we interpret Jesus' words to include but not be restricted to created glory, they would read, "Father, let the (laudatory) Glory proceed from You in praise of Your Son, so that (laudatory) Glory may proceed from Your Son in praise of You." Hence, "Let the Spirit proceed from You (and, also, be sent by You) in praise of Your Son, so that the Spirit may proceed from Your Son (and, also, be sent by Him) in praise of You."

In brief, the gift of the divine essence (by the Unoriginated to the Immediately Originated whereby they are constituted Father and Son) is the Father's intrinsic glorification of His Son. Its reception constitutes the essential

---

[48] Evidently the language of Persons must be used in all speaking of laudatory Glory, since this is definable only in terms of the Persons' actions as Persons, i.e., in terms of the order of origination.

[49] *de Trinitate* 3, 15, *p* 86.

and intrinsic glory of the Son. It is, then, something that They both glory in, though from different aspects.

For, the Unoriginated cannot laudatorily glorify the Son until the latter has received the divine essence from Him (until the Unoriginated is Father) since the perfect reception of the divine essence (imaging of the Father) is the intrinsic Personal perfection the Father praises. Hence, for the Son to glorify the Father, the Son must be able to praise that Personal excellence of the Father that constitutes Him Father, i.e., the utterly gratuitous giving of the divine essence to the Son.

Recalling the definitions of II Lyons and Florence,[50] we see that, since "the Holy Spirit proceeds from the Father and the Son," the Glory proceeds from the Father and the Son. The Spirit is constituted Person by His going forth from the Father, as the Father glorifies His Son, and by His going forth from the Son—on reception from the Father—as the Son glorifies the Father.

In detail, the Father laudatorily glorifies the Son for the Son's intrinsic excellence, which is that He is the Immediately Originated recipient of the divine essence. But since the gift the Son has from the Father is that the Spirit, i.e., the Glory, proceeds from the Son also, we must say that the Son laudatorily glorifies the Father for the Father's intrinsic excellence, which is that He is the Unoriginated Source of the divine essence. In Scriptural terms, the Son glorifies the Father even as the Father glorifies the Son, though the Son can glorify the Father only if the Father glorifies the Son first.

The Father glories in the excellence of the Son, who is intrinsically glorious, since He is the Father's perfect Image by the Father's gift; and the Son glories in the excellence of the Father, who is intrinsically glorious, simply of Himself. This glorying-in from which the Glory results is, then, the theologians' "power of spiration."

This reciprocal glorying brings about the Father's glorifying of the Son and the Son's glorifying of the Father. From both actions the Glory arises. Yet since the Son must receive His power to glorify the Father from the Father, along with all else that belongs to the Son, the Spirit can in no way proceed from the Son except insofar as this proceeding from the Son is given by the Father.

The relations of glorification are of a different kind than those constituting Father and Son (i.e., those of giving and receiving the divine essence). The doubly-directed structure of reciprocal glorification of two Persons takes place in the presence of Another who is Their Glory. The Glory with which Father and Son glorify one another goes forth from Each toward the Other. The relations here involve two Persons already constituted, as well as the Third, to be constituted by His coming forth from Both as from one principle, from the First through the (nonfree) mediation of the Second.

The relations of opposition between the Spirit and the Father-and-Son would seem to be these: In the Father's glorifying of the Son, the Glory is

---

[50] Cf. note 13 above for II Lyons and notes 12 & 16 for Florence.

opposed to the Father, who is the One from whom the Glory proceeds. In the same act, the Glory is opposed to the Son as the object of glorification, just as any person appreciatively glorified is not his own glory; and the laudatory glory he has, is not he. The Glory is directed to His object, the Son, as that 'about which' He comes to be.

So also, in the Son's glorifying of the Father, the Glory is opposed to the Son as the One from whom the Glory proceeds. And in this same act, the Glory is opposed to the Father as the object of the Son's act of glorifying, as the One "about whom" the Glory comes forth from the Son.

Hence, one cannot argue that, because the Spirit proceeds from the Father and because the Son is begotten by the Father, the Spirit might antecede the Son or that They might come forth together. The order of origination of Son and Spirit is not indeterminate nor ambiguous. The antecedent love of the Unoriginated for the Immediately Originated (i.e., the giving of the divine essence) which constitutes Them Father and Son must be regarded as completed before (logically) one can speak of this reciprocal glorification which gives rise to the Spirit.

We can offer, then, a slightly more detailed response than usual to the ancient and difficult question: How does the procession of the Spirit from the Father differ from the generation of the Son? The Spirit comes forth from the Unoriginated not by generation, which is an intrinsic glorification, a gift to the Son of the Father's excellence, but by the reciprocal actions of laudatory glorification of the Son by the Father and the Son's logically indistinguishable glorification of the Father.

This response to the question rejoins in an unexpected way a traditional one based on the different modes of procession of Eve and of Seth from Adam,[51] though going considerably beyond it. Seth proceeded from Adam by natural generation, and thus is his son. But Eve came forth from his side, in a manner known only to God. One may now see that procession by way of glorification fits this well enough, since "woman is the glory of man" (I Cor.11:7).

A better analogy can be developed from the patristic images of the Spirit as intelligible Light.[52] The Spirit shines forth from Each, being made to go forth from Both by the Father, in a way analogous to the way a single beam of light can be constituted by the reflection of light in a perfect mirror back upon its source.[53] The light proceeds from the source, yet comes forth from the mirror to irradiate the source. But both source and mirror are active principles in the emission of the one beam of light. There need be no difference in

---

[51] Cf. St. Gregory Nazianzen, Oratio (31) Theologica 5, 11 (SC 250, *pp* 294–296; PG 36, 144D–145B). The same thought is developed in a work attributed to Gregory of Nyssa, "Quid Sit Ad Imaginem Dei," PG 44, 1329C–1332A. St. Thomas' harsh verdict on this may be found in *ST* I, 93, 6, ad 2.

[52] Cf., e.g., Basil, *Saint-Esprit*, "Introduction" by B. Pruche, *pp* 64–77, and text, esp. chap 26, 64, *pp* 230–231.

[53] Basil, *Saint-Esprit*, 193–4, with note 3 on 193 concerning the choice of reading.

the quality of the light from the mirror, though this light is not the original light but is made to come forth from the mirror by the latter. And no light can come from the mirror unless the light has already come to the mirror from the source.

6. The Numbering of Glories

If we are to maintain Gregory's identification of the Spirit with uncreated (laudatory) Glory, we must deal with a difficulty arising from the fact indicated earlier that laudatory glories are numbered primarily by the persons who are their objects rather than by the excellences that are their motives. For we cannot say that the Glory that has the Son as object is a numerically different Glory from that which has the Father as object; there are not two Holy Spirits.

At the most general level, we must consider what factors render glories multiple. What aspects of glorification, when themselves of a certain multiplicity, result in an equal multiplicity of glories? Then we must analyse the particular situation in which several persons are being glorified who have the same excellence, especially when the glorifiers of one of these persons are not those who glorify another, so that there would seem to be a distinct glory for each person who is the object of glorification.

Among men, when someone is being glorified, he has but one glory regardless of the number of those who glorify him. His glory will be greater if more people contribute to it; but he does not thereby have more glories. Even though laudatory glory subsists only in the act of glorification adequately considered, the "act of glorification" is a collective act, not ordinarily the act of each single person or supposit.

An exception may occur if the one glorified possesses several distinct excellences for which distinct groups of people glorify him, so that each group has its own particular and valid reasons for glorifying him. Thus, one group might glorify St. Irenaeus as one of the Church's greatest theologians. Another, let us suppose quite different, group might glorify him for his death as martyr to Christ. Still another group might center their admiration and praise upon the charm and vigor of his literary style. So, he might be said to have three glories.

But more commonly, the different excellences are sufficiently interrelated by the simple fact of belonging to the same person that the glories they ground coalesce into one, richer, and more complex glory: the glory of one man in whom all these excellences are found harmoniously together.

Yet such coalescence need not take place. There are some, for example, who glorify Michelangelo for the Sistine chapel who do not know him as the one to be glorified for the Medici tombs, and still others who do not know he is to be glorified for the greatness of his sonnets. What is pertinent for our inquiry in such an example is that it shows us that glory is not so strictly tied to its personal object as we might first have supposed.

Whether Michelangelo the painter be known to be the same as

Michelangelo the poet or the sculptor, or not, the concrete fact that these are the same man does not determine the number of glories, but the awareness (or lack of awareness) of this sameness on the part of the glorifiers. Yet any glory given that does not spring from knowledge of the whole concrete multiplicity of excellences is an imperfect glory. Perfect glory is but one, arising only from perfect knowledge of the full excellence of the one being glorified.

Turning now to the problematic situation involving the glorification of several persons for a single excellence, we note first that the oneness of the excellence that leads to the glorification of several people is ordinarily a oneness according to conceptual class, where each person glorified is seen as possessing one concrete instance of a (logically) universal excellence. Such is the case, say, when one glorifies several men for their scientific genius or for their sanctity. Under these conditions, part of one's glorying involves the implicit recognition of the merely analogous likeness of the excellences one sees in each. Each of these saints or scientists is known as somehow unique and only in some abstractly definable way as "just like" some other.

Thus, the multiplication of glories according to the number of objects of glorification involves a recognition that one is really glorying in concretely different excellences, however hard it may be for our concepts to express the diversity.

What, then, of a situation where the excellence in two or more persons is *identically* the same, e.g., a singleness of authority, a unicity of operation, or oneness of being? St. Basil deals with this question in the extreme case of a glory given to an image; he asks if this glory is the same or other than the glory of the one whose image it is. His response is that there is no way rightly to see the glory given to the image as other than glory given the person.

Thus, if one kisses a crucifix or bows low before a statue of a saint, "the honor given the image passes through to the prototype" whose image it is.[54] Then arguing *a fortiori*, he says: "So, what the image is here by imitation, this the Son is there by nature. And just as among the results of art, the likeness is by form, so in the divine and uncomposite nature, the oneness lies in the [Persons'] sharing in divinity." Any (laudatory) glory given to the perfect Image of the Father, precisely as His Image, is a glory that has the Father as object.[55] This suggests, in turn, that, though glory is multiplied numerically according to the number of persons glorified, this multiplication is not, strictly speaking, personal.

Applying all this to the Trinity, we see that the generation of the Son is describable in two ways: the Unoriginated gives the divine essence to the Immediately Originated; or the Immediately Originated receives the divine essence from the Unoriginated. But these statements are completely convertible, in all ways equivalent to each other. Hence, the one excellence that is the reason for Their reciprocal glorying is the Father's begetting of the Son,

---

[54] *Saint-Esprit* 194–195.

[55] Or to use again (our extension of) Hilary's language: "In whatever things the Son is praised, this praise will be the Father's"—cf. above, note 49 & text.

which is identically the Son's being begotten of the Father.

Thus, if the Unoriginated, as constituted Father by this gift, glories in that perfect reception of the divine essence that constitutes the Immediately Originated as Son, by that fact He who is Son is glorying in the Father's perfect giving of the divine essence. *Who* is being glorified in this case is both Father and Son, the Father through His glorification of the Son, whose glorification is, in turn, that of the Father. The Glory that proceeds from the Glorifier of the Son cannot be even logically distinguished from the Glory that proceeds from the Glorifier of the Father.

Thus it would seem that the multiplication of laudatory glories according to the number of persons glorified is an accident of the human condition. For we, unlike the Lord, glorify someone for what he is or does, not for who he is. The concrete supposit in itself escapes our concepts and is beyond our ability truly to grasp. Our nearest approximations would lie in the glorifying of the saints—yet we glorify them by recounting their deeds, not by declaring who each is. It is noteworthy in this regard that the Scriptures do the same with respect to God. 'Who' is indicated only by the divine Names; all else we learn of from His actions. Persons in themselves, whether created or divine, in their incommunicable core, escape our power to know.

7. The Spirit's Procession from the Father through the Son

It is clear now that the theory here proposed asserts what the Church has taught: that the Glory that is the Holy Spirit proceeds as from one principle. Yet, as Fathers and Councils agree, the procession of this Glory from the one principle takes place from the Father through the Son in virtue of the reciprocity of their mutual glorification.

For, as Basil indicated,[56] the Son manifests the power of the Father by imaging it; therefore, by the Son's imaging the Father's power to breathe forth the Holy Spirit. The Spirit is the Glory of both Father and Son. Glory proceeds from Both, as from one principle; that is, the Son is, in oneness with the Father, source of the Spirit's being, though the Son is such only by the Father's gift. The Son's power to glorify the Father comes in its entirety from the Father—since there exists no difference between them except as to giving or receiving the divine essence. Yet, because the Personal differences lie in the order of origination, Glory proceeds from the Father through the Son, since the Son is the necessary object of the Father's glorifying, without which there could be no Glory.

It is to be noted that the Father does not give the Glory Itself to the Son.[57] What the Son has from the Father as the Father's gift is that the Glory come forth from the Son, that the Son be Immediate Origin, not Ultimate Origin, of the Holy Spirit. The Son glorifies the Father, then, by the Father's

---

[56] *Saint-Esprit* 230–231. Cf. also note 54 above & text.

[57] "[T]his very thing—that the Holy Spirit proceeds from the Son—the Son Himself has eternally from the Father, by whom also He is eternally generated" (*DS* 1301). Cf. *pp* 52–53 below for further discussion of this statement.

gift—the gift that (laudatory) Glory proceed from the Son. On the other hand, the Father glorifies the Son without needing any gift to Himself that this (laudatory) Glory proceed from Him.

Obviously, one may not treat the divine essence and the procession of the Holy Spirit as additive parts making up a single gift of the Unoriginated to the Immediately Originated.[58] The procession of the Spirit is not part of the gift but all of it, described in a language proper to the Persons, a language that necessarily refers to the operations of the Persons in consequent manner (the Persons must be constituted before one can speak solely of Them) rather than in the antecedent manner called for when speaking of their constitution through reference to the divine essence.

For He who is Unoriginated is sole Ultimate Source. As Source, He has two operations, two immanent actions. The Unoriginated is Father by *giving* His own essence to the Immediately Originated, (who is Son by *receiving* the Father's essence.) The other, really distinct operation of the Unoriginated, already constituted as Father, is to glorify the Immediately Originated, already constituted as Son.

For, the procession of the Spirit, as such, does not make Him who is Father to be Father and could not take place unless He is already Father with a Son to glorify, through whose Glory He is reciprocally and simultaneously glorified. Father and Son are already constituted by the antecedent giving and receiving of the divine essence. Consequently, they glory in Each Other. And the breathing forth of this Glory—not the Glory Itself—is the consequent designation of the Father's gift to the Son.[59]

From a different perspective, laudatory glorification in God is what theologians have called active spiration and is reciprocal in the manner described, so that the relational opposition that exists here has an internal structure. The Spirit is the Glory of both Father and Son, the "result" of Their act of spiration (as the Son is the "result" of the Father's act of generation). Thus, generation implies the intrinsic glorification of the Son by the gift to Him of active spiration (of the act by which He laudatorily glorifies the Father, even as the Father laudatorily glorifies Him) and the Immediately Originated is begotten by receiving it.

The Unoriginated's breathing forth of the Spirit does not make the Unoriginated to be Father; but His giving of this same operation to the

[58] Cf. Bernard Lonergan, *de Deo Trino, II, Pars Systematica*, 2nd ed., Rome: Gregorian U. P. (1964), *p* 131.

[59] According to Florence (cf. second citation in note 19), "all things" which belong to the Father have been given. Yet the Council distinguishes between the proceeding of the Spirit, which the Son has eternally from the Father, from His also being eternally generated. "[H]oc ipsum...habet" is distinguished from and set in parallel to "a quo...genitus est," as though indicating that the Son is not constituted by "hoc ipsum...habet" but, as Son, has it. If one did not advert to the need for both antecedent and consequent language when speaking of the Persons as such, this could suggest, incorrectly, a double terminus of operation in the Son: reception of the divine essence (genitus est) and having the Holy Spirit's proceeding (habet). This "aeternaliter habet" looks like a reminiscence of Jn.17:5.

Immediately Originated does. It is the *giving* of the power of spiration that makes Him who is Father to be Father. This giving, therefore, cannot be communicated to Another. But the gift that is given, which is the power of spiration itself, can be and is communicated to Him who is Son.

The gift that the Spirit proceed from the Son is the whole of the Father's gift to the Son. The Father's gift that the Glory proceed is not really distinct from the antecedent gift of the divine essence to the Son, who antecedently receives the proceeding of the Glory so as to be Son. Only from a divine Person already constituted can divine Glory, as another divine Person, proceed. So also, the Father's glorifying of the Son is the procession of the Spirit from the Father.

If the power of spiration does not make the Unoriginated to be Father, then, conversely, it cannot make the Immediately Originated to be Son. But its reception does. The Son's reception of the Spirit's proceeding (His being Image and doing what He sees the Father doing, i.e., breathing forth the Spirit) is not really distinct from the antecedent reception of the divine essence from the Father. The Spirit's proceeding from the Son is the Son's glorifying of the Father.

Note that the Spirit does not Himself glorify either Father or Son. He is the Glory with which They are glorified, not Glorifier. There are, however, many passages in the Fathers and in the Scriptures that speak of the Spirit's glorifying the Son. But these seem all (even such as Jn.16:14) to refer to the Spirit's activity on the created order.[60]

As seen above (39–41), glory among men proceeds from the one who glorifies. It is complete insofar as the glorifier has drawn, by his praises of the one glorified, all those who are competent to see the same excellence and to join in glorifying him to whom it belongs. So in God, the Spirit proceeds from the Father as the Glory with which He glorifies His Son. This Glory is complete; the Son, hearing this praise, sees the same intrinsic excellence and glorifies the Father to whom it belongs. As the Glory with which Father and Son glorify one another, i.e., precisely as reciprocal in the manner already discussed, the Glory is complete and, so, is not a Source, direct or indirect, of another Person.

The Holy Spirit, then, is wholly the Spirit of the Father and wholly the

---

[60] On the other hand, the attention of a writer may focus on something else; and "glory" and its cognates may be used without regard for the various distinctions the same writer makes at other times. Thus, in a long and difficult passage ("Adversus Macedonianos de Spiritu Sancto" in *Opera Dogmatica Minora, I*, ed. Frederick Mueller, [GN 3/1; Leiden: Brill, 1958], *pp* 108–109 [PG 45, 1327D–1329B]), Gregory of Nyssa seems to argue that the Spirit's power to glorify shows that the Spirit Himself is glory of one nature with the Father and the Son, since one cannot glorify without sharing in glory oneself. Gregory seems here to speak of each Person's glory—whether intrinsic or extrinsic is in each instance hard to tell—as that which makes Him glorious and therefore "glorifies" Him. He also seems here to use "glorify" as equivalent to "is the glory of." Though alien to our usage here, neither sense is an abuse of language. But the passage contains such a diversity of meanings as to require a protracted study, even to establish the direct sense of the passage as a whole.

Spirit of the Son, subsisting as their reciprocal Glory. Though proceeding from Them, the Glory has no further terminus beyond Them. As the Spirit of the Father, It terminates in the Son; as Spirit of the Son, It terminates in the Father. Thus there is no other Person "beyond" the Spirit. No further real relation is possible. There is no further origination of another Person. Being the Glory of Father and Son completes the processions.

It would be a serious mistake, however, to take this completion of the processions in the Godhead as a sort of closed self-centering in God. For, the Glory is sent into the world to be the principle by which both Father and Son are glorified. This created glory, the Spirit's "reflection" on the created order, is not complete till all creatures have been drawn to join the Father and the Son in their glorifying of Each Other by the Spirit. It is, then, eminently suitable, even necessary, to attribute to the Spirit all actions in the created order by which Father is glorified by the Son or the Son by the Father.

8. The Rest of Jesus' Prayer

It would be tedious to go through every passage that speaks of God's glory in the New Testament to ascertain which sense of glory is to be found in each. Yet it seems appropriate to look briefly at the rest of Jn.17. Evidently, *v* 10, "All My things are Yours and all Your things are Mine and I have been glorified in them," can play its traditional role concerning the procession of the Spirit.[61] This can be interpreted in our context as, "I have received from You all that is Yours, including Your act of glorifying Me. But this act, now being Mine, glorifies You; and the Glory is from Us both, from You as sole Origin through Me." On any interpretation, *v* 10 serves to highlight the complete reciprocity of the glorifying that is spiration, while keeping clear the primacy of the Father's action.

"The glory which You have given Me I have given to them, that they may be one even as we are one," (*v* 22) is the verse for whose analysis Gregory of Nyssa pointed out the identity of the Spirit with the Glory. What is to be noted here is that, though *v* 22 is twice the occasion for his making this identification, the identification itself is made each time in virtue of *v* 5. In Gregory's mind, *v* 22 is clearly not concerned with a giving to the Logos in the Godhead but to the Spirit's being given to Jesus in the incarnation.[62]

What, then, of: "that they may behold My glory which You have given Me, because You loved Me before the creation of the world" {Jn.17:24}, which also speaks of the Son's glory as "given"?

The comma inserted above in this portion of the verse[63] seeks to resolve an ambiguity that cannot be removed definitively. As suggested by its proximity to *v* 22 and similarity of phrasing, this would be interpreted as Gregory

---

[61] Cf. Bernard Lonergan, *de Deo Trino, I, Pars Dogmatica*, 2nd ed., Rome: Gregorian U. P. (1964), *pp* 230–236,

[62] Cf. the two citations on *pp* 33–34 above.

[63] Cf. *The Greek New Testament*, ed. K. Aland, *et al.*, 3rd ed., United Bible Societies, *ad loc.* along with the corresponding punctuation apparatus.

interpreted *v* 22: of a beholding of the Holy Spirit in His greatest work of power, uniting all believers into one in Christ and through Him to the Father. Or since, as it stands, the emphasis is on the reason for the giving, i.e., because of the eternal love the Father has had for Jesus, this glory given could be taken as that of His resurrection and His subsequent glory in all the earth. If so, the verse would be interpreted much as St. Augustine interpreted all references to glory in chapter 17.[64] But then the possible connections with *v* 5 would be too tenuous for such an interpretation either to support or to weaken Gregory's identification.

With an additional, gramatically awkward comma, however, after the second 'Me,' the giving itself would have taken place before creation. This would directly contradict at least one aspect of my theory if Jesus were referring to a giving of the Glory that is the Spirit.[65]

But given this comma, it seems to me that Jesus would here be referring to His intrinsic glory, i.e., to His divinity as such, indeed given Him before creation, by which He is Son. For there would then be no suggestion of the Spirit's being in mind at all. Jesus' use of the possessive, 'My glory,' seems out of harmony with His usual way of speaking of the Spirit to the Father. Nowhere else, at least, is there a suggestion that anyone "beholds" the Spirit (unless one would choose to take His descent in the form of a dove or in the tongues of fire as such). But a beholding of Jesus Himself in glory is mentioned often enough (cf. at the transfiguration, at the ascension, in Stephen's vision, the many scenes in *Apocalypse*).

9. The Characteristic Loves of the Spirit

At last we are in a position to consider the question that has prompted this long discussion: How does the Spirit love (characteristically) the Father and the Son; and They, the Spirit.

The characteristic loves of Father and Son for the Spirit and of the Spirit for Them, since these loves are really distinct from the loves of gift and acceptance between Father and Son, are simply identical with the procession of the Holy Spirit from the Father through the Son as from one principle and, conversely, Their breathing Him forth. These loves are characteristic and proper; the only problem is to see how they may rightly be called 'love' at all. For, if the Spirit is the Glory by which Father and Son glorify One Another—and is Himself neither Glorifier nor Glorified—how can His procession be understood as love for Them?

Firstly, we note that the reciprocal glorification of the Son by the Father and of the Father by the Son has the structure of a manifestation of mutual love. For example, the Father's glorying in the Son's intrinsic excellence is

[64] Cf. pp 57–60 below.

[65] One could say simply that the Lord is not speaking here in our theological terms and that He is not distinguishing, as we did above, between "giving the Spirit" and "giving the breathing forth of the Spirit," between giving the Glory Itself to the Son and the gift that the Glory proceed from Him. Yet the patristic method of mining this prayer of Jesus' for trinitarian doctrine would, I think, find such an argument a mere evasion.

itself a kind of love, now not antecedent to the Son's being begotten but consequent upon it.

For, the Father's glorying in His Son manifests perfect appreciation and contemplative love of the Son's excellence as Son, as one wholly like His Father and infinitely grateful for the gift. But this glorying-in is not merely a love of joy or fruition but actively wills not merely the continuation of the Son's excellence and the Father's enjoyment of it but issues in glorification, "making public" this excellence so that it is not enjoyed by the Father alone.

Since such manifestation is itself a good and is willed for the Son, this glorification is a love of the Father for Him. Like the Father's antecedent love for the Son, this love contains an implicit reference to the divine love that is the divine essence itself. Yet this consequent love is not identical with the antecedent one—for the generation of the Son is really distinct from the proceeding of the Holy Spirit. Similar things may be said, *mutatis mutandis*, about the Son's glorification of the Father.

On the other hand, these consequent loves still retain the relational opposition as to origin found in the antecedent ones. But this relational opposition appears only as the structure of Their common act of spiration, in which They remain distinct as Persons though one as principle of the Spirit. Their consequent loves belong, as such, to the procession of Their Glory, in which They act as one, and not to the first procession (of generation) by which they are constituted as distinct from Each Other. Yet, though they act as one in spiration of the Holy Spirit by their mutual glorification of One Another, they remain always Father and Son and, therefore, distinct. The consequent loves, then, of Father and Son are those that constitute the Father and the Son as but one principle of glorification while yet remaining two distinct Persons. These reciprocal loves have their being only in the procession of the Glory. The mutual willing of the Glory to Each Other is identically the love of the Father and Son for the Spirit.

The Father and the Son love the Spirit since, loving Each Other, Each wills the Glory of the Other. Hence, They love not only Each Other. Each loves the one Glory, not as His own but as the Other's. To say 'love' here implies that Father and Son will some good to the Spirit even as, conversely, the Spirit wills the corresponding good of communion to Them. But the Father and the Son do will that there be a Glory with which to glorify Each the Other, i.e., They will the Spirit's co-existence with Themselves—a good greater than which there is no other.

The Spirit's love of Father and Son is, conversely, His (nonfree) willing to eternally come-to-be in that structure of origination and oppositional relation that "defines" Him. The Spirit wills to be defined only by Their reciprocal and consequent glorification of Each Other. He wills to be, but only as Others' Glory. His being, as Person, is to be Glory for Others. He wills for them that good which is Their Glory.

From a different point of view, the Spirit's procession is precisely that in which, even as distinct Persons, Father and Son are wholly one and without distinction inasmuch as acting as the common principle of the Spirit's proceeding. This oneness of the Two in relation to the Spirit, as little as we may understand it, is in some way the unspeakable good of communion of Persons not only by oneness of essence but by inter-Personal activity.

Excursus:
The Fathers and Jn.17:5

We can now understand at least part of the response to be given to the difficult question: Why would St. Gregory of Nyssa alone have laid bare so important a scriptural identification as this one of the Spirit with a personal Glory in the Godhead? And why should even he mention it so briefly and casually and in so few passages?

Though a full response to this is not within my competence, I would suggest three things as pertinent to such a response.

1. It is not quite correct to say that there is no other evidence for this identification. Though I have found it clearly stated only in the passages from Gregory of Nyssa cited earlier, there are a number of spots where he seems to allude to it.[66] Nonethe less, this identification is not mentioned, as far as I know, by St. Gregory Nazianzen. And, as will be seen shortly, neither Hilary nor Ambrose nor Augustine shows awareness of it, though Hilary, at least, seems to have been searching for it.

2. The Fathers do use analogous terms. So, e.g., Tertullian, Basil, and others use 'light' of the Holy Spirit within the Trinity. So, also, Gregory of Nyssa, in showing that the Holy Spirit must be Glory in the Trinity since He glorifies both Father and Son, uses 'light' as the created analog to this 'glory'.[67]

3. A large part at least of the answer would seem to lie in the predominance given, in the context of anti-Arian apologetics and polemic, to the passage in Hebr 1:3, where it is said of the Son that He is "the effulgence of the glory," or perhaps: "of His [i.e., the Father's] glory," in and through whom the glory shines forth without diminishment.[68] This passage seems to have been determinative, almost exclusively, of the sense to be given to 'glory' when applied within the Trinity.

Thus, for the Cappadocians (though not for them only), the glory is the Father; the effulgence is the Son, as the image of that glory. Their primary

---

[66] The clearest of these is in the passage mentioned above in note 60 above.

[67] "Adversus Macedonianos", *p* 108. This is one possible interpretation of this complex and difficult passage. But it seems just as likely that it refers to the intrinsic glory of the Spirit, i.e., to the divine essence He shares with the Father and the Son. Basil speaks with a much greater, almost systematic clarity (cf. references in note 52 above).

[68] 'Effulgence' is the only sense of "ἀπαύγασμα" in the early Greek Fathers, according to BAG *sub voce*; 'reflection,' for obvious dogmatic reasons, is not of interest to them. Cf. also *LPGL, sub voce.*

concern, however, seems to be the conceptual inseparability of effulgence from glory, and therefore the unity of nature of the Father and the Son, rather than anything to do with the mode of constitution of the Persons.

In all such discussions, however, it is clear that the glory in question is the intrinsic glory of the Father, whose effulgence is the intrinsic glory of the Son. And since the most obvious application of the notion of laudatory glory to Christ and the Father refers to the created order, the single verse in Scripture (Jn.17:5) that seems to require laudatory glory within the Trinity itself could easily enough be overlooked or the attempt made to explain it in some other fashion.

With 'glory' pre-empted by Hebr 1:3 and by all that mass of Scriptural passages where it refers to God or to His created manifestation,[69] it seems clear enough why Gregory should deal with this identification without much interest in digging into its ramifications in detail. Neither he nor the others already wholly involved in the conflict with the Arians and related heretics would be looking for more trouble. Only a clear apologetic advantage would have led them to draw attention to a passage that would raise an immediately obvious difficulty about the divinity of Christ and the inner glory of the Father.

a) St. Hilary

The tone is very different in the great Latin Fathers, St. Hilary and St. Augustine.[70] Hilary's concern is to show how the Son can be glorified by the Father without giving a handle to the Arians for subordinating the Son to the Father. Much concerned with Arian misuse of Jn.17:3, he saw 17:5 as the basis for a strong counter-argument. Yet, by taking the glory-before-creation as the intrinsic glory of the divine nature, he is forced into a position he can neither clearly formulate nor adequately defend.[71]

As indicated earlier, the second clause of Jn.17:5 requires an interpretation of the first part of Jesus' prayer that will answer the question: What glory did Jesus have with the Father before the world began? Hence Hilary begins his analysis by highlighting this essential question: "What sort of glorification with the Father did He look for?"[72]

---

[69] Other uses of 'glory' concerning the divine, as found in the Scriptures, are those mentioned on *pp* 41–43 above. None of these would seem to have an obvious application to the sole Person of the Holy Spirit except by way of appropriation.

[70] St. Ambrose seems rarely to mention Jn.17:5. His principal treatment of it seems to be in CSEL 78, *Sancti Ambrosii Opera, Pars 8, de Fide*, ed. O. Faller, Vienna: Hoelder-Pichler-Tempsky (1962). Having distinguished between *gloria* and *claritas*, this latter being our laudatory glory (IV.10.137, *p* 205), he addresses our question (V.7.93, *p* 250). His answer is that the *claritas* of which Jesus speaks is that of man before the fall, taking *mundum* to be the world of men as in Jn.17:23.

[71] Cf. A. Fierro, *Sobre la Gloria en San Hilario*, Analecta Gregoriana, *vol* 144, Rome: Gregorian U. P. (1964), chap V, *pp* 121–180, for a detailed and persuasive effort to clear Hilary of any charge of unorthodoxy, despite the strangeness of some of his formulations, and to extract an underlying theology of real value concerning the glorification of the incarnate Word.

[72] *de Trinitate*, 3, 16, *p* 87.

Hilary answers with the sentence given in note 20 above and states that this is the glory in which He will judge the world, in which He ascended, and is enthroned and was seen in heaven by Paul and honored by Stephen.[73] One senses at once the difficulty he has generated by making the uncreated glory somehow one with the created. This difficulty recurs, writ large, when he takes the matter up again in Book 9.

His concern here is with the unity and perfection of the divine nature—how can this be preserved if the Word has taken the form of a slave? Again, stumblingly, he tries to argue that the "man taken up" is taken into the glory of the Father Himself, into unity with the Father's nature. "Id...homini (Christo) adquirebatur, ut Deus esset."[74] For, Hilary saw clearly[75] that, since the Son is to be glorified alongside and with the Father, the Father is to be glorified alongside the Son with the Son's glory. The glory of the Son is not thinkable apart from the uncreated glory of the Father Himself. But Hilary's language is at best obscure in his attempted solution,[76] and Augustine is right to set it quietly but firmly aside.[77]

What is important for us here, however, is to see that, indeed, Hilary's problem would remain and the humanity would be dissolved in the divinity, as Augustine claimed, if the glory here referred to were the intrinsic or substantive glory of the Father, that is, the divine essence. Yet Hilary argues rightly that there can be no distinction between the glory that Jesus seeks and the glory of the Father, and that this glory is a glory that belongs personally to the Father.

b) St. Augustine

Augustine starts with what seems self-evident: that the eternal and intrinsic glory of the Father in its divine perfection cannot be increased; nor has He the "form of a slave" in which a growing intrinsic glory might be His. Therefore, since any glorification implies an increase of glory, all that Jesus says

---

[73] ibid, 3, 16, *p* 88

[74] ibid, 9, 38, *p* 412

[75] ibid, 9, 39, *p* 413.

[76] ibid 9, 39–41, *pp* 414–418. Cf. also 3, 16, *p* 88. Cf. Fierro, *Gloria*, *pp* 130, 135, 139, 142, 155.

[77] *In Johannis*, Tract 105, 6 & 7, *pp* 606–607. Augustine does not mention Hilary here by name. Nonetheless, it seems clear that it is Hilary of whom he is speaking. Firstly, the strange phrasings Hilary uses in the passages just noted, if taken as they stand, would be understood as exactly the position Augustine is describing. Further, Augustine's tone is remarkably gentle and his argumentation unusually bland for setting aside an opinion that he sees as totally destroying the human nature of Christ after His ascension. This would seem to be confirmed by Augustine's remarkable silence in his own *de Trinitate* concerning Hilary's great work, mentioning him and it only twice, both times in connection with the one brief line *Aeternitas in Patre, species in Imagine, usus in Munere* that had apparently gained quasi-dogmatic authority. Describing Hilary as "of no small authority in the treatment of the Scriptures and the proclaiming of the faith," (*Sancti Aurelii Augustini de Trinitate Libri XV*, [CCL 50 & 50A], ed. W. J. Mountain, Bk 6, chap 10, 11 [*vol* 50, *p* 241] & Bk 15, chap 3, 5 [*vol* 50A, *p* 464]), Augustine knew well enough the harm and confusion he might have caused were he to have attacked Hilary's work directly; but he doubtless knew some of the ways in which Hilary's thought was being misunderstood and felt compelled to comment.

about His glorifying the Father must relate exclusively to the created order.

In particular, the Father glorifies the Son by raising Him from the dead and the Son glorifies the Father by making His power in the resurrection known to all the world. The glory, then, for which Jesus prays is His coming glory among men as predestined for Him by the Father from eternity, a glory in which the Father will share as He comes to be made rightly known to men by His glorified Son.

In Augustine's own words, Jesus prayed in Jn.17:5, "as if He were saying: It is time that I should have with You, when living at Your right hand, the glory which I have had with You, that is, that glory which I have had with You in Your predestination."[78] Or, to tie his meaning more clearly to John's text, we could paraphrase: And now, glorify Me as man (at Your right hand) with Yourself, with that future glory which I have never yet experienced but which You predestined for Me and (through My glorifying You widely among men) for Yourself before the world was.

Now, this fails, so it seems to me, for several reasons. One difficulty is that it requires an intrusion of the Pauline theme of predestination into the Gospel of John. While this is not simply alien to the latter, John's thought seems centered less on predestination than on the gratuity of election.[79]

Secondly, Augustine himself argues that this glorification refers primarily to Jesus' enthronement at the right hand of the Father. And indeed, the first clause of *v* 5 applies well enough, when taken as Augustine reads it, to Christ's ascension and enthronement. There He is seated beside the Father, sharing His glory among men with the Father. But the second clause, as Hilary saw, simply does not say what Augustine would have it say. In answer to the question: "Is this the glory that He had before the world was?" Augustine acknowledges that it is not, except solely in the sense that it was predestined for His human nature from eternity.[80]

"The glory which I had, before the world was, alongside You" is not in

---

[78] "[O]ravit dicens: [Jn.17:5], tamquam diceret: Claritatem quam habui apud te, id est, illam claritatem quam habui apud te in praedestinatione tua, tempus est ut apud te habeam etiam uiuens in dextera tua." *In Johannis*, Tract 105, 8, *p* 608.

[79] Cf. Barrett, *Gospel* who argues for predestination in *John*, yet must qualify the force of his arguments repeatedly (e.g., *pp* 95, 218–219, 366, 430–431).

[80] In one of the only two comments Augustine makes in his own *de Trinitate* on Jn.17:5 he says: "Thus the just [will go] into eternal life. What, 'however, is eternal life' if not 'that they know You...the one, true God, and Him whom You have sent, Jesus Christ'? But then [they will know Him] in that glory concerning which He says to the Father: 'Which I had with You, before the world came to be.'" (*de Trinitate*, Bk 1, chap 13, 31; *vol* 50, *pp* 78–79). (This final sentence, referring to the vision the just will have of the Father and of Jesus in the Father's glory, is ambiguous. Had Augustine said nothing else, it could easily be taken according to our understanding of this glory as the Holy Spirit, given to each nature in Christ in proportion to its capacity to receive Him. In the second of his comments, he speaks of the Spirit's glorifying the Son, but solely in the sense found in Jn.16:14, i.e., through the activity of the Apostles. (Bk 2, chap 4, 6; *p* 87). In neither case does he take any notice of the difficulties found in this verse by Hilary or by himself in *In Joannis*.

any obvious way equivalent to "the glory which You destined for me, before the world was, that I should now shortly have alongside You." The former would seem to refer to a glory already possessed by Jesus as eternal Word and Son alongside the Father in His eternity; the latter, to a glory predestined for Jesus as man, once enthroned at the Father's right hand. The question is, which of these two senses best fits our Lord's words.

Augustine helps us decide this question when he thinks to confirm his argument by a parallel in Eph.1:4, "even as He (the Father) chose us in Him (Christ) before the foundation of the world to be holy...predestining us for adoption as sons." But his argument requires that this be convertible to "even as we were holy in Him before the foundation of the world as His adopted sons." The best that could be said for this is that it seems awkward and contrived, and greatly weakens the text.

More to the point, however, is the fact that the Father "chose us...before" and "predestined us for adoption" Even Paul, with his clear notion of predestination, does not take it for granted. He does not speak as in the supposedly equivalent phrase above but mentions or alludes to predestination whenever it is pertinent to his thought. Yet in Jn.17:5, Jesus does not speak of a glory chosen for Him or promised Him or destined for Him or even to be given to Him by the Father, but a glory He had always.[81]

If, further, one takes up seriously Augustine's manner of interpretation, then other passages traditionally taken as referring to our Lord's existence "before" creation or even before His conception as man, lose their force. A merely human Jesus could then say, "Before Abraham was, I am," meaning no more than: I am now, long after Abraham in time but predestined before him. That is, before (logically speaking) God chose to create Abraham, He chose from eternity to create Me as the Messiah and then chose Abraham as My progenitor.

"In the beginning was the Word and the Word was with God"—so, God would have uttered His Word as the first of all creatures in intention but not necessarily before them in time, by predestination from eternity. Thus only the Father would have existed before the creation of the Word (whom the Arians would call 'God' with respect to all other creatures, since all things else were created through Him). So, in like fashion, for Col.1:15 & 17, Heb. 1:2–3, 10–12, Phil.2:5–8, and such OT passages as Ps.2:7, where "today" would no longer refer to the day of eternity for the Son's birth but to a day, eternally predestined by the Father, in time. In brief, by this move, Augustine slips into a mode of interpretation that the Arians could have happily taken as their own. Indeed, *all* that happens to our Lord—and to everyone else—is, Augustine holds, predestined eternally.[82] How, then, can predestination offer any special insight at this point?

This interpretation by predestination, as Augustine goes on to explain at

81 "Which I had"—literally, "which I was having continuously," for the imperfect "εἶχον."

82 The connection of Augustine's notion of predestination with the divine immutability is indicated *inter alia* in *de Trinitate* V, 16, at the end, apropos Jn.17:24.

length, both makes possible and requires an awkward (though by no means impossible) reinterpretation of the tenses of the verbs. Since in the divine predestination the future is as certain and clearly known as the past, Jesus shows that He is speaking in terms of predestination by using the past tense for all that Augustine considers to be still in the future.[83]

Thus, he notes that in *v* 1 Jesus asks the Father to glorify Him so that *then* He might glorify the Father, whereas in *vv* 4–5 He states that He *has* glorified the Father and asks that the Father *now* glorify Him (i.e., in the immediate future). To establish the sort of equivalence Augustine thinks necessary between these verses requires, then, an adjustment in the meaning of the tenses.

These objections to Augustine's interpretation are not apodictic. Some defense, even if awkward, can be found against each; and even the aggregation of awkwardnesses is not probative. What would be missing, I think, in any such defense would be a proper attention to the transcendent beauty and literary quality of the Lord's words. What John has written down is, at the least, the greatest of literature and cannot be treated as less.

This is not to deny all merit, from a literary point of view, to Augustine's interpretation. It does make good sense to say that Jesus, as man and on the verge of His sufferings, thought longingly of the goal of His life and suffering, a goal predestined and certain: the created glory promised Him as man by the Father. But His words require that one see a yet deeper longing and a greater glory being prayed for than Augustine allows.

Why should Jesus mention having had this glory in the Father's predestining before the world was? All creation could have meant little enough to the Son simply in His divinity. Why should that prospect be evoked now, when He is looking so longingly toward the future? Surely Jesus trusted the Father enough to speak in simpler fashion of "the glory which You have promised to give me at Your right hand."

Strangely, for so fine a writer and one so sensitive to the wide range of human feelings, Augustine nowhere takes account of the inconcinnity of his explanation of Jn.17:1–5 with the emotional coloring of the entire passage. The gradations and abrupt alterations of tone in the Lord's words pass without recognition.[84]

No notice is taken of the remarkable emphasis given by the repeated and carefully placed "alongside Yourself...alongside You." In particular, the point emphasized by St. Hilary and which he wrestled, not very successfully, to deal with is bypassed: that it is one thing to say "with the glory I had [e.g., by predestination] when I was with You" and it is quite a different thing to say

---

[83] *In Johannis*, Tract 105, 4–5 & 7, *pp* 605–607.

[84] In his comments on "This is eternal life, that they may know You, the one true God," he does note that the truest and greatest glory is only had in the vision of God in heaven. But though moved by Jesus' reverent love there expressed and clearly desirous of that glory, he does not notice the change in the Lord's tone as He turns with yearning towards that still greater Glory that is uncreated with the Father.

"with the glory I had with You."[85] The glory which the Son had alongside or with the Father belongs to Them both, *before* the world was.

C. Conclusion

The theological development of the "actus notionales" or, in particular, of the "amores notionales," old as it is, seems not to have gone much beyond the analyses necessary to validate such designations as "paternal Love" or "filial Love"—and rarely, indeed, this far. Here I have tried to show how each of these loves has its characteristic and proper quality *as love* given by the order of origination in the Godhead.

These characteristic loves are based on the nonpsychological structures set forth by the Councils and not on psychological analogies—though these come into play when showing that a given inter-Personal act deserves the name 'love.' The advantage of this procedure is that it enables one to speak about loves between the Persons that are not indistinguishably common to Them all. Thus, one can do justice to what is legitimate in the "communitarian" understandings of the Trinity without having to abandon the Church's tradition concerning the Persons or to resort, as do Mühlen and many others today, to considering God as mutable, suffering, etc.

There seemed to be, however, no sufficient information offered by the Councils for establishing the characteristic love of the Holy Spirit for the Father and the Son, or conversely. This led to a search for and, indeed, the finding of another, much neglected, proper name for the Holy Spirit, given in the Scriptures and reasonably referred immanently to the third Person by St. Gregory of Nyssa, albeit only in passing, and by St. Basil.

This name of the Spirit is Glory, not the intrinsic glory that is the divine essence nor the radiant glory that is the Effulgence of the Father, but that uncreated yet laudatory Glory that results from the Father's glorification of the Son and the Son's reciprocal and wholly dependent glorification of the Father. This identification of the Spirit with Glory was validated theologically by showing that there is but one Glory and that It comes forth from both Father and Son, though differently from each, proceeding from the Father through the Son.

The first fruit of all this, when analysed in terms of the characteristic loves, was to offer some clue as to how the Spirit's procession from the Father differs from that of the Son: as glorification differs from generation. Secondly, since active spiration is mutual glorification, it necessarily depends on both Father and Son; yet the *monarchia* is intact, since the Son's activity is intrinsically and totally dependent on the Father's. There is only the one Principle in the Godhead, yet the Son is more than a mere conduit for the Spirit's coming forth.

All this may seem a bit rash in view of the centuries of sometimes bitter dispute concerning the procession of the Spirit. Yet St. Gregory Nazianzen,

---

[85] *de Trinitate* 9, 39, *p* 413.

the Theologian, told his people that, nearly three centuries after the death of the last apostle, the Holy Spirit was just beginning to give a clearer vision of Himself, as He enlightened men bit by bit, with partial additions and advances, since knowledge of His divinity earlier would have burdened men excessively.[86] But Gregory's death did not end the Self-revelation of the Spirit. Is it not possible that the "burden" of disagreement about His procession may now be lightened by His action, though on the basis of what was long ago written down but only gradually understood? I hope, then, that this chapter's development—from a distinctively Greek understanding of the passage in Jn.17:1–5 as referring to the Holy Spirit—may be of help towards the resolution of the doctrinal aspects of the problem of the *Filioque*.

Thirdly, it was possible to show how all the relations in the Godhead, including those between Father and Son, can be stated in this language of glorification. This not only can clarify a seemingly endless jumble of different notions of glory in Scripture and the Fathers but offers a new perspective even on the better known relationship between Father and Son.

More importantly for the effort to gain deeper insight into created charity, we were able to see how the Spirit's coming forth from Father and from Son does indeed represent a structure of love that is recognisable as such. The Spirit's characteristic love for Father and Son is His willing their common and greatest good: that the Son have perfect Glory from the Father and that the Father, in turn, have perfect Glory from the Son. They, likewise, love the Spirit, each willing the Glory of the Other *as* belonging to the Other. Thus the relations of origin become intuitively visible as the uncreated model upon which created charity may be formed. Our conscious loves must be modeled directly, of course, on the Son's as they exist in His human nature. We would be more than a little rash, I think, to seek to form our conscious loves directly on the Trinity's in any way other than that shown in Jesus. But it is Jesus Himself who insists that we love one another as He has loved us and who adds that He loves us as the Father has loved Him, and this not simply on the created order. Having sought to unfold a small aspect of that mystery of love which transcends all the 'loves' the world designates as such, our task is now to understand how the uncreated charity is mediated to us through the one mediator between God and man, Christ Jesus.

---

[86] St. Gregory Nazianzen, Oratio (31) Theologica 5, 26–27, (SC 250, *pp* 326–330).

Chapter 4

The Love of the Trinity for Jesus and for All Creation

Even if, as we suppose, the grace of charity in man has a structure reflecting that of the characteristic loves in God, we cannot live with God's life directly and immediately. We require a Mediator. For, the structure of charity that is negated by original sin, though ultimately that of the Trinity, is immediately that of the charity of Christ, from whom and through whom ours comes. The negation is, in its essence, a privation of grace and a resultant psychic hostility to the life in Christ. Therefore, we must take one further step before we can grasp what shape or form that negation might have, and consider how the intratrinitarian loves are reflected in the grace of Christ.

Our desire in this chapter is to see how the the intelligible structure given by the *amores notionales* to the one act of divine Love, can be said to be reflected in creation and, in particular, in Jesus' love for God.[1] In the next chapter, we will consider the charity of Christ insofar as directed to us.

---

[1] The use of 'reflect' in such a context in Scripture (e.g., 2 Cor.3:18, Hebr.1:3) is at best doubtful. In many ways we might replace 'to reflect' by 'to image,' whose scriptural resonances are clear. Yet 'to image' usually implies a controlled portrayal, made by art, of some exemplar, even though it may on occasion designate the necessary, physically determined activity of reflection. 'Reflect,' on the other hand, has the advantage for our context (speaking of created things inasmuch as like divine ones) that it need not require the sharpness of focus and determinate form that belongs to 'image.' Reflections can be quite indefinite, not merely blurred but without any abiding shape or form, and usually involve a symbolically useful reduction in the number of dimensions (cf. St. Gregory Nazianzen, Oratio 28, #3 and, differently applied, Oratio 31 (5th Theological Discourse) ##32–33 in Frederick W. Norris, *Faith Gives Fullness to Reasoning: the Five Theological Orations of Gregory of Nazianzen,* with trans. by L. Wickham & F. Williams, Leiden: E. J. Brill (1991), *p* 298.

Charity—precisely because it is the one perfect and entire love into which all others must be subsumed if they are to be true and undistorted—necessarily differs in its activity in accord with the relations between the one who loves and the object of this love. We wish, then, to look at the Father's love for Jesus as man[2] and Jesus' love for the Father; and also to speak of the Spirit's love for Jesus and the Father, and Theirs for Him. We hope thence to learn the essential traits of that perfect charity that God calls us to live by. From an understanding of this, the terminus of our spiritual development, we will be enabled better to grasp the damage done to us by original sin, which directly cancels out each of these traits.

The argument of this section can be summarized as follows:

A. The Father's antecedent love for the Son, His gratuitous gift of His own essence to the Son, is reflected into the created order through His love for Jesus.

B. The Son's antecedent love for the Father, i.e., His willed reception of the gift of the divine essence, is reflected on the created order in Jesus' gratitude to the Father, manifested in His obedience.

C. The love of Father and Son for the Spirit as Their mutual Glory is reflected in His descent upon Jesus at His baptism. In the power of the Spirit, Jesus is glorified by the Father, who is in turn glorified by Jesus.

D. The Spirit's love for Father and Son is reflected in the unity constituted through common worship in the one, visible Church.

E. The Father's love for Jesus includes each of us and all of creation insofar as existing in Jesus.

A. The Father's love for Jesus

We have glimpsed something of that love of the Unoriginated for the Immediately Originated which constitutes Them Father and Son. We now wish to consider the fact, made clear all through the New Testament, that it is the Father Himself who loves Jesus, the Son made man. In some way, then, the characteristic love of the Unoriginated must be capable of 'reflection' into the created world so that by this reflection one may truly say that the Father Himself, as Father, loves Jesus and that the Father's love is not merely an appropriation to Him of the common love of all three Persons for Jesus.[3] Yet,

[2] In what follows, to avoid overburdening sentences often too long already, I shall usually use 'Son' or 'Word' when referring to the Second Person of the Trinity in His divine nature, 'Jesus' when referring to Him in His human nature, and 'Christ' when referring to Jesus in His humanity in the light of His offices, as Savior, Redeemer, King, or the like.

[3] Appropriation is the ascription of some property belonging to the divine essence to one Person (or two) because of a special likeness or similarity—not in reality but in our experience—between that property and the Person. Appropriation applies the term to this Person as if proper but without exclusion of the others. Thus 'holiness' is appropriated to the Holy Spirit, though both Father and Son are also holy; so also, 'spirit.' Likewise, wisdom is appropriated to the Son since He is the divine Word, in whom God knows all things (cf. *ST* I, 45, 6, ad 2). Appropriation serves to manifest the characteristics of the Persons by means of the essential attributes, which are often

how can one speak of the Father, in distinction from the other Persons, as loving Jesus, the Man who is also His eternal Son, since all divine actions *ad extra* are actions of the one divine nature?

Such a love may be understood, I think, in much the same way as the various sendings (*missiones*) of the Son and of the Spirit.[4] We can say that any characteristic love within the Godhead can be reflected as such into creation if, in addition to this characteristic love, God has willed to create goods in this world for the Person or Persons loved, goods that have a structure analogous to the good that is willed in the eternal love that is being reflected.[5]

Thus, we may rightly speak of a characteristic and antecedent love of the Father for Jesus insofar as: a) within the Trinity, the Father loves the Person who Jesus is; and b) on the created level, all three Persons, acting in the unity of the divine nature, will for Jesus gifts analogous to the gift that the Father has given the Son within the Trinity, gifts that are wholly gratuitous and logically prior to His human goodness, gifts that, as man, He cannot be said to deserve or even attract. We have b) only still to consider here, i.e., we seek to see how God's giving of the goods created for Jesus resembles the Father's uncreated giving in its gratuity and generosity.

Among the gifts given by the Trinity to Jesus in His humanity, gifts that reflect the Father's love for Him into the world, the foremost is the gift of the Father's essence to Him. This is not, of course, the one infinite act of divine generation. But this latter act can be and, in fact, has been reflected in the created order. For, God has given to the human nature of Jesus to be taken up forever into Personal union with the Son, whose essence is the Father's.

The Father's liberality is reflected further in that God gives to Jesus' humanity, thus united with the Son, all good that a human nature is capable of receiving.[6] So He has given Jesus the fulness of possible human likeness to God. For, Jesus is the Image of the invisible God (Col.1:15), the most perfect representation of God in the created world, in and through His human nature (Jn.14:9–10), as Head of the Church and the Source of grace.

Only the divine Love gives the Son the gift of existing at all as man. The creation of Jesus' humanity, like all acts of creation, represents a love that is gratuitous in the strongest sense. This, partly because nothing on the created level, not even the Son's humanity, can move the divine will; partly because

---

more easily graspable by our minds. Cf., *ST* I, 39, 7 & 8 and Lonergan II, 174.

[4] Cf. St. Thomas' treatment of *missio* in *ST* I, 43, 1 c. From the very meaning of the word 'send,' the one who is sent 'goes forth' from him who sends him and begins to be or act (at least in a new way) in the place whither he is sent. But within the Trinity, the Son and Spirit each goes forth, though differently, from the Father and, as sent, begins through the common action of all three Persons and for Their common purposes to be and act in our world in a new way, e.g., as did the Son when made man.

[5] It may be objected that, e.g., the Father's love for the Son, since one with the divine generation, cannot refer to anything temporal. Yet the nature of love is such that whoever loves another loves all that is related as a true good for him. Cf. also *ST* I, 43, 2 c.

[6] Cf., however, *pp* 246–253 below for some necessary qualifications on this.

until (by logical priority) this gift is given to Him, there is nothing to draw even a human will towards Him.

So, too, the gifts of original justice, of His being Redeemer and Savior, of being the channel of all grace to men, all this can only be conceived in virtue of a divine decision that is contingent on nothing created. This decision is made in total freedom; nothing in Jesus, simply as man, could claim any of these gifts for Him. Unique and incomprehensible, these are goods given without conceivable merit or hope of return. All represent different ways of sharing gratuitously the divine essence with Jesus.

B. Jesus' love for the Father

Can we speak of Jesus' love for the Father as a reflection, in the sense in which we have been using this word, into creation of the Son's characteristic love for the Father, of the love that is the Son's reception of the Father's gift, in logical antecedence to His constitution as Son?

As just seen in Section A., the Father (with the Son and Spirit) freely gives Himself to Jesus by grace (and thus can be said to dwell within Him) even though the Father is not sent into the world since there is no prior Other to send Him.[7] The only question, then, is: Given the Father's presence in Jesus by grace, does God also create some good for the Father, so present, that has a structure similar to the Son's uncreated love of the Father and that is truly Jesus' human love for the Father?

With but one qualification, we may respond affirmatively. There is in God a characteristic love with the same ordering of the Persons as in Jesus' love for the Father. The Son's love, as God, is one of total and grateful reception of the Father's gift. So Jesus' love, as man, for the Father, both as present by grace and as He is within the Trinity, is, insofar as it reflects simply the procession of the Son, pure reception. Indeed it is a reception more drastic in one sense than is the Son's characteristic love. For no created love could be antecedent in the sense required, i.e., logically prior to the reception of the gift. The gifts of creation and of grace ("the new creation") must, logically speaking, be received before the recipient can will anything at all in their regard. A created reflection of the Son's love, whatever it might be, could not be logically prior to the gift of creation. There is no relationship between the creature and the Creator that could correspond to the Son's antecedent love for the Father. Until Jesus' human nature has been created, there is no one there to receive this first gift, that of the Son's existence as man. Nor, until (by logical priority) He has received God's grace, can He choose or even wish to receive it.

One might object that the saints, at least at times, willed in total submission to receive their entire being from the Father, willing whatever the Father wills, in advance of any knowledge of what that will entailed concretely. Surely Jesus willed, from the first moment in which He could will as man at all, to

[7] Cf. *ST* I, 43, 4 ad 1 & 2.

be as God made Him, with no other gifts of grace than those bestowed on Him, to live exactly as the Father wished.[8]

But any such argument misses the essential point that the merely logical distinction that we can make concerning the order between the Son's will to receive the divine essence and His reception of it is simply other than what is proposed as a created analog. For, the Father *is* what He gives and the Son *is* what He receives, whereas the humanity of Jesus *is not* until the gift of existence has already been received. He can neither accept nor refuse anything in advance, even logically speaking, of the reception of the gift. The same is true of the gifts of grace.

Nonetheless, the Son's characteristic love for the Father is reflected in its other aspects, apart from this impossibility of a created parallel to the logical priority in question, in Jesus' love. This recipient love of Jesus for the Father is, then, a genuine though incomplete reflection. Directed by Jesus to the Father, this love depends only on the adequacy of His created knowledge of the Father as distinct from the Son Himself and from the Spirit.

Jesus' love as man, then, reflects, under human constraints and weakness, that antecedent love He has as eternal Son for the Father. In His humanity, even as in His divine nature, He loves the Father by His grateful reception of His whole being from the Father. He rejoices to be the perfect Image of the Father[9] under the conditions of human life in space and time. He assents in full to exactly that existence and growth that the Father has chosen for Him and accepts the conditions of His life and mission in simple accord with the Father's will, recognizing no other root of His being as man than this will.

Implicit in the gratitude of those who live in time is trust or hope—a quiet and simple confidence that the gift will prove to be what it claims to be, that it will not fail us unseasonably, that the giver will withdraw neither his gift nor his love. One who knows a gift to be truly given, knows the love with which it is given. But love freely given by one who is good, may not be as freely withdrawn. The love may well be limited but, within these limits, it abides. If not, if it be withdrawn without alteration on the part of the recipient, the giver is proved false. No matter how freely given, love commits itself in its gift.

Of course, one who looks only to what is given may well fear that it will prove empty or be in dread of its withdrawal; one who is embarrassed by the gift can be glad should it vanish; those who do not love the giver may see the gratuity of the gift as a perennial threat to withdraw it for bad behavior. But when, as did Jesus most perfectly, one loves the Giver Himself, the gratuity of the gift is an abiding invitation to remain with Him in simple trust: "If you keep My commandments, you will remain in My love, even as I have kept the

---

[8] Cf. Hebr.10:9.

[9] This phrase requires justification, indicating as it does a relation of a creature to *one* Person of the Trinity, even though this is not to be taken as excluding appropriate relations to the other two Persons. Jesus, like every man, is image of the Triune God. This justification is offered in the Excursus below.

commandments of My Father and I remain in His love" {Jn.15:10}.

In brief, recognizing that nothing exists that is not a gift from the Father, without any thought of His own worthiness,[10] He receives with gratitude and trust the whole of reality in whatever ways it impinges upon Him. Gratefully aware of His dependence on the Father, He recognizes and is gladly indebted to the love embodied in the gift.

C. The love of Father and Jesus for the Spirit

We saw in Section A. that the Father loves Jesus with a love that is truly attributable to the Father personally and that reflects the Father's antecedent love for the Son by its gratuity and liberality. Likewise, all that Jesus has been and done, He has accepted gratefully as free gift from the Father. But can one speak of another and different, *reciprocal* or *mutual* love by the Father for Jesus and of Jesus for the Father, a different aspect of love, one that reflects the procession of the Glory? Are the love of Father and Son for the Spirit, as They breathe Him forth, and the Spirit's love for Them, as He comes forth as Their life's Breath, reflected in Jesus' charity? And if so, how?

The Spirit is one, single, unique, and utterly simply Glory, though proceeding *from* two, really distinct Persons acting as one principle. Further, He is a single Glory that has two, really distinct Persons as objects. Any resemblance or similarity in the created world must, then, involve one, single glory (i) arising *from* many minds and hearts, and (ii) offered *both* to the Father and to the Son in His humanity. This created glory must result from the action of the entire Trinity but, as we shall now see, can be attributed to the Holy Spirit as the reflection of His love for the Others and Theirs for Him, and not merely appropriated to the Spirit. We shall consider aspect (ii) here, considering this glory insofar as it terminates in Both. Then, in Section D. we shall consider aspect (i), the created reflection of the Spirit's characteristic love for Father and Son: the "procession" of this created glory as arising from one single principle, though coming forth from many.

The Spirit proceeds from Father and Son by way of Their consequent love for Each Other, i.e., by that expressed in Their mutual glorification. Translating what we have said concerning reflection, from the generic language of love to the specific one of glorification, we can say, "The Father glorifies Jesus..." (not simply that God glorifies Him). Since the Father glorifies the Son within the Godhead, this statement will be true whenever it happens that the Trinity creates an activity among creatures of glorying-in Jesus as the perfect Son of God made perfect man and thus glorifying Him, so that a hitherto nonexistent glory of Jesus comes to be.

Because, however, the Glory proceeds from both Father and Son reciprocally, such a statement is essentially insufficient. One must add immediately: "...and Jesus, in return, glorifies the Father." This is true—given that the Son

[10] This, in both directions, i.e., He refuses no good as if He were unworthy of it; He lays claim to none as if able to demand better than He has.

glorifies the Father within the Godhead—when God creates a glorifying of the Father, by Jesus and through Him, in response to the Father's liberality in making Jesus worthy of all glory. Thus, in addition to the reflections of the Son's acceptance of the divine essence, already seen in Jesus' love, there is a reflection of His consequent love of the Father. Jesus glorifies the Father because of the Father's goodness to Him and imitates Him by doing what He sees the Father doing (Jn.5:19–20).

The existence of such a mutual love is perhaps the most obvious theme in all four Gospels. Such statements as "The Father loves Me, because I lay down My life..." (Jn.10:17) (i.e., *because of* one aspect of the goodness already given to Jesus), and conversely, "I do as the Father has commanded Me, so that the world may know that I love the Father" (Jn.14:31), and the whole of Jesus' prayer at the Last Supper (Jn.17) imply, as is now obvious, that, the Father loves the Son, already constituted, with the characteristic love of glorification and that, in the world, God creates all that belongs or contributes to the glorification of Jesus as Son of the Father, and also that the Son loves the Unoriginated as perfect Father and that God creates all that, in Jesus and through Him, belongs to or contributes to the glorification of the Father as Father.

Created glory is given by God to Jesus because of the Father's pleasure in the Son. The Father desires to make manifest to every person, human and angelic as well as divine (Eph.3:9–11), the Son's excellence as Son. This He does through Jesus' manhood, not now (logically speaking) in a further reflection of the first procession, by God's giving Jesus greater excellence, even were this possible, but in a reflection of the second procession, by making His intrinsic glory and excellence known and praised in all the world.

The Father glories in the Son as the Father's perfect Image. Thus, in the finite order, God established Jesus' humanity as perfect created image of the Father (Col.1:15; Gen.1:26).[11] He then makes Jesus glorious by making Him known to be this model on which the whole human race is made, by nature as well as by grace. God acts to display the intrinsic glory, both human and divine, of Jesus, the exemplar and most perfect of all created beings. He does this in two ways: 1. by public manifestation and announcement of the fact and 2. by bringing to light the inner attitudes of Jesus as man that are the perfect reflections of His glorification of the Father as His eternal Son.

1. The anointing of Jesus by the Spirit

It is as One sent that the Holy Spirit is the Anointing with which Jesus is anointed so as to be the Christ (i.e., the Anointed One) of the Lord. Now, St. Irenaeus, St. Athanasius, and St. Basil the Great identified this anointing with the descent of the Spirit upon Jesus at His baptism in the Jordan. St. Cyril of Jerusalem obviously thought this opinion to be that of the Tradition, as is made clear by his strong and clear assertion of this understanding of Acts. 10:38 in his instructions to his newly baptized converts.[12]

---

[11] Cf. note 8 above.

St. Gregory Nazianzen, however, denied this, as did St. Augustine and, seemingly, St. Thomas.[13] Their principal reason is that all conceivable grace was given to Jesus' humanity at the moment of His conception by the Holy Spirit, in and by the grace of union with the Son, which union they take as constituting the anointing of Jesus as the Christ. There can, then, be no increase of His grace in any way. Is it not absurd, they ask, to say that Jesus had to wait for thirty years before receiving the fulness of the Spirit?

Now, if one is speaking of the grace of union and of habitual or sanctifying grace, I do not think there can be any question that they are right. His humanity, precisely as united with the Word, is deified by the indwelling Trinity from its beginning. Further, there seem no grounds for thinking that there could be a gradual "taking over" or "penetration" of His natural powers by grace, for there is nothing in these that is resistive to or out of harmony with grace; thus, the fulness of all virtue was His from the beginning.

Yet as St. Thomas remarks,[14] there was a growth in Jesus of the greatness and difficulty of the acts that are the effects of grace. And clearly, the great supernatural goods that He merited by His actions under grace, e.g., the resurrection, glorification, and enthronement, were given Him as graces of a different sort. Actual graces are clearly evident at work in Him during His life as, for example, when He exults in the Father[15] or prays to Him at the Last Supper.

But more, even if one considered the Spirit's action at the Incarnation as alone His being sent to Jesus, one might still notice that His being sent into the world was not thereby exhausted. When one speaks of the Spirit as the mutual Glory of Father and Son, what is highlighted in the created order is indeed habitual grace, by which one knows and loves God as He is in Himself. But here we are considering the reflection of this Glory as seen in the glorification of Jesus and the Father, i.e., as the created glorification of Each through the Other.

---

[12] For details concerning the first three and Gregory Nazianzen, cf. John Egan, S.J., "When Was Jesus Anointed? The Views of Irenaeus, Basil, Athanasius and Gregory Nazianzen," (to appear). Cyril was a contemporary of Gregory Nazianzen and took part with him in the Council of 381. It is possible that the work often attributed to Cyril was due, at least in part, to his successor, John II. Cf. Cyrille de Jérusalem, *Catéchèses Mystagogiques,* SC 126, ed. A. Piedagnel, tr. P. Paris, Paris: Éditions du Cerf (1966), Cat. III, 1,9–2,4, *pp* 120–122.

[13] For St. Augustine, cf. *de Trinitate* 15, 26. St. Thomas leaves the matter ambiguous, since he does not speak of Jesus' "anointing" as such. Cf. however, *ST* I, 43, 6, ad 3, and III, 32, 1 c and 39, 6, ad 1. Gregory seems, in contrast to Augustine, to consider the anointing not to be the work of the Spirit at all but of the Son alone. If this be really his position, it does an unacceptable violence not only to the New Testament texts and the earlier tradition just mentioned but also to the very notion of anointing as the sign and quasi-sacramental conferral of the Spirit of God, found throughout the Old Testament. St. Thomas seems to do justice to both Gregory's viewpoint and Augustine's by arguing that it is the Spirit to whom the union of the Word with the humanity is properly appropriated.

[14] *ST* III, 7, 12, ad 3. Most theologians seem to have followed him in this.

[15] Mt.11:25–26.

At His baptism, Jesus is not merely manifested but glorified before Israel,[16] and before the world through the Apostles, who received from John the Baptist their witness to this anointing. By the Spirit's descent in the form of a dove, He is made present in a new way to Jesus. He does not come with an increase of divine union or habitual grace but with created glory for the Father through this glorification of His Son. Through public consecration of Jesus' Person and mission, the Spirit comes as Jesus' glory, that with which the Father glorifies Him for His public life of giving glory to the Father.

2. Jesus' glorifying of the Father

The perfection of Jesus' inner life as man is to be seen through His acts of glorification of the Father. As seen above,[17] the Son's response to the Father's gift of the divine essence is reflected in Jesus' gratitude. But gratitude shows itself in glorification, as even Seneca recognized, pagan though he was: "It is by an outpouring of feeling that we indicate that we are grateful for the benefits which have come to us, witnessing to this not only in the hearing of the giver but everywhere."[18] Immediately after quoting this, St. Thomas adds: "Recompense for a benefit can be made [even] to one living in felicity through giving him reverence and honor."

The eternal birth of the Son, then, issues in the procession of the Glory. Their reflections in Jesus' charity are seen in Jesus' knowledge of the majesty of the Father through His gifts and in Jesus' glorying in and praising of the Father in consequence, "witnessing...everywhere" to His goodness. Knowing the Father's love and willing to receive all that God wills to give Him, He responds in gratitude and glorifies the Father by being among men the worthy Son of such a Father, the Father's perfect Image living among us. God creates in Jesus those free acts of glorification and praise of the Father suitable for a perfect and wholly graced human will. And this glorying in the Father (Mt.11:25), in its reflection of the Son's consequent love, leads Jesus always to do what He sees the Father doing (Jn.5:19–20).

The Son's gratitude within the Godhead lies in the perfection with which He receives the Father's gift without any independence of the Father or of the Father's will. Since the Persons are in all things equal in majesty, one can speak of the Son's obeying the Father only by some loose figure of speech or by some implicit reference to the Son's humanity. Only so could the Father be conceived to have authority to command the Son.[19] But at the created level the matter is different: total dependence on the free will of another because of his authority is obedience; and a son's obedience is freely to choose what his father wills, from gratitude and because he is his father and has a father's authority over him.

---

[16] Jn.1:31–32, using the equivalence suggested by Jn.5:34 and 5:41.

[17] *pp* 66–68.

[18] Cited in *ST* II-II, 106, 3 ad 5: Seneca, *de Beneficiis* II, cap. 22 (Paris: Firmin-Didot [1877], ed. Nisard, 159).

[19] Cf. however, *ST*, I, 42, 4, ad 1.

Jesus acknowledges with His human will the Father's supreme dominion and right to command (Jn.12:49–50; 14:31; 10:18), for "The Father is greater than I" (Jn.14:28). He submits, then, in obedience to the Father's will (Heb. 10:9–10), even to death, even death on a cross.[20] If God permits Jesus' defeat and death, disgraced, on the cross, this is to make manifest how perfect a Son He is, even when most radically subjected to human weakness. Even in Gethsemani, in full revulsion from the horror of such suffering and death, Jesus' obedience is perfect, wholly and tenderly confident of the Father's love: "The cup which My Father has given me, shall I not drink it?" {Jn.18:11}. And He dies reciting parts of the great psalms 22, 68, and 31. This inner glory, proper to man's situation in a sinful world, is transformed into the triumphant glory merited by Jesus when God raises Him from the dead through the Glory of the Father (Rom.6:4). As in the Godhead, so also the Son in His human nature is fully worthy, from this aspect also, of the Father and truly merits, in reflection of the Father's consequent love, to be glorified.

From the mutual glorification of Father and Son, the Glory proceeds. In the world, God creates the glorification of Jesus, from Gabriel's announcement, through Jesus' sufferings, to His resurrection, ascension, and enthronement. Thus also is created the glorification of the Father through Jesus' grateful obedience, from conception till He sends the Spirit into the Church to make the Father known and loved by all men. In brief, Jesus' entire life is a glorifying of the Father for His being glorified by the Father: "Glorify Your Son that the Son may glorify You.... I glorified You on earth" (Jn.17:1, 4). This mutual love of glorification is, then, a created reflection of the breathing forth of the Spirit in the Trinity.

Excursus:
The perfect created image of the Father

The Son of God, is, within the Trinity, the perfect Image of the Father, being without diminution or distortion all that the Father is except to be Father. But there are several different ways in which one might speak of Jesus, the Son of God in His human nature, as an image of the *Father,* i.e., as image of this one Person of the Trinity.

1. Augustine and the Western tradition which followed him[21] regard every man as, by nature, an image of the Trinity. Aware that Gen.1:26–27 says only that man was created *in* or *according to* the image of God, not *as* the image, this tradition saw that phrasing as due to the necessary imperfection of

[20] Cf., e.g., Phil.2:5–11; Jn.5:30; 10:17; 14:21 & 31; 15:9–10. This is a death offered by Jesus through the eternal Spirit (Heb.9:14).

[21] The Eastern tradition emphasized man's creation in the Image of God (the Word, the Son) and only slowly took note explicitly of man's being created in the image of the entire Trinity; cf. John Egan, S.J., "Logos and Emanation in the Writings of Clement of Alexandria," *Trinification of the World: A Festschrift in Honor of Frederick E. Crowe,* edd. T. A. Dunne & J.-M. Laporte, Toronto: Regis College Press (1978), *pp* 176–209, at 176–178.

any creaturely likeness to God. Though man is an image of God, he is not a "perfect" image in the sense of one that has the same nature as its exemplar.[22]

The resemblance of any created image to the Father (or Son or Holy Spirit) must involve some created similarity to the divine Person in question, i.e., a similarity based on an intratrinitarian relation of origination.[23] According to Augustine, the various spiritual activities of the human soul provide created yet true analogs of those relations, so that the soul of man is an image, however imperfect, of the Trinity. For Aquinas,[24] the basic analog is the procession of the interior word that is the mind's act of understanding, followed by a procession of love through the action of the will. Hence one can distinguish an intellectual principle from which proceeds the word of understanding, this word itself, and the love that follows.

But whatever the particular theory, the three human elements are not only distinguishable but differentiated; and one does not automatically fall into error by speaking of one or other alone, provided he says nothing that implies a denial of the others. To speak, then, of Jesus as a created image of the Father need involve no error, provided there is no implicit denial that He is also, albeit differently, the created image of the Son and of the Holy Spirit.That Jesus is the *perfect* created image in this first sense is evident from the fact that He alone is, completely and perfectly, what man was meant to be, by nature, from the beginning.[25]

2. Thus far, we have made no distinction between Jesus and any other man. But Jesus is an image of the Father also through grace in a way superior to any other creature's graced imaging of Him.

Here it is necessary to clear away a confusion that occasionally arises. Some have too quickly assumed that a man's imaging of one Person of the Trinity (alone, or principally, or merely in a way other than that in which he images the other Persons) would require that that Person act *ad extra* differently than the Others. Now, assuredly, God's action *ad extra* is unitary. But it is far from evident that the Trinity could not create a resemblance to one Person rather than to another. Consider only the Incarnation, whereby God created a human nature that is united solely to the Son and not to either the Father or the Spirit. The Son of God alone died on the cross and rose from the dead. Further, every page of the Gospel shows us that Jesus' created

[22] Cf., e.g., St. Thomas (*ST* I, 93, 1 c), who uses 'perfect image' to indicate an image of the same nature as its exemplar, so that no perfect image, in this sense, of any or all of the Persons could exist outside the Godhead itself. 'Perfect created image' as I use the term signifies merely that all that is possible of created likeness to one of the Persons is present.

[23] Among us, this order of origination must be translated into essential properties or traits, whereas in the Trinity there is no distinction whatever in essential properties. Thus all the psychological analogies for the Persons are based on the essential elements in man, those that constitute him an image of God, a little Trinity. The best we can do is to look at what is, among us, most "personal," most truly incommunicable, i.e., the free act of the person choosing what and how he will love.

[24] *ST* I, 93, especially articles 5–7.

[25] Cf. the comments of Cabasilas and Chrysologus in Sect. 4.F below (*pp* 83–84).

relations with the Father and with the Spirit were different. Most importantly for our present question, the "imitation of Christ," so strong in the West since the late Middle Ages and much earlier in the Antiochene East involves an element of imaging that cannot be directed immediately to the Father or the Spirit.

Jesus' imaging of the Father by grace springs from His mission among us. His humanity and the graces with which it was endowed were selected to show us by their activity how to be true sons of the Father in and through Jesus and to make it possible for us by grace to "be conformed to the image of His Son,...the first-born among many brethren" (Rom.8:29). But if the Son, as man, is to show us, at the level of creation, who the Son is, then, since to be Son is to be the perfect Image of the Father, so at its own level must be Jesus' graced activity. Since Jesus is, as the Son of God, perfect Image of the Father, He is also, as the Son of man, an image of the Father, being the created image of the Image of the Father.

3. Evidently, any interpretation of Scripture given to support the assertion that the Son of man is an image of the Father must leave intact all that orthodox Christianity has already drawn from the pertinent texts to show that Jesus is the Son of God and the co-eternal Image of God the Father. So, while holding firmly that Jesus is, by His divinity, the Image of the Father but as Son of man is, like other men, an image of the Trinity, I would argue that there is more that can be said. His coming among us as man was to show us through His humanity some likeness to the Father.[26] His humanity was created not only to be able to suffer for us but to show us in a human way *who* the Son is, thereby to teach us *who* the Father is (and, indeed, who the Spirit is) so that we might know and worship the one God as the Most Holy Trinity.

Only by knowing ourselves as sons of the Father in and through His Son and not simply as sons of God, can we pray to the Father as Jesus taught us, "Our Father...." And if we can pray to Him thus, we must be in some true way like Him, as true sons, not directly but through likeness to His Son. This is twofold: like the Son of God, through His indwelling in us along with the Father and the Spirit; and like the Son of man, through that sharing in Jesus' life which the indwelling Trinity makes possible.

To illustrate: Jesus tells those who object to what He has done on the sabbath: "My Father [even] till now is working; and I am working" {Jn. 5:17}. He is reminding them that, though God rested from His work of creation on the seventh day, yet He continues to work so as to preserve and guide all things. Thus, Jesus' remark is rightly taken by His opponents as equivalent to: My Father—God, who created all—still works during His own sabbath; and I, since one with Him, am doing the same. Jesus indeed "was calling God His own Father, making Himself equal to God" {Jn.5:18}. Yet manifestly it is

[26] The strong need to distinguish sharply in every case between what Jesus says *in forma servi* and what He says *in forma Dei*, can be weakened a bit. Sometimes He speaks as the Servant and sometimes as the Son of God, but often as both, albeit differently.

Jesus as man who is under attack for the deed He did (by divine power, but through His human will and word) and for His telling the man just cured to carry away his bedding. Thus, without any clouding of the explicit assertion concerning His divinity, Jesus is "working" as man on the sabbath precisely as imaging His working as Son with the Father.

Consider, too, "I am the Way,...; no one comes to the Father except through Me." {Jn.14:6}. Since the Father is God, one does not speak falsely if he takes this to say, "No one comes to God, except through Me, who am God." One would come closer to the meaning of the text, however, were he to say, "No one comes to God, except through Me, the Son of God." Closer yet, "No one comes to the Father, who is God, except through Me, His Son and also God." But he would do better yet to say, "No one comes to the Father, who is God, except through Me, Son of God and Son of man." The human nature of the Son has also a major part in Christ's being the Way.

But what of the parts omitted in this passage as just cited?[27] Surely, the human nature of the Son is essential to Christ's being the Truth—not that He would not be the divine Truth eternally without the incarnation but that it is as man that He has revealed that Truth to us. It is as man that He spoke the truth that we needed to hear and as man that He lived as the perfect example of what He taught; and since the teaching was the Father's (Jn.7:16), the example images the Father.

D. The Spirit's love for Father and Son: the Church

The reciprocal glorification of the Father and Jesus, though the work of all three Persons, properly reflects the characteristic love of Father and Son for the Spirit. But how is the Spirit's love for Father and Son reflected in Jesus' love, that is: how does God's activity in Jesus and His world create a resemblance to the Spirit's characteristic love for Father and Son?

We saw earlier that the Spirit is that unique and utterly simple Glory of Father and Son that originates in their mutual glorification; further, He loves Father and Son by willing Himself to be as Their common Glory. But, as mentioned above,[28] the Spirit may also be said to love Them by His being the principle of the intercommunion of Father and Son in act. This He is, not by some quasi-efficient causality, as if by some action of tying or binding Them together.[29] Neither is He some sort of quasi-formal cause for their

---

[27] Augustine, (*de Trinitate* IV, 12, 24) agrees as to the Way but gives the humanity no part in Christ's being the Truth. Gregory Nazianzen, Theological Oration 4 (Oratio 30) (Norris, *Faith Gives Fullness*, 276–277) likewise ascribes His being the Way to the Son of man, though not so clearly refusing a role for the humanity in the Truth. But no harm is done, I think, to all that either of these men are concerned with in these passages if one sees all these self-designations of Jesus as also referring to His humanity as the paradigm, pattern, model, not only as to being but as to operation and activity at all levels, natural and supernatural, for all men and for all material creation.

[28] *Pp* 53–54.

[29] If nothing else, such a position would seem to imply that the Spirit's proceeding is not only

communion.[30] Rather, He makes Them one by a quasi-final causality, as a sort of goal or *finis* toward which They are intrinsically directed and with respect to which They are One: Their common Finality.

A reflection, then, of the Spirit's love requires, in addition to this love itself, a created good for both Father and Son, a good with this same structure of oneness in intercommunion through a common and intrinsic finality of those who glorify.

Father and Son are indistinguishable in Their glorifying of Each Other. So, likewise, all those who are in Christ take part by grace in Jesus' glorifying of the Father for the Father's goodness to Jesus (and to those who are in Jesus). In turn, they share in the Father's glorifying of Jesus, especially through their own imitation of Him, because of Jesus' perfection as Son of God made man. But this entry into the mutual glorification of Father and Son by created participation makes Christians, consecrated by baptism for this purpose, indistinguishably one. The reflection of the Spirit's love is, then, this issuing of created glory from many as from one single principle and, so, their being made one through their common finality.

This, then, describes the Spirit's role as Sanctifier. God creates within us that common structure of charity that gives us, as our common end and goal, to glorify the Father and the Son. And this activity is properly attributed to the Holy Spirit as reflection of His love within the Trinity.

One obtains entry into this mutual glorifying in and through Jesus alone. By being in Jesus,[31] we are made "one principle" with respect to the procession of glory. But just as the one spiration of the Holy Spirit by Father and Son does not make them less distinct as Persons, so this intercommunion among those who glorify the Father and Jesus, by which they are made one in goal and *finis*, does not destroy their personal individuality and diversity.

But is this reflection a communion in glorifying the Father and Jesus or in glorifying one another? For to be reflection, the created goods must exist as goods of the same Person(s) reached by the uncreated love in question. On the other hand, a genuine similarity of structure in the goods created for the Father and Son would seem to require that the unity be brought about between persons who are mutually glorifying each other, and that it be their glory that proceeds from this activity.

Now, the glory is one, directed both to the Father through Jesus and to Jesus by the Father, and it arises from the many people who are glorifying Them. But we can glorify Them truly only insofar as we are in Jesus. And we can be in Him only by intercommunion of glorification of one another in

---

a second procession from the Father but a sort of second principle in God, as if the Spirit were a source of the unity of Father and Son, or an agent somehow independent of Them.

[30] This is not to reject St. Thomas' theory (*ST* I, 37, 2c), since he is speaking of how Father and Son may be said to love One Another by the Spirit, not how They are constituted one Principle by the Spirit's bonding.

[31] We will consider more carefully the meaning and significance of this phrase "in Jesus" in Section E below.

diversity of persons. For, the Body lives by only one Spirit, who by one finality makes our diversity into one. For what we praise and glorify in Jesus Himself is what we must see and love and glorify, albeit so much less manifest, in one another.

This does not mean that we can see Jesus' own goodness in everyone we meet. But we can see the goodness of all those together who form His Body, the Church. This is perhaps the main reason why the Church venerates the saints—that in them the glory of Jesus and the Father shines out most visibly. Likewise, though painfully aware that we are rarely if ever in a position to recognize confirmation in grace of anyone, the Church seems always to have been at ease with praise for those who seem to be living lives of true holiness. So too, she seems always ready to accept splendor and grandeur in the ceremonials surrounding the Pope, bishops, priests, and even religious and laity, poor representatives of Jesus though many of them have obviously been.

The more who give glory, the greater is that glory; for it is not multiplied into several glories, though arising from distinct glorifications. Further, the more various those who give glory, the greater it is, as representing a wider range of judgments of the many aspects of the one excellence. What is essential is that the glorifications be authentic, i.e., that each person who gives glory be right in his judgment concerning the excellence that draws his praises.

Now, the Spirit wills to be the Glory of Father and Son, not His own. Proceeding from perfect knowledge of the divine goodness, He is the Glory that, by His public manifestation of the excellence of Each, guarantees such authenticity. Thus, it is the work of the Holy Spirit, "the Spirit of truth" (Jn.14:17; 15:26; 16:13) to make Both to be known in truth and loved and gloried in, the Son first through true knowledge (and therefore true love) of Jesus, and then of the Father through Jesus' revealing Him.

Living by one Breath and Spirit, in a common effort to seek in all the greater glory of the Father and Jesus, we are formed into one Body. This is the Body of Christ since it is in Him alone that we can fully glorify reciprocally the Father and Jesus, being made images of Jesus as the Image of the invisible Father.

The Spirit makes us enter into and participate in the one goal and *finis* of the Church: to glorify Christ as her Spouse and King and, so, glorify the Father as Jesus does, since she is His Body. She is that great mystery through which the Father glorifies Jesus, through and in which Jesus glorifies the Father. To use the striking phrase of Karl Rahner, "[T]he Church is nothing else than the visible manifestation of the Spirit in the world."[32]

[32] Karl Rahner, S.J., "The Church as the Subject of the Sending of the Spirit," in *Theological Investigations*, vol. 7, *pp* 186–192, tr. David Bourke, London: Darton, Longman, & Todd (1971), 187. Or again, "The Church is nothing else than the further projection of the historicity and of the visibility of Jesus through space and time, and every word of its message, every one of its sacramental signs, is, once more, nothing else than a part of the world in its earthiness, with which the Spirit has united itself indissolubly since the day when the Logos became flesh," 188–189. Cf.

Formed by the Spirit's drawing of believers into unity by and for her one common act of praise and glorification,[33] the Church reflects the Spirit's characteristic love for Father and Son. But this love, as seen, is also His will to be Their mutual Glory. Hence, it is not some interior and private love, but one always public and visible. So, then, is the Church. An invisible Church, composed solely of the predestined or of the justified, or some noninstitutional or nonorganizational Church, or, worst of all, whatever entity one may be speaking of in such phrases as "an experience of church"[34] is an illusive self-contradiction.

The supreme reflection of the Spirit is the (eventually) perfect, created glory of the Father and Jesus, as the latter restores all things to the Father, that He may be all and in all (I Cor.15:28). The Church exists that we, being in Jesus, may glorify the Father in Him and Him by the Father's action, through the Holy Spirit. The Church on earth is, thus, the means connaturally directed by God for the achievement of our final end, to be members of the Church in heaven, the New Jerusalem.

E. The Father's love for those living in Jesus

It will have been noticed in what we have written concerning the created reflections of the Holy Spirit that we had everywhere to consider not Jesus only but the rest of mankind, all those who are invited to glorify Him and the Father and to be made one in the Church. Even the reflections of the antecedent loves of the Father and the Son show, if thought about carefully, the same "overflow" since there is no reason to think of Jesus as man at all, were there no men. So, while we are still thinking of how the characteristic loves within the Trinity are reflected at the created level in Jesus, it will prove useful to consider how it is that we are included.

We begin with the question, how can *the Father* be truly said to love us?[35]

---

also, the text of St. Irenaeus that he quotes, "Where the Church is, there is also the Spirit of God; and where the Spirit of God is, there also is the Church and every grace."(*Adversus Haereses* III, 24, 1).

[33] Hence one can see why the Mass is the very heart of the Church and is the determinant of her morality no less than of her doctrine, as Donald J. Keefe, S.J. has cogently argued: cf., e.g., "Hacia una moralidad eucarística," *Pentecostes 34*, 5–41 (julio–septembre, 1973) or in a much shortened version: "Toward a Eucharistic Morality," *Communio 2*, 99–125 (Summer 1975)); the full argument is given in *Covenantal Theology: the eucharistic order of history*, Lanham (MD): University Press of America (1991), especially vol. I, *pp* 45–71, and vol. II, *pp* 297–315.

[34] The lack of capitalization converts 'the Church' from a proper name to a common noun. The refusal of the definite article converts the wholly specific sense of the term to some sort of putative generic, as if there were more than one example in the world of the Church. Such denigration of Catholic doctrine is done presumably in order to embrace in a single word all those who have religious convictions or experiences of whatever sort. Such a shift of language has less to do with the truth than even a Church of all and only the predestined.

[35] Note again that our question relates to a characteristic love of the Father for us. There is no possible doubt from revelation, and there should be none even from a sufficiently developed philosophy, that God loves all men and all our world.

For what could there be within the Godhead that would relate us to the Father as Jesus is related to Him, rather than to all three Persons together, who in the unity of the divine nature create both us and our world? And since it is essential that a Christian hold that all actions of the Trinity *ad extra* are common, theologians have traditionally dealt with scriptural passages that would seem to suggest otherwise by means of appropriation.

Yet the insistence of the Scripture in speaking as if it is the Father Himself who loves us should also be taken into account. To take just a few from a host of examples, we may recall St. Paul's statement, "God shows His love for us," making clear that 'God' here refers to the Father when he says shortly thereafter, "we were reconciled to God by the death of His Son" (Rom. 5:8, 10). Or consider his solemn assertion, "He [the Father] chose us in Him [Jesus] before the foundation of the world, to be holy and blameless before Him in love, predestining us for adoption as sons" {Eph. 1:4}.[36]

But it is John who insists most. Speaking of the Father, he says: "God so loved the world that He gave His only Son" (Jn.3:16). Since we are now in better position to probe our Lord's seemingly excessive language at the Last Supper,[37] we may recall some of His sayings there. Thus, He prays, "that the love with which You have loved Me may be in them, and I in them" (17:26). More direct is His statement, "The Father Himself loves you, because you have loved Me and believed..." (Jn.16:27).[38] Or again, "He who loves Me will be loved by My Father" (Jn.14:21) and "If a man loves Me, he will keep My word, and My Father will love him" (Jn.14:23). But extraordinary and quite beyond immediate comprehension, is the Lord's saying to the Father, "[You] have loved them even as You have loved Me" (Jn.17:23).

Now, I think it possible to say truly that, insofar as the Father loves us *in* Jesus, whom He loves precisely as His Father, the Father Himself does love us. St. Augustine states the matter in language much like ours:

> It is in the Son that the Father loves us, because in the Son He chose us before the creation of the world.... For He who loves the Son would not fail to love the bodily members of the Son, nor is there another cause for loving His members, except because He loves Him. But He loves the Son according to His divinity, because He has begotten Him equal to Himself; He loves Him also according to that which is man, because the only-begotten Word Himself was made flesh and, on account of the Word, the flesh of the Word is dear to Him; He loves us however because we are the members of Him whom He loves; and for this reason, that we might be such, He loved us before we existed.[39]

It is indeed *in* Jesus that the Father chose us (Eph.1:4). We are in Jesus,

---

[36] The second comma can, and perhaps should, be moved so that the passage reads, "before Him, in love predestining us..."

[37] Cf. *p* 19 above.

[38] Though the verb used here is φιλεῖν rather than ἀγαπᾶν, commentators both old and new treat the former as here equivalent to the latter. Even were a clear distinction found between them, it is not evident how this would help resolve the problem.

[39] *In Iohannis*, 110, 5–6, *pp* 625–626.

moreover, as the branches in the Vine, as the members in His Body, the living stones in the living Temple. Because we are in Jesus or called to be, we are included in the Father's love for Jesus, the reflection of His characteristic love for His eternal Son, made man for our sake.

If it be conceded that the Father does love us, as Father, we have still to ask, "In what ways or in what manner does He love us?" For, clearly, within the Trinity, neither the gift of the divine essence nor the mutual glorification of Father and Son, inasmuch as belonging to the Persons Themselves, includes us. There is no other way that we can be included in the Father's love for the Son or for the Spirit except as this love is reflected into creation by His love for Jesus. First, then, let us see in what manner He loves us in virtue of the created reflection of His antecedent love for the Son and afterwards consider what may be added through the reflection of His consequent love.

a) Because He loves us in Jesus, the Father loves us, I would argue, as He loves Jesus.[40] So, indeed, Jesus Himself said, "You loved them even as You loved Me." And if the Father's love for Jesus includes us precisely insofar as we are in Christ and as we live with His life, then the mode or manner of the Father's love for us must be the same as for Jesus in that same proportion. This means, therefore, that the Father will love us, first of all, freely and, then also, exigently, forming us to share fully in the mission of Jesus as the Christ, to labor and to suffer for the good of His Church.

The *First Letter of John*, while explaining at length the love that should exist among Christians and between them and God, twice underlines explicitly the initiative of God's love. What counts is: "not that we loved God but that He loved us and sent His Son" (I Jn.4:10). "We love, because He first loved us" (4:19). Many more times this initiative is presumed or lying just below the surface. For Paul also, the Father's love has ever had the sole initiative. His love antecedes ours from eternity. He planned for us before creation that we might be holy and blameless before Him in Jesus. Through this previsioned union with His Son, He would ransom us from our sins, because He had chosen us in the Beloved (Eph.1:4 & 6). No actuality in us but our mere possibility served as grounds for His loving us. The sole reason for His love lies in Him, in His idea of us as possible members of His Son.

This total dependence of the creature on the Father's initiative is one of the great lessons taught us by the Church's wise maintenance of the practice of infant baptism, despite whatever the abuses in practice or theological difficulties. Here is made visible, even to our dull minds, that the gift of grace is free, without the least cooperation on the part of the one receiving so great a gift. The infant cannot yet will or choose; it cannot reject or accept the grace offered. God in His pure and simple mercy chooses to make this child of

[40] We might, of course, say that the Father loves us in such a way that His love serves as the pattern and model of Jesus' love for us. Hence, the traits of Jesus' love will be found, suitably modified, in the Father's love. But we have not yet considered how Jesus loves us. When we do, we shall wish to consider how His love for us is like the Father's for Him, for this is the direction taken by the scriptural evidence, rather than the reverse.

fallen Adam His own in Christ. Yet, how often Christians are scandalized by this gratuity, which does not even require faith as a disposition but grants the faith, along with hope and charity, to one who cannot even know that a gift has been given.

Thus, baptism is an analog to what occurred in the creation of the world, lifted now to the supernatural plane. At the beginning was primeval chaos; from this He formed by His Word the beauty and goodness of our world. This is what the Father's charity towards us is like. It makes us good supernaturally by making us to exist in Jesus His Son; and only by His having chosen to do this for us can we be worthy of this gift.

The divine initiative and the gratuity of God's grace are not quite the same. Though often related concretely, the terms are not equivalent because they refer to different things: initiative to God as the source of the giving, gratuity to the giving itself.

'Initiative' signifies a certain vigor of decision on the part of one who, by his free choice, not only acts but sets in motion the activity of others. Applied to God, it emphasizes the power of His freedom to begin or to prevent any and all creaturely activity. He alone can initiate anything; He alone can make the creature exist or act or desire to act in any given way.

'Gratuity' signifies two things. It names, first of all, that quality of a gift by which it is given without hope or desire for any return or compensation and without any cost to the recipient save for the act of reception itself. Secondly, it means that the giver is free from any shadow of moral necessity. That is, one who loves gratuitously is under no obligation, of duty or office or relationship, to act in a certain way, though all acts from obligation should be done from love, i.e., willing the true good of the other. Correspondingly, acts of virtuous but nongratuitous love, e.g., in fulfilment of contract, do not call for gratitude. Applied to God's giving of His gifts, 'gratuity' implies, simultaneously and together, a giving without hope of return and the absence of anything in the creature that could obligate God or lay valid claim to His gifts.

The Father's love for us is gratuitous. He loves us in complete freedom and because He has chosen to love us, not because He finds in us anything that can command or call forth or evoke His love, still less anything we might give Him in return. Even in the eternal generation of the Son, the Father's love is (logically) antecedent to the Son's worthiness. In the reflection of that love in His love for the Son-made-man, the same is true, no longer only logically but ontologically. Far less is it possible that the Father should have loved those who are in Jesus because they were worthy of His gift. They were made worthy only by this gift, by the free initiative of His love.

In sum, the Father loves those who are in Jesus not because they are good but He makes them good because He loves them. He makes them good by forming them to share Jesus' mission. I shall say no more about this formation here, since Parts II and III will deal with it.

b) We miss the full force of Jesus' statement, "Father, You have loved them even as You have loved Me" if we neglect the love the Father has for Jesus in the created reflection of the procession of the Spirit. Looking back to Section III.C, we see that at least the following should be considered.

Insofar as we are in Jesus, we are included in the reflection of the characteristic love of mutuality that, in God, is the breathing forth of the Glory of Father and Son and that, reflected in creation, is rightly regarded as the Spirit's work. But we are made to be in Jesus by being made to live with His life as the Christ of the Lord, i.e., by being anointed as He was with His Spirit. This gift of the Spirit, too, is part of the Father's love for us, making us thereby to serve for Jesus' glory. So, we are to manifest Jesus' goodness by means of and in all the good that He confers upon us.[41]

Further, by an adoption effected through communication in the life of Jesus, a new life for us that involves an intrinsic transformation by the Holy Spirit, we are made the Father's sons. As sons, we are images of Him who is the Image of the Father. For, the Father by the Spirit makes Jesus ever more widely and perfectly known as His Image and man's exemplary cause. And, insofar as we are images of the Image, we are made part of the object of the Father's love.[42]

The Father glorifies Jesus through all the beings of the world and especially through the faith and hope and love of His fellow men. The saints, who are the finest images of the Image, are, then, those most loved by the Father. They are the best samples formed from the Exemplar, made by God to give to our dull imaginations some glimpse of the grandeur, yet also the imitability, of the inner life of Jesus. So the Father glorifies His saints in heaven to the degree and according to the manner in which they have lived in Jesus. Though over the centuries the Church's veneration of the saints has seemed scandalous to many, this glorification of the saints by the Church, inspired as it is by the Glory of the Son and and His Father, is clearly essential to her life in the Spirit.

It does not take much self-knowledge to realize how great are God's gifts to us from our conception onwards and how little is our gratitude for them. But if we live in Jesus, we enter into His gratitude to the Father in the Thanksgiving (Eucharist) offered continually by the Church, making up for our weakness by His power and generosity. Our gratitude, in Jesus, is to issue in glorification of Jesus and, through Him, of the Father. Thus, we are able to recognize Their Glory everywhere. But our gratitude, like Jesus', can prove its genuinity only by the perfection of its obedience to the Father. This obedience we live by living in Jesus, sharing this gift that the Father has given Him in such perfection.

---

[41] This good involves, chiefly, our elevation by grace and then, through the resultant healing, the gradual rectification of our whole moral life. Though not impossible to our nature itself, even though fallen, genuine moral virtue belongs primarily to grace and the *noblesse oblige* of Christ.

[42] St. Basil's insight (*p* 47) is applicable here also, though the direction is reversed, going from God to the creature.

F. The Father's love for all men

In Jesus and through Him we receive everything from the Father, who sees us either as already members of His Son or, at least, as called to be His members since sharing the same human nature as His. This matter of our common nature deserves, however, a closer look than we have yet given it.[43]

In accord with the approach we have been developing, when we speak of living in Jesus, we are referring to our own selves as being some portion of the created good given to the Son by the Father in reflection of the Father's gift to Him of the divine essence. The Father, then, loves us as part of the good He has willed for Jesus. For us to be this good that He intends for Jesus, we need to be supported not only supernaturally but also naturally by a host of created goods, things that are goods-for-us. The created good that is our life in Christ has its natural prerequisites, e.g., the human species itself[44] and *its* prerequisite, the material world.[45]

All this, then, is loved because of Jesus and for His sake. This is true not only of what surrounds us now but includes the whole history of the universe and, in particular, of man. Most especially is this true of God's dealings with His people, described in the Old Testament, which led directly toward Christ and prepared for Him.[46]

When speaking of the Father's love in creating Jesus, we passed too quickly over the nature of the good given to the Son by His becoming man. We must now return to this point.[47]

The union between Jesus and the rest of mankind is deeper and far more extensive than usually thought. Without man, there would be no Son of Man. But without Jesus, there would be no mankind at all. For,

> the nature of man was constituted from the beginning on account of the New Man. Both mind and desire were prepared for Him. We received reason that we might know Christ; desire, that we might run to Him...since He was Himself the Archetype of those who were made. The old Adam was not the model for the New, but the New Adam for the old... For Him, before whose eyes all things are before they exist, the former is the imitation of the latter and was formed according to His pattern and image.[48]

---

[43] Though not understanding well what "being in Jesus" might mean, most Christians concede that we can be in Jesus, whether this is thought to be by faith in Him or by the supernatural life of grace or by membership in His Church. Less recognized is the fact that we are already in Him, in a different way, by our very nature.

[44] This is the matter of this Section.

[45] Cf. Section G. below.

[46] This will occupy Part II of this book.

[47] In the discussion that follows, I am concerned only with the actual world and its real history, not with what God might have done otherwise. It is hazardous enough to seek to understand what He has done, without trying to determine the boundaries of what He might have done or, even, to trace the limits of divine omnipotence.

[48] Nicholas Cabasilas, *De Vita in Christo*, PG 150, 491–726 at 680–81 (my translation). The complete work is translated in: *The Life in Christ,* St. Vladimir's Seminary Press, Crestwood, NY,

The Western tradition is no different. Thus, St. Peter Chrysologus states some 900 years earlier:

> Two men gave the human race its beginning... The first Adam was made by the last... The second Adam stamped His image on the first at the time when He formed him...because this last Adam is truly the first.[49]

Jesus, then, is the Archetype of our entire race, its model and exemplar, as well as the concrete embodiment of its perfection, its fulfilment, and its goal.[50] What we need to see clearly here is that it is our nature, not just our supernatural being, that has been made in and for Jesus.

> Human nature...is not and, save for sin, never has been in any way independent of or, indeed, strictly definable apart from Christ. He is the perfect and unalterable exemplar not only of our supernatural but of our *natural* being, the ultimate and unique measure of all that is *naturally* good.[51]

Jesus, man no less truly than He is God, was subject to all that material existence necessarily entails and became, thereby, part of the history of the world. But as just seen from Cabasilas' and Chrysologus' understanding of St. Paul, Jesus is also the entire meaning of all history and its Lord. In Christ, therefore, rather than being a meaningless atom lost somewhere in a universe vastly larger than he, man is, wherever he is, the true center of the universe. For at the heart of the universe is the Heart of Christ. Through Jesus, man is not only the heart but the head of the creation. He is the goal and purpose of the world, even its source. All this is true not only of the material world but the spiritual one, since Jesus is Lord of the angels and they are, for the Christian, ministering spirits.[52]

If it be said that all this relates to man as first created, that is, in grace, unfallen, and to him only, I would reply that when Paul states that "In Him [Jesus] all things were created" (Col.1:16), he is saying much more than that all the supernatural aspects of man's world were created in Him. The whole of Adam was created in Christ, not just his life of grace, even as all of him was created for Him and through Him.

The Son, then, in taking on human nature, took up our race and our universe in their entirety since inseparable from His manhood. More importantly

---

1974. Cf. *pp* 190–191.

[49] Sermo 117, 1 & 2, in: CCL 24A, *Sancti Petri Chrysologi Collectio Sermonum, II*, ed. A. Olivar, Turnholt: Brepols (1981), *p* 709. (PL 52, 520–521).

[50] Why the Father wanted the Son to be the Archetype for a race of material-spiritual creatures remains a deep mystery, though, from the characteristic love of the Son for the Father and of Them both for the Holy Spirit, one can dimly discern some indications of its fittingness. But this is work for another generation of theologians.

[51] Paul M. Quay, S.J., "The Theological Position and Role of Ethics," *Listening: Journal of Religion and Culture 18*, 260–274 (1983), at 262.

[52] More needs to be said on this point, for the Likeness of God according to which man was created was referred by many of the Fathers to the life of grace, and thus specially related to the Holy Spirit and the holy angels.

for our purpose here, our race and our universe have come to be not only because God willed them as essential parts of the reflection of the Father's love for the Son and, indeed, of the Son's love for the Father but also of the love of Both for the Spirit, as He for Them.[53]

It is the entire Trinity that creates Jesus, who is the Son sent into the world by the Father. It is also, however, the entire Trinity that creates us and the universe, but in and for the Son so sent and so loved by the Father. There is no metaphysical possibility that the Father should love us simply for ourselves. *Only* insofar as we exist for Jesus, as contributors to His glory and to His glorifying of the Father, can we be the objects of this love. This need not, of course, imply that we are living in the grace of Christ. For, we may serve for His glory as objects of His wrath, and yet still be salvageable so as, in the future, to serve His glory as the objects of His grace.

G. The Vestiges of the Trinitarian Loves in the Subhuman Creation

The subhuman creation bears the vestiges or "footprints" of the Trinity[54] and, so, of the characteristic loves of the Persons. What we seek here, then, are those aspects of God's love for the material creation that can reasonably be appropriated to the characteristic loves proper to His inner life. What analogies or similarities of internal structure exist between the love God has for the material world and the loves within the Trinity?

That God does love His creation, not only men and angels but the merely material world as well, is evident from Scripture. For example, we read:

> You love all things that are, and loathe nothing that You have made, for You wonld not have formed anything You hated. How would anything have endured unless You willed it? Or how would anything not called forth by You have been preserved? You spare all things, for thay are Yours, O Lord who love the living. For Your immortal Spirit is in all things.[55]

Since God gives as His first gift the gift of existence, He is not only "God" and "Creator" but also "the Father," as in the first words of the Creed: "I believe in God the Father almighty, Creator of heaven and earth...." Here, evidently, creation is only appropriated to the Father since all three Persons are equally the source of created being.[56]

---

[53] I would not deny that God could have created Jesus by Himself, without a human race other than Himself and without a material universe other than Himself. But, had His humanity been so created, there could be no possibility of created glory other than that given directly by Jesus to the Father—there could be no created counterpart to the Father's glorification of the Son. (Again, this might require qualification once the role of the angels in the universe is better understood.)

[54] For the Augustinian and Thomistic development of this traditional doctrine of the traces or vestiges of the Trinity, cf. *ST* I, 45, 7c and parallels. Crucial for our work in this Section is Thomas' discussion of the ways in which these traces are to be found in creation: *ST* I, 45, 6 & 7.

[55] Wisd. 11:24–12:1. Cf. also, Ps. 104.

[56] When the Church prays: "Te Deum laudamus, Te Dominum confitemur, Te aeternum Pa-

The reasons for this appropriation are easily found. This proto-gift to the creature of its total being, alone makes any other gift possible. And the initiative, gratuity, and liberality of this gift are glimpsed as somehow like the uncreated gift of the Father to the Son.

Because God creates from nothing this good that is the world, His love is prior to any goodness other than His own. Hence, whatever created goodness He gives is given to that which stands in absolute need of this gift if it is to exist at all. Unlike our loves, His love is causative (He makes the good that He loves exist) and totally effective (the created good thereby exists exactly as He wishes it to be).[57] He makes actually to be, in itself, i.e., as other than Himself, what was merely possible. He then looks upon it and sees that it is very good (Gen.1:31). He sees that it is good because this gift is a gift of likeness to God Himself, a share in the divine goodness, and a mode of participation in the divine essence that is given an existence that is not God's own.

Logically antecedent to all creation, God knows and loves all that is: Himself. He knows—and loves accordingly—all possible ways in which His being could be shared and participated. But since, as such a participation, it is but one of infinitely many ways God's essence can be participated, it cannot force His love. Only the divine goodness itself can "move" the divine will; the goodness that moves the Creator is the divine goodness and that alone. God's love can only terminate in God Himself. Thus, His love for the creature is not what might be called a "descending" love, going out and down to the creature, infinitely below Him. His love is for the creature, but as real participation in the divine perfection, i.e., inasmuch as it exists as a reflection of His Idea of it.[58]

From nothing at all, then, God creates every existent mode of participation in His being. Each is good now because He loved it first, before it came to be. He loved it because He is good, not because of a goodness it did not yet have and could only come to have as a gift from His love for it. However good as a possible participation of His goodness, it had no goodness sufficient to draw His love; and He could have chosen an infinity of other worlds or types of being. His gift, then, is wholly free. Nothing other than His own infinite goodness can exist except insofar as He has chosen in total freedom to create it. Nor, as *Wisdom* says, could anything continue to be did He not wish it. God remains wholly free to choose that it continue to exist or not. Actual existence remains in every way God's gratuitous gift in every moment and grounds no claims upon Him. Conversely, whatever is real is loved by God, to whatever degree it is, since it is something He freely wills to exist.

On the other hand, in contrast to the Father's characteristic love for the Son, God can love the individual, material parts of the world only as parts,

---

trem omnis terra veneratur," it seems that "Patrem" is used attributively, of God as the total source of created being, and not as the Personal name of the Unoriginated.

[57] "Amor Dei est infundens et creans bonitatem in rebus," *ST* I, 20, 2 c.

[58] The ways in which God knows the divine essence to be capable of created participation through likeness or similarity constitute the divine Ideas, Cf. *ST* I, 15, 2, c.

not in themselves. Material things are those that fill space, that "have parts outside of parts"; hence, that at no point exist as a whole. They are also those things that exist in time, subject to continuous change; hence, that at no moment are fully self-identical, fully self-possessed. No material being, then, is strictly individual, so that it could exist or even be thought of in isolation from all other material things. This can be glimpsed in part in the fact of kinetic energy, dependent solely on relative motion; in the lack of an absolute zero for potential energy; in the wave-function overlap of all the particles of the whole universe in quantum theory.[59] Indeed, the need we have to be members of the Body of Christ suggests that something similar holds even at the level of the "spiritual body." Only the whole is a true counterpart to the divine Idea of things. Thus, He loves the deer or sheep, but not in such fashion as to prevent lions or wolves from devouring them. In fact, part of their goodness seems to be that they can serve as food for carnivores.[60]

When God wrought the Incarnation and created an integral human nature in Personal union with the Son, He manifested a love for the world that may be appropriated to the Son as His love for material things. For, this world exists only through Jesus and for Him.[61] He has taken it all into Himself, not only insofar as it was needed for His life on earth but also as it was from the beginning directed to Him and modelled in some way upon Him. Jesus' primacy is absolute. And even as the First Adam was modelled on the Last Adam and brought to be for His sake, so all the material order was made to support man's life in Christ.

As long as man, created in grace, was still unfallen, his world was paradise. The first heavens and the first earth were meant to be in their entirety obedient to Jesus and to all men who would live in Him, Adam first of all.[62] Man was to take up the universe into himself even as he and the world had been taken up into Christ. The world was to become an extension of man, to obey him almost as did his own body. We can surmise dimly what this means when we reflect how, even after the fall, man's bodily existence has been extended by his mind's power over the world: his vision by microscope, telescope, and TV; his hearing by radio; his physical strength and delicacy of touch by machines and tools; his locomotion by car and plane and rocket. His own body can in growing measure be prosthetically replaced. Even the

---

[59] This seems to be the insight behind the Thomistic notion of prime matter as the principle of individuation within a species—only an angel can be a complete and isolable individual, a whole species self-contained in one being.

[60] Again, however, a more developed theology concerning the angels is called for, since the fallen angels may have had some influence here. This seems the more likely since it is only due to the fall of man that tigers can eat him, lethal bacterial strains thrive in him, parasites develop their specific characteristics solely because of him. Cf. *Ch* 6.C.1 & 2 (133–135) below.

[61] Cf. *pp* 82–83.

[62] The fall of the angels has had a large effect on the material world, most especially, of course, as a result of man's fall, on those portions of the universe accessible to him, but also directly, by the demons' own activity. But more theological work needs to be done before the significance of these facts can be made concrete in terms of our present knowledge of the world.

automatic powers of his mind are being assisted by the brain-like activities of computers. But that total and graced subjection of the material world to the mind and will of man depended absolutely on his own unconditional and total obedience to God.

With the fall, not merely did man's own powers rebel within him but the material world, because still obedient to the Creator, became an alien and hostile domain for this violator of God's law. But God did not cast him off utterly. Since man cannot exist without a material universe,[63] living in time as he must, growing and developing, acting through material agency and physical strength, man was permitted to subjugate, though only partially, the world that had before been spontaneously obedient to him; and even this, only by long and painful labors.

This world, then, has served also as the material context for what St. Paul called the "new creation": man re-created in the likeness of Christ. As will be seen,[64] the new creation was to come as both completion and fulfilment of the old. So, too, the new heavens and the new earth[65] will somehow serve as the completion and fulfilment of the first heavens and the first earth, not as mere substitutes for them nor as appendages to them. For, the first heavens and the first earth were made for Christ, forming the spatio-temporal world in which man would appear and into which Jesus would come as "Heir of all things, through whom also He [the Father] made the ages" {Heb.1:2}.

Because of the fall, the material world itself, now groaning in its subjection to sinful man, needs to be set free from its enslavement to corruption and death and to be brought into the freedom given by the glory of the children of God (Rom.8:21). God's love for material things shows itself by the way these are perfected through their obedient service to man—as the endless potentialities of the dog and the cat have been bred into actuality. For, the world serves man despite his misuse of it and his abusing of its powers; and, when once he turns and begins to treat it properly, it responds once again gratefully to his care.

Both the world's angry resistances to man and its quiet submissiveness to his will serve the same purpose as did Eden: to help him towards eternal happiness in Christ. The world's reality leads man to change not only the world but himself. While he has been subjecting the earth to himself over the millennia, the world has also been entering into him through his senses and his mind, molding and shaping him at all levels of his being. Each of his conquests brings with it an alteration in man himself, as made evident by the enormous changes wrought in the workings of his mind and heart by his

---

[63] Whether he could exist without the angels is another question that must be left for future inquiry.

[64] Cf. Ch 8.B.4 (*pp* 196–200).

[65] This is the standard scriptural designation for the material creation insofar as it will be brought, after the Judgment, perfectly to manifest the glory of the new creation. Cf. Is.65:17, 66:22, Rom.8:19–22, 2 Pet.3:13. For the fulfilment of all things after the Judgment, cf. Rev.21:1 and 5.

discovery of writing, of music, of print, and of all the modes of electronic communication. These are all changes for good, yet at the same time often stimuli to greater sin. But despite the arduousness of the task, man is indeed making the universe his own and an extension of himself. If this 'larger' man is often monstrous, due to his proud sinfulness, as he cannibalizes other men for their organs and ravages the earth and seas seemingly beyond recovery, he remains by God's will the master, though one who bears responsibility for his deeds and will suffer their necessary consequences.

Since it was through His grateful obedience to the Father's will, even to suffering for the salvation of the men who tortured Him to death, that Jesus most fully reflected the Son's love for the Father,[66] we may appropriate to the Son God's subjecting the subhuman world to man's service, even when it must suffer from his foolish and arrogant abuse. It is, then, the Son who loves the world by bringing it to its perfection, even as Jesus was perfected (Heb.5:8–9), through its obedience and its service for the salvation of those who live in Jesus.

Finally, there are traces in the material world of the way in which the mutual love of Father and Son bursts forth into Their Glory, traces which are those aspects of God's love for creatures that can be appropriated to the characteristic loves between the Spirit and Those from whom He proceeds.

"The heavens declare the glory of God..." (Ps.19:1). Not only is the Bible filled with the awareness of God's glory manifested in the material creation but the poets and philosophers of the world's pagan cultures have never tired of exalting the divine glory present in storm and mountain, in sky and sea.

Since it is a participation in the divine essence, each creature shows something of God and exists as an aspect of His glory. However dim and shadowy, the created order is a likeness of that intrinsic glory which is God Himself. Likeness to Him there must be, since ultimately there is nothing else for any creature to be like. God is the sole principle of being. Anything that is not He, has whatever being it has solely from Him.[67] By likeness to Him, it serves as some small part of His created glory. For, it manifests something of His splendor and beauty and power to other creatures, which in their turn show forth other aspects of His being, all the more as the complex harmony of their interactions participates in the glorious pattern of His wholeness. More impressive yet, the endless depths of intelligibility lying beneath the many that our science has already discovered overwhelm and make dizzy the mind of anyone who gives them serious thought.

Thus ordered and oriented towards God, the material creation has no reason to be except to serve for the Son's glory in Jesus and the Father's glory through Jesus. By internal harmony and intrinsic intelligibility, the world glorifies the Father, who created it through and for Jesus; it glorifies Jesus, in and through whom it exists. For the glory of the Father, Jesus brings it back to

---

[66] Cf. *pp* 71–72 above.

[67] Thus, creation is perpetual. For a thing to continue to exist now, God must be freely giving the gift of existence now.

God from its enslavement to sinful man, not by wrenching it away from him but by overcoming his sins. For Jesus' glory, it is taken up with Him in His resurrection and enthronement. By having as its single and sole end the mutual glory of Father and Son, the world is but one. It is this finality that makes it a universe.

The world, because entirely obedient to God's will, shows that mutual glory truly, even though "as in a glass darkly." Physical law, dim image of this finality, directs the dispersed materiality of the world from within, forming it into a universe that serves the Father's glorifying of Jesus; and His, of the Father.

In Jesus, all aspects of the material world fit harmoniously together, not only in man himself but also to aid man, both in his natural operations and in his supernatural life. We are less accustomed to reflect that the entire vastness of the cosmos in space and time may, perhaps, be essential if man was to come to be at all. It has been conjectured that the Big Bang, the billions of years of spatial expansion, the immeasurable energy of stellar systems that, scattered in incomprhensible profusion, constitute the observed universe, all are but the simplest and most efficient way to produce man. Assuredly, we know of no better way.[68]

It is not, then, hard to see the grounds for appropriating to the Spirit God's glory shining out everywhere in this order and harmony of creation. This glory of the material world, manifest even to those who do not know whose glory it is, and this drawing into unity that makes the world a universe are, then, the grounds for appropriating these aspects of the material world to the loves of the Father and Son for the Spirit and He for Them.

One may note in passing how foolish is the thought that God's creating of all things for His own glory[69] is some sort of vanity or lack of love for creatures on His part. The greatest good that God can do for any creature is to make it exist in perfect accord with its divine exemplar. But if He does this, then of necessity it must give Him the greatest possible glory.

---

[68] John A. Wheeler, "Genesis and Observership," *Foundational Problems in the Special Sciences*, edd. R. E. Butts & J. Hintikka, Dordrecht: Reidel (1977), *pp* 18–19.

[69] As I Vatican defines the matter: "If anyone...should deny that the world was created for the glory of God, let him be anathema," DS 3025.

Chapter 5

The Mediation of Jesus' Charity

We have looked at the intratrinitarian loves and at the way these loves are reflected in Jesus. We saw how the Father Himself can be said to love us, at all levels of our being, in Jesus. We now turn to consider charity, once again, as it exists in its perfection in the Heart of Jesus. We have seen it there in its direction to the divine Persons; we wish now to see how this same love includes us.

A. Jesus' love for us

"As the Father has loved me, so also have I loved you." It is at this point that our absolute need for Jesus' mediation becomes most evident. Jesus mediates between God and man not only metaphysically by His incarnation nor only by His atonement for our sins upon the cross but by making visible to us what the Father's love really is. God is love (I Jn.4:8,16). Of this, Christians have no doubt. But, if we reflect on the evils let loose in the world in the name of love, we see that what love truly is, is the great mystery. But Jesus shows it to us in full and lets us see, even where we cannot understand. The Father's love is manifested in Jesus' love as He imitates the Father, for He is the created image of the Father. It is this fully human, as well as supernaturally divine, love that we are enabled by grace to share with Him.

Jesus' love for us cannot be considered a reflection in the sense we have been giving this term. We are not divine Persons. If the Father can be rightly said to love us, this is because He loves the Son and, with the Son and the Spirit, creates us and our world, in Jesus and for Him. But Jesus' human love for us is a good of the created order that reflects no intratrinitarian love since the Son's love for Himself in the Trinity is not characteristic.

As indicated earlier,[1] we will find most of what we need in what our Lord told His disciples at the Last Supper. Thus, we will finally be able to delineate the structure of this love that original sin nullifies, trait by trait, but that the Holy Spirit, once given us, pours out in our hearts.

"As the Father has loved me, so also have I loved you." Again, this trait of Jesus' love appears: doing what He sees the Father doing, for the Father's glory, now in relation to Jesus' love for His fellow men. Contrary to what one might naively expect, Jesus' love for us does not directly reflect the Son's characteristic love for the Father but rather that of the Father for the Son.

Yet surely this is not hard to understand—for how could one think of Jesus' love for us as being a simple reception of some good or gift from us? Jesus is the created image of the Father as well as the Father's uncreated Image.[2] Hence, too, the created charity of Jesus for us is like the Father's love for Jesus, the Son of man. Jesus' love for us shows, then, that same pattern of giving that reflects in creation the Father's characteristic love for His eternal Son. His love shows also the likeness of that glorification that reflects in creation the breathing forth of the Holy Spirit. Jesus, then, loves us, first, by gifts to us of intrinsic glory and, secondly, by laudatory glorification of us, as one with Him in His Church.

Jesus makes us His brothers by giving us a participation in the same created gifts that the Father has given Him. He does this through His humanity, which is not only the standard for all things human and our model but also the medium of our life of grace. Some measure of the greatness of His love can be seen from the magnitude of this gift: a sharing in Jesus' own created participation in the infinite goodness of the divine essence, His participation in the Father's gift to the eternal Son of what the Father Himself is. So Jesus divinizes us with "the life in Christ," the life of grace. He has loved us by giving to us the totality of Himself to the extent possible for human creatures to receive.

Jesus has freely chosen to offer the gift of all that He is to all these others, without exception, whom the Father so inexplicably loves. His gift is total, not only as to what it contains but as to the number of those to whom it is offered. Knowing all the weakness and the sin that has been and still is in each of us, He has chosen to love us all. He gave Himself into the hands of sinners in order to redeem sinners from death. As then, even now He gives His entire self—body, blood, soul, and divinity—to us in the Eucharist. So, the liberality of the Father's gift to the Son in the Godhead pours out, ever more visibly, into all levels below.

Since Jesus loves us as the Father has first loved Him, He gives us His gifts gratuitously, with no requirement of prior merit or worth and with no intention of any return except for their being accepted. As is true of the Father's love, this gratuity of Jesus' love is metaphysical, not merely psychological, since what He gives us cannot otherwise exist. By His entire life,

[1] *Ch* 2.C, *pp* 19–21.

[2] Cf. *Ch* 4, Excursus, *pp* 72–75.

especially by His sufferings, death, resurrection and enthronement, He has brought about a new existence, at the level of grace, for those who have no claim whatever upon it. All this He does in total freedom. For, though the Father's characteristic love for the Son is not free, yet the Father's love for Jesus in His humanity is free and so also, therefore, is Jesus' love for us wholly free.

Jesus' love for us is logically prior to our being worthy of His love.[3] It is His love that makes us worthy.[4] Jesus loves us, not as if we already shared the divine nature but that we may share it. The good that draws Him to us is previsioned only, seen as a mere possibility, consequent upon His gift. It could not cause or even invite His love unless He had already loved us. Like His Father, Jesus does not love us because we are good, but makes us good because He loves us, for this is what He sees the Father doing.

Jesus' love for us, then, is not stirred up in response to any goodness other than the Father's.[5] Hence, the initiative lies entirely with Him; none, with us. Like the Father (I Jn.4:10, 19), Jesus has first loved us. Without the prior action of His grace upon us, we cannot even begin to desire that He might love us.

This is important for a right understanding of the Catholic doctrine of human merit. This doctrine in no way implies that Jesus loves us because of any prior merits of our own. Rather, He enables us to merit because He has already chosen freely to love us. "So great is the kindness of God to all men, that He wishes those things to be our merits which are His own gifts, and that, for these things which He has lavished [on us], He will give eternal rewards."[6]

So, also, in the *Novus Ordo* for the Mass of the Latin Rite one finds the fine statement: "Blessed are You, Lord, God of the all creation, because from Your liberality we have received the bread that we offer You..." ("Benedictus es Domine, Deus universi, quia de tua largitate accepimus panem quem Tibi offerimus..."). We have nothing to offer God except what we have first received from Him, neither the bread that is the fruit of the earth and man's labor (as the rest of the prayer says) nor the Bread of heaven nor any virtue or good deed of our own.[7] Unfortunately, the now-standard ICEL translation of

[3] Since Adam's fall and the perpetuation of original sin, this priority is temporal as well as logical, that is, there is at least one period in our life during which He loves us when we actually lack such worthiness.

[4] We can only realize the greatness of this gift if we keep in mind that those in the state of grace, however far advanced or holding back, are truly worthy of both the Father's love and Jesus', in however different degrees.

[5] This may, of course, be embodied in what God has already given us.

[6] *Indiculus*, DS 248. Cf. DS 373–395 for the decrees of the Second Council of Orange, which insisted on this truth in every way possible against the Semi-Pelagians. See also the use made of these by the Council of Trent, DS 1548. Cf. also, St. Irenaeus, *Adversus Haereses* IV, 18, 6. (Irenée de Lyon, *Contre les hérésies,* SC 100, edd. A. Rousseau with B. Hemmerdinger, L. Doutreleau, & C. Mercier [1965]).

[7] Cf. DS 379 and especially 390.

this Offertory Prayer greatly weakens its sense, precisely in the aspect under consideration: "Blessed are you, Lord, God of all creation. Through your goodness we have this bread to offer...."

Thus far, we have considered only the similarity between Jesus' love for us and the Father's antecedent love for Him. But the Father also loves the Son with a consequent love, glorying in His goodness and glorifying Him within the Trinity (even as the Son does the Father), by His breathing forth with Him the Glory. A created reflection of this was established by the Father's appreciative love for Jesus, shown as He glorified Jesus by sending the Spirit upon Him and by gradually manifesting to the whole world Jesus' inner excellence as Son-made-man through the perfection of His gratitude and obedience. Conversely, the Son in His humanity does all that He does solely for the glorification of the Father. Thus, He glories in us and glorifies us by making manifest the natural and supernatural gifts that the Father has given us in Him so that the Father be the more widely glorified.

In the case of the reflections and likenesses of the first procession, what is definitive is the shar*ing* and giv*ing*, i.e., the act, and not *what* is shared or given as such. So, in this case of the reflections and similarities of the second procession, what is definitive is glorying in (having due appreciation and response to) *what* is given, in all of its goodness. To speak, then, of Jesus' consequent love for us, one that is like the Father's for Him, is to speak of the love He has for us in proportion to the good that is actually ours, by nature and by grace and as filled already with the Spirit.

Some have taken this to mean that Jesus loves His chosen ones only in proportion to their holiness. But was His filial affection for Mary a response solely to her wondrous holiness? Surely, His human will found something attractive in her as His mother? Jesus clearly loved Peter, James, and John more than the others among the Twelve. He loved the Twelve more than the Seventy. He loved Mary and Martha and Lazarus more than He loved Annas and Caiaphas. He loved Judas Iscariot more than He loved most men on the day He chose him as one of the Twelve; much more than He did when Judas kissed Him in Gethsemani.

Granted that, because of sin, we may have a very poor idea of what truly natural affection is. Yet it seems unthinkable that the natural bonds of affection should disappear because of the presence of grace,[8] for both our nature and our grace were created together in Jesus and for Him.[9] Finally, the Father glorifies Jesus in perfect truth; therefore, for all aspects of His excellence, both of nature and of grace.

When Jesus loves in this manner—surely the manner of the human heart, but a manner that today would likely be considered "discriminatory" or even "judgmental"—how is He loving us as the Father has loved Him? For, not only does the Father love Jesus more than other men; He loves Him alone in

---

[8] Cf. St. Thomas, S.T., II-II, 26, 7c.

[9] Cf. *pp* 82–84.

any man, for He loves all men only insofar as they are in Jesus.

Responding most simply, we note that holiness is a matter of grace. And though natural goods are subordinate to supernatural ones, this fact does not eliminate or require us always to ignore the natural ones. Rather, His word, "Even as the Father has loved Me, so have I loved you," implies that what Jesus loves in each being created for Him is what the Father has loved in each, though not in isolation, as we conceive things, or "in itself" or for its own sake but in Jesus.

Thus, Jesus has always loved and gloried in all the good He saw in men, natural as well as supernatural. He loved the people He met, in accordance with the good God had already given them; He sought to preserve it and to increase it by making the glory of the Father more attractive to them. But He does so not simply because people are pleasing to Him but because they manifest the goodness of the Father's gifts to Him as "first-born of all creation" (Col.1:15). It is the Father He glorifies for the goodness He sees in us.

Therefore, Jesus loves each of us as we are in Him: as part of His Body, if baptized believers; if not, at least as part of His race, progeny of the First Adam, and images, however damaged, of the Second Adam. So it is for all men's sake—indeed, for the whole, groaning creation's sake (Rom.8:21–22) —that He dies and rises and reigns in glory.

Since we are temporal beings, Jesus sees all our good as preparatory for greater gifts, as fitting us for a further growth in Him and a spiritual maturity greater than that already achieved. No matter how good we may already be, He invites us into ever closer union with Himself.[10] Since He seeks to glorify the Father as the Father has glorified Him, through each invitation that is accepted He leads us to dedicate ourselves ever more fully to the Father's greater glory. So, too, Jesus draws us to gratitude and thankfulness to the Father for all His gifts to us in Christ, leading us to an obedience from grateful love so that the Father may be glorified the more.

We must not forget, however, that the intrinsic good of creation is not to be found in a summation of isolable or disconnected packets, each with its own, individually definable goodness (not even, as is sometimes popularly supposed, in quantum physics). It is a world—more, a universe—that God has created for Jesus' glory.

Now, the reflection of the characteristic love of the Father for the Son involves God's creating the whole world—not only in this age but in the age to come—and all its people in, through, and for Jesus. To love us, then, as the Father has loved Him would seem to require that Jesus create a whole world and its people in and through and for us. Since we are speaking of Jesus' human love for us, this could be, obviously, only by distant analogy, for only God could create a world for our glory. But, even so, the very thought seems a little mad.

Yet we can understand this aspect of Jesus' love, if we recall that, as the

---

[10] Cf., e.g., the offer made the rich young man (Mk.10:17–22 and parallels).

Father had made over to Jesus the universe as His Kingdom, so Jesus has made over to us, through the apostles, the Kingdom.[11] Though, by title, His Kingdom includes the whole of creation (Rom.8:19-23), yet because of sin and death, Christ's reign is not yet complete. The Kingdom He came to establish is one that would grow and gain in power through the centuries till, at the time set by the Father, He would triumph fully over all enemies, both His and ours, destroy sin and death, and turn the Kingdom over to the Father (I Cor.15:24–28).

In the meantime, like Moses on Mount Nebo (Dt.34:1–5), we see the Promised Land, the Kingdom of the world to come, only dimly, at a distance. But our spiritual ascent enables us to discern, with ever keener vision of faith, the Kingdom of God in its fulness. As with Moses, death intervenes before we can enter. After death, however, we hope to enter this Kingdom, prepared for us by the Father's love for us in Christ from the foundation of the world (Mt.25:34). So, too, Jesus' glorification of us in an unmixed love of simple delight in our excellence through His grace must await that moment when, all sin and imperfection gone, we enter into glory. This remains our hope, that we hear Him say to each, "Well done, good and faithful servant...enter into the joy of your Master" (Mt.25:21 & 23). But we shall take possession of the Kingdom as our inheritance only when, at the end of time, we rise bodily from the dead.

This Kingdom subsists now in Christ's Church and is recognizable in her only by faith. Only at the Judgment will her full glory be manifest and recognized by all. Then Jesus will appear in glory in order to glorify the Church as His Beloved, long-espoused, at His wedding-feast with her. For, He was sent by the Father for this purpose, to establish the Church and to reveal her mystery and glory. He initiates the Church of faith so that she can become, under the Spirit's leading, the Church of glory at the Parousia—and not before. The Holy Spirit is sent to us to prepare us gradually and to make us ready to share, as members of His holy Church, in the fulness of Jesus' glory when He appears in judgment.

But this is how the Father loved Jesus, sending Him into the world of time to grow, to mature, to preach, to suffer and die, to rise, and to enter into His glory—though this is still not the definitive and total glory of the eternal Kingdom. So, in speaking of Jesus' glorifying of us, we have to talk of things only inchoate, incipient, present in seed or sprout or ear, not yet fully ripe and ready for the harvest (Mk.4:26–29).

The Kingdom exists for the glory of Jesus. Through His glory He will glorify the Father when He turns the Kingdom over to Him, once brought to

---

[11] "I make over to you, even as My Father has made over to me, a Kingdom, so that you may eat and drink at My table in My Kingdom, and sit on thrones, judging the twelve tribes of Israel" {Lk.22:29}. Cf. also Mt.19:28 and Lk.12:32, "It has pleased your Father to give to you the Kingdom." It is well in these various references to the Kingdom to keep in mind that the same word can also mean 'kingly power,' 'reign,' or 'monarchy.' The exact shade of meaning in many contexts remains open to discussion.

its perfection (I Cor.15:28). But we are in Jesus, and Jesus loves us as the Father has loved Him. The Kingdom is, then, for the glory of all whom the Father destined to be "conformed to the image of His Son", those who are justified following His call from His eternal knowledge of them (Rom.8:29–30), who were chosen for this glory from before creation (Eph.1:4).

Jesus loved His apostles by sending them to labor to bring the whole world under His dominion. The Kingdom exists, then, for their glory as part of His own. So will it be for other men, chosen to have the apostles as their exemplars and models. Strange as such language sounds at first, we can see that it is with just such a love that, in fact, Jesus has loved them—and even us.

He established for this the supernatural, still growing and developing world of the Church. He did this in and through and, indeed, for the apostles and, by their means, in and through and for all of us. He made them, indeed, exemplars and models for those in their charge[12] and through them transmitted the same office to their successors for all time to come.[13] And though about most of them next to nothing is known except that they have entered into glory already as foundation-stones of the heavenly Jerusalem, the Church has, by Jesus' will, glorified them continually.

This same love, He has for us. He makes some to be successors to the apostles. But to all He offers a similar gift: to be sanctifiers of their fellow men, to be builders of the Church universal, to be exemplars and models of charity for others, and, once beyond death, even before the resurrection, to be glorified for holiness of life under the power of the Spirit and for their grateful obedience.

So, too, Jesus makes the inner excellence of his saints shine forth before the world. "You are the light of the world" (Mt.5:14), He says to the same men whom He solemnly taught, "I am the light of the world" (Jn.8:12, 9:5). Great glory, indeed, to share Christ's titles—and not just this one, but also 'Rock' and 'Shepherd' and, above all, 'Son of God.' And today, as then, the Lord glorifies His saints, even during their earthly lifetimes, by miracles. All this, that the Father may be the more greatly glorified through the Son.

The Father sent the Spirit upon Jesus as Jesus' Glory at His baptism so that the Father might be glorified in the Son. But as Image of the Father, the Son made flesh sends the Spirit upon those who believe, as *their* intrinsic glory. Those who live in Him are made to share in His anointing by their receiving the indwelling Spirit, the Breath of the Son, and principle of the life in

---

[12] So, St. Paul insists, "You became imitators of us and of the Lord" (I Th.1:6); "You yourselves know how you ought to imitate us," (II Th. 3:7); "Be imitators of me" (I Cor.4:16); "Join in imitating me and mark those who so live as you have an example in us" (Php.3:17).

[13] St. Paul's "Set the believers an example in speech and conduct" (I Tim.4:12) is joined by Peter's "Be examples to the flock" (I Pet.5:3). Cf. also, St. Ignatius of Antioch, "To the Smyrneans" VIII.1, "To the Trallians" III.1, and "To the Magnesians" VI.1, *Ignace d'Antioche, Polycarpe de Smyrne: Lettres, Martyre de Polycarpe*, éd. P. Th. Camelot, SC 10 *bis*, Paris: Éditions du Cerf (1951),

Christ.

So Jesus has loved us, as the Father has loved Him, with a love of intrinsic glorification that the Greek Fathers spoke of as "deification," a making gods of us by giving us a participation in the divine nature through grace and the indwelling of the Holy Spirit. This deification, effected through baptism and confirmation, shows these sacraments as ways in which Jesus has chosen to glorify us in the Church so that, by living in Him, we may in turn worthily glorify the Father.

Since our life in Christ is a life lived wholly for the glory of the Father, our rebirth is appropriated to the Spirit. That is, the Spirit, who effected the union of God and man in Jesus' conception in Mary's womb, effects an analogous union by making us sons of the Father in baptism. We are reborn by the power of the Spirit of Jesus (Jn.3:5; Tit.3:5) and, so, receive our sharing in the divine nature (II Pet.1:4), made one with Jesus in His life of glorifying the Father. Thus, from this aspect also, by being the source of our new life in the Spirit, Jesus' love for us again resembles the Father's for Jesus.[14]

In the sacrament of confirmation the Spirit descends upon us invisibly as He did visibly upon Jesus at the Jordan, to lead us also out into the desert and into the world for the Father's glory. But also, confirmation is conjoined to the transition in the spiritual life that follows upon our direct sharing in the Paschal Mystery.[15] After this, Jesus sends us forth to live in and for Him, no longer by recapitulation but in the full power of the Spirit.

B. Charity in Us

Charity in us is structured according to the Great Commandment and that which "is like to it." We consider these in turn.

1. Our Love for the Trinity

The "great and first commandment" (Mt.22:38), than which there is none greater (Mk.12:31), is: "Hear, O Israel: The Lord our God, the Lord is one; and you shall love the Lord your God with all your heart and with all your soul and with all your mind and with all your strength" (Mk.12:29–30). The first imperative manifests the root of faith out of which alone charity can grow. The second imperative gives the formal content of the commandment, as comparison with the other formulations, which all omit the former imperative, indicates. Simply by being what He is, God is One who has an

[14] Though we are begotten by the Spirit's overshadowing of the Church, the Spirit is not our father any more than He is Jesus' father but is the agent sent forth by the Father (Cf. I Jn.3:9 and Brown's comments on this: *The Johannine Letters,* AB 30, *pp* 408–411). Nor is the Son our Father, for we are His brothers and members of His Body. Cf. also, Quay, *Christian Meaning, pp* 53–54.

[15] This connection between the baptism of Jesus and His sufferings is two-fold: after His baptism in the Jordan, by which He took on Himself the guilt of us all and, so, was thenceforth dedicated to the cross, He received the Spirit descending as a dove; after His sufferings and death, His Heart was pierced and poured out the water symbolizing the Spirit and, then forty days after His rising from the dead, He pours out the Spirit in full upon the disciples.

absolute claim on our love, absolute right to our obedience. By our being what we are, we are, at our best, "unprofitable servants" when we manage perfect obedience: "We have done what we were obliged to do" {Lk.17:10}.

This love of God is equated by John with keeping God's commandments, chief of which is our love for one another in charity (I Jn.5:1–3.) So, also, the command to love the Lord, who alone is our God, with undivided heart, soul, mind, and strength is followed by a second that is like it, "You shall love your neighbor as yourself" (Mt.22:39; Mk.12:31). Which of these two commandments is the greater is as explicit in John as in the Synoptics: "By this we know that we love the children of God, when we love God and obey His commandments" (I Jn.5:2).

These commandments sum up the whole of the Law and the Prophets (Mt.7:12; 22:40; Rom.13:8–10). Our Lord declared them equally basic for the New Law. But, as they stand, they are not yet equivalent to the New Law. Since the New is both explicitation and the fulfilment in Christ of the Old, what must be added is what Jesus taught us by word and example in the Paschal Mystery.

What, for good reason, strikes us all most powerfully is Jesus' transformation of the "one like" the Great Commandment: "Love your neighbor as yourself," into: "Love one another as I have loved you," so often and strongly repeated.

But the Great Commandment itself is explicitated and transformed, though perhaps less obviously. For He who told us much at the Last Supper concerning the life of charity and the structure of love, there made known to us most of what God has revealed of the inner life of the Trinity.

If we live in Christ, we share in His love for the Persons of the Trinity. We are to love Them as He, in His human nature, loves Them. We have already seen something of the ways in which Jesus loves the Father. He loves Himself as the only Son and perfect Image of the Father. He loves the Spirit as the truly adequate Glory, that which alone is worthy of the Father.

a) Through Jesus, we are enabled to love the Father as does the Son in His manhood, by the power of the Spirit. Because we have nothing except the gift itself that He is giving us, all we can do is to receive it with such gratitude that we seek nothing else but what the Father wills in giving it to us. We have no other way to offer the Father a gift in return. Our gratitude should resemble Jesus', itself the Father's gift, which found its entire nourishment (Jn.4:32–34) in doing the Father's will. Hence, our love for the Father will be most like Jesus' love for Him, when expressed as Jesus' was, by obedience "even to death on a cross."

Throughout His discourse at the Last Supper, the need for complete subjection of all wills to the will of the Father is manifest. But in the first half of chapter 15, Jesus says something strikingly new, even though one can see it implicit as early as the "But I say to you" of the Sermon on the Mount. He commands the apostles to remain in *Him*, to let *His* words remain in them, to remain in *His* love. He also lays down the condition for remaining in His love: to obey *His* commands, even as He obeys the Father's.[16] The terrible threats[17] and extraordinary promises[18] that accompany this demand for obedience confirm what is new in it: not only is Jesus declaring, with the whole of the Old Testament, that obedience to God's will is the only authentic way to show one's love for Him but also that He, Jesus, is to be loved with undivided heart, soul, mind, and strength, in equality with the Father.

Immediately after saying to His disciples, "If you keep my commandments, you will abide in my love," He adds, "just as I have kept my Father's commandments and abide in His love" (Jn.15:10). Again, in His prayer, He says, "I glorified You on earth, having accomplished the work which You gave me to do" (Jn.17:4). Though a simple carrying out of orders merits due recompense (Rom.4:4; Mt.20:1–15; Lk.17:7–10), it cannot earn love, which is by definition free. But once love has been given, then the doing of the (reasonable) will of the one who loves becomes the condition of continuance. So, Jesus declared obedience to His commands to be, indeed, a sufficient condition for remaining in His love, but also a necessary one; the same condition applies even to Him and the Father.

Only by obeying Jesus, one with the Father, can we rightly obey the Father, whose true will Jesus reveals to us in its fulness. Only so do we truly acknowledge the Father as God, by acknowledging Jesus as His Son, glorifying Both. Since we are sons of the Father only insofar as we are in Jesus, we see why faith in Him is demanded, why St. Paul insists, "Let this mind be in you which was also in Christ Jesus" {Phil.2:5}.

Willingly to receive oneself and all one's good from another is, we saw, an act of love. In Jesus, then, we love the Father as His sons, gladly receiving our whole being from the Father through Jesus and content to be loved not for ourselves but for our oneness with Jesus. We also love the Father, not only when we thus rejoice in the Father's being the ultimate Source of all our good, but when, by grace, we do what we see Jesus doing in His imitating of the Father–for it is this that Jesus commands us. Thus, we love the Father, not obeying Jesus, and the Father loves us as His sons insofar as we are like Jesus in His obedience. These loves—of the Father for us and of ours for Him in return—together issue in a reciprocal glorification. We glorify the Father through our obedience in and through Jesus. The Father glorifies us as He

[16] Much is said today of God's (or Jesus') "unconditional love for us." If this means that His love is unmerited or that it is prior to any possible fulfilment of conditions on our part, the phrase may have some use. But if it means, as too often seems to be intended, that there are no conditions to be met by us in order to remain in His love, then it is noxious indeed. Part of this error may lie in the failure to distinguish the way God loves us as sons, supernatually, and the way He loves us, also in Jesus but very differently, simply because of our nature.

[17] If one does not remain in Jesus, he bears no fruit, he can do nothing, he is cast off, dries up, and is gathered up to be burned (15:4, 5, 6).

[18] If one remains in Jesus, he bears much fruit and his fruit will remain; he will ask for whatever he wishes and it will happen, and whatever he asks the Father in Jesus' name will be given him (15:5 & 8, 16, 7, 16).

glorifies Jesus: through the action of the Spirit as His Breath and Life in us.

b) By being in Christ and living with His life, we are made one with Him and our love for Him is a love of identification with Him. Thus, though He is indeed our Brother in His humanity,[19] even this designation remains too weak an indicator of the love we are to have for Him in whom we live, by whose life we live, whose members and branches we are. And, of course, because of His oneness with the Father, He never ceases to be our Lord.

What good can be willed to Jesus by us? If He who is our exemplar and *raison d'être* is constituted such only by the sharing of His being with us, then He is formally made such only by our acceptance of this gift of His divine life. Our will to receive His gifts is a will that He be our Lord and Savior, the Lord of human history and of the universe. We will to receive, even as Jesus wills to give, a created participation in His sharing in the divine essence. Thus we render to Jesus the glory that is His as our Head and Source so that He, the Son of God, be acknowledged Son of Man and may glorify the Father through man and, so, through the whole material universe.[20]

Insofar as we live by charity, we receive and freely accept all that Jesus offers us. We do not choose to change or alter His gift by any hankering to be different, naturally or supernaturally, save to be more like Him. Different from Him in countless ways, we seek to be His hands and feet, members of His Body, the Church, one in a common life with Him. We do not pretend to have any independence of Him or any alternative norm or model for our lives. We will to receive all, in order that we may be worthy brethren to Him who is the worthy Son of the Father.

We have no claims on Jesus for His gift, for we had nothing of our own worth or merit to offer. We can do no more than receive, at most ratifying after the fact the gift made to us. We have no gift not already His to offer in return. We are constrained to simple gratitude.

Gratitude is the disposition of one who is continually and gladly aware of his dependence on another for some good he has received, without desert or merit, from this other and which the giver was free not to give. The grateful person recognizes, accepts, and is gladly indebted to the love embodied in the gift. He desires freely to respond in active love for the benefactor, by some sort of gift in return, if possible, but, where the donor lacks no good that the recipient can supply, at least by acknowledgment of the gift and by praise of the giver.

Gratitude is an opening of the heart to cast out any sense of isolated independence and to let in awareness of one's good as coming from others, so that one's own self-interest becomes the door to the just acknowledgment of the external sources of one's wellbeing. It is for these reasons that St. Ignatius Loyola saw gratitude as being the surest way to gain love and ingratitude as

---

[19] Cf. Mt.28:10; Jn.20:17; Heb.2:11–13, 17.

[20] Thus, part of Jesus' insistence on faith in Him is made clear: there is no other way in which one can know the truth of man.

one of the most abominable of vices.[21]

The love of charity that constitutes our supernatural life as such is, then, our grateful reception of Jesus' life as He offers it to us, a reception that is a living out in time of the potentialities of this divine life.

That this reception of His gift has the structure of love may perhaps be seen more clearly by looking at the matter negatively. One who declines or refuses any true gift, except on some extrinsic grounds, to this extent damages a friendship or familial love. Judgment as to just what constitutes adequate extrinsic grounds for refusal is itself a measure of the quality of love between the would-be giver and intended recipient. Again, the singular malice of the man who freely chooses to kill himself lies in his rejection of the continuous gift of his own life, gratuitously made to him by all of nature, by his fellow men, and by God.[22]

Finally, Jesus wishes to glorify us as being truly, if incompletely, worthy of Himself. We, in turn, are to rejoice in His being the Source, under the Father, of all our goodness and to glorify Him. From this mutual glorification, between Jesus and each one who lives with His life, a faint yet true resemblance to the activity of the Breath and Spirit of God is established. Through Jesus, then, we receive and are enabled to love the Holy Spirit.

Our love for the Holy Spirit is meant to be like Christ's love for the Father's Glory, who Personally anointed Him, and who dwelt within Him so that, as man, He might respond to every stirring of this Breath of the Father. The Spirit led Him up into the desert above the Jordan (Mt.4:1) to be tempted, as we, though without sin (Heb.4:15). Filled with the Spirit (Lk.4:14), He goes forth as Prophet, Priest, and King. In the Spirit, He is herald of the the Good News, He offers Himself as the sacrifice of our redemption (Heb.9:14) and, publicly declared to be "Jesus of Nazareth, King of the Jews," He enters into His Kingdom, from that moment on to extend it more fully on earth through His sending of the Spirit.

All of this, since in the Spirit, Jesus does in glorification of the Father, on earth first, then from heaven, sending the Spirit upon the disciples that they and those who believed through their witness should all glorify the Father through Jesus.

We are, then, to love the Spirit, the Glory of Both, as reflected in Their created glory in the Church, but also wherever else we can recognize the Spirit at work drawing men toward Jesus and the Father. "Since love should show itself more in deeds than in words,"[23] we will grow in love of the Spirit to the degree that we seek always and everywhere to increase the glory of Father and Son.

---

[21] *Spiritual Exercises,* Contemplatio Ad Amorem, [231–237]. Letter to Simon Rodriguez, 18 March 1542, *Monumenta Ignatiana I,* Letter 38, *p* 192.

[22] G. K. Chesterton, *Orthodoxy, Ch.* 5 (*The Collected Works* 1; San Francisco: Ignatius Press, 1986. 1st ed. 1908) 276.

[23] St. Ignatius Loyola, *Spiritual Exercises* [230].

We love the Spirit, then, by letting Him work through us to glorify the Father and the Son among men. We love Him, too, as we join with the holy angels in their continual glorifying of Father and Son in the same Spirit, especially through our share in the heavenly liturgy in the Mass. But the Spirit loves the Father and the Son by His "proceeding"—binding Them together by a common finality to be "one Principle."[24] Hence our love is not complete if it does not let itself be drawn by the Spirit into the communion with other men that is the Church.

2. The one like to it: charity for one another

When we turn our attention to the "second" commandment, the one Jesus declared to be "like to" the Great Commandment, i.e., "You shall love your neighbor as yourself" (Lev.19:18), it is evident that neither Jesus nor the Law before Him is speaking of what is usually meant by 'self-love.' Both are referring to that love of the self in truth (and of all things else) that comes from total subordination to the Great Commandment. The Lord is not saying that an adulterer, for example, should offer his own wife to be the object of other men's lust.[25]

Probably the Pharisees had already formulated the rabbinical interpretation, "Do not do to anyone what you would not wish done to you."[26] But, in the Sermon on the Mount, Jesus restores it as a *positive* command (to show love by action—the principal biblical sense of 'love') and enlarges its scope: "All things whatsoever you wish that men would do for you, thus indeed do you for them" {Mt.7:12}.

It is not hard to deduce from this (in principle; practice is another matter) that one cannot love oneself (seek the true good of the self as such) with the love of charity except insofar as one loves all people without exception. Moreover, one must take the initiative in loving, not waiting on the other. Jesus spells all this out in the same sermon (Lk.6:27–36) when He insists: "Love your enemies, do good to those who hate you, bless those who curse you, pray for those who abuse you...."

But if such teaching left the apostles in astonished incomprehension,[27] what must have been their reactions when Jesus taught them at the Last Supper that all this was not yet enough and gave them the "new commandment" (Jn.13:34), the one He called "My commandment" (Jn.15:12)! "[L]ove one another as I have loved you" {Jn.13:34}. Twice more He repeats this command (Jn.15:12, 17) but, before He does so, He solemnly asserts, "As the Father has loved Me, so have I loved you" (Jn.15:9).

---

[24] Cf. *pp* 53–55 and 75–76 above.

[25] Cf. *ST* II-II, 25, 7c.

[26] Cf. AB, *Matthew*, on 7:12, *p* 84. Also, Hillel the Elder, "That which displeases you do not do to another. This is the whole Law." (TB, Shabbath 31a). Cf. Strack-Billerbeck, I, 459–460; also *NJBC*, Englewood Cliffs (NJ): Prentice Hall (1990) #42:47.

[27] That it did so is evident, e.g., in Peter's question, "How often shall my brother sin against me, and I forgive him? As many as seven times?" (Mt.18:21).

Before we try to gain some small understanding of the new commandment, concerning which we are so much less comprehending than were the apostles, it seems useful to note that the command, "Love one another as I have loved you" when taken with, "Even as the Father has loved Me, so have I loved you," makes even more explicit Jesus' role as mediator.[28]

For, in logic, one might argue that these two commands together are equivalent to: As the Father has loved Me, so love one another. But, no. This would be a verbal logic only. The Father's love for Jesus as man is a reflection of His characteristic love for the Son, whereas our love for one another, no matter how perfectly it imitates Jesus' love for us, cannot be such a reflection.

Jesus mediates between these loves, as the New Moses, "who received the living utterances to give to us"[29] and who has the New Law, no longer on tablets of stone, "in His hand" to give to us.[30] Though we are assured that the Father Himself loves us,[31] we are given only scattered indications that we are to love one another as the Father has loved us.[32] Nowhere are we told to model our love for one another on the Father's love for Jesus.

Further, our love is to resemble, directly and explicitly, Jesus' human love, not His divine love, since it is the former that is like the Father's love for Jesus, whereas the latter is that which distinguishes the Son from the Father.

We are called, then, to love one another, not directly as the Father has loved Jesus with a love not visible to us, but as Jesus has loved us, with a love that is, in truth, "paternal" as created image of the Father's, yet that can, by grace, be understood by human hearts and minds. So, it is the Father's love that is to be shown in our love for one another through our life in Christ and even in our love for all the subhuman creation.[33]

In other words, the Father has made the Son to be of one nature with us, our Brother. Our love, then, since we are by grace to share in His divine nature, must be structurally indistinguishable from Jesus' love for His brothers and ours. Jesus as giver, however, is not the primal Source of the gift, for it is as the Image of the Father that He gives to us. Since by His grace He makes us images of Himself, we are images of the Father also. This is why we must love one another both as Christ has loved us and as the Father has loved Him.

If we take Jesus' words seriously and admit that we must come to love each other, whoever the other is, as Jesus has loved us, our only task is to recall how He has loved us that we may "go and do likewise" (Lk.10:37). Thus

---

[28] Cf. *p* 63 above.

[29] Ac.7:38

[30] Gal.3:19

[31] Jn.16:27; 14:21 & 23; 17:23.

[32] Cf. Eph.5:1; Mt.5:48; I Pet.1:15–16, which speak in very general terms of imitating God (the Father). Such passages as I Jn.4:7–12 and 19–21 seem more concerned with the motivation of our love than with its inner structure: knowing how much we have all been loved by the Father, we also must not hold back in love for one another.

[33] Cf. *Ch* 4.G, *p* 89 above and *pp* 111–112 below.

we prove to the world, and to ourselves, that His life is in us, for by no other means could such action of love be conceived. And by this, not only is Jesus glorified but also the Father (Jn.15:8).

We are, then, to share all we have, not only our external goods but our inner resources of mind and heart, still more, our faith and hope and charity, to whatever extent by God's grace we can share these with others.[34] The Father's gift of the divine essence to the Son is to find its analog even among us in our offering of the divine life to one another.

This we are called to do totally—no less than all of ourself is in question—and for all people, without exception. Not all at once and together, assuredly, but as we can and the occasion offers and the prudence given by the Holy Spirit dictates. Think, in this respect, of Mother Teresa's beginning of her major work. She did not seek to help the uncountable thousands dying in the filth of the world's slums, nor of India's only, nor even of Calcutta's. She walked only till she saw one man dying in misery, and in response to Jesus' love for her, took such care as she could of him. But then she went to the next one, and the next, until now the world knows, if it does not act well upon the knowledge, that Christ can be touched in His poor by each of us if we so will.

The range of our charity can only be the range of Jesus' love—without limits, embracing all, since Christ came for all. Charity is universal, since its motive and structure are both given by the universality of the Father's love and of Jesus'.[35] The depth of our charity must be that of Jesus', a giving to the limits of our own being, nothing being held back or in reserve that is ours to give.

In this way, then, we are to "give freely what [we] have freely received" {Mt.10:8}, not only without remuneration but without demanding prior merit or worth. For, the love that we are commanded to exercise is a love which is not restricted to or conditioned by the actual goodness of the one loved but seeks the divine goodness which might yet come to be in him. If it is already present, of course, then to that extent we rejoice in his present good and glorify Jesus and the Father through it.

Now, only the divine love can make anyone good and not, as our love, seek merely to increase or to appreciate the good present. Our response to

---

[34] This sharing is not, of course, the somewhat sentimental "sharing" in vogue today, whereby one speaks of his inmost experiences, "feelings," and life with God to anyone who wants to hear. While there are undoubtedly occasions where this latter "sharing" has its place, far more basic and far more important exercises of charity are the ways in which one helps others to come to Catholic faith, to hope in God's love on that basis, and so to risk "losing themselves" in the charity of which we speak.

[35] There have been some, who should know better, who have denied the possibility of a universal love. Their problem usually is that they cannot conceive the intensity of love they have experienced for a very few people being extended to all. But, as we have seen now *ad nauseam*, charity (and truly human love of any sort) is not a matter of feeling and emotion but of free choice in the clarity of Christ's truth. And this has no limits to its range when moved by God's grace.

Jesus' love, then, is to let Him make others good, when and as He wishes, through our words and actions. If this seems far-fetched, recall that it is just this gratuitous action of supernatural creation through human representatives that reaches its peak and its perfection in the ministration of the sacraments. Here, by what seems no more than the pouring of a little water and the saying of a few simple words, all the essential damage done by original sin is undone, and the life of God is brought into being in the infant baptized.

If, then, we are to love all those whom Jesus loves—who loves all those the Father loves—we must love those who have no claim on our love, even if they be evil and malicious and undeserving of any love. If they are not worthy of God's love, how can they be less worthy of ours, we who have all lived in sin at least till birth. The question is not whether they are loveworthy, but whether, as the parable of the Good Samaritan shows, there is some good that we can, for no reason except the love of God, offer them.[36]

Such gratuity, as we saw in speaking of the Father's antecedent love for the Son in the Trinity, logically implies an equally great initiative. So, too, the love we are commanded to live will manifest the freedom of Jesus' love for each of us. He has taken the initiative in loving us even as the Father took the initiative in loving Him as man by a wholly gratuitous, infinitely free love, given without any prior merit on Jesus' part. So, He chose to be, to live, to die, to rise for us, whether we would choose to respond or not. Thus, like Jesus, we must love "in advance," before we see what can draw our love.

The same theme recurs again and again throughout the New Testament. Recall, as one example, the invitation Jesus insists that we extend to the outcasts and those incapable of making a return to us in this world (Lk. 14:12–14). Again, "Love your enemies, do good to those who hate you,..." All reiterate from varied aspects that the love we are to have for another is not evoked by a perception of the other's virtues but is given gratuitously, like Jesus' love for us and because of this.

More, Christ's love requires of us, as every detail in the parable of the good Samaritan shows, that we show our love for our neighbor in action, even when there is danger and risk to ourselves as a result. Nor need our neighbor be one who is near to us by some human proximity or similarity, not even by a common culture or religion. He is the one to whom our love goes out because God loves him and because he is in some spiritual or temporal need and we, in some small measure, can help him if we choose.

As Jesus' glorification of us in and through His Church images the Father's glorification of Jesus in and through the entire universe,[37] so our consequent love for one another must image Jesus'. This would seem to imply that we are to glory in and glorify one another for the same goods of both nature

[36] Though those of secularist mind have doubted it, the Synoptic texts are explicit that the Great Commandment is the basis for the one like it, and the *First Letter of John* only confirms this. In addition to what we have said concerning the images of God, since Jesus has loved us because of His love for the Father, so we are to love one another for the same reason.

[37] Cf. *pp* 94–97 above.

and of grace that Jesus glories in and glorifies.[38]

We are, then, to love universally and gratuitously. We are to love particularly as well, by glorying in and glorifying every man in proportion to the intrinsic glory that God has given each. This inner excellence is not measured by its goodness considered "in itself" or by the satisfaction or pleasure we derive from it but for its relation to Jesus' glory and, through Him, to the ordering of all created good to the glory of the Father. We are to glorify one another in the Spirit.

Since our nature was created in and for Christ, we must love one another in genuine accord with the natural bonds of affection, an accord that was co-created with grace in the first Adam.[39] As Jesus loved Mary, so we are to love our mothers; and so of all other natural relationships. Only when these are separated from the love of Christ and torn loose from their inner orientation towards the Father do these loves become noxious. They are not then noxious, however, because they are merely natural but because, on their account, we have inverted the order of the commandments and given the creature the pre-eminence that belongs to God alone.

Now, any talk of glorifying one another must sound ill in a Christian ear. Our Lord would seem to have taken a very dim view of it: "How can you believe, you who receive glory from one another and the glory from the only God you do not seek?" {Jn.5:44}. And the saints insist that it is a great danger for us, weak descendants of those who would "be like God," to receive glory from our fellow men in this life.

It may, of course, be argued that what is objected to in the passage quoted and in others[40] is not the giving or even the receiving of human glory as such but the taking to oneself a glory that belongs to God alone or letting the glory received from men weigh against that which comes from Him. Surely, no Christian may rightly desire glory that terminates in himself as if his goodness were his own doing. In any case, the New Testament seems to be silent about glorifying others. On the contrary, Jesus instructs His followers so to let their light shine before men that these will see those good works and glorify the Father.

Still, not only this silence but the New Testament's generally careful reservation of 'glory' to God, except when speaking figuratively (e.g., I Ths.2:20; I Cor.12:26) or impersonally (e.g., Rom.11:13), would seem reason enough to rule out a consistent application of any argument that charity requires us to glorify one another.[41]

---

[38] Recall that to glory in someone's excellence is an internal activity whereas glorifying him is an external action. The former is the source from which the latter flows, and under most circumstances a failure to go beyond the internal activity bespeaks a failure or flaw in the one so glorying.

[39] Cf. the discussion on Cabasilas and Chrysologus, Ch 4.F, *pp* 82–84.

[40] E.g., "They did not acknowledge [their faith in Jesus] for they loved the good opinion of men more than the good opinion of God" {Jn.12:42–43}. Cf. also I Th.2:6.

[41] Cf., however, the very balanced and careful treatment of all this by St. Thomas, *ST* II-II, 132,

On the other hand, St. Paul speaks clearly of "the glory of the children of God" {Rom.8:21}. But he makes clear that this glory is a future glory, yet to be revealed to us (8:18),[42] So, too, our Lord, despite the remark mentioned above, prayed at the Last Supper not only for perfect union between the apostles but, in order to achieve it, gave them the Glory given Him by the Father (Jn.17:21–22).

Quite apart from New Testament usage of 'glory' and its cognates, the fact is that we usually lack the knowledge needed for glorification not only of others' spiritual excellence but even of their true natural excellence. If nothing else, molecular genetics has demonstrated how little we understand of gifts (or defects) of temperament and personality, how little we can grasp, even within ourselves, of what truly issues from our freedom. We seem left, then, with little ground for glorification save for external manifestations of skill and developed capabilities.

It is not good, then, to glorify ourselves, because the intrinsic glory of every excellence of body, heart, and mind comes to us as a free gift from God. Our problem with vainglory comes when we forget that these things are His gifts, given without our merit, and that it is His liberality we should glorify. To paraphrase the new Offertory Prayer: "Blessed are You, Lord, God of the universe, because from Your liberality we have received all our good, which we now offer You...." For, all that He has given us we must give back to Him through Christ Jesus, serving Him in our fellow men. We ought, indeed, to recognize and rejoice in His gifts; all the more, the greater they are. We may rejoice, even more, in His gifts to others and may thank one another and praise one another; but it is God whom we should glorify for the goods in question, since however truly they may be ours, they are infinitely more truly His.

We are, moreover, still "under construction." God has left us incomplete beings, so that by the power of His grace we may, by our free choices in accord with that grace, be completed. Truly sharing in the divine nature by grace (II Pet.1:4) we are made sharers in God's own power to create, that we may become His sons definitively and for ever. Since we do not know the final outcome for ourselves or for others now alive, any glorification touching the person himself is at best premature.[43] As we saw in connection with Jesus' consequent love for us and, indeed, could have seen in the Father's consequent love for Jesus, there is a strong relationship between such love and human temporality. As a love of good actually present, it is a love of what, in a material world, is essentially mutable and, in fact, always changing. *A fortiori* is it true of any consequent love we are to have for one another. We do, however, glorify those who have reached the goal, the Saints in heaven, even, as testified

---

especially Questions 1 and 4.

[42] It is not evident that one can press the aorists in *v* 8:30 so as to argue that God *has* already glorified those whom he has justified, though this could fit well enough with St. John's assertions that we already have eternal life within us. Cf. also, Rom.9:23.

[43] Cf. St. Ignatius Loyola, *Spiritual Exercises*, [364].

by the great feast of All Saints, those not canonized.

It is this same temporality, however, that makes it possible for us to love one another by an analogical creation of a world for others—it cannot be, if it is to be a true image of Jesus' love, a world we intend in any direct way for ourselves. As II Vatican has reminded us, the world of men is incomplete. We are to labor with Jesus, through His grace, for His glory, to build up this world.

So, too, the Kingdom of God in the Church is not yet complete. This also must be built up, in time and in space, and thus be created by Jesus' grace working through us with one another towards its completion. Whatever glory is to be ours is eschatological, made ours only when the Judgment has shown that, despite our sins, we have died in love for Him. Indeed, the dangers involved in our glorifying of one another can be obviated by recalling that Jesus' incipient glorifying of us, through the life of grace, is effected principally by His calling us into the Church, as His planting of the seed of the Kingdom in the world. Thus, we do not glorify one another as individuals, for all the reasons given and more, but as members of the Church or, at least, as our fellow men. For the work of the Spirit is union—our union with one another in the Glory of Father and Son, our glory being to have none of our own.

We participate in this union by together glorifying the Father in imitation of Jesus. For this, He sends us His Spirit to make us one with Him and with all who are in His grace, most especially in our common worship of the Father, where, having given Him thanks through Jesus' sacrifice of obedience, we are bound together ever more closely through Communion. This union, insofar as realized in the Church, is that sign of Christ's love that alone will convince all men of His having come: "By this all men will know that you are My disciples, if you have love one for another" (Jn.13:35). It is by this union "that the world may know that You [the Father] have sent Me" (17:23).

It is the Spirit who leads us to allow ourselves to be drawn into oneness by Himself. It is the Spirit's power alone that works the unity of true believers within the Church, despite all schisms and ruptures. It is His marvellous "sign" and continuing miracle through all human history, that points to her origin and manifests Him as the source of her inner strength.

Jesus has sent His Spirit upon us as members of the Church for the glorification of the Father. But He has also, in closer resemblance to the intratrinitarian loves, given to His apostles and their successors the power to do the same by means of the sacraments.

Our Lord said many things about the Spirit at the Last Supper and made many promises concerning Him. But the Apostles, before the Lord's suffering and death, having as yet no direct experience of the Spirit, were hardly able then to understand that they could love other men by giving the Spirit to them as truly as Jesus would give Him to the apostles. That experience and understanding awaited Pentecost and their power thereafter to give the Spirit through the imposition of hands.

But we all are called, if in less striking fashion, to sanctify one another. Our task is not to give shallow and deceptive external glory to one another but, so far as lies with us, the great gift of the intrinsic glory of Christ's grace. This is done most obviously by bishops when they bring the Spirit Himself upon the faithful by confirming them or by ordaining some as bishops or priests. But we all can, each in his own degree and office, sanctify others by God's own power, for Jesus' glory and, so, for the Father's.

This we can do at times sacramentally—we are all able to baptize, the ministers of the sacrament of matrimony are the couple being married, all can be called in extraordinary circumstances to distribute Communion. But we can sanctify one another also by prayer and penance, as Pope Pius XII recalled to all: "Deep mystery this...that the salvation of many depends on the prayers and voluntary penances which the members of the Mystical Body of Christ offer for this intention."[44] The universal call to holiness, spoken of so firmly and clearly by the Second Vatican Council, is made connaturally possible by the Christian family, "the domestic Church" as the same Council called it.[45]

Knowing the intrinsic glory of Christ's Church, we glorify her in faith —though care is needed lest we glorify her for reasons unworthy of her or lest we ascribe her glory to her members. We can be certain that she is filled with saints but, for the most part, they are quite invisible to our dull vision This is, I think, the most basic reason for the Church's veneration of the Saints. In their case, we have knowledge of at least their heavenly excellence, usually also of what they were while still on earth. Knowing their greatness and something of Jesus' love for them as attested by the miracles He works through their intercession and in their honor, we are left with no alternative if we have Christ's life within us: we must give ourselves not to mere private glorying but to public glorifying.

We glorify the Church best when we respect the stages and seasons of her growth. So, we glorify her saints in heaven for God's glory manifest in them; the saints on earth,[46] only for Christ's glory through His Bride, glimpsed momentarily through them. That all her members are in need of purification is obvious—it is for this that she exists. But her dignity is so great as Bride of Christ and His Body, we owe her so much as our mother by baptism and by her continual mediating of Christ's graces to us, that it is spiritually risky in the extreme to speak or act in her regard except from profound love and reverence.[47] There is something more than a little unhealthy in today's penchant

---

[44] Encyclical *Mystici Corporis*, #55.

[45] II Vatican, *Lumen Gentium*, #11; also, *Apostolicam Actuositatem*, #11. This has been carried further by Pope John Paul II; cf. *Familiaris Consortio*, #21. For the wide variety of other, normal means of helping in the sanctification of others in marriage, cf. ##55–62 of the same document.

[46] 'Glorify' seems, as indicated above, too strong a term for this; a proper reserve should limit us to 'thank' and 'praise.'

[47] The attitude called for, as we shall see in detail later (in *Ch* 17.C, Excursus, *pp* 354–358), is adumbrated in Tobit's praise of Jerusalem (Tob.13:8–18).

for speaking of the Church as though it were identical with the aggregate of its members, as if it were a merely human institution, a not very edifying one at that. However accurate our criticism may be, it is destructive if it misses those most important aspects of her being that are visible only to faith.

But precisely because Jesus directs all individual loves to the glory of the Father, and because the Father has created all things in and through and for Jesus' glory, so the creation of this inchoate glory of Christians within the Church, in faint likeness to the procession of the Glory, draws all (just as inchoately) into one. This communion of all within the Church is the ultimate "common good," one that is not distinguishable from the individual's good; it is the goal that unites all in Christ.

3. Our Love for the Subhuman Creation

A final question concerning charity in us is: How are we to love the subhuman creation if we are to love it as God loves it? How are we to love it so that we share the divine likeness in the way we love it?

If a man says, "I love steak," he is using 'love' in a very different sense than when he says, "I love my wife." The former is a love of desire for what satisfies his sensible appetites (or, should he say, "I love mathematics," his intellectual appetites). The latter is a love of benevolence directed to his wife and willing her good as his own.

Now, it would seem that sense-love can only be "concupiscent," for the senses have no internal or intrinsic power to free them from the constraints of pleasure and pain. Such love of desire manifests itself through its unconcern to preserve what is loved in the unique otherness of its own goodness. Thus, desire for food or drink or sexual release, if allowed to remain in man as solely sense appetites, have no concern for the preservation of the intrinsic goodness of what is loved except for prolonging one's own pleasures. But the converse is also true: the love of desire, by itself, is also unconcerned for one's own integral goodness.

Though sense-love for something is often linked to consumption of it, there need not be any such connection. Consumption is at most a secondary aspect if not wholly accidental. Sensible love is the desire for satisfying completion of some process resulting from stimulation of an organ (or for continuance of such satisfaction already in process.) Though hunger-pangs and thirst are only sated by the presence implied by consumption, yet even taste need not involve more than a negligible consumption. But for an intellectual love, *a fortiori* for charity, much more is needed. By the mind we can transcend the love of desire even with regard to inanimate material objects. For, out of a conviction of the goodness of the earth, one can freely love its forms and configurations, even where to our eyes ugly or cruel, appreciating it for what it is in itself, not reproaching it for what it is not. Only thus can we see truly the goodness of the world perceived through our senses and come to know it as it is, in its otherness and not merely as filtered through some satisfaction to ourselves. Only through the mind, moreover, can the sensible order be loved as showing an aspect of God's goodness and as manifesting His greatness, so as to give Him the glory.

If we, who have been created according to the Father's Image as well as in His Likeness, are to love the material world with a love structured as is His, we must love it with a love that terminates in God Himself and not in the creature. Since the creature is, essentially and before all else, a participation in the divine Being, it has nothing else as source of any of its goodness.[48] Any attempt, then, to love the creature in itself, without letting it direct our love beyond itself to its source in God, either leads us to corrupt or destroy it or, at the least, fails to grasp the beloved creature in its own truth. In either case, we do not truly love the creature but only our own partial satisfaction, seeking through the object loved our own sense of worth, power, or pleasure.

Moreover, knowing the world in its totality to be God's handiwork and His gift of love to man, still more as that which He united to Himself through the Incarnation, one has still deeper grounds to love it for His sake. Charity then calls us to look upon the subhuman creation in its own being, as other that human,[49] as the Father has created it through and for Jesus. For the earth and the universe are meant to manifest God's glory through man's proper love for them, both sensible and intellectual indeed but also by charity as expressions of the mystery of the Father's love for the Son and the Son's return of Glory to the Father.

Further, we will need to love the world not simply for what it is but for what it is meant to become. God gave it to man to work and use. So, we are called to labor to actualize its potentialities in such wise as best to show our love for God through His gift and our love for our fellow men. This implies an obligation for our own continual growth. For, no material being can possess its goodness all at once, but only spread out in time. No man can say something in an instant, even internally to himself. We reason in time, grow and develop our powers in time. What we love in creation, what our love for other men achieves in its utilization, what our own power rightly to love either men or the world, all are made so as to develop in time. Each change man makes in the world conditions the activity of those who follow him, so that his world is ever new, even with regard to what is now old.

Charity seeks to help creation grow in goodness, to call forth from chaos, as God did at the first creation, the unique goodness of this world which we must love before it has in itself any proper ground for our charity. This is the phenomenon of "induced desirability," whereby my free choice itself becomes the source of at least part of the value of the object chosen. This investing of something with value by the very act of liberty which chooses it enters into all free choice. In a good action, the person tries rather to bring into being (or at least into consciousness) the element of goodness which

---

[48] *Pp* 85–90

[49] And even in some sense as not wholly for man, for we must never forget that in ways not made wholly clear to us the world exists for the angels as well as for man. So the whole creation groans now under the lash of sinful man—and of sinful angels.

could ground such an increment of value within the real situations where this value was not grounded (or perceived). And, as mentioned, this sort of induction of value reaches its transcendent and higher-than-human perfection in charity.[50]

C. CONCLUSION: THE TRAITS OF CREATED CHARITY

What is essential to charity in us, without which it does not exist, is given by the Great Commandment and the "one like to it." To love God above all things, without division of heart or mind, and all things else for His sake, is the beginning and the end of all authentic love and of the whole moral life. As mentioned above,[51] to know what such love is and what it calls for from us in attitude and choice is given us through Jesus' mediation. As He lived these commandments in His earthly life, so are we, in our weak fashion, to do likewise by His grace. Hence, truly to love God requires that we love Him as Jesus did and does.

But Jesus' love is trinitarian in the manner we have seen, and our love is genuine insofar as we share in His. That is, we must love the Son by identification with Him, love the Father as our Father, and love the Spirit by our communion with one another in the Body of Christ, of which He is the Breath of life.

This is the structure of charity in any man. But this structure need not be visible to the one whose love it is. Thus it takes no great spiritual finesse to recognize in the Patriarchs or in Moses the traits which we shall be summarizing here, though these are only implicit and in many ways still inchoate and undeveloped. The Old Testament accounts of these men give us no indication that they had any express knowledge of the Trinity or of Jesus; what the New Testament says on this matter will be considered in its place. The prayers and actions of good pagans, not only of those mentioned in the Scriptures but of those of India or China or among the indigenous peoples of this continent, indeed, such prayers as those of Ajax and of Hector to Zeus[52] and the prayers that cultural anthropologists have found among far more primitive peoples show true evidences of the same structure. Just how charity can show itself in such diverse fashions and yet have this structure is much of the business of Part II of this book, where we shall consider the ways in which moral and spiritual growth can take place before Christ is known.

We have seen how our charity is formed, through Christ, by our relations to the Three Persons. Finally, then, we can consider what that trinitarian relationship implies for the structure of charity that is shown in Jesus' charity, which structure alone can be called unconditionally the structure of created charity.

---

[50] Cf. Paul M. Quay, S.J., "Morality by Calculation of Values," *Theology Digest 23,* 347–364, at 355

[51] Cf. *pp* 103–104 above.

[52] *Iliad* Bk 17:645–650, Bk 6:476–481.

1. The first trait of Jesus' charity, visible to believer and unbeliever alike, was His love for His Father. This was shown in His perduring choice gratefully to accept the gift of His entire being from the Father, without alteration or repining at its finitude and its consequent limitations in space and time and culture.[53] Grateful for all that the Father had given Him, He claimed no independent root of being or merit. Thankfully He accepted a life solely in accord with the Father's will, a life qualified only by the Father's desires, not by Jesus' own (Jn.6:38). Because there were no limits to His gratitude in receiving, there were no limits short of death itself to His obedience.

So we are, in Jesus, to love the Father. Knowing that our entire being is the purest of gifts, we are to be grateful for it in its entirety and in every detail. By charity we accept our life with all the limitations that the Father's will for us in Jesus' world has placed upon it. We seek no alteration of the gift but only, as creatures in time, to develop it in accordance with His desires. Able to make no return, we follow pagan Seneca's advice for one who is grateful to a benefactor so situated in felicity that there is nothing one can add to his happiness: "Do you wish to return the favor? Accept it graciously."[54] What Seneca could not add is that our gratitude to the Father, as sharing in Jesus' own, shows itself in obedience. "This is the love of God, that we keep His commandments" (I Jn.5:2–3). This obedience, moreover, is owed to Jesus Himself, since He represents the Father to us. Without obedience, our love of God is mere pretense.

2. As seen above, the Father's love for Jesus as man is the reflection of the Father's characteristic love for the Son. It is, then, the gift of all that the Father possesses that can be had by a single human nature. It is gratuitous; the Father can receive no return except Jesus' subsequent acquiescence in His gifts; He finds no grounds of prior goodness in the Son's humanity. This the Father loves, then, solely by His free decision so to love. The Father does not first love Jesus because Jesus is good but makes Him good because He loves Him.

Thus, then, does Jesus love us, for He came to show us the Father (Jn.14:8–9) and He qualified His love for us as paternal, "As the Father has loved Me, so have I loved you" (Jn.15:9). Our love of charity for the Son is one of union and identification with Jesus, for it is by His life that we live. As one with Him, then, our love must bear the same trait as His for us: "Love one another as I loved you" (13:34; 15:12).

The second fundamental trait of charity, which is this love for our fellow men, shows itself as a willingness freely to give ourselves, as well as all that is ours, for the good of others. If we give away what He has given us because others stand in need of it, we need not fear that He who gave it to us in the first place is unable to give it to us again. "You have freely received; freely

---

[53] Cf. Heinrich Schlier, "Das Bleibend Katholische," *1 Catholica*, 1/1970, 1–21 (French translation: "Le Catholicisme comme décision," *Axes 3*, oct.-nov. 1970, 9–29.)

[54] "Vis reddere beneficium? Accipe benigne." As cited in *ST* II-II, 106, 4c: Seneca, *De Beneficiis*, cap 35, (Firmin-Didot 166).

give" {Mt.10:8}. We can act this way because, through Jesus, we have been given hope and confidence in the Father who always hears us (Jn.11:41–42) and will not abandon us (Jn.8:29, 16:32). Because this love is gratuitous and free, we can give of ourselves even to those who are not loveworthy, in hope that they may become worthy of love. This gratuity becomes most evident when, even as the Father's love for us and Jesus' also, so our love for others is rebuffed. Yet like Jesus, we are not to withdraw the gift even when death is offered as its only reward.

3. Another trait of created charity is shown in, "Father,...glorify Your Son that the Son may glorify You" (Jn.17:1). The Father glorifies Jesus for the perfection of His filial obedience (Php.2:8–11). Jesus glorifies the Father for the Father's own intrinsic glory as perfect Father in giving to Jesus all that can be given. Each wills the glory of the Other, Jesus receiving His power to glorify entirely from the Father. Jesus desires to be like the Father in order to be His perfect image in this world. He does always what He sees the Father doing (Jn.5:19–20), who gives His gifts to good and bad alike, so that the goodness of the Father might be manifest to all men through Jesus, so that he who sees Jesus, sees the Father (Jn.14:9).

This trait of Christian charity is, then, an active willing of the glory of the Father. This we seek by our glorifying of Jesus, whose goodness is manifested when we do what we know that Jesus did and does. The imitation of Christ is directed, then, not to our own perfecting, though it accomplishes this, but to making Jesus so known and loved by all that all may glorify Him and, through Him, glorify the Father (I Pet.4:10–11).

By charity, then, we rejoice in whatever good we see in others, recognizing it as God's gift and giving Him the glory for it. But Jesus sought the Father's glory primarily through His labors to make Him better known among His people and more truly loved. If He came to serve rather than be served, it was that He might sanctify those He served so that the Father might be glorified through them. We are so to labor in the service of our fellows, by example as well as word, that Christ may be known and glorified. Hence comes charity's abiding desire to lead every person to sanctity, if not now, then in the future, assisting each to every suitable excellence, no matter how much this might make others greater than oneself. Rejoicing at what we have received, without envy or grief not to have what has been given to others, we praise the Father for others' gifts, making them in this way our own.

4. Hence the fourth basic trait: one's self finds its fulfilment by "disappearing" into this glorification of Christ in and through His Church. Drawn by His Spirit into oneness and intercommunion within the Church, one does not attempt to "be different from" others. The dissimilarities among us are neither perceived nor used as means to draw esteem in our own direction. Rather, as the body can live and be strong only through the diversity of organs and functions of all its parts together, so the diversities of personal capabilities and ecclesial functions within the Church are needed for her health and strength (I Cor.12). This they will be to the extent that we are united by a

common finality: the search for God's glory and not our own.

The Mass is, therefore, the focal point upon which all traits of charity converge, being brought about by the action of the Spirit[55] in order that all, together in the self-forgetfulness of perfect communion, may worship the Father through His Christ. In the Spirit, each one wills to be a member of the Body of Christ, the Church, solely for God's glory and the glory of His Son incarnate, glorifying Him in and through her as she is glorified by Him. The Spirit, then, is the Church's principle of unity, forming us as her members as He pours out the charity of God within our hearts (Rom.5:5). Through our charity He introduces us into her unity and labors to make it effective in and about us.

In sum, two traits of our charity are related to the first procession (grateful obedience to Jesus and the Father; gratuitous giving of oneself to all one's fellows) and two are related to the second procession (glorifying of Father and Son through missionary endeavor to make Christ known and loved; communion within the Church). As might be expected, the former two are those out of which alone the other two can arise in truth. If the former traits are weak, we may glory in what pleases us; but this will be only a hidden way of glorying in our own gifts, since it will be only by an extension of our love of these that we will delight in them in others. We will not be sensitive enough to God's grace truly to recognize others' gifts as rays from His glory, nor selfless enough to be made one in faith and worship within the unity of the Church. The former traits, however, if unobstructed, give rise spontaneously to the latter.

But all love requires knowledge. One must know in truth the object of one's love, either in itself or in the love which someone whom one loves bears it. Hence the traits of charity exist in someone only insofar as he stands in the truth. Our charity, as a participation in that of Jesus, can only be true to its exemplar if it shares in the truth of Jesus' charity, in the perfection of His reflecting of the intratrinitarian loves.

For, Jesus is not only the Son of the Father; He is also the Word of the Father. As the Father's Word, He is Truth itself subsistent, true because expressing without alteration by the totality of His being all that the Father is. Then, as the Word made flesh, Jesus' undistorted reflection of the Son's reception of the divine nature from the Father corresponds to the first trait of charity. Jesus' love for us shows, in turn, what love the Father has for Him and for us in Him. As the Father has given all His substance to His Word, and through the Word made flesh has given in sacrifice for evil men all He has, so charity is true in us through sharing this universality.

The Glory which is the Holy Spirit proceeds from the Father's glorying, in perfect knowledge, in the Son and the Son's in the Father. Our glorifying

---

[55] Cf. "The Mystery of the Church and of the Eucharist in the Light of the Mystery of the Holy Trinity," Joint International Commission for Theological Dialogue between the Roman Catholic Church and the Orthodox Church (August 1, 1982), *St. Vladimir's Theological Quarterly* *26*, 251–258 (#4, 1982).

of the Father through Jesus, Himself glorified among us by the Father's sending of the Spirit, would be manifest mockery were it not based on the truth of God's own majesty and power. To claim to love someone for what he neither is nor can be, is to insult him, pinning his name on a simulacrum. So also, for our communion with one another within the Church. It is through the truth of faith that we are enabled to see God's work in her and in even her least promising or merely potential members.

We will have reason later to analyse this relationship between truth and love in detail.[56] Here we need only recall that the traits of charity have this correlative and fundamental relationship to truth.

From these four basic traits, all the virtues derive in accord with concrete situations of temperament and circumstance. There is more to be said about each of the traits, in the way of refinement and explicitation. But this is better left for later, when we can deal with concrete realizations of charity. Here, we need to turn back to original sin, to explain which we have undertaken this long digression, to see how the negations of these traits have been built into us at our conception.

---

[56] Cf. end of *Ch* 9.E, *pp* 213–215 and of *Ch* 16.D, *pp* 326–331.

Chapter 6

A Theory of Original Sin

We return now to the problem of original sin as sketched out in Chapter 2. How could sin be found in a zygote or embryo, which is unable to choose well or ill? Further, if his condition is properly to be called sin, it must be worse than a mere absence of faith, hope, and charity.[1] How could the infant at birth be in a state of opposition to God, when, as the Church declared against Baius, the infant's will is not set against God or opposed to Him?

A. Preliminaries

Let us first recall briefly the data given by faith. These, taken together, constitute a great portion of the "problem" of original sin. The faith of the Church is apodictic that temptation to sin did not originate with man but with the demons.[2] Yet Adam did yield to that temptation and brought evil upon himself and on all of us, his descendants.

When we are conceived, we lack sanctifying grace and the life of Christ. The Holy Spirit is absent; so also, therefore, is charity, that love of God which the Spirit alone pours out in our hearts. The resulting condition is a state of sin, personal in each of us, not learned from bad example but innate. Nonetheless, though our wills are not turned towards God in love at our conception, neither are they set against Him (DS 1948–1949).

Since all of us, baptized infants and nonbaptized ones, saints and sinners,

[1] The mere absence of supernatural gifts defines the hypothetical 'state of pure nature.' Whether God could create a man in whom grace is merely absent, that is, in whom its absence is not also privative and damaging to his nature, is not our concern at this point.

[2] Cf. Paul M. Quay S.J., "Angels and Demons in the Teaching of IV Lateran," *Theological Studies 42,* 20–45 (1981).

all have empirically the same nature,[3] since, further, no one can be certain with the certitude of faith that he is in the state of grace without a divine revelation,[4] it seems clear that the life of charity can come or go in us without easily visible signs of its presence or absence.[5] Though our nature is made for charity, since created in the Image of the invisible God, our nature is not destroyed by the lack of charity. Man remains identifiably man even when he has lost grace.[6]

Finally, no explanation can be valid that implies that grace is in any way due to our nature or, equivalently, that mere and simple absence of grace damages our nature, though conceivably such absence might leave it less well provided for, as a nature, than otherwise.

At the beginning of our discussion,[7] I suggested that the lack of initial charity somehow brings about, progressively and necessarily, the psychic deformation of each individual that is designated 'concupiscence', a deformation that is not removed in any direct way by baptism. Hence, though the privation of grace is a central element in original sin and though the restoration of grace removes whatever is, properly speaking, sinful, there remains this damage to our nature that was an integral element in our original state of sin.[8]

Since an infant is by nature incapable of free choice, it is important to keep clearly in mind, if serious misunderstanding is to be avoided, that the discussion that follows is concerned primarily with psychic pathology, secondarily with the possibility of integral psychic health. We are concerned, therefore, solely with the psychic aspects of the human person, i.e., with the nonfree, even if sometimes voluntary, aspects of the person's conscious life.[9] More explicitly, we are concerned with the healthy and unhealthy modes of development of the feelings, emotions, drives, passions, desires—the whole host of infra-intellectual, infra-volitional, interior activities that go on within the actual or potential consciousness of the infant while still a zygote or embryo; but also with the spontaneous movements of the will—voluntary but not free—in the older infant, whether still in the womb or already born.

---

[3] 'Nature' will be used mostly in the Aristotelian sense, as "the what-it-is considered as a *principle* of operation." Hence, 'nature' is defined in terms of the basic powers to act in specific ways. These actualizations can be various while the powers remain, at least in germ, the same.

[4] DS 1540, 1566.

[5] This is not to deny that there are striking cases of the one or the other that no one can miss, however they may choose to interpret them. Nor would I wish to hold that one cannot have true certitude, at lower levels than that of faith, about the presence of grace within one.

[6] Unless explicitly stated otherwise, 'grace' will always refer in this Section to sanctifying or habitual or divinizing grace, not to actual or transient grace. Moreover, the gift of actual grace is presumed in all discussions of human freedom to choose in any manner helpful to salvation.

[7] *Pp* 15–17 above.

[8] Pope Paul VI, *Credo of the People of God*, "Original Offense," proclaimed June 30, 1968: "It is human nature so fallen, stripped of the grace that clothed it, injured in its own natural powers and subjected to the dominion of death, that is transmitted to all men...."

[9] The "subconscious," the "deep unconscious," etc. are all included, since they are defined in terms of what might become conscious under suitable conditions.

This nonfree activity strongly influences the ways in which we perceive things and think about them, and offers powerful motivation for particular responses to what we see of our world and ourselves. Yet though one's psychic structure can be helpful or hostile to a given, potentially free act, it is not ordinarily determinative of it. Unless wholly deprived of one's power to will by brain damage or psychosis, an adult is free to decide on his course of action, to do well or ill, to sin or to act virtuously, to serve God or to refuse Him, whether he is in a state marked by original sin or its residual effects (hence, with a damaged psyche) or in a state of original justice or, if such may be, of unfallen pure nature (with a psyche untouched by sin).

It would be easier for us to act virtuously in most circumstances were we unfallen. Yet the fall itself is more than adequate evidence that sin is a real possibility for man in any state[10]. God has left us truly free to set our own wills against His. Without pausing here to query concerning the state of man before the fall or immediately after, we can recognize that our state at birth is not one that makes the love of charity easy for us. In our present condition, an ascetical training is always needed in order to bring the sensory affective life under the control of the mind and will.[11]

Because of the restriction to the psychic aspects of the person, we face the difficulty of speaking sensibly about either the preconceptual or what is conceptual but without reflexive awareness. The difficulty is augmented when we attempt to speak of the infant. For we can only speak about things using words and concepts, the very things the infant either does not yet have or is only beginning to acquire. Hence we shall have to use language that, when used of older children or adults, is descriptive of intellectual and volitional attitudes, even of rational and moral ones, that depend on self-awareness although, as far as we know, the infant lacks such awareness. If, then, we talk as if the infant could reflect upon itself, this is simply because we have no other way to talk of these matters.

One might wonder how it is that we think to contribute to the understanding of the mystery of original sin by examining the human psyche. This is, after all, to a fair degree naturally accessible to us. It is even manipulable to some degree by means of psychotherapies of various sorts and by means of chemicals and drugs that affect the neural activity of the brain.

While it is true that the mystery as such cannot be adequately grasped by any natural operation of the mind, yet the faith that lets us know of the mystery in the first place is that which tells us that the effects of that mystery

[10] Cf, concerning the negative aspects of our lives that cannot be due to original sin, Karl Rahner, "The Theological Concept of Concupiscentia," *Theological Investigations 1,* tr. C. Ernst, New York: Crossroad (1982) 347–382, especially 349–350. trans. from *Schriften zur Theologie I*, Einsiedeln: Benziger (1954).

[11] The gaining of such control, a large element in the definition of psychic adulthood, is indicated not by one's first free act but by the possibility of stability in one's free choices. Though long considered to be first achieved at about fourteen years of age, the age at which one achieves such basic control will depend strongly upon the culture into which one is born. Cf. *pp* 363–366 below for details.

must be manifest in the world. Death and illness, ignorance so crass as to brutalize men, psychological aberrations, temptation and the seeming omnipresence of actual sin, of deliberate cruelties and of genuine hatreds of one's fellow men that extend far beyond what mere self-interest or simple antagonism would arouse—all these have always appeared as somehow connected with the sin of our origins, for they all exist in a world which the All-good God created and which He declared in all its visible parts, save man, to be very good. It is not from God that such evils come. Thus, we can rightly seek to analyze phenomenologically the conditions that the light of faith assures us are either part of or rooted in or caused by original sin.

Further, our analysis of the psyche will be carried out in the light of the theological positions we have been engaged with till now. We should be able to see easily enough whether a particular psychic trait is or is not helpful to a person's love of the Lord.

Here, then, I shall begin by offering a description of the way in which the privation of charity at conception might be thought to work its ill effects as the child develops in the womb and thereafter.[12] Then we shall consider a few of the notorious theological problems connected with any such efforts: to show, firstly, how things might be different were the child conceived in grace; then, to show that my suggestions for resolving various difficulties do not plunge us into far worse ones, as happened concerning these same matters to Baius and to Jansenius.

B. Psychic structures of the fallen infant

When sperm and ovum fuse, God too must act if a new human being is to be created. But though the human person is created as a being at once material and spiritual, yet, of the factors that determine his concrete nature, the first to show themselves seem to be those that are material. Physical appearance and physique, emotional structures, patterns of spontaneous reaction, and much more are built into the new person by genetic determinism. Seemingly, everything else is equally determined, but now by the maternally imposed conditions upon growth and development, e.g., by the health of the mother, the circumstances of her nourishment and exercise, sufferings of injury or disease, and her emotional life.

We know enough now of the "neural plasticity" of the human brain,[13] to say that the infant's patterns of response to all that impinges upon it—of whatever nature, biochemical, sensory, or emotional—will quickly affect the physical structure of the developing brain. The infant's intra-uterine history is, in varying degrees, built directly into the configuration of synapses in his

[12] Unless otherwise specified, I will use 'conception' in its traditional theological sense for the first coming into being of a new person, identified nowadays with the process of fertilization.

[13] Cf., e.g., Deborah L. Holmes, Jill Nagy Reich, and Joseph F. Pasternak, *The Development of Infants Born at Risk*, Hillsdale (NJ): Lawrence Erlbaum Associates (1984), *pp* 205–212. Also: R. D. Lund, *Development and Plasticity of the Brain*, New York: Oxford U. P. (1978) & G. M. Shepherd, *The Synaptic Organization of the Brain*, 2nd ed., New York: Oxford U. P. (1979).

brain; a genetically identical infant with different history of sensations and emotions will develop a different brain-structure.[14] But the spiritual aspects of the person at conception all seem to exist only in potentiality. It will be many months before he shows signs of any power of abstract thought. It will be years before he is capable of his first act of self-determination.

As the infant grows within the womb, his material powers develop rapidly. His higher ones come into activity more slowly, since they need the developed activity of the lower powers as their substrate—one cannot remember or think about what one has seen if he has as yet no eyes that see.[15] Even at birth, the child shows minimal power of intellection, hence, of freedom. Intellectual appetite is not absent; but the mind does not yet seem capable of differentiating itself spiritually from others, so that reflex knowledge of the self—a first condition for the self-appropriation needed for free choice—is yet to develop.

Most of us are simply unable to recall events that occurred while we were in the womb or in the first year or two thereafter. This is often taken as a sign that the power of memory was absent then or only inchoate, or as an indication that the mind had not yet been formed. I would suggest that neither is the case. The child is not incapable of remembering; but he has no words as yet, no labels for his concepts. Indeed, what he remembers is constantly being recalled, but nonspecifically, as the experiential foundation upon which and out of which all his concepts and words are formed. The remembering would be false if any of his primitive experiences were remembered as conceptually or verbally grasped. Only much later, when language has been acquired, will it be possible to interpret such experiences.[16]

An infant conceived without the supernatural love that is charity will

---

[14] "[D]uring the normal development of the infant nervous system, and during learning in general, external stimuli have a profound effect upon the formation, maintenance, and modulation of synapses in the brain." D. Alan Shewmon, "The Metaphysics of Brain Death, Persistent Vegetative State, and Dementia," *The Thomist 49*, 24–80, (#1, Jan. 1985), *pp* 74–75. In private communication, Shewmon has emphasized the fundamental importance of the modifications of brain-structure produced during fetal development by the brain's interaction with whatever is taking place, whether from external influences or internal formation, in the rest of the body.

[15] Yet "later" does not necessarily imply "higher." For example, the inner perfecting of the lungs comes very late, not because their functioning represents a higher power but because it is of no use until the baby is nearly ready to draw his first breath.

[16] It seems possible that an occasional dream later in life might evoke some of these prototypical experiences and so enable one to lay hold of and interpret them in terms of what one has by then conceptualized. Much of what Jung attributes to the collective unconscious, things he is convinced could not have been derived from individual personal experience, would seem to come rather from this intellectually grasped but nonverbalizable memory (with, of course, all aspects of sense memory as well). Thus his dream of the underground chamber containing the great column with the eye at the top (C. G. Jung, *Memories, Dreams, Reflections*, recorded and edited by A. Jaffe, trans. R. and C. Winston, revised ed., New York: Random House [1965], 11–13) seems at least partially explicable in terms of a boy's first erections, now known to occur within the womb at a time when his eyes are functioning (the womb, though dark, is suffused with a dim, reddish light).

still be drawn to the sensory and other goods he naturally perceives as such. But his patterns of desire and revulsion will have neither trinitarian impress nor even some general orientation towards God. Nothing in these patterns will order or structure his natural reactions so as to make them ready, once he is capable of reflection and deliberate choice, to choose in accord with the traits of charity.

The first and most radical effect of this deprivation is that, instead of having God in some way at the focus of his psychic universe, the infant will grow in the womb very much as a little animal does, as the center of his world. Drawn by pleasure, repelled by pain, he responds automatically to whatever stimuli, internal or external, trigger his genetically determined response mechanisms.

Some may argue that a little animal does not have itself at center of its consciousness, for it has no self and no reflex awareness. Further, a small child, as far as we can judge, seems primarily and intensely concerned with the world outside himself.

This difficulty exemplifies just that misunderstanding mentioned above. Of course, the little animal has no awareness of itself as such; but, for all that, its actions and focus of attention are entirely and solely determined by the animal's desires. A dog's pleasure in being with its master in cold and rain rather than away from him in a warm house and a cat's opposite preference both are nonconceptual and nonreflexive forms of seeking the individual animal's satisfaction.

So the tiny infant in the womb, though one may suspect that he becomes conscious of his world well before he becomes conscious of himself as in that world, is, in the absence of grace, governed entirely by his own needs and desires and emotions.[17] Note here that we are assuming that all of these, at least at the start, are good, and that they are corrupted, if at all, only as the effects of original sin increase. For example, the infant's instinctive love for his mother as source of warmth, nourishment, security, and firm protection can, of itself, hardly be suspect, given its importance for his survival.[18]

The situation is analogous to that shown in a famous painting of Nicholas Escher, a self-portrait done by reflection from a spherical mirror, a large, polished metal ball. Escher and the details of his room are all there; but Escher is, of optical necessity, in the exact middle. His room is depicted, distortedly but with great accuracy, splayed out circularly around him. What gives the

[17] One can find a popular (and, in part, highly controversial) introduction to what was thought a decade ago of the psychology of the child in the womb and immediately after birth in the popular account by Thomas Verny, M.D. (with John Kelly), *The Secret Life of the Unborn Child*, New York: Summit Books (Simon & Schuster), (1981), which has good references to the scientific literature on a page-by-page basis at the back. For evidence to show that some experience of maternal or sibling affection can reach the fetus, perhaps even the embryo, cf. *pp* 46–89.

[18] One might reasonably demur, arguing that an unfallen mother's care and love for her child would more than compensate for less self-centered feelings in the child. I would wish to show here that even the more optimistic view I have assumed leads to an equally grim view of original sin.

painting its peculiar power is that, no matter how Escher might have chosen otherwise to arrange things and his own position relative to them, so long as he paints what he sees in the sphere, he will necessarily be the center of all.

In this sense, the child too is the center of his world, not by willing it so or reflecting upon it but by simply being what he is, unable to be other. So long as the metal sphere of his own natural propensities and desires alone specifies the range of his loves, he will, even before he begins to grasp things intellectually, direct all things to himself as the center, the world circling around him, and God, if known at all, as a distant, even if all-inclusive, periphery.

This image of centering would be misleading if taken to assert merely that any intellectually conscious being must be a "center" of consciousness. I am not speaking of a center for perception or for thought but of the focus of all one's desires and goals; of finality, not of cognition. The infant has himself as his own goal. His interest in the world, his love for his mother, and all other psychic functions are directed solely toward his own perceived good.

The infant's psyche, then, disposes him to seek his own good as his sole ultimate end, the good of others insofar as contributing to that primary end, and God, when he comes to know of Him, only as a further good for himself. Thus the psychic structure intended to support the Great Commandment is upended, though without any free act of the infant's will. The infant is henceforth disposed to love God inasmuch as good for himself, not for God's own goodness. He is disposed to love God for his own happiness, not to love himself as beloved by God and made for Him.

Now, in none of this is there an indication of some positive psychic injury or wound. Surely in any condition, one's psyche should dispose one to love what is worthy of love. And though the infant judges what is lovable only by his own spontaneous reactions, this seems not, in an infant, a bad thing. Nonetheless, the characteristics of psychic self-centering, since opposed to the Great Commandment, cannot without qualification be labeled good; and fixation in such an attitude from conception seems a predisposition to evil. Lack of an outwardly directed relationality also implies, however unconsciously, that one regard oneself as answerable only to oneself; one makes of oneself a universal norm.

Given, then, the continuity of the infant's development, we can be certain that the embryo or fetus seeks out and loves—to the extent that we may use this word when dealing with the primitive level of affectivity he possesses when first conscious of anything—whatever he finds lovable. Conversely, he backs away from or rejects whatever he finds unattractive or repellent. Only what he sees as appealing can attract him or draw his love. These remarks, which may seem little more than tautologies, nonetheless have implications it is worth a few moments to consider.

The infant, then, begins by loving that which is lovable and shrinking in dislike from that which is not. This attitude, already months old at birth, seems to us so right and proper, so ordinary and natural, that the radical falsehood to which it leads can readily escape our attention, even sometimes when we look at it point-blank. However, the enormity of the error involved—an error that is not made, evidently, by the mind in judgment but that is a malformation of the psychic structure of love, a malformation that will automatically be the root of an infinity of errors of judgement later—can be sensed easily enough if we begin to consider what original sin produces as its corollary. Also psychically present from the beginning in the fallen infant, this corollary is: One loves what is lovable and refuses love to what is not lovable; love is given to those who are worthy of it and withheld from those who are not.

Love is given to those people who are worthy of it—well and good; it should be. Love is not to be given to those who are not worthy of it—this is the "error." It is this that nullifies the psychic support for the basic trait of charity towards others. This instinctive error of regarding one's basic and primary love for others as conditioned both positively and negatively by the lovability of the one who is to receive it is one major aspect of original sin.

But if this is natural to the infant, the question returns in force, how can it be wrong or in "error"? At worst, it would appear in the same light as the above-mentioned psychic obstacle to the Great Commandment. Yet here, I think, is something deeper, though it has its repercussions on the infant's relations to the Great Commandment also.

As the result of original sin, the infant is not psychically prepared to love gratuitously either the not-yet-lovable or the unlovable. He also senses the logical consequence that, if so, then *he* is to be loved only insofar as loveworthy. All love must be merited. And the infant is afraid that he cannot measure up.

But why should he be fearful in this way? Would not our comment about the Great Commandment lead to just the opposite conclusion: that he thinks himself already perfectly lovable and that all creation centers on him because of his very own goodness?

I think not. The fact that he directs all his activity towards his own greater good, that he is to himself his own last and ultimate end, does not mean that he ever finds himself assured of achieving what he seeks. His experiences in the womb during the last months of pregnancy would often, I suspect, counter any such assurance were it present. This will become more explicit after birth, as he acquires knowledge of rivals—others who are enough like himself to be seen as other centers of finality, as other goals for themselves. But the germ of this fear is already present as a natural instinct.

For fear is natural enough among all animals; and it is doubtful that man could naturally exist for very long without it. In particular, the infant is, of all creatures, the most helpless, the most vulnerable, the most dependent on others for its existence. It must, then, if it is to survive, fear above all else loss of its mother, whether physically or in affection. Hence, we find among infant animals, the nuzzlings, suckings, clutchings, whimperings, and other reflexes designed to keep it and its mother together. Hence, also, the fear reflexes, should she be separated from it. Such fear seems both natural and necessary.

Among the simpler mammals, enforced separation from the mother triggers instinctive and maladaptive behaviors, characteristic of panic or, later, depression, that can prove lethal to the infant if it be not succored. These reactions are generally less severe in higher forms, especially in the primates, where instinctual behaviors are less stereotyped. Even in human infants, however, extreme isolation can bring on a form of depression that will be fatal if no remedy is supplied.[19] The infant needs what might be called the "physical affection" of its mother (or mother substitute), i.e., the external signs of love, if he is to live.

One may surmise, then, that already built in to the infant in the womb is a genetically based fear of separation from his mother, added to which in the human infant is his fear of being unloveable. For if one must be lovable in order to be loved and, so, to live, then one's psychic refusal to love the unlovable, with one's consequent need to be or become lovable, will permeate the instinctive animal fear of desertion or isolation and greatly intensify it.

This immoderate fear of not being good enough to be loved would motivate the infant to act spontaneously to forestall what he fears, initiating a psychic movement to acquire the needed goodness. His fear will be a passion, seemingly instinctive, to prove himself loveworthy and to do whatever lies within his power to attract the love without which he must die. In our fallen condition, the infant's primary psychically dictated task is to make himself lovable, lest he not be loved. He seeks, therefore, to draw love by force of attractiveness rather than to receive it in its gratuity.

The mere fact that he has experientially identified the possibility of being loved with being intrinsically loveworthy constrains every child to strive to see himself as loveworthy. Because of this fundamental warping of the affectivity, to survive at all—so he is "convinced"—the infant must discover some value that is rooted in himself as such.[20] For he cannot be satisfied with a love that is not directed to him personally. It has to be *he* that is lovable. It has to

---

[19] As far as is now known, such depressions are almost fully reversible in humans. To a large extent this is true even among apes when sufficient efforts at rehabilitation are carried out over long enough times. For apes, cf. Harry F. Harlow, "Love in Infant Monkeys," *Scientific American 200*, 68–74, (June 1959). The conclusions drawn in this fascinating account need to be modified considerably in the light of further experimentation: cf. H. F. Harlow and C. Mears, *The Human Model: Primate Perspectives*, Washington DC: Winston (1979); also, Gary W. Kraemer, "Effects of Differences in Early Social Experiences on Primate Neurobiological-Behavioral Development," in *The Psychology of Attachment and Separation*, edd. M. Reite & T. Field, Orlando (FL): Academic Press (1985), *pp* 135–161. Many questions relating to bonding, isolation, and the reversibility of their consequences are still controverted, though I think there would be general consensus on what I have stated in the text.

[20] As we shall see later, once he has been born, this is easily possible for him within certain limits, e.g., he soon experiences his parent's love for his physical beauty, his animal amiability, his responsiveness to them. But some explanation is still needed: if this fear of lack of worth is natural, why is it not limited? Why is the infant not content with a limited lovability—as seems often, in fact, the case with adults? We shall return to this question later.

be *his* goodness, not only residing in him but his very own, constitutive of his being and person if he is to be proven worthy of love and life.

The vital need to be loved becomes, then, the motive force in a search for self-value. This desire for a value that is entirely one's own is insatiable. It can find no surcease till, impossibly, the infant is satisfied that the goodness of his own small self is great enough to coerce the love that is necessary for his survival. The goodness that he already possesses through the gift freely given by God and parents is necessarily insufficient for such a task. The first trait of charity is thus psychically nullified at its very root by this instinctive contradiction to the Son's attitude, both as man and as God, towards His Father.

But further, to desire that a free person's love for oneself be necessitated by one's own excellence is to desire what belongs to God alone. Only God can, by His nature, coerce any free person's love; and even He does not permit Himself to do this except in heaven. Hence the infant is, all unawares, seeking to be as God, knowing good and evil—where these are defined as what makes him lovable, in his own eyes at least, and what does not—and being his own sole beatitude.

This aspect of the psychic reversal of the Great Commandment appears more sinister than the former one. Though a psychic orientation to one's own good need not be opposed to the Great Commandment, even if offering no positive basis for it, an aggressive pursuit of essentially divine prerogatives, however unconscious, cannot be seen as innocent.

The two traits of fraternal charity associated with the generation of the Son suffer a similar unconscious reinterpretation. The psychic structures are geared to a love that is a prize or reward, won for oneself by one's own acquisition of the necessary excellences. If love can be given only according to worthiness, love for evildoers is impossible; and one loses any natural basis for seeking to share whatever good he possesses in proportion to the need of those who lack it (Ac.2:45; 4:34–35). Wonderment and gratitude for the gift of one's own being, though often felt by small children, seems more an echo of an innocence long vanished than the abiding psychic basis for the second trait of charity.

There is hardly need even to consider the aspects of charity that correspond to the procession of the Holy Spirit. For, the direct consequence of the psychic passion to win love, is the sensing of all other claimants on maternal affection as rivals. Envious stinginess grows up spontaneously. Appreciation and delight in the excellence of others, as others' and not as mere confirmation of one's own putative excellence, are cut off at their source. Indeed, if Freud is to be credited, it is not a sibling but the father himself who is perceived as the chief rival and who is murdered in desire.

Since the infant measures good solely by his instinctive grasp of what is good-for-him, even at the level of sensory cognition the psychic structures are not properly readied for their task of grasping the other simply as other.[21]

---

[21] If it is to make sense to say that one is able to know anything whatsoever, the first epistemo-

Rather, all things are perceived from the vantage point of the infant's own limited interests. Instead of attending purely to the other as other, the incipient structures of the brain increasingly serve to filter all sensation through the prior mold of the child's own mind and heart. Lacking the fourth trait of charity, he renders himself less and less capable of seeing the truth except insofar as it accords with his already exstant desires. As he learns to love, the falsehoods mentioned progressively distort his power to love rightly. Thinking wrongly about the very nature of love, all his loves are falsified.

C. ADAM-CHRIST TYPOLOGY: A THEORY OF FELT GRACE

In much that has been said above, I have appealed to the state of affairs in infants after birth. While not unjustifiable, this does leave a question as to whether what we have been considering as a part or aspect of original sin is really a defect brought about in the very act of conception or whether it is simply a generic name for various modes of developmental difficulty, serious perhaps but without the enormous theological significance of original sin.

More serious is the difficulty that, in each step of the above argument, some psychic process that seems both natural and good has been shown to have a structure that appears to be opposed to the psychic structure of some basic aspect of charity. Would not this imply that what we call "original sin" is man's natural state, a state lacking that supernatural grace of charity which by divine fiat was made a sort of wondrous but quite nonessential gift to Adam and, now, to the baptized? But, if so, man by his nature, must needs stand in fundamental opposition to God, as many a philosopher since Feuerbach has held.

1. *The experience of the grace of Christ*

What is truly natural is created as such by God and is attributable to Him. But no condition of sin, not even original sin, can be attributed to God as its cause. Now, one can raise a question about just how natural these psychic patterns in the child truly are; and I shall shortly do so. Before then, however, it is well to note the structure of the argument so far: observable or reasonably conjectured psychic patterns drawn from evidences that are

logical requisite is that what is known have 'entered' *as it is*, in its otherness, the consciousness of the knower. Whatever one's explanations for the mystery of cognition, to know some real state-of-affairs at all the knower must not merely receive it and hold it but permit it to be itself, without distorting or re-forming it by forcing it into some already extant representation of the world. The ancients thought of sensory knowledge as the receiving of a formal imprint of the object in the organ as if of a seal in wax. But in fact the senses receive actively. They process all input as it is being received; they construct, repress, discriminate, so that, e.g., we learn quickly to see objects and not mere colorations. All of this takes place spontaneously and for the most part, it seems, unconsciously. Though the senses retain an enormous independence of most other cerebral activity, in that they continue to show the world without major deformation, yet this independence is far from absolute, as sensory illusions show. For reasons to be seen (*pp* 327–328), I think that such "cross-talk" in the brain works chiefly through alteration of the power of attention rather than as a direct interference with the sensory brain structures in themselves. But this whole area needs a fair amount of further work.

equally accessible to believer and unbeliever form one term of a comparison. The other term consists of the traits of charity as derived theologically from the data of faith.

If the psychic patterns are time-conditioned but integral aspects of human nature, then they cannot, whatever the seeming, contradict the traits of charity, though these latter far transcend the former. But if those patterns are not integrally natural but in some way represent damage or corruption of the natural psyche, then it is not what we consider our natural power of reason that can show this—for, by supposition, this natural power labors under the handicap of these same grave distortions arising from the psyche—but only the light obtained from faith. Thus, we turn now to consider, through the use of scriptural typology, what man's state might have been before the fall—and what ours would have been had Adam not sinned—and then what evils were brought by Adam's sin upon himself and his progeny.[22]

Here we will follow St. Paul, whose doctrine on original sin is our primary scriptural source. Now, Paul sees Jesus as the Second Adam, rectifying superabundantly what the first Adam did wrongly (Rom.5:14–21) and bringing to spiritual completion what was only earthly preparation in the first Adam (I Cor.15:45–49). Thus, the first man Adam is "a type of the One who was to come" (Rom.5:14), who is, then, the antitype and fulfilment of Adam.

As the Last Adam, in whose likeness and for whom the first Adam was made,[23] Jesus sums up in His own life and perfectly fulfils, from the moment of His conception on, Adam's life before the fall. Thus, St. Irenaeus explains the virgin birth of Christ as a summing up and fulfilment of Adam's being taken from the still virginal earth.[24] Inverting this perspective, we may say that Adam was drawn from a virginal soil precisely in order to prefigure the virginal birth of Jesus.[25]

Further, Irenaeus regarded Adam as an "infant."[26] Since an infant's mind and attitudes could be found in Jesus only in His physical infancy, He relived

---

[22] In the absence of any clearly focussed teaching by the Church on the precise topics we shall deal with, what I propose must be considered to be no more than a speculative working hypothesis.

[23] Cf. texts from Chrysologus and Cabasilas above (*pp* 82–83), Note also the anonymous homily, found among the doubtful or spurious works of St. Epiphanius of Cyprus in PG 43, 439, 451, 462–3 (Office of Readings for Holy Saturday).

[24] Cf. text from Irenaeus, *p* 192 below.

[25] Given God's "foreknowledge" of all created things, this need not imply, though it is quite compatible with, the position that the Word would have become flesh even had man not fallen.

[26] *Demonstratio Apostolicae Praedicationis*, ##12 & 14 (cf. *Démonstration de la Prédication Apostolique*, tr. L. M. Froidevaux, Paris: Cerf [1959], SC 62), *Adv. Haer.*, IV, 38.1 & III, 22.4 and 23.5. There has been much debate as to whether Irenaeus meant that he was an infant only in mind and attitude or also physically. For an introduction to the whole question of the infancy of Adam, cf. John Lawson, *The Biblical Theology of Saint Irenaeus*, London: Epworth (1948), *pp* 203, 208, 211–213. The immediate arousal of sexual passion in both Adam and Eve that Irenaeus ascribes to them as a result of the fall seems to preclude the latter interpretation, whatever ambiguities there may be in his texts.

and fulfilled Adam's "infancy" during His own. I would suggest, then, that to Jesus, as an infant in the womb, even as to Adam at his creation, the Father made His presence felt by grace. As God would walk familiarly with Adam and Eve when the evening breeze sprang up after the heat of the day (Gen.3:8),[27] so was prefigured the way in which the Father was present to Jesus from the moment of His conception in Mary's womb.[28] From the instant of Jesus' first existence as a zygote onwards, the Father made Himself known to Him as His Father.[29]

The immediate objection, "How could a zygote experience anything?" ignores both the power of God and the essential difference between man and the whole infra-human world. For, from conception on, the soul is present as "form" of the body, making it a single, living organism, developing gradually in accord with its own genetic code. The mind, therefore, is present, inactive in us perhaps—though no one knows or, I think, can know that this is so—till the brain begins to form as the primary organ of interaction with the environment. Thereafter at least, the mind is actively learning, as the sense-organs develop, perhaps more active than ever again in the person's entire life.

Since God can act directly on the soul, needing no intermediaries, there is nothing implausible in holding that Jesus, or indeed any unfallen infant, would have had experience of God from conception onwards, somehow made aware of the greatness and the gratuity of the Father's love for Him.

The "felt love," mentioned above as essential even for the physical life of the child, would have been given to Jesus and to any unfallen child not principally by sinless parents but, as "felt grace," by God Himself. This would be that "Glory of God" of which all men have been deprived by the fall (Rom.3:23), which is the Holy Spirit acting without restriction to effect the supernatural likeness for which we were created.[30] This grace would be

---

[27] Gerhard von Rad, *Genesis*, 2nd ed., tr. J. H. Marks, London, SCM (1963), *p* 88; E. A. Speiser, *Genesis*, Anchor Bible, vol. 1, *p* 24. Garden City (NY): Doubleday (1964).

[28] In such a context one can understand more easily the praises of Mary as the new Garden of Eden, serving as Paradise to the New Adam within her. So, e.g., St. John Damascene, *In Dormitionem*, 4, 1, #8 (PG 96, 712b). By the time of Abbot Hermann of St. Martin, that briefly stated theme has developed and matured: *Tractatus de Incarnatione Christi, ch.* 8 (PL 180, 28–31).

[29] This was not, I think, conceptual knowledge. Jesus was, so far as human powers went, dependent in the womb on nature alone, even as we. One might suppose, as some of the Fathers seem to have done, that God's grace was active in Jesus to produce conceptual knowledge from conception on. Original sin's damage to our nature would have changed such a graced conceptualization, intended for all the offspring of Adam, into a nongraced inability to form concepts till the time we now regard as normal. My objections to such a theory will be given below, *pp* 246–249.

[30] This characterization of original sin is interesting, even aside from the identification of the Glory with the Spirit, which seems to fit well here. For it emphasizes, as an aspect of original justice, the manifestation of God's grace. His grace is, in its original form, something that is glorious, that shows its excellence outwardly, that manifests itself on all sides, but not as man's glory but as God's (cf. also I Cor. 11:7). In our own experience, grace is something mostly internal. When we meet someone, like Mother Teresa, who radiates the grace of God, this external manifestation—quite apart from anything miraculous—seems to us extraordinary. Though through long ac-

felt—not conceptually grasped—precisely as grace, i.e., as the Father's freely given love, making the infant sense that it has been made worthy of Him only by the gift of oneness with His Son through the Spirit's action, a love felt as wholly unmerited because radically unmeritable. An unfallen infant would indeed begin its life in a manner very different from ours.

Clearly, then, if this approach is correct, original sin is not, from any aspect, natural to man. Nor is it merely a name for natural weakness or disability. Life would be radically different for a child conceived, like our Lady, without taint of original sin. Hence, man's original state in Eden was not the same as any condition in which fallen man, before or after Christ, finds himself in this life. Had Adam and Eve not fallen, we may suppose that their children would not only have been filled with God's grace from conception on but that this grace would have been felt by each as the freely offered presence of the Father.

Some imprint of the trinitarian traits of charity would be built into the patterns of synaptic development and other features of the neural structures of the infant's brain as these formed during the nine months spent in the loving awareness of God's free choice. The psychic imprint resulting from felt grace would, then, itself be natural, though not so the imprinting, which would result from the grace of God, not owed to man nor meritable by him. This imprint would dispose the affectivity towards God so that it would be emotionally easier for the person, whose will would already be inclined towards God in a voluntary, though not yet free, manner, to come in time to choose freely in accord with His will.

Even when sin should sooner or later appear in the world, these children or their sinlessly conceived descendants would experience parental dislike or neglect as somehow secondary—distressing and terrifying, yet not traumatizing them; more serious, perhaps, than other stimuli to self-assertion or self-pity but not lethal wounds.

This experience of felt grace might have had some resemblance to any of a range of mystical states experienced by the great saints. Many saints have been granted on occasion a more or less continuous, nonconceptual awareness of God's presence, love, and protection, quiet, at the fine point of the soul, without ecstasy or other sign of physical weakness. At times, too, the Trinity makes Itself known to them, reflected somehow in the mirror of the graced soul. Or in their union with Jesus through created charity, they are enabled to know intuitively the divine Exemplar in His Son through His Spirit. These states far exceed the felt grace here postulated because they consist of a stronger and more intense union than the infant's, containing as they do the human person's freely given return of love. Yet they offer some indication of the

---

quaintance, we may think we can sense the graced goodness of some people or their ungraced wickedness, we hesitate to admit as much even to ourselves, fearing to fall into rash judgment. In Eden, Paul seems to suggest, God's own goodness streamed into this world through the grace He had given to man, manifest in ways in which it no longer, at least obviously or clearly, shows itself.

kind of experience I am hypothesizing.

The infant might have experienced, then, as something infinitely precious, throughout his whole being, the Father as present and freely—infinitely freely—choosing to love him. Yet this love would have been experienced as placing no conditions upon the infant save his own willingness to receive and to retain it. This willingness would have been something that the infant could not activate either positively or negatively, since as yet unable to place any free act. Yet God's goodness could, in analogy to the graces of conversion, large and small, that He gives to all of us, create such a willingness, not as a free act but as an inclination of the will, already turned, as suitable for a son, towards the Father in its first coming into being. Already, in the womb, the infant would have resembled Adam, who walked with God as the breeze of the evening stirred in paradise (Gen.3:8).

The gift of integrity could flow easily from this awareness of the all-sheltering, all-activating love of God for man. Even in our own gradual repossession of this gift, as we grow spiritually in Christ, this gift of spontaneous awareness of the true meaning and value of things and their true relations to the Father's will is better described as a simple awareness of Him and of all else as in Him.[31] Anything that enters consciousness that lacks its due measure, that is not rightly directed towards God, becomes a noisy, clanging dissonance that draws instant attention to its lack of harmony with His will. So we are alerted to our need to take immediate action to restore the harmony, even if at the price of temporary inner conflict.

We have all seen this sort of openness to God in people who have been living their lives holily in the Lord for long years. For the most part, they seem to find their former ways of sinning impossible. This is not to say that they could not sin if they chose, but that the meaning of the sinful project is usually so clear that they see no point to it and find nothing humanly attractive about it.

The other preternatural gifts long ascribed to Adam, in particular immortality and the absence of illness and suffering, though not deducible from this theory, yet fit within it comfortably. St. Augustine suggested[32] that the gift of immortality was not any property belonging to Adam but the effect of God's promise, once Adam had reached the terminus of the earthly life which God desired for him. A transition from this life to the next would take place, not by dissolution of the body and resurrection but by the glorification of the body without death.

On the other hand, we know how much genuine laughter and good cheer make for good health[33] and how sadness works the contrary.[34] If this be

---

[31] Cf. Quay, *Christian Meaning*, *pp* 100–105, 109.

[32] *de Genesi ad Litteram*, VI, *cc* 23–28, *##*34–39 (PL 34, 353–356).

[33] E.g., Sir.30:21–25. Cf. William F. Fry, "The Physiologic Effects of Humor, Mirth, and Laughter," *JAMA 267*, 1857–1858 (No. 13, ap.1.92) for a quick introduction to the medical literature.

[34] E.g., Sir.38:18–21; I Macc.6:8–13; II Cor.2:7 and 7:9–10. The enormous medical literature on

so with us, how much more in Eden? There even seems to be medical advantage from suitable sensory stimulation of the comatose and those in persistent vegetative state.[35] Many other aspects of psychosomatic medicine suggest, at least, that St. Thomas' notion of the gift of immortality as a supernatural force or power, divinely infused into the human soul by which it keeps the body from corruption[36] is not out of harmony with our science. Surely, a nature in which charity reigned supreme and in which all human powers were rightly ordered would be far from suffering most kinds of psychosomatic disintegration that ready us for death. On the other hand, once the proper subordination to God is gone, no fully integrated inner harmony can stand. Augustine's theory, then, that of Thomas, and a fair number of others seem not implausible in the light of present knowledge. Whatever suppositions we might reasonably make as to what God chose to do in these matters offer no manifest problems of principle.

So, as to sickness. The illnesses attendant on mere aging would vanish along with death. Those that are consequences of immoderate activity, whether by abuse of food, of drink and drugs, of sexual activity would manifestly have no occasion. The fact that, though fallen, we have such specifics as quinine for malaria, various antibiotics for different classes of infectious organisms, even the juice of aloe as a specific for burns, suggests what unfallen man could have had simply from a knowledge of nature. Doubtless, more important would have been the immunities the body could have developed on exposure to disease-causing agents without even contracting the disease. Even now, these immunities are in large part transmissible from mother to child through the mother's milk. Nothing of all this, obviously, is probative; but there is sufficient connection with our present experience to show that the preternatural gifts are in no way fantastic or improbable.

2. *The power of death*

On the basis of some such understanding of the state of original justice, it becomes possible to indicate how it is that the psychic patterns in the infant are not those proper to human nature in its integrity but represent a profound exaggeration and distortion of the natural ones.

Let us recall those data we have not yet utilized in our efforts at understanding. Adam by his sin not only brought upon himself corporeal death and, worse, the death of the soul that was the loss of all grace but incurred God's wrath and outrage, and was brought into captivity under the power of that being who rules the empire of death, that is, the devil, who through

---

psychic depresssion bears eloquent testimony to the accuracy of the scriptural insight.

[35] This matter is much debated at present. For opposed views cf. "The Effect of Intense Multisensory Stimulation on Coma Arousal and Recovery," G. Doman, R. Wilkinson, M. D. Dimancescu, & R. Pelligra, *Neuropsychological Rehabilitation 3*, 203–212 (#2. 1993) and "Evaluating sensory regulation as a method to improve awareness in patients with altered states of consciousness: a pilot study," R. L. Wood, T. B. Winkowski, J. L. Miller, L. Tierney, & L. Goldman, *Brain Injury 6*, 411–418 (# 5, 1992).

[36] *S.T.* I, 97, 1c and 3 ad 1)

Adam's fear of death held him in lifelong bondage (Heb.2:14–15). The same fate has come upon all his offspring.[37]

Because the psychic impress for felt grace finds no suitable object, the fallen infant feels himself deserted from the beginning and, though social by nature, alone in the world. Much has been written by the major philosophers of our century concerning man's keen sense of being cast out alone into an existence doomed to death. One source of their experience is evident. For, if one is so constructed as to feel God's grace yet cannot feel it, then the sense of isolation from what is most essential to one's own being must seem wellnigh absolute. One is cleft asunder at one's roots. One's ultimate expectation and one's primordial experience are contradictory.

On the one hand, God, the source of being and love and life, is experienced as "gone elsewhere," remote, unconcerned, vanished. Worse, however, Trent's teaching suggests that the infant in the womb senses that He is angry and that one would be worse off if He were present. The divine absence is felt as the only mercy that can spare one the divine displeasure. Even as Adam and Eve hid themselves from Him whose presence had hitherto been the peak of their joy, so the newly-conceived senses that, were He to come, he should have to hide, having nothing that He could love and let live. Were he worthy of His love, it would already be felt. Death is no longer a simple ending of earthly life but a fitting punishment inflicted on one not worthy to live.

Yet, the infant does not feel himself wholly alone. He feels, instead, close at hand, another presence—of someone armed with the power of death. This power to cut off at its root any love sufficient to sustain one's life is no longer to be thought of simply as the impersonal objectivity of the man experimenting on the apes in his lab. The infant senses hostility in one who hates him. Through the cold pride that demands that love be merited, the devil has power to provoke that fear of lovelessness and death that skews all the natural psychic structures from their natural functions. It is in response to this felt malevolence, lurking in the darkness left by the extinguishing of felt grace, that each infant fears inordinately and excessively his unworthiness to be loved. Accepting all unknowingly the great lie, he turns, psychically, in exactly the wrong manner, to seek love from others as though he were God. His fear is deeper and more intense than any natural fearfulness could cause.

This basic fear can, indeed, be allayed by sufficiently strong "felt love" given by the infant's parents and siblings, but cannot be extinguished thereby. This fear is the atmosphere in which the brain and its synapses are formed, before any human love can be perceived. And though such fear can be excited, say, by maternal desertion, yet it is not of necessity fatal. The infant already knows himself "deserted" far more terribly—yet he lives! Nor does the importance of parental "felt love," even though badly damaged by the scars of original and actual sin, prove the parents' love to be innocent. Better far than its absence, human love is essentially inadequate as a substitute for felt grace.

---

[37] Decree on Original Sin, Council of Trent, (DS 1511 for Adam himself, 1512 for us as his descendants).

Some may recall that Rahner held a rather benign view of concupiscence, that state of affairs left behind in us by original sin once grace has been restored to us by Christ. Rahner regarded concupiscence as merely the "spontaneous character of a conative potency" as such, insofar as its "acts anticipate and resist reflexion and free decision."[38] So he argues that concupiscence, even in its strictest theological sense, is neither good nor bad from a moral point of view, but is natural to man. Its absence or removal, therefore, is not natural to him and, hence, cannot be claimed by him as in some way due to him.[39]

Though this understanding would fit excellently the hypothetical case of a merely natural man (though Rahner had no intention so to apply it), it seems not nearly so useful if referring to supernaturally fallen man. For, while the various psychic structures that we first saw as opposing charity seemed natural enough, yet, if man was created originally so as to feel grace, the absence of this felt grace would be no mere leaving man to his natural weakness but would represent a profound derangement of all his powers through the fear of annihilation and of the death that comes from being ultimately totally unworthy to draw anyone's love or any attention save the devils'.

Rahner's explanation[40] fails, it seems, to do justice not merely to the severe Augustinian view of original sin but to the milder understanding more common in the East, which speaks of the results of original sin less in terms of intrinsic harm to human nature and more (but not exclusively) in extrinsic terms of a covering over or dirtying or defiling of the beauty of our nature by filth, all of which baptism washes away.[41] Though some such view is now popular in the West, one may note that—quite apart from the fact that the Church has, despite so many difficulties, recognized the Augustinian view as closer to her own—it is no freer of empirical and theoretical difficulties. What is washed away is not concupiscence—as visibly present in the East as in the West—but original sin, one's personal filthiness. And our moral nature itself needs at least a restoration of its original proportion and harmony, still disarranged by concupiscence.[42]

The Catholic tradition, then, is clear that the concupiscence left in us by our baptism does involve a real and profound moral disorder within us (DS 1515). Evidently, it is not a moral disorder in the sense of freely chosen misdeed but as a derangement of the psyche, including the merely spontaneous activity of the will, that inclines us to moral evil. I have suggested that this

[38] K. Rahner, "Concept of Concupiscentia," *p* 351.

[39] ibid. 371

[40] ibid. 374–382. His later position, expressed in *Foundations of Christian Faith: An Introduction to the Idea of Christianity*, tr. W. Dyck, New York: Seabury (1978), *pp* 106–115 (originally published as *Grundkurs des Glaubens: Einführung in den Begriff des Christentums,* Freiburg im Breisgau: Herder [1976]) departs much further from traditional teaching; cf. note 52 below.

[41] Both traditions are clear, of course, about the loss of charity or sanctifying grace. For a typical example, cf. Diadochus of Photike, *Œuvres spirituelles,* SC 5 ter, ed. E. des Places, Paris: Éditions du Cerf (1966), "Cent chapitres gnostiques," cap. 89, *p* 149.

[42] "Thus also the grace of God through baptism first arranges the in-the-image into the what-it-was when man came to be." Diadochus, ibid.

evil has its roots in the nullification of the psychic bases for charity. What is needed here is to connect our results with the common Christian language about concupiscence.

This is usually described as a disorder of the emotions and passions that lets them move rapidly towards illicit actions before we become fully conscious and aware of our situation. Thus, though we remain free to resist what is evil and to do what is right, we find it difficult to do so because of an emotional state that has already half-committed us to what is wrong.

Now, it is at once evident that such a notion cannot be taken *formaliter*, i.e., no psychic power of any sort can consistently opt for moral evil (or moral good), the discernment of which depends entirely on the judgment of the intellectually reflective, free agent. As Rahner points out,[43] our psychic condition can also, in suitable circumstances, carry us just as impulsively toward what is morally good. But, in fact, we are skewed towards moral evil by the remanent psychic disorder that is structurally out of harmony with the type of free activity that charity is.

Concupiscence cannot impel us, for example, to formally unchaste actions in any general way; the moral judgment is required to see what is suitable to the man of faith in the particular circumstances in which some sexual excitement is being stirred. Yet one may say with assurance that concupiscence can and does rouse men, more often than not, to sexual desires that are unsuitable for action. Conversely, most men are less frequently roused to chastity by a spontaneous movement of their nature than to lustfulness. In other words, disorder in the emotional structure of a person easily, and even of necessity, makes sound moral decisions more difficult than were the person emotionally in inner harmony with himself.

Those universal character traits that are most commonly ascribed to original sin, such as sexual lust, the yearning for ease and luxury, and the passionate drive for influence and power (cf. I Jn.2:15–17) show themselves only long after birth. Yet the inclinations and predispositions leading to them are already visible in the abnormal self-centering of original sin. One's thirst for some absolute self-worth is already activated and will manifest itself through the inordinacy of the passions as the infant grows.

Certainly, inner harmony is no proof against sin, as both Adam and Eve showed clearly. And, so long as one is sane, emotional disorders do not prevent virtue, often the more heroic for requiring so great a combat. But all this does not in any way indicate that the moral life is undamaged by emotional disorders. The moral life is more than merely the aggregate of a free agent's free choices, central as these are. The timid man, however courageous he may be in every free choice, lives a very different moral life than were he free of his fearfulness. The irascible man, however meek in his free choices, must spend much of his moral life in the effort to be ready to make these choices well, an enterprise those of other temperaments may dispense with.

---

[43] op. cit. 370–373.

Given, then, that concupiscence is a psychic disorder that is in part voluntary though not free, one can do justice to the classical understandings of it without further effort. So, too, one sees the remedy for it. By our life in Christ, we are meant in large measure to recover our integrity by sharing in His. This we do largely by a growing attentiveness to the meaning, in Christ, of whatever stirs us at any level of our being.[44] The whole of Part II, however, will be devoted to showing in detail how our growth in Christ, this recovery of integrity included, is intended by God to take place.

Even after an infant is born, baptism and the infusion of the supernatural life of grace seem to give no more than wholly unactualized and, for several years, unactualizable powers. Even in the case of our Lady, though God's extraordinary intervention gave her a fulness of (felt) grace in her very conception, nothing seems to require that this grace have been exercised by any free act of charity before the normal time for self-possession.[45]

Given the seemingly quite invisible effects of baptism on the fallen child, one might reasonably ask whether the earlier presence of grace would really have made any difference to psychic development in the womb. To my knowledge, at least, infants born more than two months before term and baptized at once do not show less damage from original sin than others. Even if the zygote be baptized—as can now be done in cases of *in vitro* fertilization[46]—I doubt that there would be any detectable difference. Original sin would leave its marks as clearly in this child as in any other. It would seem, then, that the time in a person's life when baptism is received is, at most, of secondary importance with respect to the hold of concupiscence on him.

Though grace has been restored to us by the redemption, through baptism it is restored to us "late," i.e., the child must first be conceived before it can be baptized. Baptism is a *remedy*, applied to one already in need of it. Late or not, grace comes without that special characteristic or quality which, on our theory, it had in the beginning, of being felt as grace. By God's free choice, we live under a different dispensation than our first parents. There is nothing we can do to alter this fact by the way we administer the sacraments of this dispensation. Original justice and felt grace are gone forever. But grace, once present, does desire to show its nature and inclines the will towards good, so that the first free choices of the Christian child are more likely to be good than bad.

---

[44] Cf. *p* 133 above; also Diadochus, *Œuvres*, cap. 88, *p* 148, and Quay, *Christian Meaning*, 102–107.

[45] For an excellent discussion of the Immaculate Conception as an essential component of a sound Christology of redemption and of the consequent unimportance of the purely temporal "prematurity" of this gift to Mary, cf. Karl Rahner, *Theological Investigations 1*, "The Immaculate Conception," 201–213.

[46] With what effect this might be done is not clear, since, thus far at least, whether and how the unborn are included in the present sacramental dispensation seems far from clear. St. Thomas' argument (cf. *ST* III, 68, 11 ad 1 & 3) still retains its point.

3. The transmission of original sin

Part of the Church's teaching on original sin is that Adam, by the very fact of his sin, not only lost sanctifying grace for himself but also the power to transmit it by generation to his children as their inheritance. There is no need here to trace the history of the explanations offered by theologians over the centuries for this universal transmission of original sin.[47] Suffice it to say that none of the various modes of conceiving our sinful solidarity with Adam have proved very satisfying. Though some such theories strike us as ascribing injustice to God, even those that do not still seem inadequate to the question. We just do not see what such a theory, even were it perfectly correct, contributes to explaning why original sin in us should be considered *our own* sin, as Trent requires.

The theory here proposed, however, gives some indication of what might be the case. Original sin would clearly be transmitted by generation. The conception of the child, and that alone, transmits this condition. The child is begotten without felt grace and little enough of felt love. He suffers in consequence a psychic damage that restructures his capabilities for loving in such a manner that his first fully free choice is likely to be gravely sinful, barring a special intervention of God.

St. Thomas' objection that a psychic transmission lacks a suitable connection with voluntareity has weight only against the primitive forms of these theories that he knew.[48] Clearly, the theory proposed here is based upon the true but nonfree voluntareity that arises from and interacts with the unconscious and subconscious structures of the psyche.[49]

At this point we face a crucial question: If man was created for the life of grace and meant to enter this world with a grace felt as such, are these not due to him, required by his nature as man? Conversely, if the life of charity and, more particularly, "felt grace" are in no way due to man and are not called for by his nature, how can their loss involve a necessary damage to his nature? How could being conceived without felt grace both leave a felt void in man's nature, as I have argued, and give him over to the power of death unless such grace is due to his nature—at least when, as before the fall, this was properly adapted to and supportive of this gift? In any case, whatever be said of the punishment inflicted on Adam, since God creates every person individually why does He not do for each of us what He did for Mary and create each of us without sin in a state of felt grace? Is it not unjust to deprive us of what

---

[47] For a sketch of these explanations up to the 1930's, cf. *DTC 12*, 'Péché originel,' *col.* 275–624. For more recent theories, cf. James L. Connor, "Original Sin: Contemporary Approaches," *Theological Studies 29*, 215–240 (1968) and Brian O. McDermott, S.J. "The Theology of Original Sin: Recent Developments," *Theological Studies 38*, 478–512, (1977).

[48] Cf. *ST* I-II, 81, 1 c.

[49] Not only the Council of Trent but the early anti-Pelagian decrees all indicate that man was changed for the worse not only in soul but in body, a change not restricted to his being destined to die. This corporeal deterioration is, in the theory here proposed, the immediate and ineluctable consequence of the privation of felt grace and the basis for the psychic harm.

our nature calls for when we have done no wrong and when He could do otherwise?

There are two aspects of original sin that ought to be carefully distinguished, though not separated. Firstly, there is what might be called the descriptive aspect, telling (theologically) what happened in Adam's fall, what still happens in our conception, and how these things might be explained at this level or causally interrelated. Secondly, there is what may be called the providential aspect, which seeks to understand original sin in terms of God's will and goals for man and His providence over him and over all the created order.

The descriptive aspect focusses on man. One considers the sin of Adam, shows its nature as intrinsically destructive of his divine life, and indicates how it necessarily damaged all other aspects of his being in accordance with their degree of participation in his sin, both directly and as punishment for his sin. Further, one considers the effects of his sin upon his posterity— transmitted by generation, inclining to sin yet without turning the will against God, depriving each newly conceived of sanctifying grace and, in my explanation, of felt grace.

All these are legitimate considerations; but, by restricting one's thought unduly to this descriptive aspect, one stumbles into the above-mentioned conundrums. These will not be well-resolved, I think, through still more refined arguments about what is or is not due to our nature, as if we were in a position to relate "due to our nature" to "justice" on God's part. Greater insight seems more likely through consideration of God's purposes and plans in dealing with sinful man. The questions that then arise are concerned with showing the revealed basis for the Church's making her own St. Augustine's cry, "O felix culpa!—O happy fault, that merited to have such and so great a Redeemer!" The task is to set forth what revelation indicates concerning the goodness of this dispensation in which man finds himself deprived of grace but yet unable of himself even to desire salvation.[50]

From God's vantage point, according to II Vatican, revelation and all His actions among men are directed to the salvation of man. Concretely, this means salvation from sin, not only past sin but future sin, and also from sins like those committed in Eden. Yet sin is the risk run by every kind of spiritual creature, men and angels and the great beings named principalities, thrones, cherubim, and seraphim. For, the essence of any free choice, sinful or virtuous, is given by a relating of the self to God, directly or through His creatures. God's "problem," then, is: What is (are) the good way(s) to bring a material-spiritual creature such as man, whether as Adam was before the fall or such as we are after it or in some other state, to its divinely ordained goal and to its fulfilment in accord with the Image and Likeness in which it was originally created? How best bring a creature that must somehow share in its own creation, since truly like God, to do so in the only way possible: through a genuinely free acceptance of God's will and grace?

---

[50] Cf. the canons of the Second Council of Orange, especially DS 373–377

Suppose that someone asks, "Could God create a human nature lacking a vital organ, thus doomed to death in a short time of its birth?" the answer is easy: "He can because He does so." Consider, for example, some types of Siamese twins or the results of other kinds of fetal abnormality. Obviously, however, He could not create a *race* of such men, since there could be no acts of procreation. "Well, then, could He create a human person without a utilizable mind and will?" And again the answer is "Yes, because He does it." "But can He do such things and still be just and loving? Aren't vital organs and active minds due to man, owed to his very nature?" Here the question needs to be distinguished: Can He do such things without providing for the ultimate good of each such person (so long as this good is not freely rejected)? Here the answer must be a flat "No!" But can He do such things if He does them in such a manner that each such person can achieve an everlasting good in full conformity with his nature? And here we must say "Yes, for this is what in fact He does."

Both Adam's sin and our participation in it through original sin, however explained at the descriptive level, are shown by revelation as permitted by God for the ultimate good of all of us in Jesus Christ His Son. For the great threat to our salvation is one thing only: our own pride, the terrible choice that *our* will be done rather than God's. Though there may be other ways of bringing about man's salvation than the one God has chosen, it should be obvious that the one He did choose contains endless opportunities for man to humble himself, to abase his mind in reverence before God's revealed mysteries, to accept every sort of pain, physical, emotional, and spiritual, in order humbly and out of love to put God's will ahead of his own. Further, by making His goodness manifest in human terms through His Son, He draws us powerfully towards that charity that will be our salvation. Only God can tell whether there could be any better ways to bring low our pride before we damn ourselves.

As will be seen throughout Part II, there are good reasons to think that God's providence in this present fallen-and-redeemed order acts with a mercy so great that it seems at times to obscure His justice. But unjust He is not.

On the basis of the theory I have offered, we can better understand our Lord's love for children and, especially, His teaching that His followers must become as they. For, those who have been baptized (or otherwise given the life of grace) and who have committed as yet no actual sins are truly innocent, with an innocence deeper and stronger than any we are drawn naturally to perceive in a baby. Nothing deserving condemnation remains in the baptized; and the psychic wounds that original sin inflicted have had little time to develop in an infant. The baptismal innocence of the little child is, indeed, a marvellous representation of what the Christian must become.[51] Hence, too, the Church's particular admiration for those saints who, though they sinned, never sinned gravely and never lost the grace of their baptism.

Before concluding, I should point out that the theory here proposed is

[51] How this is to be understood we will see below, *Ch* 10, Excursus, *pp* 220–225.

able to do full justice to the Immaculate Conception of our Lady—something that does not seem possible to any of the many current theories that involve "the sin of the world," whether understood as the effect of actual sins throughout human history or, in accord with Karl Rahner's development of the idea, a situation of sin common to all men in their solidarity of nature with Adam, if not of descent from him.[52] The central flaw in all these theories is that they would require that Mary not be subject to the very things that, according to the Scripture, she shared with us all: a life among the proud and sinful descendants of our first parents, who, by individual sins and by the social structures arising from these, force every human act to be a participation in some humanly hurtful situation.[53]

But if Mary was conceived in the felt grace of God, her privilege is at once apparent, whatever the condition of those around her. At the same time, we would see the rightness of the Church's instinct that she had to have had very holy parents, even though they were not sinlessly conceived.

I can remember when, in high school, I first started going to weekday Mass more or less regularly. I was somewhat disconcerted to find in my missal a feast in August in honor of St. Joachim. Now, all that was known about him was that he was the father of the Blessed Virgin Mary. Since Mary obviously had to have a father who was Jewish, they called him Joachim. But they had no knowledge of his real name. Yet, *because* he was Mary's father, he had to have been a very holy man. Now, I could accept Mary as being eminently holy because Jesus was; but extending this to her unknown father seemed to be pushing things too far. It was not at all obvious to me that his mere act of begetting Mary was sufficient reason to think him a man so holy as to be worthy of canonization and veneration from all Christians. There

[52] Towards the end of his life, Rahner's theory (cf. *Foundations*, 106–115, note 40 above) located original sin *solely* (114) in the situation of our freedom as co-determined by the guilt of a rejection of God's own offering of Himself to man at the very beginning of our race. But "How this [contemporary] individual responds to this situation...is matter for his freedom to decide, however threatening and pernicious this situation is..." (113). "[T]here are in fact objectifications of personal guilt in the world which, as the material for the free decisions of other persons, threaten these decisions, have a seductive effect upon them, and make free decisions painful" (109). One who buys a banana "is co-determined by social injustice" if the workers were economically oppressed. The buyer "now participates in this situation of guilt to his own advantage" (110–111). In consequence, though the temptation to sin arises from man's social nature and is, thus, interior to him, nonetheless this inner situation of co-determination by guilt remains external to man's freedom; the individual is not damaged in his own natural powers, though through the social aspects of his nature he can be seduced into sin. But this seduction, however inescapable, remains contingent upon the evil actions of others, not on any damage to the concrete nature of the individual so situated. Hence, not illogically, Rahner speaks of "[w]hat existence would be like without guilt, a situation which no one has experienced in the concrete..." (115). To my knowledge, he offers no explanation as to how his theory could make room for Mary's total freedom from guilt.

[53] The other major class of theories today, which identify original sin with actual sin, however deeply buried within us, manifestly need have no problem in principle with Mary's Immaculate Conception. Their problem is rather to show that they are compatible with the Church's tradition concerning infant baptism and her many seemingly explicit rejections of such doctrines.

were similar albeit lesser problems with regard to St. Anne.

I am now more at ease with the canonization of this sort of "anonymous Christian," precisely because Mary was immaculately conceived, born without trace of original sin. In terms of this theory, she lived her nine months within St. Anne's womb with the glory of God's grace suffusing her. But for so great a gift to reach its fruition and fulness, for it to terminate in an adult who could be the suitable mother of the Christ in His humanity, for her to be sinless wholly, so that not only His filial piety would not be forced to punish her but that there would be nothing to be visited by the Lord upon her Child in the first generation, this would require of her parents very extraordinary holiness. They had to be able so to love her as to confirm and assist her infant understanding of love, to preserve its direction and proper orientation, not to thwart it seriously or work against what God had wrought there.

Part II

RECAPITULATION IN CHRIST

Chapter 7

The Hermeneutic Problem

Though we hardly adverted to the fact, the ideas offered above concerning original sin as the privation at conception of felt grace were based almost entirely on the relation of type and Antitype[1] that St. Paul saw between Adam and Jesus. Since central in Paul's thought, Christians generally have accepted this sort of relationship as a possibility, even when, in practice, they denied that it could be extended to other figures in the Old Testament.

But relationships of type and Antitype are evident throughout the New Testament, even if not stated so explicitly. Indeed, I shall follow de Lubac and others in maintaining that typology is fundamental to the Catholic faith. Only by its means can the Christian understand the Old Testament in the principal way in which God intended it to be understood. For, the typical sense is part of what is called the "spiritual sense" of the Bible; and it is this spiritual sense that converts the Old Testament into a Christian book.

In this chapter, we will consider firstly Marcion's heresy: the denial that the Old Testament could in any way be a Christian book. Then we will discuss the the nature both of the literal sense and of the spiritual sense of the Old Testament, and how the latter depends on the former.[2] After consideration of typology, we will glance at other "spiritual senses," too often confused with it. We can then clarify some of the serious misunderstandings that have contributed to its loss for some centuries now in the West, and consider the criteria for ascertaining it.

---

[1] I capitalize since the only true antitype is Christ or that which in some precise way is identified with Him.

[2] The New Testament also contains a spiritual sense in addition to its literal meaning. The works I will cite of St. Thomas, de Lubac, and others offer much material on this spiritual sense also.

We will then be in position to give, in Chapter 8, a response to Marcion. There we will see how the spiritual sense may be found and used to map out in detail the earlier portions of the Christian life, those we spoke of in the Introduction as 'recapitulation' of the Old Testament.[3] It is this process of recapitulation in Christ that God has established as the remedy that is meant to heal the scars and relics of original sin. Through this recapitulation, which constitutes the earlier part of of the spiritual life, grace gradually undoes concupiscence in us, restores some semblance of integrity, and brings low our pride. Only when we have been thus prepared will we be sufficiently sensitive spiritually and free enough interiorly that the Holy Spirit may not only dwell within us but move us as He wishes for the glory of the Father through Jesus.

A. The problem: Marcion's error

Before the end of the 1st Century, serious questions had arisen for the Church concerning the Old Testament. If the New Testament contains the fulfilment of the Old, if we have in Christ Jesus and His Church all that we need for salvation, why must we keep the Old Testament? Excessively long, often barbarous in language and concept, frequently repetitive and dull, was it not clearly obsolete, even for Jews, after the Romans' destruction of Jerusalem and the Temple? What good can the Old Testament serve, at least for a Christian?[4]

The attitude from which such questions grew is already clearly visible in Pseudo-Barnabas, though not yet heretical. But before long it was to furnish Marcion with his central attack on orthodox Christianity: it is blasphemous to identify the Old Testament's Creator-God—cruel and savage, requiring His people to kill all inhabitants of Canaan, even little children, and commanding death as the punishment for a long list of crimes in no way equivalent to idolatry or murder—with "the God and Father of our Lord Jesus Christ," the God of tenderness and mercy and compassion. From such a base, it was not far to a further multiplication of deities; and soon the Roman Empire was swarming with the heresies today loosely lumped together under the designation "Christian gnosticism."

The Church's response was firm and direct. The Old Testament was to be kept, first and foremost, because it is the inspired word of God, as proved by the use made of it throughout the New Testament. Further, the older Scriptures were to be kept because they are essential to Christian faith and life. They have not only their manifest sense as commendable moral precepts and elaborate ceremonial laws, as hymns of praise and of contrition, and as chronicles of Israelite wars and rivalries, but also a spiritual sense. This spiritual sense is not readily apparent to carnal minds. To be perceived, it requires faith in Jesus as the Christ and Son of God. Its abiding importance is that it

[3] Ch. 1.C, *pp* 7 & 9–10.

[4] Even Judaism has had to wrestle to some degree with these questions, one result of which is evident in Reform Judaism. Cf. *The Story of Judaism*, Bernard J. Bamberger, 3rd ed., New York: Schocken Books (1970), 320–321.

not only grounds much of the doctrine of Christianity but, in every generation makes recapitulation in Christ intelligible and more effectively accomplished.

For various reasons, over the past several centuries Catholics have gradually forgotten about the spiritual sense. They have come to misunderstand what the term itself means and to accept in practice, without realization of the importance of this move, the position of John Calvin. Except for those specific instances in which the literal sense of the New Testament expressly asserts a spiritual sense of the Old, Calvin held the literal sense to *be* the spiritual sense.[5] The Christian could admit no other without scriptural warrant—though as a man of learning passionately interested in the Bible, Calvin rightly included in the literal sense the meaning not only of individual words, phrases, and sentences but the meaning of entire passages, sections, books, even perhaps of the entire aggregate.

The classical understanding of the two senses was thereafter, until very recently, increasingly neglected if not abandoned. Catholics had the results of 1500 years of spiritual interpretation firmly in place in the Church's doctrines and practice. But in their conflicts with Protestantism, especially with the liberal Protestantism of the 19th Century, Catholics tended to accept the latter's choice of terrain and to center on the literal sense. While not denying in principle the spiritual sense, they became increasingly unable or unwilling to make use of it in their exegetical efforts.

But Calvinist teaching was by no means the only reason for the desuetude of the spiritual sense. Well before Calvin, the classical mode of spiritual interpretation had exhausted itself and fallen into triviality if not silliness. By the time of the Reformation, there were few indeed who still had a genuine understanding of such interpretation. Moreover, since the spiritual sense, as we shall see, was given by God Himself and, thus, directly knowable only by Him, is it possible without a new revelation to find any other way to consider the matter than that traditonal mode, now seemingly defunct? Can we either avoid the now obviously arbitrary interpretations of which history tells us or justify them as being something more than mere accommodations, the sort of instructive metaphors useful for preachers but not true meanings of the text?

This failure to consider the spiritual sense represents an abandonment of more than 1500 years of essential Church teaching and of doctrines most characteristic of Christianity. For the existence of the spiritual sense is inextricably intertwined with the existence of the two Covenants, the New replacing the Old, and with the fact that Jesus comes twice as the Christ, once in the

---

[5] Though he often speaks of 'types' and of 'shadows' in a manner quite traditional, as for example in Bk II, ch 7.1–2 & 16; ch 8.31–34 of his *Institutes of the Christian Religion,* he does so apparently only insofar as the literal sense of the New Testament explicitly declares these. Cf., e.g., his *Commentary on the First Letter to the Corinthians*, ch 10, 11, where he takes *τύποι* in I Cor.10:6 as mere "examples," from which we may learn a salutary fear of sin. Note too the vigor of his attacks on those who would see Christian behavior as anything more than an integral keeping of the Torah.

weakness of our flesh 2000 years ago, once in His full majesty as Son of God in power at the end of this age. Gradually, too, many of the Church's teachings have been downplayed; drawn primarily from the spiritual sense of Scripture, they are not always evident in the literal sense. There followed necessarily a substitution of the scholar for the bishop as the chief teacher in the Church—unless one wished to deny any intrinsic link between the Scriptures and Catholic doctrine.[6]

In compensation, there has been a marvellous growth in our grasp of the literal sense, in our understanding of what the inspired authors intended to say at the time and in the circumstances in which they wrote. Most of the conflicts among scripture scholars in the past 250 years have been concerned with the proper enunciation and application of the principles that have enabled historians to achieve this.

But again, the Marcionite question has arisen, albeit in somewhat different form: Since our culture is so far removed from that of ancient Israel (or even, truth to tell, from that of the world in which Jesus lived), why should any who are not professional historians of culture or philologists specializing in ancient Near-Eastern linguistics or specialists in the anthropology of religion have any interest in the Old Testament? Admittedly, we could profit by gathering some of the lovelier poetry and the more exalted exhortations into a much shorter collection, say of the size of the New Testament (after it, too, had had its superfluous sections trimmed away); but why retain the Old Testament in its entirety? Who reads it any more except those literalists who often do not even know that it was not written in the English of the King James version?[7]

Nonetheless, many of the most learned of professional biblical scholars today, Protestant as well as Catholic, are convinced that the Old Testament (and even the New) have, in addition to the literal sense, also some sort of "more-than-literal sense."[8] But not merely are there good scholarly reasons for the Church to insist on the fact of the spiritual sense in addition to the literal. As in the 2nd Century, so now, the pastoral need is urgent. For, the cultural decline now noticed and deplored by most reflective people, whatever their

---

[6] This is the problem with which a large number of theologians and scripture scholars were forced to wrestle publicly and fruitlessly by Thomas Sheehan's notorious article "Revolution in the Church," in *The New York Review of Books*, June 14, 1984.

[7] A recent book by John Shelby Spong, *Rescuing the Bible from Fundamentalism: A Bishop Rethinks the Meaning of Scripture*, San Francisco: HarperSanFrancisco (1991), offers a striking example of neo-Marcionite teaching. More sophisticated than Marcion, Spong does not reject any book of the Scripture outright. He argues instead that, while containing a hidden truth, accessible to those who follow his lead, the literal meaning of Scripture is anti-God and anti-Jesus. The picture of God presented by most of the Old Testament he rejects in exactly Marcion's fashion; the often stern picture of Jesus given by the New is equally unacceptable to him. The words of Scripture are not God's words in any legitimate sense, but the whole is God's word, since representing the culture-bound stammerings of our forbears in the presence of the mystery of God.

[8] For the term, cf. Raymond E. Brown, "Hermeneutics," *JBC*, II: 605–623, #32 (610); for the assertion, ##48–53 (614–615). So also *NJBC*, *pp* 1146–1165.

religious views, is the direct result, I shall argue, of the loss by Christians of the spiritual understanding of Scripture, most especially of the Old Testament. But how a recovery of the spiritual sense may be effected has not been clear. Even those most convinced of the need for it, find it hard to show how it might be accomplished.

B. THE LITERAL SENSE

1. Basic notions

Before we go further, we should pause to clarify our terms, make some basic distinctions, and, in general, focus carefully the problems we have to address.

The literal sense, as this term is generally used in the Church today, is the sense that the divinely inspired writer intended to convey to his reader by the words he chose. This is, then, the same kind of sense that is found in any text composed by man through which he intends to communicate with his fellows. In brief, it is that meaning of the biblical text which anyone properly skilled can draw from the text, whether believer or unbeliever, whether aware that he is dealing with the word of God or not.[9] (Obviously, "the text" may be the smallest intelligible unit, often a single word, or any larger unit, even the diversity of books in the Old Testament taken all together with whatever unity one can discern in them).

The literal sense of the Scriptures has often been called the "historical sense" (or simply "the history"). Both 'literal' and 'historical' have their problems, since both are easily misunderstood. Thus, for Origen, great scholar though he was, metaphor lay outside what he considered the historical sense, with the awkward result that much that the Bible says could not have a literal sense. Conversely, the authors of the various "historical" books had a different understanding of what they were doing than is conveyed by our word 'history.' Yet some have thought that the historical sense could exist only in narratives or fragments of them, or where one is sure that the account is truly factual, without exaggerations, legends, or parables—or conversely, some have thought that they can be sure of these things on the grounds that the book is "historical." Usage constrains one to recognize both designations. Personally, I should prefer 'historical,' understanding this of a sense to be found *in* history, not of a sense *concerning* history or offered *as* history. But 'literal' is the term in common use today; hence, the one I shall use here.

The literal sense might also be called the 'natural sense' or the 'rational sense,' were not these words already too likely to be misunderstood from their own multiplicity of meanings. In any case, the literal sense is that

---

[9] 'Text' seems often the best translation for what is, in this context, called 'letter' by ancient authors. St. Thomas' definition is: "insofar as things are signified through words...it is in this that the literal sense exists" (*Quaestiones Quodlibetales*, VII, 6, 14 c). Or, with greater precision: "everything pertains to the literal sense which is rightly drawn from the very meaning of the words," (id. 15 c).

meaning which can be legitimately extracted from a text as what its writer intended his readers to take from it—even if he himself could not always explicitate just what this is—by anyone who is competent, whether believer or nonbeliever, using the normal powers of the human mind and its methods.

There is no need here to trace out the theological history of the literal sense, a task admirably carried through by de Lubac.[10] That this understanding is the Church's teaching, expressly formulated now in major documents of the Magisterium and crystallized out of the Tradition, may be seen by the following words of the Second Vatican Council:[11]

> In order to perceive what God Himself wished to communicate to us, the interpreter of Sacred Scripture ought attentively to investigate what the hagiographers really intended to signify.... Let the interpreter seek the sense which in his concrete situation the hagiographer, in accord with the condition of his time and culture, with the help of the literary forms used at that time, intended to express and did express. To understand rightly what the sacred author wished to state by his writing, one must pay proper attention both to the usual modes of feeling, speaking, and narrating which flourished at the time of the hagiographer and were native to him, and to those which in that age were customarily used in the mutual commerce between men.

There can be, then, no question in principle that all sound methods of coming to understand ancient documents can and should be used in seeking to grasp the literal sense of the text of the Scriptures, however unsound at times the use itself or the particular methods used may prove to have been. Today, no less than before, the various new movements in philosophical hermeneutics, linguistics, semiotics, and the like may legitimately be employed on the Scriptures to the precise extent to which they may be legitimately used elsewhere.[12] Since the Church has always taught that these are human documents, written by human authors for other human beings, there seems no possible alternative.[13]

2. *Limitations:*

Nonetheless, there remain some serious limitations *in principle* on our historical understanding of the Scriptures.

Most importantly, the methods ordinarily employed in the study of ancient cultures and their literatures do not, of themselves, deeply engage human emotions and passions. But their application to the Scriptures challenges not only our minds but our basic decisions on how we intend to live. Hence, however correct in themselves, these methods have often been employed on

[10] Henri de Lubac, S.J., *Histoire et esprit: L'intelligence de l'Écriture d'après Origène*, Paris: Aubier (1950) and *Exégèse Médiévale: les quatre sens de l'écriture*, (4 vol.), Paris: Aubier (1959–1964).

[11] Dogmatic Constitution *Dei Verbum*, #12. A more detailed development of these ideas can be found in *The Interpretation of the Bible in the Church*, Pontifical Biblical Commission, Vatican City: Libreria Editrice Vaticana (1993), II. B. 1, *pp* 78–80.

[12] For an excellent discussion of this point, cf. Pontifical Biblical Commission, *Interpretation*, I. A–E, II. A, *pp* 34–69, 73–77.

[13] Pius XII, *Divino afflante Spiritu*, (DS 3826).

the Bible in ways that reflect human sinfulness and lack of genuine love for truth.[14]

Then, too, the various methods are necessarily worked out within the framework of philosophical understanding, whether recognized as such or not, of those who have developed them. This means that the rationalisms and empiricisms of the past 350 years have in their various forms infected these methods to a greater or less degree. Hence, historical methods are often far from sound in their epistemological presuppositions. It is in its demolition of these rationalisms and intellectual self-sufficiencies, using these alone against themselves, that deconstructionism has, despite its negativity and ultimate falseness, played a most useful role.

Through it, a space has been opened for the recovery of the "Christian deconstruction" of all human words and texts, of human thought, and of all spatio-temporal being, found so movingly in St. Augustine,[15] so drily and as if taken for granted by St. Gregory Nazianzen[16] and St. Thomas Aquinas.[17] The Fathers did not have to wait for Derrida to learn that no creature's knowledge, even if infinite in extent, is like God's knowledge; that any thought expressed in words is intrinsically temporal and, hence, imperfect; that no piling up of experiences and facts can be adequate to what is.[18]

But God's Word is not in time or space, except in His manhood; and so is not subject to their conditions. We, on the other hand, are not reduced to the condition of the brutes through the temporality of our thought, for "God...made [man] in the image of His own eternity" (Wisd.2:23). Thus, despite the despair of some philosophers, we escape the constraints of a total materiality. Even in a fallen world, we are able to communicate and to perceive meaning.

The eternal and immutable Word of the Father, once incarnate, is a human "word" that sounds for a time and then falls silent so that the process of speech may continue. He died to make room for further "words," chiefly His own word in Scripture and in the Church. But He has also risen and now transcends time, even in His humanity. Thus, our time-conditioned thought and speech, always ceasing even as they come to be and never adequate to what is known or univocal with what we would say, are not, for all that, equivocal or empty of meaning. The Word remains present, in whom all

---

[14] Pierre Grelot, *The Bible, Word of God,* tr. P. Nickels, 2nd ed., New York: Desclee (1968) *pp* 204–209, 335–338, for brief and temperate discussion of this matter. The concise and balanced comments of Avery Dulles, S.J., *The Craft of Theology: From Symbol to System,* New York, Crossroad Publishing Co., 1992, *pp* 5–7 and 71–85. refer more explicitly to the major methods and approaches of recent times.

[15] *Confessions*, Bk. 11.

[16] E.g., The third and fourth Theological Discourses, SC 250, 29, 3 & 30, 17–18, *pp* 180–182 & 260–264.

[17] *Contra Gentes* I, 32–34; II, 30–31, 36 & *de Veritate* II, 11 c & ad 1.

[18] R. V. Young, "Derrida or Deity? Deconstructionism in the Presence of the Word," *Issues in the Wake of Vatican II*, Proceedings of the Eighth Convention of the Fellowship of Catholic Scholars, ed. P. L. Williams, Scranton (PA): Northeast Books (1985),105–120.

reality and all intellection of the real and all expression of the real subsists in total unity, Emmanuel, God with us, all days even to the consummation of the age.

On a smaller scale, there are endless eddies of fashionable thought, whose importance at the time seems obvious but is, as with many other long-forgotten intellectual movements before them, nonexistent or negligible.

A more particular sort of difficulty, too little noticed, is the paradox implicit in the use of all our historical methods: they seek precisely to discover and somehow enable us to enter into a mindset and cultural framework in which such search and discovery can have no meaning. Ancient Israel was blissfully unaware of the possibility of historical methodology. Our desire to recover their mentality is one of the very things that most strongly separates us from that mentality. This is not to imply a devaluing of our efforts but only to realize that what we seek must ever lie beyond us.

Another limitation arises from the overly-strong focus inherent in all scholarly effort. The enormous specialization and erudition needed for useful research into ancient Near-Eastern language and thought can have the unfortunate side-effect of weakening the scholar's abilities to perceive the more universal and broadly human aspects of the literature with which he is working.[19] Inability to deal adquately with the history of cultures in the manner, say, of Christopher Dawson and lack of the actual experience of communication of the life of faith across the boundaries of one's own culture also constitute formidable limitations to the effort to recover the full meaning of a text.

The most, then, that historical-critical methods can hope to offer us is a more or less substantial contribution to the literal sense of these documents. I say "contribution to" since no one thinks or claims to be able to recover by these methods the full and exact sense intended by the writers. Much must remain forever hidden from us, to be replaced by educated guess, reasonable conjecture, more or less plausible surmise, all of which are subject to radical revision with every major discovery of ancient inscriptions or archeological sites,[20] as well as with every new current in philosophies of history and language.

None of this is new or would be denied, at this level of generality, by any of the scholars involved. It is little more than saying that none of us has the resources, even when working with many others, to know all that he needs to know in order to discover the literal sense with the clarity we should like. But as we shall see shortly, the spiritual sense can only be found through

---

[19] Since it will be the layman who is most likely to spot the difficulty, scholarship stands to lose lay esteem more drastically for this reason than any other. Cf. the brief but valid critique of Bultmann on this basis, *Christian Reflections*, C. S. Lewis, Grand Rapids (MI): Eerdmans (1967), *pp* 152–166.

[20] How radical these revisions may be can be understood from the fact that entire civilizations, hitherto unknown but all of major importance for the biblical accounts, have been discovered: in the 1920's, the Hyksos, Mari, and Ugarit; and in 1975, Ebla with the riches of its exceedingly ancient and as yet largely undeciphered royal library.

the literal sense. If this latter remains essentially vague or uncertain, how can we ever take it as a solid basis for the spiritual sense?

The epistemological problem turns, then, into a spiritual one: Is "the clarity we should like" truly desirable? Is it a possibility for man, even in the mind of God? Can it be seen as anything more than a Kantian Idea, endlessly to be approximated but self-destroying to the degree it is achieved? Deconstructionism and Christian tradition both say no. The former, however, sees the text as a set of rationally insoluble, because radically unformulatable, problems for man's reason. The latter stands in reverence before the text and the entire world of which man and all his texts are part, since aware of standing before the mystery of God, both revealed and concealed by these lesser mysteries through which He communicates with us.

It is in no small part in response to these limitations that much of the development in more-than-literal or, truth to tell, other-than-literal senses has occurred. As will be seen shortly, the spiritual sense has not been given by man but by God alone. Hence no limitations or natural deficiencies in our methods for discovering the literal sense can serve as a basis for finding the spiritual sense; rather, every weakness in our grasp of the literal sense hinders such efforts. This fact (that the spiritual sense is not a "sense of the gaps" that may seem to be found in the literal sense, even as God is not a "God of the gaps" in current scientific explanations) serves as an excellent criterion for separating the true spiritual sense from spurious more-than-literal senses. Apparently, the lesson must once again be learned that an author's metaphors and symbolism belong to the literal sense of his text.[21]

Such realizations should generate a certain humility in all claims for final understanding of the text. Too often, however, scholarly methods lead to a certain scorn for those who think that the Bible can be accessible to all, having its literal sense available for the untrained reader. There is, of course, excellent reason, as already indicated through the Magisterial statements cited above,[22] to hold suspect the theology of any Catholic who rejects out of hand whatever is available from biblical scholarship.[23] The Church has had long and painful experience of the errors of those who have done so. Yet it remains true that, as Augustine said, though the Scriptures are deep enough to drown an elephant, they are shallow enough for a mouse to wade through.

What is involved here can be understood more easily, perhaps, by reference to the words of a blind man Jesus was healing, "I see people, because I perceive, as it were, trees walking about" {Mk.8:24}. The similarity extends to the focussing of almost any optical instrument. The image one gets from a lens not well focussed can be merely fuzzy, with the edges visually uninterpretable. Or it may be so distorted as to make impossible any sound

---

[21] Cf. W. K. Wimsatt, *Hateful Contraries: Studies in Literature and Criticism*, Lexington (KY): University of Kentucky (1966), *pp* 51–71. For an overview of the current confusions in this area, cf. *NJBC*, "Interpretation," R. E. Brown & S. M. Schneiders, 71:48–70.

[22] Especially DS 3792–3793.

[23] Cf. Pontifical Biblical Commission, *Interpretation*, I. F, *pp* 70–72.

conclusions as to what one wishes to observe. It may, even, depending on the arrangement, produce a clear but inverted image, one that could prove lethal to the observer in some circumstances if not rightly understood.

So of any text. Mysterious in its workings, the human mind can, despite all current counterarguments, extract from a text much of the sense intended, but with varying degrees of clarity and distortion. Thus, the simple faithful can indeed grasp from a basically sound translation, such as the Vulgate or many current versions into modern vernaculars, or even from a poor one, much of what the Scriptures have to say in a sense not simply false, but neither, ever, wholly true.

The uninstructed can, however, be as prideful as the scholarly and, to the extent they are so, will lose their focus or find a clear image that inverts the truth and leads to fatal contradiction with the faith. Indeed, the pride of the ignorant is more intrinsically destructive than that of the learned.[24] The learned know and accept much truth, though, if proud, with an attitude that may falsify their understanding of that truth. But one who refuses to acknowledge the obligations his ignorance places upon him to learn before he speaks or who is proud of an "independence of mind" that refuses to learn before it makes its judgments, such a man's pride cuts him off almost entirely from truth.

C. The spiritual sense

1. Basic notions

When Jesus, that first Easter afternoon, walked with the two disciples on the way to Emmaus, setting their hearts on fire as He interpreted the Scriptures for them (Lk.24:25–27, 32) or when that same evening He opened the minds of the apostles to understand the Scriptures (24:44–45), He was doing much more than pointing out to them what they already knew as good Jews from the readings in the synagogue. Already at the beginning of His ministry, He had declared that the ancient writings were then being fulfilled even as He spoke while He taught things not in those texts according to their literal sense.[25]

From the days of Jesus, then, the Church has held that the Old Testament contains, in addition to its literal or historical sense, a spiritual sense, which has been "hidden for ages in God, [but] has now been revealed" (Eph.3:9, 5).[26] For, the Christian dispensation is that which has been

[24] One should recall here the comment of St. Teresa of Avila on her preference for a learned even if not holy confessor to a holy but unlearned one. Cf., e.g., *Vida* 13, 17–18; 32, 16; *Relaciones* 3, 7.

[25] Cf., e.g., Lk.4:17–22; Mt.5:17–18.

[26] "...according to the revelation of the mystery which was kept secret for long ages but is now disclosed and through the prophetic writings is made known" Rom.16:25–26; "what has been hidden since the foundation of the world" (Mt.13:35, cf. Ps 78:2); "the mystery hidden from the ages and from the generations [of mankind]—but now it has been manifested to His saints" {Col.1:26}.

inaugurated by Jesus, who came as that Christ of the Lord who was foreseen and prepared for by the Old Testament. This doctrine, then, which affirms the existence of a spiritual sense, is not just one portion of the revelation made by Jesus and manifested in the New Testament; it forms the very core of the Church's faith.[27]

Since Scripture was given us by God to teach us what we need to know concerning our salvation and did this through human writers inspired by His Spirit, the basic meaning is the literal sense, the meaning the human author intended to convey by his words.[28] But meaning can also be conveyed by *things*, whether substantive entities or processes or by the entire course of events in the world.[29] It belongs, however, to God alone to give such meaning to things, whether by His creating them in Christ or by His providence over them. *Hence, the spiritual sense is that meaning which God has given to those things that are spoken of by the Scriptures according to their literal sense; and this meaning is Christ.*[30]

Thus any portion or aspect of reality that is spoken of by the text signifies another reality that is some aspect of Christ: the Whole Christ, Head and members, as existing in this world or in the age to come. The Christian can then speak of the literal sense of a biblical text as that sense which presents those aspects of reality which, by God's choice, signify the mysteries of Christ and His Church. Though the spiritual sense can be considered as a "deeper" meaning of the *words* of Scripture,[31] it refers primarily to the

[27] Thus, the Ponifical Biblical Commission could write in 1941, precisely in its defense of the literal sense from attack: "[I]t is a proposition of the faith, to be held as a fundamental principle, that Sacred Scripture in addition to the literal sense contains also a spiritual or typical sense" (DS 3792). For the detailed evidence, cf. de Lubac, *EM* and *HE*.

[28] St. Thomas enuntiates the principle in full generality, though he applies it only to the divine author's intent—cf. *de Potentia* 4, 1 c and *ST* I, 1, 10 c—or else identifies the intents of the human author and the divine.

[29] E.g., "Things, as they pursue their course, signify some other thing." "God uses the very course of the things that are subject to His providence for the signifying of some others." (*Quodlib.* VII, 6, 16 c). Cf. also, *de Potentia*, 4, 1 c. "The very things signified by the words also signify something" (*ST* I, 1, 10 c). Therefore, one must always know what the words actually signify before one can know what this which is signified itself signifies. Yet revelation can and does at times assert the relation between the things in question *before* one has knowledge of the literal sense.

[30] To avoid needless confusion, it should be noted here that the present-day Pontifical Biblical Commission uses a much broader definition: "[T]he spiritual sense, as understood by Christian faith, [is] the meaning expressed by the biblical texts when read under the influence of the Holy Spirit, in the context of the paschal mystery of Christ and of the new life which flows from it," *Interpretation*, II. B, *p* 81. As is evident from this definition and from the use made of it in the same document, it includes under the one name not only the spiritual sense as here defined but also the various forms of legitimate accommodation which, for our purposes, need to be carefully separated from all forms of the spiritual sense.

[31] This use of 'spiritual sense' flows from the basic meaning of this phrase if one attributes the God-given meaning of the reality spoken of by the text to the scriptural words that tell us of this reality. To avoid much repetition of such cumbersome language, and despite the risk of serious confusion from such usage (cf. note 30 above & 33 below), I shall often speak of "the spiritual

realization of what has been signified by its *persons or events.* This completion of meaning has a unique and nonreplaceable source: Jesus, the Word of God made flesh. It is this that constitutes the very center of Christian faith. The divinely revealed realities of the Old Testament (real persons, things, actions, or any real state of affairs—or what is taken or presented by the sacred author as such) are not merely predictive of or preparatory for Jesus but find their ultimate significance outside themselves in Jesus. He *is* their meaning.

Since Jesus was, and still is, true man as well as true God, discernment of the spiritual sense requires that we see how earlier realities, whatever their natural intelligibilities, gain their full import and significance only from the way they are related to the One whom the Lord has anointed. They are like shadows that gain their true significance only from the object which casts them, no matter what object one might have surmised to be casting them when looking at them alone. Jesus is that solid substance whose mere shadow constitutes all the glories of God's dealings with mankind before Jesus.[32]

Finally, it is intrinsic to the definition of the spiritual sense that, in principle, only God could assign it and only He can know it except insofar as He has chosen to reveal it.[33] Therefore, if anyone claims to know the spiritual sense of what is spoken of in a text, he is claiming that in some manner God has revealed that this is the meaning (or among the meanings) which He has given the realities there mentioned. The reverence due the divine Majesty would suggest, then, a greater circumspection in ascribing a spiritual sense to a text than has at certain periods been the case. On the other hand, often such freedom as was shown, e.g., by Origen or St. Thomas,[34] came not from too little reverence but from the conviction that God *had* revealed the matters they were concerned with. He had not revealed them directly, however, but had given into the hands of the Church the key she was to use in order to unlock the treasury of meanings He had made accessible through the texts.

---

sense of a text" but only in the way just defined. Such usage has also had a certain appeal inasmuch as the biblical words were chosen by the Spirit to present precisely this aspect of the flow of events to us.

[32] Cf. Hebr.10:1 and also the remarks in II Cor.4 concerning Moses' glory.

[33] Cf. Pius XII, "For God alone could both know this spiritual meaning and reveal it to us" (at end of DS 3828—cf. text to note 36 below). So, also, Pope John Paul II, Address of April 23, 1993, in *Interpretation*, *p* 11: "[T]he spiritual sense must offer proof of its authenticity...that it is a sense 'willed by God himself,' a spiritual meaning 'given by God' to the inspired text." This is hardly new; cf. St. Thomas: "But things are so ordered in the course of events that from them such a (spiritual) sense can be had which is His alone (to assign) who by His providence governs things, who is God alone." (*Quodlib.* VII, 6, 16 c). It is, then, incorrect to speak of the spiritual sense or any of its subdivisions as "theology" or "theological categories", unless it be solely to indicate that our mode of establishing this sense and its subdivisions or our efforts to explicate their nature are "theology." Cf., to the contrary, Grelot, *Bible*, *p* 311, and his whole chapter VI of which *p* 311 is the conclusion. This same restriction of 'spiritual sense' to theology, i.e., the result of human interpretation of the realities of which the text speaks, lays the foundation for the confusion and controversy connected with the doctrine of a *sensus plenior* of the literal sense (*Bible,* ch. VII). The text itself of *Interpretation* is silent on this need for validation.

[34] Cf. his commentaries *In Galatas,* 5, lect. 7 and *In Isaiam*, 35 (18, 807, ed. Vivès).

Nor has the Magisterium dropped or weakened this doctrine in recent times, as some have thought on the basis of Vatican condemnations of such excessive statements as the following: "The literal sense of Sacred Scripture and its explanation by so many and such great exegetes, worked out under the watchful eye of the Church,...ought to give way to the exegesis which they call symbolic and spiritual."[35] For example, Pope Pius XII stated:

> The things which...were said or done in the Old Testament have been most wisely ordered and disposed by God so that past things prefigured in a spiritual manner the things which were to be in the new covenant of grace. Wherefore, even as the exegete ought to discover and to explain the *literal* meaning, as they say, of the words, i.e., the meaning which the sacred author intended and expressed, so also the spiritual meaning, provided it is rightly established that it was given by God. For God alone could know this spiritual meaning and reveal it to us.... Catholic exegetes are to lay out and propose this spiritual sense, intended and ordered by God Himself.[36]

So also, the Second Vatican Council taught, although without using the phrase 'spiritual sense,' that the Old Testament foretold, recounted, and explained the (New Testament's) economy of salvation, that it declared in prophecy the coming of Christ, and indicated the messianic kingdom by means of types, so that, in the Old Testament, the mystery of our salvation is present in a hidden way.[37]

There has been considerable uncertainty among Catholics over the past hundred years or so as to whether this doctrine refers to the Old Testament as a whole and in all its parts or only to those sections for which the New Testament indicates such a meaning, plus, perhaps, the texts similarly interpreted by a morally complete consensus of the Fathers or by the liturgy.[38] I shall argue later that this is a dichotomy without a difference, that the doctrine refers to everything in the Bible, Old Testament and New, and that it is the New Testament along with the consensus of the Fathers and the liturgy that indicates as much. But this need not detain us here.

Though the literal sense is not the only sense of the Scriptures nor the most important, it is, however, the most basic. If one does not rightly understand what a text says, one cannot rightly know the things of which it speaks, which alone bear the spiritual sense. Yet the spiritual sense, though by no means the only reason for God's revealing Himself through the literal sense, is truly that for which this latter exists.[39]

---

[35] Pius XII, *Humani Generis* (DS 3888). Cf. also DS 3792–3793 in same sense.

[36] Pius XII, *Divino afflante Spiritu*, DS 3828.

[37] *Dei Verbum*, #15.

[38] So, the Pontifical Biblical Commission: "[N]evertheless, not every sentence or narrative contains a typical sense." (DS 3792).

[39] The distinction is similar to that so well analyzed by Bernard Lonergan ("Finality, Love, Marriage," *Theological Studies 4*, 477–510 [1943]) with regard to the ends and purposes of human sexual activity, where the more basic sense, without which no other can be truly had, is procreative; but where the more important in terms of ultimate finality and excellence is the unitive. Cf.

The existence of the spiritual sense in addition to the literal is closely related, as might be guessed, to the special characteristic that sets interpretation of the Scriptures apart from all other analyses of ancient documents. This is the fact that the Bible has two authors. Every part of Scripture, though composed and written by man, was directly intended by God to serve as part of His revelation of "Himself and the eternal decrees of His will concerning the salvation of men."[40] Since it is God who inspires the human author and directs the entire process of cultural development, writing, redaction, compilation, editing, etc. that have given us the biblical texts, each author is inerrant according to the standards of the kind of communication he is concerned with.[41] From this twofold authorship arises the possibility of two senses of the text: the one, that intended and written down by the human author, however he be defined in the complex process of the formation of one or more books of the Scripture; the other, that which God has given to the things spoken of and which He may, but need not, have made known to the human author.

2. Typology

Evidently, one portion of the meaning God has put into the things of which the Bible speaks is their natural symbolism (such as that of human sexuality in its symbolizing of marriage and family). But more important for the Christian meaning of the Bible are things' supernatural significations, given by the Spirit. These may carry the natural symbolism further, elevating it by making it speak of greater mysteries. Or, since all things spread out in time coexist with the instant of His eternity, by the free choice of His providence in governing all things well He may directly constitute one thing the meaning of something else prior to it. The thing that signifies I shall call the 'type'; the future thing that is signified, the 'Antitype'.

This terminology, even more than others in this area, is exceedingly fluid not only in the New Testament itself and in the Fathers but in their their successors down to the present day. The word 'type' itself referred originally in Greek to the impression made by a die, though it was also used on occasion for the die itself. One can use 'type,' then to speak of the strongest sort of similarity, though rarely, if ever, in the sense of a mere copy.[42] Thus in the Scriptures, it can refer to a shadow, with the Antitype being the solid substance casting it; it can indicate a promise, whose fulfilment, already known by God, gives it its intelligibility. Some have seen it also as the vital form or principle that seeks its own actualization as its Antitype. The theological tradition, however, takes 'type' with considerable freedom in varying degrees in all these and other, analogous meanings.

---

also, P. M. Quay, "Contraception and Conjugal Love," *Theological Studies 22*, 18–40 (1961), *pp* 33–34.

[40] *Dei Verbum*, #6, and also the beginning of #2. For the two-fold authorship, ibid., #11.

[41] Obviously, there is a prior question, dealt with by II Vatican (*Dei Verbum*, ##1–6) concerning what God revealed personally to those who served as the human authors. Interesting as this is, it need not be dealt with here.

[42] Cf. the article "Typos" by L. Goppelt in Kittel's *TDNT 8,* 251–256.

Like all terms that attempt to name things with many facets and aspects, 'type' has its shortcomings. The commonest equivalent for 'type' is 'figure'—but there seems to be no correspondingly common technical term for 'Antitype'. Further, the definition I have given above of the 'spiritual sense' is evidently equivalent to the 'typical sense,' and its theological utilization by us can be designated 'typology.'[43] Since St. Thomas and many others use these terms, especially 'typical sense' only for one subdivision of the spiritual sense, I shall speak of this subdivision as the 'restricted typical sense' whenever the distinction needs to be made clear.[44] Typology, then, as used here of scriptural hermeneutics, refers to man's efforts to find the meaning that God Himself has given to the things which the literal sense manifests and that, apart from His revelation, no man can know.

The mode of theological understanding that is involved in ferreting out the typical sense of the Old Testament is one that is strange and almost wholly alien to us. It is clearly a very different notion from any "typology" that seeks merely to apply, whether to doctrinal or pastoral problems, this meaning once ascertained. The latter notion gives much greater freedom to human creativity. Nonetheless, there are good reasons why 'typology' is used of both notions since, ultimately, all argument in this domain must begin with the typical sense.[45]

God's revelation to us through types ordinarily has at least the following characteristics:

In each type-Antitype pair, the reality that is the type must truly be signified by the text, but neither type nor Antitype need be identified as such by the text. Both are to be found *through* understanding of the literal sense, but not *by* such understanding. Thus, if some meaning is read into the text, understood as a human document, that does not in truth belong to its literal sense then, except for the most unlikely of coincidences, the "reality" so read in will not refer to anything of the past; in any case, it cannot serve as type of anything.[46]

---

[43] Cf. however, *HE*, *pp* 387–388, for the risks of this. Note, however, the usage of Daniélou, for whom 'typology' is the preferred term (so Brown in *JBC*, 612, #38).

[44] Cf. Sect. C.4, *pp* 162–163 with notes 49 & 55 below. The usage here is the one that seems to be most widely and consistently used. In the *Dictionary of Biblical Theology*, *pp* 177–178, Grelot restricts the term 'type' so as not to include the anagogical sense but does let it take in the moral sense; in *Bible* (289–290), though accepting anagoge as a form of typology, he hesitates about the status of the moral sense.

[45] St. Thomas notwithstanding (cf. the discussion on *pp* 176–177 below), it would seem that in our Lord's day and in the apostolic Church, theological argument was drawn much more from the spiritual sense than from the literal. If for no other reason, there was no Scripture that spoke of the Christian mysteries through its literal sense until quite some years after the resurrection. The apostles' preaching served this function, being on such matters infallible, perhaps even inspired. But such traces as we have of their preaching, say in *Acts*, show strong statements in literal language of the mysteries but interpreted and argued for almost exclusively in terms of the spiritual sense of the extant Scriptures, i.e., the Old Testament.

[46] There is to be noted, I think, a profound inconsistency between the clear and quite traditional doctrine of St. Thomas in *ST* I, 1, 9 and 10, and what he says in *ST* I, 1, 2 ad 2. This seeming fail-

The type is usually temporally prior to the Antitype in human history, though He pre-exists all history, as the One in whom, through whom, and for whom all things have been created (Col.1:16). And though we come to know the things of the present age before we learn of those of the age to come, yet most of the things of heaven do antecede us or exist concurrently with us.

The typical sense often establishes parallelisms, of a sort we shall have to consider in some detail, between certain major historical figures and Jesus. But further, it generally requires that such parallelisms exist between the entire classes which these people and Jesus represent—of whom, that is, these latter are the representatives. This sort of type, then, is a sort of collective personality—always a concrete, individual person (or particular group) but precisely as identified with or as representing those who are objectively united with this individual or group.

This representation is real, ontologically based. So, such a type is not simply the outstanding member of the class to which he belongs and which he represents, still less what ordinary English means by a "typical example." Rather, he is, in some way, the whole class. This is true also of the Antitype and, indeed, true because of the Antitype. He is neither a typical example nor merely an outstanding member of our race. For, He is our representative not merely as one who pleads our cause but as the full and perfect Exemplar of our race, the Image of God according to which we have been created and in whom alone all things subsist (Col.1:17). Further, the Father has called all men to to be really, ontologically in Christ by grace; and this union with Him, when brought about through baptism, founds His Body, the Church.

3. Subdivisions of the spiritual sense

God's revelation teaches us, through both the literal and the spiritual senses, what we need for salvation: the things we must believe and those that we must do out of love for God, and also the joy of the eternal life with God that is our goal.

Now, the Old Testament often speaks of these matters directly in the manifestly literal sense, as when teaching Israel of the Lord's uniqueness and supremacy, or when enuntiating the Ten Commandments or giving the sound advice and moral instruction of the wisdom-literature, or when nourishing Israel's hope by glimpses of a messianic age to come. The writers of the New Testament had even more to say about doctrine concerning our Lord and His Church, sin and grace and redemption; much also about morals; and vastly more than the Old Testament concerning the age to come, albeit in metaphors and fantastic images constructed for the purpose. In many places the literal sense teaches doctrinal or moral matters indirectly as well, through carefully crafted narratives or couched in a riddle or a parable. But much as the topics and styles may differ, and though they are often intermingled inextricably, they lead to no multiplication of meanings. The writer had

ure to appreciate the concreteness of history would, if pushed to its limit, undo for Thomists all that is done by the spiritual sense of the Bible.

something reasonably clear in mind which the reader was meant to understand, even if with some labor.

The spiritual sense, on the other hand, has traditionally been subdivided into three distinct senses, all of which may be simultaneously the God-given meanings of the reality spoken of by the text. These senses are defined by their relations, in this age, to matters of faith and Christian conduct and, in the age to come, to the glory of eternal life.

St. Thomas begins his exposition of the traditional approach[47] with the just mentioned distinction between what is rightly to be believed and what is rightly to be done.[48] The scriptural sense telling us of the former he calls the typical (or also 'allegorical') sense;[49] of the latter, the moral (or also 'tropological') sense. The sense which reveals the things of the age to come is called 'anagogical,' a Greek term signifying 'a leading upwards' towards the things of heaven, as they will be but also as they are now though we shall experience them in full only after the general resurrection.

Thomas goes on to argue that the things spoken of literally in the Old Testament may have any or all of these meanings. Passages in the New Testament whose literal sense speaks of the Whole Christ, Head or members, in the conditions of earthly existence have no (restricted) typical sense possible, since they already state literally what we are to believe, though they may retain in full both moral and anagogical senses. In like manner, passages whose literal sense speaks of how Christians are to behave in Christ retain only an anagogical sense in addition to the literal. Since Christ came first in the weakness of our flesh, like us in all but sin, Thomas argues that Jesus Himself in His life on earth was the (supreme) type of Christ in glory, both now and when He comes again to judge all men and bring this age to its close. But if the realities literally spoken of by some passage are the end of the age and the things of heaven; no other sense to be sought, for these are the ultimate meaning of all things.

The distinction indicated above between what is to be believed and what is to be done is, clearly, of great practical import, for a sinner need not cease to believe and those who do not believe may become habituated to many an excellent mode of action which, once brought under Christ by conversion, makes their spiritual growth much easier. Yet the distinction must not be overdriven. A phrase of the Council of Trent is both wise and suggestive: "...in matters of faith and of the modes of behavior that pertain to the building up of Christian doctrine" (DS 1507).[50] What we are to do is

---

[47] Cf. *EM 4*, 285–302 for the evidence that St. Thomas did not innovate but merely transmitted the Church's Tradition here, though with a greater clarity as to expression and structure.

[48] *Quodlib.* VII, 6, 15, c

[49] I.e., that which I have called the "restricted typical sense" in Sect. C.2, *p* 159 above. I have chosen, for reasons to be seen (185–191), to use '(unrestricted) typical sense' as equivalent to 'spiritual sense.' The difference lies in whether one restricts the terminology 'type—Antitype' to the conditions of this world only or includes the age to come and, more importantly for our purposes, on how one sees the moral life of the Christian (cf. 162, 194–196, & 225 below).

ultimately dependent on what we believe. Christian morality can only be understood through Christ, from whom we receive our nature as well as our life in grace. Hence, the only *adequate* knowledge of right conduct that man can have is through faith (without, obviously, exclusion of reason, which also comes from the divine Logos, our Lord).

Hidden in St. Thomas' presentation of these matters are a a couple of statements that call for clarification. He remarks:

> The true body of Christ itself and the things done in it are figures of the mystical body of Christ and of the things done in it, so that from Christ *we ought to draw an example of how to live* [emphasis added]...those things which are said literally of Christ as head, can be explained both allegorically, referring to His mystical body, and morally, refering to our actions, which should be reformed in accordance with Him.[51]

And already he has stated, "The moral sense pertains to the members of Christ with regard to their own actions and not inasmuch as they are considered as members."[52]

Suffice it to say that this distinction, if taken as sharply as here phrased, would cause serious problems with the doctrine of sanctifying grace and our life in Christ. One cannot reduce the latter to our receiving an "example of how to live" and seeing our own actions as being "reformed in accordance with Him."[53] The formal distinction between the members' own good acts and what they do as Christ's members must not be taken as a division, even for the purposes of interpreting a text.[54] It seems more likely, however, that Thomas sees the typical sense here as referring simply and solely to the Catholic Church in her concrete existence—one acts as a member only in terms of one's ecclesial function, which can indeed be doctrinally limned without direct discussion of morality.

There are other, important forms of the spiritual sense we shall not need here. For example, the marriage of every Christian couple has as its spiritual meaning, conferred by the grace of the sacrament, the marriage of Christ with His Church in heaven. But though this doctrine is indicated by various types, the couple's love and union are not themselves types. And even a cursory

[50] This phrase has had a long and often disputed career down to our own day. Cf. especially the controversy at I Vatican and Gasser's reports on the topic, concerning its precise meaning and bearing (*Collectio Conciliorum Recentiorum, Mansi 52*, Arnhem [1927] 1224–1225 #4 & 1316). See also, II Vatican, *Lumen Gentium,* 25, par. 1: "the faith that is to be believed and applied to behavior."

[51] ibid. ad 5.

[52] ibid., ad 2. He does, however, improve his language in *ST* I, 1, 10 c: "in the New Law...the things that have been done by the Head are signs of the things we ought to do."

[53] In point of fact, Thomas does not speak in this manner when his topic is our life in Christ. Indeed, in the same Question, ad 4, he implies as much when considering the matter from the point of view of Christ's actions on us: "The allegorical sense pertains to Christ inasmuch as he is the head of the Church Militant, justifying her and pouring in [His] grace." Cf., e.g., *ST* III, 8, 5 c & ad 1 & ad 6.

[54] Cf. below, *pp* 194–200 for detailed consideration of this point.

reading of *Hebrews* will show other sorts of spiritual sense as well. There is still work to be done in order to manifest clearly and soberly the full riches of the spiritual senses of the Scriptures.

4. Allegory and accommodation

The restricted typical sense is often referred to in the tradition as allegory or the allegorical sense. Unfortunately, 'allegory' has come to have a meaning in modern times almost contrary to that usage, being now conceived as a literary fiction in the form of prolonged metaphor or extended verbal symbolism. The spiritual sense called allegorical, on the other hand, refers solely to realities or things in the world that by God's action signify the realities of Christ and His Church.[55]

The difference needs, perhaps, some clarification. Allegory is constructed through a symbolic use of language so that the text gets its literal meaning from the success of this symbolism. What the author intends is the symbolized meaning; and he would be distressed if his reader took Christian, say, as a Danish traveller who wandered into a swamp near the British town of Despond. Allegory says nothing about the reality of the figures it employs, nor is it interested in the matter. As with any metaphor, the literal sense of an allegory is its "hidden" or symbolic meaning. On the other hand, typology is primarily concerned with the reality of which the text speaks, once the literal meaning of the text is clear, and with what this reality signifies. The details of the account, if properly interpreted, concern this reality, even when the interpretation must be restricted in large measure to the aspects expressly mentioned by the text.

Allegory is sometimes said to be spiritual because its concrete images represent abstractions or idealizations. But type and Antitype are not "spiritual" in this fashion. Types have a discernible historical basis; allegorical figures are fictions, concocted by the writer, however they may be related to historical situations. Moses, therefore, as type of Christ, does not "stand for" Jesus in the way that the characters in *A Pilgrim's Progress* stand for all that aids or imperils the Christian reader in his spiritual advance. What Moses does is not simply a literary way of describing what Christ will do. Christ is not simply a copy of the type that is His 'shadow.' That which is most important in Him (e.g., His divinity) and in His actions (e.g., the redemption), however concrete, is spiritual beyond all expectation for anyone who looks only at its representation by the type.

If, then, the restricted typical sense was often taken for our modern 'allegory' after the first generations, this is due in good measure to the fact that typology was soon taken for granted among Christians as part of the Christian's ecclesiastical culture, and simply presupposed without further

---

[55] Because confusion between these two 'allegory's is rampant even among many who, from the extent of their learning, might have been expected to be able to avoid it, I have preferred the term 'typical' in the sense explained above, even if it has to be cumbersomely qualified as 'restricted' in order to differentiate it from the general typical (spiritual) sense, all three of whose senses are based on types.

explanation. Further, since St. Paul had used our notion of allegory (Gal.4:22–30) as well as typology, it was easy for typology to degenerate from the search for the complex and profound spiritual sense into the much easier exercise of our sort of allegory, as seen already in I Clement and Pseudo-Barnabas.

Another sort of confusion has arisen in relatively recent years. Something superficially analogous to the typical sense can be found within the Old Testament itself. Later authors reflect back on what earlier ones have written, modifying and extending the original meaning of their texts considerably. Tradition-historical criticism has highlighted how the literal sense of a passage or a whole book is revised and modified and spiritualized even within the Old Testament itself.[56]

Much good work has been done, e.g., on the way Second Isaiah sees the approaching Return from the Exile in terms of the Exodus from Egypt.[57] But this is not typology.[58] Some resemblances there may be; but the essentials for the spiritual sense are missing. Thus, in the example just mentioned, Second Isaiah gives no suggestion that the *meaning* of the original Exodus is the envisioned Return. Rather, in addition to marking the similarities between the two events, he is arguing from the literal sense of the Exodus-texts, concerning what God showed of His love and power for Israel then, to what He is about to do for Israel now.

So, too, the latter half of the *Book of Wisdom* has at times been called typology. The author's meditation on the Exodus is, again, a reflection on the power and goodness of God shown therein and an ardent prayer generated by the hope that He will again rescue His people from the then current persecution in Egypt—theological argument, if one wishes, or meditative prayer based on accommodation, or perhaps other categories, but not typology. Moreover, it is Christ who is the Antitype for all that belongs to the literal sense, not the persecuted Jewish community of Alexandria, though this also was type for Him.

The typical sense, in its distinctively Christian meaning, is unique and without parallel in other religious traditions, even in Judaism. For, not only is the spiritual sense not just any figurative meaning; it is not just any identification of some earlier person or event with what might be called a new embodiment of similar traits. The typical sense is, simply and solely, the meaning God has given the realities spoken of by the biblical text, all of which realities look forward to Christ, both as the Head of His Body, the Church, and as living in His members, whether in this world or the next.[59]

---

[56] A particularly clear-sighted presentation is given by Norbert Lohfink, S.J., "Die historische und die christliche Auslegung des Alten Testaments", *Stimmen der Zeit 178*, 98–112 (1966).

[57] A useful summary and introduction may be found in Walter E. Rast, *Tradition History and the Old Testament,* Philadelphia: Fortress (1972), *pp* 63–68.

[58] Rast's definition of typology shows by its vagueness where the problem lies: "Typology—The manner in which earlier events, personages, or institutions, are seen to be recapitulated in new ways at a later time" (ibid., *p* 79).

It should be clear, then, that the interpretations of exegetes, even should these be divinely inspired,[60] and the uses made of Scripture, however orthodoxly devout and appropriate to the thought-patterns and cultural expectations of our day (or any other), are not, as such, the Antitypes of scriptural types. We ourselves may be Antitype inasmuch as members of Christ and the Church, but only insofar as the type mentioned by the text signifies us so to be.

Man, apart from the public, divine revelation already long since given, cannot reveal God to himself nor change the truth already revealed into something that "means more" to him. "Typology" defined as "one specific mode of the larger category of interpretation, one in which a present event, person, situation, or thing suggests a likeness to an event, person, situation, or things of the past" or as "the universal experience where one sees new meaning in a past event in the light of the present experience"[61] simply misconstrues the Christian notion, which, above all else, requires that this sense be revealed by God Himself. What such phrases as Cahill's really define is rather *accommodation* of the text.

Now, accommodation (the taking of what the text says as directly applicable to one's current status or experience on the basis of some more or less obvious similarity or causal connection) can be a legitimate mode of understanding, as seen by the inspired examples of it mentioned above. Through it one may see for the first time what the cause was of some past event in one's life or present experience, or understand the event as source of much that has happened to one since, or realize that the experience is no longer the unique fact of this one individual "I" but is the common experience of the Christian or of all mankind, and so on. But whatever truth such interpretation may provide, it does not represent what the human author meant by the biblical text in question or what God gave as its typical sense but is rather the spiritual fruit of one's own thought in categories drawn from the Scriptures through reflection upon them.

Accommodation is not to be scanted. Firstly, no matter what scholars say, accommodating will always be done, well or ill, by the holiest even more than by those in sin. Surely, no preacher can do without it. And, as we shall see in a moment, it is a process that, rightly understood and carried through, is not only justified by the nature and purpose of the spiritual senses, different as these are from accommodated meanings or in-reading, but required.

Today, no less than in earlier times, much if not most theology is built

---

[59] There was a sort of interpretation that can be seen as preparatory to typology, making possible, humanly speaking, God's revelation by this means, that was found in Judaism shortly before the coming of the Lord and as the final intellectual preparation for His coming. Cf., e.g., Gustave Martelet, S. J., "Sacrements, figures, et exhortation en I Cor. x, 1–11," *Rev. Sci. Rel.* *44*, 323–359, 515–559 (1956).

[60] So, St. Thomas in *ST* I, 1, 8 ad 2.

[61] P. Joseph Cahill, "Hermeneutic Implications of Typology," *The Catholic Biblical Quarterly* *44*, 266–281 (1982), *p* 267.

on accommodated meanings. Think only of liberation theology and the closely related manner of theologizing of the *communidades de base*, or of the theological currents stemming from the experience of World War II in Europe. Should one reject these out of hand solely because one can show their understanding of Scripture not to be contained in the original texts, either literally or in the spiritual sense?[62] I think not.

Just as all moral truth, as all scientific truth, as all psychic truth is not to be found in the Bible, so not all truth about the nature of man, of his experience, of his history, of his relations to God or to the Church, not even all truth about the Scripture is to be found there. God has left much to human reason in all domains. Indeed, one mark of the saint is that, even concerning his prayer and union with the Lord, he is governed by reason as well as by faith, and far more by each than by his feelings.

The study of transmission-history or redaction-criticism makes evident that an essential aspect of the development of many of the texts is just this process of accommodation, carried through by human beings, even though the final form is inspired and given meaning by the Holy Spirit. But, if confusion is to be avoided, one must see that accommodation as such never gives the meaning of the initial text nor is it ever to be regarded as part of the spiritual sense.

Still more importantly, parables, whether those of the Old Testament, e.g., *Jonah*, or those of the New, e.g., the story of the father with two sons (Lk.15:11–32) would seem to be direct invitations to accommodation. The parable is a story whose very purpose is that the hearer or reader ponder it and apply it to himself in ways such as Cahill describes.

Jean Laplace[63] has suggested that St. Ignatius would have us treat the entire Old Testament as but one long parable, from which to draw inspiration for our following of the Christ to whom it looked forward. Would not this be to degrade the Scriptures, treating them all as mere parables or holy charades? Hardly, unless one treats them as *mere* parables. What both Laplace and Ignatius would have the retreatants seek is a deeper personal assimilation of the genuine literal and typical senses of the Scripture through whatever accommodations properly grow from these through the action of grace.[64]

For, as should now be clear, accommodation, if rightly done and without illusion as to what is taking place, is one form of personal appropriation of

[62] Liberation theology, whatever its merits, shows considerable weakness in its understanding of the Old Testament narratives as supplying types for God's people now. God Himself led His people out of slavery, not without human cooperation but wholly without human initiative or intervention. There was no question of revolt or revolution; the Israelites walked out, urged on by their oppressors because of what God had done on their behalf. All this, however it be reinterpreted and accommodated in a revolutionary way, still belongs to the literal sense. Yet its relation to Christian life must somehow be made to pass through the spiritual sense. There is, of course, an abundance of excellent material in the Old Testament, e.g., Ben Sirach (34:18–22), for making many of the points directly through the literal sense that liberation theologians desire.

[63] *Les 30 Jours*, Clamart: privately published (n.d.), *pp* 45–46.

[64] For a fuller justification of Laplace's point of view, cf. Ch. 8, A, 186–187 below.

the revelation, taking place as the Holy Spirit acts upon us through the processes of mind and imagination in prayer. All of the Bible, understood both in the literal and in the varieties of the spiritual sense, is to be thus pondered and assimilated, in accord with one's opportunities and power. But true assimilation will be the weaker, the less clearly the genuine meanings of the text are grasped.

Are Christians obliged, however, to take the *contents* of the various Old Testament accommodations of earlier parts of Scripture as the divinely revealed meanings of those parts? For example, need one take as literally true all details of the plagues on Egypt that were added by the author of *Wisdom* to the account first set forth in *Exodus*?[65] Though such details are not, of themselves, impossible as additions to our knowledge, current insights into literary genres and into Jewish modes of thought at the time enable one to treat this, I think, much as a Christian treats his meditations on the Gospel. Praying on some passage, he may often use his imagination freely and receive much light and grace of insight and love. Yet such gifts do not validate the literal truth of his imaginings, which serve only as the occasion or the vehicle of the grace received. So with *Wisdom*, though here the graces of the prayer form part of God's revelation, unlike the graces given the ordinary Christian in his prayer. But this still leaves unratified in themselves the details of the imaginative vehicle.

The human author need not be thought to have been asserting his imaginings as such, but to have been using them instrumentally to draw further truth from the truths earlier revealed. The poet's freedom in the Psalms has long been recognized; the devout Jew in the first century before Christ's coming had, I think, the same liberty in his prayer. Neither was in error because of his literary artistry.

Such scriptural accommodations, since they are given us by the literal sense of the text, also have a spiritual sense, even as the rest of the Scripture. Moreover, such accommodations are themselves realities that signify Christ and His Church, at the least in the preparative sense we shall consider shortly and, quite possibly, also in the typical sense through new connections established with Moses, as in this example, or with some other type.

What of those Christian accommodations of the Bible that are not part of the New Testament itself? These do not, evidently, give a sense of the text, either literal or spiritual, except by simple accident. Yet if one does as did the author of *Wisdom* and prays over God's word humbly and in union with the Church, the Holy Spirit, who inspired the text, can surely take the occasion of this devout reflection to suggest to someone through the light of faith[66] true and holy thoughts, especially well suited to his particular personal situation, even though these be not any part of the text's inspired sense.

Thus, accommodations may well be suitable vehicles for truth, even if they are not the true meaning of the text in question, if God chooses so to

[65] Cf. e.g., Wisd.11:12–14; 16:3, 9, 21–22; 17:3–10, 15–16; 18:17–19.

[66] *EM 4*, 418

make use of them, say to stir greater reverence for the sacredness of His words. This can hardly seem scandalous when one recalls how often grace has come to the Saints in connection with the reading of great secular, even pagan, literature. Why should not the literal sense of God's own word fit even better the general human condition, showing its power by rousing us to serve God and neighbor better in our own circumstances?

The counter-argument that God would not be true to Himself if He used falsehood as a vehicle for grace needs a distinction. The argument is correct if it means that God does not lie for any conceivable good ends, and does not approve of our lying. But accommodation is not falsifying the text but using it for its resonances with one's personal experiences. To consider an extreme case, as anyone knows well who has prayed because of some newspaper story or while watching a TV "documentary," true grace can come in spite of the fact that one's prayer was on such an occasion inspired by believing some gross lie.

A more fundamental question is this: If the Old Testament has a meaning given by God Himself, a meaning that no man can find unless, as the eunuch said to Philip, someone show us (Ac.8:31), and if there has been no public revelation since the death of the last of the Apostles, then how could there be any objectively new discovery of the spiritual sense after the death of the apostle John? Surely, since the spiritual sense must be given by divine revelation, one cannot discover this for oneself by scholarship nor reveal it to oneself.

As Dodd suggested long years ago,[67] the collections of early Christian *testimonia* very likely point back to what Jesus taught His disciples of the meaning of the Scriptures on the road to Emmaus and on Easter evening, as He opened their minds to understand how Moses and the Psalms and the prophets all spoke of Him. One may presume, however, that His teaching was not a line-by-line commentary upon the entire Bible. The *testimonia* would indicate that He set forth and illustrated in some detail the central themes, thus giving the apostles the key to understanding all the rest.

Since then, the question for the Christian has not been, "What similarities to Christ can we find in this or that Old Testament text?"; still less, "What sort of allegory can we establish through symbolic meanings?" Rather, the question has been "Given that God has made each reality of which the Bible speaks a type of Christ, and this in a way exemplified in perfection by what our Lord taught His disciples on Easter, how, then, does the reality presented in this or that text speak of Christ? What is the typical assertion it is making?"

The original revelation that was given by Jesus and His Spirit contains, then, implicitly all that is legitimately given by the spiritual sense. If God has designed a key to fit a particular lock, then, even if no man has yet turned it, it is capable of opening the door. No new key is needed; we need only utilize

[67] C. H. Dodd, *According to the Scriptures—the substructure of New Testament theology*, Digswell Place: James Nisbet (1952).

the one we have in hand.

As mentioned earlier, much of what we regard as accommodation or, at best, a confusion between the spiritual sense and accommodation on the part of those who lived before Calvin was rather the effort to carry out a duty laid upon them by the incarnational aspect of Christianity. For not only did the Word become flesh. It is a commonplace that God acted continually in Israel in Old Testament times, yet that His action was in and through men in their quite human ways of thinking and acting. So too, the Bible gives us His revelation in characteristically human documents.[68] Many today see even the great miracles of the Exodus as merely natural events used by God in His providence for the benefit of His people. In any case, we can never learn too well that the world which God has created was made in and through and for Christ and is eminently suitable for His actions for the salvation of man.

5. Some misunderstandings

a) The literal or historical sense has at times been simply identified with what the human author intended; and the spiritual sense, with what the divine author intended. Such a division is, at best, unhelpful. For, on the one hand, God intends all that is written down, including, therefore, the literal sense. On the other hand, there seems no reason to say that He cannot let the human author understand the spiritual sense of what he is putting down and there are good reasons for asserting that, on occasion, He has done so.

b) The patristic use of "literal sense" or its equivalents differs significantly from ours in one respect. As a result of bad translations of the original texts or corruptions due to errors in their transmission, even such authorities as St. Augustine thought that there need not be a "literal sense" for every part of the Bible.[69] For, quite apart from the early confusion about the status of poetic imagery, the available texts asserted contradictories or known impossibilities about our world or else things patently unworthy of God.[70] Now, with God as guarantor of the text and not merely of a revelation to the writer(s),[71] it was assumed that whatever the words express is what God intended the text to mean. But if what is expressed is patently wrong, then, if one is to avoid

[68] The problem of inerrancy that has so exercised Protestants seems to gain its intractability for them from failure to see this incarnational aspect of revelation. What constitutes error is not to be judged from the standpoint of the contemporary scholar but from the point of view of the human author and his intended audience. Only in terms of his culture and context can one ascertain, firstly, what he asserted in a given passage and, secondly, what function this assertion served. The fact that we do not yet see how some few putative errors of fact in the Bible are not such in truth is surely no grave difficulty, even for those without faith, given the endlessly many more such "errors" that have over the past couple of centuries been cleared of all taint.

[69] E.g., *de Genesi ad Litteram,* I, c 1, #1 (PL 34, 247a).

[70] Cf. de Lubac, S.J., *HE, pp* 102 & 114.

[71] I do not mean by this to take a position on the question whether God always reveals something to the hagiographer, which he then puts down in his own words. I have my doubts that God does this often except with some of His prophets, at least in any fashion that the writer would think of as a revelatory experience, a vision, or a word of the Lord. God's biblical revelation, in any case, as a matter of abiding truth, is given us through the text.

attributing error to God, one must say that this passage has no literal sense but only a spiritual one.

Yet, if one were to find in a magazine today a piece beginning, "I graduated from college in 1990, when Ronald Reagan was in the midst of his third term as president. The war against Brazil was just over...," the reader would know at once that error is the least likely explanation of the objectively incorrect statements. Rather they serve as indications, within the framework of literary forms to which we are accustomed, that, despite whatever appearances of realism may be found in this text, one is reading a piece of fiction. Indications not dissimilar to these are scattered liberally through parts of the Scriptures, e.g., *Judith* and *Tobit*.

Now, in modern usage, it is precisely the literal sense of such statements that clues us in to the "code"; their manifest and public falsity is that which identifies the piece as fictional. But since God is the totally truthful author of all that is found in Scripture, the Fathers, though using these passages as indicators of a different sort of meaning, refused to grant this the status of "what the writer intended." Stated a bit differently, they restricted "the literal sense" or "the history" to whatever the text, as it stood, could truly be asserting. But if the indicators of "mystery" appeared, precisely because of their falsity they could not be taken as any meaning of the text but only as textual signposts pointing to an otherwise hidden spiritual meaning.[72]

The great tradition, however, has been that there is a literal sense, in *our* understanding of the term, for every part of Scripture as originally written, and that it is through a knowledge of this literal sense that one comes to know the spiritual sense. Evidently, however, the problems raised by a corrupt text or by mistranslation are not resolvable, by the Fathers or by us, through any improvement of terminology for the senses of Scripture.

c) But what of unreal things spoken of by the text, though taken by the human author as real or at least presented as though they were? For, some passages of Scripture seem to be pieces of ancient mythology or folk tales or other kinds of fiction. Their content, therefore, refers to things not part of the real world that God made and governs. But the fictional tale itself is real enough. God as author of all things is its source; and He governed its use by the writer who chose it. That he chose it for some particular purpose is also real. Further, he had something to say about the realities of God and our world which this fictional account could point to or embody. Divine inpiration guarantees the truth of a borrowed text not in its original form or context but in the application the inspired writer has made of it. It is, then, whatever reality the writer is talking about through such fictitious materials that is the bearer of the spiritual sense.

d) There are a few texts of St. Thomas in which he speaks of the possibility of more than one literal sense of the biblical texts.[73] As de Lubac points out,

[72] Cf. *HE*, 101–102, for Origen, Hilary, Augustine, and Jerome. The entire chapter is pertinent to the present discussion.

[73] The chief passages in St. Thomas are *ST* I, 1, 10 c (at end) and *de Potentia* 4, 1 c. Much has

however,[74] only one of these senses corresponds to the traditional definition of the literal sense that Thomas uses in most places—only one is the sense intended by the writer. A second is is a sense previsioned by the writer as a meaning that will be given the text by some readers, a meaning which he takes into account insofar as he lets the text so read as to allow such an interpretation. But this seems little more than willed ambiguity or a play on words of the sort popular in theater since *Gammer Gurton's Needle.* Finally, there is a sense that God intends as author but of which the writer has no cognizance. Since this third sense is a sense of the text only and not, rather, of the things spoken of by the text, it is not to be taken as a spiritual sense but is, as Thomas says, a literal sense. This third sense, however, requires a personal revelation from God to the reader of the text if he is to recognize it as possessing such a sense—a matter of which Thomas says nothing.

The reason mention must be made of all this, however, lies not in the question as to multiplicity of literal senses but in the fact that in the passage from *de Potentia* St. Thomas offers a definition of the literal sense that would seem at first glance to treat every legitimate accommodation of the text as its God-given literal sense.[75] Though de Lubac recognizes that Thomas is not directly concerned here with the senses of Scripture but with harmonizing various patristic opinions concerning the creation,[76] he still takes this passage as referring to the literal sense,[77] chiefly, it would seem, because it had been tied together with *ST* I, 1, 10 c in the controversy mentioned above (note 73).

But whatever one may think of Thomas' remark in the *Summa*, it is hard to see that in *de Potentia* he is speaking of anything other than accommodations:

> For this belongs to the dignity of divine Scripture that it contain under one text many senses, so that thus it may also suit the divers understandings of men, so that each one may see that he is able to find in the divine Scripture the truth which he has conceived in [his own] mind; and through this, also that it [Scripture] may be the more easily defended against unbelievers, while, if something which one wishes to understand from holy Scripture appears to be false, recourse can be had to another sense.

One notes at once that the reference is to *many* senses, which as de Lubac points out are *alternative* understandings of a text and not the simultaneous and complexly layered senses of the traditional hermeneutic. Further, since Thomas explicitly envisions the possibility that one or more of these senses might be erroneous, these cannot be seen as meanings given by God, whether as one or other kind of literal sense, if there be more than one, or as any

---

been written about these passages, with notable disagreement among the scholars. For a summary of the various positions, cf. *EM 4*, 276–285.

[74] *EM 4*, 284–285.

[75] He seems to allude, though less clearly, to the same notion in *Quodlib.* VII, 6, 14, ad 5, *In 4 Sent.* 21, 1, 2, sol. 1, ad 3 and *In 2 Sent.* 12, 1, 2, ad 7.

[76] ibid. 283.

[77] ibid. 284

spiritual sense.

Further, those of the Fathers to whom Thomas refers were seeking information from the Bible that, at least today, would not easily be thought to be in accord with the thrust and purpose of the Scriptures, as the Church has specified these.[78] Since only rarely can we so grasp the literal sense that, apart from the teaching of the Church, we can absolutely exclude other and contradictory opinions on such, at best, peripheral matters, it is not strange that Thomas, having cited both opinions, is willing to leave the matter open.

Nonetheless, he seems to be inconsistent with himself when he says that all these senses are those of the Scripture: "Every truth that can be fitted to (*aptari*) the divine Scripture while preserving the particularities of the text is its sense."[79] Perhaps, however, he regards his use of "fitted to" here and in similar passages as sufficient to distinguish these accommodated meanings from the genuine scriptural senses.

Yet, it is probably not possible in strictness of reasoning to rule out absolutely this position that sees devout accommodations as true senses, even as the supposed third kind of literal sense, of the text. Presumably, God by His foreknowledge could have designed the text so it would have all the senses seen in it by all those who would read it in the light of His Spirit—a Thomistic doctrine that early Protestants could have made much use of. But "what is asserted gratuitously may be denied gratuitously"; and I see no slightest reason in favor of such a position or for the methodological chaos that would result. If someone should marvel that so clear and vigorous a thinker as St. Thomas should weaken on occasion, he might recall that Thomas was working in the scholastic tradition of reverence not only for the Fathers but for all their opinions. And as seen, if 'sense' be taken as 'legitimate accommodation,' then Thomas is clear of self-contradiction, whatever one may think of his understanding of accommodation as God's work.

e) Underlying some of the resistances to even a sound use of modern scriptural methods is a mistrust of wholly secular methods when these are applied to the word of God. Yet, as "the Word became flesh and dwelt among us," so the revelation of God, His word to us, was "enfleshed" in human speech and thought. No literal sense of Scripture could ever be known at all without some knowledge of its language, or understood except by grasping that which it had in common with the modes and processes of human communication in its time and place. In general, the truth needed for understanding Scripture comes to us from our mostly quite secular or even sinful experience. It is not surprising, then, that there exists an aspect of the revelation made through the literal sense which can be learned by us only through secular means. To find the literal sense of the biblical books, the very need to understand the text from a literary point of view requires that we include the results of strictly historical research.

---

[78] Cf. *p* 166 above.

[79] *de Potentia*, ibid. It is this notion of "sense of Scripture" that governs Augustine's *de Doctrina Christiana*, of which more in a moment.

Related but quite different questions arise if one asks:

i) whether that which the text can convey of truth, given sufficient background knowledge even from nonscriptural sources, is part of the literal sense; or, on the other hand,

ii) whether that which the writer expects his readers to know or discover in order to understand his text, i. e., his not necessarily conscious presuppositions, is such a part.

As an example of i), if our present knowledge makes it certain that the disease of which X died, as described by the sacred text, resulted from bacterial infection Y, is this latter fact revealed or merely conveyed to us by the text when supplemented by contemporary medical science? The example itself is trivial. But analogous cases are not infrequent in biblical archeology, history, linguistics, and the like. Consider what could occur if we were to discover an authentic copy of the Book of the Chronicles of the Kings of Judah (e.g., I Kg.14:29). What effect upon our grasp of the spiritual meaning given one or other of these kings by God would this have? Would this further information about him enable us to see more of the spiritual sense he bears? Or is the spiritual meaning so given that the revealed aspects or elements are always sufficient to exhaust the meaning?

The theological distinction called for here would seem to be the same as that between defined dogma and the rationally deduced consequences thereof. Our science may give us better insight into the physical and psychic state of X implied by the text, but neither this further insight nor our science can be said to be revealed. Even if we are correct in our deduction, what we have derived is not part of the literal sense, for the writer knew nothing at all concerning bacteria; no statement involving them could have been, as such, part of what he intended to communicate.

Yet neither would our insight be an accommodation. We would not merely be finding a new way personally to appropriate the meaning of the writer's text. We would be showing forth aspects, albeit unknown to the writer, of that reality to which his text refers. We would be but drawing forth the necessary implications of what he asserted. Truths, then, that are not part of its literal sense may yet be conveyed by the literal sense of the text."[80] We are dealing in such cases with one reality under two different descriptions, one revealed, the other humanly deduced. The latter description, since it includes nonrevealed elements, may well be erroneous, though it might also, in principle, be entirely correct.

An important question arises here: would the elements of the reality of which the text speaks under our humanly derived but presumably fuller description be able to lead us to a more complete grasp of the spiritual sense?

[80] As is easily seen from, say, Hippolytus' homilies on *Daniel,* one's deductions of what is conveyed by the text can prove faulty for a thousand reasons. A similar observation can be made about what the text asserts. What we think to know about the literal sense of a passage can dramatically change on the basis of better knowledge of language, literary forms, or archeological data.

Returning to the above example, does our putative knowledge of Y let us rightly affirm that the bacteria that infested X's body bear a spiritual sense? Any such newly perceived element in the spiritual sense, since we learn of it only through the literal sense, would be based upon the latter. Yet, since the fact of Y is not part of the literal sense, can these bacteria be rightly thought to have a meaning given them by God?

I do not think a definitive answer can as yet be given to such questions since, to my knowledge, they have not been sufficiently pondered, at least in this explicit form, within the Church. On one hand, we might argue that these bacteria would have a spiritual sense since this meaning is given by God to the *reality* of which the sacred text speaks, not by the text itself. We might, then, speculate upon a possible spiritual sense for these bacteria-in-X as long as we realize that we may be wholly in error as to the reality we think we are considering. On the other hand, we might argue that the bacteria bear no spiritual meaning since, though real enough, they are not mentioned by the text, even indirectly. Yet the text is the "window" through which alone we know those *aspects* of the real to which God has given the spiritual sense. Tentatively, I would opt for this latter position as being more in accord with the way the spiritual sense is dealt with in Christian tradition.

As to ii), there are different levels of literal meaning the writer may intend. One level of meaning lies on the surface and involves no other knowledge of literary or cultural context than is required to read the language employed. It is this level that the biblical literalist[81] will frequently take as the sole meaning. But often, as in the case of a metaphor or a parable, the assertion the writer intends to make lies at a different level. His meaning cannot be found from the text alone, but requires some grasp of its context, e.g., of the literary forms in use at the time it was composed or of then-current social structures.

Evidently, an author need not be confined to only two such levels of literal meaning. He could, e.g., propose a parable entirely in metaphor, detail it in allegory. So, also, the art of the poet is, in large measure, the art of creating in a small space a whole continuum of interacting levels of meaning. But all these levels of meaning belong to the literal sense, the meaning that the author intends; and the metaphoric or parabolic or other superficial meaning must first be understood as such before it can serve its proper function and lead one, through its interaction with the context presumed by the author, to his further and principal meaning.

For our purpose here, however, we need only note the fact that, to grasp the principal literal sense intended by a scriptural writer requires that one utilize background knowledge not given, as such, by the text. This is particularly clear in the case of metaphor. Thus, on the one hand, one cannot legitimately argue that the Bible declares God to be made of stone(s) because it declares that "God is my Rock and my Fortress" (Ps.18:2). On the other hand,

[81] This is a more accurate term than the current, usually pejorative, designation "fundamentalist," which has a more honorable meaning historically than is common now.

one grasps the principal sense of the statement, "Smoke went up from His nostrils and devouring fire from His mouth" (Ps.18:8) only by grasping the author's intent to use metaphor.[82] But to grasp such an intent cannot ordinarily be effected by simply reading the words, for these speak of God's breathing forth fire and smoke but say nothing about metaphor.[83]

In a parable, for example that of the prodigal son (Lk.15:11–32), the superficial sense can often stand on its own since it may lack the obvious incongruities that alert one to the presence of metaphor. But if one takes a parable only at this level, the very heart of its teaching, that for which it was constructed in the first place, is missed.

Now, if the judgment as to the levels of meaning expressed in the texts of poem or parable or allegory is left to the intelligence of the reader, the writer must, first of all, presuppose that his reader will have not only the intelligence but also the knowledge of cultural context that will enable him to recognize the different levels that are present. The writer must also offer the hints appropriate to his literary environment that will enable the reader to recognize the literary form and style of speech and to infer the true meaning from their common knowledge of the cultural context. Only then can we grasp what the writer intends to be saying when we have grasped his language, his cultural milieu, his personal style, and much else, knowledge of which, while he was writing, he took for granted in his reader. But is this background material itself part of the reality of which the text speaks, even if only implicitly and indirectly?

Now, the presuppositions of the writer not only select the audience he has in mind; they also carve out of the total reality with which he is dealing that portion concerning which he wishes to make some assertion. They determine those aspects of the real that constitute the domain of the literal sense—what he intends his reader to understand from what he is writing. Consider only the superficial meaning of "The lion shall eat straw like the ox" (Is.11:7). This will say little to anyone who does not have some idea of the ordinary diet of lions. Can one, then, say that God has revealed that lions usually eat only flesh? No. But if the criteria for finding the spiritual sense are otherwise met, might one be able to say that in the Antitype of the lion there

---

[82] As is evident from contemporary moral theology (cf. Paul M. Quay, S.J., "The Disvalue of Ontic Evil," *TS 46*, 262–286 [1985] at 269), some care is needed not to confound 'intention' with 'intent,' i.e., 'what one intends to be doing or effecting.' The former, as used here, is equivalent to 'aim' or 'end' or 'goal' and is not directly concerned with defining a present moment's activity.

[83] If one would wish to argue that metaphor makes its presence felt simply by its imagery's being inwardly received in the dialog between text and reader, a casual reading, say, of Joseph Smith's *Doctrines and Covenants* or *The Pearl of Great Price*, where so much of what others take as metaphor concerning the divine nature is taken by him and the Latter Day Saints who have followed him as bald, physical truth, will show that something more is needed. Yet I doubt that one reader in a hundred of Ps. 18 consciously says to himself, "This is a metaphor"; and most imagine the LORD, however vaguely, as metaphorically described. Nor should we forget that in every language metaphors range from ordinarily unconscious ones, like "I see your point," to fully developed, wholly conscious constructions of great artistry.

exists some paradox corresponding to that of this newly peaceable, carnivorous eater of straw? I would say yes. For the literal sense, what the writer intends to communicate, *contains* his expectations as integral to his thought—whether at our distance we can verify his expectations or not. As dye stains cloth, his expectations permeate what he writes so that to the extent we do not fulfil them we do not understand what he is saying. They are, therefore, bearers of the spiritual sense.

For, it was by God's free choice and decision that He revealed Himself to this particular people, Israel, at a particular time, in their particular language, under these particular circumstances, through this particular writer with his own particular attitudes, ideas, cultural background, psychic traits, virtues and sins—all the concrete things that any concrete choice of action involves. These things are all charged with meaning and significance insofar as they color the writer's understanding of his text.

Already Origen argued that not only the events recounted in Scripture need to be explained and interpreted but also the fact of the writer's recounting of them and the reasons for it.[84] Why should there be such relatively detailed accounts of the wars of Joshua and so little about David's? So much about Sampson and next to nothing about Shamgar? Are the facts about an inspired writer's activity, e.g., the time when he wrote, the place, the people among whom he lived, the class of readers he had in mind, the purposes of controversy or edification that moved him to write, are these part of what is said by the text, i.e., part of the literal sense? Unless the writer is concerned directly or indirectly to make some assertion about these matters, the answer must be negative. They are merely truths conveyed by the text. Yet to the extent that knowledge of these matters, however and whencesoever obtained, was, from the time of his writing, essential to discovering what he was intending to say—so that they formed part of his communication—to this extent such truths are part of the literal sense and, as one aspect of God's revelation, bear part of "what the Spirit says to the churches" (Rev.2:7).

In sum, not all that we may learn about the matters of which the writer speaks is part of the literal sense—hence a probably negative response to i). But the concrete context of his thought, insofar as it in some way colors his writing, is part of the literal sense—hence the affirmative response to ii).

f) A difficulty more serious historically has arisen from some remarks of St. Thomas concerning theological arguments drawn from the spiritual sense. Thomas accepts the objection that "A valid argument cannot be drawn from the spiritual sense,"[85] but denies that this arises from lack of authority on the part of the spiritual sense. Rather, the difficulty arises from the very nature of similitude, in which the spiritual sense is grounded. He then explains that, from different aspects, both Christ and the devil can be compared with a lion. Hence, if the Bible says something about a lion, one cannot proceed, without more ado, to argue that what is there said applies specifically to either Christ

[84] Cf. *HE*, 107ff

[85] *Quodlib.* VII, 6, 14 ad 4. Cf. also *ST* I, 1, 10, ad 1.

or the devil. This point is important, for it has seemingly been misunderstood to mean that, even if one already knows the spiritual sense of some particular text, one may not draw a solid theological argument or matter of faith from it.[86] Yet is it not clear from the very example St. Thomas uses here that he is treating the text allegorically in our modern sense of this term?[87]

It is worth noting how heavily these remarks of Thomas rely upon Augustine's *de Doctrina Christiana,* in which Augustine makes no effort to separate the spiritual sense, as we have been using the term, from the host of purely literary metaphors, tropes, and figures of every kind. In the passage of the *Summa Theologiae* referred to above (I, 1, 10, ad 1), Thomas leans instead on a sentence from Augustine's *Letter to Vincent.*[88] But, in context, this sentence suffers from the same Origenistic treating of all tropes and literary figures as "spiritual senses." Augustine was simply pointing out that one cannot do serious theology on the basis of mere figures of speech, as the Donatists' were doing in their claim that the "spiritual sense" of a verse in the *Song of Solomon* (1:7), referred to their North African domain. Such "spiritual senses," being nothing more, at best, than accommodations of the Scripture, cannot ground a theological argument. The sentence from Augustine, then, is irrelevant to the question whether one may base a theological argument upon the spiritual sense as we have defined it (or as did Thomas when directly addressing the matter).

6. Criteria and purpose of the spiritual sense

What criteria are there, then, for discovering what the spiritual sense of a given text may be? The first is that the putative spiritual sense fit harmoniously within the framework of the Church's doctrine, since this has been derived chiefly from the spiritual senses of the Scriptures. The spiritual sense can be found only through Christian faith, by the light of the Holy Spirit as He "recognizes" His own intent and declares it. This does not mean, however, that only a Christian can find the spiritual sense of a passage. Thus, if a text reads, "Y is the spiritual sense of X," the literal sense of this is the assertion of the existence of a particular spiritual meaning Y given by God to X.[89] This is ascertainable by one without faith, who will, of course, not believe the assertion. Since the patterns of thought of a given group of believers can be analyzed naturally (rationally) in some measure, an unbeliever can in many cases, by study of the text, come to know at least part of what a believer will see as its spiritual sense. But always, antecedently, lies the faith of someone who has received from the Spirit the light to understand. The unbeliever might even, in principle, discover a spiritual meaning unseen by all believers till that time, but only if he knows enough of what Christians hold through

[86] So, among many others, Martin Luther, (*EM 4,* 381–384); surprisingly also de Lubac (*EM 4,* 277) and Grelot (*Bible,* 201).

[87] In the parallel passage in *ST* I, 1, 10 ad 1 he speaks expressly of allegory.

[88] *Sancti Aurelii Augustini Hipponensis Episcopi Epistolae,* CSEL 34/2, ed. A Goldbacher, Epist. 93, 8 (24), *p* 470 (PL 33, 334).

[89] A clear example of this occurs in Jn.11:51–52 concerning Caiaphas' remarks in 11:49–50.

faith concerning the Scriptures and the Lord.

Secondly, since only from a sufficient understanding of the literal sense can anything further be derived, the supposed spiritual sense must be shown to be a meaning plausibly possessed by the realities spoken of by the text. An accommodated treatment of the text, however useful for other purposes, cannot, of itself, yield the spiritual sense or serve to ground it.

Further, this meaning must be "spiritual" in the way the Church has always understood this term. That is, it must relate to the work of the Holy Spirit in our world. He must be shown, in one way or another, as the Glory of the Father acting through Jesus' redeeming actions as the Anointed, and as the Glory of the Son, acting through His Church, giving that life to believers by which we are made sons in Jesus, crying out "Abba, Father." Thus, the many scientific and philosophical questions that Christians have sought answers to from the Bible are, in principle, not to be found there if they lie outside the revelation of "God Himself and the eternal decrees of His will concerning the salvation of man." Given the heavily philosophical aspects of theology when developed for controversy against rationalist forms of false teaching, one should pay close attention to the validity of one's underlying philosophy, even while searching the spiritual sense for a basis of theological argumentation.

Finally, man signifies his meaning by words, but by words taken together to form sentences and longer texts which provide a context for the understanding of the individual parts, and not, in general, by words taken singly or even by isolated sentences. So, too, God gives meaning to the people and events of which the Scripture speaks not in isolation but in a context—that context of the creation of all things in and through and for Christ of which we spoke above.[90] All that God does in our world makes for unity among the things scattered and dispersed by sin. This very unity speaks of Christ, for it is "in Him," the one Person who is God and man, that "all things hold together" (Col.1:17).

Thus, in any passage such as, say, I Kgs.13:24–28, in which St. Thomas' lion appears,[91] one is not free simply to argue "from the nature of the similarity" that one may find between a lion and Christ or, in a different way, between a lion and Satan, as if this were the basis for the spiritual sense, as Thomas seems here to be saying.[92] Neither ought one give up the effort to find the spiritual sense because of inability to find a more specific similarity. Rather, the lion must be seen as but one element in the entire incident, and this incident must be taken in the context of the entire chapter 13. Even the function of this chapter in the whole book may prove necessary. In my judgment, however, only when the spiritual sense has become once again familiar in its clearest manifestations is there much hope for dealing rightly with these details.

---

[90] *Ch* 4.F & G, *pp* 82–89 and *Ch* 5.B.3, *pp* 111–112.

[91] *Quodlib.* VII, 6, 14, ad 4.

[92] "...from the very nature of the likeness in which the spiritual sense is founded"—ibid.

At this point, a perceptive reader will be saying politely, "Well and good. Suppose that all that has been said is true. Suppose we say with St. Thomas that the Scriptures were given us that we might come to know the truths that are necessary for salvation and that all that is thus necessary has been given us through the literal sense.[93] Then we may well ask what purpose the spiritual sense serves. If it merely states in obscure or figurative language what is stated clearly and conceptually elsewhere,[94] why not skip it and go to the parts that are clear? If all of the Old Testament speaks of Christ and the Church, fine; but the New Testament does it better. If, as a long tradition has it,[95] the spiritual sense cannot be used for theological argument, why should theologians bother with it?

"Perhaps it was useful to His people in Jesus' day to see that the Bible as then constituted taught about Him, albeit in a veiled and obscure manner. But we are the beneficiaries of that teaching. Why do we have to go through the discovery process as the 1st-Century Jew did? After all this talk, has one advanced a single inch towards answering Marcion? If one has the New, what does the Old add except some vivid examples of primitive but still stirring virtue, some beautiful prayers, and some interesting materials for preachers to quarry by accommodation?"

The responses to these questions that St. Thomas drew from St. Augustine seem not very helpful: to keep the reader from boredom by rousing his attention with the bafflement of mysteries, to guard him from complacency and pride by the difficulty of grasping simultaneously both senses of the text, and to protect the mysteries of the faith from the derision and scorn of unbelievers.[96]

For, if what is obscure is always elsewhere in Scripture stated clearly, then all the mysteries are somewhere available to the scornful sceptic, made more sceptical by the cloud of incomprehensible verbiage in between. The likelihood is that he will take all at the same level and reject what is not literally comprehensible as being a clear but stupid doctrine of Christian faith. And if one may judge by the history of the Church, the protection extended by the need to puzzle out the spiritual sense seems not to have made exegetes of the spiritual sense notably more humble than the rest of men nor to have prevented the uninstructed from skewing the Scriptures to their own destruction from the beginning (2 Pet.3:16). That God should have introduced mystifications for the sake of keeping the reader interested seems hardly worthy of comment.

Thomas does add another purpose: to make invisible things manifest to such beings as ourselves, tied to what is perceptible to our senses. God wishes

---

[93] Though in *Quodlib.* VII, 6, 14 ad 3 Thomas seems to say that this is true of everything said spiritually, at a later date (*ST* I, 1, 10 ad 1) he is more cautious and applies this principle only to things "necessary to faith".

[94] *Quodlib.* VII, 6, 14 ad 3

[95] Cf. *pp* 176–177 above.

[96] *Quodlib.* VII, 6, 14 ad 2.

to instruct us through symbols and other material things suited to our weakness that can lift us to the intelligible and superintelligible.[97] Thus, the spiritual senses of the text are what most easily raise us from a carnal and this-worldly understanding of human life and salvation to a truly spiritual and God-centered understanding.

But again, the Christian who takes the New Testament seriously would seem to need nothing more to accomplish just this elevation. He can recognize his own carnal understanding in the literal sense of the Old and can see clearly enough what spiritualization of these notions Christ has demanded. But, further, could he not recognize his own carnal understanding of life and of his need of Christ to save him from evil just as well from the Greek tragedians or from the death by torture that Plato considers not wholly unlikely for any perfectly just man?[98]

Now, the early Fathers, who had directly to deal with the ravages caused by Marcion and the other "gnostics," had a very different sort of response than anything so far mentioned. It is their response that I think is valid now and always for the Church. The spiritual sense of the Old Testament is, for them, something that every Christian *must* come to understand if he is to grow well as a Christian. The key was given once and for all in the New Testament. But the opening of the door has been left to the power of the Holy Spirit, who enlightens each Christian in accord with what He has already made known to the Church in prior generations. Here, then, I wish to present in the framework of our own modes of thought and reflection what I think the Fathers understood, without their ever making a systematic presentation of what they were teaching.

---

[97] *Quodlib.* VII, 6, 15 c.

[98] *The Republic*, Bk II, 361.

Chapter 8

Fulfillment and Recapitulation

It is only from Christ that the Church learned of the existence and the nature of a spiritual sense of the Old Testament; and from His Spirit, of a spiritual sense for the New Testament as well. How, then, do the New Testament and the Church's living Tradition describe what is to be accomplished through the spiritual sense? For, what it does is presumably what it was meant to do—its purpose, therefore, or a part thereof. What use does Jesus make of the spiritual sense? What use is made of it by His apostles? By the New Testament writers? By the Fathers?[1]

A. THE MODES OF FULFILLMENT

One use stands out, not necessarily as the most important but as the primitive one, the one first employed and out of which the others grew. This is the showing that the scandal of Jesus' being the Christ of the Lord was foreseen and predicted by the Scriptures. Here it is useful to recall the point made by Cardinal Ratzinger:

> Just as the two covenants are different in kind, so too is the fact of scripture not identical in the two cases. That is very plain in the New Testament writings, which understand by "scripture" only the Old Testament. This for them is and remains "scripture," the meaning of which has, they are convinced, come

[1] This last question has been answered in abundant detail and with great theological insight by de Lubac, *HE, EM I* and Jean Daniélou, *Origène*, Paris: Table Ronde (1949) and *Sacramentum Futuri: Études sur les origines de la typologie biblique*, Paris: Beauchesne (1950). Pierre Grelot, *Bible et Théologie*, Paris: Desclée (1965); *The Bible, Word of God*, tr. P. Nickels, 2nd ed., New York: Desclée (1968) has many valuable insights concerning the matters that occupy us in this chapter. there are good summaries, e.g., in the *NJBC* and in the *Dictionary of Biblical Theology*, 2nd ed., ed. X. Léon-Dufour, New York: Seabury (1973), I shall confine myself here to the briefest overview of the most basic points, apart from those topics that are somewhat new or different from the views expressed by these authors.

> to light in the Christ-event. Consequently they do not oppose to the old scripture, or set side by side with it, a new scripture, but they place in contrast to the one single scripture, i.e., the Old Testament, the Christ-event as the spirit which explains scripture....The formula "Jesus is the Christ" in fact signifies that in the historical Jesus the Christ-message of the Old Testament is fulfilled, that who Jesus is, can be understood on the basis of the Old Testament and the meaning of the Old Testament perceived in the light of the Christ-event.[2]

Thus, every Jew who heard Him would have good grounds for believing in Him through what he already believed concerning God and His ways with His people—if, indeed, the record of God's ways was understood spiritually and not fixated in the literal sense.

Though the spiritual sense reveals much more than the relations between the New Israel and the Old, yet it is the privileged sense for manifesting these relations. Not merely are they stated through it (something also done through the literal sense of the New Testament texts); it constitutes their basic intelligibility.[3] Everything of which the Old Testament speaks signifies something not only about Jesus as the Christ and the New Dispensation but, as we will see shortly, about the inner dynamic that leads from the one to the other.

But, if we look at the New Testament itself, the basic relationship to be found between literal sense and spiritual, between Old Testament and New, between Israel and the Church, between the Law and the Spirit, between the present age and the age to come, is that which is best rendered in English as 'fulfilment.'[4] Despite the somewhat static English word, however, there is always in the New Testament an aspect implied of some process taking place through time.

Thus, God fulfils His promises to His people by accomplishing great deeds for them. He fulfils the predictions of His prophet as a guarantee for the future (I Kgs.8:24, 2 Chr.36:21 ff, Is.48:3). His word is fulfilled, which goes forth to accomplish all He has sent it for (Is.55:10–11). His Law demands obedience and is fulfilled by those who obey it. His purposes are fulfilled in their accomplishment. Israel's hopes are fulfilled as God answers the prayers He has Himself stirred up in His people. So also, laws, requests, duties, desires, and destinies are all fulfilled.[5]

Throughout, however, the notion of fulfilment extends far beyond these. It implies not merely whatever was predicted or promised or proposed or aimed at as literally stated but also its unforeseeable completion through a divine and quite unexpected fulness. This is the case even if considered entirely within the context of the Old Testament taken in its literal sense. Think only

---

[2] K. Rahner & J. Ratzinger, *Revelation and Tradition*, New York: Herder & Herder (1966), 37. Translated by W. J. O'Mara from *Offenbarung und Überlieferung*, Freiburg: Herder (1965).

[3] *EM IV*, 287: "[S]aint Thomas affirme, *avec toute l'ancienne tradition*, l'équivalence de la dualité fondamentale des sens scripturaires et de la dualité des Testaments successifs" [emphasis added].

[4] The Greek verb (πληρόω) most commonly used to express this, unlike the corresponding noun (πλήρωμα), involves in all its many senses some action that fills up, completes, accomplishes, achieves, or brings to fulness and perfection.

[5] Cf. "Fulfill" by Albert Vanhoye, in *Dictionary of Biblical Theology*, 2nd ed., ed. X. Léon-Dufour, New York: Seabury (1973). Cf. also, Arndt & Gingrich, s.v. πληρόω, τελειόω, τελέω.

of Jeremiah's bewilderment when, having just heard again and finally assented to God's definitive and implacable threat utterly to destroy Judah and Jerusalem, he is told to sign a contract for a sale of property there. For in seventy years after the destruction, Jerusalem will again be inhabited and Judah will be restored (Jer.32:6–25).

Fulfilment, then, is a completion that involves two quite distinct terms. The one term, given by the earlier, literal sense, must be completed long after by a term clearly previsioned only by God and given according to the spiritual sense. Law, Prophets, Psalms must all be somehow completed by Christ (Lk.24:44).

Perhaps the simplest of the above-mentioned notions of fulfilment is that proper to a prediction. A good many predictions were made to Israel in the Old Testament that also found their fulfilment there, e.g., Moses' predictions of the plagues that would strike Egypt. The literal sense of the text is sufficient for both the prediction and its fulfilment. Biblical scholars today tend to deny that any predictions of this sort were made in the Old Testament whose fulfilment was to be found in the New Testament.[6] For, such predictions are part of the literal sense.[7] One who predicts asserts that some event will come to pass in the future. If this assertion is given simply as such by the text, then the meaning of the words is just that the event will happen. No recourse to a spiritual sense is needed; any pagan reading the words would know that a prediction was there made, whatever he might think of its predictive value.

A prediction is fulfilled when the event occurs as predicted. This counts as fulfilment, of course, only if the one who made the prediction had genuine foreknowledge of what was to be. Mere guess or conjecture, even if proved correct in the event, does not count as prediction.

Next in order of complexity is the fulfilment of a promise. Promises too, in themselves, taken formally, are part of the literal sense; and anyone who can read can ascertain, for example, that the text asserts that God promised David royal descendents. The fulfilment of a promise would seem, of its nature, also to be ascertainable from the literal sense, though this is not as easy a matter as in the case of predictions. There is, as well, a similarity of structure between the fulfilment of a prediction and that of a promise. Thus, a promise can only be fulfilled by the deliberate action of the one who promises. The same identical thing or action, brought to be by someone who knows nothing of the promise and whose action is not indirectly arranged or at least foreseen with certainty by the promiser, cannot be a fulfilment.

This relation, then, of fulfilment is not simply a relation of likeness

[6] E.g., John L. McKenzie, *NJBC*, "Aspects of Old Testament Thought," 77:178 (at *p* 1315).

[7] I use 'predict' and its cognates rather than 'prophesy' *et al.*, since the functions of a prophet extended far beyond the making of predictions. But if taken, as is often done, so as to include reference of type to Antitype, then, evidently, 'prediction' would belong to the spiritual sense. The real question here is whether prefiguration of Christ is a predicting of Him. I prefer not to use words in this way. A text so written that no human being can know without a further revelation that it contains a prediction until after the predicted event has occurred, and occurred not according to the literal sense of the prediction but spiritually, such a text is not the ordinary meaning of 'prediction'; and we have other, better words for the same idea.

between two events separated in time. One who promises does not, it is true, fulfil his promise unless there is a likeness between what is signified by the words of his promise and what he actually effects. Yet to fulfil his promise, he must initiate some process, however hidden, that will bring into being that which he intended and promised.

There is also an interior aspect that goes well beyond what is required for prediction. One who always fulfils his promises is, generally, doing more than merely "keeping his promise." The former implies that this keeping is rooted in love or affection or other personal interest in the one to whom the promise was made. Such a man is 'faithful'; and 'promise' is an essential ingredient in the notion of fidelity.

All the promises of God to man will certainly be fulfilled in accord with the divine fidelity. It is, indeed, hard not to come to regard the whole of the Old Testament as a graphic account of God's explicit and implicit promises in concrete situations to His people, promises all somehow fulfilled in Christ. Since promises relate intrinsically to the future, therefore, a divine promise involves an element of "prophecy" in our modern sense. The fulfilment of His promises includes all that was promised, though not necessarily in the way the promises were understood by the men to whom they were made, for other kinds of fulfilment may also be at work.[8]

There are, however, also implicit promises. For example, those statements asserting God's faithfulness to His people or to all those who will call on His name set up a relationship within which all the current realities take on or are given meaning for the future. In a closely related way, one can see that God's promises are not only and solely verbal declarations, or even symbolic acts; things themselves constitute promises since existing only by God's action or permission. Thus, as developed by the Council of Orange,[9] Catholicism has always seen the presence of a holy desire within us as not only the work of the Holy Spirit but as His promise that, if we respond as His grace thereby invites us to do, He will grant us a fulfilment, not always in the shape we expected but greater and of the same substance.

One may also see the Old Testament as the working out concretely of God's plan of salvation for His people.[10] 'Fulfilment,' from this point of view, is the fulfilment of God's plan, that "mystery kept hidden from ages and generations but now revealed to His saints" (Col.1:26; also: Eph. 3:5, 9; Rom.16:25–26). The ultimate fulfilment, of course, is achieved only in the age to come, when Jesus has returned in His glory and has judged the living and the dead. But the outpouring of the Holy Spirit is nonetheless a true

---

[8] Though the two notions of prediction and of promise have at times been confused with one another in the history of biblical interpretation, yet 'promise' is a far better term for describing God's relations with His people in the Old Testament than is 'prediction'. (Cf., McKenzie, *NJBC*, 77:178; Vanhoye, n. 5 above). Since the two categories are not commonly confused in daily life, the problem in the scriptural context may lie elsewhere: in thinking of the typical sense as a sort of prediction which finds its fulfilment in Christ. But, at the very least, one says much more about Him when declaring Him to be the fulfilment of all God's promises to Israel.

[9] Cf. DS 376 and 397 especially.

[10] Cf. Pierre Grelot, *Dict. Bibl. Theol.*, art. "Figure," *p* 81.

fulfilment, even if partial, of all that had prepared Israel for Jesus' first coming.

All God's actions in the history of His Chosen People gain their meaning from their relation to His plan. Perfect in all His ways, He does all that He does in conformity with His plan. He governs all things in accord with His providence, His foreseeing of all that happens. When this providence is focussed upon Israel, His governance becomes His saving action in Israel's history in accordance with His plan.[11]

These approaches in terms of God's promises or plan are surely right. They emphasize centrally important aspects of fulfilment that are found throughout the Bible. Yet, they would seem to leave the Marcionite problem just where it was. Since the literal sense of the New Testament shows us the fulfilment of the promises and tells us not only of the carrying out of God's plan through our Lord and the early Church but of what is still to come, these approaches, of themselves, do not yet justify the Christian retention of the Old Testament.[12]

So, too, the Old Testament often gives both the promises and the details of the working out of the plan and then, as the Tradition continues, sees into these more deeply, modifies them, spiritualizes them in many ways—but all this is given by the literal sense. It is not quite clear, then, why the plan and the promise could not find their fulfilment in Jesus quite apart from any supposed spiritual sense.[13] But then, again, once this has been done, what further need, save for historians, is there for the obscure details of the process?

Prediction, promise, plan, allegory—though all present in the Bible and all needed for correct interpretation—are not enough, since they lack, of themselves, a genuinely spiritual sense. God may indeed fulfil them through Christ in ways exceeding the understanding of the writers. But they are given, as such, only by the literal sense. If more is required to discover them than a correct understanding of the literal sense, then some element of typology is also present in the text. The categories of prediction, prophecy, promise, plan, and even, in large measure, type and fulfilment were, moreover, general in the ancient Near East and not, *as literary forms*, distinctive of Christianity.[14] Christians made them distinctive by using them to show the relations of the Old Testament to Jesus, both when He came in weakness and when He comes again in glory.

Let us turn, then, directly to the spiritual sense. The first of its classical subdivisions, the most basic and the most controverted, is the restricted typical sense. The moral sense flows at once, without possibility of sharp

---

[11] Obviously, the divine plan is not to be caricatured, as so many have done (some genuinely puzzled, others in order to be rid of its implications for their lives) as a sort of heavenly blueprint in which all things are predetermined and without meaningful freedom on the part of the creature. Cf. what is said on this in *Ch* 13.A, *pp* 261–263 below.

[12] Even Grelot, who uses them with careful attention to important and usually overlooked distinctions and nuances, seems not to advert to this difficulty; Cf. *Bible et Théologie*, pp 14–15.

[13] Though not asserted by Lohfink in the article cited above (*p* 164, note 57), his approach would seem to raise this as a legitimate possibility.

[14] Cf., e.g., *Bible, Word of God*, 186–190, 193, 196–198.

distinction, I shall argue, from this typical sense. The anagogical sense follows from these but, as the one furthest from the general run of human experience, is perhaps the least developed.

We take as given, then, that the persons and events of the Old Testament, as a whole and in all its parts, are so many types of Christ, in Himself personally and in all His saving works, hence, of His Church as a whole and all its members. Our question is: what is the mode of fulfilment that generates this typical relationship? That all things should be seen to refer somehow to Christ is not enough, since this is true of every mode of fulfilment. What needs explanation is the nature of the fulfilment that leads from type to Antitype. How is this fulfilment a *process* that results from some sort of dynamics on the created level?

Nor is it enough that there exist a similarity between type and Antitype, even if so extensive as to seem like allegory. One might say that David is a type of Jesus because, among other reasons, God chose to make David show forth in his own character and manner of action a personality similar to Jesus'. By his combination of strength with great charm, by the harmonious mixing of such seemingly disparate traits as his fear of the Lord, his refusal to take vengeance yet entrusting the task to Solomon, his powers of friendship, and his acute sense of justice in the leadership of men, there is much that reminds one of Jesus. Thus, when the Christ came among us, God was able to say, "All that was good and true in David as king (and in Moses and Joshua and all the great men of God in the Old Testament) is to be found, in its perfection, unmixed with sin, balanced and harmonious, in Jesus."

The equivalent to this has indeed been said, according to the literal sense, in *Colossians, Ephesians,* and *Hebrews,* and elsewhere in the New Testament. But the chief purpose and principal goal of the Old Testament must lie elsewhere. For, evidently, God could also say, "All that one sees of good and true in Aeschylus and Plato, in Gautama and in Confucius, even in Hector and Rustum, in all the heroes, real or imaginary, of every place and culture, is thus to be found in Jesus."

Now, Marcion's challenge arises in just this context, in which the typical sense is seen exclusively as prefigurative of Jesus' perfection and thus, once fulfilled, superfluous. Hence, if one is to answer Marcion, type and Antitype cannot be merely a pair of similar patterns or structures of things and events, one "carnal", the other "spiritual"; one visible, the other invisible; all separated by a gap of centuries. More is needed, and must come from the processes that link the two patterns. The imprint of a die on wax is similar to the die. But more importantly, the imprint is caused by the die. The type is caused by Christ. How?

A first and fairly common explanation reflects upon one particular kind of planning, common enough among men. One arranges things in such a way that some other person P sees or lives through a certain prearranged process. Afterwards, one may show P how that process is similar in its essential structure to something quite different in P's own life. If this latter be a serious problem for P, then the perception of this similarity can help P to objectify and resolve it. In most cases, it shows P to himself in unexpected fashion. Recall the play in *Hamlet* that caught the conscience of the king. And had Nathan hired some actors, he could have done by 'things' and actions what he did by words in telling his parable to David.[15]

Now, players act in response to lines and actions prescribed for them, with real enough emotions at times, but these also evoked by something external to the reality of the player. But God's governance acts from within each person and event, directing them by His continual and infinitely concrete and particular providence. He has directed all the realities of the world from its beginning, so that we have in the history of His first-chosen people a perennial "parable," to jar us and stir us and rouse us to love Him better by serving Him more carefully.[16] This too, however, takes place largely from a careful reading of the Old Testament in its literal sense (along with the New Testament in the same sense) and the additional meaning this "parable" has for us personally seems to be but a form of accommodation.

Yet this example does take us closer to our goal. What kind of drama has God sketched in the text of this parable that is the Old Testament? Does the drama indicate, somehow, a real and causative connection between Joshua, say, and Jesus his namesake?

There must be something in the nature of the fulfilment that we are seeking that corresponds to the traditional understanding of it as the elevating of some "carnal" being or action to its final, "spiritual" form, a form intended by the Holy Spirit, however, not the result of some human notion of spiritualization. This spiritual form does not do away with the carnal, but gives this its definitive meaning through its relation to Him towards whom it is intended by God to grow. So conceived, the spiritual sense no more downgrades or does away with the literal and historical than the spirit of man does away with his body or downgrades it by making it live and grow.

The "spiritual" in this context refers to what is to be found in Jesus, the One Anointed with the Spirit, and the "carnal" refers to man as he is, even when just and righteous, antecedent to the outpouring of the Spirit that Jesus has won for us. The spiritual is the domain of faith in Jesus as the Christ; the carnal, of even the most elevated religion that does not know Him as such, whether by ignorance or, *a fortiori*, by refusing its assent to Him. Thus, the Old Testament is spiritual because suffused with the light of Christ's coming but carnal in its literal sense, which though giving God's holy Law and words yet did not give man the power to live these things in the Spirit.

---

[15] It is this fact that shows why parables are not merely symbolic tales. They present, most often in a narrative form that could be acted out dramatically, those structures of thought and action that are hard for individuals or groups to face without the anonymity and transformation of scene and personage effected by the parable. One of their essential functions is to show a meaning in a situation that has escaped notice or been suppressed or avoided.

[16] Cf. *p* 166 above on the Bible as parable. Clearly, Laplace's treatment of the Old Testament as a parable not only need not be discarded but is of abiding value.

B. Jesus as Antitype: the Old Testament as a Christian book

If all that the Christian had were the New Testament, he would have enough for Christian faith and life. If the Old Testament is yet needed, then something else must be necessary for the Christian and yet not "necessary for salvation." This is not quite as contradictory as it seems or, if a paradox, then one of a kind familiar to both Jews and Christians. For the Jew considers that all that is needed for his right service and adoration of the Lord is given by the Hebrew Scriptures (interpreted by the Talmud), yet still knows well that more is needed, namely that he live accordingly, something God has left to his freedom. So, for the Christian. We have, through Christ and the Church, all we need for salvation. Yet, to be saved, we must live accordingly.

This suggests that, for the Christian to live the life that the New Testament opens out to him, the Old Testament, spiritually understood, provides a necessary predisposition, a sort of psychic and spiritual substrate for the activities proper to Christian faith, hope, and charity. Or, referring back to Part I, we may say that the spiritual sense of the Old Testament enables one gradually to overcome, both before and after baptism, the psychic damage done by original sin. If the Spirit is to carry him far in the love and service of Christ, perhaps it is the Old Testament that teaches him how to ready his boat and how first to unfurl his sails to this Wind. Or, to speak more scripturally, God first brought the dry bones together and covered them with flesh and skin before He had Ezechiel call upon the Spirit to give them the breath of life (Ez.37:1–14).

I shall argue here that the spiritual sense of the Old Testament, when actually lived through, not merely read or understood intellectually, readies one not only to believe in Christ and the teaching of His Church but to live in Him, with His life, to enter with Him into His suffering and death, to rise in Him to newness of life and, so, be prepared for the full activity of the Spirit of Christ. Conceived in sin, we need to labor to undo sin's wounds in us, not by a direct assault on our aberrant psyches in the modern manner, but by learning as did Israel the goodness of the Lord who loves us. Each Christian is to be, as were the first disciples of Jesus, a well-formed Jew—in Jesus, however, and not in the manner of those who lived from Jacob to Jesus—before he can live fully as a Christian.

1. The preparative sense

The faith of the Church is that Jesus is the cause, though we have yet to see how, of all the types present in Israel. He is *Ἀρχή* and *Τέλος*, Beginning and Source as well as End and Goal. How, then, is He the Image whose shadow is cast in front of Him before He steps into this world? He is the die that formed, in the soft matter of our human nature, those imprints that were His types. They were types because they were made to manifest in advance some aspect of His being. They were fulfilled by Him because already sharing in some way His own nature and action.

Genuine and important as is this prefigurative sense, there is, for the Christian, another aspect of the typical sense, even more strongly set forth by

Irenaeus and the early Fathers. This is one that manifests the *preparative* functions of the Scripture, showing how God prepared His people so that they might be ready for His coming among them. Just how this preparative aspect of the spiritual sense fits in with the traditional three we shall see shortly.[17]

St. Paul explains, in the dense and not totally linear argumentation of the *Letter to the Galatians*, that the Old Law was God's gift to Israel, still a child, to train him up as a son and heir.[18] Such training under the cold eye of the Law's severity, though seeming a slavery—a word Paul does not hesitate to use often of it—was yet established by the Father so that Israel might, once grown, be worthy of adoption as son and heir, coheir with Christ, since made son in Him who is Himself the Son.[19]

His people reached their majority and the pedagogue was sent to other work when, on the one hand, the Son came as one of them, the Seed promised to Abraham and now fulfilling God's promise to him, and when, on the other hand, Israel had at length become "a people well prepared" {Lk.1:17}.

This preparative sense offers at least a partial answer to the question: what is the dynamism that leads in time from the types to the Antitype? Under God's active governance, Israel was prepared for Jesus as the Messiah by their psycho-cultural maturation and spiritual growth as a people. The dynamic link is this process of preparation—both as set before us in the texts of the Bible and also as it occurred in the actual events and people there described.

There are some who would argue, along with Calvin,[20] that this preparation is described by and was in large part brought about through the literal sense, since it is visible to anyone reading the Old Testament. The Fathers knew better. Such a view can only be based on a faith that Jesus is the Christ—and this requires the typical sense. Jews in the days of the Fathers, as today, read essentially the same texts, perhaps found in them some account of a preparation of the people for a Messiah yet to come, but emphatically denied that the text in any way speaks literally of Jesus. One cannot speak of a process as a preparation except in terms of that for which it prepares. The Fathers did not disagree; rather, they insisted that the fault of Jews who refused to believe in Jesus was that they understood the Scriptures correctly enough but only according to the literal sense, and refused the invitation to read them according to their spiritual sense.[21]

Modern, scholarly studies of the Old Testament by faithful Christians have confirmed this. Thus, it has been shown increasingly that Israel did have

---

[17] The existence of a problem here is indicated by Grelot in his treatment of the preparative sense: "The Old Testament is not only a prefiguration of Christ but a historical preparation and an instruction as well; these two aspects of the question are not included in the Thomistic definition of the spiritual sense" (*Bible, Word of God,* 240).

[18] Gal. 3:23–4:7.

[19] As St. Irenaeus was to express it, "He who was the Son of God became the Son of Man, that man...might become the son of God." *Adv. Haer.* III, 19, 1; cf. also III,10,2.

[20] Cf. note 13 and text (*p* 185) above; also: *Institutes of the Christian Religion,* e.g., Bk II, 11.2 & 8.7.

[21] *EM IV*, 289, 409.

a belief in a life after death—but one that had practically nothing to do with the Christian understanding of heaven (or of hell) till, at the earliest, a century or so before Jesus. So, too, Israel's messianic hopes developed in directions that, without typology, cannot easily be seen as converging on Jesus.

The vicissitudes of Israel's religious and cultural history before Jesus' coming can be read without going beyond the literal sense. Under God's active providence and governance, certain processes of human growth and decline took place. These processes are evaluated in the texts through the way they are conceived by the first writers and then used by later writers. Throughout, God's providence over His people is stated so baldly as to be a perpetual stumbling block to those philosophers wishing to distinguish more sharply between primary and secondary causality.

These processes formed the particular and highly distinctive socio-religious culture and people into which Jesus was born. Without anything further than the Old Testament's literal sense and the contributions of secular history, we can know much about the influences that contributed to the formation of Jesus' personality and the framework within which His character developed. Thus, the literal sense of the Scripture tells us not how Israel was prepared for Jesus but how Israel prepared Him for what He did on earth.

All those centuries of activity become preparation only when the scriptural account is read spiritually, as showing how what is recounted readied the people and the individual for the Messiah. When so read, and because Jesus read it so, the Bible sets out Jesus' spiritual preparation for His work as well. As typical preparation, the changes in Israelite culture, especially in religious matters, took place precisely so that they could form Jesus rightly as man. It was this religion, this culture, this Scripture that formed Jesus as perfect man before the Father. Man only exists in the concrete, albeit essentially incomplete, individual. Jesus was no exception. Like us in all but sin, He lived in time and place, finite in body and in mind, shaped by His surroundings and the conditions of His people, taught to pray and to love and to serve God by the Law and the Psalms and the Prophets, taken literally indeed but also in accord with what they had to say of Him.[22]

The sequence of righteous psychic (and cultural) traits of Israel are all, then, types that bespeak the sequence of stages of Jesus' growth. Hence, according to the spiritual sense, all these are simultaneously: **a**) stages in God's preparing of Israel for Jesus as the Messiah; **b**) stages in the pattern of development of Jesus as a Jew and as the Messiah who summed up in Himself all that was good in Israel before Him.

Because Jesus, as the Messiah, is the fulfilment of all that was good in Jacob and Moses and Joshua and David and all Israel, great and small, He is the perfect Jew.[23] 'Fulfilment,' then, speaking most generally, is the process by

---

[22] At this point I am not assuming anything as to when or how this spiritual understanding of the Scriptures became His.

[23] What we noted as an objection (*p* 186 above), that He is, in somewhat similar though less immediate fashion, the fulfilment of the excellences of the great men of all peoples indicates that He

which everything of which the Old Testament speaks signifies something about Jesus as the Christ. But, correlative to this, is His containing in Himself all that came before Him and, indeed, all that was to come after Him. By this superabundant (since not even thus exhausted) fulness of being, He sums up in Himself not only the whole history of Israel but of all created being and becoming.[24]

2. *Recapitulation by Christ*

This summing up in Himself of all that He fulfilled became a central theme in the early Church's teaching against Marcion and other "gnostics." Let us turn, then, to the teaching of St. Irenaeus, who led this struggle. Above all others, he saw how this summing up of all things in Jesus, correlative to their fulfilment through Him, is that by which Jesus brings it about that all the people, all the events, all the actual writing down of the Old Testament, should be types of Himself.

This giving of meaning to the people and events mentioned in Scripture, this making of types that He would fulfil as Antitype, is the process for which St. Irenaeus used the word 'recapitulation.' Central to his thought, 'recapitulation' is for him a technical term, used often but not loosely. He takes the word from the *Letter to the Ephesians,* where St. Paul speaks of God's plan "to recapitulate *(ἀνακεφαλαιώσασθαι)* all things in Christ, things in heaven and things on earth" (1:10).

The details of Irenaeus' understanding of the term[25] and the accord or lack of accord with its scriptural sense have long been argued by scholars; I shall attempt no settlement. But Irenaeus comes as close to a definition of its fundamental meaning for him as he ever does in the following:

> There is, then, one God, the Father,...and there is one Christ Jesus our Lord, who came throughout the entire dispensation and who recapitulated in Himself all things. Among these "all things" is also man, the moulded figure of God. So, He has recapitulated man also in Himself, the Invisible become visible, the Incomprehensible, comprehensible, the Impassible, capable of suffering, the Word, man, recapitulating all things in Himself so that, just as the Word of God has the primacy among supercelestial and spiritual and invisible beings, so also He should be first among visible and corporeal beings and,

---

is also the perfect Man.

[24] Thus the New Testament indicates (through the literal sense, say, of I Cor.15 and Heb.11) that there is indeed a process that leads from Adam to Jesus. But far stronger are the assertions of Christ's causative powers in Col.1:15–16.

[25] This usage was not original with Irenaeus. Thus, he quotes St. Justin Martyr, who died for the faith when Irenaeus was a boy, as saying that, when Christ came, his whole work of redemption was "His recapitulation of His own handiwork in Himself" ("suum plasma in semetipso recapitulans," *Adv. Haer.* IV, 6. 2). From the context it is clear that Justin is asserting that Christ took into Himself everything that man is. There is nothing in us that was created and formed by God that was not to be found in Christ. The precise meaning of the phrase in *Ephesians* is subject to some discussion. 'Recapitulation' in the sense of an orator's summing up of his argument at the end of his speech is, perhaps, the most likely. But that sense, as highly figurative metaphor, cries out for further interpretation. What does it mean for Christ, as God's Word, to sum up or to pull together in brief compass the whole argument of the universe?

> taking into Himself this primacy and also giving Himself as head to the Church, He might draw all things to Himself at a suitable season. For there exists nothing disordered or untimely with Him, even as there is nothing unfitting with the Father. All things are known in advance by the Father and accomplished by the Son.[26]

Whatever, then, the nature of this process, it extends well beyond the history of man to include the entire creation.

But since Irenaeus is primarily concerned with man's salvation, 'recapitulation' often shows only part of its meaning, but this in greater detail than the above passage indicates. Thus, it implies the redoing by Christ of actions first performed by Adam (or Moses, say, or David). What Adam (or Moses or David) did wrongly or sinfully, Jesus did rightly and virtuously. What Adam (or other types) did imperfectly or stumblingly, Jesus did perfectly and, in all senses of the word, gracefully. In these contexts, the basic notion is that of going over the same ground again but with opposite outcome, of passing through the same mysteries, the same stages and structure of growth, but doing so perfectly, first correcting what was wrong so that the action could then be done as God had always desired that it be done by man. Hence, there was ever a new start, a new beginning for the entire race (or for a new Holy People or for a new kingdom of God). Hence, all that was accomplished as a result of this new beginning could be collected in the New Adam (or New Moses, or New David) and under Him, to be offered to the Father in perfect unity.[27]

Every mystery in the life of Christ represents such a fulfilment of earlier signification. Thus, Christ was born of a virgin. Why? Because God formed Adam in similar fashion (but in earthly fashion, not in the Spirit):

> From this earth, then, while it was still virgin [for it had been touched neither by rain nor plow], God took dust...and formed man.... The Lord [Jesus] recapitulated, then, this man in Himself and took up this same dispensation of corporeity as he, being born from the virgin by the will and wisdom of God.[28]

The same reasoning applies to Jesus' fast in the desert: "The corruption of man, therefore, which occurred in paradise by...eating [the fruit of the tree of the knowledge of good and evil] was done away with by [the Lord's] want of food in this world." First He fasts in order to do away with the sin of Adam, who ate what he should not have eaten, and then He eats when ministered to by angels after His temptations, in order to lead us to an angelic mode of eating and living.[29]

---

[26] *Adv. Haer.*, III, 16, 6–7

[27] For some details of this summation, cf. Lawson, op. cit., *Ch* 11 and passim.

[28] St. Irenaeus, *Demonstratio Apostolicae Praedicationis*, #32. (Cf. the more detailed presentation of the same argument in *Adv. Haer.*, III, 21, 10 or the brief reference in III, 18, 7). Irenaeus was using this against the Gnostics, who maintained, even as their followers today, that Jesus was the natural son of Joseph. What is of interest here is that this defense of the Virgin Birth hinges on the argument that, if Christ had not been born of a virgin, then the whole doctrine of recapitulation would be damaged. That alone, he judges, is sufficient refutation; nothing more need be said on that point.

[29] *Adv. Haer.*, V, 21, 2.

Jesus, then, recapitulates in Himself the whole of human history, to rectify it and validate it.

> But when He became flesh and was made man, He recapitulated the long history of men in Himself, granting us salvation in brief compass, so that what we had lost in Adam, i.e., to be, according to the image and likeness of God, this we might recover in Christ Jesus.[30]

A fortiori, then, the whole of the Old Testament, without exception and in the strongest sense, serves as type of Christ.[31] The entire moral growth of Israel from the time of Jacob onwards (indeed, of mankind from the time of Adam on) serves as type and prefiguration for Jesus' moral and spiritual growth during His life on earth (Lk.2:40 & 52).[32]

The life of Israel is type of the life of Jesus. It is precisely in this sense that He fulfils the Law and the Prophets. Not only does He keep the Law in its literal sense perfectly—none can take up His challenge, "Which of you convicts Me of sin?" (Jn.8:46). He also fulfils it spiritually. Nor is this fulfilment merely the taking to completion of the Old Testament's process of spiritualization, such as, e.g., Jeremiah's deeper understanding of what the worship of the Lord in His Temple called for in the worshipper (Jer.7)—though such completion is included.[33]

Rather, Jesus deepens the requirements of the Law and, to human eyes, makes it impossibly more difficult to keep because so much purer, so radical, requiring the cleansing and the redirecting of the very center of the heart. Yet He shows that it is all to be found within the Great Commandment, the Shema, which Israel had been reciting for more than 600 years, and the "one like it." Charity and love for God and for all men for His sake sums up the whole of the Law. Contradicting in nothing the Ten Commandments, He fulfils these by living the Beatitudes. More, He Himself exemplifies the perfection of the new Law, showing by His life and by His death, suffered out of love for those who hated Him and had Him killed, what love truly is.

After His resurrection, He declared, "All things written in the Law of Moses and in the Prophets and in the Psalms concerning Me, must be fulfilled" {Lk.24:44}. This has sometimes been taken simply as asserting that the Law and the Prophets and the Psalms made predictions concerning Jesus, fulfilled only by His death, resurrection, enthronement, and sending of the Holy Spirit. Yet, if 'fulfil' be taken in the same sense as in His Sermon on the Mount, "I have come not to abolish them [the Law and the prophets] but to fulfil them" (Mt.5:17), then any element of prediction must be, at most, secondary. Abolition is not an alternative to fulfilment for predictions.

---

[30] *Adv. Haer.*, III, 18, 1. The significance of this "in brief compass" ("in compendio") will appear shortly.

[31] Cf. Sancti Hilarii Pictaviensis, *Tractatus Mysteriorum*, in: Hilaire de Poitiers, *Traité des mystères*, SC 19, ed. J-P. Brisson, Paris: Éditions du Cerf (1947), Bk 1.1, *p* 72.

[32] Evidently, the elements of sin manifested throughout the Old Testament in God's people are rectified in Jesus' recapitulation; but they are found, all too literally, in the lives of those who are His members. Cf. below, *Ch.* 13.

[33] Cf. *pp* 190–191 above.

But He fulfilled the Law and the Prophets primarily according to the preparative sense: He recapitulated all the stages of Israel's growth under the Law. The Law was pedagogue for Israel because it was established by the Father for Jesus' living of it, as the New Israel, in order to bring the Old Israel to perfection in Himself.

The whole Old Testament, then, is type of Jesus' growth as man, up through His dying on the cross. By His rising, He makes possible our life in Him, by which we, in turn, recapitulate the Old Testament in Him, as He did it. For He recapitulated each God-intended stage of individual human life so that each person may live that stage in Him.

3. Recapitulation in Christ

The moral growth of the members of Christ, then, both individually and also collectively, results from an interior participation in Jesus' moral and spiritual growth. Irenaeus again states this simply and beautifully: Christ's light, as He came in our flesh, "hallowed our birth."[34]

> For in what manner could we participate in His [God's] adoption of sons unless we had received from Him through the Son communion with Him and unless His Word had entered into communion with us, becoming flesh? Wherefore, He passed through every age of life, thereby restoring communion with God to all [men].[35]

In an earlier passage, he has already spelled out the details of this process:

> For [Christ] came to save all by means of Himself, all, I say, who through Him are reborn unto God, infants, children, adolescents, men, and old men. He therefore passed through every age, becoming an infant for infants, thus sanctifying infants, a child for children, thus sanctifying those who are of this age, and at the same time giving them an example of piety, justice, and of due subjection to their parents. So, among men, a man, becoming a pattern to men and sanctifying them in the Lord. Likewise, He was an old man, for the old, that He might be a perfect teacher for all not only according to the manifestation of the truth but also according to age, sanctifying the old and at the same time becoming also an example to them. And then at last He came even to death itself in order that He might be the firstborn from the dead,...and the prince of life, the first of all and preceding all.[36]

If, then, we live with His life, we live with the life He actually lived, not just with the powers of His life, but in the way He actualized them.[37] Each

---

[34] *Demonstratio*, #38.

[35] *Adv. Haer.* III, 18, 7. These passages from Irenaeus, though in harmony with and suggestive of a "moral and spiritual growth" in Jesus, cannot be taken as an argument in favor of such interior growth in Him. I will discuss this latter growth in *Ch* 12,A, *pp* 244–253.

[36] *Adv. Haer.* II, 22, 4. Irenaeus speaks of Christ as an old man (*senex,* one who, according to Roman law, had reached the age of forty). He argued that our Lord lived past forty on the basis of his understanding of St. John's Gospel and of the traditions he had received from St. Polycarp the disciple of St. John, but chiefly, it seems, because he was convinced that Jesus had to live through everything that man lives through, a sound doctrine but taken with a literalism that would cause him no small difficulty if insisted on in our day of octogenarians and nonagenarians.

[37] In terms of later theology, the grace of Christ bears the stamp or form of the mysteries of

individual Christian is called to relive, in Jesus, Jesus' pattern of moral and spiritual development. Because this is done in Jesus, it is the Old Testament itself each must relive, though he can only do this rightly through the New. Living the Old Covenant as Jesus did—recapitulating it in Him—the Christian finds the Old Testament a sort of map of the spiritual terrain through which he must pass on his way to spiritual maturity. It is thus that we are to make our own the word of Irenaeus: Christ came "that there should be that which was written in the beginning: man after the image and likeness of God."[38]

Thus, the moral and spiritual development of Israel serves as type for the earlier part of the life of the Christian—earlier, since God wishes that he, like Israel, be prepared for an outpouring of the Holy Spirit, who blows whither He will. The New Testament is a sure guide thereafter according to its literal sense, but serves as type only for the life of heaven.[39]

It is worth taking a moment to point out explicitly that, through this understanding of St. Irenaeus, we have found two modes of the typical sense. One of these is well known as such, directed to enlightening us doctrinally concerning Christ and His Church, through the human and earthly analogs that we find easier to understand; it is this that is called the prefigurative sense. The preparative sense, however, is also truly typical, indeed it is also doctrinal and, as we shall see, says much about Christ and the Church. In this way, one may preserve the idea that the spiritual sense is always typical, even in the "restricted" notion of this term.[40]

The error has been to restrict type and Antitype to the restricted typical sense and not to see that this latter is but a restriction according to the focus of one's interest. Typology as a whole is not divided, in itself, into three senses. Rather, certain doctrinal aspects are of greater interest and utility in one type of theological utilization; others, in some other. But in all these "senses," we are given by the Scriptures realities that signify others which God wishes us to understand more deeply; hence, all are doctrinal, whenever we choose to advert to the fact and make use of it.

The various ideas we have been sketching were pulled together by Irenaeus in a striking passage:

> For, since the prophets themselves were members of Christ, each one of them, from that aspect in which he was a member, manifested himself as prophet, all and many preforming One and announcing the actions of One. For, just as through our members the activity of the entire body is shown, yet the figure of the entire man is not shown through one member but through all, so also all the prophets indeed prefigured but One; each of them, however, insofar as he was a member, to this extent also he fulfilled the dispensation and prophesied

the earthly life of Christ. Primary, of course, among these are the mysteries of His death and resurrection. But in no way are these the only mysteries involved. Cf. *pp* 202–204 below.

[38] *Adv. Haer.*, V, 16, 2.

[39] The Church's tradition sees in the life of infused contemplation, whether lived in action in the world or in the cloister, a sharing in advance in the life of heaven and, thus, typified by the New Testament. But since no life in this present age is even a remote substitute for heaven, the typology involved requires more careful treatment than this summary can give it here.

[40] Cf. *p* 159 above.

that activity of Christ which accorded with his nature as a member.[41]

This raises an obvious question: If the prophets of the Old Covenant were members of Christ in this strong sense, what do the Christians of the New Covenant have that is truly new? What more has Christ given us than He gave them? For, it would seem that what Irenaeus said of the prophets is functionally the same as what St. Paul told his Corinthian Christians: to represent Christ to the world through their living worthily as his members and thereby to make Him manifest and attractive to all. What difference has His presence made for us?[42] Though it calls for some explanation, the difference is enormous.

4. The gift of the Holy Spirit

Our life in Christ takes place through the infusion of His grace, an intrinsic change of the being of the Christian (and, without his explicit knowledge, of the Old Testament prophet). It is a sharing not only in Christ's life as man but, through this, in His life as God. Hence, Irenaeus and the Greek Fathers generally speak of it as the divinization of the Christian. For example, Irenaeus remarks: "The Word, which was as yet invisible, after whose image man was created, later...both revealed the image...and reestablished the likeness [in man] in a sure manner by assimilating man to the invisible Father by means of the visible Word."[43] The Christian is called to become as God, by being conformed to the image and likeness of the visible Word (Rom.8:29), who is the perfect Image of the Father; thus, ultimately, to become like the invisible Father.

Let St. Thomas express the same doctrine for the West. "The gift of grace is nothing other than a certain participation of the divine nature. Thus, it is necessarily the case that only God can deify, by communicating a having in common the goods of the divine nature."[44] Shortly after, he says: "In the very Person of Christ, the humanity causes our salvation through grace, by the divine power operating as principal agent."[45]

Thomas, however, seems never to advert to the need of the Christian to recapitulate the Old Testament in Christ. My guess as to the reason for this, strange as it is in the light of the passages just quoted and others closely related to them, is that, while seeing the effects of the sacraments as removing sin and its effects and also "for perfecting the soul in these things that pertain to the worship of God in accord with the religion of the Christian life," he ties this latter almost exclusively to Christ's sufferings and death.[46]

This grace of which we have been speaking is a created gift. It is that

---

[41] *Adv. Haer.* IV, 33, 10.

[42] This is not a question concerning personal holiness. Most Christians would not for a moment think seriously of their faith's being as strong as Abraham's or their knowledge of God as great as Moses'. Rather, it is a matter of the nature of the gifts God has freely given us.

[43] *Adv. Haer.* V, 16, 2. For more passages and details, cf. Lawson, op. cit., 155–159.

[44] *ST* I-II, 112, 1 c.

[45] ibid. ad 2.

[46] E.g., III, 62, 5 c.

power by which we are enabled to receive God when and as He gives Himself to us. But He is uncreated Grace. Thus, the one created grace—by which we can receive Him through faith, principally with our minds, and with all our powers, especially those of the will, through hope and charity—can still be receptive of very different gifts, according to the way in which God gives Himself to us.

In the Old Testament, He gave Himself to the prophets through a grace like ours indeed but only, as to faith, in the uniqueness and the unity of His nature, and as to hope, in the unshakeable firmness of His promises to His people for this world, and as to charity, in the seeking Him in all activity through the keeping of His Law.

But in the New Testament, He gives Himself more completely and more profoundly. Through faith He now gives us knowledge of His inner life as Trinity of Persons. He enables the Christian to grasp the spiritual sense of the Scripture, especially as preparatory type. He has given us His Son to redeem us from sin by His sufferings and death, and to raise us in hope through His resurrection. More, He has given us the knowledge of our redemption and makes us share in the inner life of His Son as Son. The Son comes to us Personally in the Eucharist and, in a different way, through His recapitulation, in which we share.

But most characteristically (cf. Jn.7:39), He gives us the Holy Spirit, who, as the Glory of the Father and Son, pours out His love within our hearts. For, the great and essential difference between the two Covenants lies in this giving of the Holy Spirit Himself by the Father through Jesus under the New Covenant. Not merely does the Spirit give grace, which He did to the prophets also, but He Himself is given to us. It is by His gift that we are made sons of God in Jesus so as to live by His life. It is the Spirit that makes us the adopted sons of God.[47] By His Personal presence in and among those who by His power live in Christ, He makes possible the recapitulation, quietly and unobtrusively, of the thousands of years of human history in less than a lifetime so as finally to catapult the one who has been docile to His inspiration into that ardor of charity that visibly and manifestly shows to the world Jesus as the Christ. This, which the Spirit first did with the apostles on Pentecost, He wishes to do with all Christ's disciples.

Yet such a description of Christianity seems built on a contradiction. On the one hand, the Holy Spirit has been given in power to the Church, which He guides and directs, and through her to the individual. She possesses the fulness of God's revelation, the fulness of the means of sanctification in the sacraments, the perfection of worship in the Mass. Every Catholic has received the great gift of incorporation into Christ by grace—divinization—and the sacramental anointing by the Holy Spirit. On the other hand, it is empirically evident, both to the individual Christian and to others, that even adequately instructed and believing Catholics may show little difference in their behavior, except at a very superficial cultural-religious level, from their non-Catholic, even their non-Christian neighbors, and are often morally inferior

[47] Rom.8:14–17; Gal.4:6–7. Cf. *Mystici Corporis*, #68 (DS 3807).

to these, even to those of their own age and social background.

Even in the days of the apostles, however, we find, if we read the Scriptures carefully and without prejudice, that the gentile Christians fell far short of apostolic expectations. St. Paul soon discovered the need to instruct his converts in such basics as the moral wrongness of lying with one's father's wife. He had to insist on the incompatibility of fornication with Christian life, and re-imposed much of Jewish practice concerning feast days and fasts, of seasons and holy days, on the Roman church to avoid having the Christians there rend it asunder through the misuse of their Christian freedom.

The earlier and deeper dissension among Jewish Christians concerning circumcision and the observance of the food laws—though of very different origin, involving the very process which had first led them to faith in Jesus—likewise shows that not all were fully docile to the Spirit. Even for the "people well prepared" further spiritual growth was needed before the full and true freedom of the sons of God was reached.

Yet the deep difference between Christians and their neighbors has been easily discernible in some contexts. For all their faults, Christians stood out by their charity and chastity and other virtues in the sophisticated culture of the Greco-Roman world, even though this world knew, both philosophically and religiously (through the mystery cults) much about virtue. So also, Israel, despite its sins, stood out in sharp contrast to the pagan world around it, not only when living rightly but when, as under the later kings or at the time of the Seleucid domination, many were committing abominations against the Lord.

Indeed, it seems that the above-mentioned contradiction stands out clearly only when a whole culture has long been deeply colored by Christianity and when, as this culture decays, those Christians who wish to be at peace with it become less Christian in their behavior; often, too, in their faith. At the same time, many of their neighbors still retain the older culture with its Christian aspects, even if they have no faith at all. Nor should we forget that God is continually bringing new people into the world, who have, all of them, the same difficult road to travel and who, also, are a stiff-necked and rebellious people for much of their life.

On the other hand, in our own day, Christians who take their faith seriously differ increasingly from the non-Christian world around them. In God's ordinary providence, it may only be after many years that the Christian takes his faith thus seriously and perserveres in it long enough for the difference from his non-Christian neighbors to become discernible. Nor, on first conversion to Christianity, despite the abundance of strongly felt graces usually then received, is one made perfect. Gentiles, like Jews, must learn to recapitulate the Old Testament in Jesus if they would complete the process within the span of a single human life.

Since it took Israel more than 1200 years under the Law in order to be made ready for the coming of the Spirit through Jesus, one can see how powerful is even this quiet action of the Spirit that effects this preparation in less than a lifetime. It is not, then, that the Spirit is absent or inactive because not easily seen but that His operation during the season of recapitulation of the Old Covenant is not like what He wrought in the apostles on Pentecost, when He Himself was given. For, Pentecost was the culmination of the preparation of Israel for the Christ, not its beginning.

For the Christian, then, today as earlier, Moses is still type of Christ. Reading about the wanderings in the desert or the lists of Edomite kings or the chronicle of Israelite wars still teaches us something of Christ, even though, as doctrinal prefigurations, they signify what has in large measure long since been spelled out in the solemn teachings of the Church. So, also, what is given by the preparative sense, long at work in some cultures, new in others, is necessary for all Christians who have not yet grown to adulthood in Christ, among whom, therefore, the Spirit's action is muted and not easily discerned.

In cultures already Christian, the great need is to realize that growth is required continually; the damage inflicted by original sin is only slowly overcome. This growth, however, is twofold. As we have been saying, for each individual it must, for long years, be patterned upon the growth of the Old Israel as recorded in the Scriptures. Only when one has lived through the depths of the paschal mystery and has come to know not only his own part in the crucifying of Christ but has also joined Him on the Cross and come to share, already in this age, the glory of His resurrection, is he able to receive that outpouring of the Holy Spirit that is most characteristic of the New Testament.

But there is, as well, a growth required of the culture as a whole. In Israel, as seen, a progressive spiritualizing took place. Yet this was not a progress in virtue according to its intensity, for Abraham was the first of the Patriarchs, not the last; Moses, the first to receive the Law from God; David, only the second of many kings; Isaiah and Jeremiah, predecessors of Haggai and Malachi. What was being developed was a new and more mature structure of the God-centered personality, one that, made perfect in Jesus, could recapitulate all that had preceded. So, through the Church, something similar is to take place among the nations and the cultures of the world.

On Pentecost, Christian Israel began to preach Christ to the Jews scattered among all the nations, so that Christian Jews would be God's instrument to bring the nations to Himself through Jesus. On the pattern of the Lord, who was crucified for those who crucified Him, so Jewish Christians were called by His Spirit to give themselves wholly for the spiritual good of their Roman oppressors and the other pagans, entirely undeserving of any such love. On that day, Christian Israel became the Church of Christ. Within her alone could the individual Christian's recapitulation in Christ take place since she was now not only His people but His Body.[48]

Though having to give all without reserve, Jews could only preach Christ to the gentiles by giving what they had received. And through

---

[48] No more now than then does this mean impossibility of spiritual growth or lack of all grace for those outside the Church. Part III below will deal extensively with the Church and the question of membership within her.

Christian Israel's activity from the days of the apostles onwards, we see that the Old Testament was meant to be a principal instrument for the conquest of the world for the Lord, a spiritual conquest but no less a true one.[49] Surely, in the hands of those Jews who first believed in Christ it proved marvellously effective. Yet today, most of the world remains non-Jewish and non-Christian.

5. Response to Marcion

We are at last in a position to respond to Marcion's question, "Of what use is the Old Testament to the Christian if its spiritual sense is given already through the literal sense of the New? Is not this spiritual sense then superfluous?" We may now reply: The typical sense of the Old Testament is not exhausted by prefiguration of the great dogmas of the faith—though even for this function the typical sense will be needed till the end of the world. For, the dogmas of the Church best retain their life-giving power and spiritual effectiveness when they remain integrally attached to the whole plant from which they have grown as single buds. Hence, too, it is that they most easily pass from one culture to another without distortion when they remain thus vitally united with the Scriptures. This is not to deny the need for "systematic" formulation according to the modes of understanding proper to a particular culture but only to point out that such a formulation is often indigestible within another culture unless vivified interiorly by the Scriptural sap.

More importantly, it seems, the typical sense prefigures in detail the entire inner life of Jesus as the perfect Jew; more, as the Christ of the Lord, who recapitulated in Himself all the dynamic growth and good of man. The Old Testament, according to its spiritual sense, is that portrait of the inner life of Jesus that we must learn to live if we are ever to live fully as becomes a Christian, if "we are to attain...to mature manhood, to the measure of the stature of the fulness of Christ [i.e., to the perfect Man, as measured against that adulthood given through the fulfilment brought by Christ]" (Eph.4:13).

By this prefiguration, the Old Testament completed the preparation of Israel, and is intended now to prepare the nations, for the full outpouring of the Holy Spirit. The Old Testament is intended by God to continue till the end of the age its original function, that of forming a people for the Lord. The pedagogue, no longer busy with Israel, is now seeking to teach the nations God's discipline. In each new culture, the Church must become incarnate in a long slow process, over centuries, forming its people to live worthily as God's people, in the manner typified by Israel's growth. Then, when all the world has been so formed, whatever the final decisions made within each culture for or against Christ,[50] "Then comes the end" (Mt.24:14). Yet everywhere, from the first moment of the Church's presence, by the grace of Christ individuals are meant to be formed by the Old Testament as lived through in Christ. And even as the Patriarchs, Moses, and Joshua, so there will be great saints raised up from the first converts in every culture who will live the Christian life in its manifest fulness.

---

[49] St. Ignatius of Loyola, *Spiritual Exercises*, ## 92–98.

[50] Certainly, the popular understandings of *II Thessalonians* and *Revelation* suggest that most, perhaps all, cultures will respond just as Israel did, crucifying Christ again in His members.

Rightly considered, the anagogical sense, of which we have spoken so little, is not only prefigurative of the age to come, but it leads the Christian by desire and action towards eternal life with the Lord, already begun here. This is most powerfully preparative, especially for those who, having recapitulated the Old Law in full, are now living the life that is fully characteristic of the Christian. Led by the Spirit, they are continually instructed by Him through the great message He has already given them in the Scripture, now read primarily through the spiritual sense of the New Testament but, through this, drawing much of its meaning from the anagogical sense of the Old.

Though the matter will become much clearer in the rest of the book, it is, I think, needful even here to prevent a serious misunderstanding. What I am proposing is in no way equivalent to the judaizing tendency that St. Paul had to fight so fiercely, though it may be that which, because not distinguished from it, gave the tendency its strength. The judaizers held that to become a Christian one must first be converted to Judaism and submit to circumcision—that Jesus was Christ and Savior for Jews and for gentile converts to Judaism, but not for others. What I am urging is rather that both Jews and gentiles are called to live in Jesus. By life in Him we are made Jews, circumcized in the circumcision of Christ (Col.2:10–11) without any need to pass through biblical or contemporary Judaism. In Him and by faith in Him, all are to recapitulate, through the action of His Spirit in His Church, the whole pattern of biblical Israel, as spiritually understood, in order to be able to live the characteristically Christian life: that of the sons of God, moved in all things by the gift of the Spirit.

Chapter 9

Before the Patriarchs: the Onset of Actual Sin

A. Transitional comments

Most Christian biblical scholars would admit the existence of a sufficiently limited spiritual sense. Many might even concede the *a priori* possibility of the position sketched above concerning recapitulation and the preparative aspect of the typical sense. But major questions still remain: Can this approach be put to use in some nonarbitrary way? Can it be used without irreverence as manifesting at least a part of what God Himself genuinely intended to reveal through the Scriptures? The rest of this book attempts to justify an affirmative answer to these questions, not by arguing further about exegetical and hermeneutical principles but by actually carrying out the task of finding, without arbitrariness, some portion of this spiritual sense.

As in the theory of felt grace, so here we wish to see the scriptural history from two aspects. On the one hand, our Lord recapitulates this entire history in His own life from conception on, making perfect what was incipient, righting by doing well what was done wrongly or sinfully. On the other hand, all aspects and parts of this history prefigure our Lord's life on earth and, through this, His life in glory and in the Church. Further, since all of the Old Testament prefigures Jesus' life as the fulfilment of the history of Israel and since each Christian is called by His grace to relive in Him this pattern of fulfilment before he is ready to be carried along in all things by the Holy Spirit, we must be able to show how this is to be done. How, conretely, is this pattern of fulfilment to be lived through in practice?

It is the preparative mode of typology that enables us to show this consistently. The ways in which God prepared His people, taking them from spiritual infancy to the maturity that would enable them to respond fully and rightly to Jesus when He came, typify the ways in which Jesus recapitulated

His people's maturation, thus preparing Himself for His mission as the Christ of the LORD.

In treating of original sin, we first considered the naturally ascertainable traits of the psychic structures of the infant in the womb, structures that stood in apparent opposition to the traits of created charity. Then, we showed theologically that the former traits are not wholly natural but seriously distorted. This was explained in terms of one aspect of the typical relation between Adam and Christ, by the theory of felt grace and our being deprived of it.

But even as the felt grace of Jesus' embryonic life is inaccessible to us apart from the suggestions given by the scriptural accounts of His type in Adam, so is much of the rest of His life, apart from His types throughout the Old Testament. Yet it is the way in which Jesus recapitulated Israel's history and gave it its typical sense that makes all this history normative for us. We are to live it, however, not as it eventuated nor as if we were directly typified by it—St. Thomas notwithstanding—but simply and solely in Christ, in His way, by His life shared with us by His grace. All the more, then, shall we need to look in detail at the enormous difference between the fully graced perfection of Jesus' human growth and the fallen, even though graced, development that was Israel's and that is meant to be recapitulatively our own.

Nonetheless, in this chapter I shall say very little about Jesus' recapitulation of the period under discussion—there are Christological problems that need to be dealt with first, which we will consider in Chapter 13. Here and in the next three chapters, I will concentrate on what the literal sense of the Bible offers us concerning the psycho-cultural development of God's people and their spiritual history from the point of view of its parallelism with the similar development of the individual Christian from birth onwards—and to some degree, with the non-Christian's development.[1] These are things in large measure naturally knowable from the scriptural text and from the profane sciences. They are of interest to us, obviously, because in a good many ways Jesus grew and matured as does any other child.

In the rest of Part II, I wish to sketch these interrelated modes of growth, natural and spiritual, of Israel, of Jesus, and of ourselves. I shall work as well as I can out of present understanding of the literal sense of the Old Testament. The treatment will certainly be flawed in many ways from my lack of historical-critical acumen and knowledge. But if the basic notion be valid, others can easily correct and improve it.

Because typical meanings are given the sacred text by one of its authors only, God acting by Himself alone, one has to attend much more to the Scriptures themselves than to our own historical reconstructions, based on them, save insofar as these help us to understand the literal meaning of the text. This

[1] There is, of course, a problem here, since the religious growth of the Christian, as such, takes place in Christ and is recapitulative, even if he is hardened in sin, whereas the religious development of the non-Christian in God's ordinary providence does not share in this individual recapitulation. Rather than try to separate these and other aspects abstractly, before seeing what is implied by them, I shall try now to make the process concrete, distinguishing the different aspects as the need arises.

does not mean that the historical reconstructions are false or even inadequate at their own level, and I shall be strongly dependent on them.[2] But it is God who has given to the text the meaning we are principally concerned with; and we are not likely to extract this meaning using merely the means of historical criticism, however valid.

To see the stages of the spiritual growth of God's people as set forth in the Scriptures, we need to keep in mind that the writing and editing of the scriptural books were themselves part of the history of salvation. Hence I will make an effort to take the events according to the chronological order in which the texts were written, though, if there is clear evidence of use of an appreciably earlier document or tradition, this latter text should be considered in its proper chronological position also.

B. The Infancy of the Race

Having discussed at length the state of Adam and Eve immediately after their expulsion from paradise, we turn to the period between them and the patriarchs.

The eight chapters, *Genesis* 4–11, reflect the infancy of mankind, though only in retrospect, since composed little more than three thousand years ago. But though the human infant is unique among mammals in the slowness of its growth toward maturity, this slowness is not reflected in *Genesis*, which in one instant leaps in total silence over that infancy of our race indicated to us by our profane sciences.

To judge from these, an unimaginable duration of hundreds of thousands of years, perhaps millions, stretches between the expulsion from Eden and the next item mentioned by the Scriptures, the story of Cain and Abel. This infancy of the race was long enough, it seems, that biologically distinct subspecies of man developed over those ages, perhaps two or three hundred times as long as the period from Abraham to the present. "The fulness of time" (Gal.4:4) gains new meaning in this context. This longest portion of human existence on earth, when man could not write, when no history was possible, was, like the life of the newborn infant, given over wholly to the effort to live and grow and learn the most basic features of the strange world around him.

That scriptural silence screens from view to some extent the catastrophic effects of the sin of Adam upon our race. From a condition, however primitive culturally speaking, of close union with God and of inner harmony, man is thrust out to work his own way seemingly, slowly back towards God. With mind darkened and a will whose freedom seems to have been well-nigh extinguished by the sheer pressure of the effort merely to survive, man remained under the constraints of psychic infancy far longer proportionately than even the biological growth-curve of the individual would suggest. In any case, there was nothing there to record that would be of help to us spiritually.

---

[2] For general views of this history, cf. John Bright, *A History of Israel*, Philadelphia: Westminster (1959) and Bernhard W. Anderson, *Understanding the Old Testament*, 3rd ed., Englewood Cliffs (NJ): Prentice-Hall, (1975). For greater detail, cf. *JBC* (still useful) and *NJBC* and the individual volumes in AB.

The infant cannot act on its own at all. What spiritual life it has if baptized is totally passive, a life-principle only, not yet made active. Indeed, the infant seems wholly unaware of God and, as seen, is psychologically structured so as to be ready to reject Him.

But though wholly lacking words for us, early man was, like any infant, not wholly silent. Something of the nature of those times can be glimpsed from the non-verbal communication given us by the cave-paintings of Altamira or the Dordogne. These paintings are, of course, already relatively recent, a mere 70,000 to 40,000 years ago. Strikingly realistic at the level of the individual animal's image, the whole lacks any effort at realism. The animals portrayed are those that would be the objects of a hunt, and were often painted, perhaps for magical purposes, with a spear in their back. But there is no background, no framework, and no apparent connection between the different images. The animal itself is there, filling some space on the wall in among others that often have nothing to do with it artistically or naturally, just wherever there was some space left. In some ways, this is great art; yet there is no least hint of composition, and in those cases where human beings are included, they are mere stick-figures.[3]

There is an evident fascination with these animals—rarely does one find finer animal paintings—and an amazing keenness of perception of their structure and, above all, of their movement. It is not hard to recognize there something like an infant's fixed gaze and total attention when it sees some bright and moving bauble and slowly stretches out its hand to grasp it. Yet, even later in the child's life, even after he has had an experience of some new and marvellous scene imprinted forever in full detail upon his memory, even then he draws family and pets only as stick-figures.

C. The sin of Cain

Finally, however, some ten thousand years ago as far as we can judge, men in the Middle East, though still living in caves, discovered how to raise animals for food instead of hunting them, then to grow crops and cease to forage. It is at this point only that *Genesis* offers its first light on man's story after the fall. In the story of Cain, fallen Adam's firstborn son, and of Abel, his second, the two brothers are shown as, respectively, tiller of the ground and herder of sheep. They represent the level of man's development by the time he acquired enough reflex awareness to be likened to the small child, able not only to remember and express his experiences but to converse.

Cain's sin and its aftermath are narrated immediately after the account of the expulsion from Eden,[4] despite all the millennia in between. Since the human author evidently sees Cain's action as a connatural consequence and extension of the fall, we may ask what this sin shows us of both an individual's infancy and that of the race.[5] How had original sin been

[3] It is perhaps possible, with sufficient caution, to glean something of man's early state from the cultures of the more isolated of "primitive" peoples of recent times. But the growth in our knowledge of how cultures have decayed highlights the great risks of error here.

[4] Gen.4:1–16. New Testament commentary is given in I Jn.3:12 and Hebr.11:4.

operative if to issue in such a crime in the early childhood of the race? The crime is committed, indeed, by an adult, but an adult with the psyche of a child just beyond infancy. Our concern remains more with the dynamism of the intial, inherited damage to our nature and with the ever greater structural changes wrought thereby than with questions of degree of responsibility or guilt.

Though Cain's sin seems, clearly enough, to be one of sibling rivalry, such a description is too succinct. It is indeed a sin of petulant and infantile hatred springing up against his brother simply because the latter was more acceptable to God than he. But if we recall what was said above concerning the structure of charity, we can begin to see more clearly the long-term effects of the fall.

There is no need to argue whether (or at what age) a child has the physical and mental development that would correspond to the offering of sacrifices or to examining them in ancient Near-Eastern manner for the signs of divine acceptance or rejection, nor whether he could plan out the killing of another child, luring him into the fields in order to kill him there from envy. We need only remember the remark of Saint Augustine when he recalls having seen a baby being nursed at the breast and another baby, who had been at that same breast, livid with envy: "'Innocence' is the weakness of infant limbs, not the spiritual attitude of infants."[6]

Though the breast in question was that of a mother or a wet-nurse, God's acceptance had a similar function in this sibling rivalry. It was bad enough for Cain that God should not have had regard for what he had offered Him, should not have accepted his agricultural understanding of religion and sacrifice. But far worse was the realization that what his herdsman brother did and thought *was* acceptable. Cain was not merely taken from the breast but saw Abel as his replacement there and became livid with envy.

What was involved was the threat of being unloved by God, of being cast aside by the Source of life in favor of another. The false perception of love built into him by the sin of Adam made any love given to a brother be seen as love taken from himself. His brother became his rival for an affection that was, though fear kept him from seeing it, quite large enough for both. The only solution he could see was to get rid of the rival, the one who was being accepted in his place.

Worse, what God intended as disciplinary correction was taken as a

---

[5] As indicated in the introduction to this chapter (*pp* 202–204), it is not easy to draw useful parallels between the growth of a child and of the race. Though a certain sequence of stages seems common among children, yet this sequence—and especially its correlation with the child's age—is, at best, only a sort of average over a considerable range of behaviors, one that is modified strongly, moreover, by the family and the culture. What the Bible shows depends on the age of the traditions drawn together by the writer and not merely upon the time they were written down by his predecessors or reworked by him into their present form. What I shall present, then, is a not very expert attempt to draw these parallels on a theoretically solid basis. Others of greater competence will have to correct, refine, and develop them if the basic theory is acceptable.

[6] *Confessions*, I, vii, 11: "Ita imbecillitas membrorum infantilium innocens est, non animus infantium."

threat to his very being. Having no sense of the gratuity of God's love but convinced of its dependence upon his own inner value, he could no longer see himself as worthy of any love, since it was God who was rejecting his sacrifices. Refusing to admit that it was he who was at fault, he would not accept that his offering not be regarded lovingly by the Lord when his sibling's was so regarded. Instead, then, of accepting the correction, he sulked.

I have heard from those better instructed in child psychology than I that sulking is common among small children and that it appears very early on. Having suffered some hurt or disappointment but seeing that the world goes about its ordinary business without adequate recognition of his tragedy, feeling thus that his own worth has been attacked, he turns in upon himself. To sulk is to make oneself deliberately, knowingly unlovable, flaunting one's worthlessness as a protest. At the earliest stages, this seems to be the small child's principal way to show his displeasure: by hurting the feelings of others who, he is convinced, love him, but not as he wishes to be loved.

By his sulking, the child seems to be seeking a reassurance. Recognizing indeed that he does not have that goodness that could coerce a love sufficient to rectify the situation, and standing in fear before this void, he searches for a human analog to that grace he has never felt, yet for which he was made, some equivalent to that love which can love even the unlovable.[7] But the mistake is serious, on the part of the parents, if they reassure the child of their love by assuring him that he has the worth he claims, if they lure him forth from his injured pride by the lie that he does possess a value rooted in himself greater than whatever other values were at stake for the people around him.

But what, then, can one do? All other attempts to draw forth a proper response meet a stone wall—and this despite all knowledge of the pain thereby inflicted on those he loves as well as on himself. For the child is aware that this conduct is hurting him terribly, that he yearns from the very roots of his being to show love instead of withholding it, and so, to be loved, even if with a love unmerited. But he *won't!*—and turns sharply away, and even dares to strike at the one who seeks to cajole him.

The pain is enormous in him, and may be so—he hopes—in those around him. For he wants to hurt those who do not make his grief, real or imagined, the center of their dealings with him, who can live their lives normally when he is out of sorts.

The child knows perfectly well, when he is sulking, how ridiculous he is being, but this knowledge only hardens him more stiffly as he becomes more aware of his danger in trifling thus with the very core of his own existence, in the pursuit of a reassurance that he desires above all else at the moment and which in his heart he knows he can never have in the form in which he wants it. Trifling thus with his own lovability is trifling with his life; and this, too, he somehow knows but desperately fears to consider. For, it is not a far step,

[7] This seems also to be the dynamic behind much of young people's sexual and other confidences, their "spilling their guts." They seek to be reassured that their confidant loves them anyway. There are severely pathological cases, as well, where the person goes on doing worse and worse things, ever in search of a reassurance that was, he feels, never adequately provided him as a small child by mother or father.

should the sulk ever become a free act (in a person, therefore, a good many years further along in age), for a sulk to end in suicide, the ultimate sulk.

A sulk that is freely willed would have indeed the diabolic cast ascribed by St. John to that of Cain (I Jn.3:12). For, what is desired ultimately is to be as God, wanting all grounds for being loved to be contained in oneself. The sulk is a petulant demand that all things in the child's small world come to a halt when he is hurt, that all things center upon him. The source of sulking is wounded pride, first the merely psychic attitude and nonvoluntary emotion so named, then, years later, the freely chosen self-centering to which that gives rise.

I doubt, though Augustine seemed not to, that all this can be free in the small child. But whenever a sulk is freely chosen it gains the fearsome moral quality of injured pride. This willed making of oneself unlovable, this refusal to allow love to draw one outward except on the grounds of one's own presumptive worth, this deliberate isolation of oneself from any approach from anyone else, becomes, I think, the first field of action for free choice and the first experience of sin that a child has. So, in Cain's case, even the killing of his brother is not enough to stop his sulk. He must strike out verbally at the LORD Himself with his insolent lie and counter-question.[8]

That Cain's crime is, nonetheless, a child's crime is evident from the fact that the punishment which the LORD inflicts is exile from the relative quiet of agricultural life to the life of the wanderer and nomad, a life now in humanity's past. It is, therefore, like punishing a three-year-old by dressing him again in diapers. Even this punishment seemed to him more than he could bear. But of death for Cain there is no hint.

There is no developed notion of a moral order in a small child. So, a child's actions can at times be horrible; even a very small child may gravely injure or kill another, apparently without guilt. His most fundamental, albeit minimal, moral awareness seems to be a knowledge of the wrongness of Cain's childish resentment and sulk. Cain himself seems to have been capable of true sin in his slaying of Abel only because God had told him that that is what the action he was meditating would be.[9]

The pattern seen here is not, unfortunately, always left behind with infancy. As childish malice, it is indeed despised; but the evil pattern may remain. Then it is glossed over and becomes sophisticated. But since it has not been radically rejected, it remains a sort of form or mold for future sin; and from it will grow all the ugly forms of self-pitying pride.

D. The Childhood of Mankind

Genesis is no treatise of scientific anthropology. But the human author evidently sees, in the scraps of ancient traditions he has gathered, signs of a

---

[8] Cf. von Rad, op. cit., *p* 102.

[9] The New Testament passsages that speak of Cain as belonging to the evil one and that clearly see his sin as grave seem to be considering him as though he were some contemporary adult. For the reasons mentioned just above, I think that the literal sense of the passage points to a sin that is not mortal in the moralist's sense.

true collective memory. Having begun agriculture and herding while still living in caves, men gradually find their way to higher levels of culture and collective consciousness. Cain, tiller of the soil, leaves the cave to build the city he named in honor of his first-born.[10] His descendant Jabal is the first of herdsmen to live in tents. Jubal contributes the discovery of the simplest musical instruments. In the same "generation" metals are worked by Tubal-cain into tools; and the bronze and iron ages are melted together.

Herding and farming, metal-working and music-making, life in tents or in villages are all seen as human discoveries of much earlier times than those of the writer. His acceptance of these old traditions, however, is not like the small child's taking of whatever its parents tell it as true. The writer does not simply recount sections of the epics from which he has taken one or other item, but makes use of these materials to construct a work of his own. He is careful to pass on those pieces of Israelite tradition that he uses as they have come down to him. But he is a realist, clearly aware that these achievements were all made in some historical context, by real human beings, living in society, and, indeed, not infinitely long before. No deities nor even lesser spirits were at the source of any of these human accomplishments.[11] And though he makes use here and there of mythic materials, he does so soberly, to make a point, without embroidery or fantasy, cutting them back to the few essentials he desires to use. All this points to a much later age for the writer than for his sources.

Lamech, on whom the spotlight rests momentarily, seems the epitome of the four-year-old, jealous of anyone taking his place in the light, striking back far harder than he was struck by anyone who jostles him. Savage as his words are, all we are actually shown is his boasting before his two wives, though there is no reason to think of this as mere braggadocio. But the sacred writer is more concerned to show Lamech's attitude as he seeks to excuse those petulantly impetuous killings by talking loudly of them—before those who will be impressed—as if they were proper material for boasting. In the process, he gives full vent to his passionate "conviction" that he is the sole norm for right and wrong, not seeing that he "doth protest too much."

Somewhat earlier, to judge by 4:26, about the time of the first village-dwelling, God would seem to have first made Himself known to some, belonging to a different lineage, among these distant offspring of Adam.[12] For, it was then that men, seemingly of the line of Seth, first began "to invoke the

[10] This was doubtless no more than a permanent village. Yet the relative quickness with which Jericho turned from a campsite at a ford in the Jordan to a city of gigantic fortifications millennia before Abraham (Kathleen Kenyon, *Archaeology in the Holy Land*, New York: Praeger [1970], 3rd ed., *pp* 209–212) suggests a possible reason why the author's sources may have felt no reason for a distinction.

[11] Cf., *Athanasius: Contra Gentes and De Incarnatione*, ed. & tr. R. W. Thomson, Oxford: Clarendon Press (1971), pp 33–39 & 49–53 (*Contra Gentes* ##11–13 & 18 respectively) for Athanasius' scorn for the pagans who honored as gods men far less virtuous and less technically skillful than the men who created these deities.

[12] It is doubtful, however, that the writer has any concern here with comparative chronology. His interest seems focussed, rather, on the fact, as reported, that God was invoked as the LORD from early on.

name 'the LORD'."[13] So, too, children of two years or even less can, on occasion and in deeply religious surroundings, have some true knowledge of God.

There is also shown us, as belonging to those early days of our race, another characteristic of every small child: the child's sense of living forever. He knows indeed of death, learning of it very early through the squashing of insects, the dying of flowers, the killing of animals or birds for food. He does not deny death nor does he think in some literal sense that each life goes on infinitely. But in a practical sense he sees things much as did the author of the fifth chapter of *Genesis,* a world where no one dies till after centuries and centuries, and one dies young if, like Henoch, death comes after only 365 years. Most people live on seemingly forever; life will go on like this indefinitely; it has been like this forever. Whatever the child finds about him as he grows seems to him the way the world has been from the beginning, the way, in fact, it will always remain.

Likewise, even though a child may hear from grandparents tales about his parents when they were children, even his parents seem ancient to him and full of days. Their age is not, however, gray decrepitude. The men appearing in these ancient genealogies begot their first-born only after a century or so and continued vigorous, begetting sons and daughters centuries longer. So the child is well aware of the strength and activity of his parents, though exceedingly old and wise. It is they who know things; and their word is truth, whatever rebellions there may be against their commands.

This intrinsic parental authority gives the child the first elements of religion and helps him to a certain personal contact with God. For the most part, of course, his belief is given from without, determined entirely by his parents' beliefs and practice, not yet grasped as true or false but as simply so.

Yet, these were "the times of ignorance" of God (Ac.17:30). As is clear from the story of Cain and Abel, the existence of God was no question at all; wicked and good alike take Him and His action as obvious and unquestioned. Here or there, moreover, there is an occasional indication, in the individual or in the race, of some spark of desire to "feel after God and to find Him" (Ac.17:27), some stirring, however feeble, to know God Himself. There was, then, from very early on, true but very rudimentary religion in some men, e.g., Abel, whose offering of the best of his fatlings was acceptable to God; Henoch, who walked with God and was no more because God took him; and then Noah, who walked with God.

Far more common, though, was a more highly developed but false religion, e.g., that of Cain, whose offerings from his crops were not acceptable to God; Lamech, the savage killer who fathered the arts and sciences; the similar men of Noah's day; and the builders of the city of Babel and its ziggurat. Archeologically speaking, the worship of "high gods" seems to have been common all through the Near East by 5000 B.C., with each city-state rising around its central temple-complex, first in Sumer and then throughout Mesopotamia. Even this early, the religion of the countryside must have seemed

[13] Cf. Speiser, *ad loc.*, *p* 34, for the interpretation of this assertion as referring to an early but genuine Yahwism, *pp* 37–38.

primitive to city-dwellers.

The account of the Flood, with its bit of preparatory mythology, makes clear enough that "higher" religion was not better religion in God's eyes. The over-all impression is of discord, superstition, overweening ambition, and lust, not only among men but among angels—polymorphous perversity indeed. God's judgment "that every imagination of the thoughts of his [man's] heart was only evil continually" (6:5) was repeated almost verbatim after the great chastisement of the Flood: "the imagination of man's heart is evil from his youth" (8:21). Now, however, He speaks in a tone of resignation and excuse. Man is hopelessly corrupted and cannot be expected to rise to anything much better—a better argument for some aspects of original sin than some of those more commonly offered.

Noah is presented, not as one who scratched out a bare subsistence from the land but as a prosperous farmer (5:29). Further, he is the first to plant vineyards[14] and to discover in his own person the power of wine, even as countless later children have, out of curiosity, drunk down attractive-looking liquids to their own hurt. More importantly, however, the story of Noah offers a very good picture of a small child's view that there are only good people and bad ones. Thus, Noah corresponds well to the child as he comes to the first personal contacts, with other people and with God, that he will remember distinctly in later life, and as he awakens to his first clear grasp of morality, however simple, as binding upon all men. The biblical narrator sees only utter wickedness and true virtue. What makes the wicked people evil seems to him, as to the child, to be their physical violence and wanton shedding of blood, though the implication that the "giants" were the offspring of the mismated unions between the sons of gods and the daughters of men, is probably not to be overlooked.

When the LORD tires of the wicked ones, He simply wipes them out. The just survive, all of them members of the one family. There is no sadness; there is no hint that Noah missed or regretted the loss of all his fellows or that he was lonely with none save his small family. The child, hearing the story of Noah, never questions whether he was sorry for all those people who were drowned. They were wicked and were wiped out; one doesn't feel any more sorrow for them than for other giants or goblins or witches.

As the principal wickedness was violence and bloodshed, so the principal commandment of the Noachic covenant, binding thenceforth on all men is: "Whoever sheds the blood of man, by man shall his blood be shed" (9:6).[15] This is not human vengeance given a divinely sanctioned outlet nor mere tit for tat but the recognition of murder as sacrilege, "for God made man in His own image" (9:6). This image of God in man is doubly destroyed: physically in the one murdered, spiritually in the murderer himself. For its partial restoration at the social level, God gives to man both the right and the obligation to punish the murderer by death, a power hitherto reserved entirely to

[14] Speiser, *ad loc., pp* 60–61.

[15] Though von Rad takes the prohibition against eating blood as equally as strong as this one, I would suggest that the principal function of the former is to introduce and underscore the importance of the latter prohibition.

Himself. By this delegation, He adds a further trait to His own image in man, requiring man to respond to murder as God has just done—though man's carrying out of this commandment, so far as the biblical account goes, lies well in the future. The account of the flood and the subsequent covenant are, then, the first indication of the possibility of a guilt deserving of death among the descendants of Adam. We may note for future reference that, as with the sin of Cain, the acts that offended God were not directed against Him by the evildoers but against their fellowmen.

E. The tower of Babel

A small child has no sense of impossibility. Anything is possible. Anything can be done. He has little sense that there are physical, psychological, or other limits placed on human accomplishment. If he wishes to dig a hole through to the other side of the earth, he starts to do so. If he wishes to build a tower up to the sky, to scale heaven, to impose his own judgment and will on his parents or on God, he sets about to do it.

In the account of the tower of Babel, there comes to clarity a certain pattern that has, in slow degrees, been developing from Eden onwards. "Let us build ourselves a city, and a tower with its top in the heavens, and let us make a name for ourselves, lest we be scattered abroad upon the face of the whole earth" (Gen.11:4). Here, for the first time, men are shown collaborating in a common project, albeit in what the writer regards as a manifest defiance of God.[16] They are turning their labor and skills to construct a city and a tower of such sort that they will have to be highly regarded for their achievement, regardless of whatever faults they may have—faults acknowledged in their fear that they may be scattered abroad and dispersed. Though cooperating, these men feel themselves, at heart, isolated and alone, worthy of nothing but to be scattered over the face of the entire earth. This threat of dispersal is mentioned three times in this one brief passage, once by the men themselves, twice by the writer in speaking of God's response to them, who chose precisely what they most feared as the punishment for their arrogant pretence. Something fundamental is at issue here.

Less clear, but already present earlier, one finds the same tendency in Ham, boasting to his brethren in some sort of scurrilous mocking of his naked father, in order to make himself seem important or "superior." So too, for Cain's city, and Lamech's boast to his wives of his violence, and perhaps for the list of the men first to achieve something. Fallen man wants to make himself, if not attractive to others, at least respected by them. Truth to tell, he wishes to be as important in their eyes as he is in his own.

Even Cain and Abel had their "specialties," in rivalry with one another —or so Cain perceived it—and drew from these the kind of sacrifices they offered God. Abel gave the best he had, in simplicity. Cain gave, perhaps, as a boast before the Lord of his higher culture. Back in Eden itself, after the fall,

---

[16] Thus, he carefully refrains from indicating *any* religious aspect to this city or tower, though the latter seems clearly enough to have been a ziggurat and though he shows no scruple about the pagan elements he finds even in the accounts of the patriarchs.

both Adam and Eve covered their nakedness with fig leaves, pretending that they really had no interest in these parts of their bodies and that they had none of the hot desires they already felt, with shame, within them.

The pattern, then, is this: One does something deeply shameful. Because of original sin and the privation of felt grace, he rightly thinks himself thenceforward to be unworthy of love, but wrongly thinks that he can no longer be loved by any who should know of his wrongdoing. Were the action to be known by all, this would be a sort of inner annihilation.The resultant isolation from all others would be a punishment too great to bear. Hence, one must cover one's shame—humbly, with fig leaves; petulantly, with Cain's lying retort; arrogantly, with Lamech's boast. Then, at Babel, men find the way to conceal their inner nakedness with their external achievements. Some excellence one has or can have, in oneself or from the world around, is chosen, first, as a defense against one's known but not acknowledged unworthiness of anyone's esteem or love and then, built upon this, as a means to make oneself esteemed, even loved, by others.

Ever since Babel, men have found their natural unity primarily in their common labors at technical control of the world. And always it seems that "nothing that they propose now to do will be impossible for them" (11:6). They walk about upon the moon. They discover the basic structures of the physical universe. They have started work on the genetic remaking, according to their own desires, of the human species itself. For such work, men do "have the same language and the same words" (11:1). But as soon as things of more directly personal concern arise, as has often occurred in philosophy and theology. their languages are confused and they themselves are divided and soon scattered. The culture they have so slowly and painfully developed over centuries regresses, crumbles, and soon joins the other dead and scarcely remembered cultures of the earth.

Obviously, the achievements of man are, in themselves, marvellous manifestations of God's own greatness, "who has given such power to men" (Mt.9:8). Yet, it seems that in a majority of cases, his accomplishments are, before all else, a sort of fig leaf. And how often it happens that the private lives of men of the greatest competence in various fields of thought and action are found to have been shambles and "quiet desperation." The universal condition brought about through original sin is clearly evident in this dynamic that moves from shame to cover-up to great achievements of skill and objectively recognizable excellence, that seems so closely linked to arrogance and subsequent division and dispersal.

Consider for a moment a biological analog: the larva of the caddis-fly. Looking a bit like a slender, small-bodied, little dragon-fly just a couple of inches in wingspan, the caddis-fly is often seen flitting around fresh-water ponds. Its larva is a little worm, which lives in a case that it constructs partly from the silk it can spin out and partly from the debris it finds as it crawls around the bottom of the pond or stream. Each species has a different sort of debris it prefers: some, pebbles; some, bits of grass or water-weeds; others, tiny snail's shells. Since in its larval stage, the caddis-fly is a voracious carnivore and goes about seeking other water-beasts to kill and eat and grow fat upon, one also finds in its case the tougher or indigestible parts of the bodies of its victims. But any suitable, manageable, small, tough object will do. The larva picks it up or cuts it off and binds it with a few strands of silk into its little case. The bigger the larva gets, the bigger the casing gets, being enlarged progressively at its opening, until the day when the larva seals off the entrance with silk and turns into a pupa, finally to emerge as the adult fly.

This seems not a bad image for what goes on in us. The human infant, like this larva, is able psychically to cement together, by means of the silken strands of emotion-driven association, a little case in which to live. Its primary function is camouflage and protection from what he senses as threats. But after a time he discovers that this selective binding together of small fragments of reality has a further advantage. The bits and pieces can be put together in a reconstructed little world, in which, by just ever so fortunate accident, the values, real or apparent, that the child feels within himself as his, turn out to be of central importance. And somehow, the values that he lacks or thinks he lacks turn out to be of very little worth in this reconstituted universe.

Such a casing is, of course, a very carefully camouflaged fake, a false world in which the real structures have been cut apart, shifted, and placed back again with different interrelations. The purpose of all this, usually quite unconscious, activity is to make oneself somehow uniquely valuable and love-worthy. In this fake world, the child feels safe, secure, and above all else, lovable—indeed, secure only because lovable. Spontaneously, the child has constructed this little world so that, if he looks no further than this casing, he finds himself, in relation to it, to be filled with the things that make him worthy to be loved. So, he goes through life, taking ever bigger and bigger chunks of the real and learning to fit them somehow into his value-creating world.

This process is not mere day-dreaming, which is the most obvious way to escape reality. Children easily fall into day-dreaming and even perhaps, on occasion, adults. Like a dream in sleep, the day-dream is a sort of free association of things that are buried in the subconscious or even the deep unconscious. But as an activity it resembles less that of the caddis-worm than of a spider spinning its web from its own silk alone. The caddis-larva usually spins its silk only to bind together things of greater rigidity and strength into a tough casing, concerned more with protection than with the spider's effort to catch prey with its webbing.

Harmful as day-dreaming can become if indulged, it is not very dangerous since its unreality is usually clear. One knows, at least after the event, what he has been doing. There is no room for further pretense, unless he chooses to dream his entire life away. He cannot easily fool himself after a day-dream that any of it was real. It lacks even the quasi-reality that a dream can have when one first awakes.

But when the imagination is used as the silken binding of the psychic casing and fastens securely together the various components of the world, no longer as they are conjoined in fact but in accord with the structures that will give one value, mixing in a large amount of cognitive sand and pebbles of rationalization, then one has a casing far tougher and more enduring than mere imaginings. After all, it does have great pieces of reality built in unchanged. So the whole world can be recreated and brought into conformity with one's own perceptions of oneself and one's own will.

Always fearful, like the little insect crawling about on the bottom of its pond, the child backs into his casing very quickly. But when not frightened, he is always on the alert for further items to bind into his case, to enlarge it or, most especially, to repair it should it suffer damage. Since large pieces of the real can remain intact, each piece with its own structure at least locally undamaged, though with many of its relations to other things altered or cut away, these pieces serve as tough shields against the other parts of reality that threaten one's tenderer spots. But since the pieces have been connected wrongly, no longer intrinsically related to one another but only through the will and imagination of the creature within, the bonds are weak and can give way disastrously under stress.

Every part of the person is involved in this activity, precisely because it has to be a "world." If it is not a whole universe, he cannot really feel safe in it. He has to have some sense of completeness, that he now at length has everything of importance under control, that somehow he knows, at least in principle, what is there and what is not. Like the caddis-larva, he finds danger only outside his casing but perceives none within. So he labors, not so much to improve himself as to re-do the "world" so as to seem lovable in his own eyes and in the eyes of any who are "truly perceptive." But to what end, since, to the extent in which he succeeds, his supposed lovableness is visible only to himself, for within the casing there is no one save himself alone?

All this is not confined to the small child, who is only beginning the process just described. And though it often continues as an active process well into adult life, it is usually unconscious, a setting up of defense mechanisms that let the person remain lovable in his own eyes, despite painful experiences of the scorn or contempt of others that might seem to destroy the very possibility that he could be lovable at all. All this is, then, a part of that concupiscence that, if grace does not intervene, remains as the effect of original sin in him and, even with grace, still awaits proper rectifcation in the baptized.

Yet this casing is truly protective. These psychic artifices are usually well constructed to defend the psyche from things it cannot yet adequately deal with. Thus, they help one keep his sanity. Efforts to do away with them directly, by opening them up to reveal the soft, scared creature within and to force this, unprotected, into the real world, are destructive and to be avoided unless some pathology makes lack of immediate clarity even more damaging. What is called for is, rather, whatever helps the interior rectification that enables the person to know God's love in truth, directly or through another human being, and thus himself to discard his casing as no longer useful. For the ultimate and only essential security any human being needs is to know himself truly loved by God and truly loving Him in return. This is the only thing needed, and the one without which no other can stand.

Chapter 10

The Patriarchs: God's Call and His Promise

With the LORD's call to Abram, something new begins. God freely chooses one man, of those who might be ready, to grow under the action of His grace much further and faster than those around him. The preparation for Christ enters a new phase. This is the point, then, at which the growth of the Christian can first begin visibly to diverge from that of others.

No longer is it sufficient to show merely the psychic similarities between the people of the Bible and the individual of any time or place. From here on, in addition to pointing out these similarities, we shall be interested also in a quick glance at what recapitulation might mean for the Christian at each level. Since we have still to speak of Jesus' recapitulation of this period, our overview must till then be merely descriptive and theoretically inadequate.

A. God's call to Abram

From here on, we are given, more by art than actual fact, the impression of a continuous narrative, a single story. Though a careful reading shows that we are dealing still with a collection of disconnected fragments and though many things are skipped over quickly, nonetheless henceforth all years are in some degree accounted for; a history is beginning to unfold.

Abruptly, as when the curtain goes up at the beginning of a play, God spoke to Abram.[1] There is no hint that Abram found God's speaking to him extraordinary—it was the command given that was extraordinary. Nothing implies that God did not talk to Abram every day, or even that God

[1] Even His first speaking to Noah, in the longest story of the prepatriarchal account, seems less abrupt. But that story ends, as the others there, with genealogies that are chronologically undecipherable and that serve rather to mask the unknown lapse of centuries than to declare them.

conversed only with Abram and not with his neighbors. The writer's interest lies in what God said to Abram, not in the fact that God spoke to him. As for a child, the ordinary, the uncommon, and the utterly extraordinary are not clearly distinguished—all are in some way wonderful. Adults' wonders and marvels have little significance for the child, as also for primitive religion, which rightly sees God's power as much in the existence of the grapevine as in the miracle at Cana.[2]

Abram was one whose morals were far from what we would regard as adequate for a Christian. Most Christians, in fact, when they first read about him are put off, even a bit shocked. Though there is no suggestion of malice in his behavior, moral ignorance seems present in large degree. His handing over of Sarai to the king of Egypt and his half-truths as to their relationship, seem at best, primitive. His letting Sarai mistreat and drive away the woman who was even then carrying his own first-born son (Gen.16:6) is even harder to understand. And though Abraham[3] is distressed at Sarah's insistence that he send Hagar and Ishmael out into the desert alone, he is thinking much more of his son than of Hagar (21:10–14). Yet God tells him to go ahead without scruple; He will take care of both the boy and his mother.

From recent archeological discoveries near the place of his Mesopotamian sojourn, we gather that his moral standards were simply those of his day. From the fact that God singled him out and chose him as His friend we may judge that he was a good man by those standards. Yet he showed no appreciable perception of any moral standards more developed than those—save where it was a question of faith in God and His promises. Action in accord with the LORD's will for him, whatever it was, whenever made known to him, this he accepted as unconditionally necessary and good.

Thus, the LORD promises Abram that his descendents will be as numerous as the stars of the heavens and the sands of the sea and that they will occupy all the territory his eyes can discern. Abram responds in complete faith, strong loyalty, unwavering fidelity, and total obedience to God. When God asks him for the great sacrifice, that with his own hand he slay, as a burnt offering for the LORD, the son of his old age, the son of the Promise, through whom alone all God's promises to him were to have their fulfilment, he sets about to offer it. The LORD spares him the actual execution, but he must blindly carry out the sacrifice all the way to the raising of the knife. A man who believed, he believed at whatever cost, whatever the LORD said to him. And that faith—simple faith in the Lord and simple acceptance of His promise—was accounted to Abram as righteousness.

The Scripture, though giving the evidence by which historians of culture may judge that outside the realm of faith, loyalty, and faithful obedience Abram's morals were those of his time, bypasses any question as to their quality. The writer does not ask or even suggest an answer to such questions as whether Abram was a moral man for his day or whether he was better or worse than his contemporaries. Yet the implication is clear (and Paul will

---

[2] Cf. St. Augustine, *In Joannis*, Tract. 8, 1–2.

[3] Recall God's changing of the names of Abram and Sarai (Gen.17:5, 15).

later make it explicit) that only because of his faith did he have anything that could be accounted to him as righteousness. The LORD's call for his faith was about all he could understand and respond to. It was, in any event, the only thing the LORD was concerned about. Given that, He could lead him further. Without that, he could go nowhere.

B. The religion of Abraham

Even Abram's faith, set before us often in the New Testament as the model and paradigm for our own, seems singularly uninstructed. He had begun his life, as the Scripture indicates (Jos.24:2), as a pagan worshipper of many gods. His kinsmen and neighbors worshipped these gods, and Abram seemed quite unconcerned about either the existence of these gods or their worship. Though faithful and loyal to the LORD, he seems not to have doubted the existence of the gods of his neighbors. At the least, he shows no surprise or distaste that other men should worship various gods. But he withholds his own worship from them in total fidelity to the LORD who has spoken to him.

There has been long debate among the finest scholars about the nature of the religion of the patriarchs. Whether, indeed, the God of Abraham was the same as or different from the *Pahad* of Isaac or the Might of Jacob, whether the patriarchs themselves were in any way kin to each other, even whether there were any such individuals, and whether the accounts of them have any historical content, all have been and still are strongly debated.[4]

Whatever happened historically, the Scriptures often speak of Abraham, Isaac, and Jacob as using the names of gods, independently attested as pagan deities, as titles of the LORD. Thus Abram met Melchizedech, king of Salem and priest of El Elyon, chief god among a myriad deities then worshipped by the Canaanites (Gen.14:18–20). Though 'El Elyon' is a proper name, it can also be used attributively, as Abram is shown using it here, to mean 'supreme god' or 'Most High God.' The high gods of the nations, then, are either identified with the LORD if they are taken as real, or are subsumed among His titles, if seen as unreal.[5] Yet there remains a casual tolerance for others' worship of other gods, as the account of Jacob's flight from Laban makes clear.

So far as the biblical writer is concerned, the LORD, whatever His local title, is simply God for Abraham. He is not drawn into even considering questions about other gods. His faith, childlike and unquestioning, seems simply

[4] As one, particularly important example, consider the dating and interpretation of this account of Abram's meeting with Melchizedek. For Speiser (*Genesis, pp* 100–109), this is part of perhaps the oldest fragment in *Genesis*, and was inserted to show Abram's ignoring the pagan identity of El Elyon and converting his name into a title of the LORD. Von Rad (*Genesis, pp* 173–176) sees the meeting as a fictitious and late insertion, intended to give greater religious authority to the Davidic monarchy in Jerusalem. For the earlier and much more sceptical approaches to the whole question, cf. Albrecht Alt, "Der Gott der Väter," (1929), in: *Kleine Schriften zur Geschichte des Volkes Israel,* München: Beck (1953).

[5] Scholars generally consider the designation 'El Shaddai,' the only one used of God in *Genesis* by the Priestly source, to be a similar borrowing, especially since it fits in well with the religion of Harran at that period.

to assume that any high god is God. He has so strong a sense of the LORD's uniqueness, who has spoken to him as man to man, that he takes for granted that, say, El Elyon of Melchizedek is indeed his God—who else?—venerated under a strange, local title. Abraham need not, however, have been a monotheist; henotheism is at least equally probable and, so far as I can assess the evidence, much the more probable, not only for him but for Isaac and Jacob.

C. The religion of the child

A child baptized as a small infant grows for a long time very much as a pagan child would, so far as human vision can see. Yet even so, he is capable of some first beginnings of spiritual recapitulation. As might be expected so early in life, the grace rightly to grow will be mediated principally by his family. It is the task of the family, then, to deal well with the major traits of his "pre-patriarchal" period. Sibling enmity needs to be controlled, under pain of an exile to some degree like Cain's. The family needs the deep stability that generates the sense of "foreverness." The child must sense his family to be good, however bad the neighbors may be. And he must learn to submit his will to God's, especially as expressed in the limits imposed upon him by the reality of the world around him.

Once a baptized child, say about the start of his fifth year, has reached a psychic level corresponding to the beginning of the patriarchal period, he can begin to live spiritually much as did Abraham, with an inner life that is truly his own.

God oftentimes makes Himself known to a child that was born of genuinely believing and devout parents, though not in the extraordinary way He used with Abram. God is simply evident to him. Not merely does he take His existence for granted on the basis of what his parents have said, but he himself believes in God, and he loves God. Though he may have some questions on the point, he seems not to have any problem in his prayers with the thought that God might not hear him. It does not usually occur to a child at this age, as often happens with an adult, that he might just be talking to himself.

Because these things are obvious to the child, it is very easy for him to think of God not only as creator but also as provident. He is always there. He is always watching over things. He takes care of you and your loved ones, at least if you pray to Him to do so. And He is the rewarder, who will reward the good (usually, the individual child and his parents) and punish the bad (the same child).

The child will, then, pray to God, and respond to His approaches with choices that may on occasion transcend the merely voluntary and be made in true freedom long before "the age of reason."[6] This would seem particularly

[6] We often think of "sufficient knowledge and reflection" as implying a realistic grasp of a whole situation and of the manifest consequences of an action. But freedom is related rather to knowledge of oneself as an agent, capable of orienting oneself in one manner or some other. A child is but rarely, if ever, free in this way. Nor does he have any responsibility as yet to make himself fully free. He has no abstract, conceptual notion of freedom which he could apply to all his actions or any definable subset of them. But all this does not imply that he could never, con-

the case in the way the child deals with the death or disappearance of anyone he greatly loves.

For, a child can love and be loyal with great intensity. Although he is exceedingly loyal to God and believes with great strength and conviction, he sees no necessary connection between human morality and what God wants. Whatever God wants, if the child is made to know that this is what He wants, then this is what is good. He has no reason to think otherwise, even if the result happens to be painful. Like Abram, told to leave his family and his father's house, the child will shut his eyes, screw up his face, as if that would prevent his tears from being seen, and set out. Unlike Adam and Eve, though he may often do just as he pleases, he does not decide for himself what is right and wrong, for he is already profoundly aware of his own ignorance and knows that such categories belong to adults.

But the converse is also true of a child's religion: It is simple, but it is very deep and capable of enormous sacrifice—or enormous refusal and repudiation. Precisely because God is always present both to reward the good and punish the bad, if the child fails Abram's test, he can develop an intense and lasting hatred of God. When called upon for such a sacrifice, say by the death of a father or mother or of a little brother or sister, someone deeply loved, the child can rebel against God fiercely, with a rebellion that may, apparently, continue for a lifetime.

As in the case of Abraham and the other patriarchs, there is a certain ambiguity about the way in which the baptized child of this age thinks of other gods. Depending on the nature of his religious environment and on what his parents teach him, he may simply reduce all other gods to his God. There is but the one God, the God he knows, the God of whom his parents and grandparents speak to him and to whom they pray, the God of his fathers.

Yet, I think, he has no philosophical problems with many gods, perhaps because it does not occur to him that there might really be many such. If his parents say, "Don't pray to such and such a god," he won't. But when the admonition does not relate to some idol that he can see, does he really think no such god exists? Or is it solely from loyalty to his parents and his trust in them? I suspect that in mission territories, a Catholic child could grow till adolescence without having any deep conviction about the nonexistence of other gods. But they are just not his, or not the right ones, not his parents' God.

Excursus: "Let the Little Children..."

Discussion of spiritual growth requires consideration of an interesting paradox. Already, when speaking of original sin, we have said some things about infants and children that must seem harsh to many parents. To make matters worse, we find in the Pauline writings a number of rather negative

cretely, be aware of his ability to choose and of his obligation to choose well in accord with such knowledge as he possesses.

remarks about children, though this is balanced by the Johannine corpus and, in fact, by other remarks of Paul. Moreover, we are shown our Lord, in some of the most appealing scenes in the Gospels, bringing little children to Himself, or speaking of them, with a manifest tenderness and affection that might seem quite alien to any strong doctrine of original sin.[7]

New Testament remarks about children would seem to fall into three groups: **a**) those where the word for child[8] is employed in a pejorative sense: the Christian has begun to grow up in Christ but has regressed to a child's level again; **b**) where the word is used in a neutral manner: the Christian's spiritual task is to cease to be a child and to grow to adulthood; **c**) the word takes on a strongly positive coloration: the Christian is called by God to become a child again.

a) When writing to the Galatians, Paul says of their turning back to circumcision and the food laws, "My children, I am in labor with you again, till Christ be formed in you" {Gal.4:19}. Much as there is of affection shown here, it is said in reproach. They are little children because they have not grown or matured in Christ as they should have. It is true that these gentiles were just beginning their recapitulation in Christ, individually and as a people, and hence could be called spiritual children, whatever they were doing. Surely, too, the use of "my children" here softens momentarily the harshness of the rest of the letter. Yet the sharp severity of the entire letter makes clear that, as implied here, Paul had already been in labor to bring them forth as Christians; he had succeeded; they "had been running well." He could rightly rebuke them for falling away from what they had already understood and accepted—genuine recapitulation in Christ—into a literal reliving of Jewish development.

In other passages the designation is even more clearly pejorative. Thus, in *Hebrews,* those addressed are called children because they have not yet grown up to an adult faith. They should be instructing others, not in need of further instruction themselves (Heb.5:12–13). As children, they are unskilled in the word of righteousness and cannot distinguish good from evil. So, too, Paul complains that he cannot yet give the Corinthians adult food but only milk (I Cor.3:1), for they are still walking according the the flesh, i.e., in the weakness of human ways of thinking and not in the power of the Spirit they have received.

"Do not be children in your thinking. Be babes in evil..." (I Cor.14:20).

[7] "Might seem alien" only till we recall His tenderness and affection for all sinners not obdurate in rejecting Him.

[8] The New Testament uses some six different words for 'child.' *Τέκνον* most often retains some overtone of its fundamental meaning of 'that which was brought to birth.' When so used, it lacks any pejorative tone and is then similar in many ways to the Hebraicised *υἱός* (son) signifying similarity of nature or action to that of which one is a son. Yet, *τέκνον* includes an element of weakness or inferiority that is not found in *υἱός*. Its diminutive is reserved for affectionate greeting in the *First Letter of John*, a use learned perhaps from Jesus' use of it at the Last Supper (Jn.13:33). Another diminutive, *παιδίον*, seems the word most favored by the Gospels, and is generally favorable in connotation; whereas *νήπιος*, referring primarily to infants, is more often pejorative than any other equivalent for 'child,' but again is not reserved for such usage as shown, e.g., by Lk.10:21.

Again, to be a child in thought or in spirit is not good; only a baby's incapacity for active evil is commended. Again, Paul exhorts the Christians of Ephesus to grow up "...so that we should no longer be children, tossed and carried about by every wind of doctrine" (Eph.4:14). In this world, and fairly soon, Christians are to be adult enough to hold firm in all the storms of false teaching and heresy that have blown through all periods of the Church's life. They must leave childhood behind them.

b) Yet, from this same passage one may argue that Paul somehow expects his Catholics to be children throughout their earthly life. He sees them as children who are to grow steadily "until we all attain to the unity of the faith and of the knowledge of the Son of God, to mature manhood, to the measure of the stature of the fulness of Christ" (Eph.4:13). This process is begun at baptism for his adult converts and for those still in the cradle, but is by no means finished in anyone. Paul sets no term to this growth other than "the fulness of Christ." He does not suggest that we shall achieve it on this earth. Quite the contrary: forgetting what lies behind, he strains onwards towards the heavenly goal (Phil.3:12 –14).[9] So, too, St. Peter, as if trying to clarify one of the things "hard to understand" in St. Paul, writes, "Like newborn babes, long for the pure, spiritual milk that by it you may grow up to salvation" (I Pet.2:2).

c) If one looks at the rest of the New Testament, one finds, in striking contrast to the usages we have been considering, that the Christian is not only regarded as a child because he still has much more to grow but that he must *become* a child. This is insisted on. Remember Jesus speaking to Nicodemus, "Unless a man be born again...," he will not be able to enter heaven. But nothing is said here about any process of growing up again. There is the oft repeated phrase, "Unless you are converted and become as little children, you cannot enter the Kingdom of Heaven" (Mt.18:1–4). "Let the children come to Me...for to such belongs the kingdom of heaven" (Mt.19:14).

Essential to the entire argument of this book is the fact that, through God's free gift, the children of Israel grew and developed spiritually more rapidly and fully than any other people. The post-exilic period was the time when the definitive growth to adulthood took place. By the time of our Lord, when Gabriel could declare the Jews to be a people well prepared, at least those who had been faithful and the chief beneficiaries of this growth had reached spiritual adulthood and were, therefore, no longer children in any sense we have considered. Yet, a strange reversal takes place; and we must say that under the New Law, in at least one aspect, Christians must mature enough to become as little children. Like Nicodemus, we wonder how this can be, even what it might mean. And having a later vantage point than his, we shy away half-consciously, fearing the various sorts of evil childishness that have paraded as spiritual childhood.

One can begin to understand Jesus' remarks if, in watching children, one notes that all children, whether "being good" or "bad," whether quiet and

---

[9] This theme was to become central in the spiritual writings of St. Gregory of Nyssa. Easily available now is his *The Life of Moses*, tr. A. J. Malherbe & E. Ferguson, New York: Paulist (1978); cf. Bk 1, ##5–10.

tranquil or hell-raisers, whether gentle or pugnacious, intelligent or slow, whether doing what they ought to do or the exact opposite, have one trait in common. Each is profoundly aware of being a child, of having much more yet to grow, of not yet being an adult. Indeed, the small child has a certain sense that it will be centuries before he will have grown up, so long is the child's year. Even when he is in the later grades, he will think a teacher of thirty-five aged. The universal characteristic of childhood is that the child knows that he is not adult nor equal to an adult, no matter how fiercely he may at times react against adults or resist them. Even his resistances come from his desperate need of adults' love and esteem and his intense awareness of his dependence upon them for everything, both psychic and physical.

There are many other traits of childhood, more endearing perhaps but less fundamental. The small child possesses an innocence that belongs not to lack of disordered passion, as St. Augustine pointed out, but to his lack of knowledge of actual sin. Having as yet made no free choice of evil, he is unaware of such choices in others.[10] Small children have, in consequence, a great openness to strangers who are not obviously hostile or threatening, having no thought that the stranger might seek to harm them. If abused by parent or sibling, the child has no inner defense and, crushed, assumes his own badness. Great, too, is children's confidence in adults, knowing and exaggerating their powers not only over the children themselves but the entire rest of the world. Hence, the child's weakness is generally not resented by the child, for somehow he senses that this very weakness is his strength through the affection, love, and protection it draws to him from adults.

The need for Christians to become as little children, then, whatever else it may involve, involves at least this, that they be aware that they *are* children spiritually. As they recapitulate in Christ, they grow towards adulthood. But having arrived at the adulthood that the Old Law enabled the Jews of our Lord's day to reach, they come to see that they are still children. The more adult they are, the more they realize that they are only beginning the life proper to the Spirit. In some strange way, they know themselves for the first time as Christians. Remaining babes as to malice, they must grow up in likeness to Jesus precisely inasmuch as He is the Anointed with the Spirit. Laboring with powers fully matured, they realize that all they have done or can do for Christ and the Church is no more than a child's playing, pretending to work in yard or kitchen. Like their Lord, the more mature they become, the more they become one with Him who could address the Father as 'Abba,' much as a child addresses his father.

We can now see why "our patriarch Abraham"[11] is presented as the paradigm and perfect model of faith throughout the New Testament. For if our understanding of recapitulation is correct, then Abraham was indeed a "little child." We, too, become as little children if we receive God's word in faith

[10] Hobgoblins, giants, wizards, witches, ghosts, and the like are conceived at this age as naturally wicked, differing only in their similarity to human mind and form from wild animals.

[11] *Roman Missal*, Roman Canon. This or "our father Abraham" appears in Lk.1:73 and in Rom.4:1, 12. But in these contexts it may well refer solely to carnal descent without reference to the gentiles. But the gentiles are clearly included in the *Letter of Clement*, 31:2.

and act upon it as he did, with simple trust in the Father's promises. Abraham shows us the first step in the spiritual growth of one who, through faith, begins in some externally discernable way to recapitulate in Christ.

It is this understanding that undergirds St. Paul's speaking of both children and of Abraham. If Paul reproaches his children, it is that they are weakening in their faith or trust in Christ; they are sliding back from true recapitulation into mere reliving of Judaism. But he also speaks of them as "children of the light" (Eph.5:8), as "children of God" (Phil.2:15); but most significantly he urges them to "be imitators of God, as beloved children" (Eph.5:1). In children truly loved by their father, what lies beneath this imitation is quiet trust and full confidence that what the father does is the very norm of goodness. If Paul praises Abraham's faith it is because it involves just such an attitude. Hence it is the model for the first and basic faith of every Christian. By faith one commits oneself totally to follow Jesus and to imitate Him as the perfect Image of the Father. Even so the apostles did during His earthly life. So also did those who had come to believe in Christ after growth to Jewish maturity but who had not, as yet, undergone the great purification of His suffering and death or known His resurrection.

Long, then, before we are ready for a life of entire submission to the Spirit, long before the mystical life has begun, we must become as children in the same sense that Abraham was. We must believe in the Lord as simply as he, trusting His promise of superabundant fulfilment of our natural hopes, here or hereafter. As Abraham's life makes clear, there is no competition between doing all that an adult should do and total dependence on and trust in God in the doing of it. As Abraham hoped against all hope (Rom.4:18) and came to so great a point of faith as to believe that God could raise Isaac from the dead if this were needed for Him to keep His promise (Rom.4:17; Heb.11:17–19), so the Christian is called to accept with similar faith whatever medicaments and surgery the Lord may think fit to require of him for his good.

It is worth noting that Abraham is never seen as prefiguring Christ but remains firmly set as both prefigurative and preparative type of the believer in Jesus as the Christ. Thus, it is the faith of Abraham that is common to all, whether gentile or Jew.[12] It is Isaac who is, after Adam, Abel, and Noah, the first great prefigurative type of Jesus. This typology is strongly developed on the basis of Hebr.11:17–19 by the Fathers, Antiochene no less than Alexandrian, Western as well as Eastern. Indeed, Abraham's part in the sacrifice of Isaac might appear to make him type of the Father in relation to the crucifixion of Jesus. Though this possibility is noticed by the Fathers and, perhaps, by the Scripture, it seems generally to be avoided.[13] The inverse

---

[12] Cf. *Adv. Haer.* IV, 25, 1 for Irenaeus' development of Paul's theme.

[13] Thus, Irenaeus (*Adv. Haer.* IV, 5, 4) speaks of Abraham as *following* the command of the Word to sacrifice his only and well beloved son so that the Father might in turn offer His well beloved and only Son in sacrifice for us all. It is Isaac who is the type of Christ, carrying the wood for the sacrifice, through whom we learn to carry our cross and *follow* Christ. The relation between Abraham and the Father, then, is found in the mutual exchange of gifts; as type, Abraham is shown as follower of the command of the Word on behalf of those who will be told by the

seems more acceptable: to see in the sacrifice of Isaac Abraham's sharing by anticipation in the Paschal Mystery.

Conversely, except for the literal references to Him as a baby at Bethlehem, none of the New Testament ways of referring to a child is used of Jesus. He is, rather, always and everywhere the Son, both of God and of man. Hence, when His disciples are told to love their enemies so that they may be sons of their Father in heaven (Mt.5:45), this is a command to become perfect as their heavenly Father is perfect (5:48). What is being said no longer refers solely to the recapitulative growth of a child of God but to that full life of the Spirit which is, in the language of the Eastern Church, 'the life in Christ,' anointed by the Spirit and led by Him in all things as Jesus was.[14]

With this completion of one's recapitulation and entrance into the full life of the Spirit, there is no longer a prescribed pattern to follow. Yet even after the Christian's living through the Paschal Mystery, Abraham remains a model also of that more perfect childlikeness to which Christ calls us: that easy and wholly reverent familiarity with the Father in Christ that one sees in the disciples in *Acts* and Paul's letters. It is like that of the four-year old who comes up to put his hand in any adult's, to tell him, as they walk along for a while together, of the owls he has heard in the woods or about how he plays baseball or about his new baby sister.

Only when the Holy Spirit takes over a person's life fully, does he live in the distinctively Christian manner as son of God in Jesus. Then more than ever is it clear that he has only just begun so to live in Christ; and, like a child, he has very little concrete idea of what is to come next. Only after their sharing in Christ's death and resurrection did the apostles become "My brothers" (Mt.28:10 and Jn.20:17). It was not hard for them to realize how far they were from being the adult that their older Brother, Jesus, is. So has it been for all those whom the Spirit leads.

D. Israel in Egypt

If we missed the point earlier, by the time we get well into Jacob's story, it has become inescapable that moral enlightenment is not the primary function of whatever is going on in salvation history at the time of the patriarchs. His deviousness, his willingness to take for himself despite the hurt he thereby inflicts on others, and his evident dependency on mother rather than on father, were pretty clearly disapproved of by the human author. Yet God continued to reveal Himself through him to Abraham's line. The close intimacy of His friendship with Abraham is gone, and He speaks to Jacob, as to Isaac, much less often. There is a greater stress on His protection and providence and less on His closeness.

So, too, the child, despite his faults of character, now gradually becoming

---

Word made flesh to follow Him. For all of this, cf. Jean Daniélou, *Sacramentum Futuri*, *pp* 97–111.

[14] Cf. below, *Ch* 16.E, *pp* 334–337, and above, *Ch* 1.C & D, *pp* 6–7 & 9–10.

evident to him as well as to others, continues to grow in his consciousness of the LORD in a corresponding manner. God seems not less real but less close, and there is less interest in prayer, now done largely by rote. But there is deeper conviction that God can do things for one.

Each of the patriarchs in turn takes the God of his father or his fathers as his own God. This is not, however, automatic but has conditions attached. Thus Jacob, when starting out on the long journey to get himself a wife, poured oil on the stone he had used to support his head as he slept the night before, consecrating it as a memorial because of the dream he had there received from the LORD, and said in effect, "If You will protect me and bring me back safely to this place, then You will be my God." There is, of course, the veiled threat: "If You don't bring me back this way as asked, then I won't take You as my God." But the LORD seemed not to take this transaction amiss. Boys too (for boys, quite characteristically it seems, do this much more often than girls) frequently make vows and promises to God, "If you will do this for me, I will do that for You." The veiled threat is here also, though for the most part, it is not conceived as a threat but just the other aspect of any *quid pro quo*.

Later, Jacob and his family go down into Egypt. The subsequent generations settled down in their own little world in the land of Goshen for a few hundred years. The Hyksos kings of Egypt (if we may synchronize them loosely with the Israelites' entry into Egypt—for the dating offers problems) were favorable to them because of some bonds of tribal kinship, and allowed them to take care of the large and small cattle of Egypt. It was apparently a time of relative tranquillity for them there, bound together by some minimal kind of identity, remaining, in Goshen at least, as an identifiable group that kept its own way of life, separate from the Egyptians, who employed them as shepherds.

They seemed to fit unobtrusively into their surroundings, so much so that the Scripture tells us nothing of the entire period, except its length, or of any of those who lived in it. They had, it seems, no horror of Egyptian idolatry or manner of life since, to some extent at least, they worshipped the Egyptians' gods.[15] In any case, we find no sense of antagonism to the idols of the Egyptians, nor any jealousy for their own faith in the LORD. Their separateness seems to have been imposed in large measure by their economic employment; and the attitude that kept them from being swallowed up religiously in Egypt may well have been little more than the conviction that each people ought to follow its own gods.

This long time passed under silence suggests something like the "latency period" of later childhood, a period some psychologists have thought to exist from about six till the first beginnings of puberty, during which a child loses the interest in sexual matters he had earlier. But Gesell[16] and others have

[15] Jos.24:14 speaks of Israel's fathers as "serving the gods of Egypt." This is hard to reconcile with much other data, but may well have occurred, if not *en masse*, yet enough to have been intolerable to those who sought to maintain their own tribal identities. Then, too, as they multiplied greatly over these years, they may well have spilled out from Goshen and adopted, in varying degrees, Egyptian ways.

argued that, in empirical fact, while there are fluctuations in sexual interest during later childhood, the period specified cannot be regarded as void of such interest. There are recurrent seasons of curiosity, of sex-play and self-exposure, as well as a sustained and warmly welcoming interest in babies.

Some distinctions, however, may help us see that there is truth in both views. I have very little doubt about the observational findings of Gesell. But greater care in language is needed. One must be clear, if one is not to build one's theory into the data to be used to prove it, as to the meaning of "sexual interest." Does it refer simply to curiosity about the characteristics of male and female, part of a general curiosity about all things in the world, himself and other children included? Or does it concern a "socialization" of this curiosity and a desire to make sexuality something "ordinary," by proving one's being boy or girl to one's peers? Does it refer to the processes of elimination as well as to the procreative organs? Does it imply some sort of genital stimulation?

Further, by the time the child is five or six, his family and his religious upbringing both will have begun to have an appreciable effect his spontaneous interests and desires. The more sociable and outgoing his family life and the better the religious milieu provided by his family, the more easily, ordinarily, will the child ignore too-early sexual contacts. But in some cultures, for example, the mother will manually stimulate her child sexually from early infancy. That masturbation should be common in the children of such a culture would not seem a surprise, even in "latency." In many cultures, it seems, it is not uncommon for an older child who has already learned to find some incipient sexual pleasure by one means or another to exploit younger children by manipulation or by self-exposure during or for the sake of arousal.

Those who argue for a latency period are well aware that it can be violated, sometimes with negligible results, sometimes with psychologically disastrous ones. For, such violations tend to distract the child from better things and to turn him in more on himself, and sometimes they do real harm to his psycho-sexual maturation by forcing on him things he has as yet no way to understand. In any case, such violations will skew one's interpretation of data if not taken into account. Moreover, the child's own personality and ways of responding to the actions of others, both siblings and other children, can have a large effect in this area. Since these are, in part, learned responses, it is evident that the familial and religious background needs to be taken into account.

Thus, the Bible's ambiguous silence concerning the Israelites' stay in Egypt has its parallels in later childhood. Both here and earlier, the child's interest in babies is a natural and spontaneous one, helpful for his maturing. His interest parallels the enormous interest in offspring that is central to the story of Abraham and his faith in God's promise of progeny through a son to be miraculously conceived. This interest in progeny is maintained, not now by mere genealogies but through statements about concrete individuals and

---

[16] Arnold Gesell, Frances L. Ilg, & Louise B. Ames, *The Child from Five to Ten*, revised edition, New York: Harper & Row (1977), *pp* 305–306, 311–314.

situations, through the first chapters of *Exodus*.

On the other hand, that Abraham's maturation was more rapid than that of those about him is most decisively shown in the contrast between his warm hospitality towards strangers and the attitude of the men of Sodom. As mentioned above concerning Cain and, later, the Noachic covenant, it is the violence of their eagerness to satisfy their perverse and self-indulgent desires that seems to be decisive in bringing upon them God's punishment. Yet the fact that the other Cities of the Plain were destroyed along with Sodom indicates that such sexual attitudes are intrinsically linked to this gross willingness to satisfy oneself, whatever the injury to others—much like some older children's molestation of younger ones.

A true subsidence of interest in all nongenerative aspects of sexuality, once basic curiosity has been satisfied, is, then, shown as good and desirable. The childish kinds of sexual interest and action simply disappear from view in the rest of *Genesis*. And the Israelites' serving of Egyptian gods, no models of chastity, is passed over in silence (save for the one brief remark much later on) as something to be regretted, whatever its extent, though, insofar as free from violence, nothing the LORD thought worthy of punishment.

Religiously, the Israelites may have been like pre-adolescent children, who know that Catholics, Protestants, and Jews differ in important but not well understood ways, but have no sense of hostility (or even of radical diversity) unless there is persecution by the others or an intolerance learned from their parents. The center of gravity is still firmly inside the family, and it does not really matter what outsiders do.

So, the child learns his religious identity from more or less accidental social differences. He understands a few radical distinctions in doctrine, but knows that the others are wrong and is not concerned except insofar as one of his family may be one of these others. He continues to take all in terms of his own inner life and his relation to God.

Religiously, his life tends to be quiet and regular, not very different from anyone else's. He is at home with God, though he doesn't think very much about Him and takes Him very much for granted, save in prayers and worship. For he would not skip his prayers without some sense of remorse afterward nor feel himself independent of God. Yet he rarely gives Him much reflection, though he may pray intensely to Him—but what He's like or why is of no concern.

It is interesting to note what constitutes an "enemy" at each of these stages of growth. *Genesis* gives only one glimpse of war, that of the four foreign kings against the five kings of southern Canaan (*ch* 14). Abram takes up arms and raids the retiring victors' baggage only in order to free his kinsman Lot. Even the cruel slaughter of the people of Shechem by Simeon and Levi is presented as the carrying out of a personal vendetta, not a war. Enemies, for the patriarchs, are personal, those who have done some wrong to oneself or one's kin.

Children have an enormous amount of trust. If someone comes up and slaps a child's face, but does it with a smile and some sort of formula that indicates that this is the right and proper thing to do, the way things should be if only the child knew better, then even though it hurts, the kid will take it. He is baffled and doesn't know what to make of it. He has no real defense against this sort of thing. It is hard to make a personal enemy of him—until it becomes clear to him that you are out to victimize him or others of his family. But, as in the case of Abram's raid against the kings from the east, to take as enemies those who injure one's family or tribe, that is easy. The child has no problem with this notion. Such a fight is basically fun. He will fight with great gusto. "[T]he great Gaels of Ireland...the men whom God made mad," were merely acting like children of this age, "all whose wars are merry, and all whose songs are sad."

So there is often fighting in the child's world, whose nature depends largely on the cultural context, e.g., is he growing up in North Ireland? Or in a German parish surrounded by Irish or Italian ones?

> Mostly, as children, we associated Catholicism with the fear inspired in us by the Catholic near-delinquents on our street in the middle of New York City. Once, a band of older boys encircled us on our way home and demanded to know what was our religion. Their purpose was to decide what epithets to throw at us and whether to beat us up or not. When they had exhausted every religion they knew of and we still replied with terrified negation, they asked us directly what we were. Since they had never heard the word "atheist," they let us go.[17]

So the world is divided between "we" and "they." "They" are not only different but hostile, and it's best either to avoid them or to be nice to them if you're alone, or to throw stones at them if you're more numerous. But apart from the enemies of his people and from those who are manifestly bullying him, a child will be comfortable with all sorts of people who are very much at odds with his religious convictions, even if of a wholly different culture and race.

---

[17] Ronda Chervin, *Church of Love*, Liguori (MO): Liguori Press, (1973). *pp* 120–121.

Chapter 11

The Mosaic Covenant: Adolescence and Freedom

A. Through the Saving Waters

Only once, seemingly, does the New Testament (I Cor.10:1–2) directly consider our baptism into Christ to be typified by Israel's escape from Egypt and from Pharaoh's harsh slavery, when the people marched forth dry-shod through the Red Sea[1] that would soon destroy their enemies. Yet everywhere this theme is present just beneath the surface.[2] The Last Supper is the Christian Passover meal. Jesus is the Lamb of God, who takes away the sins of the world, as John declares after His baptism. Jesus' blood marks the lintel and doorpost of the Cross, through which we enter into life, having been baptized into His death. By momentary immersion in the waters that overwhelm Satan, whoever believes (Ac.8:36–39) is born again, now spiritually, into the New People of God.[3]

Yet the passage through the Red Sea marks the point at which, according to the parallelism we have been sketching out, one leaves childhood spiritually and becomes a young adult. Leaving the slavery of Egypt means the beginning of one's full freedom and self-determination. Beginning to use one's reason in reflex awareness,[4] one acquires the power of discretion. Henceforth,

[1] The Hebrew texts read "Sea of Reeds," a phrase that would have to be used were the typology of *Exodus* sufficiently developed to deal with place names. "Red Sea" represents an interpretation of uncertain motivation by the translators of the Septuagint, whence it was carried into Old Testament works originally written in Greek (e.g., Wisd.19:7) and the New Testament.

[2] In the liturgy, of course, this connection is made explicit, indeed central. Cf., e.g., the third reading of the Easter Vigil with its prayers, the blessing of the baptismal font, and the rite for baptism itself.

[3] This major theme appears frequently, e.g. Jn.3:3–5; I Cor.1:13–15 & 3:1–2; I Pet.2:2–3.

[4] This "age of reason" is not to be confused with the much earlier "age of reason" at which Confession and Communion first become actively useful to the child. Sin, though not grave, can

reason is meant to be mistress in her own house through free choices reflexly grasped as such. One is now capable of marriage, the vows of religion, and mortal sin.[5] So, like Israel, one is able at this point to enter into covenant with the LORD.

How are these two typical meanings of the crossing of the Red Sea to be reconciled: the entry into adulthood, according to our preparative typology, or birth and first infancy, according to what Scripture implies of baptism? Is baptism restricted to adults, as the Baptists insist? Or is our parallelism incorrect? Neither, I think.

The original Passover and going forth from Egypt is the type of the Paschal mystery of Christ. Each is an historic reality, and the latter is the spiritual meaning and the fulfilment of the former. Jesus, sacrificed upon the Cross as the Paschal Lamb of the New Covenant, atones for the sins of all men and frees from eternal death all those who believe in Him. The passage through the Red Sea, then, brought about through the Passover and the deaths of Egypt's first-born, typifies the effects of Christ's death and resurrection in the liberation of Christians from sin through baptism.

Insofar as baptism is typified by the passage through the Red Sea, it is the real event of any actual baptism that fulfils the reality of this passage which is its figure. The baptism typified is the actual administration of the sacrament by a minister of the Church to some particular person, who may be of any age. There is also the new reality effected by this baptizing: the freeing from Satan's power, the infusion of grace, and birth into the Church.

But this reality of baptism does not prefigure Christ's death and rising but is their symbol, making them present by its power. By symbolizing the still-to-be-realized personal union with Christ on His cross and in His resurrection, a union that alone makes anyone spiritually adult, baptism necessarily symbolizes the spiritual reality of the birth of the Christian, coming forth from the waters of the font and, thus, his passage through the Red Sea.

We are baptized into Jesus' death, so that thereby "our old self was crucified with Him" (Rom.6:6) and buried with Him (Rom.6:3–4; Col.2:12), but also rises from these waters into newness of life in Him (Rom.6:4–5). As a new birth, baptism makes us *begin* to live the life in Christ and to grow through the recapitulative process, whatever our physical or psychic age when

---

be present very early; and already around six or seven, the child can comprehend Who and What is present in the Host and can begin to respond personally to Jesus' coming to him.

[5] So St. Thomas argues, well based in tradition (*S.T.* II-II, 88, 8 ad 2 for the first two, 88, 9 c for the last two). Here and elsewhere, he connects this capability with puberty. His argument is clearest in *Quodlibet.* III, 5, 11 c & ad 2: "After they have the use of reason, through their free will they have authority over their own lives [in contradistinction to the authority their parents had over them earlier] in these things which look to the salvation of their soul." and "at the time of puberty...then, most of all, man begins to have the free use of reason concerning these things which pertain to his salvation." Recognition of the necessarily simultaneous capability for any one of these three great acts of free commitment, as manifestations of one power come of age, would do much to help deal with the current confusion about mortal sin, fundamental option, and the like. More psychological qualification than St. Thomas offers (but in principle accepts) would, however, be needed.

baptized. But one can only be thought to have entered into Christian adulthood when he has actually lived what baptism principally symbolizes, i.e., when he has endured an equivalent of death, has become one crucified to the world and to whom the world is crucified (Gal.6:14), and has, nonetheless, been granted continued life on earth. Only then can he truly be led and blown by the Spirit whithersoever He pleases. Baptism both symbolizes and gives the power to live through the Paschal mystery; it is not itself equivalent to this living through.

Baptism, then, internally orients the Christian to a freely accepted union with Jesus in death and resurrection, a goal that is reached (in most cases[6]) only after the long action of grace involved in recapitulation. Thus, though baptism symbolizes Christian adulthood, it is always the sacrament of infancy, bringing one to birth among God's People. Even when one is baptized as an adult, one is spiritually but an infant in the Church, who must yet grow and be formed after Jesus' likeness. On the other hand, a baptism conferred in physical infancy must be personally and freely ratified as one enters adolescence and the freedom of natural adulthood. It is his struggle whether to yield this first, fully free acceptance of the implications of his baptism that marks the adolescent's spiritual development even as it did Israel's.

Hence typology would seem to encourage infant baptism. The infant should be baptized as soon as may be, so that, by the power of God's grace, his life in Christ may begin as soon as possible. This presence of grace in the baptized youngster is not useless merely because not yet personally assimilated or fully operative. It is not any less a release from the power of the devil and from original sin and an incorporation as a member of God's people. The infant possesses by grace the right orientation of his will, now intrinsically turned towards God, despite the psychic damage that remains.

To be predisposed to decide well in accord with God's will, is not useless; even a child can make some free choices. Whether and how psychic growth may be modified by the presence of grace in the infant, we do not know. One could argue that baptism makes no appreciable psychological difference to the child when living as a pre-Abrahamite, i.e., that the supernatural powers of the life of grace in Christ remain uninfluenced by his personal activity, which has only a weak and inchoate freedom. He will grow much the same in any culture which does not itself work against his growth.[7]

But we do know that the aberrant psychic growth that is concupiscence is modified for the better, all else being equal, beginning around age five, as the child reaches the psychic level of Abraham. Surely, the earlier this action

---

[6] For the early Christians, however, persecuted in a thousand ways for their faith, often their birth into the life in Christ, their union with Him in His sufferings and death, and their sharing in the newness of His risen life very nearly coincided. Many times since, and even now, the same is true for many converts from Judaism, Islam, the greater pagan cultures, and marxism.

[7] See *Ch* 18.B, *pp* 362–369 below. This does not mean that all cultures reach this level; they do not. Our own is a prime example of one that has regressed back to a level at which the child is very likely to grow in a stunted or seriously traumatized way. But the culture as such seems the dominant factor here, not baptism or its lack; the life in Christ itself does not seem directly to affect the infant's growth.

against concupiscence begins, the better. The process of recapitulation in Christ can, in any case, be well under way before adolescence. For, the period between Abraham and Moses corresponds to a stage in which the Christian child will differ in but a few, yet very important ways from the non-Christian child, though remaining like him in most.

Moreover, whatever one may hold as to the precise age when a young person becomes capable of fully free action through reflex clarity of moral perception, until this capability has been achieved in fact, no person is capable of grave sin. Thus, as St. Francis Xavier pointed out,[8] anyone baptized in infancy or childhood remains, of necessity, in the state of grace until about age fourteen.[9] Whoever, then, has been baptized in infancy is, of necessity, still blessed with the grace of a share in the supernatural life and true innocence until adolescence. Only with puberty (or later) is there sufficient habitual self-possession and freedom that the freely chosen and deliberate living of the life in Christ may begin, however early one's baptism.[10]

The waters of baptism, then, even for an infant, make him more ready for the choices that the approach to adulthood requires, even as the passage through the Red Sea manifested Israel's proximate readiness for the Covenant. Baptism is the symbol, not the reality, of this threshhold that the crossing of the Red Sea prefigures.

B. THE COVENANT AND LEGAL JUSTICE

The Hebrews went out from Egypt as a motley group of tribes (Ex.12:38) under Moses' leadership to meet the LORD at Sinai. There they received His Law, which was to constitute them His own people and possession. The LORD alone, therefore, is to be their God. Him alone are they to acknowledge and worship. This they are to do not only by sacrifices (in which they do not differ greatly from the nations around them) but by a highly specific obedience. God now reveals Himself as demanding morally right behavior as part of one's worship of Him. The LORD is a God with a moral sense.[11]

His commandments assert what man must do and, for men of a much later generation, indicate the sort of nature that man has, the sort of being that he is. More importantly, they assert the sort of God the LORD is. Morals can never henceforth be separated from faith, nor moral theology from the

---

[8] St. Francis Xavier, letter of October 22, 1548 to Francisco Henriques, *Epistolae S. Francisci Xaverii aliaque eius scripta*, 2nd ed., edd. G. Schurhammer & I. Wicki, *MHSI 67* (1944), *p* 466 (Doc. 68, #3).

[9] In this, he is following St. Thomas (*ST* II-II, 189, 5 c & ad 1), who gives fourteen for the onset of puberty in boys, but twelve in girls, Cf. note 5 above.

[10] Jesus is shown to us already with the requisite maturity at twelve (Lk.2:42), a year before He would have become "son of the Law" according to later Judaism's choice of thirteen as the age at which a boy could be made subject to the Law without being psychically crushed or overwhelmed by its obligations.

[11] Cf. C. S. Lewis' superb pages on this in: *The Problem of Pain*, "Chapter I, Introductory." London: Geoffrey Bles (1940).

Creeds, often as the attempt has been made.

The Law came down in fire and thunder and threats: "Anyone that touches the mountain will die, even an animal." No explanation is given as to why Israel should not do the things proscribed save that the Lord wants it so. The Law is His will. This is the way He is to be served.

So does His moral law seem to come down upon one shortly after puberty. Till now, God has been gentle and friendly or just "around." Suddenly He confronts the youngster in a very different guise.[12] Yet, not totally different. The Commandments given the Hebrews at Sinai, at least the final seven, did not teach them a brand new morality. The history of the Patriarchs makes clear that the content of these seven was already morally in place as what good men lived by. Honoring one's parents, shunning murder, adultery, theft, false witness, and perhaps even the coveting of what was not one's to have, were already taken as good; they were understood in much the same way, it seems, as they were in Moses' day. So, though the early adolescent knows that his parents' will is not necessarily God's will, yet if raised in a good family, there will be no surprises or serious discrepancies between what family and Church have taught him thus far and God's newly perceived moral judgment. This latter he generally still has little trouble in accepting.

What is new, however, is a sense of sin. What had been something merely bad or shameful is now revealed as an affront to the overpowering holiness of the LORD. He is terrible in His presence. His moral will is personal. As at Sinai, He imposes His law from without since, for the youngster, God is still external to him. Though He sees and observes his inmost thoughts, He does so from outside. But there is no doubt but that all of his life, waking and sleeping, down to its least details, falls under the gaze and judgment of God and is to be governed by His commands. There are no reasons given for these commands. It is sufficient that God has spoken: Do it, or else...!

Particularly troubling is his own, new, inner passion for sexual identity and activity. Though sexual interest is not new to him, its relation to God and its potential for sin is. He feels dragged by his own body into that which is sternly forbidden. Even his imagination is now subject to moral judgment, yet he sees no way to control it. That impure actions and desires can separate him from God does not usually seem doubtful to him, though a bad counsellor may dull the edge of his conscience for a time. As Israel with the golden calf or when worshipping the Baal of Peor (Num.25:1–9), unchastity is sensed as in some way the worship of a foreign god, punishable by death (Ex.32:27–29). The difference now is that spiritual death is the punishment which is inflicted if such an "apostasy" is wilful.

The crisis is not unimportant. He may do as Israel, who when encamped without leadership at the foot of Sinai and lacking things to do, spurning the LORD, ate, drank, "and rose up to play" (Exod.32:6). "Play" is the right word; for the early adolescent is not yet able, despite his preoccupation with it, to take sex seriously. Adultery, except by mere chance, is not his problem.

---

[12] This will be true, in different ways, for the well-raised Jew, Moslem, or Christian. I do not know enough about the various paganisms to guess what is true at this point among them.

Even as a bit earlier there may be the sorts of playing around with his generative powers involved in self-abuse and the first, tentative intimacies with a "date," so a bit later there can be partying and boisterous fornication in company with his peers. He may, like Israel, rebel and follow these imperious inclinations as he wishes. He may submit, but without inner assimilation of the law, as did those who stood firm at Sinai but gave themselves later to the daughters of Midian. Or he may simply be discouraged by the difficulty of the struggle and give up for a time (Nu. 13–14).

The Commandments are unique among all the ancient Near-Eastern laws in their character as peremptory and absolute injunctions: "You shall not do X." There is no longer at this stage simply a question of faith, loyalty, and fidelity as in the young child. It is a question of doing things or not doing them; one's reasons do not matter.

This aspect can seem strange to us. We ask, "If God has a moral will, how could one's reasons and motives not matter?" The response is that the first thing one must learn at this age, if the process of recapitulation is to continue well, is that moral action is, in its essence, a personal response to a personal God. If the LORD says, "Don't!", then one may not do so, whatever His reasons or our own may be, especially since, in commanding, He already knows what ours are. The subjective aspects of sin and virtue lie still in the future.

Conversely, it is very hard for the youngster at this age to get any sense of equity or epikeia. If the law says "Do this!", he does not see that he can do just the opposite without wrong-doing and even without violating the law, if he does it in accord with the intent of the lawmaker or in accord with the spirit of the law. This is especially the case when it is God's law, since God knows all the circumstances in advance and cannot have not foreseen them.

Like Moses and Phineas, then, if deeply devout, he will tend to severity of judgment and harshness of action with regard to wrongdoers, even though he himself desires and is melted by mercy shown to him. He will not think, for example, as may a modern exegete, that the golden calf was only a pedestal for the invisible LORD to stand upon and that the LORD, not the calf, was the true object of their nonetheless unacceptable worship. The youngster will simply join the sons of Levi there (Ex.32:27–29).

Justice, especially strict commutative justice, is the virtue most highly regarded by the early adolescent. A teacher may be as strict, even severe, as he likes (as was Moses with the rebels in the desert), without thereby losing the respect or even the affection of his students. But let him be ever so little unfair in his allotting of penalties or benefits, and he will lose both. Yet it is this very insistence on legal justice, justice according to the rules, that becomes for many youngsters the source of the intolerable burden of conscience known as scruples.[13]

[13] A scruple is a sort of anxious, even desperate, fear of offending God through an inability to decide what His law requires of one under the given concrete circumstances. The more one analyses the situation, the more one feels helpless to find the truth, yet seems under a tormenting obligation to make a right decision and to act.

Some people may still remember the old laws on the reception of Communion: Anyone who wished to receive had to fast, from midnight, from all food and drink, even water. But, then, what to do when you are struggling to early Mass through a snowstorm and breathe in some snowflakes? Having swallowed that trace of water, can you go to Communion or have you broken your fast? Worse yet, did you really have full advertance to what you were doing when you consented—was it really a full consent—to some impure desire or stirring? And did you confess it rightly or did you conceal some significant aspect from the confessor, who seemed to take it much too calmly? Are you concealing the full gravity of the sin even from yourself? This is essentially the same sort of intellectual process that is involved in philosophical scepticism, though with a far heavier emotional charge. As with scepticism, there is no way around this by the only methods this young person knows. He is still learning, and all he can do is to bring himself to obey his confessor till such time as he has enough experience and moral maturity to free himself with God's grace from this sort of torment.

The existence of such scruples shows one of the ways in which concupiscence has remained and grown in the person. While seeming to be rooted in piety and love for God and His law, scruples are but one, adolescent shape of that fear of death mentioned in connection with original sin (Heb.2:14). It is a fear of the LORD, who is as yet wrongly feared. The scrupulous person is, deep down, seeking to protect his own hide and not be caught hopelessly in the wrong by One whose grounds for evaluation he does not fully grasp but whose condemnation he greatly fears. He shows his descent from Adam by the covert pride of his insistence on reasoning out for himself what is good or evil when he knows how to be logical but not yet how to be reasonable.

The first three Commandments, however, were more radically new than the others. Through the very first Commandment the LORD revealed Himself as a jealous God. The Hebrews are to become His people Israel, separated from all other peoples by their being chosen to be His very own. It is not required, however, that anyone else choose to worship the LORD. Jethro was amicably allowed, without punishment or threat, to go back to his own gods. It is only Israel that may not turn to foreign gods.

So, with adolescence, comes a realization of one's religous differences from others. This need no longer be a mere factual recognition of diversity. The youngster begins to be proud of his religious background. This is not, of course, a phenomenon relating to religion alone. There was much of hero-worship at this stage in Israel, whose veneration of Moses as hero remained extraordinary in its intensity and range. Everything that came from the LORD or that was truly good in Israel had somehow to be centered on, derived from, or related to Moses. So, when the adolescent finds someone who has taken a stand for God with courage and firm reason, he is awed by him and desires to be like him. How many young people have entered the religious life or the priesthood because they have known some religious or priest whom they admired intensely!

Something similar takes place concerning one's religion and one's family. They may be valued highly and strongly defended, but now not just from familial affection. They, too, partake of the "heroic", i.e., are seen to offer fine models of the way of life the young person wishes to live or of the kind of person he desires to become. If well instructed, he then esteems the Church in large measure for what she gives in the way of cohesive strength, intellectual or artistic achievements, political or economic skill, social standing, legal structure or other cultural values. These are the things that, like the beauty of the Tabernacle or the righteousness of the Law, seem to give the service of God its grandeur and that are its connatural rewards.

C. Authority in the Desert

The youngster has by now become acutely and passionately conscious of his own selfhood as well as often miserably self-conscious, like Moses making his excuses while looking unhappily at the ground in front of the burning bush and worrying about his lack of speaking skills. Yet he knows, as did Moses, to what people he belongs or, like the various Hebrew tribes, is desirous to learn.

The ancient Hebrew had his religion, his social identity, what may pass as his politics—there wasn't much except for his interactions with the leaders at the different levels of his strongly hierarchical society—and all else given to him simply by his being one of his tribe. Through and with the giving of the Law, the LORD gradually forged, out of those many tribes, a people in which not only worship, faith, and morals were tied together but, along with these, tribal structures, family relationships, the entire culture were fused into one solid mass. The people were united in the same life and the same religious understanding of that life.[14] The varied aspects we carefully distinguish were all there present, but largely undifferentiated and still to be developed.

So, too, the adolescent already belongs to a family and a "tribe," and is, say, an irishcatholicdemocrat. But as the Hebrews had to leave behind them all that was familiar in Egypt in order to become the LORD's people, so the youngster must go out into a larger world beyond his close family and childhood friendships.

His thrust in all this, however, still remains largely tribal. He wishes to go beyond his family, i.e., his intimate family, the one in which he was nurtured; but he does so by entering a larger "family": a school, a youth organization, a gang. He has a much more elaborately structured set of relationships now, where he belongs not only to the closed, nuclear family but, as the Hebrews did, to a house and clan and tribe. Yet there are traces of an awareness of the entire people to which he belongs.[15] He and his peers belong not only to the same school or the same youth organization but to the same religion or the same country.[16]

[14] Cf. Christopher Dawson, *Religion and Culture (Gifford Lectures)*, New York: Sheed and Ward (1948), especially *pp* 47–62 and 197–218.

[15] One may wonder if the existence of gangs in their present, highly structured forms is not a result of the breakdown of the more natural units based on blood and religion and social position.

[16] This also suggests an essential difficulty with most of television: in addition to the lateral socialization that it fosters among those who watch the same programs, it brings about a "frontal"

Now, the LORD's moral will concerns not merely the individual; it is also a social will. His will for the individual person is inseparable from His will for the entire group, the tribe and people or, in our case, the Church, His new people.

Till now, the LORD may have had a moral will concerning such things as stealing cookies, vandalizing a neighbor's garden, or fighting with one's siblings. He forbade what the child already felt was bad and He commanded what he knew he really ought to do, whether God said anything about it or not. His own conscience responded fully to the prohibitions; but chiefly because these were also prohibitions by parents, who had the right to command and were right in what they commanded. God's will did not touch him, so to speak, directly, but was sensed, if at all, only as a will that one should obey one's parents. And this obedience, he really did see as good and want to do.

But at puberty, even though the youngster may still fully accept parental authority without question, there is a deep need, if he is to mature well, to distance himself from his parents, to be conscious that he is making decisions that are truly his own, for which he can both assert and accept full responsibility. He needs to act on his own. As he begins to feel the strength of his own powers and to know his own self increasingly as his own, not as "property," with which he may deal arbitrarily, but as that mystery for which he and he alone bears the full responsibility, then parents' regulations become increasingly hard to bear. At best they stand in need of justification, so that he may make them his own and impose them autonomously upon himself as rational formulations, only by accident first formulated by his parents.

The young person's whole history of sin, original and actual, and also the sins of his parents, which have, often without their recognizing it, altered their characters and made them less what they are called to be as parents, affect him in his efforts. He can easily come to resent the authority of his parents. Though God's law good and is known to be such, it may well be resisted because it has been imposed by external authority or at least has been transmitted through his parents or a seemingly impersonal Church. In its absoluteness, it may stir helpless protest. Especially in its link with scruples or in its frustration of sexual desires, it can be deeply resented. In almost any case, the young person wants to understand why these things are wrong, not knowing that understanding can only follow upon an obedient doing, not go before it.

Again he is like the Hebrews in the desert. He can accept God's current command or reject it, but there is no real way to argue about it. Not that he doesn't try. But having little experience, especially in the consequences of the forbidden matters, he can only argue about the words of the command or about the grounds of its applicability to him or about ostensible inconsistency in the one who commands: "But you said yesterday,...!" But most of it he has to take as given. There are no gray areas.[17]

---

socialization through an illusory sense of identification with the nonexistent "tribe" of those who appear on the screen (or with one that has, at best, no knowledge of one's existence except as a statistically defined source of purchases).

[17] Scruples are not gray, but terrible in their clarity of seeming internal moral contradiction.

One is God's friend or His opponent. If the former, He will do everything good for you. If the latter, He will punish you severely. Always ready for use, now as then, are the swords of Phineas and Joshua and those leaders faithful to the LORD and Moses. Or punishment will come through the bite of venomous serpents, or by pestilence, or from alien enemies. God, man, and nature are armed against the evildoer. For the adolescent, the question of good versus bad has now become life versus death, salvation versus damnation. So, death often haunts the adolescent as it haunted Israel in the desert (Num.16:41).

Yet, whatever his situation, nothing could be worse than to excuse him from the law or to set it aside (quite apart from the blasphemous usurpation involved in this latter). For one thing, it is not likely that he will really believe you or, if he does, he may well cast all religion aside.

A youngster of this age may announce, for example, that he doesn't want to continue going to a Catholic school, that he's tired of all that stuff. His parents, good Catholics themselves who have never hidden their faith and have been clear on the need to cultivate it lest it be lost, after some discussion with him, may say, "Well, it's your decision. We want what you want." There are then two terrible alternatives for the youngster. Perhaps his parents don't really believe "all that stuff" themselves but continue to talk as if they did; maybe, even, they are hypocrites. In this case, he will be strongly tempted to cast his own faith aside. Perhaps they really do believe it all. But then they have no real love for him. He has been taught how terrible is the loss of faith. To casually let him risk it in this manner seems little better than had they responded in the same fashion to his announcing, as he opened a little jar of gray powder to sprinkle in his soup, "This is rat poison. I'm tired of sticking around this lousy world."

The logical handling of clear and distinct ideas, however little based on fact, rules the adolescent world. The obscure and convoluted moral cowardice that his parents' worldliness has generated in them, he cannot yet understand. Indeed, his parents may not realize the spiritual poison they themselves have drunk. Nevertheless, psychically, even rebellion is better than finding nothing fixed that he can push against or reject. It is next to impossible for him to distance himself properly, as he must if to grow up, from blobs of soft jelly that yield to his touch and offer no resistance to his blows. Only through his sufferings and turmoil, when caught in what seems the snare of a divinely given moral law, will he, gradually or quickly, depending on temperament and upbringing, learn the true nature of his own freedom, recognize empirically when he has really exercised it and when not, and accept the responsibility to make genuinely free moral decisions. Subjection to the law is the first condition for freedom from it. But this is not done overnight. For Israel, the time between the giving of the Law and the freedom of the sons of God in Christ was some thirteen centuries.

Insofar as the youngster is not yet responsible for certain actions, he must become responsible by being held responsible; and ordinarily "punishments" remain primarily—though not wholly—disciplinary. Contrary to much contemporary psychology, at this age fear and punishment must come, not softness and permissiveness.

It is not strange, then, that the adolescent is often in revolt. At this stage, this is is not a matter of principled and planned rebellion or of attempted overthrow of established authority but of brief flare-ups and refusals, all depending on the strange new moods and feelings stirring him. Just such rebelliousness appeared in Israel in the desert. Miriam and Aaron preen themselves over God's speaking through them, presenting themselves as Moses's equals; but this is less a challenge to Moses' authority than mere pique at his marrying the Cushite woman (Num.12:1–2). Dathan and Abiram saw no reason why they could not do a better job of leading the people than Moses, arguing for equality and more democratic procedures on the grounds that "all the LORD's people is holy" (Num.16:1–3, 12–14). Korah, not content to be a Levite, wanted the powers of a priest though lacking the qualification of suitable birth (Num.16:1, 5–11, 16–19). The sons of Aaron chose to adapt liturgical practice as they thought fit (Lev.10:1–3). In like manner, the whole people, when told to fight, refused (Num.13:30; 14:9–10) or, not to fight, fought (Num.14:40–45).[18]

The early adolescent, however spontaneously courageous and generous, remains profoundly centered on himself. Israel, too, wandering through the desert, would serve the LORD generously for a time, giving freely of treasures and precious stuffs to make the Tabernacle, the Tent of Meeting, and their appurtenances. Yet whenever things went awry or danger threatened, they would lapse into self-pitying complaint. Even when things went well, except for the one brief moment after the crossing of the Red Sea, it is hard to see much of gratitude in their demeanor.

At a much later time, Hosea rebukes the Northern Kingdom (13:13) for being as a foolish child that sticks at the mouth of the womb. The LORD desires to bring them to birth and they stand fast in distrust and fear and refuse to come forth. The image fits more literally, perhaps, the period in the desert, when Moses has had his fill of their petulance and asks the LORD why He has burdened him with this people "as a nurse carries a sucking child" (Num.11:12).

There is in the adolescent a certain analogy to what happened in infancy. As one has a first birth from the womb of his mother, so at adolescence there is something like a second birth, out from the womb of the family into the world of early adulthood. Like the first birth, this second one represents a cutting off and severance from the support and matrix that has hitherto provided nourishment and comfort and protection. Like that first birth, this too begins with a wail. Recall Israel's endless complaining even when not in outright rebellion, not only about lack of water and food (Ex.15:24; 17:2–3; 16:3) but about the monotony of the miraculous sustenance then granted them (Num.11:4). Recall the complaints about the hazards of the way, about the

[18] One of the more interesting ironies of the varied ecclesiologies of democracy and dissent that have sprung up since II Vatican is their emphasis on the Church as the People of God. They seem completely to overlook the fierce wrath of the LORD against those who used just such maxims as theirs against Moses. Indeed, never again, even under the Monarchy, was Israel to have as hierarchically structured and authority-dominated a society as under Moses in the desert.

dangers of occupying the Promised Land, about almost everything (Num. 11:1). And, of course, it is always the LORD's chosen leader that is to blame.

The adolescent seems to himself at times exceedingly weak and almost incapable of surviving. Yet, if dealt with by his natural family with continued but exigent and unromanticized love, he can grow healthily in strength. There is a sense, then, in which adulthood and rebirth, even on the merely natural order are but one.

D. The Conquest and the Renewal of the Covenant

After the forty years of wandering, the Israelites under Joshua burst in upon the Promised Land of Canaan. But this conquest of the land would seem to have been longer and harder than appears on the surface. Detailed study of the text shows that not only Joshua but his successors were engaged in endless, relatively local wars and battles. It often happens that war against external enemies unites a people more closely than peace does. There was some such effect in Israel, but it should not be overestimated. The lack of open conflicts between Israelites and of rebellions against Joshua seems in large measure due to the lack of any effort to establish a strong central authority and to the independence of the various tribes as they took over the lands alloted to them.

The situation was similar to what one finds in the groups that adolescents establish for themselves, such as gangs or clubs of their own making. They are bound together, perhaps with great closeness through their common activities and the experiences they share, perhaps in opposing some common adversary, perhaps in working for some common ideal or goal, but not by any authority. The will of the group is determinative, and also fickle. The role of leadership, too, depends solely on the influence the individual exerts with his peers.

The entry into Canaan represents a coming into one's own and a realization of one's own powers and possible destiny. So, the young person may well begin to take his religion seriously, even if this be a form of atheism like the Comsomol. Moreover, just as Israel's conquest of the Holy Land under Joshua was a religious war, so youngsters of both sexes who have reached the level of (psychic) middle adolescence, are quite capable of killing people, themselves or others, for religious reasons and are easily caught up into religious warfare. (Anti-religious reasons are equally effective. Think only of the Brown Shirts or the Senderistas or Pol Pot's Marxists).

Just twenty-five years ago, such language would have been scoffed at by the majority of American intellectuals. Now, they stand appalled in the presence worldwide of these youthful killers with whom they have no way to deal, even in theory. About the best they have managed is to lump together under the label 'fundamentalists' all those who take their religion as seriously as it intrinsically requires. But the liberal nonfundamentalists, having denied the very possibility of truth in religious matters, have no categories through which to render intelligible the utterly different modes in which religious coexistence is currently being refused or rejected. Some modes are peaceable, some slaughterous; some carefully, even coldly, rational, others glowing with mystic fire; some based in deep love of what they seek to preserve and deep love for their adversaries as well, others fierce with resentment and hatred of the enemy.

All that will be worth tracing carefully later on. Here, we need note only one point. To the degree that a youngster is Christian, when he begins to take his spiritual life seriously and turns from just "being a Catholic" to working at it, what is essential is a rough and warlike beginning. He must be able and willing to break relationships that previously led him astray, to sever connections with bad companions, ultimately if need be, to cut himself off from his family, friends, social environment and culture. In brief, like the Israelites, he must do battle against those who, till then, quietly occupied his mind and heart. He now must cut all ties with any who would hinder or draw him back from his service of God.

Correlative with this is a need to have a certain success on one's own, with God's help, to feel oneself able to do battle and to win, to sever hampering ties and cloying relationships, and to be all the better for it. If one succeeds at this, he senses an internal strength and vigor that sweep opposition away as he marches forward. Think, to take perhaps the best known case, of St. Francis of Assisi, stripping off every shred of clothing so as to be able to owe nothing earthly to anyone. In such cases with the saints, recapitulation is present in its fullest degree. The merely psychic parallelism has become largely a spiritual one. But, even here, there exists a natural base: a need to push free of all obstacles to one's "cause." Even this, of course, requires much psychic development, as is evident from the many "cultures without causes," not least the Egyptian[19] and Canaanite ones.

Later on, he will often see that he has good reason to regret that he was as hard on others as he then thought he had to be. Though he acted virtuously at the time, yet, as one then still deeply infected with concupiscence, he can later see how much of sinfulness was mixed therein. Nevertheless, it seems that, at the time, this severance and willingness to break with one's whole past and those people who belonged to it is often strictly necessary.

The entire book of *Joshua* builds up to the great renewal of the Covenant at Shechem. The conquering Israelites were the children of those whom God had excluded from the land of promise and who wandered in the wilderness forty years until all the generation that had taken part in the Covenant at Sinai had died. Entering the Promised Land uncircumcised, their first act after crossing the Jordan had been to mark in their flesh the seal of faith in the LORD (Rom.4:11). All their men were then circumcised, readied for that first Passover in the new land (Josh.5:4–12) and for the labors of the holy war ahead. But now they have fought their enemies and overthrown them. Finally they are ready to stand before the LORD and to renew that Covenant which had first been made with the generation of their fathers, whose great sin was their refusal to rely the LORD's promises in order to conquer this land.

Old Testament scholars suggest that there were other Hebrew tribes, friendly to these newcomers, in some way their kin, who were already settled

[19] Akhenaton seems an almost sole exception through the 2500 years before Christ.

around Shechem. These were told of the LORD's great actions, then, and wished to become part of Israel. In this case, the renewal of the Covenant would also have constituted their reception as part of the people of the LORD. So it is with late adolescents, who, unlike their earlier selves, now easily open their groups, whether teams or gangs or clubs, to welcome all who are willing strictly to keep their rules and to prove themselves firm and faithful.

In any case, all in Israel, even the tribes that came from Egypt and had stood before the LORD at Sinai, are permitted a choice. *Before* they themselves personally enter into the Covenant with the LORD—they and not merely their fathers—they are allowed to choose between the LORD and the gods beyond the River that Abraham's fathers had worshipped, or even the gods of the people of Canaan. But, once made the LORD's people, there is no turning back. They will be His and He will be jealous in their regard. Once the land has become theirs, this land that itself forms the perennial witness to the Covenant, no further options are possible. Good and evil henceforth will be defined in terms of the Covenant and of other peoples' responses to the LORD's people.

The problem many parents have felt—that to raise their children in any particular religious belief is to predetermine their personal choice of a religion when they grow up, at least to bias them and to make them unfree in this important area—is a pseudo-problem only. For, God deals with most men as He did at Shechem with Israel. No matter how well raised in a staunch Catholic family (or in one of many other religions), each man is called by God, personally to accept Him or refuse Him, to give his life to Him or to revert to the gods of the pagans (for there is, whatever the appearances, little other option). But it is no small grace to be given an experiential basis for the choice. Only a Catholic, well raised, can discern the full range of his options with understanding. To the extent that his religious background is deficient or distorted, to this extent he does not know at least one of his alternatives, though he may be quite unaware of his ignorance.

We see in the renewing of the Covenant a sort of distant adumbration of the process of recapitulation, a sort of preparation for what the New Joshua was to do in bringing about the New Covenant, summing up in Himself all that had gone before. The Israelites at Shechem were invited to do what their fathers' generation did. What happened to the one must happen to the other. But these younger people were to take the right turn and do things correctly wherever their forebears had taken the wrong one and acted incorrectly. Joshua stood in Moses' place as the one who heard the LORD's commands for the people. They had crossed the Jordan dry-shod as their fathers did the Red Sea, not in panic but with the Ark in their midst and religiously leaving twelve stones to mark forever the event. Joshua had held out his lance till victory was won as Moses did his arms. At the LORD's command they had gone courageously into battle, against all human odds, unlike their fathers who doubted. Thus readied, they summed up all that Israel had gone through in their renewal of the Covenant of Sinai.

Chapter 12

Jesus' Recapitulation

When considering original sin, we looked at the Adam-Christ typology and considered the psychic malformations that accompany the growth of the infant in the womb. The same, nonfree, psychic damage was considered as it develops in the baby and small child. We were able to see how one conceived in original sin but baptized as an infant begins in childhood to recapitulate the life of Abraham, once he had been called by the LORD. But differences in spiritual maturation between people of the same age and even of the same culture show themselves more and more strongly in the accounts of the Exodus and the wanderings, to become yet more pronounced under Joshua and the judges.

At this point, however, the effects of the culture of Israel, their actual sins, the divergent histories of individuals over the entire range of recapitulation seen so far, make it difficult to continue to discern the universal psychic effects of original sin. Such diversity calls, even more obviously than before, for an understanding of our Lord's own growth and maturation, in terms of which alone can we make sense the spiritual growth of the Christian. Hence in Section B below, we shall consider the psychic growth and spiritual development of Jesus as seen in His recapitulation of all that took place between the fall of Adam and the death of Joshua, His namesake. But before that, we must deal with the Christological question whether we are free to attribute intellectual, moral, or spiritual growth to Jesus at all.

A. Spiritual growth of one already perfect?

A first statement of the position for which I will argue here can be made in scriptural terms. Since Jesus grew in wisdom, age, and grace, before God and man (cf. Lk.2:52), He became, as He grew older, steadily more pleasing to the Father—not, of course, in either His divine nature or Person but in His humanity. As man, He had every good and right type of human relationship to the Father and was loved the more by Him as He freely received more of the Father's gifts to Him. For, the Father's consequent love of every creature stands in direct proportion to the goodness of that creature; and what growth means is a fuller reception of that great gift of God which is the creature's progressive actualization of its potentialities.

In Jesus, His human cultural and intellectual growth ("in wisdom"), His physical and psychic maturation ("in age"), and His spiritual development ("in grace") took place together. In Him there was no disjunction, no lack of synchronization, no disorder. He grew as a human infant with the psychic maturation and development that is proper to a human infant—but to an infant that had been graced by God from His conception, in exemplary perfection, as the model for all men, beyond all other men, showing more perfectly than the first Adam the ways in which, from the beginning, God had wished man to develop. Since, as man, He was created and finite, related to the Persons of the Trinity by the real relations to Them of His human nature, He could and did grow spiritually as long as He lived on earth. *A fortiori* did His growth continue in all its psychic and biologically determined aspects.

Given, however, some recent debates in Christology, it may prove helpful to spell out this position more carefully in the rest of this section.

The Council of Chalcedon defined that "the same [Jesus Christ is] perfect in His divinity; the same, perfect also in His humanity."[1] The human and the divine are, indeed, never to be separated or divided; but neither are they ever to be mixed or altered, "never taking away the difference of the natures because of the unity but saving rather that which is proper to each nature."[2] Infinite mystery, how this can be; but clear as to what the mystery is.

It may be true that some contemporary theologies have denigrated the doctrine of Chalcedon and have tended to downplay or even deny the integral divinity of our Lord, in a manner that seems increasingly Subordinationist or Adoptionist.[3] But the greater temptation for devout Catholics has usually been to move towards a Monophysitic mixing or confusion of the two natures, thinking of Christ as compounded out of the divine and human mixed together or existing *from* the two natures rather than, in the words of the Council, "existing *in* two natures." This is as damaging to true faith as Adoptionism and more dangerous since much less obvious. For example, despite many pious uses of the term, there is no such thing as a "God-man," if this imply an essence or a nature that is both human and divine.[4] If one is speaking

[1] This phrase from Chalcedon continues to show its importance for the unity of the Church. Thus, the "Statement of Accord on Christology" (February 12, 1988) between the Coptic Church and the Roman Church uses it: Christ is "perfect in His divinity and perfect in His humanity."

[2] DS 301–302. Though Chalcedon is the Council usually mentioned in connection with current Christological debates, more directly important is III Constantinople, which amplified and extended to all of Jesus' operations, especially those of His will, the doctrine of Chalcedon (cf. DS 555–558).

[3] Some of their opponents speak of them carelessly as Arian. This is hardly the case, since Arius, though thinking the Son to be a creature, nonetheless considered Him to be vastly more than a man.

of *what* Jesus is, what kind of being Christ is, one can only say that He is two different kinds of being at once, that He exists in two natures simultaneously, being both God and also a man, yet one single Person; but not a single kind of being, a sort of supernatural minotaur.

Our question, then, is: when is a human being perfect in his humanity? To this, different answers have been given. Some theologians have considered any man as perfect only when, beyond time, he is glorified by the Father in heaven. Only then will all traces of original and actual sin have disappeared. Only then will he have reached the definitive end of every process of growth or purification or merit. Only then will all his powers be as fully actualized as ever they will be. For then he will be ravished by the beatific vision and endowed with all possible perfections of the human body, mind, and will[5] through the infusion by God of both supernatural and preternatural gifts. This "terminal perfection" exists, admittedly, only in virtue of the supernatural and other gifts added to his nature, but does *de facto* constitute the full perfection of his human nature.

But one may speak also of a "relative perfection" that exists in time, anteceding this terminal perfection: man's perfection as a temporal being at some moment in his life, as measured against the fulness of what he could then be or have been. In this sense, one may speak of a perfect infant, though the infant has not yet actualized most of his powers. Most citizens of heaven, however, are perfect in the terminal sense without having been perfect in this relative sense at all points, or even at any points, of their life on earth. Even so, terminal perfection retains a relation to history that remains forever, being less or greater and variously structured depending on how the person's life was lived under grace.

The perfection of the process that has constituted a person's life and growth up to a given moment extends somewhat the notion of relative perfection. This extension has the advantage of being less open to merely abstract consideration and more easily kept in terms of the person's history, including all his interrelations with his time and place, with his fellows, and with God. For, this perfection of life ties one in to the times and seasons of God's actions in the world. What is good and right at one time may be bad and wrong at some other. The infant should suck his mother's milk; the adolescent should not. Corporal penances can be a great aid to spiritual growth at its beginnings; they may be a major obstruction at some later time.[6] God's command to Israel to slaughter Canaanites was no longer binding upon Solomon, who, to build His Temple, might not be a "man of blood."

When applying these ideas to Christ, some theologians, afraid of anything that might seem to prejudice the Church's teaching concerning either

---

[4] Cf. DS 300. Sometimes, of course, the term is used simply as a title specifying who it is of whom one is speaking.

[5] "All possible" can only have meaning here in connection with the way God created this concrete individual and with the concrete history of his life. For, an individual's perfection must be defined in terms of the properties and potentialities of the individual in question.

[6] E.g., Letter of Sept. 20, 1548, of St. Ignatius Loyola to St. Francis Borja, *Monumenta Ignatiana: Epistolae et Instructiones 2*, Madrid: MHSI, (1904), *pp* 233–237.

Christ's divinity or His being the unique and universal Savior of mankind, have insisted that Jesus be perfect, *except for his body*, at all times with His terminal perfection. Hence, for some centuries, the greater number of theologians and spiritual writers spoke of Jesus' possession of the beatific vision as something He had from the moment of His conception. For the most part, they also denied that He could grow subjectively in knowledge,[7] freedom, or grace, since He possessed them in their absolute human fulness from the moment of His conception.[8]

They then explained the scriptural statements that seem to imply the contrary as referring only to changes in the manner and degree to which He manifested this perfect fulness externally. Many held that, even apart from the beatific vision, He knew, from His conception onwards, the totality of all things on the created order, not merely abstractly and in principle but in all the details of their concrete singularity—a knowledge that, in large measure, could not be derived from His experience but had to be infused by God. This emphasis on His infused knowledge went so far that many, including even Alexander of Hales, St. Bonaventure, Duns Scotus, and Suarez denied that Jesus ever grew in knowledge through the action of His human mind on His experience.[9]

Such positions would, however, seem to be the historical basis for the Monophysitic tendencies mentioned above. For they seem to ignore the *intent* of Chalcedon, which was, in larger part, to guarantee that the union of the two natures in the divine Person of the Son would not be taken as ground for denying the integral fulness of Christ's humanity. Since there is no question of original or actual sin in Him, one can assert every mode of perfection, except the terminal, of Him at any time. His human nature and His life were always perfect; but what argument is there to show that this was, for most of

[7] St. Thomas changed (cf. III, 9, 4 c) his earlier position concerning Christ's acquired or experiential knowledge and argues that He *does* progress in time to knowing all things that can be known by the activity of the agent intellect (III. 12. 2 c & ad 1) This sort of universal knowledge, he says (ad 1), is gained by the time He is fully mature (*in perfecta aetate*). He also introduces the notion of relative perfection and/or perfection of process (ibid. ad 2).

[8] This insistence on the terminal perfection of grace in Jesus by some of the Fathers and the medieval theologians results in a loss of its relationship to the times and seasons of God's providence over the world, especially as these relate to man's salvation. This is perhaps most clearly stated by St. Thomas, *de Veritate*, 29, 8 c: "Whatever of spiritual perfection is possible for any creature is believed to have been conferred in its entirety on the soul of Christ in the first instant of its creation." He did not change this position later: "Spiritual perfection belongs to the human nature which Christ took up, in which perfection He did not progress but had it at once from the beginning" (III, 34, 2 c) and "It was suitable that the soul of Christ be altogether perfect through this, that all its potentiality be reduced to act" (III, 11, 1 c).

[9] St. Thomas, towards the end of his career, wished to allow for genuinely human, acquired knowledge in Jesus (cf. note 7 above). But he was forced by the notion that this mode of Jesus' knowledge concerning created things must be exhaustive to hold the extraordinary opinion that He was able, by the perfection of His natural reason alone, progressively to deduce all empirical knowledge entirely from His own limited experience (III, 12, 1, ad 1 & ad 2). Since even Thomas knew of the diversity of languages, to take but one example, it is clear how very abstract indeed was his notion of knowledge of concrete beings. One might also wonder what Jesus'empirical experience amounted to in the first instant of His conception.

His spiritual powers, a terminal perfection from conception?

Interestingly, St. Thomas' arguments for the terminal perfection of all Jesus' powers, except for the agent intellect and His corporeal powers, all fail in essentially the same way: they are logically correct and built on true premisses but are irrelevant to that for which he constructed them; and this, because he considers Jesus more in terms of the metaphysics of the hypostatic union than in terms of His mission from the Father, with all that this implies of times and seasons.

Consider, for example, his argument for Jesus' possession of the beatific vision. He argues that Jesus must have had the beatific vision from the moment of His conception since all of man's potentiality for beatitude (and other graces) can be brought to actuality only through the actuality of the perfections of the human nature of Christ. Therefore, He must possess, in His humanity, the fulness of this vision, in act, for otherwise, no man could see God.[10]

Yet the most that this can show, even if taken entirely on its own terms and without disagreement about its presuppositions, is that Jesus must have possessed the beatific vision from the time of His enthronement in glory onwards. For, no man had entered heaven before this; no actualization of human beatitude had yet been called for. Similar criticisms could be made of the principle concerning his spiritual perfection mentioned above[11] and of the arguments against Jesus' growth in other ways.[12]

Another type of criticism can be offered as well. As mentioned, Thomas argues that all of Jesus' seeming growth in nonexperiential knowledge, freedom, and grace lay solely in the ever more perfect performance of the external works that He accomplished through the supposedly already perfect virtues and habits of soul conferred by an absolute fulness of grace. These works would have improved concurrently with His physical maturation.[13] Now, this position implies operations and actions of a *human* agent that do not in any way perfect the powers from which they spring.[14] Whether this is truly consistent with what St. Thomas thought concerning the unity of the material and spiritual in man, I leave to Thomistic specialists. Yet, as true man, Jesus' physical nature became ever more perfect, the child being more perfect than the infant, the adult than the child. To sunder the spiritual aspects of Jesus' life totally from His corporeal development seems to put some strain, at least, on the fundamental doctrine that the soul is immediately and of itself the

---

[10] *ST*, III, 9, 2 c & ad 2.

[11] Cf. note 7 above. enuntiated in III, 11, 1 c and 34, 2 c

[12] Cf. ST III. qq 7–13 and 34.

[13] Cf. III, 7, 12 ad 3 and III, 12, 2 c.

[14] Abstractly considered, the Aristotelian dictum "actio est in passo" is true: the perfecting produced by an agent is to be found in the recipient of its action, not in the agent itself. So, God is in no way perfected by His action in creating or redeeming. But I do not think it possible for a being that is at once material and spiritual to act so as to effect change in another being without improvement in (or damage to) the agent's active powers—and this, independently of the concomitant reaction by the being acted upon. This objection needs further development for the case of an act of purely intellectual cognition or of free choice.

form of the body.[15]

Thomas was not unaware of the problem, as is evident from his change of position allowing for Jesus an acquired intellectual knowledge. But this raised further problems as long as the rest of the older framework remained in place. Thus, Jesus' senses must have been working at the moment of His conception, at least the sense of touch, so that phantasms might be, in the same moment, presented to the agent intellect for abstraction in order to provide the knowledge needed for His free will to operate perfectly in that same first moment.[16] Apart, however, from the philosophical problems this may raise and, if by God's absolute power it could have taken place (however impossible it may seem to modern embryology), one would still have to say that Jesus was not like us in all things but sin, but that the operations of His humanity were like ours only in some strange metaphysical sense not even suggested by revelation.

The position that allows for no intrinsic growth in grace by Jesus makes grace wholly independent of the human supposit which receives it and which, being material as well as spiritual, exists essentially in time. Yet, since sanctifying grace, too, is created and finite, there would seem to be nothing in it, in itself, to prevent its growth.[17] Further, since it is in us not merely divine (insofar as it is a sharing in the Trinity's own knowledge and love) but is a *human* sharing in the divine life, made for *man* to live by, it too must have a temporal dimension and development in Jesus. If Jesus loved the Father with the love of charity, He did so in accord with the physical and psychic and mental powers that grace had taken hold of and formed for such activity.[18]

Further, if the grace of Christ receives some intrinsic modification from the particular mysteries of His earthly life and from His concrete recapitulation through them of the whole of man's history, then this grace must itself have a history in Him. As human, His mode of participating in the life of God must have changed in time, being marked by Jesus' responses to the events occurring around Him.

Such criticisms suggest not only that Jesus' mission be considered much

[15] This was defined by the ecumenical Council of Vienne (DS 900, 902).

[16] S.T. III, 34, 2, ad 3, Unfortunately, he did not live long enough to work out in full the consequences of his change of position concerning Jesus' acquired knowledge.

[17] Sanctifying grace and supernatural charity are not the measure of holiness in Jesus as they are in us. Jesus' holiness is given immediately by the grace of union. Hence, whatever one may say about His sanctifying grace, His holiness was most certainly infinite and total from His conception.

[18] Note that this position implies that, while one can speak of sanctifying grace in the angels and even compare the degree of participation in the divine life in a particular angel and a particular man, as we do when we speak of Mary's grace being greater than that of any of the angels, yet the angelic grace is different from ours, not in virtue of that in which it participates but in virtue of the sort of being that lives by this grace and the way in which such a being by its nature is made thereby to resemble God. For, even as we have several natural modes of knowing and, in consequence, of loving, so in the angels there is at least one mode of naturally knowing and loving, different essentially from any of ours. Each of these modes, then, has its own distinctive manner of being elevated to and made to operate as supernaturally human or angelic ways of knowing and loving God.

more fully than was the custom until fairly recently but also that the temporal aspects of His mission be given more detailed attention. Returning to Chalcedon, we read, "...the same [Jesus is] consubstantial with us according to [His] humanity, like us in every respect apart from sin." If one considers carefully this last phrase, paraphrased from Heb.4:15, where it refers to Jesus' being tempted (or tried or tested), most of the arguments against His growth and development seem hollow, however carefully they were wrought so as not to damage the abstract metaphysical structure of the human essence as such.

Perhaps we can gain some insight from our Lady, for she was perfect in her humanity, but without a hypostatic union. No one, to my knowledge, has ever claimed that her perfection during her life on earth was what it was to be after her assumption and glorification, or that she was immutable in her knowledge or grace because of her perfection. If one says, "Of course, but it was not she who was to actualize all supernatural good for us; her mission was different," at least the importance of the mission is acknowledged.

In Mary, too, we can see more clearly that, as I have recalled elsewhere,[19] nescience, i.e., simple lack of knowledge, is not an imperfection in a human being.[20] It is the notion that nescience is an imperfection that is, I think, the fundamental error of those who denied change in Jesus' knowledge and other perfections. Nescience would have been an imperfection in Him only had it in some way interfered with His mission. But then it would have to be called 'ignorance,' i.e., the lack of that knowledge that one *ought* to possess, which privation of knowledge all would deny of Christ. Precisely because of His mission to reveal the Father to us and to accomplish our salvation, there came the floods of infused knowledge that were His at different times. But, as indicated, it is only after His enthronement that the terminal perfection these theologians predicated of Jesus became either useful to Him or called for by His mission.

To be perfect in one's humanity, then, in the sense of Chalcedon and III Constantinople, is to be, like Mary, i) an unflawed example of our biological species, ii) who has never been subject to original sin, and iii) who has never committed any actual sin. It is, therefore, to be one who has utilized all his powers in unfailing accord with God's will for his contribution to God's work in the world, i.e., in perfect accord with his God-given mission, and has used them to that extent only.

---

[19] Paul M. Quay, S.J., "Disvalue," (cf. note 82, *p* 174), *pp* 263–264 & 283–284.

[20] I would not go as far as Karl Rahner, S. J. ("Dogmatic Reflections on the Knowledge and Self-Consciousness of Christ," *pp* 193–215 in *Theological Investigations 5*, tr. K-H. Kruger, London: Darton, Longman & Todd [1966], at *pp* 201–202.), who, if I understand him, sees nescience as a good. The space that makes freedom possible does not, in my judgment, have anything to do with nescience. Rather, true freedom for man, even as for God, in whose Image man was created, is based on a fulness of knowledge concerning one's alternatives. What is then needed is the courage to choose a particular good, even if one knows that another, also truly good, will be lost to one forever (cf. "Disvalue," *p* 285). Rahner's confusion is shown in his speaking of "a certain kind of nescience." Such specification implies that what he is really talking about is not simple non-knowing but rather, to judge by his examples, a number of very positive ways of knowing of one's ignorance of matters that one ardently desires and thinks possible to know.

Pope John Paul II makes clear that the perfection of Jesus' grace and knowledge was that relative perfection of which I have spoken above and not, during His earthly life, their terminal perfection:

> [T]here was *a real human development in Jesus*.... Infancy, childhood, adolescence and youth are the periods of his physical growth ("in age").... [T]here was also *a spiritual growth* in Jesus.... And *the Holy Spirit instilled the fullness of grace* in Christ.... However, the fullness of grace in Jesus was in proportion to His age: there was always fullness, but a fullness which increased as he grew in age. The same can be said of the *wisdom* which Christ had from the beginning in the fullness proper to the period of childhood. As He advanced in age, this fullness grew in Him to a proportionate degree.[21]

It is, then, *not* necessary that one who is perfect in his humanity have the totality of possible perfections either of body and psyche or of mind, will, or grace.[22] It *is* necessary that one who is always perfect in his humanity grow and mature, that he develop his natural and supernatural powers both through the natural processes of growth and through the graced exercise of his freedom. The temporal actualization of one's powers in complete accord with God's will is the way a *human* being glorifies God. Further, to be perfect in one's humanity means to be ever more deeply social, learning from others as well as from one's direct experience.[23]

Thus, until God becomes all in all (I Cor.15:28), saturating all human powers and potentialities, natural and supernatural, by the fulness of His self-gift to all, temporality and change are essential aspects of full and perfect humanity in this world, unless completely overridden by the direct and immediate action of God Himself. Indeed, it is by neglect of this temporal dimension, it seems to me, that Catholics generally lack a strong sense of exultation in Jesus' triumph at His glorification and the great spiritual joy that should, as a result, habitually be theirs. They often suffer a certain weakness in their hope as well, by insufficient realization that, though the grace He gives us recapitulates what has happened in His earthly life and in His sufferings and death, yet it is also and principally a sharing in His life in glory.

In the light of the above, I assume throughout this book the following:

a) Jesus in His earthly life possessed that direct and immediate consciousness of Himself as Son of God which is intrinsic to the direct and personal presence of the Logos to the human soul of Jesus that is one aspect of the hypostatic union.[24] This is, as Rahner remarked, not of itself beatifying,

---

[21] Pope John Paul II, General Audience of June 27, 1990, *L'Osservatore Romano*, (English) Weekly Edition N. 27, July 2, 1990, *p* 11 [emphasis in the original].

[22] Cf. note 5, *p* 246 above.

[23] St. Thomas denies that Jesus learned anything by being taught by men (ST, III, 12, 3 c). Again, however, his argument is beside the point; all it proves, at best, is that He learned nothing from others of the truth He was to reveal and to which He was to bear witness. Since, however, He had already spoken through the Old Testament, His learning of the Scriptures, say from Joseph and Mary, was not simply learning from men. And how, if he was to learn all the agent intellect could make known from the phantasms of experience, could He not learn, in this mode of cognition, what people had to say and think?

[24] On this matter, I would, with some qualifications as to his metaphysics, follow Karl Rahner

and cannot rightly be called (as he does) 'vision,' precisely because it is not a presence of the Self as object to the Self but is that Self-awareness that initiates and is presupposed by all objectification. What is important for our considerations here is that this Self-awareness was present indeed, from conception on, yet was not conceptual nor adequately reducible to concepts. All the operations of His mind and other human powers are rooted in this, but grew and changed without implying growth or change in this.[25]

b) Jesus possessed, as well, an infused, conceptual, articulable, hence, communicable knowledge of the Father and of all else, natural and supernatural, that was needed for or was eminently suited to His mission. All the kinds of infused knowledge (and other gifts and graces) given to His saints since Pentecost (*a fortiori*, those given to Moses and the prophets under the Old Law) were surely given Him in vastly greater measure—but, again, only in accord with their relation to a particular season of His mission.[26] Hence, this infused knowledge would not for the most part have been habitual but was always qualified in terms of time and season: what is true of the knowledge had by Christ enthroned in glory need not have been true of Jesus' knowledge in His infancy or at different times during His public life.[27]

c) Jesus had ordinary human knowledge, humanly acquired, both of sense and of intellect, in all ways like our own and with the same basic limitations. On the other hand, though I think there may have been nescience of many things in Jesus while He walked in Palestine and of still more when He was yet an infant, I should deny any ignorance in Him. Nor do I see that it was contrary to His mission to learn from others their language and their modes of thought and their cultural traits. Only what He brought new from the bosom of the Father—the things still hidden in the divine decrees for man's salvation and not already revealed in the Old Testament—were intrinsically not learnable from others.[28]

(cf. note 20 above). Cf. also, Rahner in *Lexikon für Theologie und Kirche* (2) 5:955.

[25] The precise relationship of what I have called 'felt grace' to this only slowly articulated and never adequately realized Self-awareness needs more consideration than can be given here. They cannot be identically the same—even though to be conscious of Oneself as Son of necessity implies consciousness of Oneself as from-the-Father—since Adam and Eve, Mary, and any others whom God might have chosen, had or could have had felt grace. Yet this Self-awareness might have had eminently the function that felt grace had in these others. In any case, felt grace, by definition, directly affects the feelings and psyche—something not easily incorporated into a theory of subjective Self-consciousness that is not, of itself, beatifying.

[26] This is not in accord with Rahner ("Self-Consciousness of Christ," *pp* 212–213). I see no way for the data of Scripture to be covered by only our Lord's Self-consciousness as Son along with His normal, humanly acquired knowledge. For, to point out but one of many difficulties, Rahner's position would seem to imply that consciousness of Self, i.e., of *who* He is, also includes consciousness, in some way articulable *conceptually,* of *what* He is. This in turn would seem to imply that all that He knows as God about the created order He knows as man in communicable form.

[27] Such infused knowledge could presumably supply that intimate, personal knowledge of each of us of which Pius XII spoke in *Mystici Corporis*, (DS 3812).

[28] For the acceptability of these ideas of Jesus' growth in knowledge, cf. not only "Jesus Christ, II, III," *New Catholic Encyclopedia 7, pp* 924–927; 930–938; but also, the conservative and pre-Vatican II standard text: *Sacrae Theologiae Summa III, De Verbo Incarnato*, Iesu Solano, 3rd ed. Ma-

d) Finally, Jesus' human will was drawn, in fully human fashion, to whatever good He came to know through each mode of consciousness. As His intellectual grasp of what was implicated in any given choice developed and as His conceptual Self-possession grew, so did His freedom. And as He chose ever more profoundly and in an ever greater variety of circumstances freely to act as Son of God made man, so grew His sharing as man in the divine life we call sanctifying grace. Except for the grace of the hypostatic union, all aspects of His humanity, supernatural as well as natural, developed, grew, and matured in time.

B. JESUS' SPIRITUAL DEVELOPMENT

1. Précis of the varieties of typology

It may be useful to recall briefly the difference between Jesus' personal, preparative recapitulation and the doctrinal or prefigurative typology the Scripture offers us relating to His office as the Christ of the Lord. We have already considered Jesus' time in the womb, in the Eden of Mary, in which the Spirit breathed refreshment (Ac.3:19) for the whole fallen race in Him. Yet He is the Second Adam all His life long. Like the former Adam, He falls asleep (in His death upon the cross) so that His side, too, might be opened to bring forth His bride. Analogous observations may be made in relation to Moses. In personal recapitulation, He had passed through the Mosaic stage before the age of twelve. But according to Matthew's Gospel, for example, His whole life was prefigured by the life of Moses; Jesus was the Second Moses. He escaped the tyrant by flight abroad and returned when those who sought His life were dead. He fasted forty days in the desert before proclaiming the New Law in the Sermon on the Mount, typified by God's revelation to Moses on Sinai. He fed the hungry in the wilderness with miraculously produced bread. The structure of "five books" in this Gospel correspond to the five books of the Torah; etc.

What is involved here is the diversity of the senses of the Scripture. The fulfilment—to rehearse one aspect of the distinction once again—of the prefigurative types occurs in their future. But the recapitulation of the preparative types looks to the past for the sake of the future maturation of the one recapitulating.

The New Testament itself identifies several typologies for us. We have seen something of the Adam-Christ typology, with the doctrine of original sin and grace implicit therein. We now wish to look at another typology, that between Israel and Christ. The prefigurative type of Jesus that Jacob was when considered as an individual person who, say, wrestled alone with God in order to obtain a blessing, has been commented on endlessly from patristic times but is not our concern here. The same is true for the people sprung from Jacob as the type of the Church, the Israel of God (Gal.6:16). This prefigurative mode permeates the New Testament: During His forty days in the desert, Jesus triumphed easily over the varieties of temptation to which Israel had succumbed. Through His response to the first temptation, He rectified

drid: Biblioteca de Autores Cristianos (1956), *p* 128.

the Israelites' complaining against the LORD for lack of food and water; through the second and the third, He rectified Korah's showing-off and vainglorious display as well as the ambitious thirst of Dathan and Abiram for a share in power. Here, however, we are interested in the typology of Jesus as the Christ who recapitulates in Himself when a child the history of not just the one man, Israel, but of the entire people.

We can derive little enough directly from the Gospels concerning the age at which our Lord reached one or other recapitulative level. They mention twice the mere fact of His growth (Lk.2:40, 52). The only details given between His infancy and His baptism are offered in the account of His remaining behind in Jerusalem when twelve years old (Lk.2:41–51), though it would seem, if a comparison of Mk.6:3 with Mt.13:55 be exegetically licit, that He did the same sort of work as Joseph. The Gospels, then, offer us no direct confirmation or disconfirmation of our approach.

But if we are to recapitulate the Old Testament in Jesus, must we not see how Jesus did it? One might respond that, since God's revelation hasn't given us those details, presumably we don't need them. For the baptized, recapitulation takes place in some way of itself. For it is the process by which the divine life given us heals what remains of the damage inflicted by original sin and incorporates into itself ever more of our natural selves. Its pattern of growth is intrinsic to it, "built in," "pre-programmed," in the manner common to all living things, though it always remains conditioned by our free choices.

Though all this is true, yet more is possible. We can also look at our Lord in His public life and note what He then possessed of character, development, maturity, etc. The personality He then possessed indicates what prior stages He had traversed in order to attain it. Of primary interest here is Jesus' spiritual maturation.[29]

2. Infancy and early childhood

Once born, Jesus developed as Adam should have. Irenaeus highlighted Adam's need to grow and develop, calling him an infant—not in age but in knowledge and attitude towards a world for the first time known by a human mind—therefore, without any culture, though with many animal skills.[30] Our Lord's taking up into His own infancy the vast period between the expulsion from Eden and the call of Abram rectified and corrected that dark time profoundly through the felt grace by which His brain was formed and His psyche matured free of original sin and concupiscence, as well as through the confirmatory influences of Mary's love and Joseph's.

Yet He was unable to do more than any other baby,[31] with the

---

[29] Cf. Romano Guardini, *The Lord*, trans. E. C. Briefs, Chicago: Regnery (1954), chap. 2.

[30] Cf. C. S. Lewis' description of Adam in: *The Problem of Pain,* Ch. V: The Fall of Man.

[31] One must deal cautiously with the metonymies that abound in much pious literature about Christmas: how the hands that made the world are now helpless beneath swaddling bands, and the like. True it is that He, whose hands these are, made the world—but not by means of these hands. The hands of this Baby created nothing. Nor did His human mind, created only nine months before, have anything to do with the creation of the world, except insofar as it was part of that Goal

enormous exception that He was filled from the moment of His conception with the full, felt grace of the Father's love. The brain and body, the mind and heart of this Baby were, in essence, no different from those of any other baby on earth though concretely very different because, on the one hand, of the greatness of His own grace and, on the other, the growing influence of the effects of original sin on the psycho-physical make-up of all other children than Himself.

In early childhood, before there is enough intellectual grasp of reality to set one's freedom free, Jesus was preparatively typified by Abel in the earliest stage of human development shown us in Scripture. Already there are signs of Jesus' recapitulative compression of time: He enters early childhood psychically sooner than others, i.e., while still a "herdsman," not yet at the level of agriculture. When the silence of the millenia between Adam and his sons is broken by development to this level, it is the herdsman who, less culturally advanced, is type of Christ.

We have little to go on here save that Abel was a shepherd with, one may presume, something of the patience, sagacity, and courage which the Bible, in its obvious and consistent preference for shepherds over farmers, seems to take as typical of shepherds. Since his sacrifices were accepted by God, we may suppose him to have been an upright man. Some would argue that he was more generous in his offering than his brother.[32] Abel was, then, not stingy with God and probably did not see himself as a rival to Cain. As a shepherd, filled with genuine concern for the welfare of his flock, he gave a simple love,[33] without concern for worth or return, to the dirty and cowardly animals that sheep are. Yet, grateful to God, he was willing to sacrifice them and to give their best parts to God. The one psychic trait we seem to be clearly given is his trustfulness with regard to his brother. Possibly, too, he was unwilling to defend himself when Cain assaulted him with rock or club.

Here we are not concerned with Abel's being the prefiguration of the Good Shepherd who would die at the hands of his evil brethren, though for their sake. What he shows, as a preparative type, is that Jesus in infancy was not gripped, as Cain was, by antipathy for the other infants that were his cousins and kin. Were Mary to have acted as wet-nurse for one of the other babies of Nazareth, there would have been no livid enviousness in Jesus. His focus on the Father and repose in His love not only protected Jesus from infantile jealousies but, like Abel, made Him both generous with God and grateful, trusting, and at ease with His companions and the world.

This inner security is one of the psychic traits most under threat from the psychic malformation of concupiscence. For, the ultimate and only essential security any human being needs is God's love, fully known. This is the only thing needed; the one without which no other security can stand. Though this is seen most clearly in our Lord's sufferings in Gethsemani and

---

of all creation which He Himself is as man, as He brings all things to the Father.

[32] Speiser, *Genesis*, *p* 30.

[33] Perhaps it is not, in a cultural milieu as slowly changing as herding, too much of an anachronism to recall Nathan's description of the poor man and his ewe lamb (2 Sam.12:3).

on the cross, it is visible even on the natural level, say, in a youngster from a family where he has been nurtured with strong, warm love by both parents and by siblings. This kid has no real fears. A dog three times his size may come up and startle him for a moment, but he will react with courage and coolness, raise a two-year-old's fist and order the dog away. He is wide open to the world, and shows a remarkable degree of casualness about everything, especially other people.

Such security is never absolute. Sooner or later, defects and flaws appear in him also. But he will have far less to contend with than most people. Human love, when at its best, i.e., when informed with charity and when God's grace is strongly working to purify it, gives a youngster a head-start on life. Original sin is present in this person as in all others, and will show itself, principally in temptations to pride. But to the extent that he is free of some of the worse psychic effects of the fall, especially if also strong in charity, we may gain from observation of him some inkling of what we might have been like had Adam not sinned.

As a slightly older child, Jesus was like Enoch, descended from Seth, the LORD's replacement for Abel, whom Cain slew (Gen.4:25), rather than like Cain's distant offspring Lamech. He walked with God (Gen.5:24), though God did not take Him till after His crucifixion.

Just prior to the story of Noah, as an introduction, the world is shown involved in unnatural sexual activity and inhuman violence. All through the story itself, great stress is laid on the pairing of male and female for the continuation of life on earth. As the pairs of animals were brought into the ark, so were "Noah and his wife, and his sons and their wives." But 'masculine' for Noah did not mean 'violent' but rather 'capable of laboring long and skilfully' to build an ark and 'able to exercise dominion and control over all types of animals.' 'Male' for him did not imply promiscuity but the begetting of a family. When unexpectedly uncovered, he expected modesty of glance in others and considered immodest action as deserving of a curse.

So, a boy's natural perception of and appreciation for his sexuality and masculinity, as these gradually fuse, gains its basic direction and form in early childhood. This process seems in largest measure to be tied to an identification with his father and a psychic pushing away from his mother. Jesus' sexual development as true man occurred largely, then, through His identification with Joseph and psychic separation or disassociation from Mary. What higher praise for Joseph could devotion construct than the simple fact that he is the man from whom Jesus learned to "be a man"! It was through Joseph, too, that the "male image" of the surrounding Jewish culture first reached Jesus and specified His manhood.

If parents are not in sound relationship with each other, this can adversely affect the youngster in his sexual development. Since our Lord's psychosexual maturation and virility were manifest even at twelve, the influence of Joseph upon Him must have been great, and the relations between Mary and Joseph as wondrous as any of the saints have surmised.

Jesus also learned directly from Joseph and from the surrounding culture what was expected of "carpenters." Recapitulating the events of Babel at four or so, when all things seemed possible, He did rightly what they had done wrongly. Not driven from within by fear of being unloved or unadmired to act as did the men who built the tower of Babel, He felt no call to revolutionize the construction of plows or cabinet-making. It is their total incomprehension of this fact that renders the early apocrypha about Jesus' childhood, with their accounts of childish miracles, so instantly recognizable as fictions.

3. Later childhood and adolescence

On reaching a psychic level like Abraham's, His knowledge of the Father (analogous to Abraham's faith) not only involved His natural, human, emotional as well as intellectual response and feelings to felt grace and the psychic development it produced as He grew, but also began to engage His freedom. For, as man, He had to become free since as a human infant He was not.

Totally open to the Father's will and fully submissive to its demands, He would have accepted whatever sacrifice of parents or loved ones might have been asked of Him, though, so far as we are told, none was. Yet earlier, we may have some hint of His being readied for this in Abel's sacrificing of his sheep with an attitude perhaps not entirely unlike that of a child whose parents have decided that his duckling or bunny must go lest his clumsy affection destroy it. But later, we see in the scene in the Temple at the age of twelve, the evidence that, long before, Jesus had recapitulated Abraham's sacrifice of Isaac. Despite the great external differences, what is shown here is Jesus' obedience to His Father's will at whatever cost to Mary, Joseph, and Himself.

Moses, in striking contrast to all the turmoil and agitation around him, moved with quiet firmness and reliance solely upon the LORD. It is he, already far more mature than the people about him, who was the preparative type for Jesus somewhere before the age of twelve. The difference in spiritual maturity between Moses and the people is perhaps indicated by the remark, made of him when about to approach Pharaoh to demand the Hebrews' freedom, that he was eighty years old (Ex. 7:7). That this is not mere symbolism is shown by the fact that the same verse gives the vastly less mature Aaron eighty-three years of age. In any case, these differences and, still more, that between Jesus' maturity at this level and any of His peers, of that day or now, shows not only the power and effectiveness of God's grace but, conversely, the greatness of the damage done by original sin when not countered by grace.

The first eighty years of Moses' life, apart from his youthful killing of the Egyptian and flight into exile, are presented as singularly quiet and uneventful. He matured and aged, laboring as a shepherd in the impoverished and isolated region of Midian in the Sinai Peninsula, far from any center of culture or ease, with his small family and few in-laws. So, all but three years of Jesus' life, apart from three days in Jerusalem, are shown locked into the narrowness of a small village in the mountainous back country of Galilee.

The first information that we are given about Jesus after His infancy,[34] is

[34] Recall that he was a "little child" both in His being taken to Egypt and on His return. He was presumably less than two years old when He went down and, for reasonable guesses as to His

the summary given in the former of the two verses (Lk.2:40 and 52) that bracket His being found in the Temple. Taken together, these verses set the entire incident into the context of His maturation. The former verse states simply, in the same words used of the growth of John the Baptist, that He "grew and became strong," adding, what it does not say of the Baptist, "filled with wisdom, and the favor of God was upon Him." What was occurring, was taking place spontaneously or resulting from the special action of God. In the latter verse, He "advances" or "makes progress," and matures actively. Before, He is being filled with wisdom; He advances in wisdom afterwards. Grace rests on Him before; He advances in grace thereafter.

The incident in the Temple, then, is used to mark the transition from the quiet, spontaneous growth of the child to the self-activating and free growth of the adolescent or young adult. Unafraid to strike out on His own and confident in the Father's protection, He spent at least two nights in Jerusalem, without kin or acquaintances. In the Temple? The Scripture is silent. He had become fully "His own man" and was able to maintain His own counsel. I think one can show that this transition had already taken place but was now manifested publicly by this incident. In any case, His recapitulation was more rapid (as well as much deeper) than ours. He had matured far beyond what any of us were at the age of twelve or thereabouts.

Obviously, Mary and Joseph held Him on a very loose tether. They went a whole day's journey before they tried to find Him. There are fairly evident reasons, given the nature and structure of Jewish caravans of the times, why this should have been the case. But for all that, it is clear that they were not worrying much about Him. They figured He knew how to take care of Himself, and He did. They hunted Him and found Him.[35]

During the Exodus, it was Moses, confident in God's promises and word, who calmed the fear-stricken and adolescent people. Through him, the Law was given. There is no hint that he found it surprising or difficult to keep or that he ever violated it. On the contrary, he "called out the troops" whenever the people broke loose against it. He remained the faithful one set over God's house (Heb.3:2, 5 and Num.12:7). Yet, severe as were the punishments that God had Moses inflict on Israel, never did he desert them or simply abandon them to the LORD's wrath but, rather, "withstood Him in the breach" (Ps.106:23). So, both Jesus and His precursor, John the Baptist, were born into devout Jewish families, fully cognizant of and obedient to the Law's demands, as the entire Infancy Narrative makes clear. Though neither women nor children were required to go up to Jerusalem for the Passover, Mary and Jesus both went, and Jesus is shown at twelve, while still a "boy" (Lk.2:43), as already mature and doing what the Law prescribed for adults, at least a year before he would be obligated, as an adult Jew, to the keeping of all provisions of the Law.

Jesus was here in the midst of the religious leaders of His people who

date of birth, not much older when he returned after Herod's death.

[35] There is, evidently, much in this section of the Gospel to suggest how parents might deal with their adolescent youngsters, though to develop it here, taking due account of the differences between Jesus and the best of Christian adolescents, lies well beyond our present scope.

two decades later would have Him tortured to death. Though even then He must have had some awareness of the dry rot already corroding the souls of many among them, He shows no hostility. Like Moses, however harsh His rebukes, He was never an enemy to His people. Whatever their sins, He remained faithful to them. Even on the cross, He would not desert or abandon them—"Father, forgive them; for they know not what they do" (Lk.23:34).

Moses had asked to see the LORD. God granted his request, though not letting him see His face lest he die (Ex.33:18–23 and 34:5–7). But God let him see His back after He had passed by while proclaiming His name, His mercy, and His justice. The LORD had even let Aaron, his sons, and the seventy elders approach Him in Moses' company, though not as closely, and to banquet in His presence (Ex.24:1–2, 9–11). Moses' longing to be with the LORD and to talk with Him on behalf of the people never ceased and was in no way restricted to those extraordinary occasions. He remained the constant mediator. When Moses would return from converse with the LORD in the Tent of Meeting—for "the LORD used to speak to Moses face to face, as a man speaks to his friend" (Ex.33:11)—his face would be shining with a radiance that reflected something of the glorious splendor of God's presence. Once he had delivered God's message to the people, he would veil his face because of the dread that gripped those who saw that abiding radiance (Ex.34:30–35).

At Sinai, God revealed Himself as LORD to the people, confirming the revelation of His name that He had made to Moses. In the Temple, however, Jesus reveals Him as His own Father. God had often been designated as 'Father' before this, but not as any one man's own Father. Jesus revealed Him in a new way, no longer solely as "your Father who created you [as a people], who made you and established you" (Dt.32:6).

Jesus spoke with God as a Son speaks to His Father, not merely in the Temple but at all times, and listened to His Father speaking, learning what was desired of Him moment by moment. For "morning by morning, He wakens My ear to hear as those who are taught" (Is.50:4). Thus it was that He could query, "Did you not know that it is *necessary* that I be in the house [or: about the business] of my Father?"{Lk.2:49}—necessary because the Father had so instructed Him.

When Mary and Joseph found Him in the Temple, Jesus was speaking with the teachers of the Law, yet His response to Mary's question showed that He had been also in the presence of His Father, whose House this was (Jn.2:16). There was no special radiance upon His face, but His manner was, it seems, of one with whom God has spoken. For, little as Mary and Joseph understood the answer He had given them, awe held them back from questioning Him further. They did not press Him for further explanation, then or later, but pondered what they did not understand. It was not their task to interrogate a Child to whom the Father spoke as His Son.

Moses received the LORD's first revelation to him at the burning bush on Horeb with utmost reverence, not only removing his shoes, as ordered, but hiding his face, for he dared not look at God (Ex.3:6). This uttermost reverence continued all during his life, as when he prepared himself for the reception of the Law by forty days of fasting and prayer. But, unlike the people, he showed no terror or fright before God. So, Jesus, not trembling or terrified, but in calm and confident reverence, acknowledges His Father's absolute dominion. It was through this reverence for the Father that Jesus was able to push away freely from His parents on this occasion without disobedience or tantrum, rebellion or resentment, or any of the many wrong and disordered ways that have scarred the children of men. On the other hand, this incident in Jerusalem only preludes His going back to Nazareth with His parents, to be subject to them until nearly thirty, in a town about as culturally narrow and disregarded as was Moses' Midian.

No concrete motive is given for Jesus' staying behind. If His going back quietly to Nazareth for almost two decades more shows that He was not in revolt, why, then, did He stay behind in the Temple? It is not enough to say that He was at the age when a boy naturally begins to decide for himself what he is going to do and to act on his own. This is, indeed, essential to his growing up and Jesus evidently did just that, whatever His motives may have been. But when asked *why* He so acted, He replied "Did you not know that it is necessary for me to be in the things of my Father?" {Lk.2:49}. Whatever the obscurities of this counter-question, it makes clear enough that Jesus intended to cut all ties with any who, with whatever good intentions, might hold Him back from what He knew His service of God required. What the Father had asked of Him on this occasion evidently cost no small pain to Mary and Joseph; and hence, to Jesus, who, unlike most adolescents, felt their pain as His own. Yet He seemed coolly to disregard their pain, for it could have no weight where the Father's will was clear. As with Israel under Joshua, He recognized no other norm for action than what the Father desired of Him, unafraid of the battles that would, as a result, lie ahead.[36]

[36] Cf. *p* 242 above.

Chapter 13

Actual Sin and God's Response

The references to Israel's sins that saturate the book of *Judges* seem to have been almost entirely supplied by the Deuteronomic editor. With the appearance of Samuel, things change abruptly. Sins of the whole people are mentioned only in connection with the shift to the monarchy; but sins of individuals are now manifest, frequent, and treated as of great importance—and this, long before the Deuteronomist. From this time onwards, a preoccupation with sin becomes increasingly evident in the historical books, and almost completely floods the writings of the prophets. Though the kinds of sin that were predominant changed over the centuries, the fact of sin remained the focus of the rest of the Old Testament.

So, we must pause a moment to look at those things that could not typify Christ directly but which were truly typical of us: the fall, actual sin, guilt, punishment. We can look, then, to the Old Testament to see what God thinks of our sins and in what ways He prefers to punish us at the different levels of our growth. For, the punishments He exacted from Israel changed their character in the course of time, as did their sins.

A. Off the Road: The Negative Aspect of Recapitulation

Now, anyone who recapitulated the maturation of Israel perfectly in Jesus, would do virtuously and well all that God's people did wrongly and sinfully. But no one conceived in original sin can live much beyond the age of reason without actual sin. No one then, except Jesus Himself and, through Him, His mother, recapitulates Israel's history fully. But this does not negate the existence of an ideal and detailed pattern for Christian spiritual growth which makes full allowance for the destructive effects of our sins, nor lessen its value.

This matter, however, has often been misunderstood, especially over the past thirty years. Walter Burghardt has offered a particularly clear formulation of an increasingly common notion that Christian perfection is, as it were, the heroic conquest of an icy mountain scaled by oneself and not, as it truly is, an ever-surprising adventure in the following of Christ, along with Him, but without other plan or pattern.[1] But one finds a hundred forms of this same confusion between the inflexible structure of a perfect map and the unforeseeable eventfulness of a journey.[2] A map is not a journey; but a man is stupid who, with some definite goal in mind, undertakes a journey—as distinct from a voyage of exploration—and refuses to carry a map.

The formal pattern of spiritual growth, whether as presented by Gregory of Nyssa or Cassian, by John of the Cross or Tanquerey, or as I hope to sketch it here, is a sort of map provided by the Scriptures and the Church's living Tradition. The routes of individuals vary endlessly, with a dynamics provided by grace and their own free will. The true lay of the land and the terrain are shown us by divine revelation, even though our ability to understand its symbols changes. And our equipment, resources, and seasons of readiness vary with each individual's psychic and physical endowments as given by genetics, culture, and training. It is this latter fact that accounts for the host of spiritual guidebooks produced over the centuries.

Actual sin shifts the sinner from recapitulation in Christ to a simple reliving of one or other sinful period in the life of Israel. Integral repentance brings him back to the Christ, his Way, again. If the Scripture, then, contains as much as it does concerning sin, it is to help us realize that there are characteristic patterns of deviation from the ideal even as there are diverse but characteristic ways of living in accord with the ideal. There will be, of course, more ways of deviating than of conforming. One may deviate at any point in one's journey. But if one grows as he ought, he will be following, spiritually, the Old Testament at its positive high-points: Abraham, Moses, Joshua, David, the young Solomon, the prophets, the Maccabees, and finally, the LORD in the flesh.

On the other hand, with the map the Old Testament provides, it is not hard to see what are the most likely ways of going astray at any particular spot along the road. Just as the actuarial tables of an insurance company cause no one to die yet predict with great accuracy how many will die during the year from being kicked by a horse or how many of those celebrating their fiftieth birthday will live to see their fifty-first, so the Bible shows us the patterns of sin with which, in all likelihood, we shall have to deal as we progress. In no way does the scriptural account justify any sin; it does serve to alert us to danger, to show us how to deal with the various temptations, and to offer us hope and means of recovery when we have sinned anyway.

Manifestly, then, recapitulation is not a process that takes place

---

[1] Cf. his address to the priests of the Archdiocese of Chicago, "Crisis, Cross, Confidence: A Priest for *This* Season," May 9, 1990. To judge from the rest of the talk, this may well have been a rhetorical device to show his auditors that he "was with them" in their difficulties.

[2] Because of its importance in moral theology, clarification of this sort of supposed conflict between human freedom and the truth concerning moral obligation is the principal object of the recent encyclical of Pope John Paul II, *Veritatis Splendor*, Aug. 6, 1993.

mechanically or at some predetermined rate. No Christian is under physical or psychic constraint to recapitulate the growth of Israel in and with Jesus Christ. God leaves us our freedom; and the process of recapitulation will not take place without our cooperation, late or soon, with God's grace.

Every Christian is aware that he has often failed so to live in Christ as rightly to grow and develop. Many things will draw and tempt him to center inwardly on himself. Despite all the greatly holy Christians he has known, he also knows that Christians can come to old age and still be surprisingly infantile. Nor need this be the result of brain damage brought on by the diseases of senescence. All too often, their behavior merely manifests a spiritual immaturity that has been there all along but that is now made evident through the weakening of those religious restraints that were never truly interiorized and that, with old age, lose their power. How often one runs into carefully nurtured resentments for long-past put-downs or a love for the sort of gossip that finds others' misdeeds somehow a remedy for one's own emptiness. Thus:

> Do not let me hear
> Of the wisdom of old men, but rather of their folly,
> Their fear of fear and frenzy, their fear of possession,
> Of belonging to another, or to others, or to God.[3]

or:

> Have a myriad children been quickened,
> Have a myriad children grown old,
> Grown gross and unloved and embittered,
> Grown cunning and savage and cold?
> God abides in a terrible patience,
> Unangered, unworn,
> And again for the child that was squandered
> A Child is born.[4]

Nor is it, I think, an accident that miserliness, which directly contradicts the Father's eternal giving of Himself in the generation of the Son, seems more likely to be found in the aged than in the young.

On the other hand, God does not readily abandon the creatures He has made. The grace given through baptism is a sharing in the divine life. This means that faith, hope, and charity grow by their own nature, even in poor and arid soil. Our sins can kill them; but our Lord's recapitulation was undertaken precisely in order to rectify the sinful actions of His people. Our spiritual history is never solely our own. As members of His Church, our recapitulation takes place, at whatever pace, except when we refuse it by grave sin, whether we have any awareness of it or not. Then, too, gradually to become less self-centered and more in love with God and our fellows is more in accord with our nature than is the opposite behavior. We remain free to act against our nature, but to do so goes against the grain of our being.

The rapid growth of Israel's awareness of sin at this period, along with

[3] T. S. Eliot, *East Coker*, Sect. II, (end).

[4] G. K. Chesterton, "The Nativity," in *The Collected Poems of G. K. Chesterton*, New York: Dodd, Mead & Co. (1980), *p* 139.

ever growing sinfulness, makes for a major complication in describing the maturation of Israel. The gap between those who served the LORD well and those who paid Him scant attention widens. The variety of paths followed increases. The attitudes towards sin show not only progress but also regress. Hence, we shall stop here a moment to see what God's attitude towards sin was (i.e., how He showed it to His people) in the parts of Scripture we have already seen, so that no separate treatment will be needed later.

B. The Sin of Eve and the Sin of Adam

Because of its signal importance as the source of original sin in us and also because of its crucial role in the Adam-Christ typology, the first sin of Adam calls for attention. Strangely, though Eve was the first human being to sin, her sin was not the 'original sin.' Her sin, for all its importance, did not in itself destroy the life of grace for her children and was not counted against our race as a whole. Indeed, defined doctrine concerning original sin ignores her sin altogether.

Yet, oddly enough, in *Genesis*, the drama all centers on the temptation of the woman and her sin. There is no drama at all about the woman's tempting the man: "She also gave some to her husband and he ate" (Gen.3:6). The human author has little, if any, interest in Eve as temptress. St. Paul, despite his concern with the sin of Adam, nowhere refers to Eve as a temptress, though he twice (II Cor.11:3; I Tim.2:13–14) lays stress on the fact that she was seduced or greatly deceived by the serpent. Indeed, he goes so far as to say that Adam was not deceived (I Tim.2:14). In neither passage does he have his strong teaching on original sin as the focus of his thought, though it remains vaguely in the background of his remarks in *I Timothy*, but is concerned directly with what some might see today as rather minor points of Church discipline.

Eve would seem to have been implicated in Adam's sin principally by the mere fact that she herself had fallen. Picture the situation: Adam, still in the state of integrity, is confronted with Eve, bearing one piece of the forbidden fruit, a bite already taken out of it. Whatever she then said to him, the overwhelming fact was that he was once again alone, far more now than ever he had been before her creation. The presence of moral evil filled the garden like a black smoke. She who was flesh of his flesh and bone of his bone, she whom he loved more than all the lovely earth with its other creatures, she had chosen to disobey the command of the LORD and was justly and rightly doomed. Even had she not said one word, all that Adam held dear—except the LORD—was being torn away by the one fact that she had fallen and he had not.

Because there was in him no concupiscence, her continuing physical beauty and personal charm did nothing to cover or hide the evil thing that she had made herself by her defiance of the LORD's command. He saw clearly that he was obliged to refuse her offer and, so, to lose her through death and, during what life she might still have, to endure her contemptuous loathing and mocking hatred of him for his refusal to join her. The fruit that she offered him, if we recall the mode of ancient Near-Eastern symbolism,[5] was "to be as God," deciding for himself as sole arbiter and without reference to any other will, what should be known as good and what as evil. Thus was set before him concretely the question that must come to every man: Whose will shall I follow, God's or my own, when it seems that the two are at odds?

Adam chose to join his wife, to descend to her state, rather than to obey the LORD in faith. He would not "hope against hope" that God might somehow, through Adam's own suffering and intercession, lift her again into spiritual life and bring her back, if not to himself, at least to the LORD. It is the LORD who defines his sin: "Because you have listened to the voice of your wife and have eaten..." (Gen.3:17). The sin that undid mankind was Adam's hearkening to the voice of his wife rather than to the voice of the LORD, listening to her when she suggested sin.

To understand more fully the evil involved, we need to understand what God had intended from the beginning for husband and wife. For this we must turn to the Second Adam and His bride. For it was on the cross, where the Church has always seen the action that undid the sin of Adam and its consequences,[6] that Jesus showed us what God had meant a husband to be.

Jesus died because He refused to listen to the voice of Israel, the bride of His youth.[7] Despite all her invitations and threats, He did only what His Father wished (Jn.14:31). Gracious and of a charm beyond all others, He loved people enough to respond to even their most unseasonable requests—sin alone excepted. And this exception isolated Him from all, made Him appear the enemy of all,[8] and condemned Him to death.

This, then, is the husband's task. As head of his family, not only is he to provide his wife with nurture and support but he must save her, so far as human activity under grace can do so, from spiritual harm, even more than from bodily harm. If she sins gravely, as by contraception, adultery, or abortion, he must refuse to take part in her sin and must bear the grief and pain of the resultant division between them. He is called, as Christ, to intercede for her in face of the anger of the LORD and to endure for her sake whatever suffering follows. Of course, it is rare indeed that he will himself be guiltless, so that he has an even stronger reason for bearing patiently the cross this situation lays upon him.

"Great mystery this," St. Paul would say, "Husbands, love your wives, as Christ loved the Church and gave Himself up for her, that He might sanctify her" (Eph.5:32 & 25–26). Adam's sin violated his own nature at its roots, for to be a man is, in one manner or another, to be a husband. His refusal of his

---

[5] Cf., e.g., Roland de Vaux, *La Genèse*, 2ème éd., Paris: Éditions du Cerf (1962), *p* 45.

[6] Cf. Gaston Fessard, *La dialectique des Exercices Spirituels de Saint Ignace de Loyola, tome 2*, Paris: Aubier (1966), *pp* 82–87.

[7] It was easier for Him to resist the noisy clamor of the rest of our fallen race, then still a harlot. Cf. Origen, *In Iesu Nave Homilia*, III, 5 on the Church of the gentiles "quae quondam meretrix fuit," and St. Hilary, *Tractatus Mysteriorum*, II, 9 (*Traité p* 154) and also I, 3 (*p* 80) concerning the "peccatrix ecclesia," only later to be taken to Himself through her incorporation into Israel.

[8] Cf. Wisd.2:12–20, for we all have been, of ourselves, wicked and children of wrath like the rest (Eph.2:3).

role as head—of the race indeed but also of his wife[9] (I Cor.11:3)—was the great sin that has undone us all.

Thus, in a way not ordinarily adverted to, the sin of Adam was indeed a sexual sin, i.e., one that destroyed the most essential element of his manhood and corrupted all relations between him and Eve, isolating him from her more than he had feared, before he sinned, that her sin had done. The earth, which it had been the man's task and pride to work for the sustenance of his wife and children, was now cursed so as ever to resist his efforts and to render his labor painful, dreary, and with little lasting fruit.

Hence, too, it is that Christ's sacrifice on the cross was the ultimate act of manliness. By His sacrifice of Himself, He has won for Himself His bride, without spot or wrinkle or any such thing (Eph.5:27), and wrought the definitive redemption for us all. What Adam had done most wrongly, Jesus, the second Adam, did most rightly.

Hence follows, also, the absurdity of thinking that the continuation of His sacrifice in the Mass could, even in imagination, be exercised by any woman. Not even the second Eve, who herself did rightly all that the first Eve did wrongly,[10] could act as husband and priest, though she stood at the cross, offering her Son to the Father in perfect acceptance of His will.

One can, then, begin to see the structure of every grave temptation that God permits to come upon us. The test for Adam paralleled that to which Jesus was put. Like each, was the test to which God put Abraham, or that of Israel in letting Benjamin depart. Will we have the LORD, even at the "cost" of having Him alone, yielding up to His will all else that we love, or will we not?

C. THE LAW AND THE VIRTUE OF PUNISHMENT

If we consider the actual sins that followed the fall, as shown in *Genesis*, we may be struck by what seems the precocity of sin in relation to virtue. This is the connatural effect of original sin. Yet, because of God's grace, it is more in seeming than in fact. Abel, made acceptable by God's grace, is brother to Cain, to whom God offers grace but who rejects it. Henoch walks with God at about the time of Lamech's savagery. The offspring of the sons of the gods and the daughters of men precede Noah only slightly. What gives the false impression is rather the vigor and quasi-universality of sin. Sin indeed "reigned" during this time, as Paul was to say (Rom.5:14). But there is little more to say beyond what we have mentioned already. A moral immaturity like that of Cain protected man from sentence of death until the time of Noah. But then God wiped out all men except Noah's family for their wickedness. Then through the Noachic covenant, He delegated in part His authority over all life by requiring of the whole human race that they punish murder by the death of the murderer.

---

[9] This was not then to be understood of domination, which came only as a result of the fall (Gen.3:16), but of loving governance.

[10] Cf. Irenaeus' splendid account of Mary's obdience as the recapitulation of Eve's disobedience, *Adv. Haer.*, III, 22, 4 & V, 19, 1.

Though the pride of the builders of Babel is punished only by the frustration of their efforts, God again punishes by death the men of Sodom and Lot's wife. Her punishment suggests that the desire to watch and relish the punishment of others in their wickedness is itself profoundly evil. This is far from the simple desire that justice be carried out, though often disguising itself as this latter. One does not require the ghastly details if only desiring justice. The sin of Lot's wife is the ultimate and unbridled search by the gossip for material; it will indeed turn the heart to salt. But except for the divine judgment on heinous crime, there is little to suggest that human morals were then matters of great interest to the LORD, except insofar as He wanted faith and fidelity in His chosen ones.

As we indicated earlier, the fire and cloud at Sinai, the thunders and the trembling of the earth, were all to make clear that the God who is the ruler of nature, the transcendent, all-powerful Creator, before whom all creatures must bow in awe and dread, is also a God who is interested in all the things men do among themselves in their daily lives and to one another. The God of Israel's cult is the God of Israel's moral life as well. Nowhere else among the religions of man has there been a god who has taken human beings so seriously, who has regarded them so highly.[11] The good is revealed not merely as something good-for-man, though such it is, but as what is personally desired by God for Israel, whatever the individual Israelite's reactions may be. Evil is not merely what is hurtful to man, though such it is; but is that which God hates and will not tolerate in His people, again independently of any man's judgment.

But though reinforced by the overwhelming experience of the LORD's coming down upon Sinai in fire and cloud, melting the rock and shaking the earth with thunder and the blast of the trumpet, yet the giving of the Law initiated the weaning of Israel from "experience" i.e., from their own emotional reactions to situations and people. Experience might indicate to them, on occasion, the presence and action of the LORD, as when He sent fire from heaven to consume the sacrifice Elijah offered Him on Carmel, to prove to Israel that He and not Baal is God or as when Elijah stood at the mouth of his cave at the sound of the still, small voice (1 Kgs.19:12–13). But the ultimate norm of good and bad was to be God's Law; secondarily, in concrete situations, His word to His prophets would specify the demands of the Law, but not set them aside. Israel was henceforth to live by truth and the knowledge of God through faith. They were to believe what their elders would hand on to them of the people's past experiences of the LORD's acting and speaking. The Scriptures, then, are not mere collections of secular chronicles but are the rememberings of that earlier experience given to Israel when just leaving childhood.

In fact, the Hebrews were not much interested in living by faith. Like all men since the fall, they wished to grasp with their senses and feelings the reality of the world, not realizing that that reality is primarily spiritual. Yet, in the LORD's judgment they were ready to begin; and He insisted, even though He knew how often they would fail and sin in consequence. Indeed,

[11] Cf. John L. McKenzie, S.J., *The Two-Edged Sword*, Milwaukee: Bruce (1956), *pp* 262–263.

the danger of man's sinning seems never to have deterred the LORD from demanding greater growth from him. So, He made the people wait for Moses to return from the mountain-top, though they would turn their idle time to the worship of the golden calf. He called upon them to believe that food and water would be provided even in the desert, though they complained and sulked when it was not given at the moment they demanded it. He told them that, if they were to go forward in confidence, He would defeat their enemies in Canaan, though in fact they refused. Most especially, they were to keep the first three Commandments, to which only faith could give any meaning.

As mentioned earlier, these, unlike the remaining Commandments, were totally new in content. It is they that defined the basis of the Covenant. Their special task was to separate the people of Israel from all their neighbors and to form them into the people of the LORD. The LORD alone is to be adored; any image of Him offered for worship would perforce be an idol, since nothing in the visible world truly resembles Him.[12] He is holy; His name must be treated as holy. Most especially, it is never to be defiled by using it to swear falsely, for the LORD is a God of truth and justice. He is to be worshipped for His holiness. The day of His rest from the work of creation is to be the day on which man rests from his labors in creation, entrusting all worries about his future to the LORD's care in order to give himself to God alone, in a gesture directly countering Adam's sin.

This absolute distinction that faith in the LORD establishes between good and evil, though essential, is insufficient. One must also know what things belong in each category. Israel's successive legal codes or later reformulations of its earlier ones came about in order to meet this need as the culture and the circumstances of life changed. But the basic distinction was made totally clear from the outset in a way that could not be improved upon, even though the point would have to be endlessly repeated and driven home.

The other Near-Eastern legal codes were set out as human case law, "If one commits X, he shall be punished by Y." In the Code of the Covenant, which follows immediately in *Exodus* upon the Commandments, and in later legislation, Israel follows much the same pattern. Even the last seven Commandments seem hardly original in their content. Not only was this content in place at the time of the Patriarchs, but one can find close similarities between these and the legal codes of nations that had preceded Israel. These ancient codes show that the Near-Eastern nations of that time condemned murder, adultery, bearing false witness, theft, and the like. As far as we can tell, these basic prescriptions are very close to universal among the peoples of the world as moral ideals or obligations. But among none of Israel's neighbors did these moral attitudes prevail because their gods were moral or intrinsically interested in man's morals. Despite all similarities, the pagan codes were not imposed as their gods' own personal and determinate will for man.

The Code of the Covenant is a mixture of civil and criminal legislation, heavily colored throughout by a very strong moral element. Unlike the

[12] Man was created "in" or "according to" His one true Image, the eternal Son; but only when the Son came among us Himself in the weakness of our flesh was a perfect Image of the Father made visible (cf. *Ch* 4.C Excursus, *pp* 72–75).

Commandments, the Code includes sanctions for each of its provisions. Those who obey the law will be blessed with all the many blessings mentioned (Ex.23:23ff).[13] Those who disobey are to be punished, in many cases by death and, so, blotted out from God's people.

The threats are serious; and, whatever reservations he may have, the adolescent who is rightly taught God's law knows that his own conscience ratifies the law as just. And though there is no visible flame flaring in darkness on top of the mountain, there is the almost more palpable fire of hell.

One who does good is to be rewarded; the good is worthy of reward. By his efforts, he does what God commands and merits the promised reward for doing so; God gives him his reward. A Kantian ethics of duty that would shun consideration of reward is totally alien to Israel and to Christianity. Such an ethics could only flourish when men had lost all sense of God as personal and all realization of the intrinsic nature of moral goodness as being, at root, a type of love, not the love that is mere intellectual approval, but that bond between persons, between God and man, stronger than any other.[14]

So, likewise, the man who does evil is worthy of death and is to be killed. He deserves to die. It is a good thing to kill him. It is an act of virtue, tied to the worship of the Lord, to kill those who do evil. For, grave sin is sacrilege. It is a rejection of the LORD as one's lord, a preferring to Him of something infinitely less. Flouting the LORD and breaking His law, setting one's will against His, cries out for punishment as the only proper response. God's moral will for our true good involves employment of what we wrongly regard as the greatest evils, the physical ones.

What is too often overlooked is that only when punishment is seen as a good and its infliction as virtue is it possible even to have the concept of mercy. If punishment were not due the evil action, then a choice not to punish would be simple justice, not mercy. Instead, one frequently substitutes under the splendid name of mercy some sickly and self-serving "compassion," a toleration of evil action because it could only rightly be punished if we ourselves were to be punished also.[15]

The stage of a person's growth corresponding to that of Israel when the Code of the Covenant was given is one in which, if all goes well, one comes to see for the first time that punishment, justly imposed[16] by the leadership of the community, is both right and good. Not everyone is to be be the agent of it.[17] In fact, because grave sin is sacrilegious and involves, therefore, the whole people, it is not primarily a private but a public matter.[18] In contradistinction

[13] This Code, though used much later by the Deuteronomist, belongs to the period of the Israelite settlement on the land and to the time of the Judges.

[14] Those contemporary Catholic moralists who lump traditional Catholic moral teaching with Kantian ethics under the rubric of 'deontology' show by this very fact that they have lost their comprehension of moral theology as understood in the Church.

[15] McKenzie, *Two-Edged Sword, pp* 281–285.

[16] This is, in fact, a tautology. Whatever is not just, is not punishment at all, but the venting of one's spleen or oppression or vindictiveness or sadism or some other deviation.

[17] If, in stoning the culprit, all take part in the execution in order to show the entire community's reprobation of his evil action, yet the judgment and verdict are reserved to public authority.

to the punishments God Himself inflicted on those who rebelled against Moses, these punishments are exacted by human agents acting under God's authority. Thus they are exacted for types of crime that cannot be interpreted simply as rebellion against a supreme tribal authority.

Killing those who do evil is, then, considered in itself, a good, and a good that was commanded by God fairly often during the lifetime of Moses and of Joshua, of the Judges and still under the monarchy—recall how Saul was rejected by the LORD as king because of his failure to kill off the conquered king and the better animals. One was *obliged* to punish. If he didn't, he sinned and the people suffered for it. Remember the story of Achan (Jos.7), who hid away a cloak, some money, and an ingot of gold, burying them under his tent. God's wrath was kindled against the people. And when, by revelation from the Lord, they found out who had done the evil, they took him out, along with all his wives and children, and stoned and burnt them. And the Lord's anger was turned away from Israel because they had done a good thing thereby.

The point was to drive into the very fiber of Israelite culture the distinction between what is good and what is bad, not as philosophical categories nor as man's own deciding for himself what is good and bad, but as willed or hated by God. It had to be made clear that evil really deserves all the punishment it receives. Always, the evil act is presented as something that is such because it is contrary to God's will.

The Gibeonites, who dwelt in a large and powerful city, yet sent emissaries to find a way of surrendering to Israel. They submitted themselves to the Lord's people—deceiving them by flat lies in the process—leading them to think that they came from much further away than in fact they had and that they were not inhabitants of this land promised to Israel. But once the treaty was made and the Israelites found the trick that had been played on them, they were still obligated to honor their agreement. They themselves had done wrong by acting rashly without consulting the Lord; but they were bound. And since these people were submitting themselves to the Lord through His people, as Rahab the harlot had done, there was no punishment for them, though they were made to be hewers of wood and drawers of water for Israel. Simply evil they were not, in spite of their dishonesty.

D. The *ḥerem* and Jesus

It is of first importance to understand that the invading Israelites' wars and battles were not merely religious battles and religious warfare but were punishments inflicted by the LORD upon His enemies. Israel's enemies, then, were to be those who worshipped false gods and who resisted the will of the LORD for His people. Violating the divine will, the pagans were doing evil. They were, then, to be killed by the Israelites as punishment for their wrongdoing. The ban, the anathema, the *ḥerem,* i.e., the putting to the sword of

[18] The so-called punishment of children is rather discipline, a teaching that seeks to bring about amendment of attitudes and understanding so that actions deserving of punishment will be avoided later on.

everyone, man, woman, and child, and the burning of all their possessions, retaining nothing for oneself (Jos.6:21), was a religious act. Not even animals could be kept to offer in sacrifice, for *all* this slaughter was the sacrifice.[19]

Good and bad here were judged by one very simple standard, simpler even than the Ten Commandments: Are you for us, the LORD's own people, or are you against us? Since we are His people, if you are against us, you are against Him and we will cut your throats. Those who are enemies of God's people are simply enemies of God, though not necessarily enemies of such sort as to merit eternal punishment—of which there was at that time no question—but punishable by temporal death.[20]

Today, we tend to refuse to allow ourselves to sense, much less profit from, the religious element that is found in these narratives. Scriptural commentators go to great lengths to show how all this must be understood in the context of the times and that it is, therefore, only an all too human way of putting off on God the things that we humans want to do but instinctively know to be wrong, etc. Yet profoundly and truly religious it was; and it is no less relevant for us Christians in our day than it was for them, though in the very different manner proper to Jesus' recapitulation that we shall consider in a moment.

But first, two further factors need consideration. With the slaughters we have perpetrated or countenanced in our own century, we are hardly in a position to pretend to greater moral perfection. Saturation bombing, as at Dresden in World War II, and the nuclear destruction, without warning, of Hiroshima had no justification from religion. The slaughter of infants in the wombs of their mothers was not allowed to Israel even against their enemies though we have been thus killing millions of our own children. In the meantime, we perish because we refuse to acknowledge anything to be considered truly evil except our own suffering, nor good except our own desires.

Secondly, there can be no doubt that *ḥerem* was brutal and gave rise at times to acts of great cruelty that God condemned. Yet, if one thinks about it a little, it is by no means clear that this was a more cruel form of warfare than others. Indeed, I would argue, it was less cruel than most. For all were slain together. There were no gravely wounded dying in slow agony on the battlefield. There were no distraught and grief-tormented survivors left to die of famine and cold. There were no exiles or slaves uprooted and separated forever from family and people. There were but the few, fierce moments of terror and pain, and the awareness that one was dying with one's people. Think here of the Hindu practice of suttee, the wife, most of the time quite willingly, mounting the funeral pyre of her deceased husband to be burned, unbound and fully conscious, in order to be with him in the next life—and to avoid the social isolation and misery of widowhood.

---

[19] Depending on the period and the circumstances, some minor variations, especially with regard to the animals, can be noted.

[20] A too easy extension of knowledge of hell as the punishment for unrepented mortal sin and, in particular, for refusal or rejection of the grace of faith once offered, came about through a confusion of prefigurative with preparative typology.

It may seem hard to visualize Jesus in early adolescence acting as did His type, Joshua, the son of Nun, whose name He bore, and who, the Scripture tells us, slaughtered with God's full approval, indeed, at His express command, many thousands of Canaanites, not only men but women and children. Whatever might be said about the primitive religion or culture of those earlier days, how can one picture Jesus recapitulating the killing of Canaanites, doing the job perfectly whenever Joshua failed, e.g., when the Israelites were tricked into sparing the lives of the men of Gibeon? And, then, what could our recapitulation of the same be?

But, as may be guessed from what we have already said, the question is not how many Canaanites or others He had killed by the end of this stage of growth but whether He was mature enough to have done so whenever the situation should have truly called for it and to have refrained from killing, not from fear but from moral choice, not from natural revulsion at bloodshed but from mercy.

Now, at whatever time Jesus passed through this stage in His maturing, He had certainly done so by the time He began His public life. Consider how easily and matter-of-factly He let those who were obstinate in sin go their way even if that meant dragging others with them: "They are blind, leading the blind, and both will fall into the ditch" (Mt.15:13–14). Or how He spoke of the deaths of those upon whom the tower fell or whom Pilate slaughtered: "Unless you do penance, you will all likewise perish" (Lk.13: 1–5). Or how coolly and without indication of grief, He could speak of His sending those who are on His left hand off into eternal punishment (Mt.25:41, 46). Though He speaks with anger to those whom He repeatedly threatens, "You will die in your sins" (Jn.8:21–24), He does not show any horror or cringing, as might one not yet arrived at the level of Joshua.

If one is willing to let the rest of the New Testament speak for Him, then, to take only the most striking instance, there is the truly terrible image in *Revelation* (14:10) in which the Lamb stands, quite unmoved, by the mouth of the pit as the smoke of the burning of the damned goes up forever. "The Lamb"! At the least, could not the author have spoken here, as he does elsewhere, of "the Lion of the tribe of Judah"? Yet it is of "the anger of the Lamb" (6:16–17), standing as slain for the sins of all, that he deliberately chooses to speak.

Like His namesake, Jesus had a clear vision of the goodness that punishment of God's enemies involves. The major difference lay rather in the identification of these enemies. Here, the spiritualization involved in all genuine typology is manifested: it is those who consent to a pridefulness that allies them with the demons that are truly God's enemies and the enemies of His people. Since, as long as they live on earth, such men are not beyond repentance, it was not His task to kill them but to call them back, even if by threats, through Himself to the Father.

As the angel told Joseph, Jesus was "to save His people from their sins" (Mt.1:21, Ps.130:8). But this salvation was to be more than mere forgivenness. Jesus would lead all who would follow Him into the Promised Land, not only of grace but of eternal glory (thus both the doctrinal and the anagogical prefigurative senses). But to enter and hold it means battle and warfare while still on the way to that final peace which comes only in heaven. But to fight well, one needs to know the true nature of the enemy and why this war is needed. One first must learn the gravity of sin and the rightness of punishment if mercy is to be seen as such and if one is to be moved to battle not only for one's own salvation but to bring Christ's current enemies to know and accept His mercy.

Like Joshua, too, He was unafraid to speak out publically the word of the Lord. He could threaten people with the logical consequences of their choices, or declare the equivalent of "As for me and my house...," when arguing with His enemies about their relationship to His Father.

The Gospel, again, is silent about the portion of Jesus' life corresponding to Israel's time under the judges. And again, His public life makes clear how completely He had recapitulated this period.[21] Indeed, indications are that, already at twelve, Jesus had not only submitted to the Law and had understood the need for spiritual combat but also had attained a self-possession that was decisive and stable. His decision to remain behind in the Temple showed the former two, while His decision to go down to Nazareth, to remain subject to Joseph and Mary until His early thirties, shows the stability of His choices.

E. Limping in the Service of the LORD

The *ḥerem* served another function that became visible only as Israel began to settle the land after the conquest: the protection of God's people from the seduction of idolatry. After the death of Joshua, the people began to worship the false gods of the nations they were supposed to destroy. God then punished them by raising up enemies against them (Jdg.2). They would repent; but once spared, they began again to do evil, failing to devote to destruction those whom they were supposed to kill. Instead, they kept for forced labor those they conquered and intermarried with them (Jdg.3:6), so that their own children were raised in false religions. Falling again into idolatry, they would be punished once more and their enemies would succeed against them. Brought low, they would cry out to the Lord who would take pity on them and send them a "judge," i.e., a military leader, who might also settle local disputes between them. The judge would rouse them up and lead them or, more commonly, some small fraction of them, against the enemy and, by the LORD's power, break the yoke that was weighing them down. When that judge would die, they would fall away again, be punished, would call upon the Lord, who would send them another judge to save them in His name.

The falls were as frequent as the risings. Yet, though endlessly fluctuating, the people still regarded themselves as belonging to the LORD. Apparently, they did not simply abandon Him or reject Him outright. Rather they set the idols of the nations in His shrines and worshipped these other gods

[21] It is well to recall here that we are not speaking primarily of Jesus' physical age but of His psychic age, one that ought not to have been, at this stage, greatly different from ours, were we unfallen, or, even recapitulating ideally in Him.

alongside Him. Or they would worship Him in the ways in which those other gods were worshipped rather than as the Law specified. He would not abandon His people, jealous of them as He was. Yet they never gave themselves over decisively to Him. That He should be a jealous God seemed to them unreasonable. The whole book of *Judges* is constructed so as to underline this instability.

In like manner adolescents go limping, as Elijah was to say of Israel much later on. Unable from day to day to make up their minds which way they're going to go, their good intentions are "writ in water." Whether it be a matter of chastity or faith or the use of their newly discovered reason or their relations with their families or almost anything else in their lives, inconstancy is their name.[22]

Israel at this time found the nature worship of the other Semitic peoples exceedingly congenial. The moral requirements of those peoples were few and not connected with religion, save in the sexual license that was part of their cult. Beneath this, however, lay the strong appeal of nature mysticism: a religious activity that would unite man with the gods and bring about fertility through union with the source of all fertility, a fertility of land and herds and people, with harmony and peace among them. So, the Canaanite king would unite sexually with a priestess on the "high places," a somewhat crude imitation of the powerful monarchs of Mesopotamia, who once each year united with their "goddesses" on the platforms of their great temples. The king represented the god who gave fertility; and the priestess, the people and the land. Thus man sought to enter into perfect union with nature and especially with the maternal earth.

As they mature sexually, adolescents are filled with a new and awe-struck sensitivity to the beauties and powers of nature. Sense-perception becomes measurably sharper and more refined in adolescents, readying them for an appreciation of the beauties of the opposite sex and for sexual union in marriage. They do truly perceive the world in a new way and, like the ancient Israelites, yearn to be one with this newly rediscovered nature. They may not do very well on going to Church or in praying to God, but they enjoy being "one with Him." Lying on the ground in summer, they feel the warm earth beneath them and breathe the fragrance of the field and see the blue sky above and know that they are "one with all Being." The tranquil yet exultant peace of such times is a sensible token not only of his recognition that man is, from one point of view, part of the material world but also of his awareness of the goodness of his being constituted as he is.

Nature thus romantically espoused is, however, too often divinized by the young adult and made into a god or a substitute for one. Hence come most of the pantheisms that have infested the earth and, as with the Canaanites, the deification of sex.

But nature has also its cruel and terrible side. The practical results of such romanticism will, if this be persevered in, end in bloodshed. Canaanite

[22] There are, of course, some who have been fixated, at least for a time, in the early-adolescent revolt typical of Moses' day, whose history will then be different.

religion was not unaware of this. Its goddesses, not unlike the Ugaritic Anath, were not merely sexually lustful in the ordinary ways but addicted to blood-lust and sadism, wading up to their thighs in delight in human blood stomped out of living men. These deified forces of nature and human passion were irresistible, arbitrary, and unbelievably cruel. All this is something we have tended to forget, under the influence of the Scriptures and Christian faith. We take it as obvious that nature is God's good creature, and forget how it must have appeared in the eyes of those who took it as divine.

Chapter 14

The Monarchy and the Exile

With the monarchy, Israel comes of age. So, the young Christian adult now enters the world of his people, often surrounded by alien cultures and religions, in order to make his way there. Clear-sighted at first in his assessments of what is good not only for himself but for civil society, his own weaknesses and sins come gradually to dull his vision. As he matures further, he begins to understand not merely that he may have personal enemies but that his own people are far from always being faithful and are often, so far as his spiritual growth is concerned, truly, even if at times unconsciously, his enemies. If in his career he perseveres, however weakly, in the service of the Lord, he comes to see the callous injustices perpetrated by himself and his fellows against one another as, in reality, sins against the Lord, and he begins to work against these evils. If faithful to the Lord, he will find His Law increasingly "obvious", intrinsically intelligible. Yet the Lord Himself seems in many ways increasingly to escape his understanding.

A. Saul and David

The fault of Saul, first king of Israel, was that of a man who refuses to accept adult responsibility for the exercise of his authority. At times he was rigid and cruel in its exercise, as when he ordered the death of his own son for a trivial violation of Saul's command (I Sam.14:24–30,38–44). At other times, he failed to exercise it from a probably groundless fear that he not be liked by the people. "Little in his own eyes," he forgot that the LORD had chosen him as His anointed in order to govern His people, as the LORD's delegate and not as he himself might desire.

Fixated in what is, in the adolescent, a proper concern to be liked, i.e., to learn how to get along in accord with the expectations of those with whom he is to live, Saul, like many men set in authority after him, refused true adulthood. Responsibility rested on him, as it had on Adam and, in varying degrees, on each man ever since, to govern others for their good, whether the others liked him for it or not. Saul balked when called upon to make the transit to adult manhood through his taking of that responsibility for other people's lives for which he had been made king. The strength of character requisite for any man who is to be husband and father—still more important for a king—is achieved by the freely willed carrying out of what he knows to be his duty in defiance of his fears; but Saul would not do so.

Saul was a "wimp"—in the technical sense psychologist Paul Vitz has given this term: a man whose primary psychological need is to be liked.[1] There was much of manliness in Saul; he was a brave warrior and dynamic leader. Yet, his alternations between arbitrary harshness and weak capitulation were equally signs that he did not stand firm in the LORD's will. His problem was less that he lacked prudence than that he was afraid to make obedience to God the norm of all his life. He feared to do what he knew by faith to be the one thing required under the circumstances. To do what the LORD told him through Samuel would engage him in a line of action whose end he could not foresee. Rather, relying on his own, not very clear-sighted reasoning, he sought for compromise, willing to do any good thing except the one thing needed.

Though Western culture today has its share of those perpetual adolescents who are forever in revolt against authority, more characteristic of our day is Saul's weakness. For, unlike the former, slightly less mature folk, these modern Sauls remain easily within an institution, doing well enough at their work as long as it does not require courage in acting according to one's moral convictions. Indeed, in the governments of nations and cities, of churches and religious institutes, the most likely person to have authority today is the wimp. And if civil law is in disarray or if religious doctrine and morals are rapidly dissolving, this seems in largest measure due to the wimp's inability—better, deep unwillingness—to govern and to be known publicly as one who is unafraid to exercise the full range of his authority for the common good. Our culture has accepted the wimp as leader. As a cultural phenomenon, however, this will be best discussed later.

Though Saul had not desired to be king when first called, once he had tasted power, he became ever more jealous of his authority in the very measure in which he failed to exercise it rightly. Passing from a weak man's arbitrariness to murderous suspicion and enmity, as when he had Ahimelech killed for giving aid to David and had the other priests of Nob and the whole town slaughtered, though they had had no part in the affair (I Sam.22:13–19), Saul threw away by his own weak miscalculations the very popularity for which he had sacrificed by disobedience his true authority. Forced on occasion to acknowledge David's manly goodness and fairness, he had not faith and trust enough in the LORD to overcome his own inner insecurity and to behave in like manner.

This jealousy of one's authority is also characteristic of a wimp. And if

---

[1] Paul Vitz, *Pastoral Renewal 10*, 48–47 (#3, Oct. 1985) and note 24, *p* 408 below.

this trait does not produce the greatest tyrannies, it does generate the most petty and the most diffuse. For like Saul, the wimp is relentless in tracking down those who shame him by their largeness of heart, in order to replace them with others like himself.

Saul served as the perfect foil for David, who acted like a man in all those things in which Saul remained the adolescent. When David first appears, he stands in immediate contrast to Saul through his religious reverence and quiet confidence in the LORD, whom Saul acknowledged but seemed never truly to know. Thus David, as a young shepherd, not only was roused to anger by the taunts of the Philistines but recognized them as implicit blasphemies against the LORD. Angered, he took upon himself, in the LORD's strength, what others saw as a suicidal effort to avenge them.

Once introduced to the court, David was a typical young man on the make, who had sized up his surroundings and his abilities and estimated his opportunities for getting ahead. Patient and ready to wait, he showed none of Saul's passivity, but found how to take full advantage of every situation. Men of all kinds were ready to follow him, for they found in him a leader who knew how to govern with fairness for the good of all. He lived in casual conformity with the culture of his people. Thus, he was not above demanding protection-money, so that his men in the desert might not be turned loose to raid or destroy the property of others. Yet, he was just, according to his lights. If one paid as demanded, not a sheep was stolen; his men kept their hands—and other people's hands—off one's property. So, too, he had some seven wives and ten concubines. These he took to himself only gradually, however, over the years, as his fortunes improved, not simply to provide himself with a harem.

Though he sinned grievously through lust and through pride, his life continued to be marked, before and after his gravest sins, by deep awareness of the LORD as his King and Lord, whom he wished to love and to serve in spite of his sins. In contrast to Saul, David seems to live far less from knowledge of the Law than by knowledge of the Lord of the Law. He shows little worry as to whether he is in accord with the Law or not, not because he is a scofflaw but because the Law is part of him; he has taken it into himself. It is his firmness in the LORD that sets him free. As he makes decisions for himself and for others, he takes for granted that he will be doing the things he ought to do. From a sound heart will come sound actions: "A good tree bears good fruit."

From the same firm choice that the LORD be his lord arose what seems most distinctive of David's religious life: his spontaneity in the service of the LORD. His dancing in front of the Ark, his attitude towards Shimei, who cursed him as he left Jerusalem in flight, his treatment of Saul in the cave, his responses to Jonathan, the way he set out after Nadab but responded with gratitude to Abigail's fending him off, his response to those who brought the news of the death of Saul and of Jonathan—even those nearest him could not predict his responses. He fasted and lay a week on the ground, praying that the LORD would spare the life of his infant, so that his retainers feared he might take his own life when the child died; instead, he rose and washed himself and—after worshipping in the tent of the LORD—again ate and drank as always. He wept so sorely for Absalom, who had led the great revolt against him and who, having lain publicly with all his wives and concubines, sought energetically to kill him, as to disconcert his entire army and turn their victory into seeming defeat.

It was, then, as true Son of David that Jesus disconcerted the enthusiastic crowd on Palm Sunday by stopping the triumphant procession into Jerusalem to weep over the future destruction of the city, which within the week would have Him crucified. Jesus' spiritual freedom seems the trait most easily discerned by readers of the Gospels who have no faith at all. David's spontaneity shows, in type, the freedom won for His followers by Jesus, who came to set us free from the tyranny of the Law by enabling us through His Spirit to carry out its commands without thinking about them, because going far beyond them by charity. In this way, David was what the LORD declared of him: "a man after My heart, who will do all My will" (I Sam.13:14; Ac.13:22).

None of this seems to have been a sort of subconscious comparison of every proposed action with the Law or an assumption that what he wanted would always coincide with what the Law permitted. Rather, without being able to explain it to himself or others, David had a true instinct for the "weightier demands of the Law, justice and mercy and faith," (Mt.23:23). With a man's love and loyalty to the LORD, he was determined to obey Him; but neither did he scruple about it. As every confessor soon learns, scruples are a sign of evasion of full responsibility, not only for the activity ostensibly their focus but for one's own decision about the moral quality of one's action. Instead of saying, as did David, "I have sinned before the LORD," the scrupler unconsciously seeks to avoid an acknowledgment of true guilt by scrupling about a false guilt.

Hence came the difference between David's response to prophetic reprimand and Saul's. Saul took refuge in excuses and was principally worried about what people would think about him and his kingship if Samuel would not help him cover it up. David was wholly unconcerned with whatever excuses or mitigations might have been found. He acknowledged his sins and made no slightest effort, once he had repented, to hide them from anyone.

When deciding what was right or wrong to do, David was simply unconcerned with what others might think of him. As a practical man, he did take prudent account of men's opinions—but merely as a political matter. Their opinions were their own, external to him, to be considered as one considers the condition of one's troops before a battle or the lay of the land. People's thoughts about him, good or ill, had no inner hold on him. Their evaluation and assessment of his inner self carried no weight at all and gave no moral coloration to his own convictions and decisions. These are his own and he acts upon them—or violates them by sin—but cares nothing for the raised eyebrow or the sneer. He is strong in the faith which is true knowledge of the LORD.

As should now be evident, the Christian is called upon to live through the psychic stage visible in Saul. In doing so, he must rectify what Saul did wrong—easier or harder according to one's temperament—by refusing the sins that would make a wimp of him. He is to use his authority, whatever its nature or extent, with courage and glad acceptance of the embarrassments that alone can free him from self-conscious concern for others' opinions of his actions and motives. Thus he is readied to relive, in Jesus, David's life, with alertness and attention always to the Ten Commandments, most especially the prohibition of adultery. For, as with David, such temptation does not usually strike at once but after one's first love has cooled in ardor if not in will.

B. The Later Kings

This brings one to a sort of curious saddle point. To continue to grow in the Lord, he cannot go forward with the kings of the Davidic dynasty, still less with their rivals in Israel. If he does continue in this same direction, he will find himself heading gradually downwards. Instead, he must turn, so to speak, at right angles and continue his spiritual ascent with the prophets. On its surface, this would seem to be a turning of the Christian adult from a life, admittedly a mixture of good and bad, in civil society to a life that scorns and denounces society and seeks to live apart from others in implicit contempt for their concerns and needs. Such is, needless to say, not the case; but it will be useful to see why in some detail.

Consider Solomon, the greatest of David's successors and his son. Though starting well, what Christians since the days of St. John have called 'worldliness' entangled him. Vigorous in the use of his authority from the day he took the throne, Solomon was no Saul. He was, from an early age, one who "has it made," with wealth, women, power. Clearly an administrator of extraordinary ability, the biblical accounts of his genius do not seem overdrawn when one considers the still impressive archeological remains of his reign, e.g., the great, "Bessemer" smelters for copper that he had built in the desert at Ezion-Geber[2] because there alone the wind would never cease to blow strongly into the orifices of their venturis.

But Solomon is already weak in faith; not as to belief apparently, but with small concern as to its practical exigencies. With seven hundred wives and three hundred concubines (I Kgs.11:3), Scripture asks us to consider him the wisest of men (I Kgs.10:23) —few mysteries of the faith seem harder to accept at first glance. But wisdom among the Israelites of his day was a practical virtue, not an Augustinian enlightenment of the heart. In context, so great a harem was not principally a matter of sexual satisfaction (though this motivation was not lacking)[3] but of prestige and power and politically advantageous linkages with other nations. Who but a great monarch with endless wealth could support such a ménage? And if he was as virile as the size of his harem suggests, one might think him a potent warrior against anyone who crossed him.

---

[2] Nelson Glueck, *National Geographic*, Feb. 1944. For later, dissenting opinions, *NJBC*, 74:110 & 73:69.

[3] Cf. I Kgs.11:1–2 and Sir.47:19–29.

Solomon was not much concerned about the LORD's prohibition on mixed marriages.[4] Like many a Catholic since, so long as it all gets blessed by the Church (in his case, not publicly disapproved by the priests of the temple), he saw no problem. He could, in fact, probably have gotten by with his marriages even to all those pagan wives. The harem was not his sin.[5] His sin was that he allowed these women publicly to worship their false gods on Israel's territory in shrines built for them in the very shadow of the LORD's own temple, which Solomon himself had built. At the very least, he prepared the way for idolatry among God's people. Whether he personally worshipped these idols himself or not (a matter not made clear by the text), he showed beyond doubt that such worship could be tolerated in others who were living among the people of the LORD—a level of "pluralism" in religion into which the United States has only recently sunk.[6]

Then, as since, the enjoyment of all the good things of life leads a man easily, especially one who is in a position of power, towards religious indifferentism. He may personally retain the truths of faith but considers them pretty much a private matter, in any case not important enough to let them cause any civic or familial disturbance among those for whom he bears responsibility, who are under his direct authority.

This same tendency to subordinate the practice of religion, if not one's faith itself, to the utility of the state or even to merely the convenience of the individual continues to grow under the later monarchy. Things come to the point where the kings of Judah are "personally opposed" to the killing of infants in human sacrifice. Most of them would never do it themselves.[7] But they do not wish to "impose their morals on others." They do nothing to dissuade their people from going out to the Valley of Hinnom to burn their babies alive to placate Molech or, worse perversion yet, the LORD. Yet they go without fail to the temple to worship the LORD and ask His blessing on the kingdom.

Whether they think the foreign gods really exist is not clear. In any case, they wish to play it safe, just in case. Kings and people alike are too weak in faith to act on their belief that the LORD alone governs the world —if they still do believe it at all. They are too addicted to their way of life to let it be carelessly threatened by not taking the same precautions as their pagan neighbors, culturally so far their superiors.

There seems to have been no longer any flat rejection of the Lord by direct apostasy, as in the days of the Judges. Though the foreign gods and their cults were established in the temple, the usual sacrifices to the LORD, it seems, continued to be offered (II Kgs.16:10–17; 21:4–5, 7, 21). The danger now is a sort of formalism. Religion, having become a matter of national

[4] Though implicit in the instructions for *ḥerem*, this seems first to have been made explicit in Ex.34:16.

[5] Even Moses had a pagan wife, the Cushite woman, and David also (II Sam.3:13) without any stigma of wrongdoing attaching to either.

[6] This refers to our practice. In principle, from the beginnings of this country worshippers of false gods have had the same rights as any others as long as they did not violate civil law.

[7] Ahaz (II Kgs.16:3) and Manasseh (II Kgs.21:6), however, did sacrifice their own sons.

security, is embraced not for its truth and intrinsic goodness but for its utility, from the outside only, according to its external practices. One does the religious things one is supposed to do: chiefly sacrifices and the ceremonies of the temple. But the inner life is missing.

The way in which Christianity in the United States has been permeated by such individual immorality as contraception and homosexual behavior, and by such public injustice as financial fraud and legal approval of abortion, illustrates fairly well the process that took place in Israel and Judah. How often we have known people, perhaps ourselves, who are perfect church-goers yet see no problem whatever in oppressing their workers, paying poor wages, lying easily and gravely for advantage in business or politics, engaging in a bit of carefully private adultery. There is a sinister ability at this stage to recognize God and His Law, the cult, and all the rest, while still holding it at arm's length so as to do, essentially, just what one pleases. Evidently, a genuinely Christian maturation requires, rather, an ever stronger grasp on Jesus' words, "Do not think that I have come to bring peace to the earth. I have not come to bring peace but a sword" {Mt.10:34; cf. also 10: 35–39}. "Whoever of you does not renounce all that he has cannot be My disciple" (Lk.14:33). "What shall it profit a man if he gain the whole world and suffer the loss of himself?" {Mt.16:26}. As the LORD made clear at Sinai, the moral life must be in order if He is to be rightly worshipped. A splendid church and liturgy are not enough, important as these are in themselves.

C. The Prophets and Jesus

In opposition to the well-to-do formalism and wickedness just mentioned stood the prophets. Just what they were and what they represented in Israel before Samuel is not clear. The word is used of Abraham (Gen.20:7) and the patriarchs generally (Ps.105:15); then later, of Moses and, from outside of Israel, Balaam. All these, like Samuel some centuries later, were individuals who heard the word of the LORD, to whom the Lord revealed, when and as He wished, what He was planning to do in the particular concrete circumstances or what He wanted the people to do.[8] All, with the possible exception of those mentioned in Psalm 105, were also seers, favored on occasion with visions from the LORD. Apparently more common were the "sons of the prophets," groups of ecstatics who through religious frenzy would declare what they claimed to be the word of the Lord. Both kinds, if these were truly different kinds, rose to a position of great prominence under the monarchy and were characteristic of this period.

The prophets of this period quite clearly laid the emphasis on the social dimensions of one's behavior: the trampling of the poor by the wealthy, who, though they had more than they knew what to do with already, were still filching by fraud or force the poor man's few possessions and dishonoring other men by stealing their wives. David's sins against Uriah, taking from him first his wife and then his life, foreshadowed the moral decay that had set in,

[8] Abraham and Moses, of course, were much more than this categorization would indicate. Yet the Scripture is explicit in regarding them as prophets.

even as Nathan's rebuking him for these sins highlighted one aspect of the labors of the later prophets.

The great prophets whose words we still have from Scripture, had begun, from David's time at least, to understand the Law from within. What David did without reflex understanding in interiorizing the Law, these prophets were able not only to do but to understand and express. They knew the Law, indeed, as the direct expression of the LORD's will. But through their living of His commands, they came to experience the Law not as an imposition from without, no matter how legitimate, but as that which nourished them and gave them life, "sweeter...than honey and drippings of the honeycomb" (Ps.19:10; Jer.15:16).

They came to know the Law, as did the Deuteronomist, as an expression of God's love for Israel. And they burned with zeal for Him in return. Because they had interiorized the Law, they were apt instruments to represent the LORD Himself, to speak His words, to demand fidelity. They were men in whom full submission to the Law had led to an inner knowledge both of the Holy One of Israel, who had given it, and of its being the inner law of man's nature.

There is no evidence for the position, sometimes set forth in our day, that the prophets were antinomian. True, these pre-Exilic prophets were not generally official teachers of the Law, as were the priests. But the Law was the basis for their denuntiations of the sins of Israel, though their interiorizing of the Law made it clear to them, as they then made clear to others, that the Commandments cut much deeper than a casual reading might suggest. Anyone who understood the Ten Commandments interiorly would understand the need to adapt them to the ever new situations of Israel—as they moved out of the desert, through the conquest, to agriculture, to the monarchy—and would have no difficulty in understanding the ever-accumulating strata of the Torah. But neither would he allow minor adjustments and applications to replace what was fundamental and permanent.

Already, in God's name, Samuel had denounced Saul for a sin that lay beyond a breaking of any of the Commandments taken literally, though Samuel was at pains to show that it implied a violation of the First (I Sam.15:22–23). Nathan denounced David's violations of the 6th and 5th Commandments; but Gad spoke out against his having the people numbered (2 Sam.24), something against which there was no commandment, but which implied both pride and lack of confidence in the LORD. A century later something much stronger was needed, and Elijah "arose like a fire and his word burned like a torch" (Sir.48:1), bringing famine and the sword upon the guilty. Some seventy-five years later, the prophets whose names head the biblical compilations of their preaching began their ministry. By now, the evils had become general. Social and economic injustice, idolatry, ignorance and disregard for the Law, especially among the well-to-do, were destroying both kingdoms from within. Speaking to the king was not enough; so these prophets took full advantage of a contemporary shift in the way kings had messages delivered to other nations, and went to the people.

These later prophets all had as a common theme the worthlessness of any worship, even in the temple at Jerusalem, that was not also expressed by obedience to the Law. They knew well the meaning of true worship according to all the ritual prescriptions of the Law and of custom, and what it signified about the LORD and one's own life. And they saw that a sacrifice had no value unless the offerer was at least trying to live what was signified by his sacrificial act.

Yet it would be wrong to see the prophets as opposed to any of the social institutions of Israel. Quite the contrary. They opposed relentlessly the sins, especially the injustices, that were rotting and tearing the social fabric. As no one understood the Law better than they, so no one labored more strongly for a socially sound monarchy and a religiously sound priesthood and worship.[9]

Any Christian who lives his religion reasonably well finds, as he matures spiritually, the interiorization of God's law taking place in himself. The young adolescent's carrying out of the law under threat, from fear or even, at times, from terror, gives way gradually to a straightforward obedience. Eventually, well into his adult years, he finds a sort of grateful appreciation for the strength and vigor God's law has given him and an inner understanding, having seen the results of men's various actions, of its benefits. He sees that God commands these things, not as a despot nor because He wishes to test our obedience by arbitrary commands but because He made us in such fashion that only in this way can we live and function well and fully. The Commandments have turned into the Owner's Manual of Instructions.

The Christian equivalent of the sons of the prophets are the members of the various religious institutes. If living well, they also learn to see God's law as the lifeblood of society as well as their own. They do well, then, to point out the greed too often hidden in comfortable living and, themselves, to live without comforts. But, learning from Jesus, towards whom all prophecy tended, they refrain from offering practical solutions to this world's problems, knowing that whatever they can bring to others of fuller understanding of God's truth, by word or action, will do more than any attempt to push their own opinions about practical matters.

Jesus presented Himself to His people publicly as a prophet.[10] Only those who accepted Him as a prophet were to learn of His being the Messiah and of His priesthood and kingship. Like the great prophets of the Old Law, he did not speak publicly till personally called and designated by the Father at His baptism. He brought to prophecy miracles like those of Elijah and Elisha; the training of carefully selected disciples who would gather His words, like Isaiah; celibacy and sufferings like those of Jeremiah; good news, greater even than that of Second Isaiah. But He is more than a prophet; and His knowledge and love of the Father and of the sinful people the Father loves

[9] Sacred Congregation for the Doctrine of the Faith: *Instruction on Certain Aspects of the "Theology of Liberation,"* August 6, 1984, especially *Ch* IV, and *Instruction on Christian Freedom and Liberation*, March 22, 1986, especially *Ch* III.

[10] David Noel Freedman, "Christ as Eschatological Prophet," talk given ap.25.60 at West Baden College, West Baden, IN.

completely transfigure His prophetic mission.

None of this requires the laity to become Religious, any more than the prophets wanted all Israel to become prophets. But it does mean that, as II Vatican indicates,[11] in summary of a long tradition, that the evangelical counsels are for all Christians, though embodied in different concrete forms according to one's state of life.

D. THE LAW AND WORSHIP

Jesus' interior grasp of the Law confounded even the scribes and teachers of the Law, yet He made it breathe life rather than kill by literalism. He showed, more than any of the prophets before Him, the implicit exigencies of the Law, unfolding these in the Sermon on the Mount; and was persecuted even more than Jeremiah for the purity of His preaching and practice. All this He had in full with the beginning of His public life, so that His recapitulation of the prophets from Samuel to Jeremiah—in terms of psychic readiness—had developed quietly during His life in Nazareth. Even at twelve in the temple, one senses under His quiet courtesy an independence of all human persons in His total dedication to the Father's service.

Like the prophets, Jesus had no quarrel with His people's religious institutions, even those that had no mandate from the Scriptures. Every sabbath He was in the synagogue, a post-Exilic institution promoted by the Pharisees. He taught in the temple when He would go up as prescribed by the Law for the great feast-days. All the structures that assisted the religious life of His people He loved for what they were meant to be. Consider His attitude towards the temple, built by the moral monster that was Herod the Great, an attitude that was to bring on His death. The temple was His Father's house (Jn.2:16). Its outer Court of the Gentiles was to serve as a house of prayer for all the nations (Mk.11:17) and not be turned over to the clamor and noise of a place of business and to the stabling of the animals for sacrifice. He drove out the money-changers and the animals, not because He condemned ceremonial worship or animal sacrifice, but because of His appreciation for them when rightly directed to the Father.

Law of any sort is an essentially social institution. As long as one remains shut up within adolescent individualism, he is unable to understand or appreciate the laws that bind him,[12] for they limit and constrain his freedom of action for reasons that he may often not easily discern. But an adult takes for granted that law is necessary and useful, even if some particular legislation is not. Without law—this means, law that is enforced—there is no community and no social order. Moreover, only through law imposed for the common good can one obey without abasing or demeaning oneself. Even obedience to a king was good only insofar as he ruled lawfully. Only in this way can Jesus' obedience unto death, even to the death of the cross, be seen as His free love for the Father and neither servility nor weakness.

---

[11] *Lumen Gentium*, *Ch* 5, #42.

[12] This is not to deny the possibility of a certain abstract appreciation of law as an element of that good order that will protect his interests and give greater room to his activity.

Israel's change to monarchy was, to be sure, a movement towards centralization and institutionalization of a sort common in the nations round about but not yet seen in Israel. This movement never wholly eliminated the tribal structures nor fully united the people, as becomes clear when one sees the ease with which the kingdom divided. Yet the change was distinctive and decisive; it represented a genuine coming of age, since it involved an adult willingness to be ruled by law.

But the Law is the LORD's, not man's. The king is as much subject to it as is the least of the people. In consequence, though the king was the ruler, any peasant was his equal as a man, for both were equal before the LORD, who did not stand in awe of human dignity. The distinction was social and functional but not seen as expressive of an inner quality of the person. Since the kings of the nations were endowed with quasi-divine attributes, Israel's understanding of royalty differed radically from their neighbors'. The kings of Judah and Israel were often desirous of imitating those foreign monarchs with their absolute powers; and the resentments that built from time to time against the Israelite kings grew out of a culturally rooted antagonism to such attempts. What needs to be kept in mind is that this difference from gentile rule was entirely a matter of religion. It is inconceivable that, say, a pagan prophet could have successfully imitated Elijah in his rebuke to Ahab for the murder of Naboth, still less that a monarch of quasi-divine status should have done public penance for his crime.

Not only was the government centralized, but also worship. For the first time, a temple was mentioned. Projected by David and accepted by the LORD through the prophet Nathan, though built only later by Solomon, the temple made of Jerusalem the only legitimate place to offer sacrifice. This temple, the high priest, the whole priestly class, the levites, the singers, etc. formed a third social structure in Israel, alongside the monarchy and prophecy. The three were clearly distinct, though in close interaction, much as the diocesan structures, the monasteries or friaries, and the monarchies were in the Middle Ages. The king had no recognized authority over doctrine or worship or the priestly ministry.[13]

But, as the kingdom continues, the relations between these institutions seems never to have been definitively fixed. David's devotion and initiative, coupled with Solomon's carrying through the construction of the temple to completion, must have made worship appear to some as, if not the task of the monarchy, at least subject to its supervision and control.[14] This was not the Caesaropapism of the Eastern Church, however. The offering of sacrifice had not hitherto been reserved to the priests of the LORD's shrines. Thus, Samuel offered acceptable sacrifices, though having no priestly blood. Rather, sacrifice had long been the office of the father of any family. It was this, ultimately, that enabled David to offer sacrifices before the Ark as it was brought to the

[13] Cf. II Chron.26:16–21, which interprets the leprosy of King Uzziah in terms of his overstepping these limits. Though much later than the account in II Kgs, there seems no good reason to doubt either Uzziah's attempt or people's understanding of it.

[14] David is presented in similar fashion in *Chronicles* for reasons we shall consider in *Ch* 15.A.3, *p* 295.

tent that he had prepared for it and that permitted Solomon to do so in dedicating the temple (I Kgs.8:62–64). By the time of Ahaz, however, the temple had been reduced to being a very subservient adjunct to the Court; and the king made what changes in worship he thought expedient for political purposes. As might be expected, the prophets saw this subordination as contrary to the LORD's will and stood in ever sharper opposition to both Court and temple, not in rejection of either but in repudiation of their abusive relationship.

While speaking of social structures, we might note that the army, as far as we can judge, did not feel itself a separate and potent entity in Judah because of the messianic expectations already built into the general understanding of the Davidic dynasty. Descent by carnal generation from David was, because of the LORD's promise, the one indispensable criterion for the legitimacy of the king. In Israel, on the other hand, the military frequently flexed its muscle and, under the influence of one or other prophet, its officers deposed and made monarchs. In neither kingdom, however, does there seem, despite the prophets' insistence on the goodness of peace, to have been any trace of pacifism. War remained a terrible but real necessity.

E. The Exile

The prophets had repeatedly threatened Judah and Israel with disaster if they continued in their sinful ways. The LORD is a jealous God, tolerating no rivals. If His people continued to ignore His commands and to worship the false gods of the nations, He would let loose His wrath and destroy them. Just as persistently—despite some periods of reform that was essentially superficial because led only by the piety of some few in authority—the people's reaction was mocking comment about the fathers eating sour grapes but only their children's teeth being set on edge. They refused, unmoved, to believe what the prophets predicted or to make any basic change in their manner of life. Nor was it a matter of threats alone. There were ever more serious invasions, palace revolutions, earthquakes, droughts and famines. After two hundred years, Samaria was taken, the Kingdom of Israel was destroyed, and the people were carried off and scattered all over Central Asia. But Judah still would not listen or obey.

Drawing false confidence from the LORD's promises to David and from the holiness of His temple, they refused repentance, chose not to change their ways, would not return to the LORD as their sole lord. Finally, He was left with no alternative but to chastise.

Jerusalem was destroyed, palace and temple were burned, Judah was plundered and ravaged, and the people were carried off to Babylon. "When You chasten man with rebukes for sin, You consume like a moth what is dear to him" (Ps.39:11). Forgetting God's destruction of His dwelling place at Shiloh despite Jeremiah's reminders (Jer.7:12–14),[15] they had thought that God would at least spare His temple and His city for His own Name's sake. But

[15] Or perhaps they remembered but drew far too narrow a lesson from it, not perceiving its significance for Judah (cf. Ps.78:60).

He did not. The city was wiped out, razed to the ground. He would indeed, be with this city forever, but not in any way they dreamed of—or, to be truthful, that we can dream of, for the mystery of Jerusalem, like that of its people, remains ever alive and naturally inscrutable.

"There is no prince or prophet or leader, no burnt offering or sacrifice or oblation or incense, no place to make an offering before You or to find mercy" (Dan.3:38). There was no temple: no place, then, to offer sacrifice according to the Law, which required that this be done in the temple. They could offer no legitimate sin-offering for their sins. There was no way left to propitiate Him. Worse, they were soon all taken off into the unholy lands of the false gods they had preferred to the LORD, and were swallowed up by their enemies. All that Judah had prized, all that they had achieved, all that they dreamed of, all their natural glories were wiped out together.

Except for the LORD's faithfulness, that would have been the end of the story. No other exiled nation has ever survived as a people. What happened exceeded any miracle of Elijah's. Even Ezechiel's description of the resuscitation of the valley-full of dried bones is inadequate. The other peoples of the ancient Middle East, whether victors or vanquished, have disappeared without cultural descendents, leaving nothing behind but a few artifacts to grace our museums of Near-Eastern antiquities. Even the names of many are unknown, or known only to historians. But this one tiny remnant of a nation[16]—this one tribe of Judah with some few remnants of Benjamin, perhaps traces of Simeon: those whom war and famine had spared—is carried away and dispersed and scattered throughout the Babylonian empire and then the much more extensive Persian empire. Yet, they exist to this day, a people of major influence in all the world, the descendants of those exiles from whom Christianity, Islam, and contemporary Judaism, all were to spring.

With the Exile, the LORD accomplished more things spiritually than He would seem to have wrought with all His previous centuries of labor. During the time of the Exile itself, Judah's basis of unity was transformed. Without king, without temple, without land, all the ordinary foundations for a nation were destroyed. Their political unity had disappeared along with king and nobles and civil polity.[17] Even the tribal unity grounded in physical descent began to weaken, for the evidence suggests that intermarriage and loss of records gradually made tribal and familial identities largely formal. Their language itself slowly died, as they were forced to speak the languages of their conquerors and new neighbors. For a people which had had structures, organizations, institutions, this radical destruction of their life must have seemed a total demolition.

---

[16] The count of the exiles taken from Jerusalem in the final deportation given in Jer.52:28–30 came to only 4600. Even if this refers only to adult males (cf. Roland E. Murphy, *NJBC*, #75:114) and even if the number (18,000) reported for the earlier deportations (II Kgs.24:14,16), which is much too high according to *NJBC*, #18:121, be taken at face value, we are still dealing with a total population of less than 100,000 and, most probably, of the order of 25,000.

[17] Though the Davidic dynasty lasted longer than most dynasties of which we know and though the line of descent continued, there was no further Davidic king. Several centuries later there would be the Hasmoneans and then Herod; but these claimed no connection with David.

Their religion alone kept them a people. Acquired by the LORD for Himself through the Covenant at Sinai and at Shechem, they could exist as a people only through the Covenant. But they had broken the Covenant, and now the LORD had repudiated it. A new Covenant was needed; but the LORD said little more about it than that its Law would be an interior one in the heart and that, in His mercy, He would establish it at some future time (Jer.31:31–34). So, under the guidance of Ezechiel and II Isaiah and through the priests' gathering what they could find of the Law and the earlier prophets, they sought to obtain mercy by a life as faithful as their circumstances permitted to what they could remember of His words.

Many, of course, perished or were swept away and absorbed by their conquerors. Even the small clusters that were able to cling together for support were divided in their reactions to the prophets sent by the LORD. Yet —and this is of capital importance—the few prophets and other leaders remained faithful not only to the LORD but also to their people. They sought no exemption for themselves from the Exile. They stayed with the people, even when these continued to disobey the LORD, as Jeremiah with those who insisted on going to Egypt. And it was through the prophets that the LORD worked a renewed hope in them and readied them for the Return.

Some, then, retained their faith in the LORD, remarkably more vivid and clear than before. They were more impressed by His having carried out His threats as He had promised than by the apparent successes of the gods of the gentiles. Many, if not most, held firm, strengthened by the LORD's word to Jeremiah that after seventy years He would bring them back again to their own land and reconstitute them His own people.

One may wonder here how the individual Christian could recapitulate the Exile. For the Exile seems an intrinsically social chastisement for what amounted to stubbornly persevering national apostasy. It is true that, in the history of the Church, there are many periods of exile, of faithful Christians being scattered among their enemies. In a sense, the Church was born in exile, first among unconverted Jews, then among Greeks and Romans, Armenians and Ethiops, then Gauls and Vandals and other Arian barbarians, then the Moslems, the Huns, the Avars, the various Slavic peoples, down to our century in Hitler's Germany and Communist Eastern Europe and China, much of the rest of Asia and Africa, and in the secularist and self-destructive West. Indeed, in a deeper sense it is a given of Catholic piety that the Christian is always in exile, whether he realizes it or not, as long as he lives in this world. Nevertheless, the Church has often had in one region or another long periods of growth and peace, with whole cultures founded and developed under her guidance. Thus, the socially identifiable exile seems a contingecy that is not part of the Christian life as such.[18]

But, once again, recapitulation is not a reliving analogously of some stage in the history of Israel. It is the living of some part of the life of Christ, as He took up and perfected in Himself the life Israel had been called to live.[19] If we

[18] Though there is more to say on this, it will be better said when we consider the relations of the Church to culture.

wish to consider how the Christian recapitulates this period, we need to see how Jesus lived it.

The Church's liturgy during Lent highlights the often neglected typology between Jeremiah and Jesus. Without attempting to develop this in detail, we may note what is perhaps its most striking aspect.

Jesus recapitulated in Himself the Exile, in part, by living more perfectly than did Jeremiah, His type, among those who were being punished for their sinful obduracy, even though they would kill Him, as their predecessors killed Jeremiah. Our whole race was in exile, far from what God had desired for us. The gentiles were steeped in the grossest sins, even as St. Paul described them later (Rom.1:18–32); as his next chapter makes clear, Israel was caught in the same net, though in more subtle guise. But Jesus came and lived with every type of person, though He would have to suffer for the sins of each. He would not withdraw or separate Himself from them as did the Pharisees, (i.e., 'separated ones') whose designation was earned by their self-chosen separation from the rest of the people and who came to despise the "people of the land" who did not know the 613[20] precepts of the Law, indeed who were lucky to know the Ten Commandments.

He recapitulated Ezechiel's prophetic labors when He predicted, grief-stricken, the (second) destruction of Jerusalem and the temple, and then rebuked those who still did not understand, making the events of His own life so many mysteries of which we are to inquire, as evidently John did throughout his Gospel, "What does this mean?" (Ez.24:19). Like II Isaiah, He gave hope and courage to those who had lost it: God's reign is near, the reign of His Anointed through whom sin is washed away. "Say to Jerusalem, her iniquity is pardoned...," now no longer in prophecy and in the figure of a pagan king but in reality and in the actuality of Him who is Son of God and Son of David. The Lamb of God, whose blood would seal the New Covenant that Jeremiah had foretold, had come.

Catholics, then, are called on, like the prophets, to live and suffer with their brethren in their exile. For, there is a sense in which all sufferings of a Christian who has sinned gravely and unrepentantly can count as such. There usually comes a time when God in His mercy, even as He did in Judah and Israel throughout the monarchy, lets such a man's sins catch up with him so that he must face their consequences.

One might see this activity as recapitulating only the pre-exilic punishments. But the prophets of that time, even as those who came later, were engaged in the same work. The difference was only in the degree and extent of

[19] There is, indeed, a sense that one can give to a direct "recapitulation" of Israel's sinfulnesss and weakness. Only a person of roughly David's level of psychic and spiritual maturity can sin as he did. An adolescent leader of a gang may order a killing; but his sin is not that of David. So, one can speak of the kinds and aspects of sin that are most characteristic of a given level of development. But since sin is intrinsically destructive of the person, the more frequently and more gravely one sins, the greater is the psychic damage done, even if the sins are followed by repentance. There occurs as a result a sort of "regression" to levels roughly corresponding to those passed through already.

[20] *NJBC*, #75:120.

the punishments. It is only when individuals, through their own sins and worldliness, have infected others also, so that the sins become deeply ingrained in an unrepentant people, that there will be literal exile, whether by a physical carrying away or by destruction of all visible ties with their past.

What faithful Catholics are called upon to do is to live like the prophets among their unfaithful and still misbehaving brethren. Their pain in having to live in close contact with liturgical aberration, violation of vows, familial disintegration, and false doctrine is a necessary one. They should, indeed, like the prophets, band together for support and mutual comfort; but they may not desert the shattered people left behind by abortion, drugs, and AIDS. Their own life and plans will be altered or overturned; and anger is a man's natural response to those who insist on bringing evil not only on themselves but on others. But though this anger may be supernaturalized as with the prophets, underneath there must be the charity and love that Jesus had for those with whom He was so fiercely angry. For His anger was with the coldness of heart and willful blindness that was leading His people into their most terrible exile.

Like Jeremiah and Ezechiel, like our Lord, the faithful Catholic will still have to denounce sin for what it is, and to do so not in his own name but in the Lord's. But once the catastrophe has occurred, he is called upon to do as did Ezechiel and II Isaiah and to help those who have brought about the evil to understand what has occurred and why. His task is to befriend and to stir up their hope in God, who chastises because He still loves.

Neither refusal of authority nor Thomistic literalism nor liturgical rigorism is, I think, the greatest evil brought about by Archbishop Lefebvre and his followers, but their desertion of their brethren. If they be correct in their assesment of the state of the Church, then we are indeed all exiles in Babylon. But then they should act as God's prophets and continue at all costs to remain among us to continue to announce the truth. By schism, they have separated themselves scornfully from the false worship too often seen rather than labor in servitude with their brothers. They have lost hope themselves and not awaited the Lord's own intervention to bring us all back and to rebuild the temple. And so, they do nothing that can help us hope as we sit beside the streams of Babylon and weep as we remember Zion.

Chapter 15

Judaism

The period following the Exile is one of long-tested growth, in many ways unobservable. One endures, may lash out and strike on occasion, when too closely pained or betrayed, especially by those closest and most trusted. Yet the greater pain is to see the Lord's[1] own work being resisted and corrupted and undone. Nonetheless, the purification goes on apace. No prophet is present to give reassurance as to one's direction. Perceptible support from God comes only rarely; and this little, through signs and symbols. One's chief support is simply one's being a member of a people to whose ancestors, long ago, the Lord made promises of salvation.

Yet God's attitudes concerning the new situations and difficulties in which His people find themselves are increasingly obscure. Sages and mystics puzzle greatly over them; but, in the end, the advice of the sage is merely to go on according to the Law, the visions of the mystics reveal only that sometime, somehow God will triumph against evil and glorify His people. No further understanding seems possible. One thing only is clear: the Lord is their Lord.

When a Christian is not simply reliving the life of Israel but is sharing in the recapitulation of that life by Christ, the most characteristic elements at this stage would seem to be: **a**) a long memory and much reflection upon the works of God manifested in his own life as well as upon those revealed in the Scriptures; **b**) a life centered upon the liturgy, solid in its devotion, with an ever greater reverence for God; **c**) firm adhesion to God's will through his keeping of all details of His law, often at great cost in this world's goods; **d**) unconcern with the glories of culture save for its service for the Lord in His Church; **e**) and firmness under persecution from without, coupled with

---

[1] During this period, probably during the 3rd Century B.C., God's own name (indicated in translation as 'the LORD') was replaced out of reverence by the common noun 'Lord.'

vigorous and courageous opposition to corruption within the Church.

A. The Transformation of Those Who Returned

Few of those who were carried off from Judah survived the seventy years[2] of exile save in their descendants. The people were no longer Israelites—the Northern Kingdom had vanished except for a few scattered individuals—but Jews, i.e., Judeans, dwellers in Judea and members of the tribe of Judah.[3] They had their own small enclave in the pagan world. But it was a different world. The great Semitic empires of the two previous millennia had vanished forever, leaving no trace save their ruins. The pagans now were Persians, Greeks, and Romans. A new era had opened for the whole ancient world when the Lord took Cyrus by the hand and made him conqueror.

1. The centrality of worship

The remnant that returned to the site of the Jerusalem of their fathers was a chastened people who, though still tending to compromise a bit on intermarriage with pagans, were wholly freed from idolatry themselves. They had come to realize that the Lord is the one and only God—there is no other. Their monotheism was no longer merely 'practical' (in the sense merely that they owed no allegiance to any other god). They had come to monotheism in its strongest and truest sense: the Lord alone is God. Idolatry as such was a matter of the past. This does not mean that the people never fell into it again or into other kinds of false religion; but, if they did, it was to avoid persecution or to curry favor with idolaters, not from any conviction that there might be such gods. Idolatry was seen as what it is; and the worship of alien gods was largely a dead issue.

Soon after the Return, a few prophets appeared (Haggai, Zechariah, Obadiah, Malachi, Joel)[4] whose principal concerns all lay in the area of worship: the rebuilding of the temple, the re-establishment of the priesthood and the purity of worship, and various questions relating to cult and the offering of sacrifice. Difficult though they found it to get the returning exiles to set seriously about rebuilding the temple, it and Jerusalem were rebuilt, and the worship in the temple there became central to Jewish life.

Once that worship had been re-established, the temple dominated Jewish thought and feeling, even when the people could take no direct part in its worship either because the pagans had occupied Jerusalem and the temple or because they themselves were scattered far and wide in the Diaspora. As one sees from Zech.14:20–21, the prophet looked forward to a messianic age when the pots and pans of every Jewish kitchen would share in the sacredness of the vessels used in the sacrifices in the temple. All aspects of life were to be

---

[2] The Exile began for Judah in 597; the destruction of the temple and the city and the final deportation occurred in 587. The Return is generally dated at 539 and the rebuilding of the temple was finished in 515. It is not hard to see why Jeremiah and Ezechiel, both priests, should give 'seventy years' as the round number for the length of the exile.

[3] Nonetheless, one finds, e.g., in *Joel* and *Chronicles*, that some did begin to use again the name of 'Israel' for all that was left of Gods people.

[4] Concerning Joel's inclusion here, cf. *NJBC*, 24:2 & 3.

consecrated entirely to the Lord through this unique place of worship.

2. *The attrition of time*

Well over five centuries elapsed between the Return and our Lord's coming. Yet for the entire inter-testamental period,[5] very little historical information is furnished by Scripture. *Ezra* and *Nehemiah* cover a only a few years and from very limited perspectives. Which years those were is unknown since their chronology is hotly disputed. *I* and *II Maccabees* fill in a period of some forty years in the 2nd century B.C. For the rest there are only hints here and there. Nor does extra-Scriptural Jewish tradition do much to fill the gaps. The life of faithful Jews for most of that long period would seem to have been relatively uneventful, however changing their circumstances.[6]

Despite great differences in the externals of Jewish life during the various periods, most of these years were alike in that they all were unobtrusively but decisively bringing Judaism to maturity. Much more than by idols, the faith of the Jews was being tested by the the slow attrition brought about by the mere passage of time. Except under persecution, the years passed much as the ones before them; and the troubles and concerns of the people were those that mark all human life and were limited to the particular localities where they lived, now scattered over the Near East as well as in the small community growing gradually in Judea. So, until the time of the Hasmonean revolt, life went on quietly. Whether in the Diaspora or in Judea, the Jews adapted, as well as the Law allowed, to their surroundings; and, for the first time since their pre-Mosaic stay in Egypt, their lives were 'ordinary' enough to be passed over in silence by the Scriptures.

After Malachi, the prophetic voice fell silent. There were no further prophets (unless one wishes to call such the redactors of the prophetic books and the anonymous authors who inserted bits and pieces to adapt those books to later times). God did, however, continue to reveal Himself, but now through the quasi-private forms of apocalypse and wisdom literature. Unlike the direct and public speech and action of the prophet, these newer modes of revelation consisted of written works, often anonymous or pseudonymous. Whereas the prophet acted publicly to correct current moral evils in Israel, both individual and social, the new modes sought rather to explain to each reader privately how, in the practical affairs of life, a good Jew should behave and handle his affairs under the Law or how to understand the upheavals in the pagan world, and the persecutions of the Jews that often followed, as part of the over-all struggle of the powers of darkness against the Lord. In neither

---

[5] It is so named because the Mosaic Covenant had been abrogated with the Exile and the new one that was promised through Jeremiah had not yet appeared—a major source, doubtless, of the "angst" of the devout Jew during the six-hundred-year interval between the Mosaic and the New Covenant. But there is no major interval between the portions of the Bible labeled Old Testament and New.

[6] This half-millennium comprised two centuries under the religiously tolerant Persian empire; another century under the equally tolerant Lagids of Egypt; fifty-five years under the Seleucids (called "the Greeks" in Scripture), who launched the first great persecution against Jewish religion; then, after eighty years of independence, the remaining time as a nation under the Romans, who also were quite tolerant of the Jews' religion.

wisdom literature nor apocalypse was the word of the Lord addressed directly to Israel; at most, in vision He might be heard speaking about Israel. The prophetic silence, then, painful as it was (e.g., I Macc.4:18), did not mean a total silence on God's part. It signified only that He had ceased to tell the people His concrete will concerning their particular situations. His will as expressed in the Law was sufficient.

3. The power of remembrance

Conjoined with these quieter modes of revelation was a movement among the Jews, especially the priests and levites, to gather and organize all that they could find of the writings of earlier days in that great, collective effort of memory that formed the Old Testament. Such action was needed lest Israel perish as a people, for they had no other way to survive. Without it, even the worship in the temple would not have been enough to counter the centrifugal forces of the Diaspora. The compilations that resulted were, moreover, the works of holy men, whose criteria for selecting materials were profoundly religious. As the Deuteronomist earlier had gathered and written in order to show the rightness of God's judgments on Israel, so the later compilations sought to root Jewish life in the worship of the Lord and in obedience to His Law.

The two books known as *I & II Chronicles,* compiled in this period, tell much the same story as *I & II Kings*, yet very largely reinterpret their materials in terms of cult and of the Law. This reinterpretation of the past is particularly evident in the fact that all the rather unedifying details of the lives of David and of Solomon are overlooked or glossed over, forgotten, omitted, or reinterpreted. Other kings, however, are often presented in even darker colors than in *Kings*. It seems evident, even on cursory reading, that David and Solomon fare better because of their interest in the worship of the Lord, the central and focal interest of the Chronicler. But reinterpretation cut more deeply than this. Recall the famous case in which the Chronicler attributed to Satan (I Chr.21:1) what was earlier ascribed to the LORD (II Sam.24:1). The earlier document ascribes to God directly whatever He causes or permits. The later one considers only the causes and actions to be found on the created order, those in and through all of which, in His own hidden ways, God is always working.

Characteristic of this stage was an increasing incomprehension of earlier stages. These were now seen more truly, but from a later vantage point. Earlier attitudes could no longer be grasped in their original terms. The Jews no longer understood idolatry as they had practiced it in the times of the judges or even of the late monarchy. Since the alien gods were now known simply not to exist, the worshipper of idols could only be venerating stones, sticks, or clay. Israel's earlier attitudes no longer made much sense and were of little help in interpreting what the Jews saw around them. This sort of separation from their roots and growing incapacity to comprehend how their fathers had ever behaved in those ways, perhaps contributed to the urgency of their communal act of remembering.

B. Jesus' recapitulation

If we ask how Jesus recapitulated this half millennium, we can find at least a partial answer by considering His maturity upon leaving Nazareth to begin His public life.

He, too, looked back in memory—that supernaturally enlightened memory that united His own growing up with that of His people through all their history. During these years He acquired, as man, His knowledge of the Scriptures, which had come through Him, as God and as God's Word, to man. Many have marvelled at His manner of using them: with the greatest conciseness, yet filled with new light and more than human power as, when in the desert, He responded to the devil's temptations with lightening flashes from *Deuteronomy.*

Too often overlooked, however, is the way in which He reinterpreted this remembered past—a reinterpretation that was the essential part of His teaching. He taught that divorce with remarriage is wrong while at the same time showing that, because of original sin, Moses could permit a man to divorce his wife, with the simple declaration that "From the beginning it was not so" (Mt.19:7–9). He knew Himself as "Son of Man" in a fuller sense than Ezechiel ever glimpsed and "Son of God" far beyond the understanding of the author of *Job.* He was the Christ, the Anointed of the Lord, moved at every moment by the Spirit of the Father resting within Him, a more glorious Messiah than the Jews of His day, even His own disciples, could begin to grasp till after His resurrection. He penetrated the mystery of those who were His types and could show how all the figures of Scripture were fulfilled in Him. Already He perceived the mystery of His two-fold coming, which opened the door of salvation to the gentiles and introduced the anagogical understanding of the Scriptures in distinction from the typical and moral senses.

Though Jesus was to inaugurate that worship in spirit and in truth that could not be confined to Jerusalem (Jn.4:21–24), yet He not only manifested no opposition to rightful worship offered in the temple but showed great love for it. Though the worship in the temple was to be transcended, in no way did He think it evil. Like the prophets from Haggai through Malachi, the restoration and glorification of the temple was close to His Heart; and He wept over its coming destruction when, on Palm Sunday, He looked out over the whole city and the temple spread out immediately before Him. Though this third temple—already under construction for more than forty years and not to be finished till after thirty more—had been begun by the cruel vanity of Herod the Great, not a Jew but an Idumean (Edomite), as unholy a person and as unworthy to be associated with such a work as could be imagined, yet this temple was for Jesus "My Father's house" (Jn.2:16). Already, at the age of twelve, He had stayed behind three days in the temple "in the things of my Father" {Lk.2:49}.

As during His youth, so during His public life, He did not find Galilee so far from Jerusalem as to prevent His going up to the temple for the major feasts. But not only for the major feasts, for the Gospels show Him there on other occasions also. Not only did He prefer to teach there when in

Jerusalem, but the rites and ceremonies for the temple's celebration of the Jewish feasts impregnated His teaching. Indeed, anyone ignorant of these will miss the many riches of His doctrine that were contained in His allusions to those festivals.

This formation of His mind and the shaping of the contours of His thought by the Scriptures surely began at home, as He was taught by Mary and Joseph. Later, He learned more from attending the services in the synagogue, where He went regularly on the Sabbath (Lk.4:16; Jn.18:20). Thus, His basic theological orientation would have been, however modified, that of the Pharisees.[7] This can be seen clearly enough, also, by His ways of arguing later in His life, ways which even those who opposed Him recognized as brilliant examples of their own methods, though He had had none of their training (Jn.7:15).

This Pharisaic connection shows itself in another, more basic, yet often overlooked way: Jesus, like the Pharisees, much more indeed than some of them, was one who was separated from the gentiles.[8] For, He "was not sent except to the lost sheep of the house of Israel" (Mt.15:24). Gracious as He could be to the Gentiles that came to Him, they had to seek Him out; He did not go to them of Himself. But neither is there any reason to think that He would have been any more successful with the academic types of Athens than was His faithful disciple Paul or any better treated by the splendid legal system of Rome than were Peter and Paul. Yet, in His case, it was by His choice that the gentile world ignored Him and that He remained hidden away in the "ghetto" that was Palestine. He sought nothing in the way of this world's glory, and received none. None of the dramatic events of the Gospels are recounted by pagan authors. For the same reasons, He did not seek any contact with the Sadducees, the Jews of prestige and power in Jerusalem.

It would, therefore, be an error to imagine Jesus, during His adult years at Nazareth as tempted to impatience as time passed slowly in the cultural poverty and ordinariness of life in out-of-the-way Nazareth[9] while He awaited the public manifestation of John the Baptist, the sign for Him to begin His mission. Having brought His people by means of just such ordinariness during the previous five centuries to the maturity needed to receive Him, He was not likely to have found His recapitulation of this time repugnant. 'Ordinary' need imply neither 'dull' nor 'worthless.' The seemingly dull quietude of

[7] It was their great achievement to have met the changed conditions of the times by successfully establishing the synagogue as a basic Jewish institution. In Jesus' day, however, going to the synagogue was an entirely voluntary matter of private devotion. His going, then, represented a clear acceptance of this manner of communal worship, however harsh the criticisms that He had to level at some unworthy descendants of those establishers of the synagogue.

[8] The word "Pharisee" means just that, "the Separated One." When this religious movement began to take shape in the days of the Hasmonean revolt, this implied the Pharisee's willingness not only to be separated from the pagan world around him but, much more, from his own community, his own friends, even his own family, should these have capitulated to the surrounding culture. He chose, for the sake of the Lord and for the faith of his fathers, to be isolated, if need be, and alone.

[9] Recall Nathaniel's caustic response to Philip: "Can anything good come out of Nazareth?" (Jn.1:46).

Persian and Lagid rules, concerning which we have no word save the brief interlude shown in *Ezra* and *Nehemiah*, concealed the enormous growth and development that turned the remnants of the kingdoms of Israel and Judah into the Jewish people. So also, under the easy tolerance of Jewish religion that characterized the Roman rule in Palestine in Jesus' day, His quiet years of carpentry concealed Jesus' recapitulation of all that final period of Jewish preparation for His ministry. It was at Nazareth that He, the new Israel, became also the perfect Jew.

If "no man ever spoke like this Man" (Jn.7:46), *a fortiori* no man ever prayed as Jesus did. Out of the depths of His own prayer was crystallized the *Our Father* that is the center of every Christian's prayer. His public life began with forty days of prayer and fasting in the desert, alone except for the guidance of the Spirit and the attacks of the devil. No one who has read them can forget the overpowering beauty of His long prayer at the end of the Last Supper or the sharp pain of His briefly phrased but constantly reiterated prayer during His agony in Gethsemani or, as He hung on the cross, the words of the Psalms He was praying in His dereliction and in His calm laying down of His life as He yielded it into the Father's hands.

Jesus' independence of human opinions and attitudes was, then, nothing other than His total dependence on the will of the Father. It was not an independence formed from contempt or unconcern for others' reactions, for it is clear that He felt keenly men's acceptance or rejection, their antagonism and their friendship. In every situation He was free and quietly in command, since focussed solely on the Father's love for those to whom He spoke. Though He spoke with greater suavity than any of the prophets, yet He struck to the very heart of the conscience more sharply and with even greater psychic acumen than they.[10]

C. Catholics' transformation

As part of their sharing in Jesus' recapitulation of the formation of Judaism, a similar reinterpretation of their past is easily recognizable in the reflections of older Catholics. They look back over their childhood and all their earlier life, seeing it in a new way and facing it all with the same, simple honesty that the Deuteronomist and the Chronicler displayed in recounting their sins and the sins of their fathers, about which wickedness they no longer have any illusions. They have offended the Lord; they can fully acknowledge their sins and accept their punishment; and yet, in all this, they recognize His continual mercy. They have repeatedly deserted Him; He has never, they now see, deserted them.

It is this realization that makes worship central in their lives. They are ever more deeply grateful to God for His faithfulness, whatever the difficulties of their lives, and they seek to show their gratitude in act. The Mass is indeed understood now as Eucharist[11] not only on their own behalf but on behalf of the whole community, even if they alone are present. Their inner life

[10] Cf. Mt.23; Jn.7 thru 10.

[11] I.e., Thanksgiving, *par excellence*.

is nourished through the Scriptures and all the kinds of sacramental liturgy and communally defined devotions; and their souls grow about and enter into these like a vine on a trellis. Thus, as for the Jews, out of remembrance arises their focus on worship and on moral righteousness.

Personal prayer becomes increasingly familiar to them. Like the Jews of that period, though increasingly devoted to the community of faith, they are increasingly independent of others' opinions and support. They know sin to be personal and individual, whatever its social effects; and, as the Lord explained through Ezechiel, one's actions are one's own responsibility. Like St. Thomas More, they are realistically aware that all men sin, most of them seriously, and can say with him, "I never intend (God being my good Lord) to pin my soul at another man's back,...for I know not whither he may hap to carry it."[12]

As the the passionate gathering together of the Scriptures and meditation upon them was formative of Judaism, so these Catholics' gradual assimilation of and conviction concerning the truths of the faith form them into a people apart, no longer overly impressed by the surrounding culture or desirous of making their way in a world whose hollowness and malice are now apparent to them. No matter how active they are in that world, out of love for its people and in hope for their salvation, their faith separates them ever more completely from the world (I Jn.2:15–17), even from those aspects that, although vain, are not sinful.

Under the monarchy, Israel had thought of itself as a nation reckoned among the other nations, indeed, as *the* nation, specially favored above all others by the LORD. For a half century or so, under David and Solomon, the people knew the glory of empire, even if of a small one. But soon they were divided and reduced to a pair of minor kingdoms, whose chief importance was geographical. Without knowing it, they were already in a ghetto. After the Exile, they recognized their physical smallness and their cultural isolation, came to glory in them, and chose to live in such a ghetto for the sake of the Lord.

To an even greater degree, Catholics who have matured to this point have always been forced into a ghetto—often enough by their fellow Catholics. This is not usually a constriction in living quarters but of exclusion from the exercise of their competencies in dealing with the issues that most concern their lives, their country, and the Church. Though they may think that they are bumping into invisible walls, set up to keep them out of positions of influence, more often it is they who are invisible. They are passed over and ignored by people who may have no dislike for them but who sense them as strangers to the life of the world around them.

This is not directly a matter of their own choosing. Like most men, they would like to have some effective say in the running of their world. Their exclusion results from their choice to stay close to the Lord. Those who are less mature, like the earlier Jews, think that compromise is possible—and often it

[12] R. W. Chambers *Thomas More*, Ann Arbor: University of Michigan (1958), *pp* 309–310. *The Correspondence of Sir Thomas More*, ed. E. F. Rogers, Princeton: Princeton U. P. (1947), *p* 521.

is, if one considers the matter abstractly and without realizing the intrinsic corruption of all men by sin. Hence, those less mature do not understand the somewhat distant and reserved coolness or even hostility of someone more mature towards the objects of their enthusiasms. They consider "getting ahead" a benefit not only to themselves but to the Church, and are puzzled by those who do not. They fail to see that the world lets them get ahead—unless the Lord Himself intervenes—only insofar as they serve the world's cause, first unconsciously, then with increasing awareness. But those of that maturity with which we are here concerned know clearly enough that "friendship with the world is enmity with God" (Jas.4:4) and leads ultimately to betrayal or apostasy.

Like the early Pharisees, they group together for mutual support in the work of building up the Church and in resisting the evils of the time. The resulting organizations, because their members are still spiritually imperfect, serve more for testing and perfecting their members through the inevitable struggles they will have than for having a major impact, singly, on the world. Yet, together, there is no question but that they are not only characteristic of the Church but necessary for her full health.

It may be well here to recall that those who have been reborn in Christ will not recapitulate in Christ but relive Israel's slow growth to the extent they are not living the Christian life fully and wholly in Him. Every sin, even venial, and every fault represents a movement toward the level where time is not compressed by grace.

D. The Fence Around the Law

All through Israel's history, the Law had evolved so as to codify the Lord's desires for His people in accord with their current circumstances. This tendency to codify seems to have grown stronger as repudiation of the Law became more overt under the last kings of Judah, and to have become a major preoccupation during the Exile and the century or two following the Return.

A transformation in moral life accompanied the transformation in the people's attitudes towards the uniqueness of the Lord. The later prophets did rebuke the people for marrying pagan wives and for social injustices. Yet violation of the Ten Commandments was mostly indirect, the result of human weakness in individuals rather than a religiously based contamination or rejection of the Law of the Lord. Hence, too, the tone of these prophets was vastly different from that of Jeremiah. When, moreover, the people were rebuked, they repented and took effective measures to right themselves with God. There is a sort of inner conviction and vitality for rejuvenation. Those readers who are old enough to remember the "parish missions" will have in them a good analog.

There arose at this time, however, two new attitudes with regard to the Law. The first of these showed itself in the process of "building a fence around the Law." Not only do the priests and levites not wish to violate the Law; their zeal for it extends further, even, than keeping it in all its details. They do not wish to be at risk of even a material violation of it. Thus, certain things are forbidden, not because they are wrong or in any way against the Law, but simply because, if one were allowed such actions, he would be in a position where, with another step or two, he *might* do something that would be a violation, albeit unintentional, of the Law. For the same purpose, actions were commanded that were in no way required by the Law. The religious leaders of the people did not want to come close to breaking it. They preferred to submit to an elaborate structure of regulations and to the corresponding loss of freedom of action rather than to run the risk of any unwitting violation of some provision of the Law itself. This sort of "protecting" of the Law was to become typical of the pharisaic tradition some while later and of rabbinic Judaism down to the present day.

For example, the Law forbade one to boil a kid in the milk of its mother (Ex.23:19)—an odd little fragment, twice repeated (Ex.34:26; Dt.14:21), for which no explanation is given, nor context, nor application.[13] To set up a fence around this bit of the Law, a Jew was forbidden to allow any vessel which is to contain meat (not just of kid or goat) ever to have contained milk or other dairy products (from the same sort of animal or another), and vice-versa. Therefore, one must have two sets of culinary utensils, one for meats and another for whatever might have milk in it. Then, as a fence around the fence, the two sets of utensils must be washed separately with different water, lest the milk that might come from the one set contaminate the pots intended for meat, and conversely.

By keeping these prescriptions, it seems clear enough that one will never run the least risk of boiling a kid in its mother's milk. But notice, also, what an utterly extrinsic conception of law is implied. If one wanted, for some idolatrous reason, to boil a kid in its mother's milk, having different pots and pans and wash-water in his kitchen would hardly prevent him from doing so. And if he had no such intent, it is hard to imagine, even in a pastoral society, that he would ever have done so accidentally.

This sort of approach to the Law might seem to be, at best, a sort of psychological security-blanket: one was so terrified by the punishments that were brought on Judah for its contempt of God's Law that one went to the opposite extreme. At worst, it might seem a sort of generalized, socially sanctioned scrupulosity. Perhaps. Surely, every stage in Israel's history had its characteristic temptations, and at every stage there were people who yielded to these temptations. It is not unthinkable, then, that there has been a period when the great temptation for the orthodox Jew has been to fence himself in by this fence around the Law by treating it as though it were as morally binding as the Law itself. Already our Lord had pointed out this danger to those Pharisees from Jerusalem who presumed to pass judgment on both Him and His disciples because these had not washed their hands before eating (Mk.7:5–13), an infraction only of the fence around the Law. He sought to show them how they had let their concern for the fence lead them to violate not merely the Law itself but that natural obligation to one's parents that became concrete as

[13] This prohibited practice was one practiced in the Canaanite religion of Ugarit and, presumably, elsewhere by the time of Israel's entry into Canaan.

soon as the primordial command, "Increase and multiply," was obeyed.

Yet when first introduced, the fence was not a temptation but a virtue, and a great one. The spirit behind it can be seen in Psalm 119. Alphabetic, in stanzas of eight verses that begin with the same letter, with each verse usually containing one of the terms that were seen as manifesting the different nuances of the Law: law, commandment, ordinance, precept, word, statute, promise, and testimony. It is a highly elaborated prayer, carefully and intricately wrought, a meditation on the Law as God's greatest gift to His people, something one could never sufficiently read and savor, ponder and investigate, revere and give thanks for. One is meant to search out the meaning of every nook and cranny of it. Every aspect of it is something rich and profitable to the soul. To meditate upon the Law is the finest and highest as well as the most intensely pleasurable activity a man can have. Only in such a context, I think, can one understand the building of the "fence around the Law." All this assumed, of course, that the reader was seeking to put the Law into action in his life. After the catastrophe of the Exile, none knew better than the Jews the emptiness of mere mouthing or idle reflections upon the Law.[14]

Older Catholics can well remember from their own experience how all this works. Until 1966, Catholics had had for many centuries prescribed food-laws, the best known (outside Spanish-speaking countries) being "No meat on Fridays." This served its purpose as a corporal penance and as a reminder each week of Christ's death and of each Christian's duty to share in His sufferings for the good of the whole world. It also made the faith and the Church immediately present in one's weekday life, less easily allowing a Sundays-only morality. It affected business lunches and social dinners and evening parties. More, it served to bind Catholics together as a people, easily identifiable thereby, jocularly designated as "mackerel snappers" or "fish eaters." It became a sort of badge of identity: priests often heard in the confessions of people many years away from the sacraments and with heavy burdens of sin that the one thing they'd not done was deliberately to eat meat on Friday.

One will also remember that there were scruples in plenty about just what one was allowed or not allowed, as was even more in evidence concerning the Lenten fast. There was no lack, either, of formalist legalism and mere external compliance with the rules. There were failures of charity and humility with regard to those who might be less careful or who had simply ceased to practice. That these food-laws, themselves only a sort of container for the spiritual goods sought for, should bind under grave sin has seemed to many to have been an exaggeration and distortion that injured Christian freedom and love: Why make as much or more of meat on Friday than of theft or graft or fornication?

What such criticism overlooks, as one can see in Israel's case also, is that these things are not so easily separable. It is a people fully conscious of its religious identity through a faith made visible by forceful sign and symbol that is most likely to avoid or to repent of the greater sins. Such fences around the Law are needed for further spiritual advance at this stage; and their

[14] Cf. Sir.35:1–5; Ps.50:16–20

abandonment in 1966 has represented, I think, a major injury for Catholics. After all, it was Jesus who told the Pharisees, much too caught up in such legalism, "These [justice and mercy and faith] you ought to have done without neglecting the others [the tithing of herbs—the fence around the Law]" (Mt.23:23).

Another obvious and related motive for the Jews' building of this fence was the desire to preserve and to guard the revelation that God had already made to them. This new form of fidelity was not the fidelity of Abraham, who set out, going he knew not where, or who offered up his son Isaac, even though it was through him that the Promise held and that all nations were to be blessed. Nor was it the fidelity of Elijah, left seemingly alone out of all Israel after the slaughter of the priests of Baal, who yet returned to incite Jehu to his bloody reform. Rather it was the faithfulness to God which comes from knowing that He has given us knowledge of His will and which seeks to hold fast and make secure all that has been given. It was virtue simply to keep it, in living fashion, not merely on parchment; to preserve it, though now from within, an interiorized Law that is God's gift.

Closely connected with the new attitude that generated the fence around the Law was a second, less obvious change of attitude, of particular importance in Israel's preparation for the Christ. On the one hand, there was no expectation of additional decrees from "Moses." The Law was complete. Nothing henceforth could be added to the Law.[15] This is especially clear in *Chronicles*, where the Law stands as the definitive norm for the judgments passed on each king. But on the other hand, there grew a sense that the Law, too, could be subject, without infidelity, to reinterpretation.[16] The mere fact that continued commentary was needed, even though the commentary itself was not part of the Law, indicated that the bald statements themselves were inadequate for full understanding, especially for the sake of application to new conditions or problems.

The most radical example of this is found in I Macc.2:40–41. There we are told how, having learned of the slaughter of those Jews who died rather than fight a battle on the Sabbath, Mattathias and those with him decided to fight such battles. This decision was reached without any suggestion that God had given any of them some message to that effect. They clearly had no intention to set themselves up as masters over the Law, but only to be its servants, offering their lives to preserve it. Yet the sacred account does not indicate that they saw fighting the battles of the Lord to be in any way implicit in the command to keep holy the Sabbath day. The author presents only

---

[15] Indeed, Jews are clear that the fence around the Law is not the Law itself but *halakhah*, the oral tradition of rabbinic interpretations of the Law. Though this completion of the Law bears a certain resemblance to the closing of the deposit of revelation at the end of the apostolic age, yet for Israel it was not that there *could not* be further prophets—it was just that there had been no sign of one for centuries.

[16] That this had occurred earlier seems clear: The commandment to honor one's parents was changed, it is thought, from an original, negative form. That against stealing "referred originally to the kidnapping of a free person" (von Rad, *Deuteronomy*, *p* 59). But in all likelihood, there was no knowledge in the Second Century B.C. of such alterations.

the pragmatic argument that the enemy would wipe them out if they did not change—seemingly a far cry from that earlier trust that, if they remained faithful, the Lord would surely act to vindicate their hope—just that attitude that those others had died to maintain.[17]

Some scholars have been led to see all this simply as a secularization of religion by the Hasmoneans. Yet never in Israel's history had faith been purer or more active. One might explain Mattathias' decision by arguing that he understood the Commandment from within and had so interiorized it that he could seemingly change the Commandment itself by his own practical judgment. If so, one may wonder why the account given says little that would support this. It would seem more likely that this event is tied in with a much wider alteration of attitude: that related to the nature of faith and its purification.

Recall that by the time of the Maccabean wars, there had been no prophet for nearly three hundred years. None was to come until John the Baptist, more than a century and a half later. The Maccabees themselves received neither word nor vision from the Lord.[18] God was truly now a hidden God. No one had claimed to speak His word, so far as we have record, during all that time. The Jews had to live on the memory of the Lord's great deeds, by faith. It was for a greater purity of faith and a resultant greater strength in His service, that God ceased to give them other, extraordinary support.

As at the first entry into the promised land the manna had ceased and the people had had to live from their own efforts, so now after their second entry, God's manifest interventions ceased, except in signs and symbols, and all things had to be done, in faith in God's invisible presence and with hope in His invisible providence, by ordinary human effort. But the difference from the first conquest of the land is great. Then their memory of the covenant of Sinai and the Law had rapidly faded and their practice of the Law was quickly corrupted by the surrounding paganism. Now, however, that covenant shattered, they lived in faith and hope, remembering the past better than those who had lived it, and living not only according to the Law but according to the fence around it. Their religion now permeated all their lives.

God's earlier marvellous interventions had been designed to build an immature Israel's confidence in His power and love and, hence, were externally manifest in the world. But now, His power was at work principally in the souls of men. His love for His people was now manifested by His raising up of men who were moved by their love for Him to extraordinary generosity in defense of the people, and His might was shown in the ease with which they threw aside all the world's goods for His sake.

---

[17] According to Jonathan A. Goldstein (*I Maccabees,* AB 41, Garden City (NY): Doubleday (1976), *pp* 235–237), many Jews of the time, including the author of *II Maccabees*, were strongly opposed to this decision and regarded it as a grave violation of the Commandment. They were in full sympathy with the pious Jews who had been slaughtered, seeing them in some degree as sacrificial victims whose devout deaths would bring a blessing on Israel (cf. II Macc.6:11, 9:43–48).

[18] There did appear signs of uncertain significance in the heavens at crucial moments, but there were few, if any, miracles of power.

This call to purity of faith, when all prior grounds for faith seemed gone, formed a people far more profoundly religious than ever they were earlier. It was also a people now becoming reflexly conscious that their faith was not yet complete or perfect in its understanding, that God was always greater than they knew, not only in Himself, which they had never doubted, but in His ways of acting among men and for men.

It was in this context that Mattathias had made his decision concerning the sabbath. He saw not only that God willed both the sabbath rest and the preservation of His people but also that He willed that normal human means be used to carry out His will. The manna of miraculous deliverance would no longer be found. The people should continue to pray for His assistance, even for miracles. But however great their faith, they should not so count on that aid as to fail to take whatever natural means might be appropriate. Indeed, the use of such natural means is God's normal way of giving His aid. It was not, then, that the Commandment was given a new interpretation. Rather, Mattathias realized that God willed it to be kept, but without what should henceforth properly be called 'tempting God'—a putting of Him to the test, albeit for devout motives and not in challenge—by requiring a miracle in order to survive.

The fact of Jesus' recapitulation of those troubled times can be seen from the very beginning of His public life. Thus, when the devil approached Him in the desert, He rejected precisely as tempting God the suggestion that He get His career off to a good start by drawing all eyes to Himself through miraculous showmanship. A little later, when some Pharisees complained about the disciples' plucking and eating some ears of grain on the sabbath as unlawful, an activity that was at worst an ignoring not of the Law but of some men's formulation of the fence around it, Jesus, after more direct refutation of their carping, went to the heart of the matter. "The sabbath was made for man, not man for the sabbath" (Mk.2:27), so confirming indirectly Mattathias' decision.

Jesus' rebuke did not represent any lack of reverence for God's Law nor even, as seen above, a repudiation of the idea of the fence around the Law. Simply, He was calling for renewed and practical recognition of the Law's priority over the fence. More, he insisted that what God had destined for man from the beginning, before the sin of Adam, was to have priority over the Law itself. It was in virtue of this latter priority that Jesus set aside Moses' permission for divorce and remarriage as no longer valid for any who would follow Him, because He could and would give the grace to live once more as "in the beginning."[19]

Both of the new attitudes towards the Law that we have been considering resulted from the fact that God's goodness and His love were recognized in His gift of His Law to His people. *Baruch* found the Law the very embodiment of God's mercy and presence among men (Bar.3:35–4:1). Man's love for God, in return, was to be shown by serving Him. The right way to serve Him was by doing what He wanted done, i.e., by obeying from the heart His

[19] Pope John Paul II developed this theme in great detail in the General Audiences he gave Sept. 5, 1979 to April 2, 1980 gathered together in *The Original Unity of Man and Woman*, Boston: St. Paul Editions (1981).

commands. One loved the Law as the perfect expression of His will. His goodness to Israel was manifested by His enlightening them as to His will: "Happy are we, O Israel, for we know what is pleasing to God" (Bar.4:4). It was for His sake, then, and not for the Law as such that one would die in torments rather than eat a piece of pork in contravention of the Law. Despite the fact that the Law was now more rigid than ever before in its external obervances and its exegencies, it was grasped as a reciprocal communication of love between God, who loves us and gives us His Law, and ourselves, who show our love for God by observing His Law. Indeed, just because seen as coming from His love, it had become all the more demanding and exigent. Love could be shown God only by unity of wills; therefore, by obedience to His Law.

Good Jews were habitually aware of needing God's help, of falling seven times a day, of the need of continual repentance. During the Exile they had learned that external purifications could only serve a secondary and symbolic role. As we can see from the great prayers in *Baruch* and *Daniel*, they had learned to stand before the Lord, empty-handed, appealing only to His mercy and to the greatness of His name for a forgiveness longed for but unmerited. The rituals were carried through, but as consequent upon repentance, not as if they could placate the Lord or bring about reconciliation. They were mere signs of one's need and of one's confidence that He is merciful still, trusting in God's own free choice to effect the reconciliation.

This again is not unfamiliar to Catholics at this stage. Devoted to the Lord, they seek to do His will even in small matters. They fail often enough in these latter. God is willing to let them do so in order to make them humbly dependent on His grace and to counter any tendency to contemn those who seem not as virtuous as themselves. They may occasionally sin seriously, but usually His grace restores them quickly; and their repentance is deep and sincere. Observance of His law is becoming for them a second nature. Such 'ordinariness,' as every priest soon learns, often conceals from human eyes—even from the persons themselves—a regularity and consistency in the doing of God's will and an abundance of solid virtue that show how greatly His grace has been active in our human weakness. The not inconsiderable sacrifices of convenience, of financial gain, of familial quiet, of their own good and right desires that they must make at times in order not to sin are often scarcely recognized as such by them, being seen simply as "just what anyone would do." They pray often and grow steadily in spirit, though often with more of aridity than devout feeling. The kind of people whom St. Teresa of Avila describes as living in the Third Dwelling Places[20] are recognizable here.

Others, of whom Teresa writes in the Fourth Dwelling Places, have given themselves more completely to the Lord and are more active in their charity, making little distinction between those they like and those whose sinfulness makes them hateful. They have sacrificed greatly, even heroically at times, for the Lord. To these, God makes Himself intimately known, acting upon them freely and wondrously when and as He pleases.

---

[20] "The Interior Castle," in *The Collected Works of Teresa of Avila,*, vol. 2, tr. K. Kavanaugh & O. Rodriguez. Washington (DC): Institute of Carmelite Studies (1980), *pp* 308–315.

E. Religious persecution

More than a century after Alexander the Great had conquered the Persian empire and begun the process of Hellenization of those vast regions, there came a great change. As *Esther* indicates, the Jews had felt no great antipathy to Persian culture, largely, it would seem, because the Persians left them free to decide what aspects of that culture were compatible with the Law and to act accordingly. They responded in much the same manner to the cultural splendor of the Hellenistic world, though with greater tensions and disagreements among themselves as to what accomodations were or were not licit. But they continued, on the whole, as they did under the Persians, to live their own lives with scant attention to their conquerors till the Seleucid monarchs began to persecute them.

This introduced a wholly new element into the history of Israel: persecution solely because of their religion. As noted above concerning Mattathias' decision concerning battle on the Sabbath, even then, God did not speak. The Jews, even those who were most faithful to the Lord, seemed to have been left entirely on their own. They prayed, worshipped in the temple when they could, meditated on the Law, but were left, so far as the natural eye could see, to work out by human prudence what was to be done or avoided.

Though the pagans were the chief agents of the persecution, Jewish religion was mined principally from within. Their own high priests betrayed them to the pagans and stirred these up against them. The terrifying fact was that the Jewish nation was split. Some had, for selfish reasons, gone to the Greeks to incite them against the true religious leaders of the people. Many more, it seems, submitted to the pagans on genuinely religious grounds, thinking it against their religion to oppose even unjust rulers unless these tried to force them to act directly against the Law.[21] But the real driving force behind the betrayals was an antipathy for Jewish ways, born of admiration of Greek culture and desire for the Greek way of life.[22] Fidelity was scorned as narrowness. Yet a faithful remnant, led by the Maccabees for a time, till their line too was corrupted, held on against everything, in faith, centered on true worship of the Lord in Jerusalem, no matter how corrupted by the priests of the moment.

Every least detail of the Law was now of crucial importance. Each was now something one had to be willing to die for. If he did not, he had betrayed the Law, the people whom it defined and constituted, and the Lord, who had given it into his care.

The right response to betrayal was that of Mattathias. When he sees the emissary of Antiochus coming and demanding pagan sacrifices, he seems to say, "Well, that's one of those pagans for you," and shrugs his shoulders

[21] Cf. Goldstein, op. cit., for abundant, if often somewhat speculative, details.

[22] Antiochus Epiphanes, the most cruelly determined of the persecutors, wanted homogeneity and uniformity of culture for the sake of temporal good order and, probably, for what he considered the cultural advancement of his subjects. A perfect Liberal, he was convinced that he was wise enough to bring about peace on earth, once he could get rid of the obstinately "fundamentalist" and "non-progressive" elements that the Jews represented.

despite the threat the emissary also brings. But when a Jew goes up and offers such a sacrifice, Mattathias trembles all over, draws his sword, rushes to the altar, slaughters Jew and pagan together, destroys the altar, and takes to the hills to lead a guerilla war against the pagans (I Macc.2:15–28).

His five sons, chosen by the Lord as their victories proved, dedicated themselves to the same cause and fought till death overtook them. Their successes, however, seem strangely limited to anyone accustomed to the earlier portions of the Scripture. Their victories were seldom conclusive except for the ones that set Jerusalem and the temple free; and they were often defeated.

As seen, reinterpretation of Israel's past and of the Law were characteristic of the post-exilic period. But there was a further, more drastic kind of reinterpretation also taking place: of their faith. As but one example, the ancient faith was that the Lord would save and reward the righteous during this earthly life. Even *Job* ends with a re-affirmation of this. Yet it was becoming increasingly clear, especially when persecution broke out against them precisely because of their religion, that God was manifestly refusing so to act. It was often the best and most truly religious who died unjustly and by torture, still young or else venerable with a long life of good deeds (II Macc.6 & 7). And the God of Battles did not give assured victory or continued life even to those He had chosen to lead His people. If the ancient faith was not wrong, it yet needed reinterpretation or more careful qualification. With different emphases, the authors of *II Maccabees* and of *Wisdom* explained that God was purifying His people of smaller sins and offenses so that they would not perish altogether by falling into grave ones. Both also argued that the righteous man's hope in the Lord will in fact be fulfilled, not in this life but through bodily resurrection and personal immortality and the rewards God will give to each despite temporal death.

Jesus, in the latter portion of His public life, became increasingly the object of religious persecution. The event that seems to have brought matters to a head was His driving the money-changers and sellers of animals out of the temple. For Jesus' love for the temple, spoken of briefly above, was greater than anything there indicated. Like Judas Maccabaeus and his brothers, zeal for the Lord's house consumed Him.

That enormous Court of the Gentiles should have served to overawe, by its silence and manifest centering upon the more elevated and majestic inner courts and buildings, any gentile who entered, moving him to pray to the God whose footstool this was. It had, in fact, been turned into a noisy, albeit religious, bazaar. The animals were kept in stalls around its outer wall; the tables of the pigeon-dealers and the money-changers were scattered about the vast yard itself.[23] All these served, to be sure, as an aid to the sacrifices proper to the temple; yet God's name was profaned by this manifest contempt for the gentiles and by the profiteering that made it a den of thieves.

Having stirred up the city the day before, when He entered it as Zechariah had described the Messiah's coming, His anger was recognized as more

[23] Marie-Joseph Lagrange, O,P., *Évangile selon Saint Marc*, 7th ed., Paris: J. Gabalda, (1942), *pp* 294–297.

than mere idiosyncrasy, as the holy wrath of a prophet, perhaps even of the Messiah. With an indignation that must have flared like flame, more intense than Mattathias', He drove out buyers and sellers and animals. But He was recapitulating in the Holy Spirit the Hasmonean zeal, not reliving it. He did not seek to kill those who had defiled the temple. Yet like Mattathias, He was laying His own life on the line by this rebuke to those in authority for their abuse of divine worship. But unlike him, He did not go on to stir up a revolt. He would not kill, however great the sins of His priests. It was left to them to respond, four days later, by turning Him over to the pagan oppressors of their people to be executed, so that He might redeem them as well as all Israel and all the gentiles on whose behalf He had here spoken. But very clear it was that He would not stop short, whatever the cost to His reputation or His life, before this abuse of worship—minor as it might seem when compared with the great profanations of Maccabaean days.

Though there were no Seleucid kings then constraining the Jews to deny the Lord, whether by formal idolatry or by a Hellenizing that would repudiate their Jewishness in practice, yet the same sort of betrayal of Judaism was in fact taking place, again led by the priests, the Sadducees, in a more sophisticated and, ordinarily, less violent manner.

His standing firm despite the possibility of Roman intervention is secondary in the recapitulation He displays here; He had reached that degree of maturity long before. What is primary is His dealing manfully with the corruption rotting the religious leadership itself and His seeking to overcome the resultant, widespread tolerance of irreverence towards the Lord. All this, unlike the days, say, of the late monarchy, is no longer a matter of denuntiation but of open and effective action, though in Jesus' case one might miss the difference since He did not resort to violence nor let His disciples do so.

There are many ways in which Catholics who are ready may share in this final period of preparation and purification. This variety is due not so much to the nature of the recapitulation itself as to the diversity of ways in which circumstances can act on people of very different temperaments. Moreover, it is not clear that all Catholics are subject to betrayal or religious persecution at this point in their growth or that they are not subject to them at other times. These afflictions are, at least in times of persecution, afflictions for almost all; yet they affect differently those at different stages of their recapitulation. What concerns us here is not external circumstances but further psychic maturation in Christ according to His pattern as appropriate to this level of spiritual development. Nevertheless, this maturation is often stimulated in response to the wrongdoing, great or small, intentional or not, of others.

Though the Catholic at this point in his recapitulation learns increasingly to gain strength and courage from Jesus' sufferings and death, this is not yet his passage through the paschal mystery with Christ, though the closer he gets to the term of this preparatory process, the more resemblance it will bear to that. But sufferings and great anguish were borne by Israel at this and at other stages in its history, without these being borne as Jesus bore His sufferings on the cross, in which all human pain and grief reached fulfilment.

Whether there has been an external, religious persecution or not, there have always been those in the Church who seek their own wealth or power or who tire of her particular, culturally conditioned way of life and who, in consequence, work to undo the latter or acquire the former. Some of these act from knowledge and malice. Others are more or less unconscious collaborators, knowing what they want or dislike but without any clear notion of the import and consequences of the actions they take to satisfy their desires.

Among those who remain truly devoted to Christ and His Church, there are deep cleavages concerning practical matters that embody, in the eyes of all, grave matters of principle. These divisions are analogous to that between those who followed Mattathias concerning the sabbath and those who regarded such actions as a desecration. Further, there will be the chosen fighters and others who fight but whom the Lord has not chosen for this task (I Macc.5:55–62). A brief glance at the pro-life movement in the United States at present illustrates the situation well.

The differences among those just mentioned depend largely but by no means exclusively on the directness and strength of one's love for the Lord: Is one truly fighting only for Him and His people? Or is there, as in the passage last cited, some element of vanity or self-aggrandizement? Is one responding principally to one's own fears, anguish, or suffering rather than to the truth that God's love includes all—even when this love must use the sword? The greatest temptation for the majority, perhaps, is to yield to the world's exclusion of them and to refuse the effort either to act against the evils or to build up something helpful, however small. To consent to such inaction is a hidden capitulation to bitterness and serves only to nurture resentment. This temptation is the more dangerous since it is at root a type of self-pity, one form that pride takes when hurt. Hence it leads easily to the proud self-sufficiency into which many of the later Pharisees fell rather than to the earlier ones' courage and valor in combat or their conceiving and establishing the synagogue.

The Christian is called to fight now as Jesus did, by an excess of charity, loving more those in greater need, i.e., those who seem most stubborn in malice, since these are in greater danger of damnation. But, for the time being, he is still caught—usually without realizing it—by worldliness. This is not easily recognized, since it is a sort of negative imprint of the commoner varieties of worldliness. But it can be discerned by one trait, that of contempt for those who do evil—as if the credit for not being evil oneself belonged chiefly to oneself, whatever polite statements may be made about the role of God's grace. If there is, as often happens, persistent aridity in prayer, it is likely that beneath it is some habitual sin of complaining, implicitly tied to rash judgments; or of curiosity and gossip about the evils of the day, rooted in the self-satisfaction that comes from not being such oneself or from being able to understand "what is really going on" or "what is the real cause of the trouble"; or of self-indulgence, especially in ways that hamper one's duties or are allowed as compensations for what one has to put up with.

After the religious persecution was over, there was more than a century of quiet: of deterioration among the Sadducees, of religious zeal among the Pharisees and Essenes, which latter, however, simply cut themselves off from contact with the rest of Judaism. This period of unreconciled party spirit and foreign domination served as the final preparation of Israel, the final purgation of the chosen people. One was learning then, if mature enough, the lesson St. Thomas More learned in the Tower: "Now will I let God work and leave off contention."[24] One came to know one's need, from every point of view, for salvation; to know that this salvation can come only from God in His own good time; and to wait patiently and quietly before Him, trying always to do His will in all: doing justice, loving mercy, and walking humbly with their God (Mic.6:8). When man finally learns fully that "Salvation is from the Lord" (Ps.3:8) and not from man, then Salvation comes, as Man.

What God had desired in this long process of readying Israel for His Son is seen in such saints as Anna and Simeon, fasting and waiting quietly and in hope for the Lord's Anointed (Lk.2:25–38); as Zachary and Elizabeth, who were "righteous before God, walking in all the commandments and ordinances of the Lord blameless" (Lk.1:6); their son, the greatest of the prophets, John the Baptist; Joseph and our Lady, the greatest representatives of everything good in Israel until the coming of God Himself in Jewish flesh. Undoubtedly, people around them knew that they were good Jews, both just and kind in their dealings. But for all that, they were not easily distinguished externally from their neighbors. The whole of two millennia of preparation—rather, of all the hundreds or thousands of millennia since Adam's sin—had come to fruition in this: the formation of "a people well prepared" {Lk.1:17}, among whom the holiest of our race would be unobtrusive and hardly noticeable. Israel had been formed so that, when Jesus came among us in our flesh, He might come quietly. Thus, when the Son of God became man, He was able to live both as child and as adult without standing out as an eccentric, without undue clatter, without being in some way at odds with His culture. No, the culture and the people were ready for Him.

---

[24] *A Dialog of Comfort against Tribulation*, Bk 1, *Ch* 12. *Complete Works, 12*, ed. F. Manley, New Haven: Yale University Press (1977), *p* 38.

Chapter 16

The Lord

What we have already seen of Jesus' life—mostly, the "hidden life"—was His recapitulation of Israel's life before His coming. In His public life, however, from His baptism in the Jordan onwards, He was doing rightly and perfectly what His people were doing wrongly or imperfectly at almost the same time. The maturation of Israel and Jesus' recapitulation of it had come into coincidence when He had responded to John the Baptist's proclamation that God's reign was at hand and went down into the Jordan to take up our lot as sinners and our guilt upon Himself. This was the moment of perfect synchronization, the confluence of Israel's maturation and Jesus' recapitulation of it. His recapitulation of their history in His own psychic development had overtaken the psychic growth of the people. Their preparation for His coming was practically finished, for He was there. All that remained was the short two or three years in which He gradually manifested Himself as the Messiah, and called His people to faith and discipleship.

A. The final preparation

This preparation had already been completed in John the Baptist, in whom the full maturity of Israel was to be found: "Among those born of women, none is greater than John" (Lk.7:28). Apart from his sanctification in Elizabeth's womb and his ever-growing holiness, simply as born of woman John was the greatest and most mature of the public figures of Israel. It was he who would make fully ready the "people well prepared."[1] But Jesus by His baptism was "to fulfil all righteousness" (Mt.3:15), perfecting even John's perfection. Thus, when the Holy Spirit came down in the form of a dove

[1] {Lk.1:17}. The word usually translated 'prepared' here signifies less a prior readying and more an equipping, a fitting out. That the people were "well" prepared is conveyed by the Greek perfect passive.

hovering over the waters to rest upon Him, it was that Jesus should be manifested as the first of the new order of creation. Henceforth, He was living as the Lord's Anointed, under the direct action of the Holy Spirit, who breathed where He would for the greater glory of the Father. For all others, however, "God's reign"—His governance through the manifest action of the Holy Spirit—"is near" {Mk.1:15}, but is not yet present.

We can begin to understand the enigmatic word Jesus spoke in His last moments on the cross: "It has been fulfilled" {Jn.19:30}.[2] He had recapitulated in full the life of Israel, even that of the leaders of His people at that very moment. Since His baptism, He had, moreover, developed far beyond any in Israel to a maturity of manhood that was His alone, without conceivable equal. His love, there on the cross, for the Father and for all men constituted the perfect righting of all men's sins, including the greatest one, being committed at that moment by those who hated and despised Him enough to want Him shamed and dead. The wrongness of their attitudes towards Him, the Law, Israel, the gentiles, and God, indeed the evil of every human heart from Adam on, was righted by His superabundant love for them and the Father. Perfect in gratitude to the Father, His thanksgiving was this return gift of total obedience,[3] as He rendered up His spirit to glorify the Father "through the eternal Spirit" (Heb.9:14), in fulfilment of all sacrifice and worship.

This, then, was the redemption: this recapitulation by which He undid and rectified the totality of human sinfulness and perfected the totality of human virtue. The redemption had begun from the moment of His conception. Death had been in principle overcome, the devil conquered by man, and sin obliterated. But the actualization of this liberation took place slowly, as He recapitulated what man was meant to be at every stage of his return to God. Redemption was, then, continuous through His life as He corrected, set straight, perfected, and rendered back to the Father all that original sin and actual sin had vitiated in man's graced maturation since the fall. In His passion, more psychically mature, more free, more truly human than any other man could ever be, He set all things right by showing—for the first time in the history of the universe—the perfection of the love man had been created to learn. All men have known that love is their greatest good and greatest gift. What they have not known, is what love is. It is this that Jesus showed here: what love man is to have for the Father and his fellows, in the sure hope that the Father's love for him will triumph over sin and his own death.

The Father's love for us was overwhelmingly manifest on Calvary: "He who spared not His own Son but gave Him up for us all, how will He not also give us all things with Him?" {Rom.8:32}. Yet the perfection of the Father's love for Jesus was not so manifest. To make visible the greatness of the Father's love for Him, it was necessary that Jesus be glorified, both before the world and before the Father. Thus, the redemption was completed[4] only

---

[2] It should be clear why I prefer this translation of *Τετέλεσται* to such other plausible ones as "It (His work on earth) is consummated," "It (His life and activity) is finished," "It (the redemption) has been completed," "It (our sinful debt) has been paid," or even "It (the redeeming sacrifice) has been consecrated," though resonances with each of these seem likely enough.

[3] Cf. *Ch* 4.C.2, *pp* 71–72 concerning this aspect of Jesus' love of the Father.

through Jesus' resurrection and enthronement. Through these He received the gift the Father had promised Him, that He should be glorified before men by His pouring out the Spirit upon all who believed. Through these He was glorified with that eternal Glory, which He had with the Father before the world was—the eternal anointing with the Spirit by which He is, forever, the Christ of the Lord.[5]

B. A PEOPLE WELL PREPARED?

On at least one point, however, we may have moved too rapidly. If we consider the Jewish rejection of Jesus, what might realistically be meant by saying that the people were "well prepared"? What sort of readiness is in question here?

They were not prepared in the sense that every one in the culture was ready to hear Him or had reached a suitable level of maturity. After all, there were infants and children in Israel all during His lifetime; and many were there who had early gone astray and were far less mature than God wished them to be. As the event proved clearly enough, neither were they ready for Him in the sense that they had only to see Him to accept Him or that they were constrained to receive Him. But the people were ready in the sense that their culture did not drag them back from psychic maturity or obstruct their further growth. Rather the culture of Israel, as instrument of God's grace, called them forward, to grow yet more, even till old age, in contrast with the much lower levels of maturity reached by even the best of the pagan cultures around.[6]

Jesus, then, could say what He wished to say, and be understood. He had auditors who, with the aid of proffered grace, were psychologically mature enough to grasp sufficiently and to act upon the things that He had come to say to them. "The fulness of time" {Gal.4:4} is to be taken with full seriousness. The Jewish culture of early, 1st-Century Palestine was the culture that God had chosen as the fit context for His full and definitive revelation of Himself through His Son.[7]

In some way, which has not been studied with anything like the depth of inquiry called for, Judaism of Jesus' day was the human culture *par excellence*, that which had been prepared, from Adam's fall onwards, as the only one fully suited to the entry of the Son of God into this world. Its very defects were just those that made possible the actual mode of redemption by which we are saved. The true fulfilment of every people would lie in their development of a culture in essence the same, however superficially different.[8]

---

[4] Even this completion was only relative. The final manifestation of Jesus' glory will take place only after the fulness of the gentiles has come in and He comes again to judge the world.

[5] Cf. *pp* 34–39 & 52–53 concerning His prayer at the Last Supper and *pp* 69–71 concerning His anointing by the Spirit at the Jordan.

[6] Cf. *pp* 362–372 below for a fuller analysis of this notion of the age or degree of maturity of a culture.

[7] Heinrich Schlier, op. cit., note 53. *p* 114.

[8] The meaning to be given this will be discussed on *pp* 363–366 below concerning "learnables"

It is important, then, to note that He could speak effectively to all His people, in all their diversity and according to their level of understanding. Most of those who followed Him in Galilee, drawn by the strong comfort of His teaching and their hope of miracles, turned aside when He demanded real faith; but not all: most of His apostles and many others of His disciples were faithful Galileans. Many of the Pharisees rejected Him; but not all: such friends as Nicodemus only grew stronger. The Sadducees actively and successfully sought His death; yet Joseph of Arimathea followed Him, and many others became Christians shortly after His rising. John the Baptist may have been influenced by the Essenes as much as by the Sadduceic connections of his family. And one of the apostles belonged to the revolutionary party of the Zealots. So, too, we see educated scribes and the "people of the land," those learned in the Law and the "crowd that does not know the Law"; those of upright and fervent life and those so deep in sin as to have become haunts for the demons; those who prayed even in public squares and those who were prostitutes or tax-gatherers for the Roman overlords. All these were ready, each in his own way, as is shown by the glad responses He received from some in every group. The virtues of each group He lived perfectly, and against their defects and vices He offered in perfection the example for them to follow.

Another aspect of Israel's preparation can be seen in that continuous reinterpretation and reintegration of their past, mentioned earlier, especially as that showed itself in the form of scriptural accomodation.[9] Jesus' recapitulation involved, in consequence,[10] a reinterpretation of all of Israel's experience, a reinterpretation that was also a spiritualization. Anointed with the Spirit, Jesus taught and exemplified by His life what God's Spirit had been quietly intending and carefully signifying in the Scriptures of His people. Jesus' teachings, therefore, did not lie beyond the reach of those, at least, who were willing to ask Him questions and discuss His teaching.

For example, His people had seemingly ineradicable, deeply inadequate, and often erroneous notions of what the Anointed of the Lord, the Christ, the Messiah, was to be. His own apostles shared such notions, even after His resurrection, indeed till the day when the Holy Spirit descended upon them. But He, all through His public life, had been teaching, by word and by action, what the term truly means.

This popular and quite general misconception was not, as MacKenzie rightly insisted,[11] a rendering gross and worldly of a prior spiritual notion. If anything, it was the reverse: a stage in the gradual spiritualization of an earlier, more earth-bound concept. Before the Exile, there had been a looking forward to a better king than they had had since David, through whom the LORD would rid them of the hostile nations around them. During the Exile, this developed into an awaiting of salvation through some future king of

and "developmentals."

[9] Cf. *pp* 163–168 above concerning divinely inspired accomodation, and the penetrating studies of Lohfink and others there mentioned. Of special importance is the deep spiritualization of the events of the Exodus that occurs in *Wisdom*.

[10] Cf. above *pp* 295–296, 303–306

[11] *JBC* 77:154 (same number in *NJBC*).

David's line, a salvation with cosmic overtones in a future not conceived in terms of the sons of a reigning monarch. But in the post-exilic period, there occurred not merely the collective exercise of memory of which we spoke above.[12] but also an intense looking forward to a future salvation. The Lord had not, in spite of appearances, abandoned His people to their current disarray and sinfulness. Israel still had a destiny, one that would set them over all the nations of the earth. The Jews were looking forward to this fulfilment; and the late prophets' idea of a Messiah as a king sent by the Lord gradually grew and became more closely linked to Israel's spiritual destiny.

The priests were probably not very enthusiastic at first about these notions of a future king. But there *was* going to be an Anointed of the Lord, even if not a king. After all, the high priests were the first in Israel to be anointed. By the time of the Hasmonean conflation of the offices of high priest and king, the same sort of conflation began, among some, to be made in the notions of the Messiah. But what was central to almost all notions was that the Lord Himself was going to establish His people, directly or through the action of His Anointed, as a politically independent nation on His holy land as His Kingdom forever. Moreover, the Messiah would lead this chosen people in the military and political conquest of all nations, so that the Lord might be made known in power and glorified by all. And, always in the background, were the prophecies of new heavens and a new earth. While these expectations did not much change the nature of Jewish daily life—save to make it possible by the gift of hope—somehow Israel knew that the future would be even more glorious than they expected. God would act, how they did not know, to bring it about.

Jesus' careful refusal under most circumstances to designate or let Himself be designated as the Christ, and His acceptance of this title only in contexts of humiliation and suffering are detailed in every New Testament commentary. He named Himself "Son of Man" not only in connection with that refusal but also because it was He who summed up in Himself, by recapitulating it in His own earthly life, all that man could possibly be or have been, fallen or unfallen. His resultant manifestating of the spiritual sense of the Scriptures lay at the very center of His entire mission.

Jesus' teaching on marriage, on the sabbath, on Himself as Son of Man, along with the rest of His teaching, represent not a return to a prior Golden Age but entry into the world of grace, a new creation, ever more completely destroying sin and healing the worst of its effects Even those who followed Him did not understand until He had risen that it is "the eternal Spirit," with which He had been anointed at the Jordan for His sacrifice upon the cross and through which the Father raised Him from the dead, who defines forever what the Lord's Anointed is.

In striking contrast, a contrast so great as to be considered blasphemy by the high priest, Jesus identified Himself as Son of God. He declared Himself not merely a messianic king enthroned on earth at God's right hand, nor solely as the Son of Man presented before the divine Majesty, but as true Son,

[12] *p* 295.

seated in the heavens at the Father's right.[13]

Christians (perhaps especially so today when little thought of the spiritual sense remains) have often been puzzled by the passages in the prophets promising universal peace, even among lambs and lions, in the messianic age (e.g., Is.11:6–9), with the sun shining many times brighter than now (Is.30:26), in new heavens over a new earth (Is.65:17), with the land flowing with preternatural abundances of all good things (Am.9:13; Joel.3:18) with Jerusalem built of precious stones (Is.54:11–12) and her streets paved with beryl and ruby (Tob.13:17). Even if due account be taken of symbolism and apocalyptic exaggeration, a certain uneasiness remains; and these passages are rarely preached.

The key, of course, is not found in the universal peace that reigned at the time of Jesus' birth,[14] great as has been its symbolic value. Rather, it lies in the fact of Jesus' two comings. For, God "loves all things that exist" (Wisd. 11:24): the gentiles also are to have a chance at salvation (Ac.11:18). Jesus' first coming offered salvation to the Jews by making them the ones who were to conquer the world spiritually for Him through His Church. Because He loves the nations, the time from His first coming till now—and henceforth till Judgment Day—is still preparatory, not yet the consummation. Israel was called to a greater honor than any universal temporal empire could be.

C. God's Call to Israel

All that may be true in principle. Yet, if preparation was not a matter solely for the elite handful of His disciples and scattered others, a difficulty remains. Whatever, for example, the prior uses of Scripture, can one seriously pretend that His doctrine was not most radically new? If it took the Church several centuries to find acceptable ways to express the doctrine of the Trinity, what could have been expected of a devout and faithful, 1st-Century Jew on hearing Jesus speak of Himself in terms reserved for God alone? What Christ brought and did, however deeply rooted in the Old Testament, was it not simply new and, at least in all its most important aspects, radically discontinuous with the Old?

We have seen that the mode of fulfilment that dynamically links the type to the Antitype is the preparative aspect of the spiritual sense. One element of this is the analogy between the cultural development of the human race after the fall, especially in Israel, and an infant's growth to adulthood. This approach has the great merit of making manifest how much there is in common between the two Covenants.[15] The great difficulty in such an

---

[13] Cf. Albert Vanhoye, S.J., "Structure et théologie des récits de la Passion dans les Évangiles Synoptiques," *Nouvelle Revue Théologique 89*, 135–163, (Fev. 1967) at *pp* 152–155, or *Structure and Theology of the accounts of the Passion in the Synoptic Gospels,* tr. C. H. Giblin, Collegeville (MN): Liturgical Press (1967).

[14] This is celebrated, in the words of the Roman Martyrology for the feast of Christmas: "... when all the world was at peace...: the birth of our Lord Jesus Christ according to the flesh."

[15] This is particularly the case for the nature of the faith that God desired both of Abraham and of each Christian. Cf. on this, the eloquent and perceptive passage in Grelot, *Bible, Word of*

approach is that it would seem necessarily to fail at just the point where it is most needed: the discontinuous transition from the Old Law to the New; for the child's growth, and Jesus' also, are strongly continuous.

The possibility of a solution is offered by a great page from von Balthasar.[16]

> The man obedient to his mission fulfills his own being, although he could never find this archetype and ideal of himself by penetrating to the deepest centre of his nature, his super-ego or his subconscious, or by scrutinizing his own dispositions, aspirations, talents and potentialities. Simon, fisherman, before his meeting with Christ, however thoroughly he might have searched within himself, could not possibly have found a trace of Peter. Yet the form 'Peter,' the particular mission reserved for him alone, which till then lay hid in the secret of Christ's soul and, at the moment of this encounter, was delivered over to him sternly and imperatively—was to be the fulfillment of all that, in Simon, would have sought vainly for a form ultimately valid in the eyes of God and for eternity.

Von Balthasar's analysis of vocation demonstrates that both a continuity with the old and a discontinuous transition into the new can occur simultaneously. Continuity exists at the level of man's psychic being, i.e., all that he is apart from his own freedom and God's grace. Discontinuity comes from God's own activity suddenly making itself present in the form of a call, along with the grace to accept it, and from man's freely chosen decision in response. It is the interaction of these two free, temporally locatable but instantaneous and, so, nontemporal acts that generates the most radical of discontinuities man can know. God freely offers what no man could desire of himself or even envision; man freely accepts or rejects this offer—and yet, in the new world thus instantly created, he is the same person as before so far as the "flesh" is concerned, however radically changed in his spirit.

The growth of God's people, then, was not merely a matter of internal development, analogous to the bodily and psychic growth of the individual. Though man's slow recovery after Adam did take place in accord with that analogy, yet from the moment when God first spoke to Abraham,[17] man's psychic growth was also, in many ways principally, a free response to God's calls. God's calling is integral to man's growth.[18]

God, *pp* 287–288, and the remarks of Augustine to which he refers: "The sacraments were changed, not the faith. The signs which stood for something were changed, not the things that were signified." Sermo 19 (PL 38, 133). This argument, of course, forms the heart of chapter 11 of the *Letter to the Hebrews*.

[16] Hans Urs von Balthasar, *Prayer*, tr. A. V. Littledale, New York: Sheed & Ward (1961), *p* 49. (*Das Betrachtende Gebet*, 2nd ed., Einsiedeln: Johannes Verlag [1959], *p* 51–52).

[17] Something similar was true even earlier, when God called Adam after his sin, to bring him to repentance. So, also, He called Cain, seeking both to prevent his sin and, failing that, to draw him to repentance. But in these cases, the element of mission was obscure and faint. Even His call to Noah, though in many respects like that to Abraham, lacks any sense of life-long mission.

[18] It is the neglect of both these elements, God's grace and man's free will, not merely in the exemplary case of vocation but quite generally, that vitiates almost all current theories of human development. These restrict themselves to the psychic level exclusively, yet parade as descriptions of

So Abraham was called and "went out, not knowing where he was to go" (Heb.11:8). So from the midst of the burning bush, the LORD called Moses. His calls were frequent at some times, rare at others; and in the post-exilic age not only exceedingly rare but "natural," i.e., intellectually perceived, neither externally manifested nor given by direct internal experiences such as visions, locutions, or dreams. But in all cases, He called the people as a whole by calling one man through whom He called the others. Thus He first called only Abraham's family, then the tribes of Jacob, to become under Moses a people and under Saul and David a nation and, through the prophets and mostly anonymous saints after the Exile, He formed from those first few nomads the spiritual elite of all the earth.

God called at those times in Israel's life when the people had grown sufficiently to be ready to receive a new call, i.e., when they were prepared and capable of a proper response to the call. But, as is clear, say, from the first Exodus, this does not mean that they were simply "set to go." On the contrary, many rebelled, many sinned, many refused, many fell away. What constituted their readiness was that they were mature enough not only to be able to hear, understand, and decide freely but to begin to grow still more in response to the call. For, a call from God is never merely a summons but is also a stimulus; not only a stimulus, but an offer of grace and new powers.

The same patterns were visible once again at the fulfilment. This final growth, also, did not take place simply of itself but occurred in response to God's calling. The calls were now frequent: to Zachary, to Mary, and to Joseph through angels; to John the Baptist, by God's word spoken to him in the wilderness; then to the disciples of John the Baptist, through John's preaching. Then the Father Himself called Jesus through the Holy Spirit at His baptism; then the apostles, through John's witness and Jesus' own calls to them. Finally, Jesus, both directly and through His apostles, called all Israel to a new and greater enterprise than any hitherto.

The calls went in each case to one man through whom others were called. In each case, there was a need for further, sometimes very painful growth if one accepted the call. Since these calls all had the same basic structure, this final spurt of Israel's growth and development involved the same sort of novelty as Jesus' calls to Simon and to John, to Matthew and to Saul, a newness that stemmed entirely, in each case, from Jesus' understanding of the mission to which He was calling all Israel.

The point can be made clear through recasting von Balthasar's remarks:

> The Jews, before their meeting with Christ, however thoroughly they might have searched within themselves, could not possibly have found a trace of the Church. Yet the form 'Church,' the particular mission reserved for them alone, which till then lay hid in the secret of Christ's soul and, at the moment of this encounter, was delivered over to them sternly and imperatively—was to be the fulfillment of all that, in Israel, would have sought vainly for a form ultimately valid in the eyes of God and for eternity.

---

man, whose primary difference from the animals lies precisely in what these psychologists have refused to take into account.

The abruptness and novelty of this call became indeed the occasion for many in Israel to stumble and fall. Yet He who was "set for the fall...of many in Israel" was set also for their rising (Lk.2:34) and remains forever the "glory of Your people Israel" (Lk.2:32).

Recall our Lord's parables that bear on just this point: "The Kingdom of heaven is like a king who gave a wedding feast for his son and sent his servants to call those who were invited...." {Mt.22:2–3}; "A man once gave a great banquet, and invited many...." (Lk.14:16); "When you are invited...to a wedding feast...." (Lk.14:7–11). But those who were invited and called refused to come. Even clearer, however, is the parable of the vineyard and the murderous workers in it (Mt.21:33–44). The King has been long away, but He sends His prophets and holy ones to receive the fruit. These are beaten and insulted or even killed. Finally He sends His only Son, who likewise is cast out and killed. Hence, the King sends an army to punish the evil-doers and to let out the vineyard to those who, He hopes, will yield its fruit. One aspect of this parable is the clarity with which it reminds Israel of its past resistances to God's calls,[19] each given in its season, with the sending of the Son as a last resort. No one should be surprised if He too is rejected.

Acceptance of His call would demand a new and often painful growth. Israel was called to begin to live at a level long prepared for according to potentialities still unrecognized though developed over millenia for just that moment, to live indeed a new life, now for the first time made possible, beyond all Jewish expectation. As with Simon Peter, so all were called to assent in faith to Jesus and His teaching, to acknowledge the depth of their own sinfulness, and to repent in truth. As the people had done in Moses' day, many refused. As when the spies returned from looking over the land of promise, the majority of their descendants balked at the degree of faith that Jesus required of them. They were then called, as were those who had been bitten by the fiery serpents, to repentance; hence, to believe that He whom they had had crucified was enthroned in glory at the right hand of the Father, interceding for them. Thus only could they receive the outpouring of the Holy Spirit upon them and be made God's sons through incorporation into Jesus, the Son, by the power of the Spirit (Ac.2:31–39). From this outpouring of the Spirit would come their full response to God's invitation and call, to go to the gentiles and carry, to them also, the Good News.

It is of central importance to see that Jesus' rejection by the leaders of His people and His crucifixion did not alter the call: "For the gifts and the call of God are irrevocable" (Rom.11:29). With still greater insistency Jesus called Israel through the Spirit to accept Him whom they had crucified, as their Messiah and King and LORD. Though this provided the basis for their mission, enabling them rightly to preach repentance to others, yet it did not begin to exhaust this mission. They were then to take their spiritual treasure and scatter it broadcast among the degenerate pagans of the Empire and among the barbarians beyond, to share it, seemingly to give it all away, to the nations.[20]

---

[19] This imagery, already present in Hosea (10:1) is at its strongest perhaps in Is.5:1–7, and appears frequently in Jeremiah and Ezechiel.

[20] Jesus was "hung on the tree... so that the blessing of Abraham might come to the nations in

Yet most of these could not, for centuries to come, even recognize the gift, still less be ready to receive it. Israel's call was to love the gentiles as Jesus had loved Israel, even if, as was the case with those Jews who accepted the call, by loving the gentiles the more, they would themselves be loved the less (II Cor.12:15). Only through the new powers given by the Spirit and the new life in Christ could weak human beings find such love possible.[21]

Preparation, then, there was. But let no one underestimate the greatness of the leap required or the depth of the chasm. It represented a passage from one or other kind of largely "this-worldly" hope[22] to a hope that is emphatically not of this world—though insofar as it governs our lives, it results in a fulfilment, superior to any other, even of this world's hopes. But no man can be adequately prepared to meet the Majesty of God, even in human form, without shock. Terrible is the awareness that the infinite gulf is suddenly being crossed by the Creator in order Himself to address His creature in a new and definitive way. Because of this, whatever man's choice, it is in this sense unprepared for.

St. Paul's image of the divinely planted, strong and rich and useful olive tree (Rom.11:16–24) shows what was at stake. Its roots and trunk are the patriarchs and the prophets. But some of its branches were broken off—yet after how long a growth and development!—in order that other branches, cut off from bitter, wild olive trees, might be grafted in in their place. The continuity and discontinuity of Christianity with Old Testament Judaism is manifest: the gentile branches are cut off from their own roots but are grafted in and begin to live from the roots of the cultivated tree. Thus Christianity, even among the gentiles, is Old Testament Judaism's legitimate continuation and fulfilment. The "Judaism" now so called, sprung from the stock of those who then rejected Christ's call, continues, like a broken-off branch still filled with sap, to put out leaves and shoots. But it too felt the shock of discontinuity as it was broken away from its roots, awaiting the day when "these natural branches will be grafted back into their own olive tree."

D. Those who Refused

If after so long and arduous a preparation, so many of the people best prepared rejected the Christ when He came, can those baptized as Christians hope to do better in their recapitulation? For "God has shut up all men in disobedience" {Rom.11:32} and the gentiles "too will be cut off" (Rom.11:22) if, like those Jews, they decide not to believe in Jesus or, having believed, not to act in accord with that faith. The mere fact of baptism and of membership in

Christ Jesus" {Gal.3:13–14}.

21 Grace had been offered to all men from Adam on. But this was not yet the grace to heal, within the brief compass of a single lifetime, the psychic damage inflicted on man's nature by original sin through the recapitulation of all history in Christ. Nor was it the grace to share in full Jesus' life in the Holy Spirit, either as He labored for His people on earth or as He sits enthroned in heaven at the Father's right hand.

22 'This-worldly' seems the right word, yet one must be careful to give it no pejorative meaning here, for there was much of moral grandeur and purity in this hope when at its best; cf., e.g., Ac.1:6.

the Church does not guarantee safety from the dangers of pharisaism.[23]

There are other indicators of the seriousness of this matter. The Gospels devote a surprising amount of attention to Jesus' debates with the Pharisees and their scribes, especially when one considers all the other things that the evangelists might have written down instead: what He looked like, the details of His daily life with His apostles and disciples, His other sermons and parables (for we are told of His spending whole afternoons teaching the crowds "many things" [Mk.6:34] and of the people following Him and listening for three days running), other miracles, what He told the two disciples on the way to Emmaus while their hearts were on fire within them as He explained the Scriptures to them, His other conversations and instructions given the apostles after His resurrection, and so on *ad infinitum*. How much labor, turmoil, false doctrine, and schism His Church would have been spared had He insisted on the apostles' writing down a little more of His own understanding of the truths He brought to her, say, about the procession of the Holy Spirit or about the nature of grace or of original sin.

Yet, in all four Gospels, as much space is given to His arguing with the Pharisees as to His instructions to His apostles, or even more. Many of His miracles were worked to draw them to faith. Much even of His most positive teaching (e.g., the parable of the father of the prodigal and his older brother, that of the lost sheep, the eleventh-hour laborers in the vineyard, the good Samaritan) are parts of such arguments. Willy-nilly, it behooves the Christian to look carefully at this.

It is not easy to deal with our question, given the wide range both of psychic maturation and of spiritual development within the major Jewish sects. For, whatever harsh statments one has to make about Annas and Caiaphas, it remains that Zachary and Elizabeth belonged in all likelihood to the Sadducees; and—whatever the prideful sins of Saul of Tarsus and his peers—Joseph and Mary and Jesus Himself were counted among the Pharisees. The best method, I think, is simply to direct attention to the sinful attitudes that corrupted those whom both Jesus and, later, St. Paul seemed to see as, otherwise, the most mature and religious Jews, those particular leaders of the Pharisees who hardened into enmity against Him. It is only of these Pharisees that I shall be speaking in the rest of this chapter.[24]

To judge by such men as Saul before his conversion, even the best were more or less infected with an attitude deeply hostile to Jesus and the Gospel. It is this attitude that it is crucial for the Christian to understand and, by God's grace, avoid or cast away. There were many types and degrees of moral failing among them, noted in the New Testament. But apart from passing references, it is not these that are made the subject of Jesus' special attention. But one, over-all attitude, the one that also led to Jesus' death, is in its different

[23] This word designates the hostile and sinful attitude that characterized both many of the Pharisees of our Lord's day towards Him and a great number of other people since, not the principles of the historically defined sect as a whole, which I capitalize.

[24] Jesus seems never to have sought conversation with Sadducees (apart from John the Baptist, if he may in some way be considered one). When they sought Him out, His responses were reproofs as well. As a group, they seem to have been much less ready for what He had brought.

facets highlighted repeatedly in the Gospels and in the letters of Paul.

This attitude is labeled "hypocrisy."[25] What this means may be gathered from Jesus' formulation as given in Mt.23:3, "They preach but do not practice." A different aspect is mentioned in Mk.7:8: "Abandoning the commandment of God, you hold fast the traditions of men." Or, looking at the things Jesus and Paul denounce, pharisaism is, on the one hand, a careful, even finicky, observance of all details not only of the Law but of the fence around it, coupled with a great contempt for those who do not do likewise; and on the other hand, a tradition of legal analysis that covertly catered to their own self-will and advantage, enabling them to violate the Law without breaking it.

The hidden purposes of this legalism were the usual reasons for men's sins: desire for money,[26] hope to escape the binding power of an inconvenient oath (Mt.23:16–21), and, most especially, an avid appetite for public honor, titles, and all other signs of high esteem from men.[27] These faults were not necessarily more prevalent in them than in other men. Their hypocrisy lay not in their such motivation nor in the sins that resulted but in their unwillingness to admit that they had such motives and committed such sins, that they were indeed "like the rest of men" {Lk.18:9–14}.

Less obvious to the Pharisees themselves, perhaps, was that they had come to treat the fence around the Law as morally equivalent to the Law, thus putting the core of God's moral will for man and their own traditions on the same level. Since even the Torah contained, as coming from Moses, injunctions that stemmed from later interpretation and application, the temptation here was a subtle one; and our Lord faults them for falling into it only insofar as it led to denaturing the Law itself or contempt for others. Even less easily visible but more destructive was their coming to see the Law with its fence as representing the totality of God's will for man. Thus, the inner faults of a man, his hidden lusts, his quiet hatreds, his deep contempt for "this crowd, who do not know the Law" (Jn.7:49) tended to escape his moral scrutiny; whereas the interior virtues of faith, humility, and true charity—"the weightier matters of the Law" (Mt.23:23)—could easily be ignored without qualms.

They had forgotten their fathers' understanding of the Law as God's great gift and proof of love for Israel. Ben Sirach, prosaically pragmatic as he was, agreed with *Baruch* that the Law was God's own mercy and presence among men.[28] This could have been the great theoretical problem of the Pharisees with our Lord. For, when He came, He claimed to be, Himself, God's mercy incarnate, the Law *and* the Lawgiver both, literally embodied. Yet there is no sign that they even noticed this problem.[29] Those opposed to

[25] So, in Lk.12:1, "Beware of the leaven of the Pharisees, which is hypocrisy." The term is used, insistently, seven times of them in Mt.23.

[26] This is clearest in the matter of 'corban' (Mk.7:9–12), the "devouring the houses of widows" (Mk.12:40), the failure to give alms rightly (Lk.11:41); cf. also Lk.16:14–15.

[27] Cf. Mt.23:5–7; Mk.12:38–39.

[28] Compare Bar.3:35–4:1 with, e.g., Sir.15:1, 17:11–14, 19:20.

[29] Two or three centuries later, it seems, this problem was seen by some of the rabbis. But by then, the entire context had so changed that it could hardly be regarded as the same difficulty.

Jesus had taken over the Law and the rest of Jewish religion as their own possession. The Sadducees had done this with the priesthood and the temple; the Pharisees, with the understanding and practice of the Law. Neglecting the teaching of Ps. 119 on the need of constant help from God if one is to keep His statutes and ordinances and not stray from His precepts, they considered their very real virtues to be their own, sole achievement. These things had become their property. To use our current jargon, it had become their great "value."

The Pharisees seem to have taken deep into their hearts the exultant phrase, "Happy are we, O Israel, for we know what is pleasing to God" (Bar.4:4), as if "know" meant merely intellectual knowledge and no longer the traditional Hebrew knowledge arising from action. They knew the Law well enough in the former sense; but they failed to put its harder precepts, such as love of neighbor as oneself (Lv.19:18), into action. The Pharisees wanted friends (and enemies) to praise them (or revile them) because they were the true custodians of the Law. The praise they wanted was for their being good, God-fearing keepers of the Law and the fence around it. They had grown satisfied with their religious practice and saw themselves as guides to the blind, teachers of the unlettered in the Law, masters in the discerning of God's will.[30] All this, they took more as the result of their long years of study and careful training than as gifts, ever to be sought anew from God's grace. Proud of their moral victories, content with their ability to keep much of the Law easily, they remained trapped in vainglory.[31] What was intended by its very nature for God's greater glory, since showing forth His goodness, they turned into a badge, even a banner of their own inner excellence. They worshipped no idols of gold or stone, but only themselves.

These leaders of the people sensed Jesus' newness as a threat not to the Temple or the Law, as the priests said (Jn.11:48; Ac.6:11–14), but to their own possession of the Temple or their own interpretation of the Law. What most drew the attention of these men to Jesus was the daily evidence that His understanding of the Scriptures might very soon replace theirs and, also, that their hypocrisy was under attack. After all, they had spent their lives studying the Law though they were perfectly free not to have done so. And now this Galilean, who had never sat at the feet of any recognized teacher, was, in a sense, seizing the prize which it had taken them such long effort to acquire and which they now owned, they felt, by right. They did not see that, if they had studied only for the sake of truth and for the love of God and neighbor, nothing would be lost save, perhaps, some of their status as great teachers of the Law.

Their own understanding of Judaism was at stake, an understanding that they too easily, because of their pride, identified with the reality itself. Too many among them were unwilling to relax their grip sufficiently on all the good gifts God had given them in the past to receive this new and greatest gift, by which He had become their own flesh and blood (Heb.2:14), the Gift that

[30] Cf. Rom.2:17–24.

[31] Though vainglory itself is not the sin against the Holy Spirit that brings damnation, yet it is of its nature opposed to the Glory and easily leads towards that great sin against the Light.

summed up all that had gone before and brought all gifts to completion.

Those who refused him, it is worth noting, did so by rejecting what they did not understand even though Jesus' ministry as a prophet was warranted by miracles, even as had been Moses' or Elijah's or Elisha's, and, as a teacher of the Law, by the purity of His doctrine and its consistency with the best of their own past. This rejection was, therefore, quite unlike the prophets' rejection of the deceivers and betrayers of earlier days or, more recently, by devout Catholics of teachers of false doctrine. Rather, closing upon themselves and excluding ever more rigorously the claims that charity makes even with regard to false teachers, they shut out that which would have led them to a life that fulfilled the Law and the Prophets, the new life given by the Holy Spirit in the Christ of the Lord.

But this freedom in the Spirit, by whom the love of God is poured out in our hearts, could not be had by those who blocked out His love, who refused this great and difficult step in their growth, by which they would come truly to "love [their] enemies," as they first perceived our Lord and His followers to be, to "do good to those who," they thought, might "hate" them, to "pray for those who" could provoke, at least, the Romans to "persecute" them by coming to take away their city and their holy place.[32]

There is indeed no true love of God or neighbor that does not require absolute fidelity to all that He has spoken. But neither is there any true fidelity without charity; otherwise, one has mere rigidity. As proven by the Maccabees, the love of God can demand a fidelity which is rigorous, harsh, willing to fight in battle and to die for His sake. But what marked the scribes and Pharisees was not a tenacious holding to the things of the Lord but, with that as pretext, an enmity for one whose understanding of the Scripture often implied or asserted moral fault on their part. As Jesus told them, the love of God was not in them (Jn.5:42).

Had His love been in them, this charity would have led them to inquire whether He did not think that this or that teaching of His might be subversive of the Law or of the tradition of the prophets. They would have sought an explanation and tried to get to the bottom of the problem with Him. Instead, from early on, they sought occasions to trap Him, to prove Him wrong, to put Him in a bad light before others. The spontaneous and instinctive reaction of many of them was to see this man as an enemy, to attack Him if He would not come to heel, simply to blot out the danger. This was the give-away sign of their sin: that they would not listen seriously to what He said to them. They realized that He was speaking of them; but instead of acknowledging, even to themselves, their own wrongdoing, they sought to arrest Him (Mk.12:12).

They wished to eliminate instead of to convert. If they were really convinced of their position and had any love in them instead of contempt, they would have tried to win Him over, let Him see the foolishness or the wrongness of what He was teaching. He repeatedly showed Himself willing to discuss matters with them and to explain His words, offering frequently to do so

---

[32] Cf. Lk.6:27–28 and Jn.11:48.

even though most of them steadily declined. They preferred to uphold the Law and the prophets, as they understood them, with plots and subornation rather than to listen and see whether there might not be something of value in His teachings. The action of charity was missing in them. Unwilling to love Him or anyone else who opposed their own estimate of themselves and their righteousness, they yielded to the temptation to contemn and despise Him whom they thought in error rather than to seek what they could do, for the love of God and man, to enlighten Him.

In contrast, when some of them did show a different spirit, He was receptive: "You are not far from the Kingdom of God" (Mk.12:34). There was easy dialogue if they were ready and open. Think only of Nicodemus or Joseph of Arimathea or even the teacher of the Law who drew from Him the parable of the good Samaritan (Lk.10:25–37). But most, unlike the disciples, did not want to find out more. They did not want understanding nearly as much as riddance of what disturbed them. So, unlike the disciples, they did not come to the house after an instruction to ask Him questions: "Why do you speak to them in parables?" (Mt.13:10) "Explain to us the parable of the zizania" {Mt.13:36}. Few of them bothered to hear most of His teaching, though He spoke perfect truth when He said to Annas that He had taught nothing in secret.

The sin of pharisaism would seem, then, to be the penultimate, consciously and freely willed capitulation to the psychic thrust of original sin. Despite all cultural growth, each man is confronted sooner or later by his own deep sinfulness, despite all his efforts to be truly good, and by the fact that not only does he have, in consequence, no right or claim to God's love but deserves in strict justice be punished. Man's predisposition to sin lets him see clearly only a pseudo-possibility: to make himself loveworthy wherever he senses that he is not. What is pleasant, what combines gracefully with his expectations, what lets him feel that he is indeed admirable and of value, becomes ever more luminously present; what is painful, what contradicts his spontaneous thrusts, what humiliates him by putting in doubt the necessary value of his being is thrust back out of sight. Thus reality is "restructured"—by a suitable combining of light and darkness, for it never really changes or goes away. It is this process which we earlier described with a different image.[33]

Recall briefly what was said about the process by which a child cuts reality into bits and fragments, which he then, like the larva of the caddis-fly, binds together to form a little shell, carefully camouflaged, in which to feel safe, a false world in which the real structures are replaced, in part, by imagined ones. Thus he goes through life, exploring the world with intense interest, but ever fearful, with his casing about him, into whose presumed security he is ever ready to withdraw when threatened by valuelessness. Inert matter though this casing is, it yet comes to seem like a part of his very organism. So he enlarges his world indefinitely yet always selectively. Like the caddis-worm, he will tend to leave any non-threatening reality in one piece; if it is a bit too large, he will cut it up and reconstitute it in its original order. But

[33] *Pp* 213–215.

other things must be dealt with more carefully.

If, at a later age, he is skillful enough—and it takes considerable skill—he may even be able to find a way to fit God into his casing. This is, of course, his supreme achievement because God is seen or felt as the greatest threat of all, the ultimately real and independent being, least dependent on the young person's will, yet whose love is most needed and unconsciously craved. Usually, then, only the young adult or even the older one manages to build God into his silk-bound casing so that He is no longer a threat but rather serves to manifest the value and worth of the man in whose caddis-case He has been embedded.

Of course, once a person has done this, he can no longer see God very well, since He is now on the outside, webbed into the casing and world-system. Only very occasionally, in moments of weakness, does the person notice uneasily that this smiling, immobile, easy God is not really alive at all and that the true God, the living and jealous God, has somehow escaped him and is more dangerous than ever for not taking favorably to the attempt to stick Him as an image in his casing.

Simone de Beauvoir in her *Mémoiresd'une jeune fille rangée,* [34] describes the process with terrifying realism. If half of what she says of herself is true, what a little monster she made of herself, in total self-complacency and self-esteem, centering the entire universe upon herself! Her rupture with the Church came because the priest in the confessional questioned her as to whether she was quite as sinless as she declared herself, given what he had heard of her back-biting and slandering of her teacher. From that point on, for her, God no longer existed. He had become too dangerous for her world, and there wasn't room for Him anyway.[35] On the other hand, she had not been mature enough to do as the Pharisees, who did not annihilate God but made Him their chief trophy.

Put in more scriptural terms, though the reality of the world remains always what it is, however men may regard it, yet man is able to transform the real world into his own, more agreeable world, by a suitable utilization of light and darkness. Most of men's sins depend upon this ability to cast light on certain aspects of one's own being and of what one already knows of the world while letting other aspects fall back into the darkness. Man cannot make the latter things not be, much as he may fear or dislike them. What he can do is turn off the light or let the light fall only elsewhere. His attention can be made like a searchlight, focussed into a narrow, intense beam; or it can broaden out to shed a diffuse radiance over all. Some regions of experience stand out clearly; by contrast, others are plunged into blackness though, as for our physical eye, the blackness is rarely absolute. As the magician with his mirrors, so we can remake the world pretty much as we like by suitable care

[34] Paris: Gallimard (1958), especially *pp* 135–138. Cf. also Jean Rimaud, "Sur la conversion d'une adolescente à l'athéisme," *Christus* 6, 410–423 (#23, 1959).

[35] How much of all that is literally true of her and how much is just a shrewd, psychological novel in the first person, is another question. But it has the ring of truth in any case; and her later autobiographical works, many of whose details can be checked, would seem to show the same person.

for where we let the light fall and by suitable reinterpretations of what we vaguely see or surmise to lie in the dark spaces between.

This imagery of light and darkness permeates the New Testament, especially the Pauline and Johannine writings, where it serves to lay bare the nature of the gravest sin as the free refusal of the light given by the Holy Spirit because one's evil deeds will be rebuked merely by being seen in His light. But the same imagery also describes with great accuracy what we are learning through psychology concerning the defense mechanisms set up by the subconscious and deep unconscious. These psychic mechanisms are not free and, so, are not actual sins; but in many ways they are identifiable with the still unhealed consequences of original sin.[36]

Every actual sin is the free acceptance, whether only internally or also in external act, of known falsehood. It is our free choice to cast into darkness something we know to be true, to remain in the darkness ourselves, and to do in that darkness the evil that we are pretending not to know as evil—as if our not seeing what we are doing because of this willed darkness really prevented us from knowing our sin. We pretend that the only way of knowing the evil is by seeing it, forgetting that we are responsible for the darkness that hides it. We choose the darkness, with all that this implies as to reinforcement of those psychic traits opposed to God. We choose to do the deeds of darkness, the ones that darkness itself inspires (Rom.13:12–13, Eph.4:17–19).

If the Lord has left us in such weakness that we still sin, this is to help us to humility, to make us desire to change and to grow more, to convince us that we do not yet know Him or His will as we ought. Thus, by refusing the light He seeks to shed upon our still unadmitted sins, we block our road to humility and the truth.

The analogy between the mind and the eyes, between intellectual knowing and seeing, between light and understanding, between darkness and ignorance, is ancient and universal. If our Lord spoke to the Pharisees in this language of light and darkness, He did not intend to restrict His meaning solely to what His auditors then could understand, but to open the road into "all the truth" (Jn.16:13) for those led by His Spirit. Man is, by the very nature of his mind, open to all things. He is made for light. In the light he is to look upon all that God has made; his final goal is to gaze in love upon the Father's face with Christ in His Glory with the Father.

The link, then, between love and truth is clear. It was by letting themselves despise and contemn those who were willfully ignorant and sinful, rather than by loving them enough to find out how they might help them do better, that the Pharisees first went astray. It was by a similar contempt for Jesus, refusing to inquire of Him as "little children" but letting themselves resent His untutored excellence in all that they prided themselves on, that the Pharisees came to hate the Truth, in whose light all their weaknesses and their own sins were made manifest to themselves and, in some measure, to others.

---

[36] Cf. *p* 215 above concerning defense mechanisms.

Excursus:
Freedom and the Knowledge of Truth

For man to know something, he must somehow interiorize it and bring it into himself. And this action of interiorization is his act of knowing. It is by the two-fold activity of looking in the full light upon all that is real and his interiorisation of that reality and making it his own, that he is defined as mind and that his spiritual nature is manifested.

But in this double process, he touches the real only by letting the things that enter remain as they are in their otherness. One's interiorization of what one sees must not refract the light or alter the form of that upon which one is looking. To the extent that one changes what is to be known, to that extent one knows not the reality but this creature of one's own mind, part real, part fiction, combined in some unknown manner. What is other than oneself is not rightly known if it is not known as other.[37]

Intellectual truth (truth in and for the mind) implies, consequently, an attitude of respect, of reverence for real things, material though they may be, and of love, even when they are not persons. As Louis Lavelle said of charity, "La charité est une pure attention à l'existence de l'autrui." Love, then, is a criterion for truth. But only perfect charity, such as we shall have in heaven, is total guarantee of truth. For only perfect love casts out fear (1 Jn.4:18) and lets the fearful being that fallen man is gaze with no trepidation upon all things, from the depths of its own sin and the place in hell this sin deserves to the heights of God's mercy and love, greater than all sins together.

But through the perversion of our psychic structure by original sin, we are predisposed to force what is other than ourselves into our own categories and pre-established forms. Then it is not truly the other in its otherness but, in large but unknown measure, oneself that one is knowing. In extreme cases of pride, one freely chooses to subordinate all things to one's own way of seeing. Another person is reduced to some figment of one's own construction. One destroys this other person inasmuch as he is no longer "other" in one's mind. One has denied his existence, even "killed" this other in what belongs properly to him as himself. He has been eliminated in far more serious a way than had one removed him from consciousness by paying him no attention. Willed refusal of another's otherness is the deepest sort of contempt for him. Whence, if he forces himself in his otherness too much upon one, one may destroy him by an actual deed of murder—as those particular leaders of the Pharisees did when they joined the Sadducees to kill Jesus..

Hence the malice of phariseeism, whose analogs can exist in all domains though it is, as such, found only in religion. The pharisee changes things as he interiorises them, re-making them in himself to be other than they are. Thus, he rejects the primary and authentic way in which he was created to exist in the image of God, for he re-creates the self he knows and the world, too, by

---

[37] Cf. Paul M. Quay, S.J., "Temporality and the Structure of Physics as Human Endeavor," in *Physical Sciences and History of Physics,* (Boston Studies in the Philosophy of Science, vol. 82), ed. R. S. Cohen & M. W. Wartofsky, *pp* 199–230. Dordrecht: D. Reidel (1984), at *pp* 222–225.

screening out their otherness.[38] Man is meant to be in God's image, first of all by knowledge: to know as God knows, who knows all created being precisely as other than Himself, and to share in that infinite reverence by which He lets things be without distortion. Yet for them to be, they must be in God, who makes them be only by sharing with them something of His own being, thus conforming them to Himself. Man's attempt to do the same—to make the reality of the world exist only in or through his thoughts of it, to give things existence by his willing it—is to play at being God.[39]

To put the matter a little differently, God loves all that is (Wisd.11:24). So, then, man must love. He, too, must love all that God has made. Since he can only know incompletely, he can only love partially. But what he must not do is to refuse the love that is appropriate to the particular good that constitutes the other. Only what man loves can he let into himself by true knowledge. Ultimately, knowledge and love are one. But the pharisee does not have this love for everything simply because it comes from God; instead, he tries to make all things conform to what he does love: his own good pleasure and his inner comfort, his own self or some unreal projected self.

The pharisee refuses to open himself to new things, things truly other. He thinks he knows enough and is intellectually rich and powerful enough already that he need not be further troubled. Underneath this self-sufficiency lies the fear of change. For, to know something new, a person must let himself be changed, precisely because he must permit what is other than himself become, unchanged, a part of himself. To refuse new truth is, clearly, a refusal of *becoming.* The pharisee chooses to consider himself a being who, already, fully *is*, except perhaps for some simply additive growth. He need not grow into any new way of being, nor learn from all that is still quite other than himself. Any future growth in knowledge is simply an accretion of more facts, but implies no other change in him. Such a person, then, seeks to "be as God," considering himself implicitly as one who simply is, pushing time aside as if he were the Eternal Spirit. Yet by freely shutting himself against reality, he negates the spirit of man in its essence, thus rejecting the Spirit of God in whose likeness he was created.

But why should man wish so to close himself in himself by cutting himself off from the real? Does anyone really want to be locked into the void of an empty heart? The proudly self-sufficient person probably does not even understand these questions. Others, perhaps less proud, are moved more by fear than by arrogance. For, to be opened to the real is to go out of oneself, is to depend on others, is to love them in some degree. But the security that can

[38] This may seem an odd statement, for how could the self enter as other or be altered if one knows it? Yet this is precisely the act that makes the materialist. He does not see that the "self" he knows is not the self that is knowing itself. This essential otherness of the spirit from all conceivable aspects of the material is ignored or altered mentally into a non-otherness, such as the materiality of a computer.

[39] This obviously has nothing to do with man's inventiveness or his delighting in the things that he makes, whether simple tools or completely new species through genetic engineering. For, to do any of these things well, he must first know what is, and the true principles governing its activity.

be found in temporal things is null, and man knows this well. He needs, then, to entrust himself wholly to God and His love, in full awareness of his own unworthiness to be loved, with full admission of his sins, yet with hope in God's mercy and with the determination, by His grace, to live henceforth as he ought. But the devil, he who keeps man in lifelong bondage through fear of death, having himself the power of death (Heb.2:14–15), torments him with thoughts that effective repentance and forgiveness are impossible, with fear of "the second death" (Rev.20:14), so that he may despair and see nothing else in himself except an image of that empty spirit that has wholly rejected God's truth.

St. Thomas remarked: "Error has the same intelligible structure as sin,"[40] even though it is not, ordinarily, sinful. But it is also true that sin has the same intelligible structure as error. Now, the mind, if physically unfettered, errs in its judgments only through the action of one's affectivity. All sorts of feelings, passions, emotions can operate, consciously and subconsciously, to lead into error—an assertion of something as true which is not, or of something as false which is true. If the affective element includes a person's free and deliberate choice, he sins.

Thus, the Lord's own characterization of Satan as "a liar and the father of lies" (Jn.8:44) is the most fundamental we have. The devil and all the demons are so locked into themselves by pride as to refuse all reality that does not support their rebellion—their hatred of God is hatred of all that is like Him, i.e., of all that is. By choosing to be creators of all things themselves and by asserting all that is true to be false, willing that only their own thoughts be true, they are indeed living lies. Despite the brilliance and power of those demonic minds, neither the devil nor any of the demons has a personal name.[41] By letting nothing into himself save what conforms to his hatred and contempt for God, Satan has ejected from himself all love and all truth. The lie that he has made himself to be, is a pure refusal of the existence of any other as other. His every approach to man is as to one whom he thinks to be, at root, like himself. Hence, too, his frustration with those gifted with humble love. He is, then, as Jesus called him in this same context, the "murderer from the beginning" (Jn.8:44). There is nothing like God that he does not will to corrupt into likeness to himself, i.e., to consume and, so, bring into the eternal death of hell. This is why the devil is "like a roaring lion seeking someone to devour" (I Pet.5:8). He can take another into himself only by consuming him, i.e., destroying him as other in order to turn him into more of himself.

---

[40] "Error habet rationem peccati," *de Malo*, III, 7 c.

[41] The Asmodeus in the little tale of *Tobit* constitutes no exception, given the literary genre. 'Satan' and 'the Devil,' etc. are descriptive designations: 'the prosecutor' and 'the slanderer' respectively, and so of the rest. Cf. the profound treatment of the lack of demonic personality in: Josef Ratzinger, "Abschied vom Teufel?", *Würzburger Katholisches Sonntagsblatt*, 11 & 18/3/1973.

[42] This image of the demon's rapacious hunger is well developed as a major theme by C. S. Lewis in *The Screwtape Letters*, London: G. Bles (1942).

E. Those who accepted

But even though many of the most influential Jews rejected Jesus, whether during His public life or after His resurrection, many others—who knows what percentage?—did accept Him, and loved Him greatly. We should, then, say something briefly about those Jews who formed the Christian communities in Jerusalem, Antioch, and elsewhere before any admission of gentiles, when Christianity was still an entirely Jewish matter, sociologically as well as religiously.

How the Christian is to recapitulate at this stage is perhaps best seen by a sort of reflection as in a mirror: he is to be taught by Jesus as Jesus taught the Twelve. Firstly, just by His choosing the men He chose, we are given some indication of what He was looking for and still looks for in those who are to be closest to Him.

At least six of those who were chosen were men who were already disciples of John the Baptist (or at least so interested in him as to be with him at the Jordan when Jesus came): Peter and Andrew, James and John, Philip and Bartholomew (Nathanael). They were, therefore, religious men, deeply concerned for the coming of the messianic kingdom. They had sufficient spiritual maturity and penetration to recognize that John was different from such various preparers-for-a-messiah as those who led the Essenes or the Qumran community and from the evanescent, would-be messiahs, of whom there were many at about that time.

The rest of the apostles also were Jews, though Matthew was on the fringes of Jewish society, a collaborator with and worker for the Roman conquerors of his people, a quisling, who was unclean by reason of his life among the pagans and who by his occupation was interdicted from taking any part in the religious life of his people. Yet all were products of the Old Testament growth-process; all came from the "people well prepared." All of them at least knew what was required of them, whether they were doing it or not. They had all been born into, formed by, and steeped in that culture which belonged to the fulness of time, which in the late post-exilic period had crystallized and taken firm shape in Palestine, giving the Jewish people a homogeneity that was basically new, despite the factions into which they were divided. The men He chose, then, were adult Jews, the fruit of Israel's long development as His people.

These men, each with his own personal history and individual freedom, He called, Matthew no less than Peter, drawing them towards Himself in order to be brought to the fulness of life in Him. The potentialities that were to be actualized in each were as yet invisible to the man himself and to his companions, for they were capable of actualization only by Jesus' direct action through His grace. Yet they were there, as truly human potentialities, but which could never have been fulfilled through any transmutation of his earthly surroundings or in his experience of anything other than Jesus' call. However much prepared by the witness of John the Baptist, none of these men could prevision the fulness of the glory to which he was being called. Neither could they imagine the manner of transit: their desertion or denial of Him followed by His crucifixion and, with equally jolting abruptness, by His rising from death through the Glory of the Father, in order to draw, through forgiveness, all men to Himself.

He taught them at first by means of things that drew them in accordance with their culture and religious background. The fact that John had pointed Him out as the Lamb of God and the One upon whom he had seen the Spirit come down and rest was not lost upon them. John's testimony remained, as we see from the structure of the Gospels, something that gave them major strength in their faith in Him. All that they longed for in their current stage of readiness they found in Jesus and they gave themselves ever more completely to Him.

They were drawn by His miracles. They were drawn by His power, but just as much by the authority with which He spoke and taught, even when confronted by the great authorities, not merely the scribes and Pharisees but the priests in the Temple.

He taught them—as we teach each other—by word, by explanation, by long discourses, by continual if fragmentary comment on the incidents of their life together. They listened to His sermons and talks to the people, to the things He said in synagogue, field, or mountain-side. They asked Him afterwards about the things he had said to the crowds, and He explained to them His parables and the other things they did not understand. They would argue which among them was going to be the Lord's second-in-command, once the Kingdom arrived. He would then ask them what they had been talking about on the way, making them face the true nature of what they had been saying and doing, and then teaching them further on that basis.

When Peter wanted to explain to Him that there was no need to think dim and dismal thoughts, that such things would never happen to Him, He taught him the lesson like a bolt of lightning. Whatever their situation, He would teach them accordingly, beginning with the present moment. When He engaged in His long and technical arguments with the Pharisees in Jerusalem, they were forced to listen and to learn, though some of them listened more attentively, it seems, than the others. John shows, at least, a more evident interest in this side of Jesus' teaching than does Peter.

They learned simply by watching Him, being with Him, seeing how He reacted, whether to enemies or to friends, wondering about the conditions under which He would work miracles for people. Sometimes He would explain Himself, taking pity on the multitudes because they were lying harrassed and prostrate, without a shepherd, telling them of His own mission by restricting their activity to the lost sheep of the house of Israel. Even quite unconsciously they were learning and growing.

So each Christian is called to grow through the circumstances of his following of Christ, i.e., the external events, the reactions of others, and the inner movements of his own soul that all result from what he consciously undertakes for the Lord, even more often mistakenly than the apostles' efforts. What matters now is that with firm faith in Jesus as the Christ and Son of God, as the one norm for all things human, he keep his mind and heart fixed on Him, whatever else eventuates.

Every Christian who has come thus far is invited further: to live with Jesus through the sacraments and to take on His mind increasingly through assiduous meditation on His mysteries according to the faith of the Church, learning to act in accord with the light so given, then to suffer with Him and to share in His cross while yet living in this world.

For, Jesus' crucifixion came while the apostles were still learning. Yet nothing would teach them more. If they did not despair because of this disastrous manifestation of their sinfulness but remained with Mary till Easter,[43] their joy overflowed beyond measure when He came back to them in the glory of His resurrection.

This transition is, as mentioned when we began,[44] the major one in the Christian's life, that which leads out of recapitulation into the beginning of the life of the Spirit.[45] Having shared in Christ's sufferings and death—sometimes abruptly and dramatically, sometimes very gradually and quietly—one begins, after a fairly brief transition, a life of infused knowledge and love of God and His will. Though one continues to grow, there are no longer any necessary patterns of growth. One is set free by the action of the Spirit to share the Spirit's love for Jesus and to do whatever the Spirit directs in order the more to glorify Him in the Church.[46] Each, in the way the Lord has called him—for the ways are infinitely various, as the lives of the saints make clear—manifests to the world by his obedient gratitude to the Father, who and what Jesus is, and by his glorifying of the Father and Jesus, who and what the Spirit is, so that all may know and love the Father from whom both Son and Spirit procede.

The Christian Jews of apostolic times are, thus, exemplars but not patterns, for those later Christians who have finished their recapitulation of the Old Testament and are beginning to live under the action of the Breath of God. For it was the life in the Spirit, in which no obstacles to the dominance of charity in either personal or communal life are allowed to stand and in which the true mystical life of infused contemplation begins, that was the life of those early Christians who seemed so unsurprised when Christ would appear to them or speak directly to them. Their Lord, long ago dead on the cross but now risen and glorious, constantly directs them, encourages them, tells them through His Spirit where they are to go, how long they are to stay,

---

[43] Judas did not, reminding us once again that learning for the Christian is not a matter of the mind only, for Judas learned as much in this way as the others, but of the free choice required for faith and hope and charity.

[44] Cf. *Ch* 1.C, *pp* 6–7.

[45] There seems no wholly satisfactory terminology for this latter and later stage of spiritual growth. There is an abundant vocabulary (mystical life, infused contemplation, perfection, etc.), but most designations are excessively partial, referring only to one or other aspect, often a contingent one, rather than to the essence of this new and more perfect way of living in Christ.

[46] What is now deteminative is no longer the Law, with its ramifications and its wall. The one who loves Christ well has gone far beyond the demands of the Law and its protections, seeking only how still more to please the Lord through the fulness of charity. There is a marvellous passage in Irenaeus that sets this doctrine forth as clearly as any I know: *Demonstratio, #96.*

what places they should by-pass on their apostolic journeys.

Yet the ending of recapitulation in no way implies, then or now, that further growth is either impossible or not required. Rather, the exigency for further growth is more strongly felt than ever; at last one has begun to realize how very far he is from his goal: to be wholly like Jesus, perfectly one with Him and with all those who are in Christ. As Gregory of Nyssa explains in *The Life of Moses*,[47] though one may mount without limit beyond the created order, there ever remains an infinite space above one before one might reach God. So, more than a millennium later, St. Teresa of Avila, having spoken of the step we have been considering as the one between the fourth mansion and the fifth,[48] continues on in order to set forth the endlessly greater and more abundant graces she received as she grew further in the Lord thereafter.

Often there is a time of joyful quiet, like that of the apostles between Easter and Pentecost, as the ordinary Christian enters into union with God in Christ through the Spirit. But he will not, unless a cloistered contemplative, remain long content to enjoy God's presence in repose. God will send him forth, in the strength of His Spirit, to share with all the world everything that he has heard and seen. Truth, now seen in Christ—indeed, that is Christ—can be had in fulness only through the mind that is lovingly illumined by the Spirit, set on fire by the Spirit. It is the charity poured out by the Spirit that reveals the Word, who brings us to the Father.

Sometimes one forgets the maturation and spiritual growth of the apostles after Pentecost. Perhaps this happens because the characteristics of this further growth are less familiar where the recapitulative process is not yet finished. The life of infused prayer, the mystical life properly so called, is a life still ahead of the majority of Christians, even were it true that all would eventually reach it. We hear, then, much about how Jesus formed His apostles. We hear more about how the Spirit enlightened them at Pentecost concerning the things they had already lived through, calling to their minds all that Jesus had said to them (Jn.16:13). But this was not the end of the process.

The Acts of the Apostles show many further, rather difficult, learning situations for the disciples. Peter in particular had a long ways still to grow. The sheet, let down from heaven, that contained all animals, clean and unclean, was only the first step in his learning the proper relations between Jewish Christians and the gentile ones (Ac.10:10–20, 11:5–12). Even so, he drew upon himself Paul's rebuke at Antioch for not acting rightly in this regard (Gal.2:11–14). The process of growth was never allowed to terminate in this life—this much, at least, is certain in the ancient story of Peter's leaving Rome under Nero's persecution and on his way meeting Jesus going into the city: "Quo vadis, Domine?"

---

[47] Spiritual perfection in this life, then, lies not in an attained nearness to God but in the excellence of the process by which one seeks it; cf. St. Grégoire de Nysse, *La vie de Moise*, ed. Jean Daniélou, SC 1 bis (1955) pp 2–4.

[48] This step is one which, she opines, most of her Carmelite Sisters do eventually take, though many of them after too long a wait, op. cit., "The Fifth Dwelling Places," *Ch* 1, #2, *p* 335.

Both Paul and Barnabas apparently had some lessons to learn when they went their separate ways because of the hot anger that flared up in them in their conflict about John Mark (Ac.15:37–40). A careful reading of Paul's letters makes clear, however, the much stranger fact that he had still to grow in understanding even his "own Gospel." Consider Paul's growth in his relations to his gentile Christians. He started his life as "a Hebrew born of Hebrews, as to the Law a Pharisee, as to zeal, a persecutor of the Church" (Phil.3:5–6). Not too surprisingly, then, at the start of his apostolate he dealt with His gentile Christians very much as if they had all been good Jews, apart from their ethnic origin and from circumcision. But increasingly he was talking or writing to churches that were no longer largely Jewish, with a few gentiles included, but to churches composed largely of converts from paganism.

If one looks at his letters in chronological order, one can see him more and more occupied explaining to the gentiles things they ought to have known—had they been good Jews. Since they were not, he had to spell out for them that, no, it is not right for a young man to bed down with his own father's wife, even though she was not his mother; incest is simply not permitted to the Christian, who ought to live more chastely than the pagans, not less so. He would never have had to say that to a Jewish community, which would not have tolerated any such public flaunting of incest, whatever human weakness might have yielded to in secret. But the Christian community at Corinth, to Paul's distress, really didn't see it as all that bad. They probably did not approve it, but they evidently were not making an issue of it and had no idea that such an activity could cut a man off from grace and the Church. Paul did make an issue of it, not to hurt his converts but to instruct them and train them.

So, too, he had to teach them that even ordinary fornication is gravely sinful for the Christian and to instruct them concerning other kinds of wrongdoing—all the moral matters he had assumed that the grace of conversion would make obvious to them. So, as he wrote to the largely gentile communities, increasingly he had to back up and bring in the things that he had skipped, the steps that hadn't been gone through, the things obvious to Jewish Christians but that had never dawned on gentile ones. Thus, he not only had to learn much about the attitudes of Greek and Roman pagans; more profoundly, he had to come to understand more deeply the nature of recapitulation in Christ. If, indeed, it was he who wrote the covering note for *The Letter to the Hebrews*,[49] one can understand why he should have been so uncharacteristically enthusiastic about another man's work, given its development of typology well beyond what Paul himself seems to have been aware of. But the point to notice in all this is that even Paul had to go back and pick up the things which these various gentiles had never learned; better, he had to lead them through a genuine recapitulation in Christ, going through all the stages that they had missed.

The end of *Acts* seems a good symbol of this endless growth in the Holy Spirit. Its final verses recount how Paul stayed two years in Rome, preaching

[49] Cf. Albert Vanhoye, S.J., *La situation du Christ: Hébreux 1–2*, Paris: Éditions du Cerf (1969), *pp* 17–26, 32–33.

concerning the Kingdom of God and teaching the Good News of Jesus Christ to all comers. The future remains wide open. Paul has still more to do. There is further growth ahead, as he wrestles with further problems stirred up by the differences between his Jewish and his gentile converts. The book stops; it is not ended. Its story is still unfolding. What the book is about does not end with the book but reaches onward to our day and beyond.

Thus, it does not seem possible for us to hurry our maturation and growth in Christ. It is a process through which we must grow, by the rightful activity of the life we have been called to live in the Lord. Yet, if we cannot hurry it, surely if we understand it better, we might by God's goodness do less to impede it.

F. God's words to His people and His Word

What we saw above concerning God's call to Israel through Jesus and the free responses, good and bad, made by His people serves also to explain the element of discontinuity that distinguishes the slowly developing preparative typology we have been considering from those seemingly discrete and isolated types called prefigurative.[50]

Jesus is not only the Son of God; He is also the eternal Word made flesh. The Father's Word within the Godhead, He was also, long before He joined our nature to Himself, the Word through which God's call came in each case to resound among His people. The Father is ultimately the one who calls; but a call comes to men through a word; therefore, God's call, through His Word. Thus, even the revelation of Jesus' divinity was prepared for by the long development of the theology of God's Word shown in the Scriptures. If one restricts oneself to the literal sense, it seems certain that this Word was not conceived in the Old Testament as a distinct Person. Yet from *Deuteronomy* on, through *Proverbs* and *Wisdom* especially, God's Word is often personified. It was, then, through His being the medium of God's call to Israel that Jesus was manifested not only as the Son but also as the Word of the Father, the Word that, made man and speaking in human terms, embodied that call. The Word was the Sound that signified the Father's will. As the Anointed with the Spirit, He modulated into the clarity of a determinate and particular call the humanly incomprehensible and overpowering rush of the Breath of God.

The silent Word[51] maturing as man in Bethlehem and Nazareth was the Antitype to Israel's growth. But when He became the human vehicle of the Father's call to Israel, though continuing Himself to grow as the New Israel, He became as well the Antitype of Moses. For, through Jesus, the New Moses, God's call came to men in order to make them, in a far stronger sense than before, His people.

The words of Scripture concerning Moses told of such things as we saw of Jesus' recapitulation of the Exodus during His early adolescence.[52] One

[50] Also called the 'restricted typical sense'; cf. above *Ch* 7, *p* 159, notes 49 & 55 on *pp* 161, 163. Cf also pp 253–254.

[51] The one time He spoke was itself a singular and discontinuous event, a call upon both Mary and Joseph for great growth in faith and trust.

might wonder, then, how it is that Jesus, rather than Peter, say, is the New Moses. It would seem that those aspects of the life of Moses that God chose to tell future generations—for there was obviously far more to his life than He told them—were chosen not only to throw light on our life in Christ through His recapitulation but also to show the basic structure of that call which He was about to make to Israel. Jesus is the New Moses, because it is through Him that Israel is called to a new Exodus (going forth as His emissaries to the nations), out of another slavery (to the "elemental spirits of the universe" [Gal.4:3] and to the sin necessarily deriving therefrom) and a different Egypt ("their own" land and nation), to become a new people of the Lord (His Church), moving towards a Promised Land (heaven) more holy and beloved by God than the old, following the conquest of worse enemies (the demons and those driven by them), and after the overcoming of greater odds through the spiritual conquest, for the glory of the Lord, of all the nations of the earth.[53]

At the Last Supper, Jesus, like Moses at Sinai (Ex.24:3–8) instructed those who would be the leaders of His people in their obligations under the New Covenant, teaching them His new commandment (Jn.13:34; 15:12,17) and its corollaries. Instead of the basin with the blood of oxen, "This cup which is poured out for you is the New Covenant in my Blood" (Lk.22:20). He fed them in the sacrificial banquet of communion with the Body of the Victim—but, as the Victim who is not only Way and Truth but also Life, a Body never received dead, but alive and life-giving, a Victim to be slain the next day when His blood was poured out upon the ground from the cross. There, all things came together and the Church was born from His wounded side, to be nourished by His Body and by the Blood there shed, and washed in baptism by the water from His side.

The same sort of analysis can be developed with regards to the other prefigurative types such as Joshua and David and Jeremiah. Each of these, also, was a medium of God's calling to His people; each, therefore, a typical "word," type of Jesus, God's Word and the complete Utterance of the Father to the world.

We are now on very familiar ground: the prefigurative sense that is strongly present throughout the New Testament and that reaches a sort of climax in *Hebrews*[54] resumes its commanding position. Likewise, the usage of the Fathers finds here its place, though with a difference. For there are now much tighter controls on what can pass as a genuinely spiritual (God-intended) meaning of what is spoken of by the text. Thus, many a passage in the Fathers is now seen to be a valiant but vain effort to extract some meaning from an erroneous translation or from a corrupt text or from ancient words and grammar whose significance had long since fallen completely from the memory of Israel. Then, too, the contributions of the various types of modern literary-,

---

[52] *Ch* 12, *pp* 257–260.

[53] Note how different this prefiguration is—for it is entirely spiritual, i.e., in terms of the grace of the Spirit—from a simple reduplication of the traits of Moses' life, however many of these appear here also.

[54] Cf. Heb.9 in relation to the paragraph just above, especially *vv* 15–22.

form-, and redaction-criticism, and other types of historical-critical methodology, when rightly used without a rationalistic or anti-religious bias, have given a much more detailed and accurate understanding of the literal sense—through which alone the spiritual sense may be discovered—and have corrected our grasp of it on many points.

As one small illustration of how modern scriptural studies can help better to understand the prefigurative sense, despite long disuse, it now seems clear from careful study of the earlier parts of Scripture, that many people who were not descendants of Jacob—of the tribes that had earlier come from Canaan into Egypt—tagged along in the Exodus; and others were incorporated into the people only after their arrival in Palestine. The presence of these alien lineages—for one can hardly designate them as gentiles when Israel was first becoming a people—and their inclusion in ancient Israel prefigures that openness to the nations the Lord wished for the new Israel.

The fulfilment that Christ brought to Moses' prefiguration of Him, as also His fulfilment of each other type, was similar in an important way to that by which Simon the fisherman became Saint Peter, Prince of Apostles and the Chief Shepherd of Christ's flock. In each case, a new and Spirit-filled "form" is given by Christ Himself to the figure or to the one called. This "form" is in each case a mission or, at least, an eminent suitability, effected by new powers, for a mission.

There remains, of course, an essential difference between a call from God and the process binding type to Antitype. In a divinely given vocation, the one individual, responding to grace, grows and develops from the moment of the call to its fulfilment; whereas in the case of the type, this individual, though he may receive the graces he does precisely in order to make him a suitable type, yet does not in his own life reach the fulfilment, which is Christ and not the person who is the type. As the *Letter to the Hebrews* states, after its long listing of types of Christ and of the Christian in Christ: "All these, though well attested by their faith, did not receive what was promised, since God had foreseen something better for us, that apart from us they should not be made perfect" (11:39–40).

Finally, preparative typology is that which undergirds and validates the "life in Christ," the "imitation of Christ," and similar ways of conceiving the spiritual life of the Christian. Prefigurative typology is that which asserts Christian doctrine by showing what Jesus, as the Christ of the Lord, transforms in the Spirit. The former relates principally to growth; the latter, to vocation. Thus, e.g., the masculinity of the Christian priest is prefigured by that of the priests of Israel; *a fortiori*, the Sacrifice he offers, by their offering of bloody sacrifices. The priests of the Old Law, however, were not in any direct way preparatory for the priest of the New Law. The preparatory aspect of the older priesthood helped in the forming of a people who would rightly understand sacrifice and worship through a priestly ministry but contributed little to the essential notions of Christian priesthood, save to warn the Christian priest of the danger of the worldliness his high office brings with it.

G. Transition

Soon after His sufferings, death, and resurrection, Jesus sent His Spirit upon the nascent Church as proof of His glorification. Through the Spirit, He sent the apostles and disciples out into the world with all that they knew of Him, they who had lived with Him so closely and in whom He was even then living by His Spirit. As He had promised at the Last Supper, His Spirit brought to their minds all that He had ever taught them (Jn.16:13).[55] Though the Good News was at first preached only to Jews, it was but a few years until the zeal of these Jewish Christians began to carry it to the Samaritans (Ac.8:4–25) and to various groups of gentiles (Ac.8:26–39; 10:34–48; 11:20). So the gentiles were brought to birth in Christ. The process of recapitulation in Christ began anew. Its pattern of growth and development, now largely completed within Christian Israel, was not to stop but to begin again among the gentiles.

For each individual, whether Jew or gentile, recapitulation has always been a new and unique process, starting salvation history over again at the beginning, each person beginning his life standing in Adam's naked and sullen sinfulness before God. But for our race as a whole, much has happened since Adam. The nations have, almost everywhere, grown in varying degrees towards maturity, God's grace quietly and slowly assisting them through the process that led to Cain and Abel and beyond.[56] As we saw in our response to the Marcionite problem,[57] Christ offers salvation to the nations through faith, a faith that requires their growth in Him by preparative recapitulation of the Old Testament. As Jesus told the Samaritan woman, "Salvation is from the Jews" (Jn.4:22).

We have sketched roughly the stages in spiritual maturation of the individual Christian in his sharing in Christ's recapitulation of human history. But we have said very little about the Church through which the social and communal and cultural aspects of recapitulation take place. It is this communal growth, as effected by the Church in interaction with human cultures, that we need next to consider

---

[55] Indeed, as He promised there, the Spirit announced to them the things that were yet to come. These future things were not the events the world is much concerned with. The Spirit did not make of the apostles His augurs or oracles. Even when some concrete prediction was made, it seems solely to have been as a guide to action, not a satisfying of anyone's curiosity about the future (cf., e.g., Ac.20:22–23). "The things to come" are principally those things that the anagogical sense reveals: the basic patterns for the growth of the Church on earth and the consummation of all things in heaven.

[56] Cf. below, *Ch* 18, *pp* 363–366, 369–372.

[57] *Pp* 200–201.

Part III

THE CHURCH, THE NEW ISRAEL

Chapter 17

Our Holy Mother: Recapitulation *within* the Church

As Jesus grew to maturity, He fulfilled the preparative typology of the Scriptures by recapitulating the entire history of His people up to His own day. As the Word through which the Father called Israel, He fulfiled also the prefigurative types. Of these, as implied throughout the last chapter, the most important for our present purpose is Moses. For, constantly juxtaposed to Jesus, the New Moses, is His Church, the New People of God. And just as Christ fulfilled the prefigurative types through whom God called and formed His people, so His Church has been called to fulfil in Him her type, God's first-chosen people Israel, to whom those calls were addressed.

A. The Titles of the Church

No people exists in its totality in a single moment, but is constituted by its history and concrete development in time. It is Israel in its entire history that is type of the Church. The Church herself, then, is growing in the manner prefigured by Israel. But the existence of type and Antitype implies fulfilment by and in Christ through the action of the Spirit. Hence there is a process of recapitulation for the Church herself. Thus, in a unique way, Israel is a type that is both prefigurative, since called as the result of God's choice to take this people for Himself, and preparative, manifesting all that Jesus was to recapitulate and we, through Him.

It is worth noting that one of II Vatican's most striking concrete utilizations of the typical sense of Scripture (not merely the abstract approval given in *Dei Verbum*) bears on just this point:

> He chose the Israelites as a people for Himself, with whom He established a

covenant and whom He gradually taught by manifesting Himself and the firm purpose of His will in their history and by sanctifying them for Himself. Yet all these things happened as a preparation for, and a figure of, that new and perfect covenant, which was to be ratified in Christ, and the fuller revelation to be given through the Word of God Himself made flesh.[1]

Like her type, then, the Church herself grows and matures through the growth and maturing of her members in a given people or culture. Like ancient Israel, she too develops slowly, over the course of centuries in each people to whom she comes. She too is formed in the concrete circumstances of human history among people only slowly awakening to the need for recapitulation. The Church, as God's people, is not simply a religious group or society but is the Christian people in the totality of their life and culture, as concrete and visible as was the old Israel, though it is neither common blood nor culture that makes them a people but, however diverse in those aspects, a common faith and spiritual life. As they begin their recapitulative process, the Church too, newly conceived among them, recapitulates the life of Israel under the New Moses. We shall return to these matters shortly, but first we need to remind ourselves that there are other, equally important aspects of the Church.

Of the many scriptural titles of the Church, 'the Body of Christ' has been perhaps the most favored and the one developed with the greatest richness of detail.[2] Yet the Second Vatican Council emphatically brought into prominence the typical designation, the 'New' or 'messianic People of God.' The importance attributed by the Council to this understanding of the Church is by no means misplaced, though not a few have found this shift of emphasis disconcerting, seeing in it a weakening of fundamental Catholic teaching.[3] Before going further, then, we will do well to consider the relations between these two great titles. The bond between them is to be found in the Church's further title 'the Bride of Christ.'

Israel was first designated as the Bride of the LORD at a time when she was paying Him scant attention. His people had been deeply corrupted morally and were worshipping the LORD only externally while serving the idols of the pagans. Yet it was then, just a few years before the destruction of the northern kingdom, to which principally He spoke, that He chose through

---

[1] *Lumen Gentium* #9.

[2] It was St. Paul who first declared the Church to be Christ's Body: "The Son of His love...is the head of the Body, the Church" {Col.1:13, 18; so, also, Eph.1:22–23}. Cf. Rom.12:5 and I Cor.12:12–27, which also look far beyond the local church. Medieval and later theologians tended to speak of her as the Mystical Body of Christ, a terminology earlier used rather of the Eucharist. Cf. Henri de Lubac, *Corpus Mysticum*, 2nd ed., Paris: Aubier (1949), *pp* 197–202; *Méditation sur l'église*, (no place): Aubier-Montaigne (1968), 3rd ed., *pp* 112–117. (Series *Foi Vivante*, #60, *Ch* 4, sect. 4).

[3] Their reaction was triggered mostly, I think, by a gross misconception, propagated by many theologians who ought to have known better. These were arguing that 'People of God' be taken as signifying that the Church is some sort of democracy or republic. That such a position cannot be attributed to the Council without absurdity is evident, to go no further in argument, simply from the typology upon which alone the title rests. Indeed, the great sin of Aaron, Israel's high priest, lay precisely in his yielding to the popular will (Ex.32:21–25).

Hosea to remind them that from the time He had brought them out of Egypt He had loved them as a people and had chosen them as His very own, the way a young man chooses his bride. Thus, as type for the Church, 'the Bride of the LORD' is prefigurative rather than preparative, based on God's free selection of His Bride; and the later prophets saw it as resuming all His calls to His people following upon His choice of them in Egypt.

Both designations, 'People' and 'Bride,' belong to the literal sense of the Scriptures, the one directly and prosaically, the other indirectly by means of metaphor. As one can see from Ezech.16, the metaphor of Israel as the Bride of the LORD, even when greatly elaborated and expanded, does not set aside the historical aspects of the type that is the People of God. Yet God's love for His people and His faithfulness, as also Israel's ingratitude, are given a prominence through this metaphor that are not as evident in the detailed narratives of the historical books.

Christ's Church, the New Israel, is the Lord's Bride, now come of age and ready to bear Him children. Hence, she is our Mother, who bears us virginally by the action of the Holy Spirit on behalf of the eternal Son made flesh.[4] As the Bride of Christ and our Mother, she conceives each Christian by the Holy Spirit and brings him to birth at baptism. She then nurtures and teaches him in Christ, instructing him and assisting him truly to recapitulate in Christ, calling him back whenever he falls by sin into a mere reliving of some part of Israel's life.

The bond, then, between 'the People of God' and the 'Body of Christ' is provided by an understanding of the symbolism of Christian marriage. It is this symbolism that has been God's instrument in raising marriage to the supernatural order. But, as Jesus pointed out, the essence of marriage is that man and woman, though two, become one flesh (Mt.19:4–6). So, the People of God, as Christ's Bride, is to be made one flesh with Him, His own Body (Eph.5:29–32).

But the union between Christ and His Church has not been consummated; nor will it be till after the final Judgment, when He appears in His glory to take her to Himself, every stain and defilement of sin spattered upon her by her members removed. She is now His Espoused, not yet His Wife. But, if so, then how can one speak of her being one flesh with Him?

The ambiguities introduced by the tension between descriptions of the Church as she is on earth and as she will be in heaven are well known and long pondered by theologians.[5] Nor are they to be found only in the doctrine of the Mystical Body of Christ but also in other descriptions of the Church, such as the Kingdom of God[6] and His Sheepfold.

[4] A brief analysis of the easily misunderstood complexities of this figure is given in Quay, *Christian Meaning*, *pp* 53–56.

[5] Thus, one finds them indicated in 638 A.D. by the 6th Council of Toledo (DS 493) and in the 13th Century by St. Thomas (ST III, 8, 3 c) who deals with them conjointly with other relationships of actuality and potentiality between the Church and her members. More directly, the relation between the Bride and the Body is indicated in the abrupt return of bridal imagery in II Vatican's treatment of the Body of Christ in *Lumen Gentium*, #7, last paragraph.

[6] Cf. *Lumen Gentium*, #5, first and second paragraphs, with #9, par. 2.

The simplest response we might make for the moment would be to argue that a careful reading of the key passage (Eph.5:22–33) shows that Paul does indeed find his notion of the Church as Christ's Body suggested by marital consummation, yet carefully avoids any indication that such consummation has as yet occurred between Christ and the Church. Yet this could hardly be satisfactory if one were to press *vv* 31–32. Rather, the very structure of these ambiguities, generated by their seeming oscillation between this age and the age to come, shows that we are dealing here with anagogical typology.[7] Since, however, for reasons to be seen in a moment, 'the Body of Christ' lies in largest measure outside the range of our inquiry, I shall leave to another occasion the needed development of anagogy, say what we shall need concerning the Body, and move on to the other designations already mentioned.

B. The Body of Christ

'The Body of Christ' is, I believe, the Church's sole title that has no direct Old Testament precedent. We might surmise, then, that it is this last of her great titles, unique and without type of any kind but belonging solely to the New Testament, that shows the Church as not merely a fulfilment of all that has taken place in Israel but as something utterly novel in the world.

For, the Church is the Body that is constituted by and lives with the life of Jesus given by His Spirit as its "soul."[8] But, as seen above,[9] the most striking newness of the New Covenant is the gift of the Holy Spirit Personally, first to Jesus, constituting Him Messiah, and then through the Christ to His Church.[10] Though this newness in Christ is most strikingly shown in the life the Christian is meant to live once he has gone beyond recapitulation into the full life of the Spirit, the Spirit is also active, albeit more quietly, in those not so far advanced. The fact that the Church is Christ's Body is, then, an integral and even defining element of that newness that makes the New Testament discontinuously new and not a mere continuation of the Old.[11]

Thus those who felt that a replacement of 'the Body of Christ' by 'the People of God' would be a grave impoverishment for the Church were correct. The doctrine of the Mystical Body of Christ is intrinsically the most exalted and spiritually profound of the Church's teachings about her own nature. But there is no question of replacement, as any adequate index to the Council's documents makes clear. Certainly, no other Ecumenical Council

---

[7] Cf. *Ch.* 7.D.2, *p* 161.

[8] This is the language of Leo XIII, repeated by Pius XII in *Mystici Corporis* (cf. DS 3408), because of a certain analogy with the way the soul is present in the human body. This vivifying presence of the Spirit not only makes the Body live but makes it active in the world through His charisms. It is worth noting the apparent contrast with the other scriptural (and typical) image of the Spirit dwelling within the Church as in His temple; indeed, within Jesus and within each of the faithful as in His temple.

[9] *Pp* 196–197.

[10] "[I]t [the Church] is as it were another Christ." *Mystici Corporis* #66 (DS 3806).

[11] Had the leaders of Israel accepted Jesus and, thus, been made members of His Body, though the discontinuity brought by the fulness of life in the Spirit would have remained, there would have been no cleavage into an Old Israel and a New.

has ever expressed so fully the doctrine of the Body of Christ as did II Vatican in ##7–8 of *Lumen Gentium*. But since Christians had largely lost understanding of the spiritual senses of the Scripture and this, as we shall see later,[12] to their own great harm, the Council gave greatest stress to the title that would require a renewed understanding of types and fulfilment.

It would, moreover, be a serious error so to distinguish these titles of the Church as if they constituted discrete and nonoverlapping categories. Quite the contrary. Even as each of the four Gospels speaks of the same reality yet each shows aspects not easily found in the others and where, moreover, the sublimity of St. John does not render St. Mark superfluous, so each of the Church's titles points to different but not divided aspects of her role in the life and growth of Christians.

Since we have been chiefly concerned with recapitulation by the individual Christian, we shall, for reasons that will appear as we go, begin to treat of the Church as the Body of Christ, then as His Bride. Finally, and in much greater detail, we shall consider her as the New People of God. Nonetheless, while maintaining the diversity of the descriptions indicated by the various titles, I shall make no effort to keep them wholly distinct, much less separate.

As suggested a few paragraphs back, it is through 'the Body of Christ,' that one comes best to understand the role of the Holy Spirit in providing within the Church the essential conditions necessary or helpful for the recapitulative growth of each individual Christian. For this mystery is that of our ever stronger identification with Christ, both in His earthly life and as risen, till we are united with Him in glory in heaven. This identification, by which as we share His life and His Spirit, makes us members of Christ, cells of His Body.[13] The doctrine of the Mystical Body, then, is that of the New Creation, of our fulness of life in the Spirit.[14]

Through this title, one can begin to comprehend the basic and stable spiritual structures of the Church along with their perennial functions. So, one discerns the members, organs, and tissues that, by their abiding interactions and cohesion and by their common nurture and their sharing mutually in a single life, make the body able to act in and upon the world.

Since all Christians are in Christ, even if as dead cells about to be sloughed off, the sole head of His Body, the Church, is Christ in glory. There He has preceded us and thence He animates His Body by the Holy Spirit, who pours out the love of God within each cell. Since the doctrinal emphasis

---

[12] *Ch* 20 below.

[13] St. Paul refers only to members of the Body (to head and hand and foot) and to organs (to eye and ear) but not to tissues or cells. Since he had no need to refer to these latter in order to make his point, his failure to mention them does not seem exclusive, especially since presumably neither he nor his readers had any knowledge of cells. Since this cellular analogy can provide more insight today and images of greater utility, without losing anything of what Paul was saying with his, I have chosen to speak of the individual Christian as a cell, however specialized, in Christ's Body.

[14] Our being made sons of God in Christ by the indwelling Spirit, is evidently related to this notion of membership in His Body; but it is no longer cast in terms of metaphor but in terms, however inadequate, intended to state literally the reality.

rests upon His glorious and resurrected Body, enthroned with the Father, this doctrine of His Mystical Body comes closest of all the Church's titles to offering a timeless view of her life.[15]

Christ is the Head; the Church, His Body; both together, the Whole Christ, Head and members. The members of the Church are Christ's members. These themes were endlessly and lovingly developed by St. Augustine and the other Fathers. As one brief example, we may refer to this extract from Pope St. Leo I.[16]

> Consider who has taken us into Himself, and whom we have taken into ourselves, for just as the Lord Jesus has been made our flesh by being born, so also we have been made His own body by being reborn. And so we are members of Christ and the temple of the Holy Spirit.

As cells in the Body of Him whom the Holy Spirit anointed with His own fulness, Christians too live with the life of the Spirit, through whom the love of God is poured out in their hearts (Rom.5:5) so that they, like Jesus, can address God as Abba, Father (Rom.8:15). Further, since Christ's life is typified by the Old Testament, so in Him is that of each member of His Body. It is membership in the Church that incorporates us into Christ, thus making possible our recapitulation, through which we mature into less unworthy members of the Church.

What He did, therefore, His Body must also do,[17] albeit imperfectly and often reluctantly and slowly. Each cell is to live with the common life of all the cells together, each contributing its own function and activity, and each receiving its share of the common sustenance by which all live and work.

But if the Church is the Body within which each Christian grows, each is nourished and supported through the mediation of the various organs of the Body, each of which has been constituted for a particular spiritual function. One's family, raised to the supernatural level by the sacraments of matrimony and a common baptism, is meant to represent the Church to him when young, to be that organ of the Church most completely and importantly present to him in his early growth.

C. Virginal Bride and Mother

As mentioned above, the strongest link between the understandings of the Church as God's People and as Christ's Body lies in her being Christ's Bride and, most especially, the Mother of every Christian. It is she who is the Mother of all the living—the New Eve, the Bride espoused to the New Adam, still a virgin until the consummation in heaven, yet the Mother of us all.[18]

---

[15] It might conceivably be possible to mark out stages in the life of the Church built on the physical growth of Christ's body. But it is far from easy to see how this might be done; still less, what usefulness it might have.

[16] CCL 138: *Sancti Leonis Magni Romani Pontificis Tractatus Septem et Nonaginta*, ed. A. Chevasse, Turnhout: Brepols (1973),"Tractatus XXIII (de Nativitate 3)," #5, *p* 107.

[17] II Vatican Council, *Lumen Gentium*, #7, par. 5–6.

[18] Henri de Lubac, S.J., *Méditation sur l'église*, *pp* 268–269, but indeed all of *Ch* VII and IX.

For we have already been reborn into newness of life by baptism. It is the baptismal font that is, according to the Fathers, the womb of the Church, from which she brings forth virginally, by the operation of the Holy Spirit, the members of Christ's Mystical Body even as Mary brought forth virginally, by the overshadowing of the Holy Spirit, the members of Christ's physical Body. Hence, it is also the Church, as our Mother, who nurtures and guards and helps us to grow to maturity in Christ.

The Church, then, as Mother for every Christian, is called to care for each in such a way that he can find through her that which he needs at his current stage of individual development if he is to develop further. So, the Church must always be, at once and everywhere, pre-patriarchal, patriarchal, Mosaic, monarchic, prophetic, exiled, rebuilding her devastated structures, and waiting through seemingly endless time, strong in law, devout in worship, for the coming of the Lord—yet also overflowing with the manifest charisms of the Holy Spirit. All recapitulative stages must always be at home in her and accessible to all her children, scattered as they are through the various stages of growth in Christ, in a way that is distinctively and integrally Christian. Otherwise, the Christian's growth fails to find an adequate bodily site and organic spiritual support. Being deprived of the appropriate elements of religious culture with which to interact, he will be seriously hampered in his efforts to mature through all the stages of his recapitulation. The time-scale for his growth may then be that of millennia, not of decades.

If, then, the Church should in some place and time simply reproduce one or other stage of Israel's growth, not recapitulating it but mimicking it or attempting to reconstruct it, say, as Calvin did at Geneva, all that she would do there for her children would be to help them grow at that original rate. One life would not suffice for more than an infinitesimal fraction of what is called for. A person might pass during his life from the level of Deborah, say, to that of Gideon. Recall the Roundheads. Refusing patristic tradition, they sought to live according to the Old Testament pattern not, however, through the Church and the sacraments but much as ancient Israel did. So, despite their intentions, they became, spiritually speaking, rather like Jews of Moses' or Joshua's days and ceased in some essential ways to be Christian at all.

It is not this that God wished to offer us through the Church. She must sum up rightly and through the abundance of the Spirit what nature and God's "ordinary grace" take millennia to achieve. She has taken into herself and makes present to her children all the life of God's people from the beginning, not as those events originally took place but as they were summed up in Jesus' life. It is this process of nurturing the Christian according to his spiritual needs that shows best her maternity.

She nourishes the Christian through the sacraments and the Mass; through teaching how to meditate upon the Scriptures in the light of her entire Tradition, and giving other instruction in prayer; through the influence of the saints; movements of popular devotion; involvement in the great range of the corporal works of mercy through hospitals, care for prisoners, assisting the poor both in their immediate need and in laboring for social justice and for peace; and the spiritual works of mercy, especially evangelization and truly Christian intellectual formation.

Nurturing by the Church would seem, however, more strongly emphasized by the image of the Christian as a cell in the Body or as a member of God's People since, as a part or member of the Church, he lives within her. Her maternal image evidently adds an element of personal tenderness that is lacking to either of the others. But far more important than this element and unique to the maternal symbolism is the fact that, precisely insofar as she is the Mother of Christ's People, she does *not* contain them and is not composed of them but is other than they, as a mother is other than her children. Through his awareness of the Church as his mother, the individual Christian comes to understand her, despite his oneness with her as part of her, as something distinct and different from himself. She is a complex social being that has her own dynamic center, her own principle of organization and action, elsewhere than in him. She is not only greater than he but in some way external to him.[19]

Like her type in *Ezechiel*, she who is the Bride bears children that are distinct from her, who may be adopted by the Father of the Bridegroom but are not begotten by Him upon her.[20] Hence, as a child of the Church, the Christian is not one with her; nor do his misdeeds make her evil. She remains the *holy* Catholic Church, the beloved Bride, without spot or wrinkle or any such thing (Eph.5:27), despite the terrible sins of her children.

It is this need for the Church not merely to bring us to birth in Christ but, once we are born, to act as our Mother and as Mother for all the People of God that determines the visible structures of the Church. For, insofar as the Church is Mother, she has two essential aspects that need to be seen together while held carefully distinct. On the one hand, she is alive with her own life, which has its own rhythms of growth and development, its own exigencies of work and repose. She interacts with all the world around her, universal in her interests and activity. On the other hand, she is the one who is to nurture each of her children personally and tenderly. She is meant to manifest God's love for each individual and is to focus her attention and to adapt her activity to the needs and even the pleasure of each. It is her task to teach each of us at the appropriate time that portion of the fulness of Christ's truth that he needs to know if he is to grow well in the Lord.[21]

---

[19] This externality is strongly felt also in her relations with any people to whom she comes in order to teach them of Christ—for she is the Mother of the nations, not just of individuals; cf. *Ch* 19, Sect. A, pp 381–384. The image of the Church as Bride serves an equivalent function with respect to her relations to Christ, insofar as she is other than He.

[20] Cf. Quay, *Christian Meaning, pp* 51–54 for a fuller treatment of this matter.

[21] That both these aspects coexist and interact without confusion is the mark of a healthy organism—if one may use such a term of the Church without disrespect—not merely of good organization. In an organization, the individual is subordinated to the group; he is valued for his contribution to its goals. What he does or thinks is of small concern as long as this does not hinder the soundness of structure and smooth functioning of the organization. But his personal activities cease to be tolerated as soon as they seriously interfere with the efforts of the group. The actions of the organization take cognizance of its members as persons only to the extent that it cannot function well without their contributions. Obviously, there is need for organizations within man's world—their existence is one of the marks of his humanity. But the Church is not

Both the Church's nurturing of her children and the principle of her own life function simultaneously within her. What belongs to her own characteristic life in the Spirit is universal. She knows but "one body and one Spirit,...one hope that belongs to [our] call, one Lord, one faith, one baptism, one God and Father of us all" (Eph.4:4–6). She has everywhere the same doctrine, the same moral requirements, the same sacraments, the same Mass, the same need for law, the same papacy, the same priesthood. The other aspect shows itself in her particularities of sacramental and Eucharistic rituals, in the multiplicity of legitimate theologies and catechetical styles, in the diversity of laws and even of basic types of law in the different patriarchates, in the diversity of clergy and their functions,[22] in her popular "devotions"; in brief, in all the particular structures that have made her "the institutional Church."

The universal aspects of the Church's life are universal in time—perpetual—as well as in place. Conversely, her particularities are temporal, appearing, changing, often vanishing. The Church, then, remaining ever herself, has yet her own history; and the rate of the development of her structures is rarely the rate of growth of the individual Christian.

Further, what is universal in the Church can be experienced and discovered only in and through the diverse particularities of her living forms and structures. Neither aspect can exist without the other. Though her sacraments are universal, each can be effected only by individual Christians in accordance with some particular rite for the benefit of other, equally individual Christians. Her doctrine is universal, yet it exists in this world only in the limited minds and hearts of individual believers. The papacy is universal, but can only function through the particular men who are popes. As is true of her Spouse, what is divine in her is incarnate in human nature (unlike His, of course, her humanity is smirched with her children's ignorance and sins). But it is this very materiality of her institutional being that enables her to act as our Mother.

Both the universal and perpetual on the one hand and the particular and transient on the other are essential to the Church's spiritual mission. As seen in Part II, the universal and perpetual pattern for every man's spiritual progress from conception till his entry into the fulness of the Christian life as lived in the power of the Holy Spirit is to be found in the often dull, often repellent, often seemingly unintelligible details of a few, ancient Semitic tribal histories. So, for the gentiles no less than for Israel, both aspects are essential, working together against the remanent effects of original sin. Most of what needs to be said about these spiritual functions has already been detailed in Part II. A few, further comments on the "institutional Church" may, however, be useful.

---

one of them, however much at times she may seem to be but little more.

[22] It is well to remember that priests of the second rank were instituted by the apostles or their immediate successors, even as were the deacons a few years earlier, in order to meet the particular needs of the local congregations and to deal with individuals personally. Cf. Ceslas Spicq, *Les épitres pastorales*, 4th ed., Paris: Gabalda (1969), *pp* 65–73, 541–551.

Excursus: The "Institutional Church"

a) The Problems

One perennial problem for Christians, though it has taken varied forms over the centuries, is that which has been called in recent times "the problem of the institutional Church." One thinks of the early Church in its structural simplicity, its lack of creeds and defined dogmas, the nonexistence of ecclesiastical censures and penalties, the boldness of Paul rebuking Peter at Antioch, and so on. Then one contrasts this with today's complex, publically manifest, visibly organized, sedate, tradition-bound, socially structured establishment that is called the Catholic Church.

Quite apart from the historical question as to just how unstructured or how noninstitutional the early Church was, one must admit that there were in those days no seminaries, no marriage tribunals, no papal thrones, no handbooks of moral theology, no novenas, no Codes of Canon Law. It is also true that, whether such "incrustations" are useful or not, whether they are compatible with Gospel simplicity or not, most of the institutional structures decried are entirely of human origin, devised well after our Lord's time, and could, presumably without irreparable harm, be done away with tomorrow. The question, then, is: Why can't we do without all this legalistic and juridical structure, this institutional craze for more and more dogmas, more and more declarations that this or that modern, science-based activity is sinful? At the least, can we not get rid of the papal curia and international ecclesiastical diplomacy and episcopal chanceries?

Any Catholic for whom all this is, in whatever degree, large or small, a real problem and not merely an intellectual exercise will be aware that in just the practices that give rise to his problem or, even more, in the attitudes these practices indicate, the Church impinges upon his awareness as other than he.[23] It is his Holy Mother the Church whose activities and attitudes, lying well beyond his control or even understanding, ground his problem.

As Mother of every Christian, even of those who have wandered away or scornfully rejected her, the Church is called to deal with each person individually. It is for just this purpose that she has become "institutionalized." Her essential structures have been concretized in varied manners in order to meet, as well as the Christians of each time and place have known how, the needs and the desires of the individual believer, for each of whom she is Mother.

There is no small irony, then, hidden in this problem of the

[23] The slogan, "We are the Church," stale left-over from the Council of Basel (de Lubac, *La foi chrétienne: Essai sur la structure du Symbole des Apôtres*, Paris: Aubier-Montaigne, [1969], *pp* 174–176), fails not only through its claiming for the part what belongs only to the whole (usually the right to determine some point of Christian doctrine or morality) but also because it is employed in large measure just when the part is most aware of the Church Universal as other than itself. Few are those who would insist, "We are our Mother." Indeed, the slogan seems to be used most commonly by those who are least inclined to speak of her as their Mother.

"institutional Church." For, the structures of the Church to which objection is made have come about in large measure precisely as efforts to transform and adapt the rocklike solidity of her universal and perennial nature to the local, even to the individual situation. Through parishes and their priests each Catholic can be reached—not only with the sacraments and communal worship but with individual instruction and spiritual advice. The same effort to adapt not only to the needs of individuals but to their inclinations and preferences can be seen also in the existence of Catholic schools, base communities, the Young Christian Workers, Marriage Encounter, Catholic Boy Scouts and Girl Scouts, Christian Life Communities, and the endless array of voluntary organizations of Catholic men and women.

These particularizations have, of course, been devised by individuals of varied cultures and very different degrees of Christian maturity. Human ignorance and sinfulness act as perennial limitations on the rightness of any such adaptation. Often, indeed, they render the adaptation not merely less effective but harmful. Hence, the Church Universal has, in different ways and to different degrees, reserved to herself the right to regulate the local applications. For she has often seen particular, seemingly merely extrinsic modifications or adaptations gradually distort the essentials of her life while the local church remains unaware of the damage.[24]

Correlative, then, to the Church's maternal adaptability is the adaptability required of each of her children to much that is contingent, transient, even nugatory. The "problem of the institutional Church" in large measure lies here: we do not wish so to adapt, but want all else to adapt to us. This, however, is a spiritual problem in the individual person, of which we shall speak more in a moment, not a problem with the Church.[25]

It is true, of course, that if a mother chooses to "live her own life," scanting the emotional or physical needs of her children, which may indeed often require her to renounce her own preferences and even needs, her children suffer. But it is also true that each child must learn humility enough to accept the fact that he cannot be the sole center of her attention and concern. So, as in a family, Christians may have to live with particular forms and structures of Catholic life that they find banal or unpleasant or even hurtful. What each must acknowledge is that this is basically a good thing. It humbles one's pride and forces him to recognize that even for things in no way perpetual or essential there may be no legitimate way to improve them.

---

[24] Historically, it has been the various patriarchates that have served as the chief units for such supervision.

[25] A variation upon this problem of the institutional Church will be familiar to most: "If only the old Italians (or Poles) were ousted from high places in the Church, things would be tolerable"; or "If only the nobility were done away with! or the marxist sympathizers! or the capitalists! or the liberals!" Most of this, however, is little more than a disguised form of revolt against God's permitting of others' sins and wrong-doing—or what one takes as such. One forgets that it is through just such evils that He desires to purify us and to draw us out of our own sinfulness. The temptation here is to "dream of systems so perfect that no one will have to be good." Such dreams, as should by now be clear, have no place in a Christian world.

b) The spiritual value of the "institutional Church"

Rather than focus directly on the spiritual problem underlying the "problem of the institutional Church," I prefer here to show why the Church's ministry, with all the weaknesses of her members and of her particular structures, is still the most effective of all aids in healing the wound left by original sin. It is as our Mother that she is intended by Christ to cajole us into working against the psychic self-centeredness that negates the traits of the trinitarian life for which we were created. As we come to know God's love for us through her, we cease to fear that our moral repulsiveness has cast us out into an alien world without hope.

Speaking generally, one notes that, though positive knowledge of the nature of the real world is a fundamental good for man, yet much of what moves him to the hard labor needed to gain such knowledge lies in those unyielding and sharp-edged features that disappoint his expectations, resist his desires, contradict his prior thoughts or modes of understanding, and, perhaps most of all, impose limits upon his freedom.

All our lives we are constrained by our expectations, spontaneous and often quite invisible to ourselves, that things should be or act in certain ways, expectations drawn from analogies with our already lived experience, whether through mere conditioned reflex or through the deepest level of intellectual understanding. We learn, slowly, to condition our expectations, not to act too quickly upon them, to look before we leap. Yet, because of the unending richness of the diversity and complexity of the world, we are often painfully disappointed in our expectations, for even the most genuine human understanding is unbelievably incomplete.

One could, of course, sulk like the small child or snatch what one can from life without worrying about the morality of one's acts. But one mark of adulthood is to have outgrown such childishness and to have learned to rejoice inwardly at the new, even if painful, perspectives on reality opened to one's mind and heart by such disappointed expectations.

So it is within the Church. Believing firmly in her divine origins, we may be chagrined by the all-too-human weaknesses of her children, especially those given the greater responsibilities. Expecting the pope to be, according to the demands of his office, among the holiest of men, and the other bishops likewise in their own degree, we can be deeply disappointed if we think them far from this ideal.[26] Thus, many a young man or woman has left the Church because of the harshness or greed of some bishop or priest. Some have been driven close to despair by false expectations of the way in which the sacraments should work to effect his holiness and moral integrity. Similar disillusionment can arise from one's experience of "failure" in prayer.

In any case, as for our other expectations, it is the mark of adulthood that we learn how to profit from such disappointments by further growth in understanding. If only we realized our opportunity, we would also see that much more than psychic maturity can be gained through such circumstances.

---

[26] Needless to say, it happens not infrequently that our perceptions of them can be badly mistaken. But this does not prevent the painful experience based on what we think to know.

For here, most of all, we can grow in that most basic knowledge of reality which is given by true faith. Through acceptance of this truth in full, our self-love is checked and subordinated to a growing love for Christ, provided that we resist vigorously the resentments that are, at bottom, nothing more noble than self-pity and injured pride.

As to our freedom, the very nature of real existence in the world imposes limits upon it: on what we might like to do, on what we can do, on what we ought to do; indeed, upon what we are or can or ought to become. The endless determinisms of the world, inside ourselves even more than those external to us, exist in part for the testing and forming of our freedom. What we cannot change, we must not only accept but learn how to live with gladly, as part of God's world. Even if it be a damaged part, through it our sins can be the better repented and our trust in God and firmness of faith made to grow.

Only youthful ignorance or adult stupidity can think, "I can become whatever I want!"—unless one has already wisely and drastically limited one's wants. Every particular structure, e.g., a see-saw or swing, one's family or school, one's sexuality, one's array of talents and temperament, even if first perceived as an opportunity for new activity or pleasure, before long may also be seen as a restriction upon one's freedom of choice. For, any limitation, whatever its nature, is easily experienced by fallen man as some sort of constraint upon his liberty.

The limitations imposed, then, by the universal aspects of the Church in their local embodiments help her children directly to grow beyond all claims to an unreal freedom. Her institutional structures of whatever sort invite the Christian to learn that his freedom is not absolute and that his good can only be found within the range of the possible. Some things we would, if left to ourselves, regard as impossible for us, e.g., perfect chastity outside of marriage. But the doctrine of the Church asserts the contrary; her clerical and Religious structures show what is possible with the grace of Christ; and the virtues of repentance and hope are strengthened, in case of falls, through her sacraments of Penance and the Eucharist. On the other hand, some things we may insist in our ignorance to be possible or desirable, such as the ordaining of women or the marrying of men already ordained as priests, which the Church asserts to be impossible or undesirable in principle. No one, of course, can be forced to an adult and realistic liberty. Yet the value of the Church's structures and institutions for humble growth through an ever wider perception and acceptance of reality is manifest.

The ordinary response of one conceived in sin, as he gradually awakens to his own uniqueness, is to demand that the world should somehow adapt to this unique being that he himself is. It should help him grow, help him to realize his natural powers fully, even aid and form him spiritually, in brief, make him at least a local center of the world's attention and action—another recognizable relic of original sin.

But from the nature of things, the world neither will nor can adapt itself in any appreciable measure to anyone. The smallest Christian community, that of an infant's parents, is incapable of adapting at all times and in all circumstances to all his desires, or even to all of his genuine needs. It is perfectly possible for an infant to need things desperately which mother and father simply cannot provide. Poverty, to say nothing of disease, flood, famine, and war, may prove insurmountable. More importantly, there are the child's psychic needs, many of which no one at the time may perceive or understand.

Long antecedent to any questions concerning institutions and their rightful activities and structures or of their abuses of their powers, the fundamental condition of every human being is that he can neither come to be outside of community nor can he live within a community either as its unconditional center or in complete independence of it. By the very existence of that community of which he is a part, he must be structurally related to it in ways that he has not chosen and that do not depend upon him for their mode of action. They may be accountable for him; but they can be in only a limited degree accountable to him.

The same is true of the local Christian community, still more of the whole Church. It is impossible, without destroying her, for the Church's general and universal structures to be altered so as to meet the desires of all of her subcommunities, whether local churches, parishes, families, or individuals.[27] There is no way that the Church Universal, no matter what her institutional and structural forms, however culturally varied and modified, can always adapt herself even to true needs or wholly legitimate demands, to say nothing of the desires and hopes, of the various individuals and groups within her. Her efforts to adapt to her children's needs can be rendered difficult or impossible through lack of priests and catechists, the devastation wrought by heresy, or the fierceness of persecution, to name but three reasons out of many. If, then, adaptation to the the individual cannot usually be effected beyond a certain level, maybe such adaptation is not desirable. If things cannot be, then presumably they ought not be. Hence, once again, what is called "the problem of the institutional Church" is constituted in part by her universality insofar as this requires men to relativize their self-centered concerns, draws them out of themselves, and helps them resist the urge to make all things center on themselves. We may not dismiss the Church as not our concern because she is not what we desire.

But, whatever be the adaptability that the concrete structures of the Church require of us for spiritual growth in Christ, still one may legitimately ask: what if some of the structures at a particular time and place are bad or evil structures? Did not Jesus Himself set us the example by overturning such structures?

As already indicated, adaptation need not involve conformity. Long before the transition to the life governed by the Holy Spirit, one must often recapitulate not by doing what the majority is doing, when that is bad, but by doing the opposite, accomplishing well that which is then to be done. This can on occasion involve a tearing down of what has been long established in order to rebuild it or put something else in its place. What is essential,

[27] We shall consider in c) below a second and quite different problem concerning the structures of the Church.

however, if the corrective activity is truly to serve a spiritual good, is that it be done from charity and in truth, not from yielding to the resentments and angers roused by the relics of the sin in which one was born.

We can now see better why at least an implicit understanding of recapitulation is essential in Church renewal. For, in a reformer's zeal to renew, he may set a high, truly spiritual ideal, one that is objectively wholly correct and good, and seek to wash away all that is inferior. The result is, of course, that those who need part or all of the lower levels, who could never hope to reach his high spiritual ideal without them, are automatically cut off from the aids to growth that would make the ideal possible for them. They cannot grow properly because the means of growth are now being denied them. This was the great fault of Protestant iconoclasm and the moral severity of so many of the Calvinist Reformers. It also serves to explain why the perhaps excessive humanism of the Baroque should have proved the seedbed for the great spiritual renewal of the Church during the late 16th and early 17th Centuries.

One might argue that by sweeping all these human encrustations away one clears the air and lets the full brilliance of the Gospel appear; by the shock, the tepid will be jolted out of their spiritual slumbers and brought finally to grow as they ought. This need not be wholly wrong. Growth can often be very painful, and a jolt can sometimes do much good. But not all pain is helpful for growth, any more than all changes are for the better. And if, by one's reforms, the conditions for others' further growth in Christ are destroyed, it is not clear how one can claim to be acting in accord with God's grace.

Something similar may be noted for the particular charge of "legalism." To begin with, there exists no Church legal structure established uniformly for all patriarchates. And many, if not most, of the extant structures of Church law are merely efforts to adapt the universal law of God to concrete individual situations, even to the actions of a handful of individual people.

Yet the Church must always have that firmness and consistency of structure and response that enables people to grow, whatever their level of development. There is always, then, as mentioned above,[28] a need for some form of law in the Church if there is to be the possibility for genuine recapitulation beyond early adolescence. The adolescent must be enabled to grow by being subjected to law; he must also be able to grow by pushing against that law and finding that it will not yield to him. Only so will he believe that it comes ultimately from God and far surpasses his personal interests. He must be subjected to an authority to which he can rightly submit or, if he chooses, rebel against, even if this reaction be excessive. But, above all else, he is to learn, from the grace of Christ within him, how He lived with regard to law and authority and to the particularized structures of the Judaism of His day, and do likewise.

As seen when we were speaking of the transition from recapitulation in Christ to the fulness of the life of the Spirit, law exists not only to foster growth directly through obedience and, perhaps, resistance but to be

---

[28] *Pp* 233–241.

transcended. Not only in matters of law but in regard to all the Church's structures, one who is recapitulating in Christ must learn continually to transcend their historical or literal functions and to see them all spiritually. But if the structures are not there, they cannot be transcended.

The process of transcending God's law is not an acting independently of it, still less its violation. Rather, the law is interiorized. The young adult increasingly behaves himself rightly because he sees and senses internally that it is a good thing to behave oneself according to God's commandments. His reasons for behaving himself are now part of him, not as automatic reflexes, as in a well-trained dog, but because he himself has freely chosen to live according to the law and has thus come to assimilate it as a good that expresses his real self, which is injured when he does the opposite.

This is one reason why the Church is intensely hated by many who know little or nothing of her teaching. If one wants to remake the world, whether out of mere selfishness or from some mode of altruism, thinking to rid the world of evil by one's own activity, sooner or later one is confronted with the question: What do you do about people who oppose you and resist your plans, especially at those critical junctures where it seems that, if only you could undo their opposition, you could succeed? You might, unimaginatively, do as Marxists or some of their right-wing opponents tend to do and simply kill everyone who is in the way. The alternative, more subtle and more effective, is to form a malleable people, people whose internal structure, if not completely determined by those in power, is at least capable of being molded to any shape whatever and, indeed, of being remolded indefinitely.

Now, the Church, with her divine authority and consistent trumpeting of God's commands, is the single greatest enemy of such malleability. If anything stands out sharply in the Old Testament that is in contrast with other cultures, it is the internal character, psychological individuality, of the persons formed by God in Israel. The New Testament carries this process endlessly further still. Small wonder, then, that those who want to mold people to fit their projects find the Church their enemy, even when churchmen have become malleable and willing to betray their charge.

c) The second problem of the "institutional Church"

Before ending this Excursus, we should note that there exists a second, more far reaching and dangerous "problem" with the "institutional Church": "It is not these particularized structures for adaptation that bother us. We could get along with such well enough, remaking them as needed. No, what bothers us are the structures of authority, those supposedly aboriginal Christian structures of pope and bishops and priests, of unalterable and essential dogmas, the mass of moral demands and prohibitions, stifling all creative liberty—all those things that lay claim to bind us in conscience."

The more honest anti-institutionalist will argue that all discussion of adaptation, whether by the Church or by the individual, simply shows the essential error of the institutionalist. The latter instinctively thinks of the Church as a great, elaborate, but monolithic whole; he fails wholly to see that his arguments concerning adaptation would collapse as soon as he thought of the Church as a congeries of small, highly flexible, local associations, which could meet each individual's various needs and legitimate desires, subject only to the constraints imposed by nature itself. Is not the Church of Christ, as one sees it in the New Testament and other early writings, composed of just such small, local communities, bound together only by their faith in Jesus, vigor of communal life, and some common elements of prayer and worship?

The answer to this question is, I believe, "No."[29] The anti-institutionalist positions often speak easily of the People of God, forgetting that this term was given its meaning long before their democratizing imaginings. Antecedent to any Christian meaning, according simply to the literal sense, Israel in the desert was governed, however benignly, by Moses more absolutely than by any monarch. Even then there were structures—the seventy elders, various levitical ministries, the other tribal, clan, and familial structures, and an early form of Israelite priesthood. Even the patriarchs, as biblical archeologists are demonstrating ever more fully, moved in a world with strong moral and social norms and institutions. No mere clustering of individuals was ever regarded by Scripture as a people.

In a different way, the scriptural understanding of the Body of Christ has been emptied of its genuine content through taking too seriously such political language as that concerning "the body politic" and other weak though popular metaphors. The anti-institutionalist fails to see that the Church, like any being that lives by one single life-principle (in her case, the Holy Spirit), is infinitely more than a merely conceptual aggregation of independent and disparate parts. If the local groups are wholly independent of one another, then they constitute different churches, not parts of the one, living Church. Yet, as seen, it is to the Church as Mother that the anti-institutional positions are wholly blind. Unless some universal bond exist, normative and authoritative in the way any life-principle is, the Bride of Christ becomes a harem.

These positions can lead nowhere except to total disintegration of the Church and, ultimately, of civil society as well. Historically, those groups that espoused such positions in practice—not just in theory—have endlessly divided into ever smaller and stranger sects, as did the Anabaptists and the Puritans. One eventually falls back into the world of the most primitive cultures, whose level of maturity is no higher than that of the two-year-old, where all the world is a fairyland in which all things are possible.

What is at issue in this second "problem" is not the particularities of the Church's structures but her basic nature. It is the Christian faith itself that is thus questioned. The positive grounds for the Catholic response were presented throughout Part II and developed in this Part III. But detailed replies to the current swarming of anti-institutional objections belong properly in a treatise of apologetics.

---

[29] For a modern overview of the purely historical question, cf. Jean Daniélou, *The Theology of Jewish Christianity*, tr. J. A. Baker, London: Darton, Longman, & Todd (1964), *pp* 334, 346–356.

Chapter 18

The People of God: Recapitulation *by* the Church

One splendid image of the Church from the patristic era is that of the Church as the moon, reflecting the Sun of Justice, which is Christ. Like the moon, she waxes and wanes. At times she shines so resplendently with the light of Christ that it seems almost to be her own; at other times, His light grows faint and seems to disappear, so that there is almost total darkness—only on a clear night with no clouds can one discern the tiny sliver of light still there and, marvellously, in the new moon's arms the shadowy presence of the whole disk.[1] Useful as this image is, and as heartening in those times when it seems that it is not the clouds from outside that are hiding Christ's light from men but the degradation of the Church herself by her unworthy children, and as helpful as it is in pointing out to Christians the intrinsically time-conditioned nature of the Church's life, for all this, this image misses entirely the historical aspect of the Church. The waxing and the waning of the moon are perfectly cyclic, without any history discernible except to a sophisticated astronomer.

Further, the Church, apart from her embodiment and enfleshment in peoples and cultures, is not possible save as a theological abstraction. Since no body is immaterial or exempt from space and time, the Church, as Christ's Bride, to be made one flesh with Him, must always be, like Him, incarnate in a particular people and in a determinate culture and through a cetain span of historical time.

A. The Assembly of God's People

As seen above,[2] a better, temporally structured image of the Church is

[1] Henri de Lubac, "How is the Church a Mystery?", op. cit. *Ch* 3, note 2.

[2] *Pp* 343–346.

that of the New People of God, better because not merely an image but one aspect of her definition. She is the Great Congregation of the New Israel, led by the New Moses through the desert of this world. Indeed, she is the only Israel that is in full continuity of life with the Israel of the earlier Covenant. She is the Ecclesia, the vast Assembly of the Lord,[3] drawn together from all the world into Christ by the Holy Spirit for the glory of the Father. It is this aspect of the mystery of the Church that enables us to understand something of the complex process of the growth of an entire culture in Christ and to see human history in the light of faith.

All that was said of Israel in the Old Testament serves to typify the Church, Israel's antitype through her oneness with Christ, who leads her also as the New Joshua, the New David, and the New Jeremiah. She must grow as did her type, though in Christ. This she does, in part, by the aggregate social effect of the recapitulations of all her members. For, the recapitulation of the individual within the Church has, of necessity, a strongly social aspect. It is this social aspect that we wish to consider now, no longer in terms of the momentary interactions of the individual cells of the Body of Christ but through the centuries of cultural growth. No complete disjunction may be made, of course, since the life of a body is not disjoined from the lives of its cells. Further, whole peoples and cultures have been brought into the Church through the holiness and influence of one or a few of her members.[4]

Yet, the total effect of the growth of Christians among a people is not explicable solely as a sum of of individual recapitulations nor merely as a new kind of internal influence upon the culture. Rather, there exists for the Church, as for ancient Israel, a mode of recapitulation *by* the entire People of God, whether as one universal Kingdom or, more easily discerned by human minds, as she grows in each people or cultural region. For, as the Lord espoused Israel, when once she had reached "the age for love" (Ezech.16:8), but required of her yet further growth as His bride, so must the New Israel grow, even though already espoused to Christ. She too must continue to grow if she is to be worthy of her Spouse.

This growth, when first beginning among a new people, takes place in much the same, long, slow manner needed by the outcast, wild girl whom Ezechiel described.[5] But its proper mode is that of a life in company with her Spouse, yearning for the eschaton when their union is finally to be

[3] Cf. Num.20:4, Dt.23:1ff; also called the Assembly of God (Neh.13:1). See also *Lumen Gentium*, #9.

[4] Sometimes the Church's influence has been seen as coming simply from outside a people, as an influence infiltrating, forcing its way in, or being imposed by Catholic peoples through military force or through economic, scientific, or other modes of cultural imperialism. This point of view misconceives the way in which cultural interactions, even hostile ones, take place. The Church is made present by her members, whether these are a good influence or bad; and their impact on the culture is, through that culture's own response to their presence, internal to that culture, even when that influence is bad and the net impact destructive, as long as the people themselves are not simply wiped out.

[5] Even as this description does not begin with fallen Adam or with the Deluge or Babel, so also a people's recapitulation begins at whatever level they have reached when Christianity first comes to them.

consummated. Individual recapitulation is meant to come about rapidly, by the power of the grace of Christ, in less than a lifetime, in a few decades. The social effects of such successful recapitulation take much longer to work themselves out. And slower yet, the recapitulative growth of God's People takes place at more or less the same rate as the old Israel's.

New aspects of her life are always showing themselves in the Church. The New Israel has as much of a history as does the Old. Each group on earth, each nation, each culture, each portion of mankind, must recapitulate the life of ancient Israel in and through Jesus Christ in order to enter the fulness of salvation. For, till the end, "Salvation is from the Jews.... [Yet] neither on this mountain nor in Jerusalem will [men] worship the Father" (Jn.4:22,21). Salvation has been wrought by the historical actions of the Christ and can be entered into only historically in the lives of individual men, formed in history into a single People. Each culture must grow through all the levels, with those concrete modifications unique to itself whether in terms of its natural gifts or in terms of its failures and sins.

The task of the gentiles is so to grow by the power of Christ in one culture or people after another as ultimately to render Israel jealous (Rom. 11:11). Thus, in order to share in this manifestation of the Holy Spirit, she will return to her Spouse, be grafted in again to the olive tree from which she was torn off—then will come the end and life from the dead (Rom.11:15). But, as Karl Stern pointed out, Israel will not return until the gentiles have learned to behave more like the followers of Christ they profess to be.

> [Jews'] Messianic skepticism and their very existence are a continuous reproach and sting in the flesh of the Christians. When Saint Paul says that "blindness in part has happened in Israel until the fullness of the gentiles should come in," he is not only prophesying but he is exhorting the Gentiles. Fullness is not just something numerical, it has a qualitative meaning. Unless the Gentiles come in in fullness, they cannot expect the Jews to see.[6]

Yet there is a progress from Pentecost till the present moment, one dependent on the Lord's free grace and providence, secondarily on the free will of man, and not at all on any putative Progress or ineluctable Law of Development. There will be yet more growth between now and the time when time ends as Christ returns in glory. This will be the termination of all the things of earth in their worldly existence. But it will also be the fulfilment, that towards which all things are moving, freely or perforce, the final summing up of all things in Jesus, when all typical recapitulation is finished and all things have been brought to perfect unity under their Head. Then they will be handed over by the Son when He hands over His kingship totally, through the eternal Glory, to the Father, that He may be all in all (I Cor. 15:27–28).

B. Psychic and Spiritual Ages of a Culture

Most discussions of the history of cultures make abundant use of

[6] Karl Stern, *The Pillar of Fire*, New York: Harcourt Brace (1951), *pp* 283–284.

analogies between the cultures considered and living organisms. Cultures are said to grow and develop, show vigor, reach their prime, wither, decay, and die.[7] It is possible, however, to convert these simple analogies into something stronger, into an analytical tool, a means not only of understanding but of measuring, though not in a quantifiable way, the degree of development of God's People within a culture.

1. The imitable and the developmental

There is a 'psychic age' (or 'psychic level') of a culture by which I shall indicate the degree of psychic maturity that this culture fosters or, better, that it assists its younger members to reach with comparative ease but beyond which it resists their further growth. If one should begin to grow a little beyond this level, he would meet opposition, the opposition of his entire culture. This opposition would arise from within his own self as well as from others. They do not understand where he is going or why he is acting as he does; neither does he. All he recognizes for a while is that he is being interiorly stirred or moved towards something not yet provided for by his culture.[8] We shall need to speak also of the 'spiritual age' (or 'spiritual level'), defined in similar manner for the life of charity and grace.

In a purely oral culture, and in others in proportion to their approximation to a purely oral one, mere need for survival dictates that people do very little, if anything, to alter the culture or to change it further. To live by the hard-won knowledge embedded in their tradition and to hand it on integrally is of vastly greater importance than to invent novelties. Hence, one is unlikely in the extreme to go much beyond the level of his culture, either in the technical matters relating to hunting, cooking, or tool-making, or in the moral and religious outlooks which gave rise to these latter and which, in turn, will have been, little or much, modified by them.[9]

A particular development may have taken thousands of years for the culture as a whole to reach, say, to know how to kindle fire and tame it for cooking and the hearth, to come up with the idea and practical know-how for pottery utensils, to go from stone to bronze, to go from hunting to agriculture. For pottery, say, a certain degree of sedentary life was called for, hunting and gathering being replaced by an incipient agrarian life. There was also a

---

[7] Despite his antipathy to every mode of historical determinism, Christopher Dawson is not on this point an exception. Cf., e.g., his *Progress and Religion*, Garden City (NY): Image Books (1960), (first published, New York: Sheed & Ward [1934]), *pp* 55–56, and throughout his major works.

[8] Thus, an individual's growth may be envisioned roughly as a sigmoid curve whose pitch is the steeper the lower its upper asymptote. This asymptotic upper bound or "ceiling" represents a strong limitation beyond which it is exceedingly difficult, though obviously not impossible, to grow even a little.

[9] As Dawson makes abundantly clear in the first volume of his Gifford lectures (*Religion and Culture*, New York: Sheed & Ward [1948], especially *Ch* III), a culture develops out of a particular religious vision of the world rather than the contrary. Yet there can be no doubt that the culture, if it undergoes sufficient change in its basic skills and arts, will react back vigorously upon its religious matrix, even if not always upon those who are the latter's official representatives. Cf. also, *Progress and Religion*, *pp* 65–69.

change in religion, in this transition from hunter-gatherer to farmer, from shamanism and totemism to priesthood and fertility cult. One tended increasingly to enter into the processes and movements of nature itself, on their own terms, rather than to continue simply to overpower nature, to pluck or uproot it, or to trap or spear it and drag it off to one's cave.[10] In all this long, slow growth of technology, there develops, in dynamic interaction with it and in some ways conditioned by it, the cultural, the interior, the spiritual aspects that define the culture.

Yet, any child of a pottery-making culture will be making little pots in mud almost from infancy. The idea will be part of him, even if he never gains the least technical know-how. On the other hand, by the time he has reached adulthood, he may well have learned how to improve this or that detail of the process or correct some weakness of the method. In brief, he has summed up in himself this aspect of his culture, an aspect that took hundreds or even thousands of years to develop to this point. He can be, at twenty, more sophisticated about pots and their decorations than his much more experienced grandparents.

There is a great "spottiness" to the cultural growth of which we are speaking. This maturation is shown only in certain aspects of the personality, in particular skills and cultural traits. The unity of the person guarantees, I think, that no such growth is without link to the rest of the personality; yet growth in one domain can leave most other aspects at a seemingly much more primitive level.

To spell this out a bit: when one examines any particular culture, he finds that it is very easy for a normal youngster in that society to grow up to a certain level. The Kwakiutls of the Pacific Northwest, so much discussed by anthropologists,[11] grew up easily enough till very early adolescence. Their culture was marked by an astonishing lavishness in giving, pouring out upon others blankets, food-stuffs, precious metal plates, whatever was prized in the way of possessions. This was the way one showed oneself a man (warfare was practically unknown among them, at least in part because they were physically isolated from hostile groups.) The great man was the one who gave endlessly and abundantly, who could show himself as among the most generous and liberal of all. Of course, the one to whom you had given would seek to show himself an even better man than you by giving away even more. The ultimate in this not very well disguised contest was so to bankrupt yourself by giving that those to whom you gave would be forced, if they were to save face, to give more than they could afford and be irrecoverably ruined, while you recouped all your losses. The Kwakiutl culture brought its young people easily to this stage, more or less "on schedule"; but beyond that there was little further development.

Most early adolescents in our culture would have little trouble understanding and even sympathizing with what was going on there. But a young

---

[10] E.g., Dawson, *Progress and Religion*, 88–92.

[11] Cf. Ruth Benedict, *Patterns of Culture*, New York: Penguin Books (1946), *pp* 160–205 and 225–231.

adult is likely to find very little resonance in himself with such boisterous squandering. He has outgrown it.

Thus far, the 'ages' can be used quite generally of any people or culture. If we restrict ourselves solely to Christians, then the spiritual age indicates the level of recapitulation in Christ which is characteristic of the adults in the culture. This is, of course, mediated to the child chiefly by his family though it is something that the youngster senses rather than sees. In brief, it is the level towards which the Christian child can grow with relative ease, with the support and understanding of his family and people.[12]

The psychic age of a culture into which the Church enters may correspond, say, to that of the men of Noah's day or to that of the builders of Babel or, much later, to that of Babylon or Persia or Hellenistic Greece. But there is also a psychic age that results, in part, from the direct intervention of God's grace, through His choice of a people. Thus, His call to Abraham, by rectifying in some degree or ameliorating the effects of original sin, brought about a more rapid growth in him and the people who sprang from him. There is an even greater and better psychic age possible for those who recapitulate as Christians.

The traditional distinction between the three 'dispensations,' the ways in which God has dealt with man, is clearly evident here: when He let men wander and grow on their own, when He chose some of them as His own people, and when He remade them as His New People and incorporated them into the Body of His Son. In the first dispensation, He did not publicly reveal Himself but let men grope and feel after Him in darkness. In the second, He showed Himself active in human life and affairs. Only in the third dispensation, however, can the growth of a culture be seen as recapitulation, since only here is the grace given explicitly as Christ's.

In all three cases, however, God's grace is offered and a spiritual age is possible that is measured simply and solely by the growth of the person in the charity of Christ. The spiritual age, however, is usually not in synchrony with the psychic age, because of both original and actual sin. Psychic and spiritual age stay abreast of each other only insofar as one recapitulates fully and perfectly in Christ, i.e., among the great saints. Others injure themselves and fall behind, for a time at least, by the gravity of their sins. Hence there exist in any culture many degrees and modes of lack of synchrony between psychic and spiritual age.

These distinctions call attention to still another, related one. The complex process of cultural maturation involves many things that can be learned simply by observation or by receiving instructions. There are other things,

---

[12] This provides one element of explanation for the paradox that the children of saints, e.g., Therese of Lisieux and her sisters, or the great Cappadocians (Basil the Great, Macrina, Peter, and Gregory of Nyssa) seem so often to have a headstart on holiness, yet why many holy people have had children who have gone far astray. Free will is not removed; but simultaneous high levels of both spiritual and psychic maturity (an advanced degree of genuine recapitulation) are an enormous aid to holiness in one's children, especially if this be the case for both parents.

however, that can come about only through inner development, whether psychic or free. The distinction cannot be made absolute, clearly, since any learning process whatever involves some degree of inner development. The amount of this, however, is ordinarily so small for what we may call the "learnables" that the distinction is quite workable in practice. When we deal with faith, however, it will be necessary to consider the basis of the distinction again.

It is important to see in what ways an advanced culture is "advanced." Thus, the United States today is perhaps the most advanced in all the world in terms of the sheer quantity and sophistication and maturity of its life in terms of the learnables. Nonetheless, it has regressed far behind India, say, in the developmental aspects that make possible a sound sexual and family life. It is also important to realize that the "developmentals" may easily cease to be such in reality at a given place and time and become only an external and quite learnable mimicry of themselves. Such a merely imitative development will easily collapse under stress when it no longer has a strong and sound religious support. This would seem to be the reason for the above mentioned regression with regard to sexual behavior and family life, characteristic of Western culture during this century, a regression that has led to the decay of chastity even in religious institutes and the diocesan priesthood.

2. *Spiritual and cultural regression*

It will prove useful later to have given here some further precision to this notion of 'regression.' I have spoken earlier of regression in connection with the process of individual maturation,[13] chiefly in terms of the psychic damage wrought by repeated sin, even if repented.[14] Here, however, I should like to speak of spiritual regression of a whole culture or subculture. In this case, a group of people who have grown to a certain cultural level and recapitulative age begin to lose whatever religious point of view it was that was responsible for their development to this point. So, they slide from what I labeled "developmentals" to mere "learnables."

The flowering of such cultural activity as literature, art, science, and philosophy seems essentially tied to affluence. Typically associated in both profane and sacred history with peace, material prosperity, and leisure, all these seem to require for their perfecting some time for quiet reflection and a certain freedom from anxiety about basic livelihood. Historians have often seen as something of a paradox that such periods of affluence and of greatest cultural achievement are also the periods in which spiritual decay sets in decisively and irreversibly. It should not, however, seem paradoxical from our present

---

[13] Cf. *pp* 262–264 and note 20, *p* 290 above.

[14] Part of the reason for the austerities and sometimes terrifying corporal penances of Christians has been the felt need to rectify such warpings and knottings of the psyche. In the saints, at least, it was not a prideful attempt to prove that, evil as one had been, one understood the evil and would punish oneself appropriately—Judas' sin—ignoring the redemption already wrought by the suffering of Christ; nor was it masochistic self-flagellation; but rather it was an opening to the power of the cross for the repair of the psychic damage done by one's sins. This can be rather clearly seen, I think, in the much misunderstood passage on the Alexandrian monastery's "Prison" found in the Fifth Step, concerning penitence, of *The Ladder of Divine Ascent*, St. John Climacus, tr. C. Luibheid & N. Russell, NewYork: Paulist (1982), *pp* 121–130.

point of view. Precisely the fascination with these achievements of personal development that are most easily transformed into imitable and learnable achievements of the talented or highly gifted is just what draws the minds and hearts of men away from concentration on the more sober and even unwelcome religious understandings and conduct that grounded and inspired these advances. The psychic damage of original sin shows itself here in the cultural subordinating of the world to the self rather than offering the world through and with the self to God.

'Regression' is, perhaps, a poor word for this process, since growth and maturation are strictly irreversible. No one mistakes "second childhood" with the childhood that follows upon infancy; and whatever attractiveness may remain in one who is senile, it has nothing to do with the inexhaustible charm of the youngster. 'Regression' refers rather to a breaking down in some destructive manner of the more complex psychic patterns that cultural summation and recapitulation have built up. This process, however, lets analogs of earlier and simpler patterns remain. But these are, at best, related differently among themselves and with the person in whom they exist than when first attained. One's guilty awareness of the higher levels he once knew keeps him from the relative innocence of the former stages.

Thus, when speaking of regression, I am not assuming a simple sliding backwards, a sort of passing through all the stages in reverse order. Regression represents a new road, walked sinfully, because deliberately, that leads downwards and not upwards. A people falls back to certain traits analogous to those of an earlier age but not, save perhaps through their effects on later generations,[15] to this same psychic age. Had Israel accepted the elders' lusts for Susanna as tolerable, the people would not have been acting as mere teenagers. For a culture that has once been adult but has regressed, say, to early adolescence, this degeneration from something higher is a new experience altogether. These adults in regression were once truly adolescent, but are so no longer, however childish their attitudes.

We may also note that not all the members of a culture will regress in the same way or at the same rate. Many, in fact, will actively resist the regressive movement. Thus, the members of a culture in regression will soon be spread out spiritually over a large spectrum of spiritual ages. Thence comes a gradual breakdown of inner communication within the culture and an ever greater factionalism and social conflict. This disintegration of the extant culture constitutes one of the most characteristic aspects of regression, and perhaps the one most easily perceived.

Regression is not, as indicated earlier, a mode of recapitulation, even though the various levels of recapitulation can be characterized by the kinds of sin committed and the ways in which God punishes these.[16] The Christian who regresses is doing so precisely insofar as he has by sin ceased to live in

---

[15] That subsequent generations should simply not grow up as much as their forebears and so not be part of the regression does not seem likely. For, e.g., parents who behave childishly do damage to the psyche of their children that would not occur if they were behaving in the child-like manner of Abraham.

[16] *Ch* 13.A, *pp* 261–264.

Christ (even as the Israelite, who has ceased to live according to the Law, or the pagan, who has shut his eyes to the spiritual light he has). By regressing, he becomes, not literally but by his external behavior, like those of an earlier stage, though he is mature enough to know better.

Recapitulation, both individual and cultural, once resumed through repentance, will take the false, merely imitative, developmentals and make them true ones, partly by exposing the superficiality of the former, partly and most importantly by providing the means that can bring about their interiorization and lead to true growth in the inner man. The need for this sort of transition is one reason why Christianity can, in some of its aspects, come to dramatic flourishing in a very short time after its first introduction into a culture, if the people are already habituated, even if only by imitation, to the mode of acting that belongs to the developmentals.

A culture which has never received any revelation from God that was intended to direct and govern the people of this culture as a group[17] seems *a priori* unlikely to have reached a spiritual age that is very high in comparison with one in which any portion of God's public revelation, whether through Judaism, Islam, or Christianity, has been active for some time. Though the development of a culture lacking public revelation may have resulted in considerable material and intellectual progress, such growth would have occured primarily through the learnables. The progressive summing up of the various aspects of such a culture has, as such, no other life-principle at work within it than the sin-damaged one of human nature in society.[18] Hence, the growth it encourages will be in many ways corrupt and perverse, quite apart from the simple limitations of what we have called its psychic or spiritual age.

Even without further thought, one can see that growth to human maturity will necessarily involve suffering, a suffering that, for the Christian, can be made part of his share in Christ's sufferings. The Christian will suffer more than others because he is called to grow in Christ beyond the limits of any culture whatever. Even if he does not go much beyond the limits of his own, he will still tend to reach his culture's level of maturity sooner than his companions. Every culture, having its own limited developmental age and having so many of its people who are still children or immature even by its own standards, must necessarily have an average age that is lower than that of its most adult members. Hence, those who are spiritually more mature through their longer or closer following of Christ will be opposed or rejected or persecuted

[17] I see no reason to exclude the possibility or even the likelihood of God's having spoken to individuals in all sorts of cultures, albeit privately, i.e., not using His revelation to constitute a people for Himself. Thus, when He spoke to Cain or to Noah, it was, as in shamanistic religion, for the particular good of the individual or his family, not a revelation to make His own purposes better known.

[18] This does not mean that God's grace is not at work in every culture at every period. The Church, following the Scripture, is insistent that it is: e.g., Ac.14:16–17, 17:23–31; St. Leo I, CCL 138, "Tractatus XXIII (de Nativitate 3)," #4, *p* 106 and "Tractatus XXX (de Nativitate 10)," #7, *pp* 158–159. Further, all men and all the universe are (as explained above in *Ch* 4.F & G, *pp* 82–89 and 5.B.3, *pp* 111–112) in some way in Christ. But this grace and individuals' recapitulative movement in response have only those social effects that come from the aggregation of men's weak and stumbling individual efforts.

by those who are less spiritually mature. For, these latter have no adequate way to understand from within themselves what these others are really about. Thus Aaron and Miriam came into opposition to Moses; and Sarah laughed in the tent and lied about it because her faith, great though it was in fact,[19] was not that of Abraham. If in many cultures such opposition by those of lower psychic and spiritual age seems largely absent, this is due more to the oral nature of the culture and the duress of hard living conditions than to greater virtue.

C. "Times and seasons"

Already in the earliest parts of the Bible we see that Israel led all its neighbors in that sober sort of maturity that faces directly the reality of the world and of man's position in it, since rooted firmly in its knowledge of the LORD if not always in obedience to Him. Nothing similar could be said about Israel and the cultural goods of this world. Where was Israel with respect to Egypt in social organization, art, architecture, or even in the sort of wisdom that was eventually to become a mark of the Israelite sage? Where was Israel in comparison with Babylon in the building of cities and splendid palaces and temples? Solomon himself sent abroad to Hiram, the Tyrian king, for the aid he needed for Israel's greatest efforts in this domain. Yet even when Israel was, with regard to the learnables, most primitive by our standards, it was ahead of its neighbors both in spiritual and psychic developmental maturity.

Israel matured much more rapidly than did the rest of the world because of God's continuing interventions and abundance of grace. But, with the coming of the Holy Spirit and the sending out of the apostles, the time chosen by God had come for the rest of the world to begin to catch up.

In Athens, St. Paul told his audience that the nations had been seeking God from early on, in hope that they might feel after Him and find Him (Ac.17:27). Those were the times of ignorance which God was willing to overlook (Ac.17:30). So, at Lystra in Lycaonia a little earlier, Paul had said that "In the generations that have passed away, He allowed all the nations to walk in their own ways; yet He did not leave Himself without witness" {Ac.14: 16–17}. Though Paul was speaking of what had happened over many centuries, it seems clear from the context that he was in no way restricting himself to past ages. He was concerned with his hearers right then. "In past generations" refers to all those generations up to that very moment, in which God was at last changing His way of dealing with this or that people.

Now, we falsify things if we think of time in a purely linear way, as though it were the same time for everyone, measured, say, by chronometers or by the aging of the universe or the earth's whirling on its axis. We too easily forget that the time which matters most is the time that God is working with, which is different for all the different races and peoples on the face of the earth. Each culture, even as each individual, has its own times, known only to God. And, at any given time, each culture is different in the level it

[19] Cf. the testimony given her in this regard in Heb.11:11.

has reached, in its openness or closedness, in its readiness—in God's plan, not ours—to hear the Good News. This pattern is already visible in Israel's growth considered in relationship to that of the nations.

When the earth had circled the sun many millions of times and when ancient Mesopotamian culture had reached a certain level, God found one gentile in Ur whom He judged ready to mature more rapidly, whom He then enjoined: "Leave your people and your fathers' house!" But the other people of Ur and those of the other nations continued their own growth, but a growth much slower than that for which Abram had been chosen. To be chosen by God means always to be called to greater maturity and holiness of life. What is important here is simply the fact of the diversity of rates of growth, a diversity determined entirely by God's free choice, without regard to the merits of those called or left behind.

With the coming of our Lord, Israel was called to enter God's new time, into that rapid growth in Christ that was a recapitulation like that of the disciples and that flowering of charity that was given by life in the Spirit. With the coming of the Church to each other people, this people too is brought from its own slow growth into one first like the old Israel's, then the New.

So, when Paul was speaking at Athens, it had just become *their* time. God was now, for the first time, no longer allowing this people to walk in its own way. Culturally, Athens had matured to the point that at least some of its people were sufficiently prepared for the particular call the Lord had reserved for them alone in the history of the world. He had then sent them another witness to Himself beyond the good seasons and rains and abundant harvests, this Paul, witness to His Son who had become man and had been crucified for their sins and risen to glory. And with this good news came the announcement of the divine will, that men everywhere are now to repent their sins, in view of the coming judgment. As Paul's own missionary activity makes clear, this "now" is not the same "everywhere." The history of man's salvation is not synchronous among different peoples.

Paul sets out the same idea in his letter to the Roman Christians (Rom. 3:25): "[I]n His divine forbearance He had passed over former sins." A new season, however, had come. God was no longer going simply to pass over any sins. He would now show Himself the Just One, pre-eminently just, precisely by forgiving their sins through His Son, who had had to pay the full cost of that forgiveness.

We tend today, under the impact of the exact sciences and the "instant communications" of radio and TV, of FAX and computer networks, to think of the times of all peoples as but one. We conceive time as some universal duration, flowing onward, whatever its real nature may be, the same for everyone and the whole of nature. But it is not in fact the same for everyone, nor does it simply flow on uniformly. Even the time used by physicists today can be dilated and curved.

The nations grow without synchronization among them, at least from any human point of view. Part of the human race grows rapidly while the other parts do not. The particular temporal relationship between any two peoples can itself change in the course of time, so that those who outstripped others for a while may themselves later be outstripped. "The first shall be last; and the last, first." Indeed, only when speaking at the most abstract level, can we even speak of "*the* human race" when we are discussing the history of man's salvation.

All this is visible even in the Old Testament. Consider the story of Balaam (Num.22). Israel had received the Law forty years earlier and was about to enter the Promised Land. They came like a storm, to the east of the Jordan, and had wiped out the Amorites and then moved on towards Moab. Balak, king of Moab, in terror seeks for someone who can put a curse on Israel, for he had despaired of any other way to fend them off.

Balak, therefore, sent messengers and presents to Balaam, a seer and diviner, living far away near the Euphrates. On receiving Balak's message, Balaam replied that he could only respond in accord with what "the LORD speaks to me" (22:8). God came to him that night and told him what he should do. The next morning he told the messengers: "The LORD has refused to let me go with you" (22:13). The rest of the story recounts how the LORD, the God of the heavens and all the earth, blessed His own people through this gentile diviner who had been summoned to curse them.

The significance of all this for our present purposes is that it shows this gentile seer as one with whom the LORD Himself spoke familiarly, before any message from Balak about Israel, and whom He had been using as His mouthpiece. In Balaam we find a typical person from the pre-patriarchal or perhaps early patriarchal stage of development. When God spoke to Balaam, He spoke in much the manner in which He spoke to Abram. The LORD here, also, simply commands with clarity a definite action. First He says, "Do not go with them" i.e., Balak's messengers; and Balaam refused to go. The king was angered and, in yet deeper fear, sent the messengers back with more gold and silver and bade him come anyway, "and let no one hold you back." This time God tells him to go, "But do only what I tell you to do." Balaam's lack of surprise also reminds us of Abram's; even the strongly personal bond between the LORD and Abram seems faintly reflected in Balaam's speaking of Him as "the LORD, my God" (22:18).

Israel at that time was already being structured by the Covenant and the Law into a well formed tribal society, whose bond of unity was their common worship of the LORD of the Covenant, in spite of the considerable diversity of their kinship relations. The spiritual maturity of Israel was already greater than that of the surrounding peoples. Balaam stood at a much lower level. Had he been more faithful, though, he might have led his own tribe to grow more rapidly than, say, the Moabites, who at the still lower level, seen in Balak, were far back in the pre-patriarchal age, lost in superstition and with minimal knowledge of God. Here we find a threefold lack of synchrony at one and the same physical time.

Anyone reading the Scriptures will find many such passages in each Testament. As mentioned already, the promise was made to Abraham in order to initiate this lack of synchrony. This is the purpose for which God chooses

Israel. This asynchronous relation does not, however, imply that the more primitive are necessarily the worse, morally or religiously. Think only a moment about the widow of Zarephath and the greatness of her generosity and faith, praised by Jesus Himself, in contrast to such religiously more advanced (in a cultural sense) countrymen of Elijah as Ahab.

In like manner, we cannot presume that all those of a given age in a given culture will have reached the same level of maturity. This fact complicates life considerably for those whose tasks depend in some critical way upon the exact degree of maturity reached by those for whose benefit they labor.[20]

The notion of time of which we have been speaking is particularly strong in the New Testament and is there called "season"; *kairos* in Greek.[21] *Kairos* is the right time, time not just in its duration or flow or mere continuance, but time as appropriate, suitable, seasonable, when something can and, indeed, ought to happen—as opposed to other times when the same thing could not happen, or at least not happen fittingly or rightly. Perhaps the world is not yet ripe for its happening. Or its season may have come and is now gone; the right time is past. What might have been done can no longer be done. The opportunity has been missed. Thus the Israelites, who sinned by lack of confidence after the return of Joshua, Caleb and the other scouts and spent the night lamenting and grumbling in their tents when once told of God's anger and the punishment He had decided on, decided they would then, at length, do what He had asked. But the season had passed. He did not want them to go into the Promised Land then. They were roundly defeated when they tried to do so anyway.

D. Synagogue vs. Church

As mentioned, when once the Church was forced to leave the synagogue if she was to carry the Good News to the nations, the season of Judaism passed and the season of the gentiles began (Lk.21:24). Israel had developed spiritually, under the power of the LORD's choice, far beyond any of the nations. But when Judaism blocked and obstructed the spread of the Good News, the call of God went out to the pagans through Christian Israel.

The break between the synagogue and the Church did not occur because

---

[20] This has been, from the days of St. Ignatius Loyola, a key problem for those who think of directing someone through the full thirty days or so of the Spiritual Exercises: is the proposed exercitant truly mature enough, and mature enough in the right ways, to profit sufficiently from this arduous undertaking to make it worth both his and his director's time and effort? It is also one of the inescapable impossibilities built into the very notion of a 'Catholic program of sex education'—how can a *program* tailor its offerings to each individual, given the enormous differences at a given age of physical, psychic, and spiritual growth, to say nothing of differences in ethnic and family background, intelligence, previous history, knowledge and experience of the faith, and so on, *ad infinitum*? A sufficiently carefully wrought program concerning the Christian virtue of chastity, if developed within the larger framework of charity and Christian morality in general, would seem the only truly helpful way of dealing with whatever aspects of sexuality might be suitable.

[21] This is evidently related to, but distinct from, the notion of the Lord's "hour," that brief period that is the season of all seasons, the Paschal season, when He wrought our redemption.

the Jewish leaders of Jesus' day rejected Him and had Him crucified. He died for all the sins of all men, theirs included. There were none of His followers who did not have to repent after His resurrection and to accept His forgiveness.[22] And, except for the five hundred or so who actually saw him after the resurrection, the same great act of faith had been asked of each Christian Jew as of those Sadduceic priests and Pharisaic leaders of the synagogue who had refused to believe in Him.

What seems to have been at work among the Pharisees, who became the sole leaders of the people after the destruction of Jerusalem by the Romans,[23] was the conviction that no messianic salvation could come to the gentiles except insofar as the gentiles should become converts to Judaism, submitting to circumcision and the Law. Even for many Christian Pharisees this remained a stumbling block and point of contention. Hence Paul's running battle with those "Judaizers" who did not understand that, though "salvation is from the Jews" forever, yet, because of the nature of faith, no gentile who believed in Christ needed first to convert to Judaism in order to share all the fruits of the redemption. This rooting of messianic salvation in faith rather than in circumcision was already implicit in what Jesus preached during His public life[24] and was doubtless sensed already by His Pharisaic opponents. Their rejection of it (Ac.22:1–24) constituted a complete refusal of the Church's missions to both the Jew and the gentile alike.

Thus the Church became the community of all believers; the synagogue, only of the circumcised. The synagogue now set itself up as an institution in competition with the Church for the minds and hearts of Jews. Through this institutionalized perseverance in the rejection of the Christ, the synagogue became fixated at a certain level of growth and made herself incapable of the undistorted completion of the recapitulation of her own history to which Christ had invited her.

In his long doctrinal discussion (Rom.9:1–11:36) of the relations between non-Christian Jews and Christians, whether Jews or gentiles, part of which we discussed earlier in a different context,[25] St. Paul is keenly aware of the lack of synchronization between God's seasons already spoken of, but he projects it into the future. The gentile is the wild olive branch (Rom. 11:16–24), broken off from its own stock (its own religion, culture, and people), now grafted in to the trunk that is Israel, from whose holy roots, the patriarchs and the prophets, it draws its life. Hence, the gentiles may not glory, because if they, the wild olive branches, have been grafted in, they can be broken off far more easily than were the natural branches. And the natural branches can be grafted

---

[22] His mother Mary, alone sinless, had nothing to repent. But she was no less indebted to His sufferings and death for her redemption than anyone else. Only, the full effects of the redemption, before it had been accomplished, were lavished on her from her conception onwards through God's foreknowledge of Jesus' cross. What was singular in her case was the greatness of the prior gifts, not the fact of them; for the salvation of Adam and Eve, of Abraham and of Moses, and of all the just of the world before Christ was also the fruit of Christ's death alone.

[23] Those Sadducees who had not become Christians disappeared with the Temple.

[24] Cf., e.g., Mk.7:1–23, 11:17; Lk.7:1–10; Mt.23:15 and almost everywhere in *John*.

[25] *Ch* 16, *pp* 320–321.

in again much more easily into what was their own than the gentiles, should these be broken off.

Paul is a messenger of Christ to the gentiles, in part, so that he may, through the outpouring of the graces of the Spirit upon them, provoke the Jews to jealousy (11:13–14). Then they will want what the gentiles have and will turn to Christ to claim the fulness of their own inheritance. Paul's hope is to rouse them to grow the seemingly small amount that remains for them if they are to be grafted back into their own tree, from which they broke themselves off by rejecting not only Jesus but the Holy Spirit, "incarnated" in His Church. In brief, through the Church's recapitulation among the nations, their growth was to be speeded up so that, overtaking and passing the synagogue, they might by holiness of life in the Spirit make the splendor and glory of Christ's grace visible to all. Then the synagogue would be able to recognize the wrong turn it had taken in scorning the pagans.

It is this final Return from this ultimate Exile that dominates Paul's thought here, as he asks rhetorically, "If their rejection means the reconciliation of the world, what will their acceptance mean but life from the dead?" (Rom.11:15). The return of the Jews as a people—not merely as individuals, one or two at a time—and their conversion to their Messiah, is the greatest event that can yet happen to the Church before the Lord's coming in glory at the end of the age. If the relatively small group of Christian Jews in the 1st Century has so reshaped the world, it is not easy to limit the spiritual power God will show when the greater number of them come in. "If their trespass is the world's wealth and their failure is the gentiles' wealth, how much more will their fulness be?" {Rom. 11:12}.

Since still alive, though broken off, some growth has continued in Judaism. But that growth has often been distorted and warped and damaging, not only religiously but even at a cultural level.[26] The life of explicit faith, hope, and charity which constitute the life in Christ and which make possible the transition to the life led by the Holy Spirit is missing. Hence, Jewish belief in the God of their fathers seems to have been ever more rapidly disappearing. Hope for a personal Messiah has faded among many who still believe in God.[27] Instead of a universal charity that is ready to forgive all enemies, even before they truly seek forgiveness, there seems more often to be, even in some of those who believe and hope, a calculating, coldly implacable readiness to retaliate in kind. What has become characteristic of secular Judaism as it appears in the state of Israel today is a hard, cruel imposition of the will of the government, despite at times the strong opposition of its own people, and, worst sign of all, some forty years of deliberate lies, not only to enemies but to friends.[28] All this would seem to indicate a slow but lethal drying up of the

---

[26] The increase of genetic disease, brought on by the obligation to marry within Judaism coupled with the small admixture of new genes to the Jewish gene-pool through conversions, would seem, even at the biological level, to point to a divinely constituted admonition that perhaps the Christian Jews' opening to the nations was rightly grounded.

[27] Bernard J. Bamberger, *The Story of Judaism*, 3rd ed., New York: Schocken (1970), *pp* 443 and 449 and his earlier sections on Reform Judaism.

[28] For what is hard and cruel, cf. the statements of Sept. 4, 1991 by Israeli Prime Minister Yitz-

spiritual sap in the broken branch.

But someday, their recapitulation finished, at least some of the nations will make the charity of Christ clearly visible, a charity that fully and explicitly loves all Jews. When gentile Christians live, at long last, fully and truly in Christ and not contrary to Him, God's grace will unblock Israel. This unblocking will allow her to grow again, now in brief recapitulation, correcting through repentance what is awry, revivifying what has died, and in Christ forgiving all enemies. So Israel will be yet again first in the Lord's affections, as somehow always; for God's free gifts and call, as Paul insists (Rom.11:29), are never revoked or made void. Once grafted in to her own trunk and roots again, the hindered growth will resume and quickly bring forth the sweet fruit her Lord desires.

It might be well to mention that Paul's exhortation to his gentile Christians in that same chapter is not some curious but long obsolete relic of the early days of Christianity but is needed constantly in the Church. Christianity too often has been growing in seemingly no better fashion than Judaism.[29] Gentile Christians have been steadily tempted to refuse to recognize Israel's initial spiritual pre-eminence, or even to ignore or despise the Jews as a fallen people. Fallen they may be; but Christian gentiles can be broken off yet more easily and fall further, as we may see today in much of the so-called Christian West, now in deep regression and in many ways worse off spiritually than Judah under Manasseh. True, the Church and the synagogue have not been growing at the same speeds. Even in her weakest days in a particular culture, the Church has been honored by her Lord with great saints, led fully by the Holy Spirit and working wonders of charity all around them. Nonetheless, gentile Christians must never forget that their Lord and God, along with the greatest of His saints, those who will never be surpassed, were all Jews: Mary and Joseph, the apostles, John the Baptist, and Stephen.

E. Recapitulation and the Transformation of Culture

When God begins to draw to Himself a new people from among the

hak Shamir in defense of the terrorist tactics of the Stern Gang. As to lies, one need only recall the case of Jonathan Pollard, the government funding of an undercover effort to buy out parts of the Christian quarter of Jerusalem, the unnamed colonel involved in the Iran-Contra case, or the question of the source of enriched uranium. Documentation on a broad range of such matters can be found in: Victor Ostrovsky & Claire Hoy, *By Way of Deception: the Making and Unmaking of a Mossad Officer*, New York: St. Martin's (1990). What is said here is not at all to be taken as a comparison with gentile governments, which are in many cases as bad or worse. My concern is only with the degree of spiritual life that still remains in the broken branches and its conformity with the life of the trunk and roots.

[29] How far some Christian peoples have to grow in their recapitulation has been shown by the evils that Catholics have at times inflicted upon Jews, acting much as one can find Israel doing to Edom under the monarchy, kin though they were. However, given current forgetfulness of the facts, it is also of importance to recall that Nazism was, in principle, as hostile to Christianity as to Judaism, recognizing in both of these an irreconcilable opposition to its atheistic worship of *das Volk*. The key difference was that the Jews formed, in central Europe, a much smaller and more easily identifiable target. The Nazis' basic orientation was made unmistakeable, however, once they had overrun Poland and Ukraine.

pagan nations, the Church begins through these new converts to raise the cultural "ceiling," laboring to lift this people above their current level of cultural development. This she does, not directly but by bringing them to a genuine recapitulation, through which their spiritual age increases.

Thus, as the Church spreads from one people or culture to another through the centuries, in each she takes root (Sir.24:9–12). As she enters a culture, she begins, most manifestly through the lives of her most saintly, to carry through again the process the LORD wrought first in Israel, rectifying what is evil in the culture, remedying what is deficient, improving what is already growing well. Those who grow more rapidly unite by the strength of their charity into organs within the Church and society at large that not only aid and foster the growth of other individuals but invigorate the whole Body.

Yet this cultural recapitulation in Christ, even as that first preparation for Him, seems always to become ever more strongly entangled in sin; and the culture's adulthood seems always an adulthood deferred or in some way frozen or blocked. A blindness comes in part upon gentile Christians, too, in each culture so that they must wait, with Israel, until "the fulness of the gentiles comes in" {Rom.11:25}.

Thus, both Christians and those Jews who have not accepted Jesus as the Christ and Son of God await together His coming in glory. We and they both wait for the Messiah to be manifested in the fulness of His Glory, no longer to draw men from their sins but to judge us all according to our deeds (Heb.9:27–28). His first coming left us all our freedom, to believe or not, to obey in accordance with our faith or not. His next coming will leave no further choices. The delay of His second coming is to enable the nations also to be saved and to be grafted into the stock of the patriarchs and prophets, to let each gentile become through recapitulation, in the span of a few years, like those Jews of His own day who received Him. So, the gentile Christians are called to join with the apostles and other Jewish Christians to go forth to bear witness to Christ so that, through the action of the Holy Spirit, all the world may live in Jesus. Their labors must continue until all is ready, as the Father judges readiness, for Jesus' second coming. Then will be the full conversion and return of Israel, resurrection from the dead, and life with Him forever.

Clearly, then, Christian apostolate cannot be defined solely in terms of preaching the Good News so as to bring about the conversion of individuals to Christ and their incorporation into His Church. Also needed is the development, mostly through these converts, of their culture, so that it becomes a more suitable and effective medium for assisting new generations to mature more easily and fully in the Lord. This does not mean that anyone's salvation is determined by his culture or lack of it. But, as creatures of flesh, we find that even the externals of our lives serve as instruments of grace or of temptation: the so-called external graces, such as hearing a missionary announce the Good News,[30] and the external objects or situations we call

[30] The small space devoted to external grace in Blasius Beraza's enormous *Tractatus de Gratia Christi*, Bilbao: Elexpuru (1916), #63, *p* 47, to say nothing of the extrinsicist, even occasionalist, treatment he gives it, indicates clearly enough that this is an area in need of much deeper theological reflection than it has yet received. Needless to say, he makes no connection with temptation or

snares or occasions of sin.

This point is often overlooked. Protestantism, in its often iconoclastic zeal for naked faith and a gospel pure of human supports, has always been hostile to any notion of external grace. Yet it is hard to see how hearing a sermon or reading the Bible is any less external or any more intrinsically supernatural than gazing upon an icon or participating in a Corpus Christi procession. Others, chiefly theologians and philosophers infected by Kantian attitudes, would argue that, since the weakness is entirely our own, we should never speak of anything in the world as a snare or a temptation. This latter point is not wholly wrong; but it does miss the embodied and enfleshed nature of mankind—and overlooks the strong language used by our Lord and St. Paul.[31]

All of this suggests that the Church exists, in part, to rectify cultures and to bring them to their natural fulfilment. As indicated above, it is peoples, not cultures, that are grafted into God's olive tree. Their cultures, however, must be at least as much transformed by Christ as Old Testament Jewish culture was called to be. This can only be achieved through their supernatural fulfilment in the Church, through a transformation of the natural processes of cultural development into true recapitulation. An integrally and totally Catholic culture—none has ever existed or will exist, this side of the Day of Judgment[32]—would serve as a paradigm of what every culture is meant to be. To the extent that any culture is less than that, it is as warped and impoverished as is any individual who, to an analogous degree, is lacking in likeness to Christ. Yet it is *as* Church that the growth takes place in the Lord, and *as* culture that it will have all sorts of human and even sinful and destructive components. Hence, the cultural mission of the Church is paramount and indispensable in her ministry, if 'culture' be conceived, say, in Dawson's broadly general sense and not in one of its many restricted senses, e.g., intellectual or aesthetic refinement, or the general way of life of one or other class or group characterized by such refinement, or the way of life of the dominant group within a people.

This understood, one can say that it is by the formation of Christian culture that the Church's ministry is carried out. For, the Church's task is to bring all things into subjection to Christ (II Cor.10:3–6) so that all things may be united, by the power of the Holy Spirit, in glorifying the Father through the Son. Since her own recapitulation within a people is part of her leading of all men through recapitulation into their living fully in the Spirit thereafter, this growth of human culture is an essential element in her primary function. The Church's bond with culture springs directly from a culture's relation to the recapitulation of the individual.

Thus, sound cultural growth is not secondary in her life, for she is Bride and Body of Him who is to fill all things. The Church cannot avoid, if she is

occasions of sin. *The New Catholic Encyclopedia* deals briefly but competently with the latter two (*13*, 246–247 & 1002–3), but gives hardly four lines to external grace in our sense here (*6*, 679).

[31] Cf. Mt.18:6–9 and Rom.14:15–21 for starters.

[32] The closest approximations would seem to be the first Jewish Christian community in Jerusalem and the early churches in Antioch and in Philippi.

truly to be God's People in this world, being passionately interested in the healthy growth of human culture. It is essential to her apostolate.

F. The Parables of Growth

Recapitulation by the Church includes, no less than does that of an individual, a rectification of what is wrong or deficient in its environing culture. This comes about in part through a twofold process interior to the person or the Church. On the one hand, one absorbs and takes into himself from the day of his birth all elements of his cultural environment that he finds congenial and that are not somehow shunted aside by his elders. On the other hand, as he grows older, he begins to winnow these elements on the basis of his fundamental convictions; he selects from them what he thinks suitable, and deliberately ignores or rejects much else. This process of cultural absorption and selection is not optional; it is an essential aspect of any human life. For the Christian, of course, the power rightly to effect this winnowing comes from God's grace, and the fundamental convictions that guide the process arise from his faith and from the rest of his life in Christ at the stage of spiritual maturity he has reached.

Traditionally treated under the rubric of 'avoiding worldliness,' this selectivity in the absorption of elements from one's cultural environment[33] involves a largely unconscious utilization of familiar cultural elements, modified only when this generates a conflict with one's convictions. Obviously, in the case of individuals, the social pressures to conform, if not to the majority fashion, at least to the generic, culturally defined ways of seeing the world, are powerful. More grave sins are probably committed for such reasons of worldliness than because of weakness of the flesh or the direct assaults of the devils, for non-Christian worldviews are many and persuasive.

The Church must exercise a similar selectivity. She, also, has responsibilities not only to winnow out but to accept and improve elements from her cultural environment. These responsibilities are heavier and even of a different kind than those weighing on individuals. Hence, our Lord Himself has given her the guidance she needs in His many parables concerning the nature of the growth of the Kingdom of God.

The kingdom of God is like a mustard seed, like a vine, like yeast in dough, like good seed among which cockle has been scattered, like a grain of wheat that grows up day and night, etc. Too often Christians take these parables as referring to themselves individually and to the growth of God's grace within their souls, but miss the chief point of the parables, which is to tell us about the Kingdom of God as it is extended upon earth, the Church in her growth.

A long tradition exists, based on the Lord's statement, "The Kingdom of

---

[33] This environment may be constituted by a single homogeneous culture, as for one growing up among a relatively isolated people or in a strongly bonded community, or it may include elements from various cultures. These in turn may be ones long co-existent, even if hostile to each other, provided they are socially sufficiently kept apart, or they may represent an incursion of some alien culture into a people already formed.

God is within you" (Lk.17:21), to legitimate the individualized interpretation of those parables. But even if this somewhat dubious translation be accepted or, at least, the tradition that grew from it, this does not permit one to push out of its place the primary meaning. Yet, there is a legitimate application of these parables to the individual, for recapitulation by the Church in a cultural region can only take place if the individual cells are recapitulating within her.[34]

Now, in each parable, growth takes place that is rightly described as the growth of the mustard plant, of the stalk of wheat, of the vine. But whence comes this highly specific growth? It is the principle of life hidden in the seed that brings about the growth that is characteristic of the species and without which there would be no growth at all. Nevertheless, even biologically identical strains of vine in different plots of a single small vineyard in Burgundy produce fine wines in each; yet in only one do soil and sun combine to produce "Le Chambertin." The seed determines the species; but the soil and the climate determine the quality of the individual plant and its fruit.

The plant looks nothing like the seed. It has become what it is by sinking rootlets into the well-manured and dark soil, whence it has selectively absorbed most of the material needed for its structure. All this additional substance the seedling has drawn from the air and the soil, activated by the light of the sun—all, however, from outside the seedling itself, by the power of the life it has within it. It does not take in everything that the soil has; most of the soil remains there, inert and unchanged. It can happen, too, that what the plant does absorb from an unhealthy or poisonous ground will destroy it; and both earth and air conceal active agents of destruction, cut-worms and blights, fumes and flying pests.

So it is with the Church as she enters into a people and their culture. She takes in from them all the natural elements of her being, absorbing from the midst of every sort of rottenness and decay almost all she needs for her visible existence, but growing steadily and strongly in her own characteristic patterns because animated by the one principle of life which is the Spirit of Christ. All things human are mixed together on earth in a mucky soil far darker and more ill-smelling than any compost-heap. But the Church draws out of that all that she needs for growth except for the hidden principle of her own life and except for the human agents, martyrs and missionaries, whom she scatters abroad as seeds.

The Church takes from a culture its arts, its crafts, its styles of thought and patterns of action, all that this people have been accomplishing by natural growth through all the long millennia in which the Lord has allowed them "to walk in their own ways" (Ac.14:16). During all this season, He lets their natural culture grow as it will, twistedly, distortedly, often terribly, yet also beautifully—for even sin does not, in this life, wholly corrupt man's nature,

[34] These parables of the Kingdom should not be confused with the parable of the Sower who casts abroad the good seed which is the announcement of the Kingdom and its mysteries and where the different ways of growing refer to the different responses individuals give to the Gospel, once accepted.

which still retains some semblance of God's Image.

But when He chooses at last to let warmth of His Spirit blow upon a people, like the winds in spring, bringing the rain of His grace, then scattering the clouds so that the radiance of the Sun of Justice may cause the seeds of the Gospel there planted to germinate, then that life sprouts. The new little shoot that is the Church takes from the dark soil those things compatible with the life given by the Spirit and that she can transform by Christ's life into her own substance. She absorbs these things spontaneously, by osmosis, in their particular culturally conditioned form because that is the form in which she finds what she needs for continued growth.

Hence, if any claimant to the title 'Church' today looks much like the "Early Church," so beloved by reformers of every age, the one thing we would know instantly about her would be that she is not the Church of Christ. It is the Lord Himself who pointed out how little the mustard plant, in whose branches all the birds of the air build their nests, looks like the least of all the seeds. It is precisely the infinitely varied inculturations of the Catholic Church that make her visibly and manifestly a candidate, at least, for being that Church which is animated by the same life-principle as the primitive Christian community.

Yet inculturation is not a task that she can well go about consciously or work at expressly. Its processes take place primarily in her roots, hidden in the darkness of the soil, drawing the nourishment she needs for her earthly structures without explicit awareness. For no one can stand so far apart from his own incultured self as to see the totality of his own culture with sufficient clarity for this task. Nor can he evaluate not only its actual strengths and weaknesses but also its potentialities in response to God's grace. Still less can one grasp God's plan for this people and their culture. Inculturation as a conscious and rationally thought-out process is but one, and not the finest, trait of modern Western rationalism.

Chapter 19

To All the Nations

When the Church begins to live among a particular people, she makes concrete in a new way, unique to this people, the fulfilment of her type in ancient Israel.[1] Her implanting among them implies very little if anything about the psychic age this people has already reached. Christianity has come to peoples at any and every stage of their cultural development. Surely, given the high level of culture of the peoples of the Mediterranean world of the first few Christian centuries, one may not assume that the peoples among whom the Church grows most successfully are culturally primitive. Whatever a people's age and type of cultural development may be, recapitulation proceeds apace from the time at which the Church enters and is accepted. In principle, moreover, wherever this people then is, culturally speaking, there is no upper limit to the raising of their spiritual age short of the full maturity of the manhood of Christ.

A. Recapitulation in Each People Anew

If the recapitulative process has not long been noted simply on empirical grounds, it is that it has not been rightly distinguished from psychic maturation. Thus, it may be helpful to consider the relationship between these two processes in Christianity as this came to Europe through Greece and Rome, whose high cultures are familiar to all. Lofty as were some of the insights of Aeschylus and Euripedes, of Plato and of Aristotle, they seem to have been without spiritual effect on the life of Greece before Christ. The ideas of justice and fairness in government, proper to Rome and there marvellously developed,[2] had begun to show their weak ineffectiveness in the spiritual

---

[1] Again, the Church as antitype is to be distinguished from her individual members, many of whom at every period will grow beyond recapitulation into the fulness of the Christian life in the Spirit.

domain well before Pilate, Felix, and Festus. Spiritually the Church had to begin among these highly cultured peoples in the pattern we see in *Genesis*.

Nor could any steps be skipped—for, no matter what one pretends, they will not be. A "skipping" is merely a concealment of a spiritual immaturity not being faced and, therefore, not being grown beyond.[3] Even St. Paul had to learn this the hard way, as we saw from those glimpses of recapitulation by the early gentile churches that the New Testament shows us.[4]

The Gospel was first preached by Paul to the Greeks without reference to the Law, except to attack the iniquity of those who set it against his preaching of Christ. His teaching was, as a result, misconstrued and misapplied by his converts because these new Christians were not a "people well prepared." He had increasingly to explain things to them that he had optimistically overlooked, for they had not developed enough spiritually to grasp the moral implications of what they had been taught. So, he was forced to go back, as with the Corinthians, to teach things already known at the patriarchal level. He had to tell them that it is not tolerable that a man sleep with his father's wife (remember how far back it was that Ruben's similar incest had drawn on him a blessing from Jacob no better than a curse). In writing to the Romans, he takes no chances but denounces vigorously, in the very first chapter, the idolatry that had not been a Jewish problem for more than 500 years; the homosexual sins that had wiped out Sodom nearly two millennia earlier and that were then rapidly corrupting Roman society; as well as other vices already abhorrent to the patriarchs.

Toward the end of *Romans*, there is a long disquisition on those who were "strong" or "weak" with regard to Jewish food-laws, observances of feasts and fasts, and liturgical days and seasons. The weak still felt themselves bound in conscience by Jewish practice in these and similar matters, and judged as wrongdoers the strong, who knew that the Christian was not so obliged. The strong, in return, despised the weak for their scruples and lack of understanding. Paul rebukes both the one and the other. More important than freedom with regard to such religious practice and more important than any ritual obligation was the commandment of mutual charity. Each group in its own way had missed a step in recapitulation: the weak had still to learn from David or possibly the Maccabees about freedom of conscience; the strong, from post-Exilic Judaism in general about community and respect for those whose consciences kept them bound.

None of the Roman Christians, then, if they were in the company of those with weaker consciences, could permit themselves to use their freedom on such occasions, but had to follow along with Jewish observances, though taking care to keep their liberty of spirit.[5] For all practical purposes, much of

---

[2] Cf. I Macc.8:1–16 for its praise of Roman governance. No other nation is given such an encomium in all of Scripture.

[3] Perhaps the major fault of the modern psychologizing tendencies as practiced within communities of vowed religious is that they represent an effort to manipulate some people into what other people regard as Christian adulthood—to coerce them into reaching it—without the pain and long effort of inner and truly recapitulative growth.

[4] *Ch* 16.E above, *pp* 334–337.

the ceremonial burden of Judaism was laid upon the shoulders of the strong gentile Christians in Rome because of this need for charity towards those who were weaker.

But the truly mature, thus taught by Paul, still more by the Spirit of his Master, learned how to put up with these less mature Christians and gave up some of their own freedom of action for the sake of charity. Or better stated, in the true freedom that love gives, they chose freely to protect the weaker consciences of their brethren. They would not use their liberty in such fashion that it could destroy their brothers. For, Paul does speak, in just this passage, of the ruin of those for whom Christ died, of their condemnation if, by the example of the strong, they violate their consciences in these matters. This is strong language that we tend all too easily to ignore. It throws a very different light on his notion of mortal sin than is fashionable to admit among moral theologians in our day.

In this regard, one may note the singular lack of concern for other Catholics' consciences that in recent years has marked those liturgical innovators who have set "the spirit of Vatican II" against papal directives. One might argue that those who have held back from these novelties did so from weak consciences and that the innovators were strong in conscience. Yet the willingness of these latter to impose their preferred practices by surrepticiously juggling circumstances and catching the others by surprise would seem to indicate that those among the innovators who understand what they are doing have lost this basic Christian attitude and are spiritually at risk for their lack of concern for the salvation of those they have scandalized.[6]

Be this as it may, the principal point is that even St. Paul had to go back and pick up the things which his various gentile churches had never learned. Better, he had to lead them through a genuine recapitulation in Christ, going through all the stages that they had missed.

The Church, then, in every people chosen by the Lord must grow through this same sort of process, learning anew among them how to submit to God in fundamental faith and allegiance, to wrestle with Him, to obey His Law, to destroy false religion, to develop a sense of oneness as a nation

---

[5] Note the difference in his treatment of these weak consciences from that he accorded the Pharisees, whose consciences are not so much weak as hardened and *installées*. In this he was but echoing the differences of manner Jesus showed when He spoke to those who were hostile from an exaggerated but sincere love for the Law and to those whose motivation sprang from pride.

[6] Women appear who will distribute Communion when priests are visibly available. The Creed is replaced by newly fabricated statements of belief or dropped altogether; and unrecognized Eucharistic Prayers are used without warning to concelebrants or congregation. The bread for the Mass is discovered, too late, to have been sweetened and spiced, to be heavily greasy or filled with sesame seeds. Such underhandedness is wrong not merely because it is dishonest; often it puts concelebrants in a situation where they do act contrary to their consciences. Not seeing at the instant how to deal with the matter, they may, through a certain cowardice and fear of stirring up a row in the middle of what is most sacred, go along with what they are convinced is sinful. Nothing better shows the wrongness of such liturgical practice, though it has paraded as Catholic renewal, than this total unconcern, even contempt, for the consciences of those whom the innovators consider weak of conscience. Cf. also, Paul V. Mankowski, S.J., "In Praise of Conformity—why priests should stop fooling around with the liturgy," *Crisis* 9, 23–27 (#2, Feb. 1991).

because of prior oneness in faith, to grow in cult and ritual, to interiorize the Law, to persevere, to battle for the Lord and His people—all this interspersed with many defeats and perhaps exile. Finally, each "national church" will be called to let go of all that has made it distinctive and unique in order to enter into Christ's sufferings. Each must die to its own culture (as defined by its learnables) and its own past, even as Jesus called Judaism to do. All this, however, takes place only so that it may rise with Him and find—also risen with Him—all that was good of its past, now glorified in some degree even on earth.

New things in the history of man's salvation did not suddenly cease at Pentecost or when divine revelation ended at the death of the apostle John. The Church's recapitulation among the cultures of the world, like that of individuals, though rooted in a common pattern, yet manifests the action of the Spirit, giving glory to Jesus and to the Father through Him, in that endless diversity through which alone His fullest likeness can be expressed. Recapitulation is not a recycling of the same old things over and over again like a broken dishwasher. Each new cycle among a new people writes a truly new chapter in the history of salvation.

The history of the New Israel, with all its relatively distinct sub-histories in the different peoples of the world, is as much a part of that history as is that of the old Israel. Indeed, as part of what the biblical history is meant to accomplish, the history of the Church is as essential as is that of the old Israel, though, as typified rather than type, it lacks the definitive and normative character that God chose for the latter. The realization on the practical order of this insight, that we too are living a history which is unique, which, though it bears the imprint and pattern of the old, is nonetheless essentially new, a history not seen ever before on earth nor to be seen again, is one of the most striking results of II Vatican.

Thus, all the nations of the world are to be called towards spiritual maturity in and through the Church's recapitulation among them, each at its own pace and in its own season, chosen not by man but by God. Whatever their psychic age and whatever their prior spiritual preparation, they must begin to live consciously in Christ. As a people, they must live through, in their own new and distinctive fashion, the spiritual life of ancient Israel.

B. The Cross and the Death of Cultures

When the Church comes to a people, she comes to them from elsewhere, through messengers from some other people in whom she has already taken root. She comes, then, but not only in accord with her purpose to make Christ truly known and to inaugurate true recapitulation for all who accept Him. Also, with or without conscious intent, she brings the characteristic traits belonging to the culture of the bearers of her message. For, the Church is always, like ancient Israel under Moses, concretely embodied among particular peoples. She is never, nor is she meant to be, a disincarnate set of profound religious truths and norms, a Gospel pure of human contaminants. The results of faith and of cultural development are inseparable in her, even though the faith is but one and the cultural developments diverse.

The processes initiated by this importation of elements of an alien culture and their resultant effects can be good or bad or, more often, of mixed worth. In any case, the inescapable cultural interaction results in humanly unforeseeable developments or declines. But before discussing these matters, it seems necessary to comment on the total extinction of some cultures by Christians.

1. Christian destructiveness

Though Christian greed and contemptuous pride have been responsible for the wiping out of peoples, languages, and cultures, this is not a distinctively Christian problem except in the sense that greed and obtuseness and the wiping out of the innocent are graver evils in Christians than in others.

War seems to have been the primary destroyer of peoples and cultures,[7] wars often fought from human greed, pride, simple destructiveness. These can be traced as far back as we can trace anything. Long before Israel began to wipe out some of the peoples of the ancient Near East, Ebla and its highly developed culture had been ravaged and destroyed. The ancient world is full of the ruins of vanished peoples, some as great as the Hittite empire, others mere isolated tribes.

As is the death of an individual, the death of a people is an evil, however caused. But whether such killing, when caused by men, is also *morally* evil depends on the innocence of those killed, the motives of the killers, and the circumstances of time and place.[8] In any case, the magnitude, if not of sin, then of the evils brought on by the destruction—given what the Church has held about the unity of mankind, the dignity of every man, the charity and justice that are to be extended to all—makes a genuine problem for Christians. How can Catholics explain exterminations of whole peoples, by Catholics, so as to leave no trace save perhaps on the consciences of the slaughterers, in such dramatic violation of what the Church professes?

Though at times one might seem to be forced to appeal to the mystery of God's decrees—"Jacob I loved, but Esau I hated" (Rom.9:13)—such a response misses much of what is involved not only in wars but in any cultural interactions, and in particular that of Christian preaching and conversion.

The sinfulness of a deliberate destruction of an alien people and their culture by Christians would depend principally on what it involves of unjust treatment of the innocent. Now, as for the individual, so for a Christian

---

[7] The cause need not be a human cause at all. Pestilence has destroyed or weakened beyond recovery many a people. We have seen in our own day in sub-Saharan Africa the disastrous results of changes of weather-patterns with consequent famines. The preservation of the affected peoples has been due solely to massive outside assistance. Earthquakes and vulcanism have played their part on occasion. There are destructions by human agencies morally less questionable than war, e.g., the loss of the Cornish language and traditions through unconscious pressures to adapt to the more prosperous and numerous people around, or the loss of desire to propagate, as seemingly among present-day Germans.

[8] For a clarification of today's considerable confusion concerning types of evil, cf. Quay, "Disvalue" (note 82, *p* 174).

people, there will be a season for a recapitulation of each stage of Israel's development. For the people, this will often be much closer to a literal reliving of the typical stages. Thus, when they are at the recapitulative level of Joshua and the Israelites during their conquest of Canaan or even at the level of David, their way of dealing with the vices of the pagans will be considerably more direct than either the secular humanist's toleration or the zeal of a fully Christian missionary. As I argued earlier, it is at least conceivable that ancient Israel's understanding of the *ḥerem* as the LORD's just punishment upon the wicked was not itself mere Israelite wickedness.[9] Neither should we forget the childish sentimentality and refusal to acknowledge that there is such a thing as guilt that has made the modern West lose almost entirely its sense of punishment as a virtue.

The corresponding destruction of cultural goods along with cultural evils may be unfortunate for the world as a whole, but is, morally speaking, a relatively minor matter. Those capable of such actions are hardly likely to be discriminating enough even to see a question. In any case, even the largest and most powerful and influential cultures, sooner or later die out, if not before the glory of the final coming of Christ, then at that moment. A greater problem for the Christian lies in the killings of Christians by fellow Christians—something more frequent when recapitulating (or merely living through) Israel's life under the judges or early monarchy.

All the natural elements of any human culture, high or low, remain mere compost—that from which true life can spring, in which it can grow, from which it can draw sustenance; but they are not the life. Without the supernatural seed, there is no plant. All temporal goods must be given up (not contemned or despised) if they are to be saved through the action of God's Spirit in us, while He selects and chooses and purifies in ways that seem to us not simply mysterious but even arbitrary or capricious as He permits men to act in their freedom contrary to every good. Nor does it help much to note that, at times, something of a vanished culture remains and is taken up, purified, and preserved by the Church for future generations. Important as these cultural questions are, it is not they that are the immediate goal of God's action through the Church. So, one must hope; but one does not hope for what one sees (Rom.8:24–25).

A couple of related points might be mentioned before going further. Much of the deploring of vanished cultures would seem to come less from fine sensitivity to the physical and moral evils mentioned than from a Rousseauvian romanticizing of those cultures and a perverse blindness to their vices. There is also a kind of moral snobbishness that would like to visit, or at least read about, all the exotic details of the manners and beliefs of such curious and interesting folk. What is being deplored may well be, then, not some particular moral iniquity introduced or perpetrated by Christians—for other

[9] Cf. *pp* 270–273 for *ḥerem*. It may be useful here to note that the conquest of Mexico by the Spaniards, despite the *leyenda negra*, saved far more Indian lives than it destroyed. The Aztecs' hideous human sacrifices and the selling of the dismembered corpses of the victims as meat in the market places might indicate a culture not worth saving—though the Aztecs themselves, once converted, contributed notably to the culture of present-day Mexico.

moral iniquities, equally bad but more familiar, often are known and not deplored—but the loss of some real or projected pleasure to the one deploring.

In essence, then, both the question concerning the loss to our race of the goods of vanished cultures and that concerning the wrongdoing of Christians when they have been the agents in cultural destruction or, more rarely, in the extermination of peoples are no different than the one this whole book has been addressing; and they will have exactly the same explanation. This can be no surprise since, in the last analysis, there is only one theological problem, the problem of evil, of which this is but one, more specific form.

2. *India and Christianity*

The history of the great culture of India offers an excellent example of the kinds of cultural interaction generated by the preaching of the Gospel. Christianity came, not for the first time but in a second or third wave, in the 16th Century, through the medium of men, whether as soldiers, merchants, or missionaries, whose personal incorporation of then Western culture was profound.

This arrival of the Church, considered in all its concreteness, need not be regarded as having improved Indian culture in most or even many aspects.[10] St. Francis Xavier's fierce denuntiations of Portuguese oppression, both on the spot and in his personal letters to King John III, make clear enough that most of the "Christianizers" were causing grave scandal to the non-Christians and were headed, barring a great conversion of heart, to eternal damnation. His protests probably did some good, as did the interventions of other missionaries thereafter. Yet one can also argue that the foreign conquest and rule did much to aggravate an all too ready subservience already present in Hindu culture. The desire for nationhood and for personal freedom was very possibly an import from a very modestly Christian Europe. Yet had Britain retained even less of Christian influence than it had, Gandhi's non-violence would have been given very short shrift, as the events in Tien Anmen Square in July of 1989 have shown. But even the rightness of the importation of secular, Western notions of democratic government can be and has been denied by many.

The best of Indian culture, however, its philosophical and religious components, stood to gain greatly from Christianity. It has done so to some extent; but in characteristically Hindu fashion, through syncretism. Many things in Hinduism today, even as many things in contemporary Judaism and secular humanism, have come about as not always conscious borrowings from the Church.[11] Those, moreover, who argue that Hinduism contains almost all that Christianity prizes seem able to give some plausibility to their point only by extracting what is best, when judged by Christian norms, from the different schools of Hindu thought and the writings of its many sages, though these are all quite at odds with each other. The synthesis is brought about only

---

[10] The rotting of religion and culture in the West today must at least make one inquire as to whether at least the spores of the decay were not already present in those who came to India.

[11] Mahatma Gandhi is one, however, who was quite conscious of his debt to Christ, if not to the Church, and willing publicly to acknowledge it, both in words and in his life.

through the careful selectivity of those who search among them with Christian eyes. This fact alone, however, would seem sufficient to indicate that Christianity is not hostile to what is good in Hinduism.

On the other hand, Christianity does demand radical changes in Indian culture. Just the one doctrine of God's creating the world from nothing has the most profound of implications for all that is Indian; indeed, it spells the death of Hindu religion. Hinduism is not capable of ingesting, without bursting asunder, the uniqueness and historical intelligibility of a material universe that is really other than God, that is truly His creature. Hinduism cannot see how the intrinsically temporal flow of created becoming can bear true and indeed salvific meaning in its unique and nonrepeatable events.

Thus, one hears the questions, even from Indian Catholics: Why should Israelite history be more of a norm than any other? Indeed, if one looks carefully, is not Hinduism much more spiritual than the Old Testament taken as a whole? Why concede special status to Judaism in preference to religious cultures greater than it?

The simplest answer, of course, is simply that God so chose. This would seem to be the Bible's answer when the question is raised (Dt.7:7–8). And will the pot say to the potter, "Why have you made me thus?" (Rom.9:20). But closer to the underlying nature of the specifically Hindu difficulty, I think, is the concreteness of any human existence. Jesus was not an avatar, but was the Word made flesh, God made man. To be man, He had to exist as one individual, with one sexual constitution,[12] live in but one period of human time, be a member of a determinate people, culture, and linguistic context. All the rest that has happened on earth is necessarily either preparatory for His coming or in consequence of it.[13] Perhaps this same lack of appreciation for human history contributes to a desire sometimes expressed for a liturgical life more sensitive to Hindu sensibilities than rooted in the concrete development of some of the pre-16th-Century liturgies of early Indian Christianity.

The greater temptation, however, would seem to be to yield to the Hindu thirst for an *experience* of the Transcendent, apart from any specific mediation by the material concreteness of Christ, the Church, the sacraments, and the rest of Christian life. The ultimately individualistic aspect of this search for trancendent experience seems to ground much of Christian India's current fascination with Western psychologies.

3. *The culture and the Spirit*

A newly Christian people must, then, come to live by an inner principle of life that is, in truth, no longer "their own" in the sense of something that

---

[12] This highlights an implicitly pagan aspect of some feminist ideology: the failure to understand that the material world cannot share in redemption except insofar as Jesus is material—and therefore one, concrete individual, of one determinate sex. He could not redeem man except as man—which meant as *either* a woman *or* a man, not both nor neither.

[13] Cf. Heinrich Schlier's "Das bleibend Katholische" (note 53, *p* 114 above) where from a different perspective he considers the uniqueness of and repetitiveness of God's decision in Christ. What God did in Christ is unique and unrepeatable; nonetheless, it is constantly being relived and constantly summing up in itself all prior repetitions.

has from the beginning formed and generated their specific manner of life. Yet this new life is most intimately "their own" since Christ's life has, through the coming of the Holy Spirit, become truly theirs. In this seeming conundrum lie most of the problems of missiology. Yet, as a people become more strongly Christian, they will be able to recognize in their earlier culture the traces of God's work among them as He readied them for the coming of His Son in His Church.

As an Epilog to Karl Stern's spiritual autobiography, he transcribes a letter he wrote to his brother, a fervent Zionist, living on a kibbutz in Israel, to make some attempt to explain to him Karl's conversion to Catholicism. What he touches on there with regard to Judaism is what I am trying to say here of the whole of the world.

> If the Jews at the time of Christ, in view of the Roman occupation, had refused the "national solution" as He Himself did, they would have died as a nation but they would have died in Christ! They might have gone out into the world preaching the Gospel, or they might have lived a life of non-violence toward the Roman conqueror. In either case they would have lost their life as a nation in order to gain it. They would have transcended their racial destiny, and it is difficult to think what tremendous historical impulse would have come from a nation thus transfigured.[14]

Each culture that comes under the influence of Christianity, Judaism having been the first, must come to the point where a choice must be made: Will it deny itself and take up its cross daily and follow Jesus? Will it seek its own life and, so, lose it? Or will it lose its life for His sake and for the Gospel and, so, find it?[15] If it dies for Christ, it will rise, forgive those who contributed wrongfully to its death, and go forth to witness in its own, wondrously new way to Christ's glory and the Father's. Each culture, with its entire human richness of religion, philosophy, science, art, amusements, institutions, all, must allow itself to die, in and with Christ on the cross, through the action of charity for the sake of others. Those others, because they think of Christianity as an enemy, since sensing that it will require their death in turn, will seek to kill the Christians and destroy their Church. In so dying, these Christians will be Christ's members, nailed again to the cross in them. Doing this for His love and for love of all His people is also that which will do the most to preserve, not for themselves but for the rest of mankind in the future, what God has found good in their culture.

So the Christian Jews of the Church's first generation went out to carry the great Good News to all the world and suffered martyrdom in large numbers for their efforts. So Rome, when once converted, sent forth missionaries to evangelize the barbarian tribes that were then ravaging it and that were to bring on the Dark Ages of the 9th and 10th Centuries. What had been required of Israel was also to be demanded of the gentiles. Every race, people, culture must die by offering itself, and offering Christ through itself, to a world that wants a temporal messiah only, that wants him on its own terms,

---

[14] *Pillar of Fire*, *pp* 289–290.

[15] Mk.8:34–35.

according to its own cultural ideals, and in such a way that it may be enriched and grow but not have to forgive and die. The missionary people, if faithful to its task, will not offer such a messiah or promise him and, so, will win hatred for itself as well as undying love from its converts.

C. Eternal and temporal welfare

Conceived as I have sketched it, missionary effort is something uniquely and distinctively Christian. The missionary is one who, despite his human weakness and sins, seeks by all his life and action to do what Jesus told the apostles just before His ascension: "You will be My witnesses (*martyres*) both in Jerusalem and in all Judaea and Samaria, and even to the end of the earth" {Ac.1:8}. This is, then, something different from proselytism, which conceals a subconscious desire to add "one more for our side."[16]

1. Missionary work and charity

Every Christian is called to bear witness to Christ, at times even by the shedding of his blood. Yet missionary work in its fulness is primarily a matter for those who have passed beyond recapitulation into the life in the Spirit. The Breath of God then blows them whither He will for the greater glory of the Father and the Son.[17] Thus, there cannot be, for missionary work in its perfection, a pattern that the missionary's action must follow, a pattern such as the Old Testament provides for recapitulation. On the other hand, not only is there much for the missionary to understand concerning the process of recapitulation in the people to whom he speaks but there is also much for him to learn, under the guidance of the Spirit, in the manner we have seen in St. Peter and St. Paul.[18] Finally, the spiritual senses of the New Testament, which we have utilized often in this Part, will throw ever new light on his mission and call him to ever greater maturity in Christ. Failure to distinguish these various aspects has contributed considerably to making missiology cloudy and ill-defined in its methods and subject matter.

All this can be clearly seen in St. Paul. He is intensely aware that what he is doing is no longer a recapitulation of what has preceeded but is a response, both in success and in seeming failure, to direction by the Holy Spirit. The same seems to have been true of those missionary journeys of early Christians of which we catch a glimpse occasionally.[19]

---

[16] There were, of course, some not very successful efforts at carrying knowledge of the LORD and His Law to the pagans by the Jews of our Lord's day (Mt.23:15). There was a brief flowering of Judaism among the Khazars as that people reached their zenith in southern Russia in the 9th Century. But, on the whole, Judaism has spread by transplantation of families or communities and waited for the gentiles to seek admission rather than gone out to make converts of all—even though the LORD is God of all.

[17] This is no argument, of course, against sending young men to mission territory while still in their years of recapitulation so as to learn, while still young enough, the languages and the cultures of those among whom they are eventually to work. The rigors of the life, moreover, help considerably to a mortification and denial of self-interest that greatly speed their growth.

[18] *Pp* 334–337.

[19] Cf. III Jn 5–8, Phm 7; also, Daniélou, *Jewish Christianity*, *pp* 350–351.

If the spiritual requisites for missionary work are so high, it is due simply to the difference already mentioned between proselytism, on the one hand, and love for Christ and those of His people who do not yet know Him, on the other. The missionary's task is set by the overflow of his charity. As Paul reminds his people in Corinth, though an apostle, he has no title to lord it over their faith; they are not his conquest; he is not their lord. He brought them the faith through love for Christ, first and foremost, wanting Him to be known and loved by all men. He spoke to them as witness to Jesus' working out of our salvation. If people did not believe, he made no effort to force the issue but went elsewhere.[20]

Central, then, to missionary work is the demand of charity (the love of God, the passion to glorify the Father in Christ through the Spirit, and of our neighbors for God's sake). This work is directed, if it be genuine, to others' good, not one's own. I remember a train trip once, non-stop, from Philadelphia to New York. Suddenly a young man stood up at the far end of the car and began to "preach Jesus" as his young woman companion looked on admiringly. There was an acute sense of discomfort throughout the car as people fixed their attention resolutely on their newspapers or on the scenery. After a few minutes, he sat down or went to another car—I don't recall. But I do remember that, though I was in reasonable agreement with most of what he said, I was as uncomfortable as anyone else. The problem was that he was doing this because it seemed to him an excellent thing to do—but he had not waited on God's grace. He had not acted from that love for his auditors which would have sought simply to win them to Christ and not merely to preach Christ at them. His witness was, without his realizing it, rather to the fine quality of his own religious convictions than to the Lord.

This is not to say that the less mature Christian should not seek, as well as he knows how, to draw people to Christ. Often God in his love for the person addressed will supply, just for that time, the sometimes quite extraordinary grace that the would-be missionary needs truly to get beyond himself. But humble recognition of one's own sinfulness and inadequacy is needed. The history of the Church is filled with the accounts of the harm done by zealous missionaries, whose zeal was not for the Lord. Intolerantly impatient for the pagans to cease their iniquitous ways, they were less concerned that Jesus be known and loved and served. On the other hand, when the latter motive dominated wholly as, say, with St. Peter Claver, centuries of faithful Catholics followed despite the worst of conditions. Only when the fearfulness generated by original sin and one's self-centering longing for love have been largely overcome by recapitulation and one has entered into full life in the Spirit or when the power of concupiscence has been suspended temporarily by special grace, is one truly free to assist his neighbor spiritually as is appropriate.

Now, to help someone to know and love and follow Christ is the greatest good we can do him. But it is not by any means the only good we can do him; and we are not entitled to omit the lesser good except insofar as it

[20] Conflict arose only when those who did not believe began to raise obstacles for those who did or were still inquiring.

conflicts with the greater. Hence, the connection between the corporal works of mercy that have been so characteristic of mission work and the preaching of the Good News of Jesus Christ is an intrinsic one. Saving the baby girls abandoned in the streets of China, feeding the people of the Sahel in their famines, caring for the sick in leprosaria, in hospitals, in jungle clearings, gathering together and giving some rudiments of education and a sense of family to orphans, laboring to bring peace between families, tribes, or hostile classes of society—all of this, though secondary, is essentially connected with the preaching of Christ, for it witnesses to the reality of the love of Christ in those who claim to be His witnesses.

Since missionary work is the necessary fruit of charity, a Christian community but little interested in mission activity shows itself at risk. A community, say, like the Jerusalem church of the 5th and 6th Centuries, which stays contentedly within itself and declines to bring Christ to others even though tolerating those who do, no matter how flourishing it may seem and no matter how devout many of its members may be, this Christianity dies.[21] For it is called to spend itself in communicating this life to those who lack it even at the risk of its own earthly livelihood and life. Each local church, as St. Paul was constantly reminding those he founded, must constantly be giving away what it has in order to spread the good odor of Christ everywhere.

It may be objected that there have been Catholic peoples who have clearly rotted away as Christians even while assiduously working for the spread of the Gospel. Despite the logical flaw in this if taken as an objection, what it alleges is factual, as observation of the condition of the Church in several countries over the past forty years should make clear. The reason, however, for the seeming contradiction between the great charity called for by missionary work and the decay of Catholic life is the phenomenon pointed out earlier:[22] the hidden substitution of what only requires learning or imitation for what calls for personal development and spiritual maturation. Missionary charity requires a maximum of spiritual growth, yet its external activities are among the most easily imitated. Wanderlust, the enjoyment of the challenge of change and adventure, and natural sympathy for the evil plight of many of one's fellows can easily motivate such activity. Not that such motives are to be despised—but they are incapable of maintaining a vigorous and spiritually effective Christian life in any missionaries in whom they substitute for genuine charity.

The same thing happens at their own level with individuals. Catholics who are "not interested" in the missions are at grave risk for their own salvation. If charity is alive in a man, he must go out and let it act for other men under pain of dying spiritually, a death not by crucifixion, which is life-giving, but of weakness, decay, and sin. The individual Catholic who tries to solve his problems or his family's problems while choosing to remain isolated within himself, or even within his family or his society or his culture, who thinks that he must solve these problems first before he tries to be of help to

[21] J. Lebreton & J. Zeiller, *The History of the Primitive Church*, tr. E. C. Messenger, New York: Macmillan (1942–1947), *pp* 499–503 with 1006–1008.

[22] *Pp* 363–366.

others, loses quickly his outward thrust and stifles the Spirit by refusing to allow Him to operate in His own way. A Christian cannot draw a line for God and stop short. If one is alive as a Christian in the strong sense, having completed his recapitulation and begun to live fully in the Holy Spirit, and yet refuses to "go to the gentiles," he may soon cease to be a Christian at all.

So, the Church—here, I am talking not only of the Church as a whole but of national and local churches as well—must be going out constantly with the integral message of the Gospel. But, if integral, the message will often be rejected. It would be very easy for all mankind to accept a message, if visibly confirmed by its effects, that entry into the Church would bring about social justice, health of body and mind, peace, culture and education, and other basic temporal goods: "each man under his own vine and under his own fig tree."[23] These things are not hard for men to labor for, even should they involve considerable pain and suffering in the effort.

But Jesus did not come in His own day and does not today come as a temporal messiah. He is not today directly concerned with freeing the oppressed from their oppressors any more than He was then concerned with freeing the Jews from the Romans or in setting slaves free from their masters. So, He is not now directly concerned with overturning unjust social structures that give license to kill the innocent by abortion or euthanasia, or that subject the poor to the oppressive greed of the rich, or that foster wars for the sake of economic gain, any more than He then fought against Greco-Roman infanticide or the gladiatorial games. Indeed, before He comes in judgment, He does not intervene so as to prevent all sin, any more than He then prevented sin, who wrought our redemption as the victim of the gravest of sins. He comes simply to change the heart of each person, in some season known to Himself alone, so that this heart may, at last, be found repentant and contrite, set free from sin, at least by the time death comes.

The change of heart that Christ desires, coupled with some minimal knowledge of God's laws and of the workings of the natural world, will prevent this individual from oppressing or enslaving others, from aborting or killing of the innocent, from centering upon himself through unchastity, gluttony, and drugs. Rather, it will lead him to do all that he can to help others because of his love for Christ. But the change of heart may come too late to make much external difference, even in the life of the individual; and his knowledge of what is truly good for another may be acquired too late to prevent his doing the other great harm, albeit with the best of motives. Thus, in the life of a society, it may take centuries before individual changes of heart make a clearly detectable cultural change that manifests the social fruit of the individuals' conversions.

Hence, no temporal goods can ever rightly be the primary object of the Church's activity, whether the missionary's or the Christian's "back home."

---

[23] From the glorious days of peace under Solomon (I Kgs.5:5), through both pre- and post-Exilic prophets (Mic.4:4; Zch.3:10), through the days of the Maccabees (I Macc.14:12), this phrase expressed the most basic Jewish conception of God's blessing for His people. The extravagant imagery of endless wealth and power in apocalyptic literature was related rather to the glory of God, manifested through His people's salvation, than to the daily life the pious Jew longed for.

Yet, just as our Lord used every occasion to cure and feed and instruct those who were in need, so the Church and her missionaries and all her children must seek, from hearts opening ever wider to the exigencies of the divine life within, to alleviate for others the miseries of this life and to provide whatever good is possible.

Even when those to whom the Church is preaching Christ are resistant, the Christian should labor at their temporal welfare for as long, at least, as such preaching continues. One does not stop trying to help them temporally because they are resistant but only because one turns elsewhere to meet greater obligations to one's fellow Christians or to a more receptive people. In any case, the temporal welfare of one's fellow men is to be sought, wherever possible without loss of greater good, since one is following and preaching Jesus, who healed the sick and fed the hungry and even provided better wine for the wedding feast.[24]

2. *Inculturation*

"Inculturation," as one aspect of missionary activity, is governed by the same principles. Adaptation to the new culture is never a goal in itself. This culture may have to be profoundly altered, even dissolved. Yet some inculturation is necessary if one is to speak to these people out of love for them in Christ. The only proof needed is the depth of the inculturation of the Word when He became flesh. To refuse this inculturation is to show an implicit contempt for those to whom one speaks. For, their culture is part of them, and so must be dealt with with the respect that Christian love owes them.[25] No matter how disgusting to a good physician his patients' diseases may be or the ways in which they became infected, his efforts must be to heal; and surgery, if needed, gives him no right to inflict any more pain than is necessary. As indicated above, moreover,[26] God's revelation, not the missionary's own culture, is the norm for judging a culture foreign to him.

This charity of genuine inculturation is far from the attitudes of those who, unhappy with the Church or the faith, go hunting elsewhere for something that may satisfy them. That was, in type, what Esau did; and he lost to Jacob his inheritance and the Promise. But the Church is not a hunter, to track down and kill animals to feast on. She does not go out consciously

---

[24] Pope John Paul II has noted (*Centesimus Annus*, #19, 36), as have many others, the identity of purpose of secularist capitalism and marxism, both of which are concerned with a temporal messianism. Such capitalists think the final age is already here and are puzzled that things don't work out better than they do. The marxists desperately seek to overthrow all that has been established in hopes of being able to build the kingdom on their own terms without God. Both groups, though preferring different means, seem equally convinced that, once those opposed to rational solutions are sidelined, a bit more planning will set things right.

[25] Despite common parlance, one need not have much respect for another's opinions (or culture) if these are filled with error, but must have great love for and, therefore, great reverence for the person whose false opinions these are. And if one listens with such reverence, one will come to understand better both what the other is saying and why he says it. Thus one will be better able to correct the errors and may well learn much more of truth despite the wrongness of the assertions.

[26] *Ch* 18, 376–380.

hunting things in her surroundings with which to improve her own status, as do those who envy the pagans their *satori* and their mystical experiences of insight or emptiness. Her nourishment is of a different sort and she has no need of meats from "gentile" sources to enrich what the Lord has given her.

The Jews were often tempted to such borrowings for their worship of the Lord: the golden calves, the sacred pillars, the "passing of their infants through fire," the altar like "the altar that was at Damascus" (2 Kgs.16:10–16). But whenever they thus "went hunting," they fell into sin and were punished. Yet their unconscious borrowings seemed generally to have pleased God. What they took in spontaneously, without even knowing that they were borrowing, simply because they wished to give the LORD the best they had—all this He accepted gladly. But this best was no longer defined by them as the particularly attractive elements from their neighbors' religions but as the best portions from their own (already acculturated) life.

Such selective absorption from one's culture is rightly initiated and carried through only in this unnoticed operation of God's grace, working in the world according to the times and seasons that He alone knows. All goes rotten if men seek on their own to modify their practice of religion by deliberately adopting traits from the mentality of the surrounding "gentiles" or by a deliberate borrowing of their practices.

For example, after the Exile, when the Jews set about to restore the Temple and their public worship of the Lord, they took in without realizing it all sorts of elements from Persia and Mesopotamia. Judaism in the strict sense begins with this return from the Exile, a culture quite drastically distinct in its human traits from the culture of their grandfathers some seventy years before, precisely because they had absorbed into their ordinary lives so many new ways of thinking and acting from the pagans among whom they had been scattered. Even as they lamented that they could not sing the song of the LORD in a strange land, by the mere fact of living or, for most, being raised among alien peoples, they were absorbing from those cultures all sorts of new elements which they carried back with them to Palestine quite unconsciously and which they built into the House of the Lord and their worship of the King of Heaven (a Persian title for Him that they had taken over).

Chapter 20

Marcion's Revenge: the Disappearance of the Old Testament

Obviously, the regression of cultures should be, if anything, a still greater matter of concern to the Church than their development. For, their regression implies a serious loss of contact with whatever was sound in their religious past. If the culture is one belonging to the earliest dispensation, that of natural cultural development before public revelation, then the regression will be analogous, say, to the rotting away of the cultures of Greece and Rome. The Church's concern will then be to graft these cultures, as completely as possible, into the trunk of the patriarchs and prophets, in and through Christ. If, however, the regression is that of an already developed Christian culture, such as the gradual decay of Christian life in the West since the beginnings of the Renaissance, her concern must be with her very survival in a culture already either severed from her or poisoned by some alien substance. In any case, this last mentioned regression is worth another glance, since it is in its midst that we are living.

A. Substitution of Learning for Recapitulation

Before going further, we will do well to give some attention to the fact of our cultural regression—for there are some today who would deny it. This will also permit us to note the historical context in which the very notion of culture arose and developed. For, enormously useful as this notion is, that context shows us much about the regression with which we are concerned.

1. The fact of the regression of the West

Western intellectuals have been fascinated, for well over 500 years now, first with the diversity, then with the internal structure and the history of particular cultures, and most recently with the laws governing the rise and fall of any culture whatever.[1] New disciplines resulted, especially philosophy of history and cultural anthropology, which grew vigorously and came gradually to take to themselves the task of adequately explaining man to himself, of saying what can be said about the meaning of human existence, a task formerly reserved to divine revelation.

This was no accident. The passion to develop a philosophy of history, to weigh and balance cultures, and to understand the causes at work in their development—a passion that is itself a highly specific and characteristic trait of our modern Western culture—seems to have arisen largely from the efforts of the academic establishment (principally, the Renaissance universities and their graduates) to mediate, transcend, and eventually to relativize the conflicting claims of the Church and the torn-off members of the Body of Christ. This process gradually became, with the Enlightenment, an effort to escape from an understanding of the world rooted in divine revelation. Thence arose philosophy of history.[2] As a philosophical movement, it was seeking a substitute for the Christian view, since this latter finds no definitive solution in time for man's woes and no intelligibility to his history that remains solely within this world. But if one would cut away the supramundane and yet would not regard the life of the entire race as "a tale told by an idiot, full of sound and fury, signifying nothing," then the intelligibility must be extracted somehow from man himself and his world.

Despite the best efforts of novelists and philosophers, however, it has been hard to convince people that meaning and intelligibility of an exclusively intramundane sort can be drawn from the lives of single individuals. The "life of quiet desperation" lived by the Jewish bourgeoisie of turn-of-the-century Vienna has by now become the life of Western man generally.

Hence, at least part of the drive towards the study of the history of cultures came from the size of the unit, from the hope that what seemed random and happenstance at the level of the individual might show some true pattern as one took the average over an entire culture. But even this did not suffice. Since, as Dawson persuasively demonstrated, a culture arises from a religion, not the religion as some sort of by-product of the culture, to gain the intelligibility sought one must turn to the comparison of many cultures and many religions, standing above or apart from them all in order to grasp the overall intelligibility of their rise and fall in time.

---

[1] Such interest is found already in the mid-13th Century in individuals such as Roger Bacon (cf. *EM IV*, 318–319). But only slowly did it become part of the general intellectual life of the West. Commerce, war, and missionary activity all contributed to making the late-medieval West well aware of other peoples. Moreover, the different cultures then known had been in large measure a perennial even if sometimes marginal part of European consciousness. This relative familiarity coupled with the extraordinary fact that the great civilizations with which Europe had vital contact were all formed by "the religions of the Book"—the only exceptions being the civilizations of India and China, with which at that time there was minimal contact—brought it about that the focus was on the diversity of peoples rather than on the differences in their cultures as such. But with Europe's discoveries in Africa and East Asia, and of the Americas, Western interest increasingly shifted, partly under the impact of novelty, partly under the influences that explain the regression we are discussing, to what we now subsume under the term 'culture.'

[2] Gerhart Niemeyer, *Imprimis 6*, no. 10, (October, 1977)

The great explanatory systems that resulted were not exercises of idle speculation. "Knowledge is power," the slogan runs. Understanding was sought in order to control, direct, and improve human cultures. These explanatory systems were gnostic responses to the Christian faith, i.e., each a *gnosis*, a hitherto hidden knowledge that would bring salvation from human miseries. Yet, despite the fact that these efforts contributed much to our understanding of ourselves through the detailed investigations of human cultures carried out by anthropologists, linguists, and specialists in the other social disciplines, the promise of all these explanatory systems seems always to have withered before fruition.

If one takes into account that what some rejoice in as progress others abominate as degeneracy, one can see that the major thinkers in this domain are in agreement that Western culture is in serious decline. From Hegel and Marx through Spengler to Toynbee, Jaspers, and Dawson, almost all attest to the virulence of the disease that ravages the traditional Christian culture of the West. A reasonable consensus has been reached even as to the more obvious causes, or many of them, for this state of affairs though, again, limned sadly by some as decadence, with exultant defiance by others as freedom. Toynbee gives little more ground for optimism than Spengler, despite his difference of manner; and Spengler is not really more grim than Hegel, the grandfather both of Marxism and of Nazism. Thus, the faith of the secular humanist in an ineluctable progress has come to resemble nothing so much as Faustus' petulant reliance on the word of Mephistopheles; and the underlying despair is the same in each.

Devout Catholic that he was, Christopher Dawson seemed, nevertheless, no less gloomy in his assessment of the current state of Western culture. "The events of the last few years," he remarked after World War II in 1947,

> portend either the end of human history or a turning point in it. They have warned us in letters of fire that our civilization has been tried in the balance and found wanting—that there is an absolute limit to the progress that can be achieved by the perfectionment of scientific techniques detached from spiritual aims and moral values.[3]

With the dramatic breakdown of the Communist empire and the ever more striking growth of our scientific and technical knowledge, especially in genetics and communications, many will pooh-pooh such dismal assessments. But they may only do so by ignoring people's inner lives and their growing miseries of both psychic and spiritual nature, some of which we have already mentioned, more of which we will consider shortly as we consider the causes of this regression.

I will argue that two related yet distinguishable processes have concurred in bringing about our current regression. Neither one nor both would have been sufficient, however, had it not been for the loss of the Old Testament as an integrally Christian book.

The first such process is intimately tied in with the development of the university. The second process is the gradual unsexing of the Christian West

[3] *Religion and Culture*, p 215.

through the search for total individual autonomy.[4] The former process rendered both theologians and their theology inhospitable to, indeed uncomprehending of, the spiritual sense of Scripture. The latter process, in good measure a result of the former, though feeding back into it and reinforcing it at all stages, was able to pass itself off as Christian during its crucial earlier stages only through the absence of what the spiritual sense had to say of Christian marriage.

2. The rise of the university

The cultural triumphs of European Christianity, though rooted in the cultures of the ancient world, were genuinely native to the Church in her growth among the new peoples. The medieval syntheses of philosophy and theology, the development of modern science and scientific technology, the flowering of Western architecture, art, music, and literature, the Western notion of the university, all were distinctively Christian achievements. But, as in all cultures, these very successes have served to draw men away from the harder tasks of personal growth and the further spiritual development of their people. The "learnables" have gradually taken the place of the "developmentals." The primary locus and principal agent of this transformation, I would suggest, has been the university.[5]

With the displacement of the cathedral schools by the universities in the 12th Century, the formative and developmental aspects of learning, included as essential to the attainment of Christian wisdom, began gradually to weaken.[6] They were replaced by the practical knowledges directed to the instruction of professionals—law, both canon and civil, medicine, and the theology that was coming to have some importance for the better schooled among the clergy—trainings arduous enough in their own right, yet not deeply formative of the person. Thus, the universities brought to birth the professional, intellectual classes, lay and clerical, that have had the dominant role in the shaping of Western culture ever since.

What is perhaps not as well understood is the importance of the shift that took place in the very meaning of 'theology' with that ascendancy of scholasticism that accompanied the emergence of the universities. Even at the time and, with much better justification, for a century and a half before and during the Reformation, scholastic theology was severely criticized for being nothing but book-learning like the philosophy that had become its vehicle, derived from an endless analysis of the details of such texts as the *Sentences* of Peter Lombard. Its partisans were derided for their endless commenting on

[4] To the extent that the self becomes autonomous, i.e., independent of any human control or claims upon oneself other than those one has originated, sexuality is withered. For sexuality is essentially relational and the natural soil out of which all communal relations grow. To become autonomous, then, means to strip one's sexuality of everything except mere physical excitement.

[5] By 'university' I refer not only to the institutions of higher learning so named but also to the vast throng of people who have been formed by them.

[6] In the cathedral schools, though learning was often bookish, yet this learning was intended as but a part of the life of the student and as only one element in the development of Christian wisdom. The purpose of the studies was to nourish worship and meditation and charity. The knowledge that was sought and prized was that given by God in contemplation.

commentaries, with nothing of reality entering in and nothing new to be found except more complex terminology. Long before the Reformation, also, the scholastic method was criticized for replacing personal knowledge of God and the divine mysteries, which required spiritual maturity and long growth in prayer, by the vain logic and philosophy of men.

Whatever the validity of the particular charges, there was a change taking place in the role accorded to the human mind and reason within theology itself. In the patristic understanding, theology was an experiential knowledge of God, given in and through faith as this suffused and activated all the natural powers of man.[7] But in the universities theology came to be seen—whether philosophical or biblical in its method—as a demonstrative science of divine truths, derived by the activity of the human reason working upon data provided in part by man's natural powers, partly by faith. Theologians, in their zeal to refute the adversaries of Christian teaching, had too readily accepted their ground for the debate. For, once theology was thus reconceived, even an atheist could be a sound theologian if he chose to work with the full set of data offered by revelation. There was in principle no intrinsic check upon the ever more detailed logical analyses or upon the ever more widely ranging and, eventually, sceptical questionings of the theologian.

In spite of the amazingly powerful developmental elements displayed by its early practitioners, scholasticism focussed on the training of the mind rather than on the formation of the man. The university gradually transformed theology from a developmental to a learnable. This in-built weakness was held in check by such great scholastics as St. Albert the Great, St. Bonaventure, and St. Thomas. But these men, as members of the new and fervent Mendicant Orders, had been initiated into the developmental life of recapitulative growth in the faith well before their university teaching and research. The secular clergy who so stoutly resisted them at the University of Paris sensed, if they could not well articulate, the difference—and ultimately they won, not by obtaining the exclusion of the Religious but by changing the attitudes of the Religious to conform to their own.

In such an atmosphere it is not surprising that the spiritual sense, so extensively used by Aquinas and by Bonaventure in their commentaries on the Old Testament and so well analyzed by Thomas, wilted like a plant without water. It soon became little more than simplified accomodations and standardized preacher's tropes, increasingly disregarded by careful and rigorous thinkers. Even Thomas seems not to have grasped explicitly the central role of recapitulation in Christ for the Christian life.[8]

The flourishing of the critical and systematic intelligence in all the professions led quickly enough to the university's becoming the authority for both canon law and for theology, as well as for the other professions. At first, this influence involved little more than others' simple consultation with those expert in their field. But, by the time of the Reformation, the universities

[7] For a brief but excellent treatment of this point, cf. Georges Chantraine, *Vraie et fausse liberté du théologien: un essai*, Paris: Desclée de Brouwer (1969), *pp* 21–68.

[8] Consider, e.g., how his arguments in *ST* I-II. 107. 1 ad 2 could have been strengthed and integrated had he been thinking in terms of recapitulation.

were receiving and accepting a much more active role, as one may see by their willingness to offer their judgments when asked by King Henry VIII of England in the matter of his marriage to Catherine. With the division of the West into Catholic and Protestant, the university came slowly to feel itself neither as a forum for the contestants nor as one of them but as the proper arbiter of their struggle and the competent settler of religious disputes. The Papacy took pains to assert its authority in these matters, not least by condemning large numbers of theological propositions defended by university faculties. But as mentioned earlier,[9] the restriction of all controversy to the literal sense of the Bible was cutting at its root the right of the Magisterium to judge theological positions.

Already, long before this, back in the 14th Century, the new professional classes had found that their training in critical thought and in that aggressive spirit of inquiry typified by the *disputationes quodlibetales*—well, if jokingly, described as arguments *de omni re scibili et quibusdam aliis*[10]—did not serve for union of minds and hearts. Endless great and minor schisms and wars were but symptoms of the growing inner disunity of the culture. In particular, the Church's constant need for renewal and reform ceased to be met as the higher clergy either followed the universities or turned to the new humanism of the Renaissance—itself made possible only by the large number of university-trained intellectuals—leaving unassuaged ordinary Christians' religious thirst and desires for reform. These desires, coupled to growing regional diversities, easily fed the sectarianism of which we shall have more to say in a moment.

For centuries, then, the clergy and better schooled Catholic laity have been taught, rightly enough to a point, to appreciate the arts and sciences of their day, to develop their minds' critical powers, and to think through their faith systematically on the basis, say, of St. Augustine or St. Thomas. In ever greater measure, however, this has been accomplished by a schooling, which, even had it not had so rationalistic a flavor, increasingly lacked the recapitulative element needed for personal Christian maturation and was ignorant of, if not hostile to, a theological understanding of that element. What had been learned in the strongly developmental context of the family or the guild or even the army or the royal court has been remitted increasingly to the university. The result—all too reminiscent of ancient Athens—has been an ever higher percentage of Christians who are more cultivated in mind and sensibility and technical skills than in faith and practical charity.

Christopher Dawson assessed the condition of Western culture in 1947 as follows:

> We are faced with a spiritual conflict of the most acute kind, a sort of social schizophrenia which divides the soul of society between a non-moral will to power served by inhuman techniques and a religious faith and a moral idealism which have no power to influence human life.[11]

This religion impotent to affect human life is, as can be seen from the

---

[9] Cf. *pp* 147–148, 176–177.

[10] I.e., *concerning everything knowable and various other matters.*

[11] *Religion and Culture, p* 217.

Scriptures, the sort of religion that is highly characteristic of periods of spiritual regression. The religion in question is impotent because it is regressing. Further, this impotence in its leaders brings on regression throughout the culture, a regression not at first in the learnables, which may well grow more rapidly than ever as men concentrate on them excessively, but in the developmentals. But the decay in these latter will eventually damage the learnables as well.

If one looks at the history of Israel, one can see that all religion in accord with God's call, even when fairly primitive, affected human life profoundly, even if slowly and not always perceptibly. On the other hand, all turnings away from true worship and service of the LORD had a stronger and more visible effect, indeed, the only effect that most men noticed, then or since. Yet those effects have long since been washed away without having other influence on the world than that exercised by the seemingly futile opposition of the great prophets, whose words still have power to change the hearts of all who believe. The religion of the majority of the priests and of the prophets—those called by Jeremiah "false prophets"—was, even when sincere, quite incapable of affecting matters usefully. And as quiet as was the maturing of Judaism, its power to influence human life is still being exercised. Yet it was only with the coming of the Holy Spirit upon the apostles that a religion appeared that was intent upon changing all the world and that had the evident power to do so.

In sum, the weakening of this power among Christians during the period of which we are speaking[12] can be traced in large measure to the social dominance of the academic disciplines and the consequent over-emphasis on schooling[13] at the expense of the practice of one's faith and of recapitulative development. This academically generated weakness is, if not the ultimate source of our religious and cultural decline, its most visible symptom, a symptom that, like a high fever, is itself causative of much of the harm. This over-emphasis on the intellectual life, however, is excessive not in the esteem it has for the mind, which cannot be over-esteemed and which as a result of the present regression is both insufficiently and wrongly esteemed, but in the lack of esteem it has for the more arduous development that can take place only through doing the will of the Lord in accord with true faith.

Dawson's comment about "a religious faith and a moral idealism which have no power to influence human life" points, I think, to the root of the bleakness on all sides today. The great practical works of charity of our own day, such as the pro-life movement, the Catholic Worker, the original Cana Conference, the work begun by Mother Teresa for those dying in destitution in Calcutta, and the communities of L'Arche established for the mentally and physically handicapped by Jean Vanier, while finding some small resonances

---

[12] The weakening in question has been localized in the West principally in those strata of Christian society that have been most influenced by the universities. During this same period, however, the missionary activity of the Church, throughout the Americas and in Africa and Asia, has flourished more vigorously than at any time since its first centuries. Cf. *Ch.* 19.C, *pp* 390–395.

[13] The weakness here spoken of was long since pointed to by the popular understanding of 'academic' as that which is pedantic, impractical, and ineffectual.

among those academics who have been disappointed by the emasculation of our culture, seem all to have in common that they have grown up in independence of, even defiance of, the regnant academic cultural world. They seem to have sensed that any religion, especially Catholicism, that would allow itself to be bound by the chains that a gnostic academicism would impose on it, even were it somehow possible to retain intact its faith and worship, would have no chance of influencing positively the life of any group of men.

Yet it is the university that has been, I think, the major power in the growth of the modern world. Since the university's greatest occupational hazard is gnosticism, a seeking of salvation through and by the mind alone rather than by the charity that the Spirit gives, it is not hard to see why Christian academics may have had so little influence for good on the culture as a whole. On the other hand, when they have overcome the gnostic temptations and reached a certain fulness of Christian maturity, they have generally been rebuffed, not only by non-Christian academics but, often more vigorously, by their Christian fellows and excluded from direct participation in the formation of policy and in the training of younger scholars.

The proper response to all such situations is clear. Since charity is the love that grows from faith and that gains its courage from hope, the Christian academic must live a life so governed by the full truth of faith and so invigorated by hope in the Lord, in whose rebuffs and repudiations he gladly shares, that his recapitulation is accomplished in relatively few years. Thus, he may begin the life of infused contemplation and all-consuming charity before retirement. Then indeed, his religion will have influence on the world, not perhaps as he would have desired but as the Lord desires.

Many Christians schooled in the universities or even teaching in them have lived lives of great charity, as personal acquaintance today makes evident and as the roster of university-educated saints since the 13th Century attests—though their number seems to decrease with each century. There is no intrinsic incompatibility between the academy and the Church; concentration on teaching and learning can be conjoined, however great the difficulty, with recapitulation in Christ. But let no one underestimate the difficulty.

B. The Emasculation of Western Christendom

But would not a truly Christian culture be proof against the substitution of intellectual achievement for integral recapitulation, important as this process has been? Some further causal factor seems necessary for a sound understanding of the regression of Christianity in the West. Without denying what I have said concerning this substitution of what is merely imitable for what is spiritually developmental, I think it worthwhile to push the analysis further, following a line of argument suggested by psychologist Paul Vitz.[14]

He argues that, toward the end of the 15th Century, a cultural shift began in Western Europe that was implicitly a revolt against Christian fatherhood. By the beginning of the Enlightenment, that cultural movement had

[14] Panel discussion, Allies for Faith and Renewal Conference, May 1985. Personal communications, June 1986 and December 1990.

triumphed and the revolt continued, now against fatherhood itself. This shift, too, succeeded; and between the two World Wars, the attack came to be directed against manhood as such. There was first, then, a discarding of what was Christian in fatherhood, then of what was paternal in manhood, then of what was male *tout court*. Feminism would not, then, be the agent of this last revolt but a somewhat desperate response to the vanishing of true manhood from those whose Christianity and fatherliness had already grown dim and weak and warped.

Vitz characterizes the driving force behind these shifts as an ever stronger assertion of the autonomy of the ego, a movement largely led by Luther, Zwingli, and, later, Calvin. The common element was the breaking of the communal bonds of the Church's traditional understanding of divine revelation in favor of each individual's own interpretation of God's word. The religious upheaval led quickly to scepticism, as with Montaigne and Pomponazzi, followed by that popularized Cartesianism that cut the mind off from all else in the world—making it a pure spirit localized somehow in a body—and, effectively, from God through this denial of the knowability of His works. Such scepticism, having separated the autonomous ego from God, moved on to deny Him outright by atheism—rejecting Him who is the Father of all. By the time of the French Revolution, this had become an antipathy and assault against all authority, for all true authority is ultimately paternal.

Vitz is well aware, of course, that other elements were also at work. For example, the printing press played no small role in the process. Printing made the book a readily available personal possession, encouraging a withdrawal into privacy, one person alone with a text.[15] Protestants naturally made much greater use of the press than did Catholics for, in some ways, Protestantism is a natural outcome of the demand that every man have his own Bible. What the Reformers added, of course, was not only a permission but an injunction for each man to have it and read it and interpret it for himself, as guided by the Spirit, independently of the Church's tradition. The privatization of religion was, then, in its origin, a Protestant boast and brag, not an imposition by a State worn out by sectarian violence.

I think, however, that the beginning of the first shift can be seen a good century and a half before the Reformation. Even before the need to repair the devastation wrought by the Black Death in the mid-14th Century, the spiritual lassitude of clergy and religious and the growing prosperity of the city-states of the early Renaissance were contributing to a new attitude developing rapidly by the end of that century. Men's spontaneous desires to set things straight and to bring about a greater prosperity became stronger; and this, in an environment where the first thing to be "set straight" was the Church.

The life of the Church in the Middle Ages, as in every age, was marred by the splitting off of sects. But from the 13th Century on, what increasingly marked the medieval sects, whatever their doctrinal aberrations, was their separatism. In contrast with patristic times, the divisions did not come

[15] Deconstructionism has at least the merit of indicating some of the ambiguity intrinsic to the transition from knowledge of a text to knowledge of its author's meaning—*a fortiori*, to knowledge of the author himself.

principally from erroneous doctrines.[16] Rather the false doctrines arose from a separation already desired.[17] What animated these sects and gave them their principal influence was their growing dissatisfaction with the abuses in the medieval Church. These movements grew in influence until by the 15th Century the great pre-Reformation sects of Waldensians, Lollards, and Hussites had achieved an abiding presence and importance.

Papal and clerical authority were under steady attack, not only by such sectaries but by the powerful conciliarist movement, which showed its true nature most clearly at the rump Council of Basel. More significant yet from our point of view were such separatist doctrines as that only those in the state of grace could validly have authority in the Church or administer the sacraments. Hence, the true Church was said to consist only of the righteous or of the predestined—some form of wholly invisible church.

The sectaries did, of course, gather together visibly, forming congregations of greater material poverty and simplicity and, for a while at least, of seemingly purer Christian inspiration. But this congregational emphasis, strongly masculine in its psychic structure, through which all matters could be dealt with in good, male, rational and cooperative fashion, was a grave threat to the feminine mode of being of what had been till then "our Holy Mother," the Church.

Except for the Cathar sects, the separatist heresies seem not to have attacked doctrinally the sacramental nature of marriage. Yet, within the framework of thought and feeling created by the sacramental understanding of marriage, attitudes towards the Church were closely linked to attitudes towards marriage and to the whole domain of sexuality.[18] Hence, the mere fact of the wide influence of these various movements that preferred to separate from the Church rather than to continue the difficult task of dealing with the misdeeds of her children, augured ill for marriage.

Applicable to that entire period from the early 1300's on are some remarks of Walter Ong concerning the Reformation:

> The real, deeply felt, but little understood difficulties of separatists were and are not with...authoritarianism but with the mitigated, mediated authority, the symbol of which must be feminine, the initial experience of which each human being ordinarily knows in his relations with his mother. The Church which the separatist berated he saw, significantly, not as a cruel father but as an outcast mother.[19]

---

[16] The Cathars were a major exception; but their roots went back to earlier centuries.

[17] Christopher Dawson argued that even in patristic times this was true. The spirit of schism with which he is concerned, however, might better be called a spirit of social conflict (also his own term). For 'schism' more properly relates to a division that arises from conflict over religious authority and its proper exercise. Cf. his *The Judgment of the Nations*, New York: Sheed & Ward (1942), *pp* 171–172, his *The Formation of Christendom*, New York: Sheed & Ward (1967), *pp* 5–6, and "Dawson on Religious Controversy and the Spirit of Schism," (unsigned), *The Dawson Newsletter 4*, 3–6 (#1, Spring 1985).

[18] That understanding of sexuality, including the sacramental understanding of marriage, as part of the mystery of Christ and His Church is what I sought to sketch in my *Christian Meaning of Human Sexuality*.

The separatists were willing to put up with a God and Father whose authority was exercised tyrannically and terribly but of whom one could have clear and distinct ideas, whose will was made evident by His word, and with whom one's relationships were definite and well specified. One's relations with God were pictured not only as with someone other than oneself but as with one external to oneself, even though privy to all one's inner life. He was, moreover, suitably distant and increasingly unneeded as well, for the later separatists' various notions of predestination meant ultimately that one did not have to work to please Him; if He was not pleased already, there was no hope. All this seemed psychically preferable to the continued struggle with the femininity of the Church and her merely intermediary authority—for indeed she has none of her own.

The separatist movements were a kind of characteristically male revolt against a Church that, as feminine, was the abode of the mysteries of religion, the locus of what was not graspable by men's natural reason. They wished to be set free from the Church, not so much, however, because of the mysteries of her doctrine as because of the mysteries of her being. How could she be the ransomed Bride of Christ, without spot or wrinkle (Eph.5:27), if she showed herself so weak in checking the corruption of her members, so vacillating in reform, so frustratingly feminine?

The Reformation appears as a sort of final despair in the face of the seriously irresponsible and sinful behavior of many of the Church's members, especially those in the highest offices. Precisely, however, as such, it represented an abdication of Christ's mode of responsibility for her whom He had had to redeem for Himself by death upon the cross. The Reformers, indeed, refused longer to accept any responsibility for her. She was branded the Great Harlot, the Whore of Babylon, who once had been Christ's Bride but who had defiled herself beyond recognition.

True reform was most certainly needed. But in the midst of the seemingly insurmountable difficulties, the Reformers showed themselves unwilling to accept their role as one with Christ in His suffering for His Bride, whom, in her sinful members, He would neither yield to—as did the first Adam—nor desert. Rather, yielding to impatience and fallen man's excessive desire for power, they sought, because of their lack of Christ-like manliness, to set things straight by power, even by force.

Because the psychic link between wife and Church is so strong, not only was the Church to be reformed and set straight; so would men come to deal with their wives. The first step of weak human nature to justify its abandonment of the marital duties of a Christian father was, then, a 'macho' one. A man thought to exercise his authority for the benefit of wife and children (and of the Church) by making his power felt, and eventually became a tyrant to both wife and Church.

All this represented a redefining of the Christian husband's responsibility for his wife and children. Responsibility for their temporal welfare was

---

[19] Walter J. Ong, "The Lady and the Issue," *Cross Currents* 2, 17–26 (#3 Spring, 1952), *pp* 17–18.

accepted; the despair centered on their spiritual welfare, ultimately not under his control since dependent on their freedom and God's free grace. This redefined masculinity tended to deal with an errant wife either by "beating some sense into her" or by casting her out to "let her go her own way." Such masculinity would rightly not consent, as Adam had done, to her sins; but neither did these men any longer understand Christ's sufferings on her behalf.

As mentioned a few paragraphs back, till the end of the 15th Century all Christians still believed—whatever their actual practice—that Christian marriage is a sacrament. Its special nature was much debated; but always, whatever the rest of one's theory, one essential aspect was that marriage is intended to manifest Christ's love for His Church and hers for Him.[20] Since all sacramental grace was widely seen as directly connected to Christ's sacrifice, marriage also had to be sacrificial, though it symbolized not His sufferings but the love He showed while dying in order to win His Bride and make her worthy of Himself.[21]

Hence, Christian marriage requires that a man be faithful, like Christ and in Christ, even should this amount at times to crucifixion. Christ accepted to be frustrated and "done in" by the weakness and sinfulness of His Bride. It was thus that He purified and saved her.[22] So, too, if wives are to obey their husbands, their husbands must love their wives even as Christ loved His Church and gave Himself up for her (Eph.4:24–25).[23]

All this changed dramatically with Luther. He rejected out of hand the sacramental nature of marriage, seeing this as a merely natural institution, good in itself but, since the Fall, intrinsically corrupted by concupiscence. Far from being a sacred union, as the Church taught, every act of marital intercourse was, according to Luther, a grave sin, meriting damnation. Only by God's gratuitous mercy, were the justified saved, not from the sin but from its just punishment. Yet marriage, so Luther taught, was enjoined on most, if not all, men by God though it remained a merely human arrangement,on the same level as those for the acquisition of raiment or food or housing. Not surprisingly, then, its regulation lay entirely under the control of the State, not of the Church, with which it had no essential link.

Luther saw marriage, therefore, as a purely secular matter. The scriptural passages that were thought traditionally to support a sacramental notion were swept away by the fierceness of his doctrine of the uncontrollability of sexual passion and its intrinsic sinfulness due to the Fall. The words of St. Paul, he agreed, referred to a great Christian mystery; but this had nothing to do with

---

[20] This doctrine, inherited from the New Testament itself and the Fathers' developments of its teaching, was not seriously challenged in the Middle Ages except by the Cathar sects, who regarded all material things as evil, especially procreation. For the Catholic and quasi-universal teaching of the early period, cf., e.g., *S.T.* Suppl., 42, 2c. Nearly two centuries later, the doctrine is, if anything, clearer: e.g., from the Decree of Union with the Armenian Church in 1439 (DS 1327).

[21] E.g., *S.T.* Suppl., 42, 1, ad 3.

[22] Cf. *Ch* 13.B, *pp* 264–266 above, concerning Adam's obligation with regard to Eve.

[23] The psychological rightness of these scriptural injunctions has been set out profoundly and simply in: Paul Vitz, "Husbands, Love Your Wives," *Pastoral Renewal 8*, 48–47 (#4, November 1983).

the marital life of Christians in the present dispensation. Nonetheless, Luther's teachings on family life and, despite a hot temper, his own married life seem to have been exemplary—though conceived in secular, not Christian terms. He was a Christian who was also a good husband and father; but according to his doctrinal understanding, neither he nor any other man, insofar as father or husband, was living Christianly.

The same tendencies to an authoritarian masculinity, to a male ego that would set the world right, still new in the 15th Century but growing, can also be described, as Bireley has noted,[24] as an ever greater desire for a well-ordered and completely ordered society. With this appeared a greater willingness to discipline, forcibly if need be, the unruly and disorderly, chiefly the peasants and lower classes or whoever did not fit in well with the masculinized vision of order that was in possession, until they should live the sort of well-ordered lives desired by the authorities. Needless to say, hidden in this lay both a contempt for those in need of such discipline and a fear of them. This was the beginning of the tendency that would issue, on the one hand, in Calvin's Geneva, in Cromwell's Covenanters, and in Puritan New England and, on the other hand, in Christian Europe's first absolute monarchies.

Well before the scientific revolution and the Enlightenment, then, the Machiavellian, Calvinist, or similar passion for a well-ordered society was animated in its depths by a vision of good order as a way for men to avoid the messiness and inconvenience of the feminine elements in ordinary living. By it, they sought to impose a masculine clarity of mind upon the feminine receptivity of the actual world in a manner already premonitory of the later application of scientific methodologies to human beings and human society. Nor was it long before the same secularizing attitudes that the Reform had let loose began to be applied by men, flushed with their success in the early stages of modern science, to their relations with women and to all human relations.

For, men spontaneously desire to be free to think their thoughts and to devise their schemes and to carry out their contests and power-struggles without being held back by the dull and pedestrian duties of pleasing a wife and making some effort to meet her expectations—except through sexual intercourse—and of raising children. These duties required still more effort if one was to act as a Christian oneself in the process and to help one's family do so as well. Only through revelation, I think, and a humble living of it in faith can most men—*a fortiori* a whole culture—learn to be neither macho nor wimp,[25] neither authoritarian tyrant within the home nor weak figurehead for an "authority" that has, in truth, ceased to be paternal.

It is, then, not hard to see how the Reformation was indeed a prime example and causative factor in the process described by Vitz. Moreover, the long process of which we have been speaking serves as an integral portion of

[24] Robert Bireley, *The Counter-Reformation Prince: Anti-Machiavellianism or Catholic Statecraft in Early Modern Europe*, Chapel Hill: University of North Carolina Press (1990), *pp* 30–33, 59–62, 217–242.

[25] Cf. above, note 2 and text, *p* 277 for Vitz's use of this as a technical term. As he remarks in the same article, "The wimp needs to be loved at all costs, and the typical cost of this need is the truth."

what psychiatrist Karl Stern has called, apropos the beginnings of the 17th Century's scientific rationalism, the Western world's "flight from woman."

Stern's psychoanalytic study of the cultural regression of the West[26] begins only with Descartes, when already the sceptical period had begun and Christian fatherhood had already suffered defeat. What he seeks to show is that the polar "male" and "female" traits that are each present both in men and women, though with a very different emphasis in each sex, have been split asunder in modern times.[27]

Doubt, methodical or other, is a connatural solvent for personal relationships and social bonds. The increasingly autonomous ego was soon chafed under the varied tyrannies flowing from the overthrow of the Christian understanding of fatherhood, and set about to cast them off as an intolerable degradation for the human spirit. Their replacement was accompanied by the far more radical rejection of fatherhood that was implicit in Deism. The authoritarianism that Protestantism brought to the father of a family, that appeared in the social tyrannies that resulted, also underlay the separatist images of God as Father. Thus it was guaranteed that the same assault would be unleashed against the divine Fatherhood as against human fatherhood. By the end of the 18th Century, this attack had been made explicit in the virulence of the rationalist atheisms that soon followed and that are now dominant among the intellectuals of the West.

The privatization of religion began to serve as a sort of solace to believers. Only so did one not have to be deeply bothered interiorly by the false doctrines, the perverse behavior, the deliberate maliciousness of others. One had one's own religion, one's own way of life, and it was right. So, too, the earlier concern for good public order was gradually transformed among most men into a desire for nothing much higher than not to be bothered in one's life and enjoyments by the demands of familial responsibility. For the secular enjoyment of marriage, fatherhood increasingly was felt as a constraint by unwanted dependencies.

What had been the natural strength of a man, to have sons and daughters to carry on his work, his name, his line, his kinships, became bonds preventing him from doing what he would like to do, hindrances upon a mobility ever more physically and socially possible and attractive. Responsibility for children was a nuisance and a bondage, and indeed a limitation even upon his enjoyment of women. Hence, we see Jean-Jacques Rousseau as the model and epitome of this stage of cultural deterioration. Such, a generation later, was Goethe, who could not bring himself to stay in town when his mistress/wife would give birth to a child. Neither, much as he thought he loved her, could he bring himself even to enter the room where for a week she lay dying or to speak, even from the hallway, one word of comfort or love to her.

Erik Erikson has pointed out the sad consequences in a marriage if the

---

[26] Karl Stern, *The Flight from Woman*, New York: Farrar, Straus & Giroux (1965).

[27] This arose, psychoanalytically speaking, from ever worse relations between the infant and his mother. But a secular increase in such harmful relations evidently itself calls out for explanation, one which Stern locates, without much detail, in the modern loss of sound religious faith.

husband has not reached that level of psychic maturation Erikson labels 'generativity.'[28] Such a man is not yet ready psychically to take responsibility for another person's life. He will not (perhaps psychically, cannot) tolerate that anyone "cling" to him in a way that lays hold of his conscience; he feels too weak to carry the burden. Responsibility involves the free acceptance of not well foreseen restrictions upon one's activities as well as obligations to act when one might rather not, all determined by the objective good of another. To accept responsibility for another's life means, then, to engage oneself by a moral bond, by an obligation in conscience, to act or to refrain from acting as determined not by one's own desires but by the genuine and integral good of another. Since this good embraces all of time and eternity as well, however clear one's goal may be, the means are often fearsomely unclear when both parties are continually changing in an ever changing world.

By accepting responsibility for a wife, a man accepts a risk of failing as well as an opportunity—but also obligation—to mature yet more through the exercise of his powers in new and fuller ways. All this requires a loosening of the grip of his own spontaneous desires and an uncentering of his choices from his own preferences. He cannot take responsibility for a wife, an adult like himself, without being committed to interpersonal and mutual self-revelation of a sort that lets her have confidence enough to manifest her own understandings and needs. If, later, he is responsible for children, still less can he demand or even accept that his spontaneous desires be normative. He must be able to love much more as God does, for a long while without any return of unselfish love from his children, willing to seek their good even at the cost of their rejecting him. He will at times be made to feel all his weakness and limitations, for he does not know, at least for a while, what to do or how to deal with these refractory youngsters who are upsetting things and requiring his intervention while refusing it.

Matters only grew worse in the bourgeois culture of 19th Century Germany and France and in the corresponding life of Victorian England and Scandanavia.[29] Thence it was but a short step to refusal of true responsibility for any other person. Today, as Stern points out, the so-called First World has found the formula, through technological progress, for the male without dependents to indulge himself in pleasures in an ever more childish and regressive manner. It is this that has brought about that unsexing of men that is manifested by the social acceptance of masturbation, pornography, and homosexual activity—now a mere "alternate lifestyle"—and by feminism. This is the pre-patriarchal world come to life again, far more regressively with us now than with the mob in Gibea when, "committing abomination and wantonness in Israel" (Jdg.20:6), they acted like those who had assaulted the angels at Lot's door some 800 years before.

The ever greater regimentations characteristic of the 20th Century show,

[28] Cf., e.g., Erik H. Erikson, *Childhood and Society*, 2nd ed.,, New York: W. W. Norton (1963), 166–168.

[29] Stern analyses Ibsen's *Hedda Gabler* in this context; but the point is set out with still more biting and sardonic ruthlessness in *Peer Gynt*, with its striking parallelism, even unconscious parody, to Part II of Goethe's *Faust*.

however, that the search for the perfect, rationally ordered society has not ended. The ideological leaders of Marxism, Fascism, Nazism, American Liberalism, and the like have differed from their predecessors principally in their employment of technology and organization upon what had hitherto been the preserve of the personal and humane. As if human relationships were the results merely of animal instinct or of biochemistry, men with an intellectually constructed ideal vision of how society ought to be have set about to reconstruct either the whole social order (as in Maoist China or Marxist Kampuchea), or the basic structures of any society (as in the drive for homosexual "marriage"), or even the nature of the individual person (as in the coupling of *in vitro* fertilization with genetic engineering). These are indeed legitimate descendants of the 13th Century schismatics, though with their visions of a godly Christian society replaced by atheistic ideologies.

The male "addiction" to power that Stern finds the dominant psychic trait of modern men has also shown itself in its scientific and technological subjugation of nature and in its increasing contempt for what it has subjugated: the material and the individual. Hence, in men's personal lives, there has been a movement to mere use of all that is receptive, concrete, or feminine, along with concommitant contempt for what is so used. Women themselves have been increasingly despised, though unconsciously feared or resented. They were to be seduced, not out of affection or mere attraction but just to prove oneself, to see how it can be done, what variations are possible. Increasingly, sexual relations with women have been seen not as an element in love but as mere material, along with love itself, for countering a man's insecurity and for satisfaction of intellectual curiosity.

Over the last six centuries, then, the husband who sought to symbolize in his marriage something of Christ's relations with His Church has become in succession the earth-bound husband and father, the macho mate who provides sustenance but whose life is centered elsewhere, the paramour, the philanderer, and the wimp. Psychologically, the process was, as Vitz describes it, the gradual setting loose in the world of the totally autonomous ego.

Such assertion of one's "autonomous self" is evidently but the retention and amplification of the infant's sinfully aberrant psyche, now freely willed by the adult. The psychic traits of such a "self" are the central ones among the residues of original sin. Whatever the autonomous self may choose, it does not truly show gratitude for its own being nor glorify anyone other than itself. Underlying these traits as their cause is the self's making itself the sole center of the universe. For, a genuine autonomy of the self would require unconditioned existence; and man still wishes to be as God. The demand for autonomy is the self-contradictory demand for an absolute masculinity, a non-relational and sterile mimicry of the Father in Satan's scoffing manner. This demand is also, in essence, the refusal of femininity, a fear of it, and a flight from it.

Hence, too, every genuine feminism—not simply movements for the righting of injustices against women but the angry claim to an autonomous female self—shows itself in a radical hostility to the feminine. Since, of all things feminine, the Church is the most feminine, the first target for feminist hostility will be the Church. Though rightly but, I think, inadequately described as springing from anger at men or fierce disgust with them, feminism includes as well a self-directed anger, roused by some sense of internal connivance with the men at whom the anger and disgust are directed. This anger, then, rejects the feminine and seeks either to destroy it or to replace it. It is not only men but women who have been fleeing from woman these past six centuries—the women fleeing, however, because of the men.

From such, now wholly autonomous, egos, the contemporary situation results. Women are for men, but men are not to be bound to women; no-fault divorce has come to the rescue. Men are not to be bound to children; hence, if contraception fails, the mothers can be persuaded or frightened into aborting their infants. Even government has become mere self-will, either of ruthless ideologues in search of their abstractly concocted, ideal worlds or of equally ruthless seekers for the simpler and baser pleasures of personal aggrandizement. An atomic individualism reigns. But, as Orwell made palpable in his *1984*, total individualism and total tyranny are not only not incompatible but require each other.

The draining away of Christian manliness in the West has, of course, been noted by others but has been attributed to society's decreasing need for such typically masculine functions as hunting, farming, and fighting. This putative social emasculation, however, has small plausibility when one considers that, except for a quarter-century, most of these functions were absent from the cities of post-exilic Judaism without such effects. Rather, I would argue, the emasculation has come from a gradual cutting away of Christianity's religious roots in that post-Exilic Judaism.

C. Loss of Christian Understanding of the Old Testament

Again, however, the point can be made that the tendency towards the absolute individualism of an autonomous ego has been present in everyone from the time of Adam's sin. Why did it triumph so dramatically in the West despite the Christian culture in which it arose? The flight from woman, while not unique to this regression of the West, seems not to have taken place in any other major Christian culture. Why, then, has it occurred in this one? Why, if the university was a Christian invention, did not its Christian faith countervail its tendency to substitute the imitable for the developmental?

The answer that I would suggest to these questions can be stated in two ways. Firstly, during just this period we find Christians gradually weakening in their knowledge of the divinely revealed and guaranteed plan for their spiritual maturation and personal development. Alternatively, as a culture we have been recapitulating that loss of contact with our spiritual roots experienced in Israel under the late monarchy, when knowledge of the writings that were to become the Scriptures had all but vanished.

God had given a spiritual sense to the Old Testament so that out of its soil true Christians might grow and that the principle effects of original sin might be healed through our recapitulation in Jesus of the life of Israel. The disappearance, then, of the Christian understanding of the Old Testament, this loss of knowledge of the spiritual sense of the Scriptures, was, I would argue, the principal causative element, not otherwise present in the Church's history, for the regression of the West over the last 600 years.

If this thesis should seem too novel to be plausible, recall that this understanding of the Bible is not a luxury for the learned but is a central and essential part of Christian faith. It was the spiritual sense alone that distinguished the Christian Jew's understanding of Scripture from his non-Christian brother's. It was this divinely given intelligibility of history that Irenaeus, Origen, and the other Fathers opposed to the gnosticisms of their day. It is the same intelligibility that can overcome the academic gnosticisms of our own.

It was through the realities of Israelite history described in the Bible,[30] that God formed men and women "well prepared," among whom Joseph, Mary, and Jesus could live truly as members of their culture. The whole life of the Chosen People, from Abraham till our Lord's day, was needed to bring about the manliness and womanliness of the those among whom God's Son, made man, and His sinless and virginal mother could walk at ease, exemplary in their human goodness but not glaringly conspicuous.

But the manliness of Christ was not for Himself but for us. As seen throughout Part II, the Old Testament was to provide the necessary and universal pattern for human moral and spiritual growth in Christ for every Christian, whatever his culture. The Old Testament, understood recapitulatively, is the sole pedagogue (Gal.3:23–26) that forms the Christian for the fulness of the life of the Spirit, the freedom in charity of the sons of God. Only through the spiritual sense could Christians be rightly taught how to recapitulate in Christ His re-living of the Old Testament in the Holy Spirit. And only by sharing in His recapitulation can His followers, in less than a lifetime, not merely learn what true manhood and womanhood are but become true men and women, who live in the likeness of Christ.

Here we need merely summarize the general pattern of correlation we have already seen.

The drive towards individual autonomy is easily discernable in the gnostic temptation of the academy: let each man there be not merely his own expert but his own truth.[31] That the temptation has been yielded to is evident in the fragmentation of academic departments, not only in the relatively harmless manner based on the multiplication of specialties but in the profound and irreconcilable divergences between theologies, philosophies, indeed, of entire worldviews, that have splintered each of the humanities. In our own times, 'academic freedom,' originally a legal concept for freeing academic

---

[30] This is not to deny the influence of those realities that were not chosen by God to be written down and that, in consequence, could not serve as types. But the importance of the typical realities was vastly greater, as is attested by the building up of the many strata and progressive reworkings of the text.

[31] The literature on the weaknesses of the university is limitless. For recent views, cf., e.g., Allan Bloom, *The Closing of the American Mind*, New York: Simon & Schuster (1987). Roger Kimball, *Tenured Radicals: How Politics Has Corrupted Our Higher Education*, New York: Harper & Row (1990). Dinesh D'Souza, *Illiberal Education: the Politics of Race and Sex on Campus*, New York: The Free Press (1991).

administrators from extraneous pressures, has become the guarantee that faculty be accountable to no one for their teaching except to their fellow faculty members. In Catholic universities, professors of theology at times presume to define for their students—against papal teaching—what the 'genuine' doctrines of the Church are, in a sort of derisive mimicry of papal teaching authority. Nor when faculty are being hired, is much interest shown in what effect they may have on the spiritual growth of the students, as this is ordinarily understood within the Church.

There is a tight correlation, as well, between the academy and the loss of manhood. Visible enough in Athens and in Alexandria, as among Moslems in their more opulent days, this is not so much caused by the entry of women into the university, as it is witnessed to by this.[32] The ineffectiveness of the university for true building up of the Christian life has been a matter of concern and of general awareness since at least 1350. The popular slogan, "Those who can, do; those who can't, teach," though unjust to many, yet catches much of what is "academic." The childish captiousness of many a professor, the growing unwillingness to hold students rightly accountable for learning and understanding, the triviality of much research, all point to a relationship that has lost most aspects of the fatherhood that is rightly sought in any teacher of young adults.

True though it is that the mind conceives and that it brings to birth new ideas and theories, often after hard labor, yet it is the father that initiates a young man into the adult world and helps him grow in intellectual adequacy to deal with it. The professor's task is less midwifery, at least once beyond the stage of mere instruction, than it is to assist the young person who wishes to advance human knowledge to face the need for the long training and toughness of mind that are necessary and to induct him, with suitable professional dispositions, into the society of his peers. But this professorial relationship, if not to be in some degree degrading of the student, must contain a strong element of not only of professional selflessness and competence but of the manly, sometimes stern affection of genuine fatherhood.

This latter does not cease with begetting the child but only then begins; and a father's responsibility grows the greater for the youngster's formation as the latter approaches maturity. Though to the degree a father is successful, the young person becomes independent of his progenitor, yet the father is not absolved of his responsibilities before that point has been reached. So, in his proper sphere, should the professor be. No wonder that students have rejected *in loco parentis*, since it is a rare professor that seems willing or even able to act in parental capacity for them.

Now, the damage done by an academic approach to the faith through the growth of Western university culture seems to have come in large measure from the late scholasticism that increasingly ignored or misunderstood the spiritual senses of the Bible.[33] Teaching about the spiritual senses in the lecture

[32] Cf. Walter J. Ong, *Fighting for Life: Contest, Sexuality, and Consciousness*, Ithaca: Cornell U. P. (1981) for extended treatment of this point.

[33] Despite what many have thought, St. Thomas was firmly committed to the elucidation of the spiritual sense in the explanation of the Scriptures, as is made evident by his extensive com-

hall, apart from the life of prayer and quiet service that had been its accompaniment in the monastic and cathedral schools, made the theology based on it ever more like the scholastic theology that was then seen as its great adversary. For, both were becoming increasingly mere studies of texts and the particularities of isolated arguments, ideas, words.

At the very least, the six centuries or so of "sexual revolution"—of the unsexing of the West—were contemporaneous with the loss, first of proper understanding and then even of awareness of the spiritual sense of the Scriptures.[34] This loss of the spiritual sense was, as indicated by Vitz, a breaking of the communal bonds of the religious tradition of the West in favor of the autonomous ego and the concomitant loss of manhood. Nor was there anything distinctive about the first Protestant neglect of the spiritual sense. For several centuries the established practice in the universities excluded theological argument based on what they erroneously called the spiritual sense.[35] Further, the Reformers' insistence on 'private interpretation' of Scripture, which broke, in principle at least, with any normative tradition in hermeneutics, would not have been thinkable to anyone convinced of the the divine origin of the accomodations then passing as the spiritual sense. But this conviction once gone, why should one not hold that no Christian could be bound in conscience by what other men, even the whole Church, have seen in the Bible. It is small wonder—even without Calvin's denials—that the spiritual sense disappeared from Protestantism. But it is just this exaggerated autonomy of the individual that, in its historical development was to become "the flight from woman."

We have already seen some of the strong correlations to be found between our strictly religious deterioration and the gradual loss of a Christian understanding and living of the Old Testament. It is worth considering one more. The elements of the sacramental understanding of Christian marriage, whose importance in this whole process we have seen, are found explicitly in many places in the New Testament[36] and, so, were available in principle to both Luther and Calvin. Yet the perception of the Church not merely as Christ's Bride but, as such, to be imaged by the wife in a human marriage in her relations to her husband, depends on a clear grasp of the various spiritual senses. As seen above,[37] the anagogical sense is needed as well as the preparative and the prefigurative to match the fulness the Church had given to her teaching. Thus, St. Paul had been able to present Christian marriage as the type of the union between Christ and the Church precisely because he knew this as the spiritual sense of Gen.2:24. On this basis, Christians before the Reformation had taken Paul's words in Eph.5:22–33 to show that by Christian marriage a couple is graced so as to be able to symbolize the union between

---

mentaries on the Old Testament. Nor should one forget that his systematic theology was in large measure motivated by the needs of controversy and defense of the faith against attacks of the Aristotelians. The rationalist scholasticism we have been speaking of cannot claim him for itself.

[34] The classic and carefully detailed exposition of this process of loss can be found in de Lubac, *EM IV*, *pp* 325–344, 369–427 and passim.

[35] *Ch.* 7.A above, *p* 147.

[36] E.g., Eph.5:22–33; I Cor.11:3–9; Rev. 19:7–8, 21:2–3 & 9–10 especially.

[37] *Ch* 17.A, *pp* 345–346.

Christ and the Church. But those who would not acknowledge a theological argument based on the spiritual sense, gave such an understanding short shrift.

Luther accepted in principle the spiritual sense of Scripture and, indeed, saw Christ as the key to a right understanding of everything in the Old Testament. Under the strain of his personal problems, however, the unresolved ambiguities in the medieval teaching that he inherited showed the inadequacy of the Scholastics' systematizations. If the spiritual sense is too arbitrary or ambiguous to be used in theological argument,[38] then out with it in any discussion of the doctrinal questions concerning Christian marriage!

It is in Calvin, however, that one sees the consequences of such teaching deduced with a merciless if not always rigorous logic. His scornful dismissal of the sacramentality of marriage[39] reiterates Luther's. "Marriage is a good and holy ordinance of God." But in the same way, "farming, building, cobbling, and barbering are lawful ordinances of God and yet are not sacraments. For it is required that a sacrament be not only a work of God but an outward ceremony appointed by God to confirm a promise [i.e., made to us by His word[40]]. Even children can discern that there exists no such thing in matrimony."[41] A clearer refusal of the spiritual sense would be hard to find.

St. Paul's words in *Ephesians* are for Calvin nothing more than an imaginative comparison, a parable only. Hence, even as the mustard seed is not a sacrament, though the Kingdom of God is like to it, so marriage is no sacrament though it is meant to encourage husbands to love their wives tenderly after the example of Christ's love for the Church.[42] Paul's reference to Gen.2 shows only the closeness of this latter union, but has nothing to do with the carnal union between spouses.

A man clearly determined to focus all things on Christ, yet all that Calvin touched turned into a sort of caricature of the Old Testament. At one level, by rejecting all that is not literal and at the same time rejecting Marcion, he made the Old Testament dominant by its mere size. But the more basic fact is that, for Calvin, Christ did not replace the Law by the Holy Spirit but simply renewed it, purified it of accretions, adding nothing new to it.[43] Calvin would not see in the Law a meaning that went beyond the Law. Yet the spiritual

---

[38] In this, as we have seen (*pp* 177–178 above), he was a good Thomist (e.g., *Quodlib.*, 7, 6, 14, ad 4; *ST* I, 1, 10, ad 1) and Augustinian as well: (Ep. 93, ad Vincent., cap. 8, PL 33, 334).

[39] *Institutes* IV, 19, 34–37.

[40] *Institutes* IV, 14, 1–6.

[41] *Institutes* IV, 19, 34; translation from *Calvin: Institutes of the Christian Religion,* ed. J. T. McNeill, trans. F. L. Battles, Philadelphia: Westminster Press (1960), vol 2, *p* 1481.

[42] He seems not to notice that the parallelism needed for a conclusive argument would require instead, "though Christ's love for the Church is like to it"—a wording that might have alerted him to the presence of error.

[43] Cf. again his commentary on the First Letter to the Corinthians, 10:1. That Christ did indeed perfect and bring the Law to completion was traditional doctrine (cf. St. Thomas, *ST* I-II, 107, 1 ad 2 for one example), but the notion of perfection is very different in the two men. For Catholicism, the grace of Christ, though the purest and most unmerited of gifts, is a gift of intrinsic power and life; hence, the perfecting of the Law involves not only a keeping of it flawlessly but a spiritual transcending of it by the life in the fulness of the Spirit.

sense alone could tell Christians that the Law not only meant what it literally commanded but also signified the New Law, i.e., the grace of the Holy Spirit,[44] present in the heart through faith in Christ, in preparation for whom the Old Law was given. Not accepting the spiritual sense except where it is given as the literal sense of the New Testament, Calvin could see no objectively real progress from the Old Testament to the New. Thus he demonstrated, contrary to his intentions, that the difference between Judaism and Christianity is manifested, as the Church had always taught, in the denial or the affirmation of the spiritual sense of Scripture.

The loss of the spiritual sense meant, then, the loss of the Old Testament as a *Christian* book. The two Testaments were cleft increasingly asunder. Either the genuine newness of the New seemed to render the Old superfluous—Marcion redivivus—or the attempt literally to relive the Old made the New basically unintelligible. For the heretics of the 15th and 16th Centuries, the latter path was followed, so that for Protestants the Old Testament remained till a century and a half ago very much a book-for-Christians, even though not a Christian book. Catholics and some strains of Lutheranism increasingly took the former path, so that for them the Old Testament gradually ceased to exist.

Calvin's teaching, even more than Luther's (who, if anything, had overemphasized the New Testament, especially St. Paul as he understood him), showed clearly enough the masculinizing power of the Old Testament. Thus, if Protestants who still really believe what they find in their Bibles often show a more easy and integrated masculinity (or femininity) than many Catholics, or if Orthodox Jews as a people tend to be more resistant to cultural influences that are hostile to their religion than many Catholics or Protestants, this can be traced to greater formation by the Old Testament.

But when this has not been lived as Israel had done, still less as Jesus had, such masculinity is not integral. Containing some profound distortions in its relations with the feminine—whether this be the femininity of their wives or of the Church or of the material universe—it showed itself, as seen above, as domineering and excessively abstract, "macho"[45] and authoritarian. Without the spiritual sense of the Old Testament that guided everywhere St. Paul's own understanding, even when he was making no mention of it, Calvinist doctrines on original sin, human nature, and predestination took on a monstrous appearance that they had not shown in Luther's teaching.[46]

As a result, toward the end of the 17th Century northern Europe began to revolt against the worship of a God of such seeming cruelty as the Reformers', though having no adequate knowledge of any other. The same sort of reaction took place roughly a century later in this country. Without the

---

[44] Cf. *ST* I-II, 106, 1

[45] As this word suggests, the Old Testament has fared better in Latin American Catholicism than, say, in that of the United States.

[46] This was, of course, due in large part to Calvin's removing of Luther's inconsistencies and ambiguities and his setting forth of the doctrines with uncompromising clarity.

spiritual sense, Christians could not moderate the sharpness of the verbal formulations of the biblical texts by means of the Church's fuller explanations, these often not being verifiable by the literal sense alone. If the only sense is the literal sense, her Tradition could be at best a tool for investigating earlier generations' opinions about what the scriptural writers might have had in mind.

The Protestant refusal of a normative Tradition asserting a God-given spiritual understanding of the Scriptures brought it about that the Reformation and post-Reformation controversies were fought out on the basis of the literal sense alone, the only sense admitted by all sides. Thus, Catholics also gradually lost their awareness of the spiritual sense, so that for a century or two prior to II Vatican, many an honest Catholic, when challenged by a Protestant friend, "Where's that in the Bible?" has been forced to appeal in often incoherent fashion to a completely independent "church tradition" for his response. For neither the one party nor the other has knowledge of any other intelligibility in Scripture other than "what it says."

In Catholic regions of Europe, the traditional understandings still permeated the culture, and the Baroque can be seen as a sort of Counter-Reformational glorying in the Catholic retention of all the senses of the Bible. A true grasp of the spiritual sense was still seen on occasion, as for example in the *Spiritual Exercises* of St. Ignatius Loyola[47] and in St. John of the Cross.[48] But this was "spirituality." The genuine spiritual sense, already so greatly weakened through theological literalism and confused with mere accomodations was, for the most part, still talked about; but genuine understanding was gone. Theology, preoccupied, first with Protestantism and, then, with the subtler heresies of Baius and Janssens, fought its battles, as St. Thomas and Luther had required, on the basis of the literal sense alone, this sense itself increasingly under attack from the Enlightenment.

Indeed, to take the Old Testament "literally," when once it had been cut off both from the Church and from Jewish traditions, which still retained contact with its original sense and context, meant that Calvinism could not possibly understand even the literal sense of the Bible rightly. Much of the impact, even shock, produced among Liberal Protestants by their "higher criticism" came from its gradual rectification of the Reformers' quite unhistorical understandings of the literal sense of many parts of the Bible.

Further, this restriction to the literal sense led logically to the predominance of the scientific study of the biblical texts; for, the new sciences of linguistics, archeology, and the history of cultures were the appropriate disciplines for tracking down the literal meanings of any texts whatever. But in a Europe in which science was seen as the weapon of choice against all intellectual traditions, it is not surprising that an exclusively scientific study of the Bible led increasingly to the rejection of whatever in it was deemed incompatible with current scientific theory. By this very fact, of course, the sort of

[47] The "Call of the Temporal King" [91–98] is a particularly splendid example, showing in its brief compass the whole process of spiritualization that was accomplished by Jesus.

[48] *EM IV, pp* 500–505.

knowledge of Scripture that comes only through virtuous freedom and recapitulation became ever more academically unacceptable; the teachables and learnables replaced almost entirely the developmentals in this most crucial of all areas.

If, then, one let oneself be shut up within the New Testament alone (as was the Catholic tendency), though he still had the Holy Spirit, the Church, the sacraments, the feminine, as well as the Father and His Son, yet he had lost sight of the need, and even the possibility, for recapitulation. For, without a Christian Old Testament, there can be no consciousness of recapitulation. The liturgical cycle, the Jesuit emphasis on the efficacy of the mysteries of Christ's life, and similar movements helped to slow down this forgetfulness and gradual loss. But what the Fathers had taught of spiritual growth in terms of purgative, illuminative, and unitive ways was increasingly turned inwards and separated, at least concretely, from the recapitulative aspects of the life in Christ. Hence much of the treatment of the former ways reduced to consideration of virtues and vices in a quasi-philosophical manner. So, too, the relations between the active and the contemplative lives, taken increasingly without reference to recapitulation, tended to make a genuine spiritual life a matter solely for monks and nuns.

Due to this loss of the understanding of recapitulation and the preparative typology on which its rests, a great moral softness has come about among Western Catholics. The moral exigencies for spiritual growth have been both greatly watered down and also distorted, since missing increasingly those elements not made clearly visible in the New Testament. As everyone today has heard *ad nauseam*, the New Testament says nothing expressly condemning contraception or usury or abortion or a host of matters the Old Testament and the Church's Tradition have dealt with; and Jesus said even less. All these matters, of course, had been dealt with centuries before. Whatever a Jew of Jesus' day might have done in practice, he had few doubts about what the LORD's Law required of him. And our Lord, having already spent a millennium teaching these things to His people before His incarnation, apparently saw no good reason to repeat it all over again in the three short years of His earthly life.

A goodly percentage of the college-trained Christians in this country, along with many of their clergy, have been among those most visibly affected by that moral softness, one that is rotting away observance even of the Commandments. These Christians limply deplore, if they do not defend, ever grosser and more frequent blasphemies by artists, writers, and the media. Not even to notice that the Second Commandment is being violated suggests that none of the Commandments really registers, as such, with these Christians. This is, in fact, evident in their frequent lack of concern about the violation of the Fifth Commandment through abortion and euthanasia and their "compassionate" condonations of the varied and often perverse violations of the Sixth Commandment. They have regressed, like those successful and influential secularists whom they admire for their high positions in the world, to a childish or infantile level. Further confirmation, if needed, can be seen in the growing minimalism with respect to the Lord's Day, where not only is less and less required or expected by the clergy but more is not even desired. Unlike the Reformers, they ignore, if not reject, not only the maternity of the Church but the Lordship and the Fatherhood of God. Small wonder, then, that "Catholic" feminists' repudiation of the First Commandment has received so little rebuke from their bishops.

But if the Old Testment is shunted aside and a youngster is raised solely on Jn.13–17, sublime as this replacement is, it cannot be rightly understood. The new commandment to love will be known—but what behavior it requires of one will not be. What love means in this context can not be grasped except very imperfectly. As just seen, its connection with the Ten Commandments—for Jesus and for Paul still the basis of all moral life and that which one "must...do to inherit eternal life" (Mk.10:17–19)—has become, for many, very dim. The sentimentality of the last two centuries seems the only alternative for one who does not wish to let his faith be reduced to rationalism. And even were it true that all that is given by the spiritual sense of the Old Testament is said literally by the New, this literal meaning would not be intelligible or interpretable without the experience or, at least, sound theological understanding of recapitulation .

In brief, with the concentration on the literal sense of the Bible by Catholic exegetes, from the late 17th Century till now, Catholics also have lost sight of that which makes the Old Testament a truly Christian book. It is still useful in preaching, providing illustrative stories and some devout accomodations. But the true state of affairs is shown, I think, by the degree to which even the current, bowdlerized versions of the Psalms have been replaced in liturgical use by textually ever more saccharine songs, and by the number of priests who have discarded the Psalter as essential to their life of prayer.

If indeed the spiritual senses of the Scripture are part of Catholic faith, then St. Paul's threat to the gentile Christians of Rome may be working itself out in our regard. "[Y]ou stand fast only through faith...."—a faith we have allowed to wither away—"For if God did not spare the natural branches, neither will He spare you....[O]therwise, you too will be cut off" (Rom.11:20–22).

D. For the future...

But however bad things may be, the Holy Spirit continues in the Church. Jesus remains with us all days till the consummation of the age. Indeed, even to the human eye, things are not so bad as to seem utterly hopeless. As Bl. Pierre Favre, the first Jesuit priest, indicated in his spiritual journal, discouragement can come from failing to notice all the little green shoots springing up under the dead and decaying leaves.[49] Even in the decadent West, the Church is still growing, putting out new twigs and buds, some flowers and fruit, even if at times somewhat shriveled. And who will dare predict what will come from the new freedom of religion in the Communist

[49] *Memoriale*, #330, in *Fabri Monumenta*, Madrid (1914), *pp* 489–696; Pierre Favre, *Mémorial* ed. M. de Certeau, S.J. (no place): Desclée De Brouwer (1960).

world of the East? Or from the rapidly growing churches of Africa and India?

Despite the grave psychic damage inflicted by the use of drugs, perverse sexual activity, the daily slaughter both of infants in the womb and of the decrepit aged and ill, and the amoral pursuit of power and wealth, the Spirit continues His work, stirring up the Church to glorify the Father through Jesus in ever new ways. One may think of such new things as the rise of the secular institutes, especially Opus Dei, such renewal of the religious life as Mother Teresa's Sisters, the charismatic renewal, the pro-life movement, to say nothing of more local activities of great Catholic vigor.

What will happen, in the Lord's own time and according to His unknown decrees governing the seasons for the nations, we do not know. It seems not impossible that, as happened in the England of St. Thomas More's day, the Christian soil is all to be turned under again in order to make it the richer and more ready for a second spring. Our recapitulation as a people may be about to inflict on us the terrible mercy of catastrophic war and exile, as happened when the people of Israel started sacrificing their infants to the LORD. God may grant us, as seems increasingly probable, the greater and still more terrible grace of persecution and martyrdom, for the blood of the martyrs remains forever the seed of Christians.

But whatever the future may be, what lies with us to do is once more to make manifest to all men that primary aspect of revelation and that basic part of Catholic faith which is the spiritual sense shown to us through the Scripture. The proof of its message will appear, as our Lord told the apostles at the Last Supper, in the vigor of Catholics' charity: "By this all men will know that you are my disciples, if you have love for one another" (Jn.13:35). The power of the Gospel still resides in the outpouring of charity that is characteristic of the life of the Spirit. This does not come early in anyone's life; and all too often, very late or never. But once Catholics have a clearer vision of their life in Christ and have come to understand how the difficulties of the spiritual life can be enlightened by the Bible—in brief, as recapitulation becomes a conscious aspect of their lives—one may hope that the Lord's grace will come more abundantly to their aid.

It is essential, however, to remember that recapitulation is a sharing in the inner life of Jesus. As a vital process, recapitulation cannot be reduced to any set of techniques. It will take place, in those who do not obstruct it by serious sin, whether the person has ever heard of spiritual growth or of recapitulation or not. Essential for it is supernatural faith in Christ, even if, as with many believers today, it is a faith badly instructed and in serious error in its explicit formulations. To the extent, however, that its understanding is false, even genuine faith is slow and faltering in its recapitulation.[50] Hence comes the crucial importance, for the individual no less than for the culture, of his correct understanding the spiritual senses of the Scripture and of letting them

[50] Yet, as one often sees in fact, the Holy Spirit teaches those whose faith is, as a supernatural virtue, still alive to reinterpret, usually quite unconsciously, false doctrines they have inherited so as to give them a genuinely Catholic meaning. There is perhaps no better evidence of the truth of the Catholic faith.

illumine his faith and life.

The application of all of this to the life of the individual, insofar as it can be spelled out in a general fashion, is matter for some other book, one on spirituality, i.e., the applied and practical theology of the temporal development of the life of charity. More work also needs to be done on those aspects of the senses of Scripture that we have only touched upon here, especially the anagogical sense that is meant, above all others, to nourish our hope and give us the joyful strength we need to serve the Lord as we ought.

Epilogue

What, then, about Alfred Shatkin's question with which I began?

Firstly, according to the basic notions of either Judaism or Christianity, every man retains his freedom under God's ordinary grace. Hypocrisy is in no way the prerogative only of Pharisees. Whatever the intrinsic worth and efficacy of their religion, men remain free to corrupt it, merely pretend to live it, use it as a screen to hide their own evil-doing from others and even from themselves.

Secondly, however, depending on the measure of God's graces at different times and on Christians' own understanding of their faith and their generosity, they grow at very different rates in their recapitulation. Often they will still behave, when adult in years, in ways that belong to pre-Davidic Israel or to the late monarchy. And of course, as sinners, their sins may well partake of similar barbarity. Their baptism inaugurated and made possible their recapitulative maturation; it does not bring it to its fulfilment. For this, not only is grace needed but their own free choices, under grace, to submit to the moral demands of what they believe. (It is here, I suspect, that Alfred is likely to balk and to argue that if one really believed the doctrine, he would necessarily show it by his actions. To which, I think, the proper response is that two millennia of convinced Christians and nigh on four millennia of devout Jews are unanimous in declaring that, whatever the explanation, experience proves that more is needed than true faith).

It is perhaps particularly relevant to Alfred's concern to note that, even if every Catholic recapitulated rightly and well, the great majority would, at any one time, still be somewhere in the process of recapitulation and not yet living the full life of the Spirit. This follows from the length of the process in comparison with the length of a human life and from the fact that the psychic damage suffered at conception is only gradually and partially healed.

Thirdly, it needs to be asked not only why Catholics are so often and in so many ways no better or even worse than the non-Catholics in their surrounding culture but also why so many of them are profoundly better, if 'better' be defined in terms of a total and self-sacrificing love for any and all men. Karl Stern, who suffered more terribly than either Alfred or I could possibly do from the former question after his escape from Nazism,[1] nonetheless saw that:

> The Catholic Church is a church of the multitude. Consequently the outsider, approaching her, faces a thick layer of mediocrity.... Whoever has experienced supernatural charity during the persecution on the Continent may stumble across a bigoted or anti-semitic priest—and with one such experience the vision of the Church seems forever gone.... Thus, it took us some time before we saw the immense hidden treasure of anonymous sanctity in the Church; the spiritual power that flows to and from thousands of unknown souls every day. The stream of sacrifices made, for supernatural motives, by a multitude of working-class people, by religious in their communities, by priests and lay-people alike. In one superficial respect there is again a strange resemblance between the Jewish people and the Church: the misdeeds of one member are more broadcast than the sanc[t]ity of a hundred others.[2]

Then, too, while one may discuss the question raised, as we have done, as to why Catholics show outwardly so little of the treasures they claim to possess, there is perhaps a better question: why are they not worse than they are, considering the gifts they have betrayed by their sins? For, the greater the gifts, the greater the sin. Further, granted the effects of original sin in all men, is it so strange that God's redemptive plan should make use of these very defects, and of men's actual sins as well, as "the rod of His anger" or of His discipline for His children?

With all the qualifications the reader is now able to provide, the Judaism of the Old Testament may be described as the religion that told men how they were to live to become good men—not only men with whom God would be pleased but whom He could fittingly adopt as His sons in Christ. Christianity is the religion that, as its first and absolutely essential action, picks up the fragments of the shattered lives of those—all of us—who have failed to do what we were commanded, have done much to displease Him, and have rendered ourselves totally unfit and unworthy to be His sons.[3]

His response through Christ is mercy. The Old Testament tells us what sin is, concretely, by showing something of its true ugliness and God's loathing for it. The New Testament and the Church complete that picture with the knowledge of hell. But they also set before us what God has been willing to do, indeed, to undergo, not to prevent us from sinning in the first place, but to bring us to repentance and to forgive us our sins while yet remaining the Just and Holy One. The first business of the New Testament is repentance and contrition for our sins and acceptance of the forgiveness God offers. But

---

[1] Stern, *Pillar of Fire, pp* 242–248.

[2] ibid. *pp* 247–248.

[3] Note how often every stratum of the New Testament speaks of freeing us from our sins as *the* grace Christ won for us.

then we must offer the same forgiveness to all other sinners—i.e., all men, without exception—even as He offered His to us. Only so can we bear His likeness, for this is what He is like. If we would live with Christ's life, we must be willing to die His death, forgiving those who have injured us most grievously.

Hence, we can see why the Pharisees, in so many ways the best among the Jews, were those at greatest risk of eternal damnation: they were those least inclined to forgive. The Sadducees, they opposed or used as the occasion offered. The publicans and prostitutes, the "people of the land," and those who did not know much about the Law they were tempted to despise or brush aside. The Romans and other gentiles could be quietly hated or condescengingly tolerated. And the crucifix shows the attitude of their leaders towards Jesus because He had called them to acknowledge that they too had sinned and, therefore, not only had need of God's mercy but, as one with all other sinners, needed to offer mercy as well. This was their deepest hypocrisy: that they were unforgiving and contemptuous of those whose actions they very rightly despised and condemned, though they also had sinned.

The problem of evil, then, is the problem of love. How can God best lead the sinful and still free-willed creature, created for perfect love, to such love? The evil of sin, the free act of choice of what one knows to be wrong, is, mysteriously, an act of disordered love, putting some created good, one's own putative autonomy or some other beloved creature, before the Uncreated Love that died to show us both how we are loved by Him and how to love Him in return. Psychic evils are predispositions to love wrongly, in us as a result of original sin and our actual sins. Both the psychic evils, once recognized as such, and physical evils of similar origin are intended to draw us out of ourselves, acknowledging our weakness and need. Recapitulation in Christ gradually heals the scars of sin but, more importantly, trains us in genuine love, vigorous and strong, that seeks with clear vision and without sentimentality the true good of others. Eventually, we may learn to love as Jesus did upon the cross, and as He still loves us: "the Lamb standing as slain" (Rev.5:6, 9, 12) forever.

Most of us do not realize how deficient we are in love for each other or for God. But there is only one ultimate standard of comparison: the love of the Father for the Son, the Son's love for the Father, and the Holy Spirit's proceeding as the mutual Glory of Them both. It is that we might be saved from the hell of an eternal refusal of Their love that we must suffer and grow —and, thus, that we might ratify, by our own free choice, our being made in the Image and Likeness of that eternal Love for whom we were created from the beginning.

Index of Spiritual Citations

Index of Authors Cited

Index of Subjects

GENERAL THEOLOGICAL SEMINARY
NEW YORK

DATE DUE

Printed in USA